8 50

C. W. Horn

CONFUCIANISM IN ACTION

STANFORD STUDIES IN THE CIVILIZATIONS
OF EASTERN ASIA

Editors

ARTHUR F. WRIGHT   GEORGE SANSOM   JOHN D. GOHEEN
ROBERT H. BROWER   MARY CLABAUGH WRIGHT

*Earlier volumes published under the auspices
of the Committee on Chinese Thought of
the Association for Asian Studies*

ARTHUR F. WRIGHT, *Editor*
Studies in Chinese Thought
Chicago, 1953

JOHN K. FAIRBANK, *Editor*
Chinese Thought and Institutions
Chicago, 1957

Ou-yang Hsiu, 1007–72
Adapted from a portrait by T'ang Yin, 1470–1523

CONFUCIANISM IN ACTION

Edited by

DAVID S. NIVISON *and* ARTHUR F. WRIGHT

With Contributions by

WM. THEODORE DE BARY	HUI-CHEN WANG LIU
JOHN WHITNEY HALL	DAVID S. NIVISON
CHARLES O. HUCKER	BENJAMIN SCHWARTZ
JOSEPH R. LEVENSON	DONALD H. SHIVELY
JAMES T. C. LIU	DENIS TWITCHETT
C. K. YANG	

STANFORD UNIVERSITY PRESS · STANFORD, CALIFORNIA · 1959

Stanford University Press
Stanford, California

© 1959 by the Board of Trustees of the
Leland Stanford Junior University
All rights reserved

Library of Congress Catalog Card Number: 59-7433
Printed in the United States of America

Published with the assistance of the Ford Foundation

To the Honored Memory of

ROBERT REDFIELD
1897–1958

". . . In folk society the
moral rules bend, but men
cannot make them afresh.
In civilization the old moral
orders suffer, but new states
of mind are developed by
which the moral order is,
to some significant degree,
taken in charge. The story
of the moral order is at-
tainment of some autonomy
through much adversity."

Preface

This volume of studies is part of a continuing effort to examine Chinese traditions of thought against the history of characteristic Chinese institutions and patterns of behavior, in the hope of acquiring a better grasp of China's enduring but ever-changing civilization. The papers in this volume were presented at the 1957 and 1958 conferences sponsored by the Committee on Chinese Thought, founded in 1951 and now a standing committee of the Association for Asian Studies.

Two earlier conferences were sponsored by the University of Chicago Program of Comparative Studies of Cultures and Civilizations, directed by Milton Singer and the late Robert Redfield, to whose wise and kindly guidance the Committee owes a great debt. Two volumes were the result of those conferences: *Studies in Chinese Thought* (Chicago, 1953), edited by Arthur F. Wright, and *Chinese Thought and Institutions* (Chicago, 1957), edited by John K. Fairbank. In the past two years, further conferences, made possible by support from the Rockefeller Foundation, have explored the problems of Confucianism.

The papers in this volume are primarily concerned with three areas of Chinese life in which Confucian ideas have been prominent: familial institutions, bureaucratic behavior, and the power relations between monarch and the literati. In addition, two papers examine Japanese Confucianism, with particular attention to the political and educational role of professional Confucianists. The studies in this volume deal, not with the reflections of the philosopher in his study, but with men active in society and in government, and with the values and beliefs we can see them applying. We have indeed been concerned with ideas; but with ideas, always, which are focused upon and seen in action.

A companion volume, *The Confucian Persuasion*, edited by Arthur F. Wright, is in press; its emphasis is on Confucian values in art and literature, in historical concept-formation, and in the ideology of popular rebellions and of political and social protest. The variety of content in this and other volumes produced by the Committee illustrates the way in which our work has been conducted: each scholar has built on his own knowledge and interests and has been encouraged to apply his own methods.

In deciding to concentrate on Confucianism, however, the Committee has indeed had a guiding motive. For we have found "Confucian" and "Confucianism" applied almost indiscriminately to phenomena scat-

tered over vast reaches of time and culture: to the imperial ideology of
the Han, the reforms of Tokugawa Ieyasu, the outlook of certain modern Chinese politicians, the current village institutions of Annam. Such
usage was clearly more than untidy semantics. It reflected the primitive level of our general understanding of this tradition. It assumed
certain continuities and uniformities which the user would have been
at a loss to specify with any precision; it blurred the varieties, the mu-
tations within the tradition that had yet to be isolated and defined.
Here, then, was a problem that seemed to cry for sustained and disciplined attention.

This abuse of the word Confucian is, we feel, closely related to a
very widespread misconception of Chinese civilization—to wit, the
image of a society whose ideas and institutions were in a perpetual
harmonious balance. Such an image has had a perennial charm for
Western man; it has colored most popular books on China and has
insinuated itself into scholarly studies, but it gives no clue to what made
the Chinese people persistently creative or what inspired them to build
the most stable polity known to history.

The papers in this volume and *The Confucian Persuasion* will, we
hope, present a more believable account of Chinese creativity, by docu-
menting some of the concrete problems with which the Chinese have
struggled down the centuries, and by analyzing some of the vexing tensions and conflicts of thought that have stood at the very center of their
way of life.

Whatever success these volumes may have will be mainly to the
credit of the learning and sensitivity of the individual authors. But at
each step of the way we have had invaluable assistance from many
others. Dr. Francis X. Sutton of the Ford Foundation filled with distinction the difficult role of outside critic at our 1957 conference, and
Professor Richard Rudner of Michigan State University in a similar
role contributed notably to the success of our 1958 meeting. Mr. Kai-yu
Hsu of Stanford University served as rapporteur at both conferences.
Mrs. Mary H. Johnson, as the Committee's secretary, was devoted and
effective in the handling of conference and editorial detail; and Mr.
Jesse G. Bell, Jr., of the Stanford University Press, gave us many invaluable editorial suggestions. Dr. Susan Han Marsh prepared the
index.

THE EDITORS

Stanford, California
February 26, 1959

Contents

	xiii	Contributors
DAVID S. NIVISON	3	Introduction
WM. THEODORE DE BARY	25	Some Common Tendencies in Neo-Confucianism
BENJAMIN SCHWARTZ	50	Some Polarities in Confucian Thought
HUI-CHEN WANG LIU	63	An Analysis of Chinese Clan Rules: Confucian Theories in Action
DENIS TWITCHETT	97	The Fan Clan's Charitable Estate, 1050–1760
C. K. YANG	134	Some Characteristics of Chinese Bureaucratic Behavior
JAMES T. C. LIU	165	Some Classifications of Bureaucrats in Chinese Historiography
CHARLES O. HUCKER	182	Confucianism and the Chinese Censorial System
DAVID S. NIVISON	209	Ho-shen and His Accusers: Ideology and Political Behavior in the Eighteenth Century
JOSEPH R. LEVENSON	244	The Suggestiveness of Vestiges: Confucianism and Monarchy at the Last
JOHN WHITNEY HALL	268	The Confucian Teacher in Tokugawa Japan
DONALD H. SHIVELY	302	Motoda Eifu: Confucian Lecturer to the Meiji Emperor
	335	Notes
	375	Index

Contributors

WILLIAM THEODORE DE BARY took his B.A. at Columbia in 1941. After naval service in the Pacific and postwar study at Yenching and Lingnan universities in China, he completed his Ph.D. at Columbia in 1953. He is now Associate Professor of Chinese and Japanese and Chairman of the General Education Program in Oriental Studies, Columbia College. His writings include a study and translation of the seventeenth-century Chinese thinker Huang Tsung-hsi and a volume of stories from the Japanese of Saikaku, *Five Women Who Loved Love* (Tokyo, 1956); he has edited three recent volumes published by the Columbia University Press: *Sources of the Japanese Tradition* (1958), *Sources of the Indian Tradition* (1958), and *Approaches to the Oriental Classics* (1959).

JOHN WHITNEY HALL received his doctorate from Harvard in 1950. He is now Associate Professor of History and Director of the Center for Japanese Studies at the University of Michigan. He is the author of *Japanese History, a Guide to Japanese Research and Reference Materials* (Ann Arbor, 1954), of *Tanuma Okitsugu, Forerunner of Modern Japan* (Cambridge, Mass., 1955), and of numerous articles on Japanese institutional history. He is presently engaged in a study of the institutional structure of the daimyo domain of Okayama.

CHARLES O. HUCKER, Professor of Oriental Studies and Chairman of the Committee on Oriental Studies at the University of Arizona, is a specialist in China's early modern history and traditional political institutions. He was formerly on the faculty of the Department of Oriental Languages and Literatures of the University of Chicago. In 1952–54 he was a postdoctoral research fellow of Academia Sinica in Taiwan and at Kyoto University in Japan. His writings include monographs on the Ming dynasty government and on political and intellectual movements of the late Ming period.

JOSEPH R. LEVENSON received his Ph.D. from Harvard, where he was a member of the Society of Fellows. He is now Associate Professor of History at the University of California. His research has been primarily in the field of Chinese intellectual history. He is the author of *Liang Ch'i-ch'ao and the Mind of Modern China* and *Confucian China and Its Modern Fate: The Problem of Intellectual Continuity*.

JAMES T. C. (TZU-CHIEN) LIU was trained in political science at Tsinghua and Yenching universities, and began graduate work in history at Yenching. After World War II he served as a historical consultant to the International Military Tribunal, Tokyo. His present interest is the political thought, institutions, and behavior of the Sung period. His publications on this period include contributions to *Chinese Thought and Institutions*, to the Sung History Project (Paris), and to *Tōhōgaku* (Tokyo), and a book, *Wang An-shih and His Times*, to be published shortly by the Harvard University Press. He has been connected with the University of Washington, Yale University, and the University of Pittsburgh, where he is now Professor of History and coordinator of interdepartmental majors in Far Eastern studies.

HUI-CHEN WANG LIU was trained in sociology at Yenching University. After two years as a staff member of the Chinese mission in Japan after World War II, she resumed her studies at the University of Washington, Columbia University, and finally the University of Pittsburgh, where she took her Ph.D. Her thesis, revised for publication in the Monograph Series of the Association for Asian Studies, will appear in 1959 as *The Clan Rules in Traditional China*. She is currently Lecturer in Chinese Language at the University of Pittsburgh.

DAVID S. NIVISON obtained his professional training in Far Eastern languages at Harvard, receiving the doctorate there in 1953. For a number of years he has been teaching at Stanford University, where he is now Associate Professor of Philosophy and Chinese. He is the author of several articles dealing with modern Chinese intellectual history and of a forthcoming volume on the eighteenth-century philosopher of history Chang Hsüeh-ch'eng.

BENJAMIN SCHWARTZ, following wartime service in the Pacific, took his Ph.D. at Harvard, where he is now Associate Professor of History. He is best known for his two books on the development of the Communist movement in China, *Chinese Communism and the Rise of Mao* and *A Documentary History of Chinese Communism* (with C. Brandt and J. K. Fairbank). His primary interest, however, is in the whole range of intellectual history in China and Japan, and his current research is in this broad field.

DONALD H. SHIVELY was born in Kyoto and received his training at Harvard, where he was a member of the Society of Fellows. He is now Associate Professor of Oriental Languages at the University of California, Berkeley. He was editor of the *Journal of Asian Studies* from 1955 to 1959, and among his publications are *The Love Suicide at Amijima* and articles on literature, drama, and other topics in the cultural history of Japan.

DENIS TWITCHETT studied at London and Cambridge universities and received his doctorate from Cambridge with a thesis on the T'ang financial system. After further study in Tokyo, he became Lecturer in Far Eastern History at London University. He is now University Lecturer in Classical Chinese at Cambridge. His primary interest is in the economic and institutional history of medieval China, on which he has published a number of articles and reviews.

C. K. YANG (YANG CH'ING-K'UN) took his M.A. in sociology at Yenching University, Peiping, in 1934 and his Ph.D. in the same subject at the University of Michigan in 1939. He taught at the University of Washington, 1944–48, became Chairman of the Sociology Department at Lingnan University at Canton in 1948, and since returning to the United States has become Professor of Sociology at the University of Pittsburgh. Aside from publications in Chinese, he is the author of *A North China Local Market Economy*, *Meet the U.S.A.*, and several manuscripts awaiting publication.

CONFUCIANISM IN ACTION

David S. Nivison

INTRODUCTION

What is Confucianism? When we look at the volumes which have been written on China and its historic culture, it is plain that this vast subject cannot be discussed in any depth without reference to Confucian ideas and Confucian values. Yet it is perilously easy for writers to treat Confucianism as if its content were self-evident, simple, and unchanging.

The indiscriminate use of the term Confucian leads rather easily to one of two evils. In many a discussion, all Chinese things, people, ideas, acts, institutions turn out to be Confucian ones, no matter how varied they are seen to be; as a result, "Confucian" comes to mean simply "Chinese"; its use adds nothing to what we already knew. The word becomes a useless counter, empty of content; and although it is used in many a learned pseudo-explanation, it scarcely amounts to more than a comforting noise. Or worse: the word Confucian, applied to everything indiscriminately, is felt to have content, albeit this content is fuzzily conceived. All Chinese entities, all elements of Chinese culture and history, are wafted into one vast limbo of hazy similarity. All are Confucian; and the variety, the sharpness, the individuality which distinguishes one idea, institution, mode of behavior from another is lost sight of. All could have been accounted for from an examination of one or another of the Confucian classics, or from some idea intuited from the welter of Chinese historical and cultural fact. Confucianism lacks any internal variety, does not change with time, and within the world of Chinese history and culture it includes everything.

If Confucianism is to be a useful thing to talk about, surely we must be able to divide it into parts, and to know what it is not.

In the first place, it is nonsense to say that "Confucian" really means simply "Chinese." Taoism, some forms of Buddhism, pure Legalism, and Taiping mysticism, to name but a few credos, are indisputably Chinese; they are not Confucian. In the second place, Confucianism is no monolith, no repository of the unchanging truth, impervious to time and tide. Han Confucianism, Sung Neo-Confucianism, and Tokugawa

Confucianism are not one philosophy, but many, compounded under three labels; and there are other varieties, often similar to these, but not identical. Most of the papers in this volume are concerned with some aspect of Neo-Confucianism, a movement dating from the late T'ang. And Neo-Confucian thought is not only significantly different from what went before, but very far from a unified philosophy itself. Neo-Confucianism, like Confucianism, is a catch-all term, covering all manner of conflict and variety. There is the variety of a multitude of philosophical schools with subtle differences in metaphysical and psychological theory. More important (because more consequential), there is the variety caused by the inexorable pressures of social and political reality—the variety that results when a cluster of ideas is adapted to very different human problems and activities. This second kind of variety is amply revealed in this volume.

Two broad distinctions will guide this introductory discussion. First, we shall consider Neo-Confucianism as an attempt to recapture what was thought to be the "vision" of its founder, a vision of an ancient utopian past; and as an attempt to apply this vision to the reform of contemporary life. Second, we shall examine "Confucianism" as the point of view of a class—the gentry-literati, the scholar-official—for there is an excellent case to be made, from the studies of Mr. Levenson, Mr. Twitchett, Mrs. Liu, Mr. Yang, and others in this book, that this is what it was. Seen in this light, how does Confucianism work? Here we shall be concerned with one of the most puzzling and most compelling problems in Chinese intellectual history: the relation of Neo-Confucian ideas to the development of state power.

THE NEO-CONFUCIAN VISION

Mr. de Bary ascribes to Neo-Confucianism in China and Japan a number of characteristics, which he has given names: fundamentalism, restorationism, humanism, rationalism, historical-mindedness. He is trying, if I understand him, to give a very general description of one kind of Confucianism in such a way as to show (1) that it has certain characteristics which other Chinese philosophies and views of the world do not have; and (2) that it is a philosophy with a great deal of internal variety to it. I shall not discuss here what Mr. de Bary means by "rationalism"; the term is of course frequently applied to this tradition. "Humanism" is a useful term of characterization, for the various things it could mean—a primary concern with man and social values, a recommendation of humaneness in the ruling of men—are all undeniably Confucian.

But the other three characteristics—fundamentalism, restorationism, and historical-mindedness—seem to me particularly worth comment. Confucians were historical-minded in looking to the past for moral lessons and moral insights, and simply for models for present behavior and present institutions. They were fundamentalist in regarding certain texts, the Classics, from that past—telling of it and reflecting its characteristics—as authoritative, and in being often disposed to take these texts fairly literally. And they were restorationist in seriously wanting to bring back into existence, in all important respects, the golden age of which the Classics spoke. To use Mr. Schwartz's expression, Neo-Confucian leaders were intensely serious about recapturing an original vision and giving it reality in the present time.

It will be objected that this is a characteristic not of Neo-Confucianism, but of all Confucianism. This I think is not quite true. There was a reformist drive among Confucian writers and statesmen of the late T'ang and Sung which is not to be found in earlier centuries. The Han Confucians commonly gave classical accounts of past history an extraordinarily allegorical interpretation, to the point of seeing in the Classics a new, not hitherto existing social and political order, a utopia of the future. For the Sung and later, on the contrary, the "original vision" of Confucius was a glimpse, a sensing, of a perfect human order which had once been, a utopia of the past.

It was not the mere fact that the Neo-Confucians wanted to restore something that marks them off, but the content of their vision, and the enthusiasm that they felt for it. This content is not merely classical. To discover it, we need to look at writings of the visionaries themselves. One of these men is the eleventh-century statesman, historian, and essayist Ou-yang Hsiu, whose portrait, by the Ming painter T'ang Yin, appears at the front of this volume. Ou-yang Hsiu, as our conference discussions repeatedly made evident to us, exercised a critical influence over the entire subsequent history of Neo-Confucian thought. His vision of the classical golden age was of course only one of many; but it is well worth analyzing, for it exhibits and assumes some of the most basic Neo-Confucian conceptions about men, society, and the state.

Down to the end of the Three Royal Dynasties, government followed one principle, and rites and music reached everywhere in the world. After the Three Dynasties, government was divided and followed two separate principles, and "rites and music" became an expression without reality.[1]

Thus does Ou-yang Hsiu open his introduction to the "Monograph on Rites and Music" in the "New T'ang History." What does he mean by this epigram? In antiquity, he explains, every detail of human life was arranged by the setting of sumptuary standards and the devising of rituals and ritual objects. In his widely known "Essay on Fundamentals" ("Pen Lun"), Ou-yang expatiated lovingly on this ancient ritual utopia:

In ancient times, when Yao, Shun, and the founders of the Three Dynasties governed the world, they established the well-field [*ching-t'ien*] pattern of land tenure, registered the population, and distributed fields proportionately, so that any man able to plow would have a field to work. They collected a tenth of the produce, and adjusted labor service and taxes to spur on those who were not diligent, so that all men would devote themselves entirely to farming, and have no leisure for other occupations. Fearing, moreover, that the people might become tired and lazy, and enter upon evildoing, they instituted sacrifices of meat and wine to nourish their bodies, and made stringed and wind instruments, ceremonial platters and tureens, to please their ears and eyes, using the time when they were resting from their labors to teach them the rites.

Ceremonial hunts, marriage and funeral rites, drinking festivals, and archery contests were established, "not only to keep the people from becoming disorderly, but also to teach them, so that they would come to understand the distinction between noble and humble, old and young, and all the great principles of morality." Institutions and ceremonials were devised for every detail and every need of human life, and were made beautiful so that men would enjoy them and accept them easily; in this way, scope was given to men to express their natural impulses, but in a measured and orderly way. But still these wise rulers feared that they had not done enough; and so they established schools at every level of government and society, "choosing the most intelligent among the people to study in them and having them discuss their lessons with one another, in order to stimulate those who were dull and inattentive." "Ah," exclaimed Ou-yang Hsiu, emerging from his revery, "How perfect it was!"[2]

This rhapsody conveys something of the emotive intensity of Neo-Confucian social utopianism; but Ou-yang's "One single principle of government" and the all-pervasiveness of "rites" have an additional significance. For Ou-yang in the "New T'ang History," "rites" are not merely the central part of the sages' dispensation to the people; they are everything, from the well-field system and tithing to the ordered behavior of teachers and students. To govern, in the golden age, was not to enforce dehumanized rules of behavior upon the people, but to give meaning to "goodness" by providing a rich complex of patterns for family life and then to teach the people to love these patterns. To govern is the same thing as to impart moral instruction: *chih* and *chiao* are identical. A ruler's moral teaching was easy to grasp because it was never abstract, but always pointed at what was most familiar—for nothing the people did was not a part of the "rites."

Those who used them to teach the people to be filial and kind, friendly and respectful to elder brothers, loyal and faithful, could do so without ever going beyond such matters as their dwelling places, their work, their clothing and food; plainly it was just these ordinary things with which those who governed the people must have been concerned every day. This is what I mean by saying that there was but one principle of government, so that rites and music reached everywhere.

All this changed. The Ch'in swept away the old order of things, and established a centralized empire; succeeding dynasties followed the Ch'in's methods of government, and even when there was a ruler who wanted to reform the world and turn back to antiquity, he was unable to do so, but found himself slowed to a stop by the habitual ways of his time. What occupied China's rulers now was "the keeping of tax registers, the trying of criminal cases, and providing support for the army." These things, it was said, were the elements of "administration"; it was by these that the people were "governed." The old rituals, which had existed for and among the people, now became the concern of certain special officials, who produced and enacted them only on certain grand ceremonial occasions; it was by this means that the people were "taught." Hence, Ou-yang Hsiu says, government was "divided," since its active, coercive aspect (in effect the formal operation of the state bureaucracy) was no longer identifiable with a beautiful, morally edifying aspect, a universally applicable system of rites. The rites themselves were now empty, lifeless, merely an antique relic of what once was. Their details were now scarcely understood even by the official experts in such matters; they were never seen at all by the ordinary man, and their real meaning was no longer known to anyone. Though the government might make a fetish of court ceremony and the study of ancient ritual, the living tradition, the rites' transforming power for good over the people, was gone.[3]

Ou-yang Hsiu's vision is no specific reform program. Over details of reform there was not only endless difference among Sung Confucians, but bitter political conflict. His vision, however, deserves attention for the obvious fervor with which he felt it, and for its underlying assumptions—assumptions which were widely shared.

Let us look closely at some of these assumptions.

First, what is to be restored is an integrated human order, exhibiting an identity of state with society and a unity of value and formal function. If the restoration is accomplished, people will cease to strive selfishly; they will be "transformed," will come to be devoted only to virtue. Human life will be whole, morally and aesthetically alive.

Second, this envisioned order is contrasted with the actual political order: a government by force, military and legal; a dirty political world in which the motives of fame and gain are dominant. Here we can see an instance of that struggle between theory and practice which Mr. Liu examines—a struggle, as he puts it, which went on incessantly between Confucianism as a morally oriented body of thought and the state as a power structure.

Third, there is the stress on rites, considered as embodying both the content of righteousness and a therapy producing it, together with an almost magical, mystical force for *chiao-hua*, moral transformation of the world. What this transformation was thought to bring about, as we can see from glimpses of the vision in such men as Chu Hsi and Wang Yang-ming, was a universal turning away from fame and gain, a state of things in which all men, concerned only with the perfecting of their virtue, were as contented with their places in the scheme of things as if they were the members of one family.

Fourth, an organic analogy is implicit in this way of talking about unity and the moral effect of the rites. Ou-yang Hsiu makes it quite explicit: China, he says in the "Essay on Fundamentals," is to be doctored as a doctor treats his patient, by nourishing its vital force, its *ch'i*; and this *ch'i* of society is precisely the spirit of harmony, universal satisfaction, and selfless love of virtue which the rites engender. Only by attending to *ch'i* could men succeed with such undertakings as the elimination of Buddhism.[4] The modern world, other writers were to argue, was not yet "good" enough for a return to the much admired well-field system of antiquity.

Ou-yang Hsiu's seemingly casual analogy of the doctor and his patient, like Plato's, is of great interest, for it explicitly and very naturally links his political and social idealism with a very compelling idea which accounts for at least half of all Neo-Confucian intellectual preoccupations: the cultivation of the moral self.

Personal self-cultivation for Neo-Confucian moralists provides the model for the total "cultivation" of society. It integrates one's nature, eliminates "double-mindedness," so that the values one subscribes to and one's spontaneous feelings, actions, and thoughts coincide. It eliminates hidden base motives, leads to and is perfected by sincerity in ritual. It makes a man's moral nature sound, preventing him from being affected by "external" temptations (as society is led astray by Buddhism).

Moreover, it is essential to literary activity—an important point, since the Neo-Confucian movement was developed and carried on by men whose claim to prestige and position was their mastery of literary tradition, and their ability to read and write well. How does one learn to write? The cultivation of self and the reform of society provided the guiding ideas. There is the idea of wholeness: that there should be no hiatus between "mind and hand," motive and expression. The result will be literary naturalness and freshness, an end of hackneyed language. There is the ideal of selflessness: that writing should not be for ulterior motives, not for "fame and gain." There is the longing look back to the inimitable beauty of the golden age. And finally, the idea that good writing can't be schemed or forced but must result from a total cultivation of mind and moral nature.

Clearly, then, individual moral self-cultivation is a step toward the reform of society as a whole, particularly if the cultivators are men of influence. An emperor whose mind is "rectified" not only will have the courage and the vision to make needed institutional changes, but will recognize cultivated men and (this was always, as Mr. Schwartz says, in the Confucian program) put them in positions from which they can exert the maximum moral influence on the rest of the world.

Mr. Schwartz's "polarities," alternative emphases which he finds continually ordering the range of choice of the Confucian thinker or statesman, are evident in these conceptions. There is at one pole the interest in governing the world, reforming society and state; at the other, the interest in cultivating the self, nourishing one's own virtue or powers. Within each emphasis there is the contrast between the "inner" and the "outer," between spirit and overt behavior, virtue and rite. Ou-yang Hsiu's antithesis of *chih* (government) and *chiao* (instruction, doctrine) catches the age-old dualism of action and knowledge. In all these ideas there is a characteristic holism: cultivation of whatever kind had to be total, and it always aimed at a closing of gaps, some sort of "making whole." Self-cultivation, specifically, meant an overcoming of the paralyzing discord between the individual's values and his actual behavior, overt, emotional, and psychic. The idea of reform meant closing the gulf between ideal and reality. Ou-yang Hsiu's utopian nostalgia may justly be called totalitarian; for what he regretted was the fact that the state structure and the workings of human society had become two separate things.

Let us now consider how the Neo-Confucian vision applies to some of the papers in this volume.

The two papers that describe clan institutions—the study of clan rules by Mrs. Liu, and the detailed history of the charitable estates of the Fan clan by Mr. Twitchett—have a special relevance to the Neo-Confucian vision. As we have seen, community rituals and mores were very important to Ou-yang Hsiu, as producing a spirit of harmony (like the harmony in an ideal family) which he evidently felt would be spread over the whole of society. Profound social disturbances occurred after the middle of the T'ang: the growth of cities, the dislocation of populations due to wars and uprisings, basic changes in the mode of peasant landholding and taxation, and the breaking up, especially in the north, of powerful family structures. Efforts were accordingly made by idealistic reformers in the early Sung to revive strong clan organizations among the people, to compensate for the scattering of clan members over widely separated areas.

Initiative for the strengthening of clan institutions came typically from literati clan members, who in many cases obtained some measure of state support or official approval for their efforts. These efforts took many forms—drawing up rituals for the ancestral temples, financing the construction of clan buildings, establishing schools, composing clan regulations and genealogies, and in some instances devising completely new institutions such as the charitable estates—which were patterned, if Mr. Twitchett is correct, on a Buddhist rather than a Confucian institutional model. In this way the literati were able to work some of their ideas, derived from the "great" or classical tradition which was theirs, into the "little" traditions of community life and peasant mores. Even the charitable estates were explicitly designed to foster what the visionaries regarded as the animating spirit of ancient society: the fields were in the first instance for the support of ancestral temples and rituals; the equal disbursements among members were designed to foster a feeling of solidarity and common interest as well as provide for the needy (this last function itself an important feature of the Mencian sort of utopia).

Here, as in their attempts to reform and reanimate the state, the literati visionaries were not in an idealist void. They too were clan members; and a clan, even in a single community, might include peasants, landlords, officials, and shopkeepers or artisans as well—rocky soil for nurturing a vision, and as it turned out, too rocky. It proved quite impossible to spread the spirit of affection of the immediate family over an entire clan with all its occupational and economic disparity. Well-to-do members tried to take advantage of the less fortunate; regulations for the handling of the estates, the distribution of responsibilities, and the disbursal of funds had to be made constantly more detailed and more rigorous. Clan regulations that evolved in this way were much more severe in the restraints they imposed, and had an ideological tone much tougher and quite different from those which were purely literati creations. On the other hand, while Neo-Confucian moralists were extremely strict in forbidding the remarriage of widows and in insisting on absolute obedience to parents, clan rules were in these matters much more lenient than moral purists. Here the rules seem to reflect the actual moral code of the peasantry.

Clans sometimes became fairly effective organs of social control, to the extent that the state occasionally delegated to them some of its police power. The state was wary, however, of allowing the clans to acquire independent power; and where this possibility became imminent, the literati-bureaucrats, for all their clan interests, instinctively sided with the state; for the vision condemned above all else division in society, whether caused by personal selfish interests or by the interests of larger groups. The emergence of separate local centers of power was never what the literati wanted, in spite of reformers' idealistic talk of reviving features of ancient feudal decentralization. At the same time, the clan's wishes could not be ignored. While it was to the clan's interest to have some of its members acquire official rank, the clan's desire to avoid involvement with government was, inevitably, a pressure upon any member in office to avoid a dangerous political course into which he might be led by following his conscience as a Confucian minister; and as Mr. Yang shows, a bureaucrat found himself under constant pressure from clan connections to abuse his office in order to help his relatives, or to strive improperly to advance himself. In such ways we see the bright vision of the Confucian idealist not only colliding with a hard and very different social reality, but actually tending to produce developments that conflicted with that vision.

We have in Mr. Hall's and Mr. Shively's papers on Japan another case in which the Neo-Confucian vision of a golden past was confronted with a very alien reality. It was surely a very different sort of confrontation: among other things, as Mr. de Bary makes plain, the golden age to which the Japanese Confucian thinker harked back was not a native one, not Japanese but Chinese. We would expect this to be embarrassing, in view of the great stress placed by men like Ou-yang Hsiu on the value of a living tradition of rites deriving from antiquity. Here we find a powerful reason for that ostensibly strange alliance between the *jusha* (Confucianist) and the Shintoist. Confucianism always craved native, local roots and indigenous rituals. Shinto had both.

The *jusha*, moreover, unlike his Chinese counterpart, was not a typical member of a ruling elite; he occupied a tenuous position on the lower fringe of the Japanese elite. In this position he was confronted not with a society and state which had "degenerated" from an ancient ideal order, but with a vigorous society and political structure quite unprepared to acknowledge automatically his claims to moral authority, and demanding of him, if he were to be successful, tangible services and useful knowledge. In a sense he had trouble meeting this demand: his learning, based as it was on Chinese books, was not always directly relevant to Japanese problems; and in his political counseling, he had little of the wide sense of the possible we see in the Chinese bureaucrat.

More important, Neo-Confucianism in the Tokugawa lacked the compelling force it had had when the vision was a new thing in the Sung.
It was less a force for reform, apparently, than a scheme for rationalizing
the existing political order and supplying political authorities with a
useful ideology of duty to parents and rulers.

To a large extent, of course, this is the role Neo-Confucian ethics
had come to play in China by the seventeenth century, or at least by
the eighteenth. Unlike the *jusha*, however, the Confucian-educated
bureaucrats in China, while individually dependent on the throne for
their position, were collectively indispensable to it, and even as individuals they regularly had great power. A particularly sharp contrast
is afforded by cases in which a Confucian tutor exercised great influence
over a ruler. In China this was likely to indicate a high degree of literati
dominance in the total scene; Ch'eng I, in the eleventh century, came
close to equating the respect he would have the emperor pay his Confucian mentors with imperial respect and even subservience to the literati as a class. Another sometime tutor to an imperial minor, Motoda
Eifu in Meiji Japan, we may fairly take as a surviving example of the
Tokugawa *jusha*, and one who was favored with a position surpassing
that of any of his predecessors. Yet, as Mr. Shively describes him, Motoda, unlike Ch'eng I, was hardly an official of power and consequence.
And we obviously do not find behind Motoda a reformist party fired
with a vision, working through him and upon the ruler to effect broad
changes in society and state. The Meiji emperor, indeed, seems at times
scarcely a real ruler. Motoda was greatly respected for his sincerity,
and may indeed have exerted a profound influence on the emperor's
thinking; yet one suspects that for a long time his unwitting role was to
keep his imperial disciple preoccupied with other than practical matters,
while the substantial problems of state were decided by the tough-
minded oligarchs, Ito, Yamagata, and others, men who may have been
prepared to use the Confucian code of social ethics for popular indoctrination, but who were hardly devoted to it.

Why, one asks, should the Confucian social and ethical philosophy
have seemed pertinent and useful to the Japanese state in its transformation during the Meiji emperor's reign, while in China it seemed to stand
in the way of modernization? Both Mr. de Bary and Mr. Levenson, in
different ways, raise this question.

Perhaps the old social vision retained to the very end in China more
of a compelling hold on imaginations than it ever acquired in Japan—
a vision which, as in Ou-yang Hsiu, filled out men's lives to the last nook
and cranny. It may be a measure of the dying power of the vision that
for some of the keenest-minded at the end of China's empire the only

way to move forward seemed to be to construct utopian pictures of society, such as K'ang Yu-wei's radical "Great Union," which would be new, yet somehow still Confucian. If necessary, the old sacred names could be dispensed with; but the new vision must retain the quality of wholeness, the picture of a human order free of all divisiveness, all dirty striving after "fame and gain," and bound together by all-embracing bonds of affection. Far-reaching (indeed, far-fetched) attempts were made, by K'ang Yu-wei and T'an Ssu-t'ung, to breathe life into this vision. And by "working at Confucianism for a social purpose," as Mr. Levenson says, they were after all doing something not utterly different from what Ou-yang Hsiu had urged. Yet somehow it didn't work. The Confucian way of talking by this time may have come to be too much associated—even in the minds of those who most longed to make Confucianism work—with actual ways of thinking and social habits which the vision itself condemned.

The problem of diagnosing Confucianism's last illness in China remains perplexing. But what seems to me the most salient point in Mr. Levenson's paper is, I am convinced, an insight of really fundamental value for our understanding of the Chinese state. This is his analysis of what is so unreal about the "love-death" of Confucianism and monarchy. The alert reader will notice how much some of the other papers, written later (my own included), owe to this insight. The problem it illumines is the relationship between the scholar-official and the throne. To this question we now turn.

THE SCHOLAR-OFFICIAL AND THE STATE

The emperor institution, Mr. Levenson argues, was not entirely a Confucian institution. In the old, the real empire, the court with its imperial household officials, eunuchs, and elite guards stood in a strange relationship to the civil bureaucracy and the social class of gentry-literati who filled it. Each needed the other, leaned on the other. The throne needed the scholar-bureaucrats' cooperation and acquiescence to govern at all. And the scholar-bureaucrats relied on the throne to maintain a stable political order within which they could enjoy a high status and through which they could enrich themselves, gradually destroying the structure and undermining the state in the process.

Each needed the other. Yet each was dangerous to the other, pulled against the other, struggled to restrain the other. The lore of ministerial loyalty and of respect owed by the prince to his servitors gives something to both sides and makes of the emperor institution a Confucian thing, yet marks the tension between them. But surely Levenson is right in saying that on the whole the myths of an ideal past—the "model emperor lore"—were an implied reproach to present rulers who needed to rule by law and force, and needed, also, extravagance and display.

The suggestion is unmistakable. The Neo-Confucian vision described above was the inspiration of articulate members of the socially important families we call the gentry, the families which produced schoolteachers and philosophers, degree-holders — and bureaucrats. How does this vision look when we try regarding it not as a utopian ideal, but as the ideological weapon of a social class with a specific political role?

The question sharply put is the relationship between Neo-Confucianism and despotic power.

The power of the state apparatus and of the emperor steadily increased in the later centuries. The history of Chinese thought by itself cannot, of course, explain completely this rise of despotism. Certainly related to it was the economic condition of the literati, the existence or nonexistence of enormously powerful families, the increase in the number of potential bureaucrats upon whom the state could draw, and the personality of powerful emperors, as well as some of the harsher accidents of military history. Sometimes, too, the development of institutions appears to follow a logic of its own, and it is clear that a purely institutional study of the development and exercise of Chinese imperial power would have great value. But institutions are fashioned and operated by men with purposes, guided by ideals and fears.

The values and ideological commitments of the literati would therefore seem to be directly relevant to this institutional change. The Confucian gentleman, moreover, thought of himself ideally as a *ch'en*, a "minister" to his "prince"; it was in this capacity that he hoped to realize himself most fully. His vision seemed at almost every point to imply criticism of some feature of public life or political practice. We might expect either (1) that the articulate defender of the vision, the scholar-gentleman, would succeed in remaking the state in the image of his idea; or (2) failing that, that his philosophy would remain (for it did endure) a perpetual vantage point against the claims of emperors to be all-wise as well as all-powerful, a perpetual inspiration for and justification for criticism and remonstrance against present-day degenerate political ways—that it would always, in short, lend intellectual strength to the social strength of the gentleman class as a counterweight to the political structure and the power of the court. Did either of these things happen?

It can hardly be claimed that the state was actually transfigured. Indeed, only the most extreme idealistic reformers claimed that it should be, literally. But can it be said at least that the state was remolded into something significantly nearer to what the Confucians wished it to become? There is evidence in several of our papers that makes this view difficult: over and over we see the values that coincide with literati interests, or that reflect a vision such as Ou-yang Hsiu's, pitted against other values which (following Mr. Levenson) we would ascribe to the emperor and the state structure, with the latter winning out. Mr. Liu has sketched the long history of the opposition between two sets of standards for bureaucratic behavior, broadly an antithesis between a moral criterion and an efficiency criterion for office. The Han conception of a "rigorous" official was deformed, in the hands of Confucian moralistic historians, into the conception of an abusive and venal bureaucrat. But the encyclopedias and the actual operation of official rating schemes reveal that with the unified empires of T'ang and Sung, the criterion of efficiency in administration became the decisive one at the level of actual government operation, if not in the pages of the histories. The picture is complex, for the moral criterion continued to be recognized, verbally, as the primary one—even though men continued to get promoted for their efficiency rather than for their moral purity, as long as they were not too brazen about bribe-taking.

As Mr. Liu suggests, the tension here was a tension between the moral orientation of the literati and the practical needs of the state as a power structure. Mr. Hucker's paper brings out the conflict between literati and imperial interests more sharply. He examines the history of the institutions of remonstrance and surveillance, which are of crucial importance in the relationship between minister and prince. The modern (Ming) censorate combined, he points out, two functions which were institutionally separate prior to the Mongol dynasty: surveillance of the bureaucracy, and remonstrance to the throne. The first is Legalist in origin and spirit, the second Confucian; for Legalism meant insistence on rigid conformity to law in administration, whereas Confucianism specified that the *tao* and the welfare of the world take precedence over the ruler's will and the power of the state. The legal-bureaucratic structure from Han on was a Legalist-Confucian synthesis—Legalist in its forms and its rigor, and in its stress on form, Confucian in the values and ideology it reverenced and brought to bear when it safely could.

After Sung the Confucian side of this balance was weakened and the Legalist strengthened: the remonstrance function was made merely an appendage of the surveillance function. During the Ming, imperial reprisals against outspokenness on the part of remonstrators were extremely severe. Moreover, Hucker argues, the content of remonstrances came to stress "Legalist" values: the safety of the state, the strength of the dynasty, and the authority of the ruler rather than the welfare of the people. And surveillance itself became more Legalist than ever:

the number of censors increased greatly, and they became more and more enthusiastic in their search for errors, for any bureaucratic departure from the highly detailed administrative code. The Censorate was more and more obviously an arm of the monarch against the rest of the bureaucracy. Memorials of Ming censors make it clear that the throne's rigorist, power-oriented point of view, far from being blunted by Confucian idealism, actually penetrated far down into the bureaucracy. Hucker indeed finds an ultimately Confucian character in the Ming censor in the sincerity of his loyalty to the throne; but it is plainly a Confucianism of almost complete, despairing surrender to the "ruler-father."

If the material in my own paper means what it appears to, the imperial triumph was consummated in the Ch'ing. The literati were taught (and apparently most of them believed) that running the state was the court's business, not theirs; that criticism of the monarch was inconceivable, so inconceivable that even feeling critical must be regarded as a moral failure on the part of the critic to "identify his likes and dislikes with those of his prince"; and that any sort of political collaboration among members of the bureaucracy was evidence of disloyalty or at best venality. Still, the very fact that emperors were preoccupied with driving home these ideological lessons indicates that suppressed conflicts of outlook between the bureaucracy and the throne remained.

Mr. Yang's paper has much that is to the same point, but it also introduces difficulties which, I think, make it impossible to regard the bureaucracy, the literati, and the holders of an anti-rigorist, Confucian-idealist point of view as in any real sense a single cohesive group opposed to the power orientation of the throne.

Mr. Yang offers his paper both as a contribution to our knowledge of China and as a small but important amendment to the sociological theory of bureaucracy. Weber ascribes to bureaucracy four characteristics, all tending to maximize its effectiveness and predictability: (1) it exhibits a hierarchy of authority; (2) the bureaucrat operates within a formal structure of legal rules; (3) he maintains a high degree of impersonality in all his official acts; and (4) he is characteristically a trained specialist at some particular task. But the Chinese bureaucrat does not fit the model; whatever his responsibilities at a given time, he was not a trained specialist, nor was he supposed to be. On the contrary, his qualification for office, and the qualification tested in the state examinations, was his mastery of a body of *general* knowledge about society, proprieties, and moral norms governing human relationships—i.e., his knowledge of the Classics.

If we accept Mr. Yang's analysis, we might interpret this generalism of the Chinese bureaucrat, distinguishing him from the usual bureaucratic type, as a mark of the strength of the literati interest and viewpoint, able in this important way to qualify the usual tendencies of a power structure. The bureaucrat was trained to be sensitive to pressures from the society of which he was a part; and this in turn caused his behavior constantly to deviate from the other bureaucratic ideals of formality and impersonality. We can picture the bureaucrat as a scholar-gentleman, with his roots in society, sensitive to the varied complexities of individual social and family situations and adapting the law and his own behavior to fit them, accommodating himself to state power (without which there would be no bureaucracy and no bureaucrat), but checking it simply by being what he was.

Perhaps this picture is a true one. But it is also true that, no matter how he behaved, the bureaucrat who tried to state his ideals of official conduct is frequently found to stress the principles of impersonality and of conformity to formal rules. Moreover, the similarity between the points of view of the bureaucrat and the throne went very deep. The lower limit of the official bureaucratic hierarchy (in the Ch'ing) was the office of county magistrate. Below him, as Mr. Yang shows, the yamen aides and operatives constituted a staff of true specialists, often technically trained, but among these, business was characteristically carried on by direct, informal personal arrangement, with endless opportunity for the formation of cliques, corruption, and improper influence. The magistrate, almost helplessly trying to hold his staff to his own formal standards, reminds one of nothing so much as the Yung-cheng Emperor (reigned 1723–35), lecturing his officials at the top of the bureaucracy and warning them to subordinate their interests to his, to deal with him individually and not to form "factions" or undermine his decisions.

The situation cannot be described simply in terms of a clash between subversive Confucianism and authoritarian "Legalism"; for the bureaucrat was pulled in both directions. Indeed, one of the most striking things in Mr. Yang's paper is the extent to which he is able to show the bureaucratic values of formality and impersonality to have been taken up into Confucian ethics. A conscientious official such as Wang Hui-tsu, caught between conflicting obligations to family, friends, and emperor, shunned the normal way out—the way of nepotism, bribe taking, and the struggle to advance oneself by influence and alliances. Revulsion against just this sort of behavior among officials had been one of the basic motivations for the Neo-Confucian revival; and so Wang recommended that the official make the necessary personal sacrifices to conform to strict bureaucratic standards, precisely the standards making for efficient exercise of imperial authority. The degree to which writers on bureaucratic ethics came to echo the throne's point of view is truly surprising. One of these, for example, warns officials almost exactly as did both the Yung-cheng Emperor and the Ch'ien-lung Emperor (reigned 1736–96), not to assume that a colleague who has been promoted has obtained his promotion through the influence of a clique, or that a degraded official has received a political stabbing, but to credit higher authority in its wisdom with having given the man what he deserved. It would seem that instead of staying the official against the throne, the Neo-Confucian vision had driven him into the emperor's arms.

We must therefore reconsider the possibility that the despotism of the later empire was actually a consequence of the Neo-Confucian movement, possibly even an intended consequence of that movement; in a word, that Neo-Confucian idealism was in some special way ideologically conducive to despotism. Is this possible?

It seems plain that after the beginning of the Ming dynasty in 1368, and especially by the time of the Yung-lo reign (1403–24), the emperor and his advisers assumed that indoctrination of the bureaucracy in the ethical ideas of Chu Hsi (1130–1200) would be a mainstay of the state—assumed this to the extent of making his teachings orthodox and instilling them through the examination and school system. Furthermore, Neo-Confucian visionaries dreamed of a restoration of the sort of human condition they thought had existed in antiquity under the rule of sage-emperors. In the later Neo-Confucian empire, especially in the Ming and Ch'ing, the court insistently maintained that the reigning emperor—patent booby though he might be—was in fact a sage. Mr. Hucker has pointed to the increasingly obsequious language that had to be used in addressing the Ming emperor. This pose plainly implied that if the vision hadn't quite been realized, this was not the emperor's fault, but that of those below, perhaps of the very ones who were critical. Moreover, to a very large extent, this claim was acknowledged by the Neo-Confucian intellectuals; for they offered a vision of a harmonious, noncompetitive world devoted to virtue, as a reproach to the existing political and social order of which they themselves were a part. Thereby they were self-condemned, for they were forced to suspect their own discontent of being an instance of the modern decadence they deplored, of hiding a suppressed desire in themselves to attract attention, justify themselves, or get ahead. Their visionary reproach to the existing order became the substance for self-reproach.

Chu Hsi, in some of his pieces of advice to students, caught this twist of idealistic Confucian thought very subtly; it was this talent that made him so marvelously useful to the state. And we find much the same streak in Ou-yang Hsiu.

Ou-yang Hsiu was a man of many parts: statesman, reformer and visionary, poet, prose stylist, and historian, the author of one history (of the Five Dynasties) and one of two editors-in-chief of a second, the "New T'ang History." These were political histories of fairly recent times, constantly concerned with the lives and doings of emperors and officials and their relation to one another, with types of men and situations familiar to Ou-yang and his contemporaries from their own political experience.

Ou-yang himself was centrally involved in a conflict among factions in the bureaucracy in the 1030's and 1040's. The leader of the reform party (of Neo-Confucian visionaries) was Fan Chung-yen, the same Fan who started Mr. Twitchett's "charitable estates." Ou-yang in 1033 wrote a forceful letter to Fan when the latter was an official remonstrator, urging him to action and chiding him for not speaking out. Subsequently Fan and his party were outplayed and disgraced. Ou-yang came vigorously and openly to Fan's support and as a result suffered exile (i.e., demotion to a minor and remote post) along with others of the reform faction.

En route, he wrote letters to Yin Shu, a close friend and fellow exile, in which he tried to draw lessons from their experience. People marvel, said Ou-yang, at the rise and fall of Fan's party; this merely shows their historical naïveté. This sort of thing happened constantly in ancient times, and the only question then asked was whether or not the partisans were right. But men who are in the right and who have met defeat are not, he declared, to be admired for their fortitude or pitied for their misfortunes; fortitude in a good man should be taken for granted, and as for misfortunes, we are far better off than the ancients, who used to be chopped in two, boiled alive, and worse. If the histories include accounts of people who have gone to death bravely maintaining the right, it is not at all to excite admiration for such conduct, but merely to warn modern degenerates and cowards that there are some situations in which this just has to be done. In Ou-yang's view, the proper concern of an exile was with resignation and self-cultivation; above all, he must shun self-pity and resentment. For his own part, he would devote himself to his duties in penance for his "indolence" at the capital.[5]

What has happened, in brief, is that the visionary ideal of selfless individual conduct has tended in Ou-yang Hsiu's thinking to shift responsibility downward from the ruler and his advisers to the individual bureaucrat. The old ethical code has been supplanted. When the good man meets misfortune (mistreatment at court), when something goes wrong with the world around him, the first thing he should do is to suspect himself of an impure attitude and try to mend it by self-cultivation.

Ou-yang Hsiu's letter to Yin was a long way from the fine achievement of political indoctrination in the Ch'ing, however. It took centuries during which more and more power was concentrated in the emperor's hands and the ordinary bureaucrat's economic position became more and more dependent on the state, for the authoritarian potentialities of Neo-Confucian idealism to develop fully. Meanwhile, the vision was indeed an inspiration to protest, and Ou-yang Hsiu was no political coward. He took it for granted that the emperor should delegate authority to ministers and then respect them. The old ideal of the man of principle speaking up in criticism to his prince was strong with him; in his letter to Fan we find him saying,

Although the remonstrator's position is relatively humble, it is like that of the prime minister; for if the emperor says "That is not good," the prime minister may say "It is good"; if the emperor says "That is so," he may say "It is not so." . . . Likewise, if the emperor says "That is right," the remonstrator may say "It is wrong"; and if the emperor says "This ought to be done," he may reply "It ought not to be done" . . .[6]

It is hardly to be wondered at that the Yung-cheng Emperor found it necessary to box Ou-yang Hsiu's ears posthumously.[7]

Indeed the great Chu Hsi also, in spite of the heavy stress in his moral philosophy on the individual's duty to parents and rulers, had a keen eye for the failings of the great and could be very sharp-tongued about pointing them out. The general impression of him as a man utterly preoccupied with personal ethics and with metaphysical ideas remote from the real world, is an image he owes to the careful work of imperial editors of the early Ming. Actually Chu picked the institutions of his day apart realistically, and sometimes spoke bluntly.

A very revealing incident of this sort occurred in the summer of 1180—revealing not only because it puts Chu in a fairer perspective, but because of the light it throws on the relationship between the literati and imperial power. There was, it seems, a drought, and the emperor was driven (in a traditional gesture of penitence before this affliction from Heaven) to issue a general request for "honest advice." Chu, a mere prefect at the time, was angered by the throne's constant reliance on court favorites whom he considered worthless, and took this opportunity to submit a blistering criticism of the emperor. Worthy officials there were, said Chu, but

Your majesty consults intimately with only two or three favorites. On the one hand, these men confuse your majesty's mind and purpose, with the result that your majesty does not have confidence in the great Way of your royal predecessors, but instead takes delight in base counsels of expediency, failing to appreciate the good advice of upright men and being satisfied with the vulgar viewpoint of personal intimates of low character. On the other hand, they gather around themselves men who shamelessly seek to serve their own interests. These men, according to their status as military or civilian officials, become the protégés of your favorites, who then proceed to assist secretly anyone they are pleased with, and place them in good positions, while secretly slandering those they dislike, openly taking steps to get rid of them. . . . Many of your majesty's officials . . . owe their position to these favorites and follow their cue in every move they make.

There is talk of partisanship here, and Chu, in regarding partisan behavior as selfish, divisive, and bad, is undoubtedly closer to the implications of Neo-Confucian idealism than was Ou-yang Hsiu (who boldly defended the thesis that factions in the bureaucracy were sometimes good). But this doctrine that officials should never join together, which was in the Ch'ing to become a club held by the throne over the heads of its servitors, Chu in the twelfth century surprisingly turned against the emperor himself: it is he who was tainted with "partisanship" and guilty of abetting it.

Chu's following remarks would have made a beautiful analysis of the political situation in the 1780's and 1790's, and would as surely have driven the Ch'ien-lung Emperor into a murderous fury:

An independent man, if there should be one, would only withdraw and preserve his own honor, without ever daring to offer a word of criticism. Those who hold justice especially dear may perhaps express some concern for the situation, and may speak out against one or two members of this crowd, but not only are they unable to do such men any serious harm, indeed never at all do they dare to speak plainly and point out the root of the trouble.

And the "root of the trouble," Chu said explicitly, was that the emperor's mind was not properly cultivated: he did not really know right from wrong. Chu then pointed out as a fact something that eighteenth-century emperors later warned their officials never to suggest even as a possibility: that these evil favorites were actually usurping the throne's authority—that appointments and decisions which seemed to be the emperor's were really theirs. In these circumstances, Chu asked, how could good men do other than despair? How could the state be restored to health and the foreign enemy defeated?

The emperor was angry, but decided against punishing or even dismissing Chu: for, said one of his advisers, "The more your majesty shows your hatred of fame-seekers like this, the more numerous will their admirers be. If you do anything, will it not just serve to enhance his prestige?"[8] Here was surely a revealing admission, and a clear indication that in the Sung at least the court had to reckon with a literati class which had real strength.

The relation between Confucian idealism and despotic imperial power during the long history of the later empire was, we can see, highly complex, but we can try to summarize it. The holism in the Neo-Confucian vision, the idea that a harmony of feeling should unite all levels of society and state, was partly (or potentially) a reproach to state power, to rulers. Mr. Levenson is right in saying that the lore of the sage-emperor was an implied rebuke to imperfect living emperors. But the vision had another aspect: a regret that the gap, the tension, between the ruler with his power apparatus and its values of efficiency and utility, and the scholar or bureaucrat with his commitment to rites, tradition, and the ideal of "transforming" the people, existed at all. Tension meant lack of mental composure somewhere; it meant the presence of an impulse to follow one's own interest—the poison of society.

For this tension both sides could be deemed at fault; but with the emperor claiming the status of sage—a claim made easier by the political necessity of constantly calling him one—the weight of condemnation fell on the literati-officials, with the Neo-Confucian idealists (themselves literati-officials) doing the condemning and the emperor and his aides piously quoting them. For the idealistic vision had always been a reproach not only to the ruler and his latter-day mode of governing by a structure of law and force, but also to those who were involved in this structure, the bureaucrats who had surrendered to "expediency." It was among them, the visionaries felt, more than anywhere, that the lack of the ancient selfless devotion to virtue was visible.

What happened, then, was this: very gradually, while always actually looking to its own interest and sensitive to its power position, the throne assumed the mantle of reform itself, and pressed reform—not reform of the government structure, but personal reform, the personal cultivation of virtue—upon the entire bureaucratic class. This it did, and with special vigor from the fourteenth century on, through a Neo-Confucianism now become a state-enforced orthodoxy, with its meddlesome interest in the redrawing of institutions and its tendency to make a virtue of righteous and loyal criticism thoughtfully edited out. Idealistic scholar-bureaucrats were peculiarly vulnerable to this treatment, because reformers had always chiefly hoped to realize their vision by working through the ruler. Now they had him—and he them. The heavens were out of joint: they accepted the guilt, which had once been by common consent the ruler's, not only because they had to but because their convictions drove them to. They sometimes felt guilty even when they saw nothing wrong in what they had done or thought—even when they were abused. We have seen this in Ou-yang Hsiu; and surely Mr. Hucker's censor Tso Kuang-tou, screaming from his dungeon that he had not been able to repay his "ruler-father," was guilt-ridden also, precisely because he could not help feeling self-justified.

At the same time, however, the moral initiative, the ability to use the critical force of the vision, shifted away from the scholar and the official to the throne. And this is not surprising. As Mr. Levenson argues, official corruption, the building up of private wealth, the perpetual pursuit of "fame and gain," were not mere blemishes in the "official way"; they were part of its essence, without which, for all its touted Confucian ideals, the bureaucracy as a counterweight to the throne scarcely existed. The throne could not eradicate these ways, but it must try to check them; this it did both by strategic handling of its officials and by Legalistic rigor, and also by using that part of the vision itself which had been directed against the dirtiness of bureaucratic life. So fortified, the throne was increasingly able to dismiss even the most high-minded criticism of itself as basely motivated. Even Chu Hsi was a "fame-seeker."

And so the great paradox of Neo-Confucianism is that, having started as a protest against the existing order of things, it ended as a state-sponsored system of thought for keeping in humbled silence the very ones who might have protested. The protest potential of Neo-Confucian idealism was never eradicated, and from time to time it did find devious expression; but its eruptions were nearly always directed at moral decadence in society and bureaucratic life, or alleged bad tendencies in thought and writing, or—at most, and rarely—at supposed moral failings in some powerful official or clique, rather than at the throne or the institutions of the state itself.

Neo-Confucianism was a movement of thought in great ferment in the Sung, exhibiting great variety of opinion and range of interest. In the Ming, it was rigidified and its character as a state ideology was defined, but sharp clashes between the officials and the throne, as Mr. Hucker shows, occurred repeatedly—clashes in which the specific point of disagreement was often trivial, but in which the fundamental question of moral dominance, of whether the throne was to be the teacher of the literati or the literati the mentors of the throne, was crucially important. And in the Ch'ing, by the eighteenth century, Chinese despotism had become as perfect as human things become; not only was the emperor's command of political power unqualified, but his moral authority, even his intellectual authority, was paramount, and the literati now accepted this situation as natural and right.

In retrospect, it seems that nothing else could have happened. There were many reasons why the literati lost the independent power and prestige they had enjoyed: stern and impersonal institutional forces and the fickle whims of political fortune played their part. But the fate of Confucian utopia was the fate that history so often metes out to bright illusions—to the hopes of the Roman Republic, of Rousseau, of Marx. The Neo-Confucian visionaries wanted a utopian totalitarianism, minus the trappings and sinews, the harsh reality, of power. What they got was not what they had wanted. But it was what we might have expected.

Wm. Theodore de Bary

SOME COMMON TENDENCIES IN NEO-CONFUCIANISM

The present paper consists of some very general reflections on the meaning and use of the term "Confucian" as applied to the later development of this school of thought in China and Japan. In a loose sense it may be considered an attempt at a rough definition or description of Neo-Confucianism. That such an attempt is justified is suggested by our own perplexity in defining the scope and character of the inquiry which this Committee has launched upon. The fact that at times we have been tempted to speak of "Confucianisms" in the plural, in order to stress the diversity of both Confucian thought and the social contexts in which it functioned, draws attention to our dilemma without really pointing a way out. That is, it serves to put us on guard against simplistic characterizations of Confucianism, but leaves unanswered the basic question: What do various schools of thought have in common which we seek to designate by using the term "Confucian," whether in the singular or plural?

Moreover, quite apart from the importance of this question as a matter of basic terminology in dealing with intellectual history, it arises constantly in attempts to characterize traditional Chinese and Japanese culture in relation to other cultures or in the framework of world history. The fact that all East Asian societies have a Confucian tradition, and have encountered common problems in adjusting from this tradition to the needs of the modern world, inevitably calls forth from world historians and students of comparative culture, as well as from Far Eastern specialists, generalizations which involve the term "Confucian."

I do not propose to examine the use of the term in this very broad sense, but rather to work back toward a clearer definition of its meaning in intellectual history by disengaging it, for the moment, from some of its wider associations. To illustrate my purpose, let me cite a few examples of the use of the term "Confucian" in recent studies by John Fairbank, who for some time has been wrestling with some of the problems that are involved here. Discussing the failure of China in the nineteenth century to respond more rapidly to the challenge of the West, he says: "China's comparative failure in its varied aspects may perhaps be summed up as the failure of the traditional "Confucian" social and political order, as represented in its ruling class."[1] Here he seems to be reaffirming a judgment made earlier in his *United States and China*: ". . . the movement for modernization in China was obstructed at every turn by the narrow ignorance and prejudice of the Confucian literati. This lack of responsiveness in China, during the decades when Japan was being rapidly modernized, provides one of the great contrasts of history and when fully understood may offer one of its great lessons."[2]

Now even without fully understanding all factors involved, I believe that the contrast suggested here between China and Japan is illuminating for our purposes. For there can be no doubt that a clearly recognizable form of Confucianism was a powerful ingredient in the thinking and training of the Japanese statesmen who succeeded where their Chinese contemporaries failed. If, then, Confucianism seems to have contributed as both an intellectual force and an ethical system to the success in Japan, to what extent can we hold it responsible for the failure in China?[3] If the leaders of the Meiji Restoration subscribed to Sakuma Shōzan's formula "Eastern [i.e., Confucian] ethics and Western science" and found it suited to their purposes, was it inevitable that the *t'i-yung* rationalization of the Chinese self-strengtheners should have failed them?

Similar questions arise when we consider the adaptability of Confucian ethics to the requirements of modern nationalism. Thus, Mr. Fairbank states in regard to China: "While the revival of a kind of Confucian idealism in the period of the [T'ung-chih] restoration infused a degree of morale into the upper levels of the bureaucracy, the ancient ethical teaching could make little direct contribution to nationalism as a new incentive or focus of mass loyalty."[4] When, however, we consider the very important role which Confucian ethics played in the great upsurge of Japanese nationalism in the Meiji period and after, both among the leaders of the new regime and through the mass indoctrination inaugurated by the Imperial Rescript on Education in 1890, we cannot help asking why in the one case Confucian ethics appears to have made a positive contribution to modern nationalism, while in the other it is seen as essentially an obstacle to it. To resolve our apparent dilemma, it seems to me, we should have to consider whether Confucianism, as such, was really the crucial factor in either of these situations. For example, we might find ourselves asking whether, in Mr. Fairbank's references to the "traditional Confucian social and political order" and the "Confucian literati," any special significance attaches to the characterization of this order and these men as "Confucian" rather than simply as "Chinese."

To answer these questions, of course, we must have a clearer idea both of what is essential to Confucianism and what the specific historical factors are which affected its development in each case. This latter aspect of the problem extends far beyond our scope here. We may, however, be able to shed some light on those common elements in the Chinese and Japanese intellectual traditions which mark them as, to some degree, "Confucian." By "common elements" I do not mean to suggest a kind of common denominator or consensus on basic doctrine. To arrive at this would involve a job of compilation, interpretation, and classification beyond even the ambitions of Ch'ing scholarship or Mr. Adler's *Syntopicon*. For our purposes it is enough to identify as Confucianists those who accept the authority of the Confucian classics as providing the most reliable guide to the conduct of life and government. Granting a considerable divergence in the interpretation of certain texts and teachings by different Confucianists, I think we can further discern certain tendencies that are characteristic of the Confucian tradition during the later centuries of its development. First, however, we must explain in what sense we speak of Confucianism as a tradition, and particularly what type of authority was involved in the acceptance and perpetuation of this tradition. The authoritarian character of Confucianism has seemed to many students of modern China and Japan to be the most significant aspect of its influence. Forgive me for citing Mr. Fairbank again, in a passage where he seeks to explain the appeal of Marxist theory to Japanese intellectuals in recent times:

The many and diverse reasons for the acceptance of Marxist theory in Japan may be suggested briefly under two main heads. First is the tradition of ideological orthodoxy. Confucianism in Japan, as in China, had been the official tool of government. By it the scholar-administrator had been taught to think deductively from the authority of abstract principles. To some extent the ideology of the state, summed up pre-eminently in Confucianism, had commanded an emotional adherence similar to that given religion in the West. The state had been comparatively more dominant over the individual and his thinking. It had regularly used history both to buttress authority and sanction its exercise. There was little precedent for a Western type of historical pluralism. Thus the influence of tradition was to give Japanese scholars a craving for a comprehensive historical scheme, an authoritative doctrine of history.[5]

Essentially the same view of Confucianism is put forward by a modern Japanese authority, Kishimoto Hideo:

For two and one-half centuries, the Japanese government confined its people within its own national borders and indoctrinated them with Confucian precepts. Confucianism implanted in their minds a tendency toward unquestioning obedience to their superiors. One could not expect to find in Confucianism any development of independent thinking.[6]

Now this view of Confucianism would not be so very widespread if there were not a great deal of substance to it. There can be no doubt that Confucianism enjoined men to accept the authority of father, teacher, and ruler, and that the ruler had an especially important role in intellectual matters as well as political. Confucius and his followers, assuming that the ruler of a country had a decisive influence over the thinking and conduct of the people, not only through educational policy in the ordinary sense but also through the example of state policy and administration, encouraged the ruler to accept the responsibility of a teacher toward them. This, together with the undoubted contribution of Confucian ethics to social stability, and of Confucian learning to the training of public officials, was reason enough for the intimate alliance between Confucianism and political power in China and Japan.

We must be careful, however, not to assume that the role of Confucianism as an intellectual force can be described solely in terms of its function as "an official tool of government." The "ideological orthodoxy" of which Mr. Fairbank speaks, referring to the influence of Confucianism on the Japanese scholar, is by no means as uncomplicated a phenomenon as the mere tendency of uneducated masses to accept political direction. Intellectual matters, by their very nature, are less susceptible of control. Without going very far into what for the institutional historian is the very rich and still largely unexplored field of the corporate relations between state power and intellectual forces, we may suggest at least a few of the factors which would have to be considered in any assessment of the government's part in maintaining ideological orthodoxy.

First of all, we must recognize within what limits the state attempted to impose or enforce orthodoxy. In China the principal means employed, apart from the purely formal honors paid to Confucius, his descendants, and noted Confucian scholars of later times (which, depending on the circumstances, only served to exploit the prestige of the state for the benefit of the teaching, or vice versa), was the sanctioning of the Confucian classics, and of Chu Hsi as their interpreter, for the civil service examinations and for the instruction offered in a limited number of official schools.[7] Undeniably these means ensured that the great majority of educated men, aspiring for office, would gain at least some grounding in the official doctrine. But it is a question whether this training had any deep effect on the thinking of thinking men—that is,

whether its influence was more than skin-deep. Certainly we have endless complaints from the more articulate and serious-minded Confucianists that the examination system was a mere formality, a mechanical
exercise in composition and memory work. At the same time, we find
many graduates of this system in the Ming and Ch'ing dynasties who
fulfilled the formal requirements and yet, in their writings, showed considerable independence of the Chu Hsi orthodoxy enshrined in the examinations. The ramifications of this question are, of course, considerable, but at the very least we have reason to doubt the automatic effect
of the system in obtaining uniformity or conformity of thought. To be
sure, it made for a certain negative uniformity in the sense that, because
so much of the educated man's time was devoted to this type of activity,
he was less free and less eager to investigate other branches of learning
and thought (this was one reason given by the Jesuits, for instance, to
explain why Western science attracted so few Chinese scholars). That
this was a crucial factor, however, seems doubtful in view of the number of scholars who for various reasons purposely avoided the civil
service system, looked upon the official orthodoxy with suspicion or
distaste, and still gave no evidence of transcending the traditional
bounds of Chinese thought.

Because of the great concentration of power in the Chinese court
and the despotic uses to which it was sometimes put, we are likely to
think of this power as being constantly exerted in support of ideological
orthodoxy and to suppress any semblance of heterodoxy. We think of
the so-called literary inquisition in the Ch'ien-lung period, the suppression of private academies in the Ming, the celebrated cases of individual
persecution—then perhaps we fill in the picture with our own picture of
totalitarian control in the forms developed today, and superimposing it
on the past, assume that the same intense and pervasive pressures
operated to stultify thought.

Here I would not hope to draw a sharply contrasting picture. My
own impression, however, for whatever it might be worth in a matter
that defies systematic proof, is that whereas the pressures to conform
to a minimal set of beliefs and values were indeed pervasive, the application of force was comparatively infrequent. What is more significant, if I am right, is that these acts of persecution rarely had as their
aim the support of a specific ideological orthodoxy or the suppression of
heterodoxy. Most often the grounds for persecution are political: the
man or school attacked is accused of complicity in a plot or factional
conspiracy against the state or the dynasty; there is an allegation of
lèse majesté, often involving the use of taboo words; there is some suspicion or insinuation of disrespect for the ruler or the dynasty. I am

aware of only a few isolated cases in which the issue appears to be a strictly intellectual one (i.e., nonconformity to Chu Hsi orthodoxy).

Moreover, we can point to numerous cases of intellectual nonconformity in the Ming and Ch'ing periods wherein official disapproval seems not to have made itself very strongly felt. During the latter part of the Ming period, the Wang Yang-ming school continued to flourish among intellectuals despite official suppressions during the sixteenth century of some of the academies in which it was taught. At the beginning of the seventeenth century heterodoxy flourished in the form of a syncretism of the Three Doctrines (Confucianism, Taoism, and Buddhism), and only such an extreme iconoclast as Li Chih (1527–1602) suffered actual persecution. In the early Ch'ing such dissenters as Li Kung (1659–1733) and Yen Yüan (1635–1704) disputed the metaphysics of Chu Hsi with impunity, and the similar views of the great Tai Chen (1724–77) did not disqualify him from holding important scholarly positions under the Manchu regime. By contrast, the severest measures were taken posthumously against the surviving works and reputation of Lü Liu-liang (1629–83), more orthodox in his philosophy but considered a menace for his anti-Manchu feelings.

It would appear, then, that Chinese rulers were far more sensitive to the expression of attitudes which might endanger their rule than they were to expressions of purely intellectual dissent unassociated with political opposition. It should be remembered also that the emperors, and the imperial family generally, were often less exclusively devoted to Confucianism than the members of the bureaucracy (many emperors were followers and patrons of Buddhism); and that the bureaucrats themselves were probably less strongly attached to Confucianism than those whose allegiance to it was of a more intellectual nature. All this, of course, does not add up to a large measure of intellectual freedom in China, but it certainly raises doubts about the extent to which Confucianism may be considered an enforced ideology.

In Japan it was even less possible than in China to maintain complete ideological uniformity, or to ensure that Confucianism would be kept within the precise bounds set for it by the Shogunate. The Tokugawa could establish Chu Hsi philosophy as the approved teaching in official schools, both in Edo at the Confucian college run by the Hayashi family and at the various *han* schools, but this type of education served no such vital function in a feudal military government as it did in the civil administration of China. There was indeed no civil service system to speak of, and warrior aristocrats whose status in society and position in the government were largely dependent on birth and family relationships were not compelled to qualify themselves in Confucian studies as a means of personal advancement. Also, since this type of instruction was not keyed to a uniform examination system such as prevailed in China, the greater political autonomy of the Japanese *han* was reflected in a greater diversity in the intellectual atmosphere of their schools. To a degree unparalleled in China (though still within certain limits) this situation provided an actual institutional basis for the dissemination of non-conformist ideas. A man whose views differed markedly from the official school did not find that all employment was closed to him; it was often possible to enter the service of a feudal lord who was either sympathetic to his ideas or at least willing to give them a trial in the hope that they might serve a practical purpose in the strengthening of his own *han*. Even writers openly condemned by the Shogunate were only exiled from Edo to some more remote region, where they often continued to write and study, either under a kind of loose surveillance by the local lord or sometimes even with his tacit approval and support.

The case of Yamaga Sokō (1632–85) illustrates this situation very well. The first scholar of importance openly to repudiate Chu Hsi orthodoxy, Yamaga preached his philosophical revolt for many years to his students without suffering at the hands of the government. Finally he actually dared to publish his views in writing. This act brought immediate retaliation by the government, which could not afford to let its intellectual authority be so brazenly challenged, but still its response only took the usual form of suppressing the book and exiling the author. In the custody of the Lord of Akō, though Yamaga's means of expression were more limited, he could still pursue his studies and write works which exerted a great influence on later generations. Nor is his simply an isolated case. Other nonconformists, not always so influential as Yamaga, ran afoul of the Shogunate without losing all opportunity to propagate their ideas, and they (such men as Kumazawa Banzan [1619–91], Hirata Atsutane [1776–1843], the later Mito school men, Sakuma Shōzan [1811–64], and Yoshida Shōin [1831–60], to name just a few) contributed much to the intellectual ferment which prepared Japan for her role in the modern world.[8]

On the other hand, we may take the example of Ogyū Sorai (1666–1728) as roughly paralleling that of the nonconformist Tai Chen in China. There was certainly no question that he had broken completely with the established orthodoxy, yet as a loyal supporter of the Bakufu, Ogyū was not only tolerated by the Tokugawa but listened to with respect in political and cultural matters. Here again is an indication that ideological conformity in itself was of much less concern to Japan's rulers than political reliability. The Tokugawa could tolerate teachers and schools that were independent (men such as Nakae Tōju [1608–48] of the Wang Yang-ming school and schools such as the Kogaku-ha of Itō Jinsai [1627–1705], but not those who appeared to usurp or undermine the authority of the Shogunate. For this reason it was a far more serious offense to publish one's views on political questions (to offer a program of reform, for instance, without being specifically invited to do so by the authorities) than to write a work setting forth a new metaphysics.

Clearly, then, the disapproval of the Shogunate in intellectual matters did not necessarily involve thoroughgoing suppression of dissent or any sustained effort to mold people's minds to suit a preconceived pattern. As a matter of fact, ideological purity proved difficult to impose even in the nominal strongholds of orthodoxy. From the beginning even those most closely identified with the establishment of Neo-Confucianism in Japan were somewhat less than pure in their adherence to the philosophy of Chu Hsi. Fujiwara Seika (1561–1619), though firmly opposed to Buddhism and Taoism, was definitely eclectic in his attitude toward the Lu-Wang school. Hayashi Razan (1583–1657), the founder of the official school, put much more stress on orthodoxy, but he nevertheless reduced Chu Hsi's dualism of principle (ri) and ether (ki) to a monism of ri; while Kaibara Ekken (1630–1714), one of the most effective exponents of Chu Hsi's teaching in the seventeenth century, did precisely the reverse by reducing it to a monism of ki. Yamazaki Ansai (1618–82), another pillar of the Chu Hsi school, worked so hard at a synthesis of Neo-Confucianism and Shinto that he ended up with a hybrid metaphysics which Chu Hsi would have had difficulty recognizing as in any way his own. With such confusion among the early exponents of Neo-Confucianism, it is hardly to be wondered at that the official Hayashi family school should have had difficulty in maintaining any kind of purity of thought in its own ranks. By the early eighteenth century the most vigorous defender of orthodoxy against the increasingly popular schools of Itō Jinsai and Ogyū Sorai was not a member of the Hayashi school but an independent, Muro Kyūso (1658–1734). And by the late eighteenth century the Hayashi school itself was so infiltrated by unorthodox teachings that the Shogunate took it over and attempted a housecleaning, while ordering the various han schools to do the same. Significantly, the measures taken to tighten the reins of orthodoxy in the 1790's did not apply to private schools such as the Kogaku-ha and the Kokugaku-ha, and even in the official schools the prohibition on heterodox teachings seems not to have been rigidly enforced.[9]

What these remarks are meant to bring out is not, of course, that the state had an insignificant role in the propagation, perpetuation, and formulation of Confucian thought in Japan or in China, but only that in both countries there were definite limits to the aims and the effectiveness of state-maintained "ideological orthodoxy." Personally, I should welcome a study of the workings of "thought control" in China and Japan which does not proceed from the assumption that regimes which are reactionary in their thinking (as the Tokugawa certainly was) are inevitably repressive of all independent thought. But be that as it may, the significant thing here is that neither in China nor in Japan did Confucianism remain set within the narrow mold of a state-imposed orthodoxy, and that intellectually speaking it had a life of its own which must be understood on its own terms.

We must remember that Neo-Confucianism took its rise among intellectuals and commanded the adherence of other intellectuals in circumstances in which the influence of the state, if it counted at all, counted adversely. State orthodoxy, such as it was, did not work in favor of the Ch'eng-Chu school in the Southern Sung, yet its influence spread rapidly. In the Yüan dynasty the endorsement of the state came late, after Neo-Confucianism had already gained ascendency among scholars for reasons which have no immediate connection with bureaucratic functions or purposes. In other words, the Ch'eng-Chu teaching satisfied an intellectual need of the times (not excluding the need for a political philosophy) before it came to be exploited in the interests of the state or taken up as a means of advancing men's political careers. In Japan likewise Neo-Confucianism commanded the intellectual respect of Zen monks well before it was adopted by the Tokugawa for its own uses. Granted that the eventual adoption of this philosophy by these states greatly strengthened its position, still we cannot ignore its intrinsic appeal or value as a philosophical system, or deny that Neo-Confucianism as a historical movement had a kind of inner life, a power of recreation and preservation from within, which sustained it for centuries even against the sterilizing effect of state control. Just how to characterize or define this vital essence I am not able to say at this point. Nevertheless, to judge from my own rather superficial study of Neo-Confucianism in these two very different cultural and social environments, it does appear to have certain persistent features that may help us to get at the bases of its continuing vitality.

It should be emphasized that our problem here is not necessarily to identify what is "new" in Neo-Confucianism. There is no question but that the influence of Buddhism and Taoism can be seen in certain aspects of Neo-Confucian metaphysics and mental discipline. Even in the famous motto of the Sung political reformer Fan Chung-yen, "To be first in worrying about the world's troubles and last in the enjoyment of its pleasures,"[10] one can detect overtones of the Boddhisattva ideal of seek-

ing the salvation of others before passing to one's own reward as a
Buddha. Still, what is "new" here, though it may be what is most distinctive in comparison with earlier forms of Confucianism, does not
necessarily represent what is most central or vital to Neo-Confucianism.
The motive power may well have been generated within the Confucian
tradition itself and only incidentally manifested in these novel forms.

First of all, borrowing a term from the Western tradition and adapting it slightly, I suggest that a kind of fundamentalism was a persistent
and probably essential element in Neo-Confucianism. Next there is
what I am tempted to call "revivalism," since it involves an attempt to
revive or restore a system of belief and practice which has suffered a
decline. To avoid the extrinsic connotations of "revivalism" in American usage—the spectacular emotional manifestations of the camp-meet-
ing type of Christianity—I shall designate this tendency rather as "restorationism." To these two I add at least three other tendencies that
are characteristic of the Confucian tradition as a whole and that had
special significance in this later period: historical-mindedness, rationalism, and humanism. I do not doubt that other features could also be
distinguished. For the five listed here I claim only two virtues: they are
suitably general, and they are meaningful in relation to the rival systems
of thought with which Neo-Confucianism had to contend.

What I have called "fundamentalism" and "restorationism" are
closely related and must be taken together. By "fundamentalism" I
refer to the kind of thinking exemplified very early by Han Yü (768–
824), the precursor of the Confucian revival in the Sung, who strongly
reaffirmed what he considered to be the fundamental ethical precepts
of Confucius by simply stating and restating these precepts as self-
evident—i.e., without making any serious attempt to justify or reinterpret
them in the light of subsequent developments in Chinese thought. What
I call "restorationism" goes beyond this. Ou-yang Hsiu (1007–72),
among others in the early Sung, expresses the attitude I have in mind
in his "Essay on Fundamentals" ("Pen-lun"). He makes the point that
men have been upholding Confucian ethical principles against Buddhism for years without making any headway among the mass of the
people because the whole social and cultural environment is indis-
posed to Confucianism. Civilization is in such an advanced state of
decay that one cannot hope to reassert Confucian principles without
first remaking society and resurrecting institutions from the hallowed
past which are more in harmony with the Confucian ideal. The leaders
of the Confucian revival in the early Sung proclaimed this purpose in the
slogan "Return to the Past" or "Restore the Old Order" (*fu-ku*), and
talked a great deal about those of the Confucian classics (notably the

books of Rites) which purported to describe the institutions of the sage-kings. Thus they stressed the formal or institutional element in the Confucian tradition, not merely the ethical. The latter, they insisted, could never stand alone. The ethical principles and ideals of Confucius were meaningless unless put into action, unless given tangible form; and they were not viable unless sustained by a social order conducive to them.

With this type of Confucian restorationism in the Sung I have already dealt to some extent in my paper for the first of these conferences.[11] It will be sufficient here to point out the distinction between this sort of thing and the Confucian fundamentalism out of which it developed. Wang An-shih (1021–86), of course, made the most famous serious and practical attempt to reform society and achieve the ideals of those who looked for a Restoration of the Old Order. This celebrated episode is also an excellent example of the tensions which developed between these related tendencies in Confucian thought: that is, the strain which Wang's determined pursuit of his social goals put upon the traditional political ethics of the Confucian school.

After Wang An-shih's fall, it is true, enthusiasm for this type of Confucian restoration—or more correctly, optimism concerning its attainability—waned among Neo-Confucian scholars. There is no movement in later dynasties representing such a powerful wave of political idealism among scholars or such a concerted drive for the accomplishment of its goals. But to the extent that Confucian thinkers concerned themselves with political problems at all, and considered the need for institutional reform rather than simply the need for self-reformation and personal cultivation on the part of rulers, the idea continued to reappear and to stimulate proposals for basic change. Huang Tsung-hsi (1610–95), in the seventeenth century, is clearly fired with the same vision of a wholesale restoration in his "Plan for the Prince" (*Ming-i tai-fang lu*), though like Wang An-shih he concedes that times have changed sufficiently to preclude reviving the ancient feudal system in every detail. Ku Yen-wu (1613–82) also thinks of a modified return to the feudal order of the past, to be effected by decentralizing the administrative system and allowing more scope to the individual *chün-tzu*. Among other scholars in the early Ch'ing, the tendency to think in terms of a return to the past is still strong; Liang Ch'i-ch'ao (1873–1929) in his "Outline of Ch'ing Thought" (*Ch'ing-tai hsueh-shu kai-lun*) goes so far as to assert that *fu-ku* is the guiding aim of Ch'ing thought. In this situation, however, the "return to the past" clearly has altered significance, reflecting other tendencies at work within Neo-Confucianism which we shall discuss later.[12]

In Japan, during these same years, *fu-ku* in its original sense as a restoration of the ancient order continued to attract attention. Ogyū Sorai, probably Japan's outstanding Confucian scholar and student of things Chinese as well as an adviser to the Shogunate, made this the central idea in his teaching, and his school is identified according to the traditional system of classification as the Fukko-gakuha (*fukko*, of course, being the Japanese reading for the same characters as *fu-ku* in Chinese).[13] Having studied and finally rejected Chu Hsi philosophy, as well as other forms of Neo-Confucian teaching which placed primary stress on personal ethics or metaphysics, Ogyū turned to the study of institutions. For him, as for the early Sung reformers, Confucianism in its fullness could not be sought in the *Analects* alone, or in the commentaries of the Ch'eng-Chu school, but had to be found in the entire political and social system of the sage-kings as it was described in the Confucian classics as a whole, including the texts on history, ritual, and so on. This idea had an immense effect on non-Confucian thinkers influenced by Ogyū. If, at the beginning of history, the truth in all its fullness has been revealed by the sage-kings and embodied in an ideal social order which could be understood through the study of history, was it not reasonable to think that truth of the same sort could be recovered from the records of Japan's own sage-emperors (who had been clothed by Confucian-minded Japanese historians of the eighth century with all the wisdom and virtue of China's sage-kings)? This was the notion that Ogyū inspired in Kada Azumamaro (1669–1736), and which Kada put forward in a memorial to the Shogun asking for the establishment of a school to study the ancient learning of Japan. Though his request was not acted upon, the basic idea was followed up by Kada's successors in the School of National Learning (Kokugaku-ha) who led the Shinto revival in the eighteenth century.

If in this case, however, the spirit of restorationism was transplanted and enjoyed a separate existence outside the Confucian tradition, in other cases it provided a link between traditions. Satō Nobuhiro (or Shinen, 1769–1850), drawing upon both the Confucian and Shinto traditions, as well as some knowledge of the West gained through the school of Dutch learning, produced an ambitious plan of national reorganization in his book "Restoration of the Ancient Order" (*Fukko-sho*) and similar works. His ideal is still the complete, rationally controlled social order of the distant past, but the drastic reforms, totalitarian scope, and imperialistic aims of his plan have no analogue except in the modern totalitarian systems.

Finally, we should not fail to mention that *fukko* was also a prominent slogan in the early years of the Meiji Restoration among samurai-reformers who, like Satō, drew inspiration from both the Confucian and Shinto traditions.[14] In other words, the Restoration was not meant simply as a restoration of the imperial house to actual rulership, but also as a promise that the idealized social order of the ancient past would be reestablished in a form appropriate to modern requirements. It did not take long, of course, for this idea to become submerged in the drive for a "renovation" along Western lines.[15]

Before leaving this element of restoration, I should perhaps make clear how much significance I attach to it. Certainly I do not mean to suggest that the history of Neo-Confucianism can be written in these terms. The cases I have referred to are exceptional ones, not typical; they represent only a strong undercurrent in Neo-Confucian thinking, not the main stream. Nevertheless we should recognize that these men and these trends are by no means insignificant in the intellectual history of their times. At the very least they demonstrate that latter-day Confucianism contained vital seeds which bore fruit outside the preserve of narrow orthodoxy. Furthermore, by recognizing such elements for what they are while still conscious that they were overshadowed by more powerful ones, we shall find that these latter, more central, tendencies emerge with heightened significance for our understanding of Confucianism as a whole.

In this light, for instance, we gain a renewed appreciation of ritual as a basic element in the Confucian way of life. If institutional change proved so difficult at court and the idealized government of the books of Rites seemed unachievable in the present circumstances, it was still possible to accomplish some of the social objectives of the Confucianists —to create a social environment embodying and conducing to Confucian ethical values—through the infiltration into every household and school of the Confucian rules of social intercourse. Chu Hsi himself wrote extensively on this subject, and there are few Confucianists after him who do not insist upon the necessity of authentic ritual and ceremonial traditions to the moral health of society, especially to its preservation from the baneful effects of popular customs and superstitious practices. The widespread dissemination of such compilations as Chu Hsi's collected utterances on family ritual (the *Chu Tzu Chia-li,* which figures so often in Hui-chen Wang Liu's paper on Chinese family rules) during the Ming and Ch'ing dynasties, is evidence of the way in which Neo-Confucianism had its widest and deepest influence on Chinese society simply through the more intensive application of traditional elements rather than through the elaboration of new concepts and institutions.

The same trend is found reflected in other countries which came under Neo-Confucian influence, sometimes in exaggerated form. John

Meskill's recent translation of the *P'yohae-rok*,[16] the journal of the Korean Ch'oe Pu who was shipwrecked on the Chinese coast in the fifteenth century, gives a striking example of this. Again and again Ch'oe, in trying to demonstrate his superiority as a Confucian gentleman to a disaffected crew, or his "civilized" character to Chinese suspicious of him as a Japanese pirate, makes a point of his strict adherence to Confucian ceremonial and quotes the *Chu Tzu Chia-li* almost as if it were his Bible. Ch'oe would seem a wholly implausible or comic figure unless we recognized the seriousness with which Neo-Confucianists viewed ritual as one of the most practical and constructive of activities as well as the most civilized and refined.[17]

The other characteristics or tendencies of Confucianism which I have mentioned are humanism, rationalism, and historical-mindedness. Since in general the importance of these is well understood, I shall be more brief in discussing them. The fundamental humanism of Confucius' own teaching—the fact that it centers most directly upon man and his place in society, rather than upon any supernatural order or divine law—is evident. In Neo-Confucianism this emphasis upon the human personality and the problems of human society is strongly reasserted against the Buddhist and Taoist view of the universe as essentially indifferent to the values of man and the fate of human society. Most specifically this attitude is reflected in the doctrine of the moral nature of man and the essential goodness of man, which virtually all schools of Neo-Confucianism upheld (though they interpreted it differently) and which they pointed to as their point of basic difference with Buddhism. In Japan the introduction of Neo-Confucianism was followed by a new interest in a whole range of human and social problems to which little thought had been given during the centuries of Buddhist dominance. That this flowering of humanistic culture in the Tokugawa period is a direct consequence of Neo-Confucian influence alone seems unlikely, since a whole new set of political, economic, and social forces was at work to much the same end. The point remains, nonetheless, that Neo-Confucianism proved congenial to this new climate and contributed its share to the stimulation of effort along these lines.

We are perhaps justified further in pointing to the special function of Confucianism in Japan as a humanizing force in a slightly different sense, that is in "humanizing" or liberalizing the samurai class. Much has been made of the part Confucian ethics played in the formation of *bushidō,* the way of the warrior; but this was only one aspect of a much larger process by which the Japanese warrior was "civilized," so to speak, through the influence of the humanistic and civil-bureaucratic traditions of Confucianism. The union of military power, as represented by the Shogunate and samurai class, with the civil arts, as the Tokugawa encouraged them through humanistic studies of the Confucian type, is both a leading theme and a major development of this period. Hayashi Razan, the Confucian adviser to Ieyasu, and Yamaga Sokō, the pioneer exponent of *bushidō* whose intellectual interests nevertheless ranged far beyond it, both symbolize this trend of momentous significance—the conversion of the samurai class from a purely military aristocracy to one of increasing political and intellectual leadership. This development helps to explain why the samurai, instead of becoming a wholly idle and effete class during the long Tokugawa peace, could in the end furnish the brains of the Restoration movement, take the initiative in dismantling feudalism itself, and play an important role in Japan's subsequent modernization.

The next tendency, Confucian rationalism, does not involve a conscious exaltation of reason as opposed to faith or intuition (none of the early masters seems to have acknowledged such an explicit dichotomy). It derives rather from three basic attitudes found in Confucius and the classical Confucianists; first, that the universe is characterized by order, regularity, and a harmonious integration of its parts; second, that it is possible for man to discern this order underlying things and events; and third, that to devote oneself to what the "Great Learning" calls the systematic study of "things" (i.e., man, his institutions and history, and the Classics), and in this way to contribute to the accumulation of knowledge, is the high calling of the "noble man" (*chün-tzu*), the occupation which will enable men to live in harmony with themselves and the universe. Buddhism, by contrast, employed reason to destroy reason, to demonstrate the insubstantiality and ephemerality of all things, to prove that there is nothing in the universe, including the moral order, not subject to the law of incessant change. Thus it was the task of Neo-Confucianism to meet the challenge of Buddhist skepticism by dealing with the question of change and reestablishing Confucian confidence in an ordered universe on a secure metaphysical foundation. (This was not, of course, the first such challenge or response in the history of Confucianism; the process was already well launched in Han times, prompted chiefly by Taoism.) The importance of this element in Neo-Confucianism is clearly exemplified by the Ch'eng-Chu school, which became known as the school of reason or principle (*li*), since it stressed the objective reason or principle in all things as the basis of learning and conduct. The influence of the Ch'eng-Chu teaching, both as the official orthodoxy and as a leading school of thought in its own right, was set squarely against the grosser forms of superstition associated with Chinese religious cults, which sometimes made a powerful appeal to Chinese emperors.

In Japan this aspect of Neo-Confucianism is manifested in a particularly striking manner by the attempts of Hayashi Razan to provide a rational interpretation of the legends setting forth the divine origins of Japan and the founding of the dynasty by Jimmu Tenno. Essentially the same spirit moves Yamazaki Ansai in his syncretism of Shinto and Neo-Confucianism, which, however forced and implausible, nevertheless testifies to the strong rationalistic drive and cogency of Neo-Confucian metaphysical thought. In later Japanese Confucianists, too, notably in Arai Hakuseki (1657–1725), we find a strong critical attitude toward the mythological elements in Japanese history.

This type of rationalism, since it stressed the intelligibility of things and the objective investigation of them, naturally drew attention to things themselves as well as to the principles they embodied. In this respect the seeds of a kind of empiricism were latent in Confucian rationalism, the outgrowth of which became most fully manifest in the empirical philosophers and critical scholarship of the seventeenth and eighteenth centuries in China. The fact, however, that this empirical strain in Chinese thought never made itself felt in the field of natural science in any sustained and systematic way is, I think, sufficiently recognized to need no further comment here.[18]

In Japan, there are indications that this empiricism was carried into a somewhat wider range of intellectual inquiry. Kaibara Ekken, who shared an interest in botany and biology already seen among Chinese students of materia medica like Li Shih-chen, the compiler of the massive *Pen-ts'ao kang-mu* (1590), went further to develop the importance of nature as a central feature of his own philosophy. Carrying on in this same line of thought and inquiry were others like Miura Baien (1723–89) and Kaiho Seiryō (1755–1817), whose independence of the strict Neo-Confucian tradition does not lessen the debt they owe to Neo-Confucian rationalism for the spirit of inquiry which they applied to the development of natural sciences and social sciences. Miura's philosophy of *jōri* represented a kind of logical or dialectical order in nature combining the Neo-Confucian concept of reason or principle (*ri*) with a specifically organic conception of the structural patterns found everywhere in nature (*jō*, literally the branches of a tree). Similarly, Kaiho, who made the laws of economics his special study, described both the social order and the natural in terms of "the laws of nature" (literally, the "principles of heaven-and-earth," *tenchi-no-ri*), an expression that bears the marks of Neo-Confucian terminology and suggests a further exploration of the rationally ordered universe of the Sung philosophers. Finally, we should not neglect to mention the contribution of Neo-Confucian rationalism and empiricism to the Shinto revival, which, though it came to repudiate this very rationalism, nevertheless borrowed from it the philological method for the study of scripture which gave intellectual respectability to the reassessment of the Shinto tradition undertaken by men like Kamo Mabuchi (1697–1769) and Motoori Norinaga (1730–1801).

Despite these glimmerings, the significant fact concerning Confucian rationalism and empiricism in China and Japan is that they were not carried further. I believe that this can be at least partially explained in terms of two other tendencies I have mentioned, Confucian fundamentalism and historical-mindedness. It should never be forgotten that the rationalism of the Ch'eng-Chu school subserved another, more basic aim: the reassertion and reestablishment of Confucian ethics. The order which the Neo-Confucianists found in the universe was in the final analysis more fundamentally moral than it was rational. From their point of view, of course, no such distinction was necessary. But when we study what they meant by principle (*li*) we cannot avoid the conclusion that it was moral principles above all which they wished to rescue from the consuming fires of Buddhist skepticism and nihilism, as represented especially by Nagarjuna's dialectics of negation. This is why in Chu Hsi's metaphysics there is such a complete identification of the cosmic and moral orders. This is why the term "things," though in a general sense it embraces the objects of nature, most often is used by the Neo-Confucianists in the sense of "affairs," that is, the affairs of men living together, the events of history which exemplify the workings of the moral law in human society.

The "investigation of things," then, was more properly the examination of moral problems than the kind of experimentation and inquiry we associate with natural science. For Chu Hsi, who stressed objective learning, the directive to investigate "things" was carried out mainly in scriptural and historical studies, but to a lesser extent also in the study of contemporary social problems. For Wang Yang-ming, whose approach was more intuitive, it involved examining the psychological or spiritual bases of human action, of the moral life. Taking these two thinkers as significant types in the later development of Confucianism, we can see why Confucian rationalism should have expended itself in the service of historical study (as in the great endeavors of Ch'ing historical scholarship) or in a preoccupation with the practical life in a restricted sphere which still reflected the limits of traditional ethical cultivation (as in Yen Yüan and especially Li Kung, for whom practical studies tended to center around the classical Six Arts). The further question of why Confucian rationalism was unable to disengage itself from such practical concerns and maintain itself on a higher level of abstraction is a fascinating subject of speculation and study. Here we must be content with noting the fact that it remained true to Confucius' primary concern with the relation of self-cultivation to social order, and developed very little in the direction of what for Confucius was a secondary aim: the pursuit of knowledge for its own sake.[19]

The importance of Confucian historical-mindedness should already be apparent. Basically, of course, it springs from what I call the fundamentalist urge to turn to the past for values which are thought to have an irreplaceable function even in later times, and also from what I have called the restorationist or revivalist spirit, which seeks to restore the whole social and institutional order of ancient times as inseparable from the fundamental ethical teachings of Confucianism. In both cases there is a need to study the past and especially to study scripture. This need, moreover, is reinforced by Confucian humanism, which attaches a value to human history, and Confucian rationalism, which sees a meaning, an order, a pattern, in human history. Indeed, so obvious is the place of historical study in Confucianism that we might be inclined simply to have it subsumed under these other categories. I list it separately, however, primarily because it is one of the main features that distinguish the Confucian tradition from the religious and philosophical traditions that arose in India—and to some degree also from Islam, where, despite the importance attached to the chronicling of individual events, there is such an absolute insistence on the inscrutability of Allah's will that to see a regularity or pattern in history is to imply a limitation on Allah's perfect freedom to deal with men as he pleases.[20]

In China, after the spread of Neo-Confucian thought, there is a noticeable increase in historical studies and especially in the writing of general history, which is seen as exemplifying more clearly the grand design of history and the inescapability of the moral law. Of course, Confucian historiography had not altogether disappeared during the centuries of Confucian decline, but there is a noticeable stimulation of historical writing on the grand scale in the Sung, with Ou-yang Hsiu, Ssu-ma Kuang (1019–86), Chu Hsi, Cheng Ch'iao (1104–60), Ma Tuan-lin (thirteenth century), and Wang Ying-lin (1223–96), among others, leading the effort to recapitulate and reassess the whole course of Chinese history.

In Japan there is an even more striking efflorescence of historical writing associated with the rise of Neo-Confucianism, when contrasted with the dearth of genuine historical scholarship during centuries of

Buddhist dominance after the first general histories, the *Kojiki* and the *Nihongi,* were written under Chinese inspiration in the eighth century.[21] There is first of all Kitabatake Chikafusa's *Jinnō Shōtō-ki* (ca. 1340), which, though Shintoistic, is inspired to a considerable degree by Confucian models and legitimacy theory. There is next Hayashi Razan's conscious imitation of Ssu-ma Kuang in his attempt to provide the Shogunate with a general history for guidance in government, the *Honchō tsugan* ("General Mirror of Our State"), which was finally completed in 1670, after Hayashi's death. There is the concurrent project of the Mito school of Neo-Confucianism, the "History of Great Japan" (*Dai-Nihon-shi*), the first portions of which came out in 1715. And in this same general wave of historical consciousness there are the efforts of the great scholar-statesman Arai Hakuseki, after his retirement from office, to prepare a more critical version of Japanese history than the Hayashi school had turned out or than he expected the Mito school to produce.

A significant feature of Neo-Confucian historical-mindedness, however, is that just as it had tended to absorb Confucian rationalism—that is, just as the rationalistic and empirical strain in Neo-Confucianism was absorbed largely in studies of a historical nature—so in the long run did this historical interest and effort tend to subserve what I consider the primary drive in Neo-Confucianism, the fundamentalist urge to recover and set forth the basic ethico-political principles of the Confucian tradition. To my knowledge there is no important school of Chinese or Japanese historiography in this general period which does not partake of the moral didacticism of traditional historiography. They might differ on what they considered significant in history and in Confucian teaching, they might apply themselves to very different subjects and materials, but always they kept in mind that history was a guide to moral and political action, and never, so far as I am aware, did history come to have a value in itself or aspire to a kind of detachment and objectivity which rose above all doctrinal considerations. Even the relatively "detached" and critical historian Tsui Shu (1740–1816) was convinced that when all of the spurious accretions to the tradition had been cleared away by critical scholarship, the essential truths of Confucius' teaching would be restored to their original purity.

We therefore return in the end to fundamentalism as, first and last, the most significant factor in Neo-Confucianism. At first sight this might seem no more than obvious, or perhaps even tautological. But if we reexamine the development of Neo-Confucianism as a whole through many centuries in China and Japan, we come to a deeper appreciation of its significance both in relation to the vitality of Neo-Confucianism, such as it was, and to the problem of orthodoxy, the core of the intellectual tradition we have been discussing. The urge to reassert what is most essential in Confucianism was not something felt by Han Yü and his early Sung followers alone. The reestablishment (as they saw it) of Confucian ethics as the basis of individual morality and the cement of Chinese society was not a task to be performed once and for all, leaving nothing more to be done in later ages than to applaud a great work well done. After the Sung there may have been no basic change or striking development in the body of Confucian doctrine which served to regulate the daily lives of the people;[22] in the intellectual sphere, however, there was a continuing need to defend and define this body of doctrine, as well as again and again to reconcile to it the intellectual tendencies which Neo-Confucianism itself had set in motion. Here it may be recalled that in the Ch'eng-Chu school we observed Confucian rationalism at work to provide a metaphysical substructure (or superstructure) primarily for the support of Confucian ethics—that is, for what was seen as most fundamental and essential in Confucianism. In the Lu-Wang school of the Mind, however, we observe a reaction to this type of rationalism precisely on the ground that it is a distortion of the original teaching. Whatever other influences may have affected this reaction, particularly the influence of Buddhism, it seems clear that Wang Yang-ming thought of himself, not as attempting a reconciliation of Confucianism with Buddhism, but rather as defending and reasserting the centrality of individual moral action against a system so top-heavy with book learning and so paralyzed by dead formalism that it could not serve the ordinary man as a guide to the conduct of life.

In turn, however, Wang Yang-ming's stress on individual intuition—innate knowledge of the good—bred in the more extreme wing of his school, which had wide influence in the late Ming dynasty, a rejection of all formal and traditional standards of Confucian morality, a positive contempt for book learning as an intellectual discipline, and a conscious desire to arrive at a syncretism of Buddhism and Taoism with Confucianism.

Against this development, as is well known, still another series of reactions took place. First of all there was the Tung-lin school, whose spokesmen deplored the general breakdown of Confucian morality among the educated, which they saw as contributing to the breakdown of political morality at court. Whether or not these would-be political reformers were invariably on the side of virtue in the battles they waged at court, the fact is that as a school of thought they were basically conservative, the exponents of a return to traditional standards of morality. Some identified themselves with the Chu Hsi school and attacked Wang

Yang-ming himself; others were closer to Wang Yang-ming but deplored the excesses of certain of his followers. Together, however, they insisted upon the primacy of individual moral cultivation, on the *chün-tzu*'s need for self-reformation as the precondition of political reform.

The methods of self-examination and the personal philosophies of Tung-lin scholars still reflected the deep influence of both the rationalist and idealist schools. In the Ch'ing dynasty, however, the continuing reaction against the so-called "empty speculation and introspection" of the Ming led to a further break with the immediate past and a further attempt to get back to the fundamentals of Confucianism. One aspect of the immediate reaction was a reaffirmation of Chu Hsi orthodoxy, especially in official circles. But in other circles it led to a complete rejection of Chu Hsi's metaphysics (as in Yen Yüan, Li Kung, and Tai Chen) or a rejection of Neo-Confucian metaphysics altogether (as in Ku Yen-wu and many other members of the School of Han Learning). Here again the common tendency was to get back to what was fundamental and discard theories that seemed to obscure the original teachings; in the Yen-Li school, which stressed practical action, the aim was to correct Chu Hsi's dualism and set forth a monism believed to be more in harmony with Mencius' doctrine of the goodness of human nature; in the Han school, which stressed objective scholarship and a simple personal ethics, it was to get back beyond Neo-Confucianism and all metaphysical speculation to the original deposit of truth. In both cases a basic objection to the Neo-Confucian theories attacked was that they bore the taint of Buddhism, and Juan Yüan (1764–1894), summing up the accomplishments of the Han school in his preface to the *Han-hsüeh shih-ch'eng chi* of Chiang Fan (1761–1831), praises it primarily for purging Confucianism of Buddhist and Taoist influences and restoring the teaching to its original purity. That even in this process Ch'ing philosophy and scholarship did not step beyond the limits of Neo-Confucianism, as Fung Yu-lan points out in his *History of Chinese Philosophy*,[23] suggests that they were still obeying the basic impulses of rationalism and historicism as put to the service of Confucian fundamentalism. And it is in this sense that Liang Ch'i-ch'ao could say, in the quotation cited earlier, that "return to the past" was the guiding aim of Ch'ing thought and scholarship.

In Japan we find the same process at work. Other factors affected it, of course, factors peculiar to Japan and to the Tokugawa period; nevertheless, to the extent that Confucianism was a distinctive and recognizable force in Tokugawa life (a fact almost universally acknowledged by historians), it tended to follow the same inner tendencies as in China. From the beginning, despite the deep impression made by the well-rounded and well-articulated system of Neo-Confucian metaphysics, the early exponents of this movement in Japan placed the greatest emphasis on what they understood to be the fundamental ethical doctrines of the school, and in particular attempted to adapt these doctrines to the still unformulated code of the samurai.

This is already evident in such "orthodox" exponents of Neo-Confucian teaching as Yamazaki Ansai and Kaibara Ekken, who are known especially for the effectiveness of their efforts to inculcate Confucian ethical precepts on a wide scale. The same tendency is further intensified in the Japanese representatives of the Wang Yang-ming school: Nakae Tōju, renowned for his exemplary virtue, and Kumazawa Banzan, who was admired above all as a model samurai. Indeed, the strong ethical strain in Neo-Confucian thought represented by these two men proved perhaps its most significant influence on the leaders of the later Restoration movement, who were strongly attracted to Wang's doctrine of the unity of knowledge and action as exemplified by the scholar-statesman Kumazawa.

But then, before even a century of Tokugawa rule and official orthodoxy had passed, there was a rather powerful eruption of Confucian fundamentalism and revivalism in the form of three independent scholars who attracted wide attention and a large following. These are the aforementioned Yamaga Sokō, Itō Jinsai, and Ogyū Sorai. All three subjected the Sung philosophers to strong attack, as Ch'ing scholars had, on the charge of being infected by Buddhism and Taoism and having adulterated the true teachings of the Confucian school. All three demanded a return to the past, to the fundamentals of Confucianism. Yamaga's provocative "Essentials of the Sage's Teaching" (*Seikyō Yōroku*) identified the essential truths as the simple ethical principles of Confucius, and on these principles, considered as a guide to the everyday conduct of life, Yamaga proceeded to formulate his system of *bushidō* (referred to by him as *shidō* or *bukyō*). The more bourgeois Itō Jinsai exalted Confucius and Mencius as the only true teachers of Confucianism, and devoted himself to the study and exposition of the humanistic ethical ideals of the *Analects* and Mencius. Ogyū Sorai, for his part, rejected both Ch'eng-Chu metaphysics and the idea that Confucianism could be reduced simply to the ethical maxims of Confucius and Mencius. For him a "fundamental" Confucianism embraced the institutional structure of the sage-kings just as much as it did moral philosophy.

For our purposes we need not trace here the later history of Confucian thought in the Tokugawa period. It is enough to point out that the kind of basic Confucian ethics exemplified and expounded by the men already discussed was what lived on, what formed the far from inert residue of Neo-Confucianism at the end of the Tokugawa period. Where the official Hayashi school demonstrated the sterility of the state orthodoxy, these other thinkers either by example or by explicit teaching had redefined for themselves the true orthodoxy, orthodoxy as it had meaning for active intellectuals as well as for educated men of action. And they did this, as Ch'ing thinkers and scholars did, by constantly returning to the past. That is, in Japan as in China Confucianism continued to live on, but it made progress always by turning back, it matured by drinking deeper of the ancient springs of its youth, it came into its own only by divesting itself of the successive increments to its inheritance.

In the nature of the case, then, there is a very real question whether in Japan, any more than in China, Confucianism could have progressed further on its own unaided resources. For the plain fact is that the Confucian ethical core of which we have been speaking was perpetuated in the late Tokugawa to a considerable extent by schools that were no longer strictly Confucian; indeed, it was only through a powerful alliance with Shinto that Confucianism was still able to make itself felt in the Meiji period. This alliance, achieved in the final Tokugawa synthesis of the later Mito school and eloquently set forth in the *Shin-ron* of Aizawa Seishisai (1782–1863), was actually long in the making. In the early days of Neo-Confucianism in Japan, Hayashi Razan had seen in Shinto a religion compatible with Confucianism and a source of support in the struggle he waged at court to displace the Buddhist clergy as the advisers of the Shogunate. In effect Hayashi subscribed to the original Neo-Confucian belief that Buddhism was fundamentally irreconcilable with Confucianism, but he sensed the importance of traditional religion (as indeed Confucius himself had) and devoted himself to long study of the native cult. Almost all the prominent Tokugawa Confucianists I have mentioned contributed to this rapprochement in some phase of their work—Fujiwara Seika, Hayashi Razan, Yamazaki Ansai, Kaibara Ekken, Nakae Tōju, Yamaga Sokō, and many others.

Yet it is hardly likely that any of these men—much less the leaders of the Shinto revival, who regarded Neo-Confucianism with resentment and hostility—fully appreciated the potentialities of this alliance. Neo-Shinto, like primitive Shinto, had one serious deficiency—it lacked an explicit moral philosophy and code of ethics. Confucianism had both, and the genius of the later Mito school converted them into the strong element of discipline that was needed to give direction to Shinto emotionalism and fanaticism. To Japanese Confucianism, on the other hand, the union provided something no less indispensable—a sense of the future, a sense of destiny. No longer did it have to expend its energies in constantly turning back upon itself, or seek renewal in vain from within. Now with the promises which the Sun Goddess had made to the Japanese people, and which Aizawa proclaimed at the dawn of the new age, a future was assured to Confucian ethics as the divinely sanctioned basis of the Japanese national polity. Henceforth Confucianism would serve, not just as a philosophy for the educated, a code for the warrior-aristocrat, a system of social ethics maintained by the Shogunate, but as the common basis of action for a people conscious of their special mission in a larger world.

While this consciousness remained alive, Confucianism was far from dead or dormant, though it might indeed undergo considerable transformation. In China, where such a consciousness was noticeably lacking, there was unquestionably a corresponding lack of dynamism and vitality in Confucianism, though the precise relationship of these two factors is still not easy to discern or describe. We know that on the very eve of China's forcible opening to the West, and within a decade of Aizawa's appeal to the Japanese nation to rise up and meet the challenge of the West, the aforementioned Juan Yüan, a leading figure of his day in China, was still describing the triumph of Ch'ing scholarship in terms of the old, never-to-be-forgotten struggle with Buddhism. From the hindsight of history, with the subsequent fate of the Manchu dynasty and Confucianism looming so large in our minds, we cannot help but feel that Ch'ing Confucianism was too immobilized by its past to provide the intellectual or ideological leadership which the times required. And this feeling is only confirmed by the desperate attempts of certain Confucianists, no doubt much impressed by the dynamism and sense of national cohesion which Japan seemed to derive from its form of religious nationalism, somehow to win the same advantages for Confucianism in China by establishing it as a national religion. The failure of this attempt, and all the other failures of the Confucian-minded leadership of Manchu China, strongly suggest that Neo-Confucianism had already spent itself reaching back to the sources of its inspiration. In this sense, then, as Mr. Fairbank rightly implies in our opening quotations, Confucianism shared in the responsibility for China's inability in the nineteenth century to cope with the staggering problems of modernization.

If this much is granted, it may seem pointless to ask the further question: Does this mean that the original vision of Confucius too had exhausted itself, that it had nothing more to offer China and the world? It is commonly taken to mean just that, but perhaps we have judged the issue too narrowly and from too short a range. For one thing, Confucianism has survived earlier periods of eclipse and near-extinction; it can look back through many centuries to the momentary triumph and eventual defeat of opposing forces. For another, though the Neo-Confucianists' obsession with the past proved a serious weakness, we are hardly justified in concluding from this that the original Confucian teaching itself was wholly bankrupt. Indeed, the very fact that it has exerted such a powerful attraction through the ages would lead rather to the presumption that there was something in Confucianism central to the life of the Chinese people—and perhaps central to human life— that would keep it alive in some form despite its failure as a self-sufficient system of thought and conduct. Finally, world trends adverse to Confucianism in the recent past may yield to others more compatible with it. Thus the failure of Confucianism to adjust in China to the nineteenth- and twentieth-century world of intense nationalism may be no index of its viability in a possible future age of internationalism. Times change. Confucian family values came under strong attack during the past century for running counter to the "modern" trends toward individualism, the emancipation of women and youth, the requirements of industrialization and urbanization, and so on. Today in New York, a citadel of modern civilization, subway cards and posters proclaim a new era in which civic and welfare agencies, alarmed over juvenile delinquency, attempt a massive reindoctrination in the values of family life, family worship, and family solidarity. Here the emphasis, for the moment at least, is all on parental responsibility rather than filial. But who knows—the day may yet come when that subway poster is graced by an apt quotation from the Classic of Filial Piety!

While thus making allowance for the fact that almost anything is possible in a rapidly changing world, one conclusion still seems inescapable—that Confucianism can never again stand by itself, looking only to its past. It cannot reassume its traditional form or maintain the characteristic Neo-Confucian pretense of self-sufficiency. If it is to live again, it must acquire the capacity to face the future, and today this means the future of the whole world, not just of Chinese civilization.

Benjamin Schwartz

SOME POLARITIES IN
CONFUCIAN THOUGHT

One of the striking insights that have emerged from the comparative study of thought is the realization that what might be called the problem of founders and followers is both universal and perennial. Whether we deal with Confucianism or Buddhism, Christianity or Marxism, we are soon confronted with certain characteristic questions. How do the interpretations of the followers relate themselves to the original or "primitive" teachings of the founders? Or, conversely, can the original teachings of the founders be extricated from the interpretations of the followers? Questions of this nature come up even in an intellectual tradition as close to our own time as Marxism, where all the utterances of the founder are extant and available. Everywhere we find claims that certain interpretations represent the true tradition while others are partial or total distortions. Everywhere we find generations which revolt against what they regard as the formalized, unauthentic perversions of the original vision and which attempt to recapture that vision in its pristine freshness—only to be accused of one-sidedness and distortion by their successors within the tradition.

Often, when confronted with the incubus of interpretations, schools, and sects which has accumulated over the ages, one is tempted to give up the search for any underlying unity. The social historian may be quite content to study later interpretations in terms of the interests and preoccupations of given times and places without attempting to relate these interpretations to the original doctrine or to the tradition as a whole. In China, for example, one might treat the Neo-Confucian developments of the Sung period simply as a manifestation of the social and cultural situation of that period.

Important as it is to place a given mode of thought in its historical setting, an exclusively historical approach eliminates a whole living dimension of the intellectual situation. The Neo-Confucianists were not interested in creating "Neo-Confucianism"; they were deadly serious in their effort to recapture the original Confucian vision. It would be unsafe to assume that in carrying out their attempt to relate their own preoccupation to the Confucian tradition as a whole they were necessarily greater fools or knaves than we. Their thought must be understood *both* in the context of the times *and* in terms of the *Problematik* inherent in the tradition as a whole. There are, of course, tendencies that bear no relationship—or only a tenuous relationship—to the tradition and that nevertheless insist on appropriating the name. The outer limits of any stream of thought are seldom obvious, and certain tendencies may hover on the edge between the stream in question and other streams. Within the Chinese world of ideas Confucianism seems to blend at one of its edges with Taoism and at the other with Legalism. In order to discern the limits, however, we must have some grasp of the *Problematik* of the tradition as a whole; and to achieve such a grasp, we must have the courage to be ahistorical—at least provisionally. We must be willing to confront ideas with each other across the centuries, suspending for a moment our concern with specific historical contexts. We must be willing to confront Confucius with Wang Yang-ming and Wang An-shih with Ku Yen-wu.

The founder himself is seldom an academic philosopher bent on building a rigidly coherent system. More often than not, he is simply a man seized with an overwhelming vision which he must proclaim. He is not necessarily concerned with the mutual consistency of all his utterances, and on many problems his thought may be fruitfully ambiguous. Therein may lie one of the secrets of his greatness. Nor is he generally concerned with aspects of reality which do not impinge on his vision. It is generally the followers who assume the burden of defending the vision against hostile challenge and who must attempt to relate the vision to those aspects of experience which the founder has left out of account. If the vision is accepted by a whole society and becomes an "official" philosophy, the problem of relating it to new realities becomes particularly acute. Such a problem arose when Confucianism became the official philosophy of a centralized bureaucratic state—a state which hardly embodied the Master's own vision of the ideal polity. In the course of defending and applying the vision, many of the problems implicit in it become explicit and many of its inner polarities come to the surface.

Confucianism was such a vision and such a philosophy. In the following pages I shall use the metaphor of polarity to deal with certain themes within Confucianism which seem to me to be of some importance. We cannot use words such as antithesis, contradiction, and dichotomy because the alternatives in question were regarded by the Master and by most orthodox Confucianists not as antithetical but as inseparably complementary. And yet, over the course of the centuries it became obvious that tensions existed between the poles in question; that some men gravitated to or toward one pole rather than the other in spite of their nominal commitment to both.

SELF-CULTIVATION AND THE ORDERING OF SOCIETY

A central polarity in such works as the *Analects* is the polarity of self-cultivation (*hsiu-shen, hsiu-chi*) leading to personal self-realization (the attainment of the highest virtues of *jen* or *cheng,* and the ordering and harmonizing of the world (*chih-kuo p'ing t'ien-hsia*). This polarity could fully concern only those with a vocation for political and cultural leadership—the superior men, or *chün-tzu.* It is, of course, true that Confucius speaks of "teaching" the people (e.g., in *Analects,* Book XIII, chap. ix); what they are to be taught, however, is presumably no more than the rudiments of proper family relationships. They are hardly in a position to achieve the extensive cultivation required for the achievement of full self-realization, and it is obvious that only those in public office can do anything substantial to order human society.

In the *Analects* and in the *Great Learning* the two aims form two parts of an indivisible whole. In the latter work we find a logical progression from one to another; and Confucius himself states that "he (the superior man) cultivates himself in order to give rest to the people" (*Analects,* Book XIV, chap. xlv). The superior man can achieve complete self-realization only in his public vocation. It might indeed be stated that a commitment to public service—even when such service is unattainable—forms one of the basic criteria distinguishing the Confucian ideal of self-cultivation from some competing ideals in the Chinese world. Conversely, society can be harmonized and set in order only when men who have approached the ideal of self-realization are in public office. Here we find what may seem to many the extravagantly "idealistic" view of government so peculiar to Confucianism—a view which sees in government primarily an agency for bringing to bear on society as a whole the moral influence of superior men through the power of moral example and of education.

Theory was one thing, practice another. The central tragedy of the Master's own life was his failure to find any opportunity to fulfill his public vocation in a manner in keeping with his superior attainments in the realm of self-cultivation. The superior man is not always blessed with "times" (*shih*) propitious for the public employment of his talents. The times will remain out of joint so long as superior men are not in positions of responsibility, but such positions are not to be attained when the times are out of joint. There is here an element of fate which lies beyond human control. Confucius himself, however, offers a concrete model of how the superior man behaves in such periods. He does not give up his attempts to fulfill his vocation. Beyond that, he contents himself with achieving as high a degree of self-cultivation as possible, while fulfilling his role as teacher and preserver of the Way.

This tragic motif in the life of Confucius was to be repeated in the lives of innumerable idealistic Confucian gentlemen down through the centuries. Within the centralized bureaucratic state of the post-Ch'in period, the times were frequently unfavorable in the eyes of truly dedicated *chün-tzu*. We do not assume that such "idealists" were more numerous in China than elsewhere. In China as elsewhere, however, it was usually the idealist who worried himself about the yawning abyss between the ideal and the actual. Men soon came to wonder whether it was in fact possible to pursue the goals of self-cultivation and of setting the world in order with equal hopes of success. Furthermore, as the bureaucratic machinery of the imperial state became more articulated and complex, there soon emerged, on the level of practice, the problem of whether the self-cultivation of the superior man, which was based primarily on his conscientious adherence to the prescriptions of proper behavior (*li*), was qualification enough for an official post which seemed to call for training in professional statecraft and various specialized skills. Did not the "ordering of society" require some sort of professional science of government? Self-cultivation in private life was all very well, but how could its influence be brought to bear within this type of state?

A debate involving this issue came to a head in the controversies of Wang An-shih and his enemies during the Northern Sung dynasty. While this debate was undoubtedly strongly enmeshed with social and economic interests, in this paper we are concerned with its ideological aspects. Again, it must be stressed that neither side in the debate ever explicitly renounced either pole of our polarity. If Wang An-shih was convinced that society could be improved only by reforming its wayward institutions and enacting new laws, if he was convinced that professional statecraft was essential, he never on that account renounced the aim of self-realization. His opponents, while attacking his emphasis on professional specialization and his reliance on institutional machinery, for the most part maintained their dedication to the perfection of society. There were, to be sure, borderline cases—men like the mystical Chou Tun-i (1017–73), who renounced all public office to devote himself exclusively to a life of philosophic meditation and self-cultivation—but the typical statesman had a foot in both camps. Wang An-shih's more prominent enemies, for example, for all their emphasis on the virtues of self-cultivation and moral excellence as a means of ordering society, had definite notions in the realm of what might be called state policy (*chih-shu*). These notions will be discussed in greater detail below. At this point it need simply be noted that those who stressed self-cultivation were not all indifferent to the institutional setting of society or the proper policies of state. One even finds among them "feudal utopians"—men like Liu Chih (eleventh century) and many Sung Neo-Confucians—who look back to the idealized social order of the Chou period as the only order in which the self-cultivation of the *chün-tzu* can be made a force for the salvation of society.

While both sides claim commitment to both poles, however, they tend to accuse each other (often quite rightly) of glaring one-sidedness. In the eyes of his opponents Wang An-shih was a man indifferent to his own moral cultivation and the moral cultivation of his subordinates, a man who relied on machinery to achieve the goals of society. His goal, furthermore, was not the Confucian "ordering of society" but the Legalist goal of "wealth and power." To Wang An-shih, his opponents were selfishly absorbed in their own self-cultivation at best, or in their own interests at worst, and unwilling to support the institutional reforms that were indispensable to social order and harmony.

THE INNER AND OUTER REALMS

The polarity of self-cultivation and the ordering of society concerns the ideals of the superior man—his life aims. The polarity of the "inner" (*nei*) and "outer" (*wai*) concerns the two realms of reality which bear most immediately on the achievement of these ideals. The two polarities are intimately related, but their relationship is complex. One cannot assume that even those overwhelmingly concerned with self-cultivation will be exclusively concerned with the "inner" realm, or their adversaries with the "outer."

The first elucidation of this polarity can be found in the famous debate of Mencius and Kao-tzu which appears in Book VI of *Mencius*. The key problem is the relation of the "inner" realm to the "outer" in accounting for the bases of human culture. Both realms are touched on in the sayings of Confucius, but nothing is said of the relation between them. Living in a later century, when the vision of the Master had already come under serious challenge, men like Mencius and Kao-tzu were forced to deal explicitly with problems which remain implicit in the *Analects*. The polarity which first emerged in this debate was then carried forward in the discussions of Hsün-tzu.

The outer realm is the objective social and cultural order, and in the first instance, the *li*, the binding tissue of objective prescriptions, rules, rites, and mores which holds that order together. The social order in question is specifically the ideal social order which in Confucius' judgment had been realized in actuality during the early Chou period. Interestingly enough, Mencius, Kao-tzu and Hsün-tzu all accepted the nature of this objective order as an unquestioned datum. The point on which they differed was the relation of this outer realm to the inner, the innate spiritual and moral capacities of the individual human being considered in isolation from the objective, normative cultural order. Was the outer realm an outgrowth of capacities and potentialities present in the inner realm, or was the moral content of the inner realm largely a product of culture? The question was by no means an academic one. Men had strayed from the Way; how was one to go about leading them back?

To Mencius, the good social order was the outer manifestation of spiritual and moral capacities innate in the individual human being. In Western terminology we might say that the natural law is imprinted on the human heart. To Kao-tzu the individual human being considered in isolation was nothing but a collection of rudimentary biological appetites. The objective cultural order could not be explained in terms of the capacities of the individual; on the contrary, the social and cultural order had an autonomous life of its own (as many modern schools of sociology believe it has), and human capacities were a result of the "internalization" of the values inherent in the order. Hsün-tzu goes still further: not only can one not explain human culture in terms of the innate capacities of the individual, but the individual's propensities actually run counter to the aims of higher culture (it is in this sense that human nature is bad), and it is only with considerable difficulty that he is transformed into a child of culture.

It is interesting to note that in dealing with the outer realm all three men concerned themselves primarily with the *li*. Although the *li*, to be sure, are part of the outer realm, they are only a part. Even in the *Analects* we have some discussion of *hsing*, penal law, and of *cheng*, government in the sense of state policy and concern for proper institutions. Yet Confucius himself, like Mencius and Kao-tzu, was overwhelmingly concerned with the *li*, for although the *li* are part of the outer realm they represent an essentially moral force. To the extent that the *li* can be successfully implemented, penal law and institutional devices can be de-emphasized. Hsün-tzu had essentially the same attitude; where he differed with Mencius was over the type of "educational" philosophy required in order to realize the moral order. Whereas Mencius felt that a gentle regimen was all that was required in order to get men to behave properly, Hsün-tzu called for draconian educational methods emphasizing discipline and a detailed and explicit working out of the rules of behavior. To both, however, education in the *li* was a central factor.

Hsün-tzu, however, was by no means willing to rely wholly on the *li*. His conception of the outer realm embraces the four categories *li*, *yüeh*, *hsing*, and *cheng*—"rites," music, penal law, and government. He tends in particular to place a high valuation on the coercive force of penal law as a supplement to *li* in achieving social order and harmony.

In the generation immediately following Hsün-tzu we find a decided shift of commitment from rites and music to laws and government. This shift was the work of the so-called Legalists, two of whom—Han Fei-tzu and Li Ssu—were reputedly disciples of Hsün-tzu. The Legalists departed altogether from Confucianism: not only were they completely indifferent to the inner realm and committed to the outer realm to the extent of championing brute force and institutional conditioning, but their very ends were no longer Confucian ends. Their goal was a wealthy and powerful state, not the Confucian vision of an ordered world of peace, harmony, and simple contentment. In a world where the great powers of the Warring States period were girding themselves for the final battle, they offered themselves as experts in the arts of enriching and strengthening the state. They strove to create a "rationalized" military and state machine, and to bring the masses into line by a severe system of penal law on the one hand and incentive awards for good performance on the other. From their point of view the whole fabric of the *li* was entirely irrational and irrelevant.

The distinction between means and ends which we have just made must be underlined if we are to understand the controversies stirred up by such figures as Wang An-shih. To the more orthodox line of Sung Confucianists any heavy reliance on laws and institutions was evidence of the desire to achieve Legalist ends. The Legalist philosophers and the Ch'in dynasty had established a close association between the two. In their view, Wang was clearly a Legalist; his insistence on new laws and institutions put him on the outer side of the outer realm. However, he and the other Sung "utilitarians" argued in effect that they were not Legalists since their end was to "order society" in terms of the Confucian image of the good order. Confucius himself, after all, had not entirely neglected laws and institutions.

Wang's case was somewhat weakened by the fact that many of his proposed reforms were in fact aimed at "wealth and power." He argued, however, that his emphasis on wealth was tied to the legitimate Confucian goal of assuring the people's livelihood, and that the defense of the realm was necessary to the achievement of peace and harmony. His opponents argued that he had committed himself to both Legalist means and Legalist ends.

It must be emphasized again that just as Wang An-shih's opponents by no means renounced the goal of "ordering the world," neither did they reject all concern for the outer realm. They were, of course, deeply committed to the objective prescriptions of the *li*, which they regarded as the sine qua non of self-cultivation. Beyond this, many of them had very positive ideas about how the state should be governed. One must here draw a distinction between a concern for the general institutional setting of human behavior and the belief that human behavior can be completely conditioned by institutional devices and laws. Confucius' own judgments take for granted an acceptance of the institutional framework of the early Chou period, but he does not assume that the presence of the framework guarantees the presence of the Way. What is desired is an institutional framework which will facilitate the influence of men of superior cultivation on society as a whole.

The "feudal utopians" found the solution in an idealized Chou feudalism: a state in which decision-making power is dispersed among many local rulers, each of whom confronts his Confucian ministers on a face-to-face basis and can thus be brought under their moral influence. The whole notion of the ruling class as an agency of moral example becomes more plausible within this context. On the other hand, the more realistic opponents of Wang An-shih—men like Chu Hsi—while regretfully conceding that the idealized Chou order could not be revived, opposed further tendencies toward bureaucratization in the form of new laws, institutional reform, and further intervention of the state in the economy. Positively, they did their utmost to increase the influence of self-cultivation as a force in government. In their view of self-cultivation, they tended to emphasize the resources of the inner realm.

Their economic policy followed the teachings of Confucius and Mencius: i.e., they accepted the notion that the uncultivated masses could be led to good social and ethical behavior only by the guarantee of a minimal level of economic security. In their opinion, this economic security could best be brought about by a "light government" policy. If government would refrain from heavy taxes, excessive corvée demands, ambitious military ventures, and displays of pomp and luxury, the people would be able to create its own economic welfare, and it might then be led by a virtuous ruling class to conform to the Way.

In spite of this type of concern with objective considerations, most of Wang An-shih's opponents (Ssu-ma Kuang is an exception) sided with Mencius in his view of the inner and outer realms. They were presumably concerned only with those factors in the outer realm which they saw as inhibiting the outflow of the spiritual forces latent in the inner realm. Only the more extreme among them turned away from all concern with the outer.

KNOWLEDGE AND ACTION

A third polarity that can be discerned within the Confucian tradition is the well-known polarity of knowledge and action. Here again we have no neat antithesis; here again the Master saw the two poles as complementary. Over the course of time, however, we find not only differences of emphasis, but also widely divergent notions of the nature and content of knowledge and the nature and content of action.

In the *Analects* knowledge (*chih*) and learning (*hsüeh*), are basic values. In attempting to revive the ideal order of the early Chou, Confucius necessarily stressed the knowledge of its elements: the order could be restored only to the extent that its culture, its institutions, and its *li* were known. The nature of this knowledge was not theoretical and abstract but concrete and factual. Confucius' good society was not like Plato's Republic—an ideal construct built up step by step by a systematic process of deductive reasoning and then contrasted to all merely "conventional" social orders. His good society had been realized in the flux of history. To know this order one had to know the facts about it. The type of knowledge required was empirical and "scholarly."

Nevertheless, the knowledge in question was by no means a chaotic heaping up of miscellaneous facts. There was the constant assertion that embedded in these facts was a coherent, underlying unity which could be apprehended by the perceptive disciple. "My Way," states Confucius, "is that of an all-pervading unity" (*Analects*, Book IV, chap. xv). Confucius himself did not extract any system from his separate reflections on the Way; he shied away from what might be considered ontological questions, and it was left to his followers to deal with these questions. Even such early works as the *Great Learning* and *The Doctrine of the Mean* attempt to furnish an abstract and reasonably logical account of the broad underlying principles of the Way. Presumably this effort to elucidate general principles was made at a time when the Master's thought required some sort of defense against hostile challenge. When Mencius and Hsün-tzu devoted a great deal of attention to the question of "human nature" in spite of the Master's silence on this subject, they were not simply repudiating the Master's soberly "positivistic" approach. Those who were challenging Confucius' dicta were also challenging what they regarded as his unstated assumptions. By the same token, the Master's defenders felt obliged to clarify and defend these unstated assumptions.

When we turn to the Neo-Confucian philosophers of the Sung dynasty, we find that they confronted the challenge of Buddhist metaphysics in addition to the challenge of native anti-Confucian philosophies. They simply assumed that if there was an "all-pervading unity" underlying the Master's teachings, the philosophic principles involved could be abstracted from the knowledge of the facts for purposes of philosophic reflection. On the other hand, to Tai Chen (1724–77) and other "radical empiricists" of the Ch'ing period this effort to deal with general philosophic principles without regard to concrete facts implied a belief in a sort of self-contained realm of ideal essences. Tai Chen believed that only by clinging compulsively to the facts could one be in contact with the Way, which was inextricably imbedded in them. The discussion of abstractions apart from concrete facts was merely "empty talk."

The issue of the content of knowledge also becomes deeply enmeshed with the attitudes toward the inner and outer realms. The Neo-Confucian philosophers of the Chu Hsi school were deeply committed to the importance of self-cultivation. Since the inner realm was the realm of human nature (*hsing*), they were naturally very concerned with the attributes of the *hsing*. It was precisely the inner realm of the *hsing*, however, which bound man to the cosmos as a whole. "What heaven confers," states the *Doctrine of the Mean*, "is the *hsing*." Even writers like Hsün-tzu who denigrated the *hsing* conceived of it as part of the "heavenly" or cosmic order. Mahayana Buddhist philosophy probably reinforced this association. Thus to achieve a true comprehension of the *hsing* one must understand the ultimate nature of reality. Here we find a possible source of the Neo-Confucian concern with metaphysical knowledge.

This knowledge of the principles underlying the cosmos and the *hsing* was of course by no means knowledge for the sake of knowledge. Like Spinoza, the Sung Neo-Confucianists sought the kind of intellectual enlightenment that would free the spirit from the bonds of the affects. Chu Hsi himself conceived this knowledge still more broadly. He saw it, in fact, as being encyclopedic: the ultimate organizing principles of reality could be found not only in the inner realm which attaches man to the cosmos but also behind the outer realm of rites, music, law, and government with which man must be concerned. Among the late Neo-Confucianists, however, the Neo-Confucian emphasis on the inner realm became decidedly more pronounced and "knowledge" tended to become overwhelmingly a concern with metaphysical problems.

On the other hand, those who were concerned primarily with the outer realm—men otherwise as different in their outlooks as Wang

An-shih in the Northern Sung and Ku Yen-wu of the early Ch'ing—
regarded knowledge of history, of the development of institutions, of
the "li," and even of law as the central focus of real knowledge. To
Wang An-shih such knowledge was the knowledge most relevant to his
goal of ordering society. Ku Yen-wu's position was more complex. Although, like Wang, he stressed "practical statesmanship" (*ching-shih*)
and the bulk of his scholarly investigations involved the outer realm,
his conception of good statesmanship was substantially that of Wang's
opponents. He favored an institutional setting which would make the
self-cultivation of the *chün-tzu* a dominant force in human society. He
did not feel, however, that individual self-cultivation required a deep
concern for ultimate metaphysical problems. Self-cultivation was primarily a matter of moral training: "In your action be guided by a sense
of shame; in your learning be comprehensive." The relationship between knowledge and the goal of self-cultivation has here become
somewhat tenuous.

In the century following Ku Yen-wu the acquisition of knowledge
came to be exalted in some quarters almost as an end in itself, without
reference to the goals of either self-cultivation or the ordering of society. The school of empirical research (*k'ao-cheng*) conceived of
knowledge essentially as precise factual knowledge of the cultural
heritage. Its members refused to discuss abstract principles apart from
the facts, and in this regard considered themselves closer to the Master
than their metaphysically inclined predecessors. In their divorce of
knowledge from all the larger concerns of Confucianism, however, they
certainly drifted far from the Master's original intent.

The Sung controversies also disclose divergent views of the nature
and content of action. The enemies of Chu Hsi and Wang Yang-ming
saw them as primarily engrossed in their own self-cultivation even
when they were deeply immersed in public activities—and with some
justice, since both viewed the arena of public action primarily as a field
for exercising their own moral musculatures, as it were. To Wang
An-shih and his school, by contrast, action was primarily "social action"
—the framing and administration of new laws which would affect society
as a whole and not merely a given official's own arena of action. Chu
Hsi and Wang Yang-ming were both capable and vigorous officials who
performed most spectacularly in the positions they occupied, and both
were very much concerned with their own performance as officials.
Chu Hsi would indeed have argued that the example of a noble and
capable official who does his job well is more important to the ordering of society than elaborate blueprints of institutional change.

It is important to emphasize that an orientation toward the pole of action in the Confucian tradition was not necessarily an orientation toward the general type of social and political action which modern men tend to regard as "practical." The Tung-lin party of the late Ming period, which was deeply concerned with the social and political situation of its own times and firmly dedicated to moral action, conceived of such action largely in terms of exhorting the ruling class to honor the prescriptions of the *li*; it was markedly indifferent to laws and institutions.

Divergent conceptions of the nature and content of knowledge and action necessarily lead to divergent conceptions of the relations between the two. To Wang Yang-ming, Chu Hsi's notion that only a knowledge of all the principles underlying the myriad phenomena of reality could lead to self-realization was a snare and a delusion: clearly the intellectual baggage of Chu Hsi's latter-day disciples bore little relationship to their day-to-day behavior. (One is reminded of Kierkegaard's disgust with the Hegelian university docents who could devise philosophies of universal history but were unable to introduce any elevation into their own squalid lives.) According to Wang, man manifests his spirit by acting in the concrete situations which confront him. It is ridiculous to suppose that a whole system of universal knowledge must intervene between man and his action.

This belief did not lead Wang Yang-ming to a repudiation of knowledge, but it did lead him to a radical redefinition of its content. There was nothing to be gained in seeking knowledge of the sum total of discrete general principles underlying all the phenomena of nature and human society; men should rather seek to know the mystic One Reality which is latent in the human spirit and which makes itself manifest whenever a man of superior spiritual insight faces up to the moral requirements of the concrete situation which confronts him. Ostensibly, to adopt this view is to reject the whole outer realm (except in so far as the situation which the Sage confronts may be considered outer), and to espouse a form of transcendental individualism which might easily break out of the bounds of Confucian objective morality altogether. Wang himself was not so radical. He continued to accept the "five relationships" and their outward manifestation, the prescriptions of the *li*. He assumed a happy coincidence between the intuitive impulses of the individual conscience and Confucian objective morality. The outer realm of the *li*, as he saw it, emerged directly from the inner realm of the human heart. Actually, among some of Wang's later followers—particularly the heterodox Li Chih (1527–1602)—the tendency to break out of the bounds of Confucian objective morality does indeed emerge.

I have here dealt in a very tentative and topical manner with three polarities within Confucian thought which seem to have an enduring importance within the tradition as a whole. The judgments expressed are preliminary judgments and are certainly open to further scrutiny. There are undoubtedly many other themes of equal importance. The aim of this paper has been to communicate some sense of the turbulent inner life to be found within a tradition which has often been portrayed in the West as a collection of trite copybook maxims blandly accepted in toto by innumerable generations of "scholar-officials." Confucianism has its own *Problematik* which we have only begun to explore.

In line with my purpose I have stressed the variety of alternatives available within the tradition. This does not mean that there is no common core of assumptions shared by almost all who call themselves Confucianists nor that there are no bounds (indistinct as these bounds may be) between Confucianism and other streams of thought.

Finally, it must again be stressed that no attempt has been made in this paper to link ideas to interest factors. However much the intellectual issues discussed may have become enmeshed with individual and group interests, no apology is required for an attempt to achieve an understanding of the ideas *qua* ideas.

Hui-chen Wang Liu

AN ANALYSIS OF
CHINESE CLAN RULES:
CONFUCIAN THEORIES IN ACTION

The purpose of this paper is to examine the clan rules in Chinese genealogies from the viewpoint of Confucian theories in action—in other words, to examine how and with what effect the clan rules transmitted and applied the Confucian teachings to successive generations in the various clans. The data are found in the collection of genealogies in the East Asiatic Library, Columbia University. My earlier study of the clan rules[1] dealt chiefly with social control, and to a lesser extent with value schemes and group organization; the present paper is concerned above all with value schemes and their complex ramifications. For my earlier study I used only genealogies printed during the Republican years 1912–36, in order to include some account of modern changes within the surviving tradition; the present paper draws upon the entire collection, including the genealogies printed during the Ch'ing period.

The term clan rule designates any formal instruction, injunction, regulation, stipulation, or similar passage found in a genealogy which explicitly prescribes the conduct of clan members.

The forms of the clan rules vary. Some are merely collections of famous quotations, imperial injunctions, excerpts from the penal code, or mottoes stated by ancestral members of the clan. Others address themselves to such concrete matters as management of the ancestral hall, regulation of common property, and common clan activities. However, the majority of them follow a standard arrangement of articles or short paragraphs, each on a given topic indicated by a caption, an itemized heading, or the first sentence.

In general, these articles extol virtuous and desirable conduct on the one hand, and condemn deviations and offenses on the other. Some lay down more concrete specifications for the conduct of family, clan, individual, and social life. A number of clan rules, though not the majority, stipulate measures of punishment. The predominant emphases of all the clan rules are two: first, upon the ideal of orderly and harmonious life in kinship groups; and second, upon the observance of proper status relationships among kinsmen.

The clan rules are basically instructions. They depend on moral persuasion, and they derive their sanction from authority, that is, from such impersonal authorities as Confucianism and the law of the state as well as such personal authorities as the clan's ancestors, its formal and informal leaders, and its family heads. The punitive provisions in some of the clan rules—oral censure, ritual discipline, cash fines, corporal punishment, denial of clan privileges, expulsion from the clan group, and legal indictment—are paradoxically less punitive than protective. They are designed to warn the offender, to see to it that there will be no need for the law to punish him except as a last resort.

The clan rules, as guidance toward ideal conduct, could not be very effective beyond a certain point, depending upon how well a given clan was organized and operated. It seems that even the clans which were sufficiently well organized and wealthy enough to have their genealogies printed did not have the necessary organizational strength and appeal to make the clan rules rigidly binding upon their members. The clan rules nonetheless had an impressive normative influence, even upon members with little education.[2]

After the earlier aristocratic clans declined toward the end of the T'ang period, the importance of the primary group was rediscovered by the Sung Confucianists, who reinstituted the clan system as a means of promoting self-cultivation, rectifying social customs, and stabilizing society. The purposes stated by these pioneers are worth quoting. Chang Tsai of the Northern Sung period said:

To control the heart of the people needs the gathering of clan members and the promotion of good customs so that the people will not forget their origins. To achieve this purpose requires genealogy, clan organization, and the ancient system of *tsung-tzu* [head of the leading lineage by primogeniture as the clan head]. Without *tsung-tzu*, people do not know where their own lines of descent come from. Though this system has lapsed, genealogies have kept its spirit alive. If there is no genealogy, the families do not know their origins and cannot be kept together very long. Without a control among the kin, even the sentiment between parents and children tends to be weak.[3]

Chu Hsi, one of the great masters of Neo-Confucianism in the Southern Sung, has cited Ch'eng I, the Northern Sung philosopher, as saying:

Without the *tsung-tzu* as the clan head, the imperial court has no hereditary officials to depend on. If the system of *tsung-tzu* is revived, people will learn to respect their ancestors and value their origins, and then the court will naturally command more respect. In ancient times, young people looked up to their fathers and elder brothers. Now the reverse is true, because people no longer respect their origins. . . . Only recognition of the relationship between superior and subordinate, between high and low, can ensure order and obedience without confusion. How can people live properly without some means of control?

Furthermore, the system of *tsung-tzu* follows the principle of nature. For example, a tree has its trunk, coming up straight from its root, as well as its side branches. A waterway, however long, has its main stream among other divergent streams. This is natural. What is needed now is for a few families of leading officials to try to revive the *tsung-tzu* system, that is, the system of keeping families together. One way of achieving this objective is to follow the precedent of the T'ang period by establishing ancestral halls and clan estates, so that the ancestral inheritance remains intact and can be managed by one chosen person. The clan members should always assemble at a monthly meeting.[4]

At the time of the Northern Sung, pioneer efforts were made to improve upon genealogies and to strengthen clan organizations. Ou-yang Hsiu and Su Hsün were responsible for laying down the standards by which genealogies should be compiled. Fan Chung-yen set an example by establishing *i-t'ien* or charitable lands and *i-chuang* or charitable estates to aid poor clan members. Ssu-ma Kuang in his writings drew attention to family upbringing, manners, and training. These pioneer efforts gained an increasing following during the Southern Sung period.

However, the Sung genealogies, being a new growth, were relatively few in number. Mostly, they limited themselves to genealogical tables and did not incorporate clan rules as such. The full development of genealogies took place during the Ming period, owing to a number of factors: the state's interest in stabilizing the social order; the emphasis of the law upon the privileges and responsibilities of clans; the interest of scholar-officials in clan matters; the spread of learning among the common people; and the growing financial strength of the clans particularly in the provinces of Anhwei, Kiangsu, Kiangsi, Chekiang, Fukien, and Kwangtung, where revenue was derived from commercial as well as agricultural sources.[5] The development of printing was probably another factor. Underlying many of these factors was the widening and deepening influence of Neo-Confucianism with its emphasis on family discipline and individual self-cultivation. It was perhaps in the later part of the Ming period that clan rules became a standard feature in the fully developed genealogies.

This trend continued without basic change into the Ch'ing period. Several Ch'ing genealogies among the present data contain clan rules of Ming date.[6] Many other Ch'ing genealogies added new items to the old clan rules: new compositions, new compilations of old quotations, imperial injunctions, excerpts from the laws, borrowed passages from the rules of other clans.[7] These Ch'ing genealogies, on the whole, suggest that the elaboration and revision of clan rules reached a saturation point around 1880. The clan rules of subsequent date show no significant change in substance. It may be of interest to mention in passing that the rules of a Moslem clan named Chu in Chen-chiang, Kiangsu province, save for an introductory mention of the five pillars of Islam, is not distinguishable in the least from numerous other clan rules compiled after 1800.[8] Even after 1912, the overwhelming majority of the clan rules still abide by the old models. A few of them responded to modernization by limited adjustments deleting obsolete provisions and adding some modern features, but these adjustments were little more than futile efforts to keep an old heritage alive.[9]

The principal function of the clan rules is to exercise social control upon the clan's individual members, and especially to provide normative orientation, with concrete specifications for proper conduct and detailed description of desirable and undesirable behavior. The rules derived mainly from the Confucian teachings; but to these they added a second layer of more specific teachings, amounting to a sort of value scheme that was more directly applicable to behavior in and beyond the kinship groups than the broader tenets of Confucianism. It is this value scheme that interests us here.

THE VALUE SCHEME IN THE CLAN RULES

The generalization that the clan rules merely follow and pass on the Confucian teachings and adhere to the Confucian value scheme is an inadequate one, for it tends to obscure the flexibility of the rules, and their tendency toward making adjustments and modifications within the broad limits of Confucianism. One clan rule concedes that "there is more than one way to achieve the essence of good family life."[10] Another recognizes that "rituals are originally based upon human feelings and hence their observance should not be compulsory" regardless of circumstances.[11] Several clan rules adopt the principle that both "consultation of the old, set ways and consideration of their present applicability" are desirable.[12] Another, the work of an old lady and probably based upon her life experience rather than upon the Confucian theories, says that "studying books should not make one follow the books in a deadly rigid manner; and in managing a family one should not adhere to deadly fixed rules."[13]

The above quotations, a few examples among many, show that the clan rules were prepared to select, restate, and reinterpret the Confucian teachings to adjust them to the realities of life. Sometimes no adjustment was necessary; sometimes only a slight adjustment would do; sometimes traditional Confucianism had to give way altogether. In short, the value scheme in the clan rules resulted from a complicated process of two-way adjustment between doctrine and practical experience.

In the following pages, we shall consider four aspects of this complicated process. The first is the ideological make-up of the clan rules. The Confucian teachings are by no means the only component in the rules. Actually the ancient classics of Confucianism, though basic, are less in evidence than the later Confucianist teachings, especially those of the Neo-Confucianists from the Sung to the early Ch'ing period, with their admixture of Buddhism, Taoism, and folk religion.

The second aspect is the influence of the state. The law of the state, which incorporated some Confucian principles, is the legal basis of the clan rules. Many of the imperial injunctions on moral conduct, by which the state transmitted and applied such Confucian teachings as it deemed especially important, were embodied in clan rules. At the same time a suspicious attitude toward the state, the fruit of the people's practical experience in their relationship with the government, also found expression in the clan rules.

The third aspect is the influence of scholar-officials. Men of this class generally gave their clan organizations strong support and moral leadership, and usually were among the actual compilers of the clan rules. These scholar-officials combined the scholar's idealistic interests with the realistic interests of members of the ruling class. On the one hand, they were devoted to Confucian teachings; on the other, they had their responsibilities as family heads and community leaders. On the one hand, they knew that the clan rules could be made effective only by a strong clan organization, requiring the active participation of many more scholar-officials and members of their families; on the other, they realized painfully that the conduct of many upper-class members left much to be desired. On the one hand, they were loyal to the state; on the other hand, they were responsible to the clan and inclined to avoid government interference. These mixed motives are evident in the clan rules.

The fourth and last essential aspect in the value scheme of the clan rules is their response to prevailing social customs. The clan rules deal with what is as well as with what should be; and they necessarily pass judgment on at least some of the social customs with which they are concerned. This judgment is not a simple matter of approval or disapproval; it may be a persistent resistance, a permissive tolerance, an ambivalent acceptance, or a tacit approval. It must also be emphasized that the rules were directed above all to the clan's less educated and uneducated members. One clan rule, for example, states that it renounces the difficult classical language used in the famous rules of the past in favor of the simple, plain language that most people can understand.[14] Furthermore, the clan rules necessarily drew upon the kind of practical experience that was largely shared by the scholar-officials and the common people alike, so that in this sense, too, they may be said to have responded to the customs of the common people.

CONFUCIAN TEACHINGS IN THE CLAN RULES

Among the numerous ancient classics cited by the clan rules, the most important one is the *Li-chi* ("Book of Rituals"), especially the section entitled "Nei-tse" ("Domestic Rules"). Next in importance are the other classics on *li*, notably the *I-li*, the *Chou-li*, and the *Erh-ya*. Other passages come from the *Hsiao-ching* ("Classic of Filial Piety") and the *Analects* of Confucius. It is evident that the clan rules place their strongest emphasis upon *li*. In the words of the "Nei-tse," quoted by some clan rules, "*li* serves to determine the closeness or distance of relations, to settle what is the proper conduct in doubtful circumstances, to distinguish kin from non-kin, and to clarify what is right and wrong."[15] The term *li*, sometimes translated as "propriety," refers not merely to rituals, ceremonies, and manners, but more important than that, to proper conduct and its ethical basis. It signifies both the conventions and the principles which regulate all group life, and particularly the life of kinship groups. Take the ancestral hall and the activities there, for example; one clan rule explains, "The ancestral hall is established, first for the remembrance of the ancestors; second, for the purpose of uniting the sentiment of clan members; and third, for the sake of teaching those to come the virtues of filial piety and sincerity."[16]

When the clan rules cite other classics such as the Book of Changes, the Book of Poetry, and the Spring and Autumn Annals, they are concerned mainly with bringing metaphysical interpretations, aesthetic sanction, and historical precedents to the support of the approved conventions and principles called *li*.

The clan rules quote several other pre-Han works, among them the *Hsün-tzu* and the *Kuan-tzu*. The Confucianist philosopher Hsün-tzu stressed the restraining aspects of *li* and pointed to the need for punitive regulations. His work paved the way for the clan rules to cite the *Kuan-tzu* on the desirability of supporting *li* with institutional and legal controls. Many Han writings are also quoted, especially the following: Chia I, *Hsin-shu*; Liu Hsi, *Shih-ming*; Pan Ku, *Po-hu-t'ung*; Wang Ch'ung, *Lun-heng*; Yang Hsiung, *Fa-yen*; and Ying Shao, *Feng-su*

T'ung-i. These books have two characteristics in common: (1) they
develop the Confucian doctrines on *li* to include an emphasis upon
ming-chieh (integrity); and (2) they advance the concept of *kang-chi*
(governing principles and discipline) as being necessary for all organized groups. In short, in Han Confucian teachings, the basic emphasis on *li* took two forms: voluntary control by self-respect and disciplinary restraint by institutions.

Besides the above, the clan rules often quote some writings of the
period between Han and T'ang which deal with the family. Among
these are Pan Chao's *Nü Chieh* ("Instructions for Women"), a classic
on the proper conduct of ladies, and Yen Chih-t'ui's *Yen-shih Chia-
hsün* ("Family Instructions") probably the earliest systematically compiled work of the kind. While Yen's book in the main follows Confucianism, it also provides in detail more practical ways of behaving and
treating people. Liu P'ien's work, also on family instructions, reflects
the aristocratic mode of living during the T'ang period.

The Sung Neo-Confucianists in reviving Confucianism developed
it to a new height. They amplified the significance of self-respect and
stressed self-cultivation in accordance with the metaphysical concepts
of *li* (principles) and *hsing* (nature). They implemented the principle
of disciplinary restraint by strengthening institutional control, particularly in the family and by extension in the clan, to a greater degree than
before. As we have seen, it is the Neo-Confucianist teachings that
occupy the foremost place in the clan rules.

Many clan rules quote with reverence the *Chia-li* ("Family Rituals")
by Chu Hsi and *Chia-i* ("Family Manners") by Ssu-ma Kuang. Fan
Chung-yen is highly praised for originating the system of the charitable estate, which provides regular relief and aid to poor clan members;
and the "Rules of the Charitable Estate of the Fan Clan" is cited in many
of the clan rules. Almost equal in fame was the "Chih Chia Ke-yen"
("Motto on Family Discipline") composed by Chu Yung-ch'un (better
known by his courtesy name, Po-lu), an early Ch'ing scholar who remained loyal to the Ming and adhered consistently to Chu Hsi. (A number of clan rules mistakenly attribute the "Chih Chia Ke-yen" to Chu Hsi
himself.)

Some clan rules include all or part of the *hsiang-yüeh* (community
pact), a system devised during the Northern Sung period by Lü Ta-lin
and his brothers, who formulated it in four principles: mutual encouragement of virtue, mutual rectification of faults, mutual friendship
through observing proper etiquette, and mutual aid in case of trouble.
It was widely adopted during the Southern Sung period. Especially
popular was *Chu-tzu Tseng-sun Lü-shih Hsiang-yüeh* ("A Revision of

the Lü Community Pact by Chu Hsi"). In the Ming period, Wang Yang-ming officially issued his remodeled community pact known as "Nan Kan Hsiang-yüeh" and put it into effect in southern Kiangsi in combination with a system of community surveillance of crime. From then on, the community pact system was followed in many areas.[17]

A fairly large number of clan rules include elaborate collections of quotations from famous scholars and scholar-officials, mainly from the Sung period to the early Ch'ing. Of the sixty frequently cited, more than forty are named in the *Ssu Ch'ao Hsüeh-an*, a kind of cyclopedia listing the various Confucian schools of learning and their notable scholars during the Sung, Yüan, Ming, and Ch'ing dynasties.[18] The quotations generally follow the Sung emphasis on *li*, self-respect, self-cultivation, and disciplinary restraint both self-imposed and institutional. These were the paramount Confucian (or rather, Neo-Confucian) values during the Ch'ing period when these clan rules were compiled.

This brief survey has shown the selective accumulation of the Confucianist teachings in the clan rules. One clan rule that illustrates this selective accumulation very nicely requires the clan in its meetings to hear lectures on the following: (1) the community pact; (2) imperial injunctions on moral conduct; (3) factual instances of filial piety, other merits, and demerits; (4) Chu Hsi's *Chia-li* ("Family Rituals"); (5) other writings on family discipline and self-cultivation by famous authors; and (6) the clan rule itself. After the lecture, the clan meeting should proceed to reward meritorious conduct and punish offenses among the members.[19] This example, which is one among many, demonstrates that the classics and the early writings, though upheld as the basic sources of the clan rules, are not as useful as the Neo-Confucianist teachings which deal specifically and directly with the family, the clan, and proper behavior beyond the kinship group.

The Confucian teachings in the clan rules became more or less conventionally fixed during the course of the eighteenth century. In this regard, it is pertinent to mention the encyclopedia, *Ku Chin T'u-shu Chi-ch'eng*, completed in 1725, which covers numerous kinship and social relations in its various sections, notably in its section on family norms ("Chia-fan-tien"). We find that the clan rules deal with a number of topics covered by this section of the encyclopedia: parents, father and son, mother and son, discipline of children, sons of the wife and sons of concubines, adoption, adopted heirs, womanhood, grandchildren, brotherhood, man and wife, clan relations, and domestic servants. In other topics, however, the clan rules fail to take much interest: among these are grandfather and grandson, wet nurse, sisterhood, sister-in-law and brother, uncle and nephew, aunt and nephew. Significantly, the clan rules are almost unanimously silent on the relationship between mother and daughter-in-law, which has a special heading in this section of the encyclopedia, and in general they express far less interest than the encyclopedia in relationships between various maternal relatives.[20]

This comparison definitely underscores the family-centered, patriarchal nature and the hierarchical emphasis of the clan rules. However, there is another point of comparison which is even more important. The encyclopedia quotes the ancient classics and writings on Confucian theory extensively; but the clan rules prefer to quote from more recent writings of a more practical kind. The availablity of the encyclopedia probably enriched the contents of the clan rules; but the Confucian materials selected from it were primarily those that seemed most relevant to family and clan activities in daily life.

There is further evidence that clan rules took their ultimate form in the course of the eighteenth century. Ch'en Hung-mou, a leading scholar-official active in the government during the early years of the Ch'ien-lung reign (1736–96), edited several compilations of Confucian writings of a utilitarian nature. His compilations, collectively known as the *Wu Chung I-kuei* ("The Five Collections of Rules"), consist of the *Yang Cheng I-kuei* ("Rules on Proper Upbringing"), the *Hsün Su I-kuei* ("Rules on Social Customs"), the *Chiao Nü I-kuei* ("Rules on Teaching Girls"), and two other sets of rules on the conduct of government officials.[21] One clan rule says that the *Wu Chung I-kuei* should be kept handy for constant reference.[22] The reason is not hard to find. Both this compilation and many clan rules share the same purpose, namely, to transmit and apply the Confucian teachings in practical matters. The appearance of this compilation probably contributed to the growth of the clan rules into generally accepted and even fixed models.

As might be expected, the Neo-Confucianist teachings found in the clan rules contain some minor admixtures of Buddhism and Taoism. One clan rule goes to the extreme of quoting many Buddhist and Taoist sayings and equating them with comparable Confucian teachings.[23] Several others admit the value of borrowing some good teachings from Buddhism. One says:

Han-shan said to his fellow Buddhist Shih-te: "People slander me, trespass against me, envy me, laugh at me, cause me harm, cheat me, and humiliate me. What should I do?" Shih-te replied, "I would just yield to them, tolerate them, suffer from them, be patient with them, avoid them, let them do what they wish, pay no attention to them, and wait to see what will happen to them several years later." Though this is a Buddhist saying, there is useful knowledge in it and it can be used as a principle in dealing with people.[24]

Other clan rules accept some Buddhist concepts but give them a Confucian interpretation. One of these rules reads as follows:

The Buddhists say that if you want to know about previous lives, look at the sufferings of this life. If you want to know about the next life, look at what is being done in this life. This is an excellent statement. However, what Buddhists refer to as previous lives and the lives to come stems from their theory of rebirth and transmigration of souls. I think what has happened before yesterday—the father, and the ancestors—are really the previous lives, and that what will happen after today—the sons and the grandsons—are really the lives to come.

A friend spoke to me of rebirth and emancipation. I answered that a family which has accumulated goodness will have lasting fortunes, while a family which has accumulated demerits will have misfortunes in the future. Is this not what we Confucianists believe in and an equivalent to the Buddhist theory of rebirth? A gentleman neither worries nor fears. He lives at peace and leaves the rest to destiny. Is this not what we Confucianists believe to be emancipation?[25]

A few clan rules advise their members to read *T'ai-shang Kan-ying P'ien* and follow *Kung Kuo Ke*; both are known to be colored by Taoism. However, these admixtures of Buddhism, and to a lesser extent of Taoism, caused no significant change in the value scheme of the clan rules. As will be shown later, the clan rules are generally opposed to the prevailing practices of organized religions. Adhering to the Confucian teachings in the main, they accept or reject certain religious influences largely on grounds of whether such influences strengthen or weaken the Confucian values they uphold.

STATE INFLUENCE IN THE CLAN RULES

The traditional Chinese state was interested in maintaining order through both the law and moral education. It relied to a certain extent upon the clan rules, which incorporate excerpts from the penal code in their texts, to transmit the law to clan members, as well as to uphold law-abiding conduct in general. Above all, however, the clan rules served as an instrument for passing along the *sheng-yü*, imperial injunctions on moral conduct. The *sheng-yü* are often termed "imperial instructions" or "educational edicts" on the grounds that they lie in the area of moral education; it seems more accurate to describe them as injunctions, for they were proclaimed by the Emperor and had the force of law.

These imperial injunctions had a complicated background. Mixing the Neo-Confucianist emphasis upon moral education and the state interest in controlling the social order, the Ming government instituted the *li-chia* neighborhood unit system to impose collective responsibility, the appointment of *lao-jen* (elders) to supervise village communities, and community meetings at the *shen-ming t'ing* (pavilion of moral education) and *ching-shan t'ing* (pavilion in honor of moral conduct) to encourage good conduct. Essential in all these institutions were the Six Injunctions proclaimed by the Emperor T'ai-tsu, the founder of the dynasty. This elaborate system of local control was disrupted around 1430 but revived briefly under the Wan-li reign (1573–1619).[26]

While in the beginning the Ch'ing government did not institute a system of local control as elaborate as that of the Ming, it did authorize the revival of the Six Injunctions in 1652, not long after its conquest of China proper. The Six Injunctions, together with commentaries on them, also spread to the Liu-ch'iu Islands and from there to Tokugawa Japan, where they were honored with many editions.[27] However, the Ch'ing government did not find the Ming document entirely satisfactory. The K'ang-hsi Emperor proclaimed his own Sixteen Injunctions in 1670 and his son, the Yung-cheng Emperor, issued in 1724 the 10,000-word *Sheng-yü Kuang Hsün* as the official commentary on the Sixteen Injunctions. From time to time, enthusiastic local government officials circulated their own editions of these texts. Other interested officials compiled and printed additional explanations (some of them in the colloquial language), illustrations,[28] and historical examples.

The Ch'ing government required local magistrates to give lectures on the imperial injunctions, but most magistrates did so only occasionally and in a very perfunctory manner.[29] The clan rules seem to have provided a much more effective channel of communicating the imperial injunctions to the clan groups.

The Six Injunctions read as follows:

1. Render filial piety to your parents.
2. Respect your seniors by generation and age.
3. Remain in harmony with clan and community members.
4. Teach and discipline your sons and grandsons.
5. Attend to your proper vocation.
6. Do not do what the law forbids.

It may be seen that the Six Injunctions emphasize family responsibilities more than clan activities; family security more than clan welfare; conformity to conventions more than self-cultivation; and obedience to law more than other Confucian virtues.

The Sixteen Injunctions read as follows:

1. Be steadfast in filial piety and brotherhood.
2. Be close to fellow clan members.

3. Be kind to community people.
4. Take care of farming productivity.
5. Be industrious and thrifty.
6. Support schools.
7. Abjure heretical religions.
8. Learn the law and statutes.
9. Follow the rituals in showing deference to others.
10. Attend to your proper vocation.
11. Instruct sons and younger ones.
12. Forbid false accusation.
13. Do not harbor outlaws.
14. Pay taxes.
15. Organize *pao-chia* neighborhood units to maintain local order.
16. Resolve enmities.

The Sixteen Injunctions are more comprehensive and more specific than the Six Injunctions. There are several close parallels between the Sixteen Injunctions and the clan rules. First, both follow the same sequence of arrangement in putting the general principles of desirable behavior at the beginning and the specific provisions on concrete matters—either desirable or, in most cases, undesirable conduct—toward the end. Second, while both the Sixteen Injunctions and many clan rules deal with intra-clan and community relations, their strongest emphasis is upon family order and family security. Third, those of the Sixteen Injunctions (7, 8, 12, 13, 14, 15) that stress obedience to the law and other required obligations to the state are reflected faithfully in many clan rules, sometimes in the identical wording.

Government efforts in moral education were by no means limited to the imperial injunctions. The K'ang-hsi, Yung-cheng, and Ch'ien-lung Emperors each issued a number of supplementary edicts giving further specifications and direct applications of the injunctions to particular cases. These edicts were largely of two kinds. The first kind censured certain influential, wealthy, and aggressive elements for engaging in various undesirable practices. Some edicts denounced those gentry who imposed their will upon the community;[30] others decried indulgence in luxury, especially in the matter of expensive funerals and weddings.[31] Clan organizations also had their faults; well-organized clans, as several edicts pointed out, were apt to start litigation against other people and even to engage in feuds with other clans.[32] The second category of edicts appealed to important elements in the community and the clan groups to assume leadership in upholding Confucian principles against undesirable religious influences. One edict after another called upon local leaders to combat belief in geomancy and witchcraft.[33]

Several edicts deplored the joining of religious orders, the holding of religious services in mixed company, and the practice of permitting women to visit temples.[34] The government took a particularly serious view of large pilgrimages across provincial boundaries, which might endanger state security.[35] Though the clan rules rarely cite these edicts specifically, they reflect an acceptance of the government's wishes by expressing the same views.

These edicts raise the question: What was the Ch'ing government's attitude toward organized clans on the whole? The government realized that it could not depend upon local government officials alone to propagate the imperial injunctions or to enforce moral education in general.[36] The suggestion that the *pao-chia* neighborhood units assume this responsibility did not seem feasible.[37] The alternative was to call upon the clan groups, especially the scholar-official leaders among them.

A memorial in 1736 pointed out significantly that the improvement of social customs and the spread of moral education must begin with the officials and their families. Unfortunately, it went on, many officials and their families were so selfish that they did not look after their clan members. Though the government sometimes commended a few officials who had donated land to their clans for the relief of clan members, this was hardly enough. This memorial suggested that a clan with more than 1,000 members should have a clan head with power to instruct and guide the members; that a clan with a record of several years without litigation should receive government commendation; and that individuals who made outstanding contributions to their clan, especially in relief during famine years, should be similarly rewarded and even given official titles. On the other hand, the government should punish both officials and scholars who mistreated their clan members. Only through such measures would it be possible to have the clan groups promote moral behavior.[38]

Though the government did wish to have the clan groups move in the direction suggested by this memorial, it did not want to regulate clan activities in such a formal manner. Furthermore, there was another consideration: from the viewpoint of the state, it might not be entirely desirable to have really strong clan organizations. Some clans in Kiangsi and Kwangtung provinces had already built up in the mid-eighteenth century unusually large memberships by including groups of the same surname who were not necessarily related by blood. Such clan organizations had not only extensive common properties but also great social influence. Looking upon such clans with political suspicion, the government compelled them to limit their membership to nearby kin and to limit their property holdings.[39] In fact, when a memorial presented in 1768 again suggested the system of assigning official powers to the heads of large clan groups, the Ch'ien-lung Emperor rejected it with a reprimand, pointing out that large clans often caused trouble by fighting with other clans or by dominating the community, and that to give clan heads official power would be tantamount to a revival of feudalism.[40] In short, the Ch'ing government wanted the clans to promote moral education within their existing structure but did not want them to become too influential. This limitation was also tacitly accepted by the clan rules.

So far, our discussion has separated the state from the scholar-officials. In reality, these two elements were closely related. The wishes of the state, as expressed by the imperial injunctions and the numerous edicts on moral education, were often the result of advice given by a few scholar-officials who were particularly interested in these matters. As we have seen, however, these scholar-officials served two masters. On the one hand, as officials working for the government, they saw the desirability of having clan organizations promote moral education and take care of their members without troubling the government. On the other hand, as clan leaders and thinking in terms of the clan's security, they wished to avoid involvement with the government, whether in the form of litigation, or in the form of government supervision of clan activities. For this reason, the compilers of clan rules gladly went along with the government in keeping the clan organization as it was.

The attitude of avoiding the government is clearly seen in three injunctions which the clan rules generally give to their members. These three injunctions stem not so much from the imperial injunctions or from Confucian teachings as from the practical experience of the people in general. In other words, they reflect the effects of government operations upon the people. The first injunction is not to discuss political matters. An early Ch'ing genealogy contains a Ming clan rule which warns that political gossip is unbecoming to a cultivated man, that criticism of local government officials is neither loyal nor kind, and that ignoring this advice may bring disaster.[41] Though such specific formulations are not numerous, practically all clan rules refrain from mentioning politics.

The second injunction is to pay taxes promptly, primarily in order to keep clear of the government. Prompt payment of taxes is both necessary and desirable—necessary because paying taxes is the duty of subjects who should be loyal to the government and grateful for its protection, desirable (and here the language of the rule is far more emphatic) because of the hardship which comes with the collection of tax arrears.[42]

The third injunction is to avoid litigation. The Confucian precept that clan groups should settle disputes among themselves is naturally a point, but by no means the only point here. Many clan rules base their advice on experience rather than on theory. They point out that the clerks in the local government are like "tigers and wolves," that many magistrates are unreliable and unpredictable and some of them are corrupt and cruel, and that litigation is invariably time-consuming and, as a result, financially ruinous. It is for these practical reasons that one should avoid litigation as much as possible and use clan arbitration to settle disputes.[43]

Confucian theory assumed that one who cultivated himself and disciplined his family should be able to influence society at large and contribute his share of leadership to government administration. While this assumption applied to a significant extent to the scholar-officials in government service, it was by no means applicable to the common people or private citizens, as can be seen from the clans' eagerness to avoid government interference. Despite the Confucian theory, the state definitely exerted a negative influence upon the clan rules; that is, the rules reflect a distinct conflict of interest between the clan and the state. As might be expected, the clan rules do not admit this discrepancy. At most, they try to justify a certain degree of dissociation from the government by stretching the meanings of such virtues as loyalty and honesty and by emphasizing the desirability of law-abiding conduct according to the imperial injunctions, regardless of how the law and the government happen to be operating. In any case, what the clan rules value are principally order and security for the family and for the clan.

SCHOLAR-OFFICIAL INTERESTS IN THE CLAN RULES

Idealistic Interests

The idealism of the scholar-officials in the clan organizations should not be underestimated. In the first place, they assumed the responsibility of moral leadership. Through the clan organizations they supported, the clan rules they compiled, and other clan activities in which they played a prominent part, they helped to instill Confucian values in the people under their influence.[44] Their function has been stated in many ways in the clan rules. One such statement is often cited:

Once a scholar has earned his degree, Heaven places the destiny of the common people in his hands. If Heaven does not want to save the people, why should Heaven bring up scholar-officials? If scholar-officials do not save the people, what is the use of their being officials?[45]

A true Confucian scholar-official has important roles, even when he does not happen to be in office. Another common quotation explains what the scholar-officials' interests should be and should not be:

The local gentry [*hsiang-shen*, principally former officials and close relatives of officials] is the hope of the country. By living at home and promoting good, a gentleman can move and influence the district and the neighborhood. He can also help train the coming generation. His substantial and moral contributions are a hundred times greater than those of a mere scholar. The best thing for a gentleman to do is to uphold the worthy, to make known what is good, and to exercise his leadership in improving social customs. Short of this ideal, he should at least keep himself upright, discipline those close to him, and maintain his integrity in peace and quiet. There is less to be said for those who look around for land and houses to buy. Even worse are those who trample upon weak and helpless people.[46]

Some scholar-officials went beyond this requirement of moral leadership and made concrete contributions to their clan organizations. They selected responsible clan officers, built ancestral halls and acquired ritual lands to support them, compiled genealogies and clan rules, promoted cordial relations within the clan and the community, established charitable granaries for relief purposes, set up charitable schools to educate the poor youths of the clan, rewarded members for exemplary conduct, and restrained those who had misbehaved—all with the aim of creating a morally uplifting and practically gratifying way of life.[47]

One clan rule records a donation of charitable land in the following words:

My father, Hsün-ch'in, had always admired the way Fan Chung-yen helped the clan [with charitable estates]. During his twenty years of government service, he saved money from his salary, after providing for his parents, and used the money to help poor clan members. After his retirement, he studied the rituals at home, contributed ritual lands, provided graveyards for those without descendants, aided orphans, and helped widows. He did not finish these tasks before he died. On his deathbed, he expressed regret that no charitable estate had yet been established and no charitable school had yet been set up for the clan. This was more than thirty years ago. I am now about fifty years of age, old, sick, and unable to do much. Deeply sorrowful that the wishes of my late father have not been realized, I now donate five *mou* of the land he left me to the clan as charitable land.[48]

Such efforts from father to son and even through several generations sometimes led to the building up of large charitable estates, as another clan rule shows:

Hsün Shu of the Han period and Ying Chan of the Chin period, in dividing their properties to provide for their clan members, earned unanimous praise. The term "charitable estate," however, originated much later with Fan

Chung-yen of the Sung period. . . . We, the Chao clan, moved from Chiang-yin to Ch'ang-shu in the time of our ancestor Sung-yün. We have remained together for ten generations and behaved toward each other with loyalty and kindness. Now, clan members have multiplied, and many are in need. My late father, Wen-piao, donated more than 400 *mou* of land to the clan, but this has been sufficient only for the purpose of helping to pay for weddings and funerals. A charitable estate in order to be registered with the government as such must have 1,000 *mou*. I tried to save money for thirty years but could not reach the objective. Unfortunately, my eldest son had studied hard and died early, leaving no one to assist me in this task. Nevertheless, this wish has never left my mind for a single day. I now put down the tentative regulations of our charitable estate in the hope that coming generations will join in this common effort.[49]

For clans that did not have charitable estates, the donation of ritual land served many useful purposes. Sometimes the donation was made by a single scholar-official, as in the following case:

Thanks to the benefits bestowed by our ancestors, I was fortunate enough to get government degrees. I felt that I should not keep my salary from many years of government service to myself. Originally, in proposing the building of the ancestral hall, the buying of ritual land, and aid for the aged and the orphans in the clan, I intended to contribute some 3,000 taels of silver. I did not anticipate that a severe famine, together with deficits in the treasury, would lead to my contributing more than 5,000 taels for relief in the area in which I served as an official. Consequently, my properties were sold, my family was reduced to poverty, and my intention to help the clan was no longer matched by my ability to do so. In spite of the difficulty, I have decided to give up the 250 *mou* of land on which the living of my family normally depends. This property is worth approximately 1,000 taels. I have turned in the registration of the land and the names of the tenants, so that the land shall be recorded [as clan property] for the use of the ancestral hall in accordance with common decision of the clan members. The use of the rental income shall of course depend upon the amount of the two harvests each year. However, it shall be generally as follows: one-third to defray the expenses of the spring and autumn rituals; one-third as savings to earn interest in order to build the ancestral hall; and the remaining one-third for the relief of the poor and the aged, for helping pay for weddings and funerals, and for clan rewards. All these outlays shall be made twice a year. It is hoped that the whole clan will understand my humble wishes, give more attention to education, and distinguish themselves in filial piety and brotherly love.[50]

It was not easy for many clans to own common property in land. Even building and maintaining an ancestral hall took great efforts. One clan rule testifies to this fact:

We, the Shen clan, had an ancestral hall which was donated by our ancestors I-chai and Fu-chai. I-chai, after his first government degree, became secretary in the Secretariat-Chancellery. After many years of service, he was a

circuit intendant of defense in Shantung province. Fu-chai, after the same
degree, took the examination at the Directorate of Education and became a
government school administrator. When they came home, they planned for
the ancestral hall. Without much savings from their salaries, they could do
no more than buy a house outside the West Gate, which was then used as
our ancestral hall. Owing to subsequent difficulties, only its main hall could
be reserved for the tablets of our ancestors; the other rooms were leased or
rented to meet the annual expenses of the rituals. Later on, during the reign
of Tao-kuang, as no one managed it, the tenants simply took it over. After
repeated negotiations by Chiu-fu, the former clan head, the clan's property
rights were restored but not without costing a great deal of money. This expense was met by the former clan head and my late father, who each contributed 100,000 coins, and by small contributions from other members. It
was by no means easy. From then on, the ancestral hall was registered with
the local government. In 1851, the tablet of our foremost ancestor was placed
in it, and the spring and autumn rituals were performed. The ancestral hall
was finally in good order. Yet it was soon destroyed during the Taiping Rebellion. Now, after the government has recaptured the area, our clan members have to plan for its restoration.[51]

The pattern of group life promoted and the values advocated by
the scholar-officials had a pervading effect among the general populace
and made many features of the clan organization lasting. This has been
confirmed by contemporary field surveys. Even in such areas as Manchuria, where, owing to relatively recent settlement, formal clan organization was generally lacking, a meeting of clan members sometimes adopted certain regulations in the absence of a written clan rule.
Where there was no clan head, influential leaders were called upon to
mediate in disputes between fellow members and to promote clan
welfare.[52]

In conclusion, it should be emphasized that the idealism of even
the most idealistic scholar-officials was not morally doctrinaire; it took
into consideration many realistic aspects of life. An essential task in the
compilation of clan rules is to narrow the gap between theories and
reality by adjusting the theories within permissible limits and applying
them as far as may be practicable. The clan rules, collectively speaking,
represent efforts to specify the Confucian virtues in the light of actual
conditions.

Realistic Interests

Compiled as they were by scholar-officials, the clan rules naturally
devote more space to the interests of upper-class families than to the
interests of ordinary members. Most rules, for example, include sections on training in proper manners, the importance of dignity, strict
segregation of the sexes, and how to deal with domestic servants. Above
all, the rules are concerned with the achievement and perpetuation of

scholar-official status. Many quote Chu Hsi to the effect that a family's first duty is to educate its members for official careers, with a view to raising the family's social position.[53] Though the vocation of scholar is unanimously upheld as the best, a few clan rules express some reservations about it. They point out that not all scholars succeed in getting higher degrees and becoming government officials. In fact, many scholars after having earned their first degree find it necessary to earn a living by teaching, a vocation which is not only financially unsatisfactory but sometimes demeaning.[54] Other frustrated scholars who turn to such irregular activities as contacting and negotiating with government offices on behalf of other people are in effect tampering with justice and should be prohibited from doing so.[55] Nevertheless, the majority of clan rules insist that a scholar, though frustrated, has many advantages. He is addressed as "sir," he has the privilege of calling on gentry families, he may have the opportunity of becoming a private staff member under an official, and he can apply his knowledge to such vocations or pursuits as bookkeeping, letter-writing, fortune-telling, astronomy, geomancy, medicine, and the arts. Moreover, scholarship has intrinsic moral value in self-cultivation.[56]

The scholar-official status, comprising both power and wealth, is as important to the clan as it is to the family. Many clan rules urge the use of the clan's common fund for the promotion of education. The rules of wealthy clans provide for assistance to promising young members who are financially in need of help, either through a charitable school or otherwise. Individual rules set aside funds for essay contests, permit students to use rooms in the ancestral hall as studies, provide assistance to candidates in the government examinations, and specify rewards for the successful candidates.[57] One clan rule is especially remarkable. It stipulates that any poor scholar in the clan who keeps on studying, whether he is working as a tutor or not, shall receive an annual stipend of 16,000 coins if he is preparing to take an examination, and half this amount if he is not.[58] This stipulation is noteworthy for both its encouragement of hopeful scholars and its comfort to frustrated ones.

The active promotion of education in the clan group is variously motivated. The altruism of Confucian scholars is one motive, but not a strong one. The immediate motivation is the prestige of the clan, which will be greatly enhanced by an increase in the number of its scholars, and especially its scholar-officials.[59] There is also a long-range motivation: the wish to have more educated members to take the lead in clan activities, to spread Confucian moral education, and to strengthen the clan organization.

This long-range motivation can be best understood in the context of ancestral rites, the most important clan activity in terms of holding the group together. According to the clan rules, only a small number of select members are entitled on ritual occasions to such privileges as toasting with sacrificial wine and attending the commensal banquet afterwards. These select members are those who have made some contribution to either the clan's welfare or its prestige. They include the clan officers, members whose conduct has been highly exemplary, and venerable elders, but they consist mainly of scholar-officials and those who have donated money and land to the clan. The special honor accorded them at the ancestral rites serves more purposes than one—to induce them to engage in additional clan activities, to show appreciation of their contributions so far, to encourage them to give more, and to inspire other members to become scholar-officials and active leaders in clan functions.[60]

If there had been no clan organization, the transmission and application of Confucian theories would perhaps have been limited to the individual families of scholar-officials. On the other hand, to keep the clan organization going, the active interest and financial support of scholar-official members were indispensable. Ideally a clan had certain properties in addition to its essential properties. The essential properties were those dedicated to the ancestral cult such as the ancestral hall, the ancestral graveyard, and ritual land to provide the expenses required by the rites. The additional properties were those devoted to welfare functions such as charitable land, school land, educational land, and charitable granaries for emergency relief. The main source of all these common properties was the generous endowment of a few scholar-official members, while the rest came from surplus income of previously donated land under good management and miscellaneous donations from the membership at large.[61]

A number of clan rules stipulate various measures for raising support from scholar-official members—for example, a voluntary or required contribution upon receiving a civil service appointment, earning a degree, acquiring land, or inheriting an estate.[62] Such measures were especially helpful in rehabilitating clans that had suffered from disruptions, notably those caused by the Taiping Rebellion.[63] Yet the formal existence of these regulations did not necessarily secure the support they aimed at. Of the 151 clans that were well enough organized to have genealogies printed from 1912 to 1936, only about one-third had some kind of common land, and few of these had more than 100 *mou*.[64] Only twelve clans had large charitable estates. One clan rule laments the fact that in a very wealthy area such as Soochow only a dozen or so clans had charitable estates larger than 1,000 *mou*.[65] As we have seen, the most generous endowment of common land often came from an individual family, with the father's example inspiring the son to follow suit.[66] This indicates that the appeals the clan rules made to their scholar-official members were not always answered.

During the Yung-cheng period, the Ch'ing government tried to encourage scholar-officials to donate their property to their clans for the benefit of poor clan members in return for public commendation and merit rating in the civil service. However, this encouragement did not produce the desired results. As a memorial of 1736 pointed out,

It has always been true that the improvement of social customs depends upon the initiative of leading families and large clans and that the implementation of moral education should begin with the officials. Among the scholar-officials in recent times, some have done well for their clans and communities. However, many have been selfish. Some of these selfish scholar-officials provide their own families with many comforts but leave their brothers and cousins in poverty and in need. Some of them have many servants, expensive carriages, and horses, while they pay no attention to their clan members who have neither enough clothing nor sufficient food. . . . When scholar-official families so comport themselves, how can the common people be blamed for trespassing against and disputing with one another?[67]

The records of a few charitable estates show notable success in overcoming many difficulties of management and in maintaining the system of relief over a long period of time.[68] These few, however, are outstanding exceptions. Much more often the failure of scholar-officials to respond adequately to the welfare needs of their clan left the clan organization with no alternative but to limit the scope of its activities, to the disadvantage of poor members. For example, numerous clan rules fail to mention any concrete measure to assist poor widows except a vague appeal to their close kin for voluntary help as a moral obligation. A number of clan rules require a fee for participation in ancestral rites. Some clan rules even insist on a donation before permitting memorial tablets of deceased members to be placed in the ancestral hall.[69] Under these circumstances, poor members could not help losing interest in the clan organization. To borrow the words of the anthropologist Redfield, there was a class barrier "preventing the cultural influence of the ceremonial centers from filtering down to the rural masses."[70] The transmission and application of the Confucian heritage became limited largely to the privileged and relatively well-to-do.

Even more detrimental to clan cohesion than the scholar-officials' inadequate support were the deviations in the conduct of their family members.[71] The clan rules reflect a painful awareness of certain common deviations; there are numerous prohibitions, for example, against concubinage not for the justifiable purpose of begetting an heir, against indulgence in luxuries, and against conspicuous consumption in funerals and weddings.[72] The clan rules condemn the young members of wealthy families for not being industrious and thrifty, for wasteful hobbies, and for forming gangs with bad company.[73] Gambling, drinking, and visiting prostitutes are regarded as ruinous.[74] Opium smoking is banned in the relatively recent clan rules.[75] The use of power and prestige to take advantage of fellow clan members is another kind of misconduct generally forbidden.[76]

The very fact that these deviations are so often mentioned is probably an indication of their frequency. The corrupting influence of a comfortable life seems to be stronger than the influence of the Confucian teachings and mores. Against socially undesirable tendencies, the moral appeals of the clan rules fought a losing battle. One clan rule goes so far as to observe that a family would do well to reside forty *li* away from the city, so that its members could not often go to the market place and expose themselves to corrupting influences.[77] This suggests the existence of a conflict between the Confucian value scheme and the city mode of living; the Confucian value scheme seems to be primarily the projection of primary group life in rural communities, while the city mode of living, at least from the Confucianist viewpoint, usually leads people astray.

Basically the clan rules, in transmitting and applying Confucian theories, suffered from an insoluble dilemma: the necessity of depending on scholar-official leadership, and the fact that this leadership was exercised by only a very few idealistic scholar-officials while their many colleagues contented themselves with a less demanding interpretation of proper Confucian conduct.

The Interpretation of Confucian Values

The scholar-officials had an active interest in interpreting Confucian values for the benefit of clan members. Their interpretations as seen in the clan rules tend to combine theoretical teachings and practical experience, ideals and realities. By way of illustration we shall consider the five leading areas of interpretation: parent-children relationships, relationships between brothers, marriage relationships, clan relationships, and finally community relationships and friendship.

In parent-children relationships, a number of clan rules extol the value of filial piety on lofty philosophical grounds. For example, one rule says: "Filial piety is a matter of intuitive knowledge and ability, and in fact exists in man's nature itself. Failure to render filial piety to parents is a crime against Heaven."[78] However, the leading justification for filial piety in the majority of clan rules is reasonable, humane, and practical. It holds that since the parents have done so much in rearing their children, it is only fair for children to express their gratitude in return by respecting, pleasing, and taking care of their parents.[79]

What, then, constitutes filial piety in behavioral terms? The clan rules do not approve of going to such extremes as the famous historical example of cutting out a piece of one's own flesh as medicine to cure the illness of a parent.[80] They confine themselves generally to an ideal on the one hand and a minimum requirement on the other. The ideal is to give the parents, in addition to their daily sustenance, a psychological satisfaction by understanding, anticipating, and meeting their wishes. Even when the parents happen to be senile, harsh, mistaken, or hard to please, a good son defers to them without showing displeasure, meanwhile trying tactfully to dissuade them from making serious mistakes or at least to shield them from their mistakes. The minimum requirement is to show due respect and to provide for the parents. Failure to exert efforts toward the ideal is not regarded as an offense, but failure to meet the minimum requirement is condemned as filial impiety.[81] According to field surveys, this minimum requirement has been the norm of conduct among the common people.[82]

To the value of filial piety, the clan rules add a realistic qualification. It is necessary for the parents to recognize the growing importance of their sons when they come of age and are ready to take over the family affairs. It is also desirable for the parents to exercise their authority without partiality or abuse, but for the well-being of all family members. In other words, parental authority, though supreme in the family, is not absolute. It is qualified by the value of mutual kindness and understanding. In fact, a number of clan rules maintain that it would be advisable for the parents to be patient and tolerant in overlooking minor faults.[83] Field surveys indicate that this advice agrees with the norm of conduct among the common people. The common people usually consult their grown-up sons.[84] They also consider it justifiable to disobey parental orders which are improper.[85]

Filial piety has a value greater than itself; the clan rules regard it as the basic element in all subordinate-superior relationships. Many rules project the spirit of filial piety into respect for elder brothers, for senior clan members, and for superiors in general.[86] One rule, for example, follows the *Hsiao-ching* in suggesting that sobriety in life, self-respect in official conduct, and honesty to friends are all necessary attributes of a pious son. In short, a pious son is an ideal gentleman.[87]

Actually, however, the value of brotherly love is not on the same basis as filial piety. An elder brother is only a leader among equals, with no authority to regard his younger brothers as subordinates. Hence, the clan rules uphold brotherly love mainly by appealing to the extension of filial piety, to sentimental affinity, and to the practical advantages of brothers' co-operating with one another. The behavioral content of brotherly love as given by the clan rules clearly underscores its co-operative nature: affection and kindness on the part of elder brothers, respect and deference on the part of younger brothers. Essentially this means that brothers should compromise and not quarrel.[88] One clan rule puts it plainly: "There will be no insoluble difficulty among brothers if one of them suppresses his anger and makes up with a few kind words."[89] Another rule warns that "one who tries to correct his brother's mistake should never be so overanxious as to hurt his brother's feelings, since this would not help the situation at all."[90]

Brotherly love is essential to the realization of the ideal of the large joint family in which several generations live together. Not only did the clan rules extol this ideal, but the state gave such families official commendations. On the other hand, many clan rules recognize the almost inevitable frictions in large joint families. These frictions stem from many factors: the varying earning powers of brothers, the sharing of goods and services in the household, disputes over inheritance, favoritism of parents, and especially jealousy and resentment between sisters-in-law. The root of all these frictions is the fact that each component conjugal unit has an equal share in the common family property and resources.[91]

The provisions of the clan rules vary on how to deal with these frictions. Some idealistic rules advocate the elimination or suppression of disharmony by moral persuasion and ethical control. On the other hand, a few realistic rules frankly admit the desirability of breaking up a large joint family when disharmony prevails, a course of action suggested long before by the famous *Yüan Shih Shih-fan* ("Social Code of the Yüan Family") of the Sung period. One exceptional rule has a modern ring: it criticizes the large joint family for discouraging the talent and initiative of its individual members.[92] However, the majority of clan rules are in favor of a compromise between the ideal and the reality. They suggest that each conjugal unit may cook and dine separately while continuing to live with the others in the same household. In this manner, brotherly love can still be maintained.[93] By implication, each unit may generally manage its own expenditures from whatever sources it has. This majority opinion is again in accord with the prevailing practice among the common people as revealed by recent field surveys. Apart from the common property of the joint family, each brother or his wife has usually held a "small property" of his or her own. Ordinarily, brothers have refrained from breaking up the joint family as long as their parents lived.[94] The Confucian values of filial piety and brotherly love have probably helped a great many families to live together within three generations in a tolerably harmonious atmosphere.

As for marriage relationships, the clan rules invariably stress the wife's virtuous qualities as being essential to the family welfare. Both for moralistic reasons and for reasons of social prestige, the clan rules insist that marriage should be arranged with a family of spotless background and matching social status. Some clan rules based upon experience have added two qualifications to this general proposition. First, they quote Hu Yüan of the Sung period in saying that "a wife should come from a family of slightly lower position and a daughter should be married off to a family of slightly better circumstances," so that married women will be satisfied. Second, they warn that social status should not be mistakenly equated with wealth and influence. Marriages motivated by considerations of wealth and influence frequently result in disputes and unhappy relations between the two families. Furthermore, wealthy and influential families often produce conceited and quarrelsome girls. The clan rules urge their members to look for girls with virtuous qualities, adding that such girls are likely to be found in families of high moral standing.[95]

After marriage, according to the clan rules, a woman should follow the spirit of the "Domestic Rules" in the *Li-chi*. Ideally she should observe female seclusion and sex segregation, take her place next to her husband in the family hierarchy, identify her interest with the entire family rather than with her conjugal unit only, and fulfill her duties toward all other family members. In case her husband is over forty years of age and she has not had an heir for him, she should agree to his taking a concubine. In return, a wife is entitled to the respect befitting her status and to protection by the family and clan against mistreatment by her husband.[96] On the mistreatment of a wife by her mother-in-law, however, the clan rules are silent.[97]

The rules generally forbid a wife to assume power over her husband, although a wife will be highly praised for assuming family responsibility, taking care of the family's needs, and raising her sons from childhood when her husband happens to be stupid, ill-behaved, or dead. The stipulation against a wife's assuming power under normal circumstances is dictated by the very nature of family organization. She must be made to subordinate herself to her parents-in-law and to get along well with her sisters-in-law for the sake of family order and harmony.[98] If she should assume power over her husband, she would tend to favor her own conjugal unit over other component units in the family, and she might even disregard the interest of the whole family in favor of her own family by birth. This general proposition does not really preclude a wife's assuming control of domestic matters so long as what she does is not in conflict with family order, family harmony, and family interest. As a recent study points out, traditionally and also nowadays, in many families it is the wife who keeps the keys of the chest and controls the domestic economy.[99]

With regard to clan relationships, one value which all clan rules highly cherish is that of clan leadership. According to the ancient classics, the leader should be chosen in accordance with the feudal principal of primogeniture—the heir of the eldest line of descent, called the *tsung-tzu*. The clan rules, however, have realistically departed from this principle. Some rules keep the *tsung-tzu* as a titular head mainly for ceremonial occasions,[100] but others never even mention the title. The formal leadership of the clan is generally invested by the rules in the *tsu-chang* or clan head. A man chosen for this position, according to the rules, should have a fairly high generation-age status and a respectable enough record in the way of fairness, honesty, integrity, capability, and experience to command the respect of most clan members. He need not be wealthy or a scholar-official,[101] but if he is, so much the better.[102] The system of clan heads functioned with considerable effectiveness in rural areas until quite recently. A clan head, even when he was old, weak, and poor, still enjoyed respect and mediated between clan members.[103] For such a person often embodied the kind of practical Confucian virtues which both the clan rules and the common people valued.

Another important value in clan relationships was cordiality and mutual respect among members. The main difficulty was class differentiation. Theoretically, the relationship between members was governed by their respective generation-age status; in reality, however, members of lower generation-age status might have higher social positions. The clan rules had to find a realistic solution to this problem. As one clan rule explains,

Close and remote kin all belong to one indivisible body. Good and bad members are of the same descent. The clan relationship forbids deviation and wrong conduct; the sentiment of oneness requires mutual respect and kindness. However, social customs have deteriorated and good feelings have become less and less apparent than before. Most people base their claims on the prestige of their families.

They remain friendly to one another only in consideration of individual fortunes. If their wealth is about equal, they call each other brothers. If not, they do not see each other. Because of some disagreement, they would humiliate senior clan members or trample upon helpless members or minority members, without regarding this conduct as wrong. Because of some trivial irritating words, a junior member offends a senior member and considers himself to be the stronger of the two. Some clan members live close to one another, yet do not offer to one another congratulations or condolences on appropriate occasions. Though some clan members live in the same neighborhood, they do not help each other in emergencies.[104]

Such attitudes are detrimental to clan cohesion; at the same time, they are understandable and frequently encountered. The best solution the clan rules can offer is for those with better social positions to respect those with a higher generation-age status, and also for the latter to make due allowance for the former.[105] The value of cordiality and mutual respect is thus redefined by the clan rules in terms of social reality.

Finally, with regard to community relationships, the clan rules betray a discrepancy between their moral ideals and their practical advice. They uphold the value of mutual help among community people and neighbors but fail to specify when and how such help is to be given. In emphasizing community harmony, the clan rules generally give the advice that one should defer to community people, tolerate one's neighbors, and be tactful toward all. This amounts to recommending a desirable minimum of involvement in community affairs.[106] One clan rule frankly states: "Avoid being a witness or a guarantor and you will have no worry in your life," and "As an old saying goes, 'Many good deeds are not as good as none.'"[107] Though this statement is exceptionally outspoken, many other clan rules in less obvious words express the same lukewarm attitude toward community life.

The clan rules look upon community relationships essentially from the family and the clan standpoint. The following is a typical example:

When someone in the clan suffers humiliation and mistreatment from outsiders, the clan members shall use reason to obtain justice. . . . However, when a clan member disobeys the clan rules, indulges himself in misconduct, arbitrarily dominates the community, infringes upon property of other people, or violates the law, the whole clan shall spare no effort to correct his mistakes. If he reforms, he deserves respect; if he disregards advice three times in succession and his misconduct might implicate other clan members, he should be brought to the ancestral hall to be reprimanded by the clan head or sent to the government for due punishment. The name of such an offender shall not be entered in the genealogy and upon his death he shall not be buried in the clan cemetery.[108]

The clan rules contribute to good community relations mainly by their negative restraining influence upon the aggressive misconduct of their members.[109]

On the question of friendship, the clan rules are emphatically against keeping bad company, and especially against having friends who fritter away their time in entertainment, amusement, and unbecoming activities. They advise that one should not have too many friends, since this would entail too much expense and not enough benefits. Instead, one should keep a few well-chosen friends who are reliable and have good moral qualities. But even with such desirable friends, caution is still the watchword. One clan rule after another explains that though friendship is one of the five cardinal relationships honored by Confucian ethics, the members should be careful about it. The way to treat good friends is to be neither too intimate nor too stern, but to be sincere and respectful.[110] Several clan rules offer the frank suggestion, however, that in dealing with friends one should be "squarely" upright but at the same time "roundly" circumspect, emphasizing one quality or the other as the situation may require.[111]

According to Confucian theory, as mentioned earlier, one should extend one's moral influence beyond the family and the clan to the community and society at large. By contrast, the value scheme of the clan rules is rather strictly family- and clan-oriented.[112] The cohesion and consolidation of the clan group, while desirable, undeniably led to tension in the community between the clan and other groups, notably the poor tenants on the clan property and especially the members of competing clans. At worst, the strong we-group feeling of the clans must have made for community disharmony, lasting resentment, and even inter-clan feuds.

Furthermore, in overemphasizing family and clan control over individuals, the clan rules point toward a kind of personality characterized by modesty, caution, and restraint. This type of personality was well suited to the stable social order in traditional China, which was rigid in structure and conventional in mores, but it was scarcely active, resolute, and energetic enough to fulfill the original Confucian ideal of leadership in the service of the community and the state.[113]

In the preceding pages, we have seen how the scholar-officials' idealistic interests mingled with realistic considerations in their interpretation of Confucian values. In some cases, the clan rules strengthened the Confucian theories by making them more specific and applicable; in others, they modified the Confucian teachings just enough to make them reasonably workable in the face of admitted difficulties. In a few instances, the clan rules in effect abandoned the Confucian teachings altogether. They no doubt made significant contributions in spreading this adapted version of Confucian doctrine, but they did so at the price of weakening the vitality and narrowing the outlook of traditional Confucianism.

The clan rules are interested more in promoting ideal social customs than in discussing prevailing social customs; nevertheless, they cannot ignore the existence of the latter, many of which clearly do not quite agree with the Confucian teachings. In this connection we shall here consider the clan rules' pronouncements on two issues: first, the religious customs which prevailed among both the scholar-official class and the common people; and second, the remarriage of widows, which during the Ch'ing period was condoned only among the poor.

Neo-Confucianism took a somewhat ambivalent position with regard to Buddhism and Taoism. It was opposed to such of their practices and customs as conflicted or tended to compete with Confucianism; but at the same time it absorbed certain of their religious concepts on the philosophical level which were acceptable from the Confucian viewpoint. The clan rules in following the Neo-Confucianist teachings generally maintained the same attitude. They raise four major objections to religious practices.[114] First, they make a distinction between acceptable religion and improper heretical beliefs. The acceptable religions are Buddhism and Taoism. Some clan rules admit that these religions are law-abiding and not without beneficial teachings, but it is generally argued that they are overly profound and abstract, and hence beyond the comprehension of the common people.[115] The improper and heretical beliefs are those which lead people to believe mistakenly in gods, demons, promised good fortunes, and threatened misfortunes. Especially dangerous are the subversive secret sects, which the law explicitly forbids.[116]

Second, the clan rules theoretically permit no religion to subvert the family and the clan institutions. Many of the rules forbid their members to join religious orders on the ground that parents do not rear their children for such a purpose.[117] Other rules advise their members not to employ Buddhist or Taoist priests to pray for one's deceased parents because this would impiously suggest that the parents have sinned.[118] The presence of priests at funerals is also viewed as contaminating the Confucian rites.[119]

Third, the rules are most severe in condemning the practice of holding religious services in mixed company, which violates the principle of sex segregation. It is regarded as revoltingly vulgar for females to brush shoulders with strangers, and especially for them to make pilgrimages to temples.[120]

Finally, the clan rules express mild skepticism about the magic powers claimed by various religions. Some rules raise the question whether prayers and offerings are not a form of bribery in the hope of buying good fortune, pointing out that if they are, the deities are hardly

worthy of their names. Other rules give the rational advice that for
illness one should spend one's money on medicines instead of on prayers
and superstitious offerings.[121]

The attitude on religious practices in the clan rules largely parallels
that of the state. A memorial of 1655, soon after the Manchu conquest
of China proper, criticized the spread of religions, especially Buddhism,
during the Ming period at the expense of the Confucian rites. It condemned the wasteful practice of burning offerings at funeral services,
the error of asking priests to pray for good fortune in the alleged after-
life, the use of precious resources to build temples and pagodas, and
noisy religious gatherings. The memorial also recalled that the first
emperor of the Ming had forbidden sending children into religious
orders.[122] The Sixteen Injunctions proclaimed by the Emperor K'ang-
hsi explicitly prohibited heretical beliefs. By government order many
heretical shrines and images were destroyed. One edict after another
was issued during the reign of Ch'ien-lung against sorcery, prayers for
the cure of illness, pilgrimage across provincial boundaries, secret sects,
the use of Buddhist priests in funeral services, and women's visits to
temples.[123] While the government made some allowance for the common people in the matter of following prevailing social customs, it
adopted a stern attitude toward scholar-officials who actively spread
unorthodox beliefs.[124] The prohibition of secret sects with rebellious
tendencies was of course strictly enforced for reasons of state security.

There is nonetheless an appreciable distance between the attitude
of the clan rules and that of the government. The clan rules express
their objections to religious practices in relatively mild language, and
rarely stipulate any punishment for disregarding these objections. In
a few cases, they actually sanction placing Buddhist images next to the
ancestral tablets and inviting Buddhist or Taoist monks to be the care-
takers of ancestral halls.[125] It is well known that the common people
remained largely syncretic and polytheistic in their beliefs and customs.[126]

The clan rules are ambivalent on the popular belief in geomancy—
the belief in "wind and water," which holds that the burial site of an
ancestor, because of its topographical location and geological composition, will have mysterious latent effects upon the good fortune or
misfortune of the descendants. In many instances this belief had become inseparable from the prevailing customs of the ancestral cult and
closely identified with the family interest. A few clan rules express disbelief in it; a few others openly affirm it. A large number of them,
however, sidestep the main issue of belief or disbelief and concentrate
on lesser issues. They suggest that one should not spend too much

time or money in looking for good geomantic sites, since such sites are often found accidentally; that burials should not be postponed for a long period while a good site is being sought; and that buried bodies should not be shifted to another site which is believed by a geomantic practitioner to be better.[127] This last point was also emphasized by an imperial edict in 1735.[128]

The clan rules on the whole tolerate many religious practices. Their disapproval of religions in general is broad and vague; their objections to some religious practices are mild or ambivalent; and even more significantly, on many other religious customs they are altogether silent. Although the Confucian teachings on religion were occasionally reasserted in their original purity, in general they gave ground to prevailing social customs.

The remarriage of widows offers another interesting illustration of the relationship between the clan rules and social customs. It was a few of the leading Sung Confucianists who first insisted that "losing chastity is a serious matter, while death by starvation is by comparison a small matter." At the beginning of the Ming period, the government adopted the policy of rewarding chaste widows with official commendation. The Yung-cheng Emperor of the Ch'ing period encouraged the building of memorial halls in honor of chastity and filial piety. With such government encouragement, and with the spread of Neo-Confucian teachings, the scholar-official class came to regard the remarriage of widows as infamous.[129]

Many poor families however did permit the remarriage of widows and in some cases even collected money from the prospective husband. A large number of clan rules do not discuss the remarriage of widows (except to forbid the remarriage of a widow to a clan member, or particularly to a brother of her deceased husband, in accordance with the state law)[130]—probably because the practice was considered beyond hope of correction. A few rules give a realistic appraisal of the problem.[131] They admit that "although the principle of chastity requires a woman to be faithful to her husband forever, even after his death, such conduct cannot be expected of, or imposed upon, every widow." These clan rules argue that though it is disgraceful for widows to remarry, adultery without remarriage would be far more shameful.[132] In approving remarriage reluctantly, several clan rules add the condition that widows who remarry must leave their family property and children behind to be taken care of by kind members in the clan.[133]

Confucian morality permeated society. Though the poor permitted the remarriage of widows, they did so only on practical grounds and for lack of alternatives.[134] In most cases the clan organization was unable to take care of widows whose families could not provide for them. Though a number of clan rules prohibit mistreatment, pressure, and other aggressive acts against helpless widows, and some provide mild punishment for such acts, many rules stipulate no punishment at all. The few clans which were able to give relief to poor widows from their charitable estates are the exceptions. Ironically, many clan rules show an eagerness to reap prestige for the clan from a widow of distinguished chastity by authorizing the use of common funds to solicit a government commendation for her and to build her a commemorative arch.[135] Indeed, a chaste widow apparently got more consideration from the clan after her death than during her lifetime. It is reasonable to suggest, though, that if the clan organizations had been better able to protect and provide for poor widows, the clan rules might have been readier to prohibit remarriage in accordance with Neo-Confucianist doctrine.

Once again we find the clan rules, while adhering to Confucian theories in the main, making a concession to prevailing social customs. Such concessions were not made lightly. They were permissible only when clan rule compilers considered them to be matters of minor importance and when neither the Confucian theories, nor the existing circumstances, nor the clan institutions, were capable of furnishing a better solution.

CONCLUSION: THE GREAT TRADITION AND THE LITTLE TRADITIONS

The foregoing analysis has shown that the clan rules represent a second-layer value scheme in operation, beneath the idealistic value scheme of Confucian theory and above the *ad hoc* expediency of everyday family, clan, and social life. They form a sort of subdivision within Confucianism, mixed with the influence exerted by the state, upheld by the inspiration of certain model scholar-officials, compromised to a certain extent by practical considerations, and mainly dependent upon the amount of support they can derive from other scholar-officials and their families.

The clan rules appear to have been effective in helping people to live in accordance with Confucian ideals and to place a high value upon the Confucian virtues. However, the tremendous emphasis upon conformity also helped to produce a type of personality more introspective and circumspect, and less energetic and active, than what the Confucian theories originally visualized. The clan rules necessarily modified Confucian teachings in the light of practical experience. Their efforts to arrive at a really satisfactory synthesis, however, were limited—not only by the uncompromising nature of many of the Confucian theories, but also by certain weaknesses in the clan organization. These limitations unquestionably made the clan rules less effective in influencing the common people than they might otherwise have been. Nevertheless, not a few values upheld by the clan rules were generally accepted.

Taking the clan rules as a point of departure and looking in both directions—their modifications of the Confucian theories on the one hand, and their effects upon the common people on the other—we find a state of affairs that fits very well into the conceptual scheme of great tradition and little traditions proposed by Redfield. The great tradition and the little traditions are dependent on each other in a given civilization. The great tradition belongs to a reflective minority; it is consciously cultivated and handed down through schools and temples, by philosophers, theologians, teachers, and literary men. The little tradition develops and keeps itself going in the lives of the majority of unlettered people, especially those in village communities, who take it for granted for the most part and make no conscious effort to analyze it or refine it. Within the great tradition are several subdivisions. The two traditions act upon and bring about modifications in each other.[136]

In terms of this conceptual scheme, we may identify Confucianism as the great tradition, and the clan rules collectively as both one of the subdivisions of the great tradition and a channel of communication between it and the little traditions. Precisely because it is a channel of communication, the instrument of a deliberate effort to spread the great tradition in the hope of modifying the little traditions, it has produced modifications within the great tradition itself by drawing upon, accepting, and tolerating some aspects of the little traditions; and it has also produced effects upon the little traditions in getting some aspects of the great tradition more firmly established.

One question should be raised: Under what conditions does this communication and modification process take place? Redfield has discussed one such condition; we shall add two others. First, the great tradition and the little traditions must have a fairly large common basis. Redfield makes this point by describing the general characteristics of the peasant attitude: the state of mind at once practical and reverent, the inseparable mixture of prudence and piety, the chosen mode of sobriety, the values of decorum and decency, and the restraint placed upon the showing of emotion.[137] Obviously the Confucian virtues—morality, rituals, self-cultivation, and self-restraint—are elaborations of the same characteristics.

Second, if the great tradition is to adopt some modifications from or draw closer to the little traditions, there must already be some elements in the great tradition which point in the same direction. This is a condition which this paper has repeatedly emphasized. We may illustrate it by yet another example. It is well known that the common people in China have always tried to avoid the government as much as they could. We have seen the clan rules adopt the same attitude, a negative disinterestedness in social and political activities outside the clan except on the part of those few who succeed in becoming prominent scholar-officials, a modification which is at variance with a cardinal assumption of Confucian political theory. But this modification is not due to the influence of the little traditions or the practical experience of the common people alone. Perhaps even more important was the influence of the state, through the law, the imperial injunctions, and other edicts, which, though formally associated with the great tradition, tended to discourage social and political activities. Also influential in this respect was the narrow familism developed by the scholar-officials, again a natural outgrowth of the great tradition, with its emphasis on the family and the clan.

Third, for the great tradition to have any effect upon the little traditions, there must already exist a functional basis for that effect within the little traditions. This is a contribution of Professor Niida's analysis of field survey data. The best example is parental authority in the family hierarchy. The Confucian ethics emphasize it, and this emphasis has definitely had effects upon the common people. However, it is not the only explanation for the universal acceptance of parental authority. Functionally, the necessity of regulating the use of labor within the family has the same result.[138] The effect of the great tradition is to reinforce and deepen, rather than to create, the value of honoring parental authority.

Because these three conditions were fulfilled, the clan rules were able to serve as a channel of communication between the Confucian theories and the common people, and hence as an instrument for modifying both the Confucian heritage and the ways of the unlettered.

Denis Twitchett

THE FAN CLAN'S CHARITABLE ESTATE, 1050–1760

There is little doubt that the Chinese extended family system has been a determining factor in the growth of a specifically Chinese society. The family was always conceived as the basic and indivisible unit of social organization, and all political philosophies stressed the importance of a stable and strong family system as the foundation for a stable social order. The Confucian thinkers, to whom social stability was an object of paramount importance, always paid due attention to the family, and in the course of time, as Confucianism became the accepted orthodoxy of the scholar class, Confucianism and the clan and family systems came to be identified in the popular mind.

One of the most urgent tasks confronting the social historian writing on China is to provide a dynamic picture of the developments in clan organization over the past two millennia. Too many writers have assumed that it is enough to draw superficial parallels between the attitudes and conventions concerning family life to be found in the classics and the facts observed by modern sociologists in China or even in Chinese communities overseas, and then to label Chinese society "static." In fact the changes which have taken place within the broad framework of social continuity have been very great. The history of these changes, the development of new family institutions, the changes in official and personal attitudes toward the clan and family, and the multiplication of regional forms of organization must be better understood before we can begin to write a history of Chinese society.

The present paper is an attempt to clarify some questions concerning the very important matter of joint clan property. In recent times, joint clan properties of various types have been an important means of preserving the unity of clans, and of maintaining some of their members' social status as members of the literati class. It is sometimes forgotten that these institutions are comparatively recent innovations—at least by the yardstick of Chinese history—beginning only in the eleventh century, and that the close-knit clan which we tend to think of as the norm is to a very large extent the product of Sung times, just as the more extreme expressions of Confucian familism begin with the Neo-Confucians. The most important among the institutions which constituted joint clan properties were the *i-t'ien* (charitable lands) or *i-chuang* (charitable estates). These were trust properties held in the name of a clan, endowed out of the charity of clan members, and inalienable. They produced an income to relieve needy clan members and to help pay those expenses—weddings, funerals, and the cost of education—which could easily cripple a poor family of gentry status.

This institution was first set up in the middle of the eleventh century by the famous statesman Fan Chung-yen (989–1052) as one means by which to produce an ideal Confucian social order, and was widely imitated until Republican times. We are particularly fortunate in that the Fan clan has left a very full and detailed family record, the *Fan Shih Chia-sheng*,[1] from which a continuous history of the clan from the time of Fan Chung-yen to the date of publication in 1758 or 1759 can easily be compiled. Since the charitable estate system was a source of great family pride, the compilers have given it very full treatment, three whole chapters being devoted to its workings. The following study is based for the most part on the material in these chapters, and is an attempt, first, to give an account of the administration of an important but not outstanding clan over a period of seven centuries, together with an assessment of the part played by the charitable estate and other joint properties in maintaining its clan unity; and second, to present an example of the sort of historical material which can be extracted from the records of large Chinese clans. Although the innumerable family records and genealogies of this type contain immense quantities of historical data, they have so far been used merely as sources for describing institutions rather than for compiling a dynamic history of the families concerned.[2] Like all other institutionalized historical material, these works must be read with their self-imposed limitations in mind, but for certain purposes they provide much information which is not elsewhere available, and they deserve to be more widely used.

THE FAN CLAN BEFORE FAN CHUNG-YEN

The lineage of the Fan family as it is conceived in the *Fan Shih Chia-sheng* begins effectively with Fan Li-ping, who rose to high office during the 680's, enjoying a brief period as Great Minister before being murdered by the Empress Wu in 689 for "having selected rebellious persons." He is said to have been a native of Huai-chou (modern Honei, Honan).[3] His son rose to be prefect of an important city, but his descendants are recorded as holding no posts or official rank, and the family seems to have been of minor importance.[4] At some time they migrated to the north, and in the ninth century they were living at Pin-chou (modern Ta-hsing, Chihli). Fan Li-ping's sixth-generation descendant Fan Sui entered government service, and after serving as registrar of Yu-chou (Peking) in the 860's, was appointed in 871 as deputy magistrate of Li-shui County in Ch'u-chou (modern place of the same name in Chekiang). When the empire fell into chaos after the rebellion of Huang Ch'ao, he was unable to return to his home and settled in Su-chou.[5]

With the fall of the T'ang, Fan Sui's son Fan Meng-ling took service under the kings of Wu-yüeh, and his sons followed him. His fourth son, Fan Tsan-shih, was a precocious scholar who rose to high honorary rank. He in turn had four sons, all of whom held office under Wu-yüeh. The third of these, Fan Yung, was the father of Fan Chung-yen.[6]

In 978, when Wu-yüeh at last submitted to the Sung, the Fan family, together with their former royal masters the Ch'ien clan, entered the service of the new dynasty. However, they were posted to various parts of the empire, and all the family records were lost.[7] Fan Yung served in a succession of provincial military posts, and died in office when Fan Chung-yen was only two years old (one year by European reckoning).

The family was thus a gentry clan of modest importance, with a long record of official employment, who had been dispersed by the troubles at the end of the ninth century, and had consolidated their position by regional service during the Five Dynasties. It seems likely that they were only moderately well-to-do, for they had long been cut off from their original clan home, and the Su-chou region was too long-settled to offer great opportunities for the acquisition of wealth under the comparatively stable government of the Wu-yüeh state. Moreover, the dispersal of the family in the early Sung must once again have weakened its unity.

FAN CHUNG-YEN AND THE FOUNDATION OF THE CHARITABLE ESTATE

When Fan Yung died in 990, his widow remarried into the Chu clan of Ch'ang-pai in northern Shantung, and took her son with her into the new family. He was brought up as a member of the family, and passed the *chin-shih* examination under his adoptive name of Chu Yüeh.[8] He learned that he was not a true son of the Chu clan only when, having reprimanded his adoptive brothers for their immoderate behavior, he was told that it was no business of his since he was not a full clan member.[9] He reacted very violently to this news and visited Su-chou in order to be reaccepted as a member of the Fan family. However, far from welcoming him, certain of the clan members made difficulties about

taking him back into the clan, and it is said that he was eventually received only on giving a promise that he wished no more than to restore
his true surname and would make no further claim upon them.[10] In 1017
he memorialized the throne for permission to resume the surname Fan,
and this was granted.[11]

His career in government was long, and although his major reformist
doctrines were never accepted, successful.[12] He amassed considerable
wealth toward the end of his life, but continued to live in a frugal and
restrained simplicity, while doing his utmost to assist not only his own
Fan clan, but also his adoptive family, the Chus, for several of whom he
secured employment by grace.[13] His deep conviction of the family bond
and the obligation laid upon the individual to act in the common interest
is well expressed in the following, which is said to have been addressed
to the junior members of his clan:

Our clan in Wu-chung (i.e., Su-chou) is very numerous; some among them
are close, and others distant, relatives. Yet, if we regard them from the viewpoint of our ancestors, all are equally descendants without distinction of the
degree of relationship. How should I not feel shame over their suffering from
cold and hunger? Moreover, "virtue" has been accumulating from our ancestors for more than a century, but has for the first time brought forth its fruits
in myself. Now that I have achieved high office, if I should alone enjoy my
riches and honorable position without thought for my fellow clansmen, how
shall I in future days be able to face our ancestors in the next life, and how
should I be able to enter the ancestral temple?[14]

From this passage it is easy to see his semi-religious conception of the
family as a continuous organism, in which the individual member is the
product of the accumulated virtue—for good or ill—of his ancestors, and
himself either adds to or substracts from this sum by his own deeds.
This attitude, which was long-established in Confucian thought, had
been strengthened by the introduction of the Buddhist doctrine of
karma. The deep conviction of this fundamental relationship underlies
much of Fan Chung-yen's writing, and helps explain the violence of his
reaction to the news that he was not in fact a true member of the clan
in which he had grown up. It is more, however, than a purely personal
attitude, for during the early Sung period there seems to have been a
general movement towards a tightening of the clan system.[15] This
movement stressed the importance of the clan system as a means of
achieving good social order and a general spirit of conformism, a
spirit which would lead to acceptance of the responsibilities stemming
from the ruler-subject relationship by analogy with the strengthened
senior-junior relationship stressed in the clan system. This rather practical approach to the problem was also connected with an attempt to

reinforce the quasi-religious aspect of the clan as a perpetual corporate cult group, and this tendency found its final expression in the Neo-Confucians' remolding of the family rites.

The reason for this stress upon the family in Sung times is not difficult to discover. The old aristocracy, who had been above all the transmitters of family conformism during the middle ages and early T'ang, disintegrated as a social group after An Lu-shan's rebellion, and in the ninth and tenth centuries were replaced by a ruling class drawn from a much more varied social background. The disorders of this period led to an awareness of the need for stable local institutions as a basis on which a solid governmental system could be erected, and the clans of the gentry were an obvious unit with which to begin. At the same time, the official class, who were no longer able to rely upon hereditary employment, were forced to seek available means of consolidating their own position, and again strengthening of the family ties was the obvious means to hand.

Thus it is hardly surprising that Fan Chung-yen devoted his resources and energies to the well-being and prosperity of his family, to ensure that in the future they would not be forced by economic necessity to take up demeaning professions or to allow such offenses against correct behavior as the remarriage of widows and the consequent loss of their sons to the clan, as had happened in his own case.

This in itself was nothing very original. There are many examples in the histories, ancient and modern, of persons who devoted their wealth and income to the support of relatives. It is almost a cliché in the biographies of virtuous men that they should donate their salaries to their poorer relatives while themselves living in frugal simplicity, so that "when they died there was no property to leave to their heirs, and not even the wherewithal for the coffin."[16] The fundamental moral and social attitude underlying such acts of charity as these is, of course, the very attitude that impelled Fan Chung-yen to institute the charitable estate.

However, the actual nature of the donation is quite different. The earlier acts of charity seem to have been simple gifts made to family members during the lifetime of the donor. Fan Chung-yen himself made such simple charitable gifts to the family at Su-chou.[17] But his plan for the charitable estate was much more sophisticated, for here the gift was invested in an inalienable trust property of over 3,000 *mou* held in the name of the clan, the income from which would provide a permanent reserve for charitable purposes. As the *I-t'ien Chi* of Ch'ien Kung-fu (1023–74) says, after drawing a comparison with Yen-tzu, who gave all his salary to his family, "If we consider the righteousness of

Wen-cheng [Fan Chung-yen], it equals that of Yen-tzu in quality. But
Yen-tzu's benevolence ceased with his death, while Wen-cheng's righteousness survived after his own death."[18] Obviously the investment of
charity to provide a permanent income was a great advance which
attracted wide attention, and was copied by many families.

In one sense this development is closely bound up with the contemporary changes in economic life. During the late T'ang, Five Dynasties, and early Sung more and more landed properties came to be held
as investments producing a steady income in rents. The trend in this
direction followed the relaxation of the old laws which had strictly
limited the rights of the individual to dispose freely of landed property;
it was also connected with the increase in surplus wealth which followed
improvements in agricultural techniques and the growth of commerce,
and with the sudden broadening of the base of the ruling class to include many families of lowly origins who had an urgent need for economic security. The charitable estate was merely a rather special kind
of family estate in so far as it was designed to strengthen the economic
foundations of the family.

But the ordinary *chuang-yüan* estate in the Sung period was held in
the name of a single owner and like all landed property was liable to
fragmentation on his death, since Chinese inheritance law did not
recognize primogeniture; whereas the charitable estate was held in the
name of a perpetual corporation—the cult group participating in the
common ancestral rites—and thus fragmentation was avoided. This
development again could not have taken place under the rigid equalization (*chün-t'ien*) laws of the early T'ang, for these had been based
on the assumption that land ownership was merely personal tenure on
a longer or shorter basis, the actual possession and disposal rights in
land remaining theoretically in the hands of the emperor.

However, there was one accepted exception to this rule already
under the T'ang, and it is here, rather than in the estates of Sung times,
that we should seek the original model from which the charitable
estate was developed. This was the *ch'ang-chu t'ien*, the permanent
endowments in land held by the Buddhist monastic communities. It
is surprising that this connection has never yet been recognized, for
the parallel is very close. The properties were each composed of invested donations, and each was held in the name of a perpetual
corporation and managed on behalf of the corporate body by members
chosen for the task.

It may seem surprising to see a Buddhist origin for an institution
which has been widely considered a manifestation of Confucian clan-

consciousness, and whose founder was later enshrined in the state Confucian temple. However, it is clear that the Fans had extensive connections with Buddhism. The Su-chou area, and all the region ruled by the kings of Wu-yüeh, was a stronghold of Buddhism in early Sung times, and the founder of the Su-chou branch of the clan, Fan Sui, with his immediate descendants, was buried in a monastery on T'ien-p'ing shan.[19] But much more significant is the fact that Fan Chung-yen himself was educated in a monastery, the famous Li-ch'üan ssu on Mount Ch'ang-pai near the home of his adoptive clan.[20] By a happy chance we know that this monastery had a long history of property administration going well back into the eighth century.[21] Although the education Fan Chung-yen received was probably a conventional Confucian one, it is almost certain that he had the opportunity of witnessing the management of a Buddhist estate during his most impressionable years, before he was suddenly and violently confronted with the evidence of the poverty of his own clan.

Moreover, his deeply emotional response to the family relationship, which is borne out by many of the anecdotes attached to his name, would naturally incline him to see the clan as a continuing religious community, analogous to the Buddhist community, the *samgha*.

This connection with Buddhism did not cease with Fan Chung-yen's childhood. In 1044 he requested permission to take over the former shrine for Yüan-lu kung on T'ien-p'ing shan west of Su-chou, which contained the tombs of his ancestors, to rename it Pai-yün ssu, and to use it as his private chapel (*kung-tê ssu*).[22] In a sense this was simply an act of filial piety, since the monks said prayers for the ancestors, but this in itself shows Fan's respect for Buddhism.

His son, Fan Shun-jen, who more than anybody was responsible for the survival and expansion of the charitable estate, was also closely connected with Buddhism. He in turn established a private chapel at the tomb of Fan Chung-yen in 1056, and received imperial permission to ordain a monk each year to conduct the ancestral prayers. When he in turn rose to the highest rank, he obtained permission to increase the number of monks ordained annually.[23]

The strong connection of the monks with the family sacrifices during these early years is also borne out by another of Shun-jen's schemes. In 1079 he set up a thousand *mou* of ritual land (*chi-t'ien*) attached to the T'ien-p'ing shan family chapel, whose income was specifically designed to defray the cost of the annual sacrifices. This land and its income were placed not under the charitable estate as might have been expected, but under the monks of the chapel. In 1109 Fan Cheng-ch'ing established a separate endowment of "incense land" (*hsiang-huo t'ien*) whose income was to pay for Buddhist ceremonies on behalf of the deceased members of the clan.[24]

The charitable aspect of the estate's organization coincided with the Buddhist emphasis on charity, and several instances of specifically Buddhist-inspired charity are recorded in the "biographies of notable women members." One wife insisted that her dowry land (*lien-t'ien*) should be used for the support of needy family members.[25]

During the centuries covered by the *Fan Shih Chia-sheng* a steady trickle of family members—an average of one or two per generation—were ordained as monks. It would be interesting to know whether they became monks in the family temples, but no such information is given, since on taking full vows a monk ceased to figure on the family register.

The family connection with Buddhism even survived the hardening of the official attitude toward the church during Ch'ien-lung, for members were ordained in this reign, and in 1744 a further endowment of "incense land" was added to the estate.[26]

There is thus evidence of a strong and lasting link between the clan and Buddhism. If, as I have suggested, the Buddhist *ch'ang-chu t'ien* provided a model for the charitable estate, there was one very important difference between the perpetual corporation represented by the *samgha* and that formed by the common descent group of the clan. Whereas the *samgha* was of more or less constant size, the number of its ordinations and members being strictly controlled by law, the clan group was constantly increasing in size. Moreover, new members of a Buddhist community often brought with them considerable property, much of which was taken into the common treasury of the community. The individual monks in general had little individual property over which they retained control, and depended entirely on the community investments and the charity of the faithful laity for their support. The family, however, was a much less tightly knit community, and in fact functioned as a community only in the two limited fields of joint worship and mutual assistance. Each of its constituent families was financially independent, having its own properties of greater or lesser size. Since the charitable estate rules as laid down by Fan Chung-yen stipulate a fixed grant to all family members not currently serving in an official post, it is obvious that unless some means were found to increase either the size or the productivity of the investments, sooner or later the natural increase of the family would reach a point at which the income would be insufficient for the grants. Hence the charitable estate as originally conceived was inherently unstable by comparison with the *ch'ang-chu t'ien* on which it was modeled, and it was perhaps because the *samgha* properties did not suffer from this instability that Fan Chung-yen did not visualize the problem and avert it by limiting grants to those members who were actually in need.

Later charitable estates which in other respects imitated the Fan clan's model devised means of meeting this problem: first, by limiting grants to impecunious family members, and second, by reinvesting surplus income in additional lands or by employing the income for loans at interest.[27] The latter was by far the most profitable means of providing additional income—in one instance it increased a family's property from 10 to 200 *mou* within a decade[28]—but was specifically banned by the Fan family rules. The only reinvestment which these seem to have visualized, and this only in the later rules, was the advancing of money for mortgage on the security of lands.[29] This is undoubtedly a reflection of the Confucian anti-commercial attitude, and it is interesting to contrast it with that of the Buddhists, who did not hesitate to use their funds for loans and similar transactions.

According to the *Nien-p'u* of Fan Chung-yen compiled by Lou Ho (1137–1213), the formal foundation of the charitable estate took place in the tenth month of 1049, but it seems preferable to follow another account by which the property is said to have been acquired gradually during the forties.[30] Elsewhere we are told that Fan formulated the scheme long before, but that for twenty years he had not the resources to put it into effect.[31] His younger relatives are said to have suggested that he should buy a property near Loyang for his retirement. His reply is worth quoting as revealing something of his attitude:

If a man takes pleasure in virtuous conduct and righteousness, he can put aside all concern over his physical body. How mush less need he be concerned about where he lives! Now I have passed sixty, and have little longer to live. Were I to establish a residence with gardens and grounds, what pleasure could I look forward to in living there? My concern is not that I shall retire and have no place in which to live, but that my rank is high and it will prove difficult to retire. At Loyang the estates of grand officials look out the one over the other. Those who own them can never go on enjoying them forever—should I alone be able to do so? And should I be able to enjoy such a life and feel happy about it afterwards? No, my surplus salary and rewards should go to support my clan. If you respect my words do not give any more thought to the matter.[32]

In 1050 he drew up the first rules of administration, which are worth quoting in full.

1. Every branch (*fang*) by turns shall calculate the number of its members, and one *sheng* of rice shall be granted [daily] to each person. All these grants shall be made in polished rice. If they are paid out in hulled rice, the amount shall be increased proportionately as a temporary expedient. [When

granting hulled rice, one *tou* shall be equivalent to eight *sheng* of polished rice. The total grant per month in respect of each individual will be three *tou* of polished rice.]

2. Male and female children of five years of age and above shall be included in the total.

3. Female servants who have borne children in the family (i.e., by members of the family) who have reached fifteen years of age, or who are themselves fifty years of age or more, are permitted to be granted rice.

4. For winter clothing each individual shall receive one length [of silk]. Children if less than ten and more than five years of age shall each be granted half a length.

5. In each branch it is permitted to issue rice for a single slave. But they shall not be granted clothing.

6. Whenever good fortune or ill is encountered [which would alter the family circumstances], or whenever there is any increase or decrease of numbers, it should be entered in the registers immediately.

7. Each branch of a family should establish an entitlement list for requesting grain issues [*ch'ing-mi li-tzu*]. At the end of every month the manager [*chang-kuan jen*] shall consider and sanction these requests. It is forbidden to make prior arrangements, or to exceed the monthly allowance in making grants. The manager himself should also establish a register to check and control them, and this register should record a quota for each branch based on the number of its members. Should the manager make any wasteful expenditure or make advance payments to anybody, the branches are permitted to review the matter and force him to pay an indemnity.

8. On the marriage of daughters a grant of thirty strings of cash shall be made. In the case of a second marriage twenty strings. [These shall be paid in cash at the rate of seventy-seven cash per hundred. All the following cases should accord with this rule.]

9. On taking a wife a grant of twenty strings shall be made. In the case of a second marriage there will be no grant.

10. In the case of members who become officials, each time they return to the family to await a vacant post, to await selection, or to perform mourning for their parents, or where they are employed in official posts in Szechuan, Kwangtung, or Fukien and leave their families in their home village, they shall be allowed rice and silk, and money grants on occasions of good or ill fortune in accordance with the general rule for the various branches. Even when an official is employed in a post near to his home, if he leaves his family behind for some good reason, grants will still be made to them according to this rule.

11. Regarding payments for mourning and funerals in the different branches: in the case of a senior member when mourning begins a grant of ten strings shall be made, and a further fifteen strings at the time of the interment. For more junior members, five strings and ten strings at interment. In the case of low-ranking members or of young persons under the age of nineteen years, seven strings to cover both mourning and burial. For those under fifteen years, three strings; and for those under ten years, two strings. No grant shall be made in the case of persons under seven years of age, or in the case of slaves or servants.

12. If there should be any among the relatives of the clan by marriage living in the district who should be in poverty or dire need, or who should have fallen into unexpected difficulties or should have met with a year of dearth and been unable to provide for themselves, the branches should jointly discuss the case to arrive at the facts and then arrange to provide assistance from the grain of the charitable lands.

13. Regarding the stock of rice to be kept in charge (of the charitable estate) from year to year: as from the tenth month 1050 the monthly grant of provisions shall be made, together with that of silk for winter clothing. It is agreed that as from 1051, during each year when there is a full harvest, grain rations for two years shall be hulled and stored. If a year of dearth occurs, no grants shall be made apart from the issue of provisions. If there should be a surplus over and above the reserve of two years' rations, funeral and mourning expenses will be granted first, and then marriage expenses. If there is still a surplus left, winter clothing may be granted. However, if the surplus is not very large, such things as good or ill fortune (i.e., marriages or mourning) shall be jointly discussed, and the amount available divided up and granted in equitable proportions. Or if no grants are to be made [to all entitled to them] they shall be made first to those who have suffered misfortune (mourning) and then to those who have encountered good fortune (marriages). In cases where more than one person has suffered bereavement at the same time, senior members shall take precedence over junior members in the making of grants. Where the relative seniority of those concerned is the same, the grant shall be made on the basis of priority of the bereavement or burial. If, after paying out the above-mentioned rations and allowances for marriages and burials, there should still remain a surplus, this must not be sold off, but must be hulled so as to provide a store of rations for three or more years. If there be any anxiety about grain in store going stale, after the day when the autumn harvest is completed it may be sold off and exchanged for fresh rice.

All members of the clan branches shall together carefully comply with the above rules.

1050, 10th month.

Fan, Academician of the Tzu-cheng Hall, Vice-minister of Rites, Prefect of Hang-chou.

Sealed.[33]

These basic rules are very simple, and planned purely with the idea of providing support and insurance for clan members against unexpected financial burdens. The management was left in the hands of a manager (*chang-kuan jen*), the manner of whose appointment is left very vague. The memorial of 1064 presented by Fan Shun-jen (see below) tells us that Fan Chung-yen "looked among the junior members of the various branches, and selected one to manage [the charitable estate]."[34] His powers were restricted to collecting rent in grain, maintaining an adequate stock of grain as security against crop failure, and distributing the various amounts to which members were entitled. It is worth noting that he was expressly forbidden to sell off surplus grain, though it is difficult to visualize how the money and silk involved in the grants were to be obtained except by sale of grain, unless the rents were collected in cash as well as in kind, which is unlikely.

After Fan Chung-yen's death in 1052 the family found it very difficult to enforce the rules[35]—partly, perhaps, because a number of family members held quite high office and were sufficiently powerful to infringe on the charitable estate, but largely because the family lacked adequate disciplinary powers. The clan, especially a clan like the Fan, who had been reunified almost entirely by the efforts of one man, did not have the authority to threaten an offender with more than formal censure, exclusion from the rites, possibly corporal punishment or a fine if they were more than normally well-organized, and as a last resort expulsion from the clan. The standard of such discipline depended to a very large extent on the personal authority of the clan head. Unfortunately when Fan Chung-yen died, the new nominal clan head, his eldest son Fan Shun-yu, was a permanent invalid, and until his death in 1063 the clan organization was very weak.[36] Since it is certain that the power of selecting a manager lay with the clan head, authority over the management of the estate undoubtedly suffered.

In 1064, Fan Shun-jen (1027–1101), the second son of Fan Chung-yen, replaced Fan Shun-yu as family head, and immediately took action to restore the authority of the charitable estate by memorializing the throne requesting official recognition of the estate and of its rules, and asking permission to bring offenders before the local magistrate for trial. His memorial reads:

I, Fan Shun-jen, Magistrate of Hsiang-i County in K'ai-feng fu, submit that I humbly bear in mind that my father, Fan Chung-yen, at the time when he was formerly employed as Academician of the Tzu-cheng Hall, established lands of more than ten *ch'ing* in the two counties of Wu-hsien and Chang-ch'ou in Su-chou. The rents obtained from these were to provide food and clothing and the necessary expenses for marriage, mourning and burial for all members considered to belong to any of the branches of the clan descended from our distant ancestor. These lands were called the charitable estate. He looked among the branches of the clan and selected a junior member to manage [the estate], and subsequently established rules of administration which he caused the branches to obey implicitly.

At present, however, among the junior members of the various branches there are some persons who do not obey these rules. The local prefect and magistrate have never yet received a detailed edict [covering the question], and thus the clan have had difficulty in asserting their rights. For five or seven years [the administration] has by degrees fallen into decay, so as to cause those descendents who are hungry and cold to lack the means of support.

It is my humble hope that the Court will especially send down a directive to Su-chou that, if there are any among the junior members of the various branches related to us who offend against the rules of administration, it is permitted to have the officials attend to the matter.

I humbly await an edict.

An edict ordering that the policy suggested in this memorial should be put into force was duly forwarded by the Secretariat to Su-chou in the fourth month of 1064.[37]

The promulgation of this order meant that the trust estate was no longer merely a private arrangement within the clan backed by family discipline, but was now a recognized legal institution backed by the rigor of the law. This step was possible partly because of the considerable posthumous reputation of Fan Chung-yen, partly because his descendants were themselves in influential positions. Fan Shun-jen himself was embarked on a political career which was to rival that of his father in importance, and in 1064 may have judged the time ripe to ask a favor of the new Emperor Ying-tsung, who shortly afterwards summoned him to the capital to an important post in the Censorate.[38] It is certain that this type of edict on a private matter was a rare privilege, but it would be most interesting to know whether other clans who established charitable estates could claim such recognition by analogy.[39]

Very soon after its founding the Fan clan's institution was imitated by other clans. Ch'ien Kung-fu's *I-t'ien Chi*, which must have been written soon after the setting up of the charitable estate, since its author died in 1074, says that "his pattern was adopted far and wide," though this is perhaps hyperbole in keeping with the rest of the document.[40] Almost immediately after Fan Chung-yen's death, Wu Kuei (1012–69) set up a charitable estate out of his surplus salary, again as a result of a long-established ambition.[41] It is also worth noting the case of Liu Hui, who is reported to have set up a similar institution of precisely the same type at Ch'ien-shan (Kiangsi) shortly after the death of Fan Chung-yen, and who is claimed by Yü Yüeh to have been of equal importance as originator of the institution.[42] Another eleventh-century estate, that of Han Chih, was also set up within twenty years of Fan Chung-yen's death.[43] By the end of the Northern Sung charitable estates are reported set up as far afield as Fukien, Hupeh, Shantung, and Kiangsi, as well as in the Kiangsu-Anhwei region, which remained the stronghold of the system until recent times. In the Southern Sung the institution continued to spread in Kiangsi, Chekiang, Szechuan, Hunan, Hupeh, and even Kwangsi.[44] By late Sung or early Yüan times the system is mentioned as a commonplace in some of the decisions in the *Ming-kung Shu-p'an Ch'ing-ming Chi*, and in the *Yüan Shih Shih-fan*. Many of these estates are said to have been "imitations of Fan Wen-cheng's charitable estate" or to have "employed the rules of administration of Fan Wen-cheng's charitable estate."[45]

Not all of these estates flourished, however, and the troubles of the Fan estate were by no means solved by official recognition in 1064. Having obtained official backing and revived the charitable estate, the family gave very careful attention to the rules of administration, and from the supplementary rulings added during the latter part of the eleventh and early twelfth centuries we may see the development of a complex system of clan legislation. It is quite clear that the guiding intelligence behind these developments was Fan Shun-jen, although toward the end of his life, when the return to power of the partisans of Wang An-shih led to his banishment to Yung-chou, his younger brothers Fan Shun-li and Fan Shun-tsui also came to exert some influence.[46] During this period we have no evidence about the selection of managers, but presumably junior members were selected as laid down in Fan Chun-jen's memorial, while the direction of policy remained in the hands of the ritual head of the clan.

Whereas the original rules laid down by Fan Chung-yen were concerned only with the basic policies of providing maintenance and making grants to assist with the expense of weddings and funerals, the new rules extended the area in which the family trust was to assist in maintaining the position of the clan. The supplementary rules laid down in 1073 by Fan Shun-jen were a particularly important step forward. They read as follows:

14. Any member of the clan who succeeds in being entered for the Triennial Examinations shall be granted ten strings of cash [to be granted in cash at the rate of seventy-seven cash per hundred; the following clauses to accord with this]. Those taking the examination for the second time shall have the amount reduced by half. In all cases payment shall be made only when the candidate actually goes to take the examination. Should a person having received this grant fail to take the examination without good reason, he shall refund the money.

15. Any junior member who allows persons to cut and take timber or bamboo growing in the vicinity of the graves shall be reported to the local authorities by the manager for trial.

16. From among those of the junior members who have retired from office or who have been entered for the examinations and have followed the life of a scholar, two persons shall be selected as teachers for the clan. They shall be granted five *tan* of hulled grain per month. [If the price of rice should rise above one string of cash for one *tan*, they shall be granted only one string of cash in lieu of each *tan* to which they are entitled.] It shall also be permissible to select persons who have not retired from office or entered for the examinations, so long as they have become well known to everybody as having led a cultured life. All family members shall discuss such cases.

[But family members who have no son or younger brother to enter school may not participate in the discussion.] If the pupils number less than six, the teacher will be paid only three *tan*. If they number up to eight, he shall be paid four *tan*. If the number reaches ten, he shall be paid the full amount. [The various branches may estimate their resources, and pay cash with which to supplement the teachers' salaries.][47]

The second clause is designed to deal with the constant problem of desecration of the family graves.[48] The other two rules, by subsidizing education in the family and by paying the expense of potential examination candidates, took a very important step in ensuring that the clan should continue to produce potential members of the official class. This very farsighted policy may well have taken account of the growing feeling against employment by "privilege" (*yin*) or "favor" (*en*). This movement, in which Fan Chung-yen had taken a part (although this did not prevent him from making extensive use of privilege on behalf of his own family), had been gathering momentum from the beginning of the eleventh century, and had begun to produce measures designed to limit the exercise of privileged employment.[49]

Fan Shun-jen is credited in his biography with having added extensively to the lands of the charitable estate, but this is not strictly correct.[50] His only actual gift of land to the clan was one thousand *mou* of ritual land (*chi-t'ien*), which he established close to T'ien-p'ing shan in 1079.[51] The purpose of ritual land was to provide income which would prevent the annual drain on the pockets of clan members caused by the ancestral sacrifices and by the entertainment and feast which followed them. The later ritual lands were normally administered by the ancestral hall, but in the case of the Fans the income was placed at the disposal of the family chapel (Pai-yün ssu). The origin of the *chi-t'ien* system is by no means clear. It is frequently linked in later times with the name of Chu Hsi, but this attribution is based on a passage in a work which is uncertainly attributed to his authorship,[52] and which in any case only sets out a rather unusual plan for the endowment of sacrificial rites by the establishment of a fixed proportion of bequeathed property as *chi-t'ien* for rites on behalf of the deceased.[53] Not only was this plan never widely adopted, but several mentions of *chi-t'ien* considerably earlier than Chu Hsi in date are to be found. The present instance is one of the earliest. Again the institution may well have had a Buddhist origin. Special endowments for ceremonies on behalf of the dead and for other specific purposes were not uncommon.

In 1083 Fan Shun-jen laid down new rules covering the administration of the property. Family members were forbidden to become tenants of the charitable estate's lands, or to become tenants under the cover of nominees, since this might easily have led to difficult and embarrassing situations if the manager had to collect rents from a family member of superior status. The procedure for dealing with frauds by the managers was tightened up. At the same time arrangements were made for the payment of the managers, which was made dependent upon the full collection of rents and full payment of entitlements. This provision of a salary argues that the duties of administration had become a full-time occupation.[54]

In 1095 Fan Chun-jen added further rules which forbade the charitable estate to grant mortgages on the lands of clan members—again to prevent embarrassing situations in which the contractual relation might conflict with the family relationship. Other rules strictly limited the grants to persons actually resident in Su-chou, an obvious measure for the preservation of clan unity, and forbade grants on behalf of large numbers of slaves and dependents. These rules suggest that family members had been taking advantage of loopholes in the rules to maintain extravagant households out of the common funds.[55]

In the next year (1096) a rule was inserted to maintain the authority of the manager, as representative of the clan community, over individual members of higher status than himself. To prevent his abusing this new position of authority, the rule gave members the right of appeal to the head of the clan in case the manager should be engaged in fraud or dishonesty.[56] This same year another rule was added, forbidding the estate, even if it should be in financial difficulties, from contracting debts at interest.[57] This was clearly a measure to preserve the endowments of the estate intact, even at the expense of temporary hardship to clan members.

In 1098 a long series of supplementary rules was issued under the joint authority of the three surviving sons of Fan Chung-yen. Since the senior son, Fan Shun-jen, was at this time in banishment in the far south, the other two were presumably responsible for the new rules, and since two rules refer to the actions of the clan head, it is possible that they took the opportunity of his absence to write in some limitation on the authority of the ritual head over the management. The clan head was forbidden to make extraordinary grants from the charitable estate funds, and arrangements were made for a clan assembly to decide on any matter not covered by the rules, whose decision was to be enforced even without the assent of the clan head. Otherwise the rules of 1098 comprise detailed rules against the abuse of the buildings belonging to the charitable estate, on the issue of rice, and on the registration of children with the family.[58] These rules raise for the first time the important question of the charitable estate buildings. Just as *chuang* alone could designate either a whole estate or simply the estate buildings, so *i-chuang* was not only the general term covering the whole clan property, including its lands, but also a restricted term referring to the buildings of the administration, in particular its granaries and stores.[59] Among the clan buildings was the *i-chai*, a communally owned building for the residence of poor members. At first, according to the *Fan Shih Chia-sheng*, the charitable estate building was inside the *i-chai*, which took up a fairly extensive site in Su-chou city.[60] This site also included the great assembly hall Sui-han t'ang, the secondary Chung-hou t'ang, and the ancestral hall in honor of Fan Chung-yen, besides a large garden.[61] Probably poor family members were allowed to reside in the side rooms of the ancestral halls, and in many smaller pavilions and wings which are shown in the conventional pictures of the charitable estate site (though these are admittedly of late Ming date). The providing of shelter as well as food was an important part of the charitable function of the estate.

Another rule prescribed the kind of paper and the sort of signature for documents dealing with the business of the charitable estates. Apparently senior members of the family, debarred in 1098 from deliberately interfering with the manager, had used anonymous documents on special papers to secure special consideration for their proposals.[62]

In 1106 we have a rare glimpse of the type of external business in which the charitable estate participated. Although the estate was forbidden to take out mortgages on lands belonging to its members, it apparently did make loans on mortgage to outsiders, for in 1106 a rule was imposed to regulate the use of sums repaid on the redemption of mortgaged lands. Presumably, then, the family had accumulated sufficient surplus funds to invest in mortgaging lands, thus raising interest with the maximum security.[63]

In 1107 a strict rule was imposed against the adoption of children of a different surname.[64] This practice was not only against all Confucian morality, but also against the law. However, the law had not been strictly enforced, especially during the late T'ang, Five Dynasties, and early Sung, and here we may perhaps see another effect of the hardening of the general attitude toward clan relations.[65]

This problem, which involved a loosening of the strict boundary of the family relationship, was connected with that of persons who left the clan home to reside elsewhere; yet another rule on this subject was added in 1113. It seems almost certain that the members of the clan living away from Su-chou were constantly interfering with the family and attempting to gain benefits throughout Sung times.[66] Abuse of the *i-chai* buildings again seems to have occurred, for in 1115 clan members were forbidden to rent rooms among themselves. It is clear that the more powerful members were attempting to convert the public clan property represented by these buildings into personal possessions of their own, which could be used for personal profit.[67]

The above rules represent the gradual development of a system of administrative laws which were clearly supplemented as new situations arose and new abuses developed. The main threats to this administration were apparently weak management, the power of individual members, and interference from remote relatives living away from Su-chou. One rule after another seeks to provide adequate disciplinary powers, to bolster up the influence of the managers, to prevent the true clan lineage from confusion by the introduction of adopted sons or by intrusion from relatives not resident in Su-chou, and to gradually limit and control expenditure by the estate. Whether or not these objects were all achieved, it is clear that far from being theoretical, the rules were pragmatic rules developed for given situations.

In 1117 all the foregoing rules were codified together under the direction of Fan Cheng-t'u and inscribed on a stone by the manager Fan Chih-yin—the first manager whose name is recorded. This stele was set up at the family temple Chung-lieh miao, which stood next to the Buddhist chapel Pai-yün ssu on T'ien-p'ing shan.[68]

THE DECADENCE AND RESTORATION OF THE CHARITABLE ESTATE DURING THE SOUTHERN SUNG

Shortly after the family had brought the regulations for the administration of their properties to such an advanced level, the whole of China was thrown into an upheaval by the invasion of the Chin, and the subsequent loss of northern China by the Sung. Little information survives on the fate of the family properties during the twelfth century, but the family suffered severely during the wars, especially those direct descendants of Fan Chung-yen who lived in Honan. The Shih-lang branch, descended from the third son Fan Shun-tsui, was virtually wiped out, or at least completely cut off from the clan in Su-chou. Among those who fell into the hands of the invaders was Fan Cheng-t'u, who had been so influential in the family administration in the early years of the century.

The effects of the invasion upon the clan in Su-chou are graphically described in a postscript added to Ch'ien Kung-fu's *I-tien Chi* in 1139 by Fan Chih-fang:

Formerly, in the time of Chung-hsüan kung [i.e., Fan Shun-jen], his kinsmen heard him discourse upon the subject. He said, "When formerly Wencheng founded the Charitable Land, he did not speak about so many *tou* of grain, or so many lengths of silk. He spoke above all of being able to keep the clansmen fed and clothed, and it was in this that his real purpose lay."

At that time I was still small, and had yet no great experience. After three generations, at the end of the Hsüan-ho period the dynasty migrated to the south to escape disorder (1125). In 1135 I was recalled from Lin-hai to the provisional capital. In the spring of 1136 I was sent on a mission to Huai-shang, and first passed through P'ing-chiang [i.e., Su-chou]. At that time the charitable residence [*i-chai*] had been burned and destroyed, and the clan members were living scattered among the local villages. One morning I assembled the scattered remnants at the grave mounds. There were still some 200 persons old and young who paid their respects with a kindly and respectful manner. All those who had lived together or were close relatives I looked up in the family genealogy [*chia-p'u*]. There were more than ten descendants in the generation with Liang as the standard first character in their personal names [i.e., the fifth generation descendants from Fan Chung-yen] descended from the "Lord of Li-shui fu" [i.e., Fan Sui]. Afterwards, seeing the way in which Wen-cheng kung had exerted his thoughts, I became aware of the wisdom of what Chung-hsüan kung had said.[69]

Fan Chih-fang and his immediate successors seem to have been able to do little to restore their fortunes. Although a high proportion of descendants down to the sixth generation continued to enter government service by protection or grace, most of them remained in relatively lowly positions, and there can have been no great surplus available for the assistance of the clan.

In 1195 the three brothers in the senior line of the family (the Chien-pu branch)—the former Han-lin scholar Fan Liang-ch'i (1140–97); Fan Chih-ju (1151–1216), *chin-shih* of 1172, who was embarked on a highly successful official career; and Fan Liang-sui (1154–1232), a retired scholar and prolific poet who lived at Ch'ü-t'ang—planned together to restore the estate, and for this purpose lodged a request with the judicial intendant, Ho I, and the prefect of Su-chou, Cheng Jo-yung, to effect a just settlement and completely restore their lands.[70] This was done, presumably on the authority of the recognition of the estate implied by the 1063 edict. The clan decided to rebuild the granary, the Sui-han t'ang, and the charitable residence (*i-chai*), and the rules were again engraved on the stele.[71]

Fan Liang-ch'i, as senior member of the family, acted as manager in 1195 while the reestablishment of the estate was being completed,[72] and for the next decade two managers (*chang-chuang*) were appointed annually to administer the property.[73] The resumption of the charitable work of the estate was reported in 1196. In the next year Fan Liang-sui made a gift of an additional 500 *mou* of land to the estate. He was encouraged to do this by his wife, who had already donated her dowry land (*lien-t'ien*) to assist the family in their difficulties.[74] In 1208 eighteen members of the family subscribed an additional ten *mou* to help pay for funeral and mourning expenses in the family.[75] By this time (1208–9) the estate seems to have been restored to a condition of relative prosperity. Not only were regular managers appointed annually, but the charitable residence (*i-chai*) was rebuilt, decorated, and extended by the provision of two buildings for hire, while the granary buildings were also enlarged.[76] It seems possible, though the sources are vague, that at this same period the estate building was separated from the *i-chai* in the city of Su-chou, and reestablished on T'ien-p'ing shan.[77]

In 1210, Fan Chih-ju, who had risen to the post of Policy Critic of the Left and Han-lin lecturer-in-waiting, took the opportunity to request not only confirmation of the edict of 1064 and of the old rules to which this edict gave legal backing, but confirmation of judicial backing for a long and complicated series of amended rules which he had drawn up in the same year. The emperor gave his permission for a new edict, and this official confirmation of the new detailed rules marks the complete restoration of the charitable estate.[78]

The new amended rules are of great interest, for the rulings themselves are prefaced in the manner of an official edict with accounts of the straits into which the family had fallen. Family members are reported to have cut and stolen timber from the ancestral grave mounds, grazed their goats over the ancestral graves, and infringed on the property of the family chapel, driving out the monks and converting the buildings to dwellings, appropriating its lands as vegetable plots and gardens, and employing its servants for personal labor. They had taken possession of the lands of the charitable estate, farmed them under the names of the tenants whom they had forcibly evicted, and driven away the tenants by blocking the irrigation ditches and preventing the use of irrigation machinery. (Since most of the land was reclaimed *yü-t'ien*, irrigation was essential to farming.)[79] Others had bribed the managers or brought in unruly clansmen living away from Su-chou to force the managers to open up the granaries at improper times, and had stolen large quantities of grain. In addition these rules confirm the inroads made upon the property by outsiders, and the impositions levied upon it by unscrupulous local officials during its period of decadence.

Another important difference marks the amended rules off from the older ones. Each of the new clauses provides a specific punishment for a given offense. In nearly every case such punishments were collective deprivation of entitlement to grants from the charitable estate, affecting the whole branch (*fang*) to which the offender belonged. This principle of collective punishment and collective responsibility was obviously a device to ensure the cooperation of the heads of branches and individual families (*chia*) in enforcing the rules, rather than relying upon the less direct discipline of the clan head. These heavy fines gave the clan a set of adequate sanctions to back up their own internal organization without the trouble and expense of taking an offender to trial. An even more severe form of clan discipline, erasure from the family register, was ordered to be imposed on members who brought shame on the family by repeated offenses against the criminal law. Such exclusion from the family not only meant deprivation of all benefits from the clan, but also involved the offender in a very invidious social situation, for he ceased to belong to a clan and thus had no regular place in society. This was the most severe penalty which the clan could normally impose.

Although there is some internal evidence that the rules are not in fact the original supplementary rules of 1210, but an amended version of them completed no earlier than 1276, it is safe to say that apart from minor emendations Fan Chih-ju's supplementary rules of administration, as drawn up in 1210 and recognized by the authorities, provided a detailed code of administration which remained unaltered until 1678.[80]

The confirmation of official recognition of the charitable estate rules was celebrated in a long inscription written at Fan Chih-ju's request by his fellow Han-lin lecturer-in-waiting Liu Chü.[81] This provides us with the tantalizingly vague information that the clan, which had numbered only 90 persons at its foundation in 1049,[82] and some 200 in 1139,[83] now included "several hundreds and tens of persons." It is clear that the temporary setback to the family's prosperity following the exile of Fan Shun-jen and the Chin conquest had been made up, and that its numbers were increasing steadily. This increase in itself suggests a very good reason for the tightening up of the rules of administration.

When the charitable estate was first established, the income in rents had been 800 bushels (*hu*) of grain[84]—enough to provide the annual grant of rice for 222 persons. Clearly this must have left a large annual surplus, since most of the adult male members were serving officials who would have ceased to draw their entitlement. By the thirteenth century, however, the *yin* privilege—appointment by hereditary right—which derived from the exalted clan members of the eleventh century, was wearing thin, and in any case the exercise of such privileged means of entry into official service was gradually being restricted. As a result clan members could no longer depend almost automatically on a career in the bureaucracy, whatever their talents. The accompanying table shows the rapidity of this decline in official careers.

The Chung-hsüan Branch
(Direct descendants of Fan Shun-jen)

Generation	Male descendants	Died prematurely	Official careers	Entry method	Percentage of officials among members reaching maturity
2	1	–	1	1 *yin**	100
3	5	1	4	3 *yin** 1 examination	100
4	13	3	10	4 *yin** 6 *en***	100
5	23	2	11	3 *yin** 8 *en***	52
6	17	–	3	1 *yin** 2 *en***	17.6
7	13	1	1	1 *en***	8.3
8	5	–	–		0
9	5	–	–		0

* By hereditary right.   ** By special grace.

The branch analyzed in the table does not reveal the decline in its extreme form, since it had two prime ministers in successive generations to begin it (Fan Chung-yen, Fan Shun-jen) and thus had exceptional claims to privileged treatment. Yet after six generations it ceased to produce serving officials.

With this rapid decline in the proportion of serving officials, which began to show its full effect about the end of the twelfth century, the calls upon the charitable estate for grants must have increased severalfold. The income, however, cannot have grown to the same degree, and any accumulation which may have been made in the early years was undoubtedly wiped out during the mid-twelfth century. The only significant addition to the 3,000 *mou* originally donated by Fan Chung-yen was the gift of 500 *mou* made by Fan Liang-sui in 1197. Assuming that the rents were levied at the same rate as that which can be deduced for the earlier period—that is, 2.66 *tou* per *mou*—the total income would have been only 931 *tan*, sufficient only for the bare rations of 260 persons without any allowance for the greatly increased number of weddings and funerals consequent on the natural increase of the clan. It is possible, of course, that the rents had risen slightly, for a contemporary inscription from Su-chou dated 1196 shows average rents of 2.9 *tou* and 3.7 *tou*.[85] Even if the rents reached the high level of 1 *tan* per *mou*, they could have provided only bare support for 777 persons. The financial position of the estate must therefore have been rather unstable, especially in view of the general deterioration of the reclaimed *yü-t'ien* lands which made up most of the estate.[86] This deterioration intensified during the thirteenth century, and it is possible that the productivity of the charitable estate's lands was actually declining. Crop failures occurred in both 1208 and 1209, and this situation may have had its effect upon the financial position of the estate.[87]

Small parcels of land were added to the estate between 1214 and 1217, but these were hill lands destined to become grave land and had no effect in increasing the production of the properties.[88] In 1240 the financial troubles besetting the estate were still severe. In that year, however, the central government gave instructions to the counties in which the charitable lands were situated, ordering a total remission of taxes amounting to 1,073 *tan* 6 *tou* of grain in respect of 897 *mou* in Wu-hsien and 2,271 *mou* in Ch'ang-shu County.[89] Unfortunately the *Chia-sheng* does not make it clear whether the family themselves requested this remission of taxes, or whether this was a spontaneous action on the part of the government. Neither does it say explicitly whether the remission was a single act of grace, or whether it was to be permanent. But the documents do give the reason why the estate was singled out for favored treatment: "The Censorate has decided that Fan Wen-cheng's charitable estate is a means for the improvement of social customs."[90] In 1243 the family are recorded as making an approach to the Censorate for a remission of taxes to apply not only to the charitable estate, but to the family chapel and tombs. The statement is again very laconic, but it seems possible that this second memorial was an attempt to extend the exemption to the considerable ritual lands which did not form a part of the charitable estate.[91]

The acceptance by the government of the principle that the charitable estate was a beneficial institution and a good example for the improvement of social organization, and that it therefore merited privileged treatment in financial matters, was a most important step in the secure foundation of the estate. The immediate effect of the exemption must have been to greatly increase the annual income from the lands, and to make possible the implementation of the detailed rules on personal grants. But its broader implications were far more important. There seems little doubt that the charitable estate survived above all because of the general good will of the authorities, who wished to honor the memory of its illustrious founder, and who saw in it a practical policy for promoting the clan unity which was such an important feature of

Confucian social theory. Without such external support, an estate of this type, bound by its rules to give support to an ever-increasing number of clan members, would inevitably find itself in difficulties after a few generations unless its endowments were increased, or some new form of investment discovered.

During this period, when the estate was restored to a condition of prosperity, the pattern of management also underwent some slight changes. In the first years after the reestablishment in 1195 the managers were changed every year. As time went on this method was changed, and from 1208 onwards managers were usually appointed for up to five consecutive terms in office, the terms being made to overlap so that one of the managers at least had had previous experience in the work.[92] After 1231 annual reappointment of new managers was resumed for a time, possibly to prevent managers from unduly consolidating their personal power and influence, possibly to avoid inter-branch rivalry. But a group of more or less professional clan administrators again emerged, and from 1242 until the break in the record in 1260, a handful of members of the Yu-ch'eng, Ch'ao-ch'ing, and Ssu-li branches filled over 80 per cent of the appointments.[93]

The emergence of a group of semi-permanent managers within the family, most of whom were not employed in any bureaucratic post and must have seen in family administration an alternative outlet for their abilities, was obviously a move toward greater efficiency, closely connected with the reshaping of the rules and the confirmation of official support. But the tendency brought some dangers with it. In 1251 the first offense against the rules is recorded, the manager Fan Shih-lien being dismissed for having conspired with the tenant farmers to misappropriate grain belonging to the estate.[94] Fan Shih-lien had a long record of service dating back to 1234; nearly all the recorded cases of corruption occur at the end of long periods of service. The danger of improper practices being accepted after long use was clearly implicit in the growth of semi-professional administrators and the decline of general participation in management.

CHANGES IN THE PATTERN OF MANAGEMENT

In 1260 the "Annual Record" breaks down, and nothing is recorded until 1274. The account is resumed in this year by recording a major change in the administration of the estate. The local prefect Ch'ien Shuo-yu memorialized the throne for permission to build a temple in honor of Fan Chung-yen adjoining the charitable residence in Su-chou. This was done, and he further endowed the charitable estate with 300 *mou* of land to provide funds for the spring and autumn sacrifices in

Chung-yen's honor. The senior member of the family, Fan Shih-k'uei, was put in charge of the temple, and concurrently given control over the accounts of the charitable estate as a whole.[95]

From this time onwards the head of the charitable estate organization was no longer an elected manager or managers, but the *chu-feng*, the ritual head of the clan. By this move the unity of the clan as a ritual community and as the common proprietor of the charitable estate was greatly strengthened. The *chu-feng* could not be selected from such a wide field as a simple manager, for to fulfill his ritual duties he had to be the senior surviving member of the clan, and although he was removable in case of grave misconduct—indeed this sometimes happened[96]—he normally remained in office until his death or retirement. From 1274 to the end of the record in 1758, leaving aside temporary withdrawal from office because of mourning obligations, absence on official duty or at the examinations, etc., the great majority of *chu-feng* served until their death. Their tenure of office was in several cases over thirty years and in two cases over forty years.[97]

Since the *chu-feng* had to have seniority within the clan, the position went almost automatically to a member of the senior branch, the Chien-pu fang, direct descendants of Fan Chung-yen's eldest son.[98] Until 1636 there was a regular succession from one generation of the Chien-pu branch to the next, broken only by the occasional appointment of a provisional *chu-feng* who assumed office when the actual *chu-feng* was unable to perform his duties. This provisional *chu-feng* was at first normally a member of the next generation in the Chien-pu branch, often a son of the holder or the obvious candidate to succeed him. In one case, after the *chu-feng* had been dismissed for defalcation, an obviously junior member was appointed for two years, to allow time for a settlement and selection of a new *chu-feng*.[99] In the sixteenth and seventeenth centuries the second (Yu-ch'eng) branch and the tenth (Ju-lin) branch began to produce candidates for provisional *chu-feng*, and after 1636 these branches monopolized the post of *chu-feng* itself, for reasons which are far from clear. This period, however, ended in wholesale corruption; after 1669 the Chien-pu branch resumed control, and the succession reverted to normal.

The assumption of control over the clan lands by the ritual head unified the administration of the family estates in one important way. Prior to this the various properties which belonged to the clan as a ritual community, but not to the charitable estate, had been managed separately. These additional lands, most important of which were the ritual lands, but which also included the grave land and various lands set aside for specific ritual purposes, were already directly or indirectly under the control of the ritual head. Transferring the charitable estates to his control brought all the clan holdings under a single head.

From 1276 the system of control by the *chu-feng* was elaborated by the appointment of a controller (*ti-kuan*) and two auditors (*chu-chi*) to assist him in the everyday business of the estate.[100] There is no information on the means by which they were appointed, but there is little doubt that they were chosen for their business ability. Although the record is by no means complete before the fifteenth century, it seems that they too were appointed either for life or for very long terms.

In 1275 the Mongol forces overran Su-chou, and a number of the family, including its head, Fan Shih-k'uei, were killed.[101] Under the new dynasty the prestige of the family declined still further. The *Chiasheng* lists thirteen family members who took service under the invaders, but none of these rose to a post equivalent to county magistrate.[102] Only two members passed those official examinations held in the course of the dynasty, and the only member to achieve the *chin-shih* degree was never subsequently employed. The majority of those who obtained posts were employed as Confucian teachers in local schools in Kiangsu, Chekiang, Kiangsi, and Anhwei. There is little doubt that there was a strong family tradition of Confucian studies, for the family not only maintained its own teachers, but also were closely identified with the prefectural school in Su-chou.[103]

The origin of the charitable school (*i-hsüeh*) belonging to the family is obscure. Although some sources state that it was established at the same time as the charitable estate,[104] there seems to be no evidence that this was so, and although teachers had been subsidized by the clan ever since 1073, a charitable school does not seem to have been founded before 1277. In that year a school of considerable size was built to the south of T'ien-p'ing shan, and family members were selected as instructors, not only for the young members of the clan, but for "students coming from all the four quarters."[105] The clan endowed this school with 150 *mou* of agricultural and hillside land to provide an income for its upkeep. This income was to cover "the teachers' salaries and rites, and the expenses of brushes and stationery for the pupils."[106] The management of this endowment, and the organization of the work as a whole, was carried out by the charitable estate on behalf of the clan. The income proved to be more than adequate, for in 1285 there was a surplus which was devoted to the repair of the family chapel.[107]

In general, however, financial problems continued to press the clan. The favored tax position established under the Sung was challenged by local officials under the new dynasty, and for the first few years of Mongol rule the estate was subject to abuse by the petty underlings of the local counties.[108] In 1290 the controller of the estate lodged a complaint in the capital, asking the government to enforce the policy that apart from the basic taxes (*na-shui*), all impositions (*k'o-che*) and services (*cha-i*) due on the lands of the charitable estates should be remitted. An edict was duly promulgated granting this request and giving exemption from deficiencies outstanding.[109] From the full text of the memorial it seems that local people had attempted through their village elders to take the opportunity of the change of dynasty to approach the prefectural authorities and have the charitable estate's privileged tax position abolished.[110]

Even after the edict of 1290 was issued, the local authorities do not seem to have enforced it. In 1294 the controller was again complaining that after the promulgation of the edict in 1290 the personnel of the counties had changed, and that although the provincial administration still honored the order, the minor officials of Ch'ang-shu county had been causing trouble to the estate by the imposition of "enforced purchases."[111] He again requested a permanent exemption from all forms of tax and levy apart from the basic *ti-shui* and *shang-shui* taxes.

In 1298 still another edict gave a permanent favorable position to the charitable estate and the charitable school, and forbade local officials to trouble these institutions, which "helped in instructing the generation and in spreading good behavior."[112] In 1304 the local governor-general Tung Chia-i again memorialized requesting preferential treatment for the estate and school, and the subsequent edict ordered the local authorities to proclaim the order so that all persons should be aware of it.[113] A further confirmatory order was issued in 1310 by the Board of Rites.[114]

In the early fourteenth century the reputation of Fan Chung-yen seems to have stood high, and successive local officials in Su-chou exerted their influence on behalf of the clan.[115] In 1311 the next in succession as ritual head, Fan Kuo-chün, visited the tomb of Fan Chung-yen in Loyang, performed the sacrifices, and reestablished the lands attached to the tomb. The provincial governor gave orders that the local authorities were to make regular offerings and to look after the clan properties in the district.[116] In 1312, 1317, and 1327 local governors in the Su-chou area requested the bestowal of honors and favors on the estate, and in 1317 insignia of merit were bestowed upon the clan "to encourage future generations to promote good customs."[117]

This specially favored position of the estate, which derived from its being an institution which was widely imitated and honored as an example, undoubtedly stood it in good stead at this period, for the region experienced a disastrous series of crop failures in 1319, 1322, 1323, 1324, and 1328, by which the income from the estate was seriously reduced.[118]

The position of the family as Confucian teachers was further consolidated in 1346, when two local governors, Chao Cheng-hsi and Wu-Ping-i, rebuilt the ancestral temple of Wen-cheng kung and received official permission to transform it into a school named after him, the Wen-cheng Shu-yüan. Three hundred *mou* of official land was provided to produce an income to support it, and members of the Fan clan were to provide the teachers and continue the rites to Fan Chung-yen.[119]

DECLINE OF THE CLAN UNDER THE MING

The restoration of Chinese rule under the Ming had no favorable effect upon the fortunes of the clan. A great deal of mystery surrounds the events of the last quarter of the fourteenth century. The crucial event for the family was the confiscation of two thousand *mou* of land belonging to the charitable estate in 1384, allegedly following the rendering of erroneous tax lists by the auditor Fan Yüan-hou.[120] It seems unlikely, however, that non-payment of taxes would have led to such wholesale confiscation of property, and it is significant that about the same time a great many members of the family were banished to various distant regions of the empire. It is possible that we should seek some political cause for both these events, but until fresh evidence is forthcoming I prefer to leave the reason for the family's disgrace an open question.[121]

This blow to the clan was a severe one, and during the next century the clan fortunes reached their lowest ebb. Perhaps the best evidence of this is the change in the pattern of migration within the family. In Sung and Yüan times migration of family branches was rather rare (amounting to perhaps four or five persons per generation), and was in almost every case the result of official posting to some more or less distant region.[122] In the first thirty-five years of the Ming, however, thirty new branches were scattered all over China from Liaotung to Yunnan.[123] Some of these clan members were banished to garrison duties or assigned to the various guards, and so do not represent voluntary departures from Su-chou. But many other cases indicate that the protection of the clan organization at Su-chou was no longer enough to prevent hardship or to outweigh the attractions of setting up an independent family elsewhere. Particularly significant is the sudden appearance in the early fifteenth century of the hitherto unknown practice of husbands marrying out of the clan, and going to live in the households of their in-laws. No fewer than seven marriages of this type are recorded in the early fifteenth century, and stray cases continue to occur throughout the period of clan poverty, which lasted until roughly 1630.[124]

Another evidence of declining fortune may be seen in the records of marriages. Whereas in Sung times a high proportion of wives are named in the record as daughters of serving officials, or as coming from specified clans, in the Yüan period such cases became rare, and in the Ming practically unknown, the only information given being the maiden name.[125]

There are also indications that the family members, since the number able to enter the bureaucracy was severely restricted as the examination system became more strict, began to enter other fields of activity. The members who achieved entry into the bureaucracy never numbered more than 2 per cent of the total males in Ming or Ch'ing times, and the percentage of actively employed officials was of course still smaller. One outlet for the unsuccessful scholars in the family remained teaching, but here again the openings were limited, especially in a region which produced a very high percentage of the empire's intelligentsia. One member, Fan Hsi-i, was promoted from the clerical service in 1431,[126] and presumably some of the family may have filled subordinate posts in local government as bookkeepers, secretaries, scribes, and so forth. Several of the migrating groups are said to have gone to such and such a city to trade, and in one case the person concerned was the eldest son of the ritual head, so that this was far from being a desperate step to be taken only by the less fortunate members of the family. Unfortunately the *Chia-sheng* is very vague on this topic, but it would be surprising if such a well-established clan had taken no part in the great commercial activity which grew up in Su-chou during the Ming.

Another new development in the family was the growth of a strong tradition of medicine. Several members from late Yüan and Ming times are mentioned in their biographies as having "had skill in medicine" or as having served in the palace medical service. This tradition, which was concentrated in the Ju-lin and Ch'ao-ch'ing branches, persisted down to the end of the sixteenth century.[127]

It is clear that both clan cohesion and the *literati* tradition of official service were broken down to some extent in this period. The clan property administration, which played an important part in promoting cohesion and social conformism through vocational education, was also reduced to disorder. The charitable estate, reduced to one-third of its former size by confiscation of lands, seems to have been subjected to the full rigors of taxation during the early Ming, and the family administration was slackened considerably. In 1416, the ritual head of the clan, Fan Yüan-shao, being called to the capital to take the examinations

126DENIS TWITCHETT

(which he duly failed), mortgaged away another three hundred *mou* of the charitable estate to pay his expenses. As a result, beginning in 1417 new subordinate officers called registrars (*tien-chi*) were appointed to the estate to tighten up its management.[128]

The threat to the family properties during the early Ming was the result not only of economic pressure and the unsympathetic policies of the government, but of pressures from within the clan. When few clan members held influential posts, government support for the clan administration was almost invariably withdrawn. It was at these times, when members were without official stipends, that they sought economic security by acquiring land. Hence the process of deterioration was a cumulative one, and the rapid decline of the family in the early fifteenth century was the result of a complex of causes.

THE REVIVAL OF THE CHARITABLE ESTATE

Fortunately, although external factors could provoke a breakdown of the family administration, renewed government support could quite easily restore the situation. The fame of Fan Chung-yen and of his charitable foundation were still sufficient to influence local officials, and under the direction of successive local officials the depredations of powerful clan members upon the common property were made good. In 1426 the provincial inspector Hu Chi restored the clan temple, re-established the rules of administration, and recovered lands lost to the clan through sale by dishonest clan members.[129] In 1432 the provincial inspector Chou Shen and the prefect K'uang Chung recovered lands mortgaged away by dishonest clan members or appropriated by powerful ones, and returned them to the charitable estate.[130] A land register for the estate was drawn up in separate copies held by the ritual head, the controller and the accountant, and the resident manager of the T'ien-p'ing shan family temple. These recorded in minute detail the size of all lands and the names of all tenants, and took four years to compile.[131] However, complete restoration of the lands (apart from those confiscated) was not made until 1453, when the magistrate of Su-hsien, Yang Lung, recovered the last of the lands from powerful clan members.[132] From this time onwards the lands remained more or less constant in size, gradually increasing by small donations, such as the 89 *mou* presented in 1457 by the controller Fan Hsi-p'in.[133]

Throughout Ming times local officials, both in Su-chou and at the burial place of Fan Chung-yen in Loyang, continued to honor his memory by assisting with repairs to buildings, arranging for the performance of rites in his honor, and presenting inscriptions to the various halls and ancestral shrines.[134]

After 1461 the tax-exempt position of the estate was also gradually restored. In that year exemption from all labor services and from *Ma-i* was granted.[135] In 1538 it was decided to rationalize the land levy, abolishing the graduated rates at which it had formerly been collected in favor of an overall general rate.[136] Although the charitable estate remained theoretically privileged, this measure led to such a sharp increase in taxation that the funds of the estate were entirely exhausted, and the managers had to pay the excess out of their own resources, nearly ruining their families.[137] But in 1556 this decision was rescinded, and it was decided to collect the land levy on the estate at 50 per cent of the normal rate.[138] In 1569 further exemptions were granted, and the outstanding taxes due from the estate were canceled.[139]

The estate remained in financial difficulties, however, and not entirely because of increased taxation or the natural increase in the number of clan members and the consequent demands made on the charitable funds. In 1471 the controller was reported to the local authorities and dismissed for misappropriating grain belonging to the estate.[140] In 1541 the ritual head Fan Ch'i-i, who had held office for twenty-one years, was impeached before the local authorities for stealing the grain from rents, pawning the clan's sacrificial vessels, and generally acting to the detriment of the family charities. His depredations may be connected with the plight into which the family was thrown when the taxes were suddenly increased in 1538.[141] In 1580 again the managers were forced to pawn two of the family treasures, pieces of calligraphy by Fan Chung-yen and Fan Shun-jen, which they were unable to redeem after ten years.[142]

The unity of the family was also seriously threatened. When the genealogy was recompiled in 1577, the editors stated that the whole lineage had fallen into confusion during the preceding century.

It seems to have been impossible to build up any adequate reserves, for in 1608 a single year of disastrous crop failure again found the estate unable to meet the claims made upon it by clan members. The ritual head, fearing complete ruin if a second year of famine followed, resigned his post; ultimately a member who had risen to high rank after being the first *chin-shih* produced by the family for more than half a century paid for the relief out of his own funds.[143]

The eventual recovery of the clan owed a great deal to this man, Fan Yün-lin,[144] who proved the most considerable benefactor to the family since Fan Shun-jen. In 1625 he bought back 500 *mou* of land in Wu-hsien which had been lost, and in 1631 he presented yet another 500 *mou* in Ch'ang-shu hsien. These lands were specially registered, and the local authorities provided certificates of tax exemption on them.

Yün-lin was posthumously honored by the institution of special rites on his behalf in the family temple.[145]

The beginning of the Ch'ing dynasty again brought difficulty with local officials, who refused to recognize the privileges accorded the estate under the Ming and attempted to levy tax at the full normal rate on its lands.[146] In 1662, probably judging that the new emperor might look favorably on such a request, the clan reported this situation and asked for a restoration of its privileges. In response, the throne decided that the charitable estate not only was to be granted favorable treatment and total exemption from labor services and miscellaneous levies, but was to be allowed extra time in which to pay its taxes.[147]

The pattern of management of the estate had remained constant since the middle of the fifteenth century, when the number of controllers, auditors, and registrars was reduced to one apiece.[148] In early Ch'ing times management was again reformed, following nine years of flagrant mismanagement by Fan An-kung, who had been instrumental in getting the estate's taxes remitted in 1660. He took advantage of this concession to turn the estate to his own profit, keeping back the rents and refusing to make grants, and when the clan members began to resent his actions, bringing in ruffians from the city to take possession of the lands. In 1669 he was reported to the authorities and punished, and the ritual head was appointed in his place with three controllers, three accountants, and three registrars.[149] The restoration of the estate to working order took several years, and was made more difficult by crop failures in 1670, 1671, and 1672, by which time the resources of the estate had been completely dissipated, so that the the ritual head and the managers had to pay the taxes out of their own pockets.[150]

This might well have precipitated another crisis in the family fortunes, but fortunately help again came from outside. A distant branch of the family, which had been settled in the far northeast since early Ming times, defected to the Manchus at a very early date, providing one of the first Grand Secretaries in 1636, and produced a whole crop of distinguished officials during the K'ang-hsi period.[151] One of these men, Fan Ch'eng-mo, happened to pass through Su-chou in 1669 on his way to take up an appointment in Chekiang. He was anxious to resume relations with his ancestral clan in Su-chou, and visited the family temple. During 1671–72 he paid for repairs to various family buildings and also repurchased the sites of the ancestral temples which had been sold off by Fan An-kung.[152] This assistance came at a most opportune moment, and although Fan Ch'eng-mo was shortly afterwards killed in the rising in Fukien,[153] members of his branch of the family continued to give support to the family in Su-chou on a considerable scale.[154] In 1673 the administration of the estate reverted to normal, and the taxes were paid off in full. The number of administrators was reduced to two controllers, auditors, and registrars instead of three.[155] In 1674 the lands misappropriated and sold by Fan An-kung were completely restored, and registered with the local authorities.[156] The administration of the estate was finally restored to prosperity by the enactment in 1678 of a new series of detailed supplementary rules of administration, the first since 1210.[157] These were presented in a memorial for approval, and duly received official backing. No really new principle emerges from these rules, but the renewal of such activity really marks the beginning of a new phase in the history of the family, a phase of steady and continuous expansion which continued until comparatively recently.

The rest of the record shows a steady growth of the estates,[158] further detailed rules for their administration,[159] the expansion of the buildings held in common, and an increase in the complexity of the staff of the estate.[160] By 1682 there was again a surplus of rent grain which could be put to other purposes, and by the beginning of the eighteenth century there seems to have been a considerable accumulated surplus, which was at least occasionally plowed back into the estate by the purchase of additional lands.[161] The tax position of the estate also continued to improve.[162] The general esteem in which the family was held was finally consolidated in 1715 when Fan Chung-yen was admitted to the State Confucian Temple,[163] and in 1751 and 1757 when the Ch'ien-lung emperor on his progress to the south paid state visits to the charitable estate and to the family tombs on T'ien-p'ing shan.[164]

These developments in early Ch'ing times are of considerable complexity, but there were no new departures from the general pattern already established, and detailed consideration of them must await another occasion. It is perhaps worth drawing attention to one aspect, however. In spite of the continual increase in the size of the family properties, the consolidation of the clan administration, the assistance of powerful distant relatives, and other favorable factors such as the great and growing prosperity of the Su-chou region as a whole, the number of family members who managed to enter official careers remained extremely small. In the middle of the eighteenth century, when the family as a whole numbered some 2,000 persons, not more than half a dozen were ever in the official service at any one time, and some members were clearly engaged in trade and other profssions.[165] The reunification of the clan as a cult community did not lead to its consolidating its social status or cause all its members to conform to one social pattern.

CONCLUSION

The history of the Fan clan's internal administration throws some interesting sidelights on the clan stability and continuity which have been held to characterize traditional Chinese society, and also on the role of clan common properties, which have been represented as a most important means of attaining such continuity and stability.

The Fan family started with everything in their favor, with two great ministers in successive generations, large endowments of land in a stable and productive area, a strong sense of family community interest which happened to coincide with a general upsurge of clan-consciousness in society in general, several generations of intelligent and progressive clan leadership, adequate family rules. In addition they received government recognition of the clan estates as a legal entity, and of their special status as a model institution founded by a notable social innovator and a famous Confucian figure. Every contingency was provided for. The endowments protected clan members against actual want, and against the heavy expenses of funerals and weddings. The charitable school and the grants for education and for entering the state examinations protected members against the possibility of losing their status as educated members of the literati class. If we accept the conventional picture of a self-perpetuating "gentry," we would expect this clan, barring political accidents, to continue to produce a steady stream of officials, and to maintain its clan cohesion over a long period.

In fact, nothing of the sort occurred. Within seven generations after the founder, the percentage of family members reaching government office had fallen from 100 per cent to roughly 5 per cent, and it afterwards declined to a steady 2 per cent of the total male members of the clan. The clan was so far from remaining a cohesive organization that the advantages of leaving it came to outweigh the advantages of remaining with it and migration occurred on a large scale.

What forces in fact tended to split up a clan and to destroy its unity and social position? The most important factor was the economic problem posed by the Chinese inheritance system, which led to the continual fragmentation and diminution of family holdings. Division of properties among all the sons entailed an inevitable decline in the economic status of the individual member unless new property was continually acquired. A second factor was the difficulty of maintaining social status through official service. This became more and more a question of preparing one's sons to achieve success in the examinations, which depended to a certain extent upon the family's possessing sufficient resources to underwrite a lengthy education.

The first and more important of these problems the charitable estate and the clan system could not deal with at all; it remained the problem of the individual family (*chia*). All that the charitable estate could do was to remove a certain amount of clan property from the process of fragmentation and division, and attempt to keep it an independent and inalienable property. But although it was more or less successful in this limited end, the system did not affect the bulk of the productive land in the clan as a whole, which continued to be divided as before. Thus the economic instability of the clan was not seriously modified by the estate.

The second problem is more complex, for the history of the Fan clan stretches over a period in which there were considerable changes in the mechanism of selecting officials. In the time of Fan Chung-yen a very high proportion of the bureaucracy entered the service either by hereditary privilege (*yin*) or by special grace (*en*), and although examination candidates were highly esteemed it was by no means a foregone conclusion that they would be employed. From the eleventh century *yin* and *en* declined in importance, and the clan had the foresight to ensure against their loss of hereditary privilege by bolstering up the family education system, and eventually by establishing a charitable school for clan members. This was an attempt to replace purely hereditary privilege by providing training facilities in a family which had a strong tradition of learning.

Unfortunately, late Sung times saw an enormous expansion of schools, both public and private, and by early Ming, when the clan's need for scholars to restore its prestige was acute, educational facilities, and the possibility of social mobility generally, were very good. This minimized the advantage held by the sons of a literary family, who might indeed be in a disadvantageous position if the father was employed in a busy post and had not the considerable leisure necessary for the prolonged drudgery of a conventional classical education. The clan community was thus unable to capitalize on the clan's strong tradition of learning.

Since the charitable estate did not confer either economic stability or the permanent advantage of an official career on clan members, what was its contribution to the clan, and why was it so widely imitated? The answer lies in the great change that took place in the clan organization, of which the development of the charitable estate was but one aspect. The new respect for the clan organization which arose in Sung times led first to an increased sense of obligation toward the clan community on the part of its members, then to the proliferation of clan institutions (such as ancestral halls, charitable schools, charitable estates), and gradually to an ever-widening conception of what constituted the clan—

a conception which ended in the absurdity of many clans from Kwangtung and Kwangsi claiming as clansmen all local residents with the same
surname. The functions of charity and ritual performance, which had
previously been performed by wealthy individual members on behalf
of a comparatively restricted family circle, now had to be extended to a
larger community. Moreover, the new stress on the continuity of ritual
produced a pressing need for some economic foundation for clan institutions more solid than individual fortunes, which would never survive
more than a very few generations. This the charitable estate provided.

Had this idea been extended to family holdings of land and turned
into something very similar to a system of entail, it might well have had
the revolutionary effect of enabling the new landowning class that arose
in Sung times to establish themselves as a separate and permanent
hereditary "gentry" of landowners. But, as it happened, the division of
inheritance continued, and the charitable estate had its effect at the
noneconomic level of the clan community. What stability it afforded,
then, was stability for the clan as a ritual group; by works of charity and
by the proper performance of rites, it constantly reminded the clan
members of their part as members of the larger community, and of the
social obligations toward their relatives which this involved. This sense
of mutual responsibility was of course in itself an important factor in
producing stability within the clan.

However, the record of the Fan clan illustrates certain pitfalls even
within this limited conception of the role of a charitable estate. Two
of these, the attempt to grant an income to all family members out of
the estate, and the failure to reinvest surplus income to allow for the
growth of the clan community, were peculiar to the Fan estate, which
was a pioneer project of its kind. Later estates abandoned general grants
and developed methods of reinvestment, and these developments appear to have affected the Fan clan in their turn. But the most important
failure which is shown in the record is the failure of family morale, and
the constant inroads made upon the common property by powerful
clan members. The pressure to obtain landed property, which was
exerted most strongly when the majority of members held no office and
thus had no other source of lands than purchase or encroachment, became greater as the clan's official influence declined, and there can be
little doubt that the charitable estate survived through twenty-two generations largely owing to assistance from sources outside the clan. In
particular, it survived by official recognition, and by continual support
from well-disposed local officials. Since the attitude of these officials
was conditioned largely by the reputation of the estate itself as a model
institution and of its founder as a Confucian paragon, this situation

was far from normal, and we need express no surprise that similar estates established in other clans during the Sung can show no such long and continuous record.

Despite these failings, however, the charitable estate played an important if limited role in Chinese social organization. By institutionalizing clan-consciousness and channeling it into specific works of charity, supporting the indigent, providing a reserve income for members, and paying for education within the clan, the estate could help maintain a very limited degree of social homogeneity by preserving members from utter impoverishment or recourse to some shameful profession. But in spite of the claims which have been made on its behalf, I see little reason to believe that it exerted any decisive influence on the shaping of Chinese traditional society, and no reason whatever to believe that it assisted in the growth of a hypothetical permanent and self-contained "gentry."

C. K. Yang

SOME CHARACTERISTICS OF
CHINESE BUREAUCRATIC BEHAVIOR

When the imperial political order arose to replace feudalism in China, rule based on the hereditary status system yielded to the development of a monocratic (centrally controlled) organization of appointed officials, a development which continued for the next two thousand years. It was to this organization (considered as a form of "patrimonial bureaucracy") that Max Weber attributed the enduring stability of the Chinese state, and to its absence that he ascribed the quick demise of ephemeral empires.[1] The purpose of this paper is to consider several major characteristics of the Chinese bureaucracy systematically with a view to establishing it as an empirical type, and in so doing to throw some light on the basic nature of bureaucracy in general.

In the absence of a systematic empirical typology of bureaucracy, we shall take as a point of departure what Weber considered to be the universal qualities of bureaucracies. His theoretical construct contains four basic features: specialization of functions, a hierarchy of authority (preferably monocratically structured), a system of formal norms or rules, and impersonality.[2] According to Weber, these factors imparted to the bureaucratic apparatus a high degree of rationality in terms of precision and predictability of means toward an organizational goal, and it was this inexorable rationality that enabled bureaucracy to triumph over such other structures as patriarchism, patrimonialism, and feudalism.[3]

If we grant the logical validity of Weber's construct, any significant development of the rational qualities of a given bureaucratic system approaching his "ideal type" would require a commensurate development of rational behavior, rational attitudes, and rational motivations, on the part of the bureaucrat. But since incompatible values and functional requirements from the general social system constantly exert disconcerting influences upon the bureaucrat's behavior, the rational features of the bureaucratic structure are constantly being modified. In other words, bureaucracy is a subsystem in the general social system, and must shape its own characteristics in response to the latter's functional-structural requirements. Hence the differences between bureaucracies in different social settings.[4]

In China, the bureaucracy developed in a social system characterized by a diffuse social pattern, local self-sufficiency, local homogeneity but national heterogeneity, emphasis on the primary group with its network of intimate personal relations, and the importance of an informal moral order.

The Confucian ideology, which provided the leading motivational values for the general social system, was shaped with close reference to these characteristics. Although the practical requirements of government compelled the development of certain rational features, pressure from the structural characteristics of the social system tended to force these features away from the rational ideal and into conformity with the social environment. Confucianism came to be adopted as the official ideology of the bureaucracy precisely because it was so well suited to such a social system[5] as compared with Legalism, the formal and impersonal characteristics of which were ostensibly much more conducive to the development of an efficient bureaucracy.

In this sense, traditional China may be thought of as having two major structural components: a national bureaucratic superstructure emphasizing centralization, standardization, formalism, a monocratically organized hierarchy of authority, and the norm of impersonality; and a vast substratum of heterogeneous local communities based on a morally oriented social order and the informal primary group. This huge conglomeration of local communities was tenuously held together by its common acceptance of the Confucian ideology, a national bureaucracy, and a weakly organized national economy. By exerting influence upon the behavior of the bureaucrat, the functional requirements of this vast substratum constantly tended to modify the operation of the bureaucratic structure. This is illustrated in Wang Hui-tsu's (1731–1807) remarks on the "rule of isolation" (*kuan fang*), by which a magistrate's aides could be cut off from personal contacts with the outside world while they served in residence with the yamen:

The rule of isolation must be avoided, and the way to avoid it is by faithful observation of the imperial mandates. Friendship ranks among the five cardinal relations, but the relationship between host [official] and guest [aide] is only one type of friendship. Sacrificing all other friendships out of devotion to one's host is surely not the conduct of a morally erect man. However, if we should take advantage of the fact that the host does not impose the rule of isolation to relax our self-discipline and soil our own reputation, we would invite contempt from the host, with the result that we would be compelled to accept isolation. Therefore, when relatives and friends come [to the ya-

men] to visit, we must inform the host of their names; and if we leave the
yamen on business, we must let him know our specific destination. If our
every move is made clearly and openly, thus proving our reliability to our
host, he will not dare to hint at imposing the rule of isolation.[6]

This illustration shows that the pressure of the general social system
upon the bureaucratic subsystem was so great that contact between the
two systems at times had to be forcibly severed in order to keep officials
from being distracted by their informal and personal relations with
friends and kinsmen.

In the following pages we shall analyze several aspects of Chinese
bureaucratic behavior in the light of the general social structure of
China in the nineteenth and early twentieth century when the traditional
bureaucratic system and social order were still in operation. The sources
employed are mostly products of the nineteenth century; some were
originally written earlier but retained their influence in the nineteenth
century. For example, Ch'en Hung-mou's (1696–1771) *Ts'ung-cheng
I-kuei* ("The Administrative Tradition"), although primarily the work
of Ming and early Ch'ing administrators, remained an important reference for officials throughout the nineteenth century and into the twentieth. The *Ch'in-pan Chou Hsien Shih-i* ("Imperial Directive on Prefectural and County Affairs") was issued by the Yung-cheng emperor
in the first part of the eighteenth century, but was reprinted and distributed to the bureaucracy in the 1850's in the Hsien-feng reign.

Though various levels of the bureaucracy will be discussed, we shall
emphasize local administration at the *hsien* level. This limitation does
not seriously restrict us, since the *hsien* level was of fundamental importance administratively, and its problems were a sort of index to the problems that occurred higher up in the bureaucratic structure. As Wang
Hui-tsu said:

The empire represents the totality of all the prefectures and counties . . .
Above the prefects and county magistrates are the governors and high dignitaries who help to administer the state with their complex offices. But it is
the prefectural and county administrations that deal directly with the people.
The duties of offices above the prefect and county magistrate consist in regulating and improving the administration of prefectures and counties.[7]

THE BUREAUCRAT AS A GENERALIST

An important characteristic of bureaucracy, as distinguished from
other types of administrative structure, is its stress on specialization of
functions. It is Weber's belief that this emphasis helped enable bureaucracy to achieve a higher degree of rationality and efficiency in attaining
specific goals than the historical counterparts it displaced.[8]

The logical soundness of this broad principle can hardly be questioned; yet in applying it to the Chinese bureaucracy, we are confronted with a certain ambiguity in the term "specialization." In the popular conception, specialization means the assigning of workers to technically differentiated tasks, as in dividing the government into technically separate departments, each with its own expertly trained staff.

In actual practice, however, the nature of specialization varies considerably with (1) administrative levels and (2) types of organizational goals. The head of a department, especially a large one, has to coordinate the activities of many specialized officials, perhaps performing many types of tasks himself at critical points, such as personally drafting an important statement to his superiors or to the public. Again, the head of an administrative area, e.g., a county, a prefecture, or a province, oversees the operation of all specialized departments and occasionally deals with the business of certain departments directly when necessary.[9] Neither the head of a department nor the head of an administrative area is preoccupied exclusively with a single task. His coordinating duties may be regarded as a specialized function claiming his main attention, but his decision-making role demands that he be acquainted with the nature of many specialized tasks and capable of performing some of them at critical points. As a coordinator of tasks and a decision-maker, such an administrator may be regarded as a *generalist* with a broad knowledge of social relations.

He is not, strictly speaking, an expert. In the bureaucratic structure, it is generally not until we get down to the rank of operatives and clerical workers, the actual producers of work, that we see specialization according to the commonly accepted conception.

In terms of organizational goals, the principle of specialization applies better to areas in which administrative policies are highly specific than to areas in which the organizational goal is broadly defined or diffuse. In the former, the position of the specialist is clearly defined by decisions handed down from above; in the latter, the position of the specialist is only of limited importance. The heads of complex departments or administrative areas usually deal with the second type of goal. Here once again it is the generalist rather than the expert who commands an important position. In analyzing Chinese bureaucracy, these conceptual considerations must be kept in view.

Examining the Chinese bureaucracy in this light, we find that it was men with general knowledge and ability who provided the backbone for the administration of the far-flung empire by filling the hierarchy of positions from county magistracies to provincial governor-generalships. Even the men in control of more or less specialized departments in the provincial and central governments were officials with a generalist orientation, and most specialists at the provincial level and below enjoyed little or no formal status in the bureaucratic hierarchy (see pp. 160–63).

It is well known that the scholar-official, who was destined for all sorts of bureaucratic positions, at times including military posts, was equipped with a general stock of knowledge from the Confucian classics, rather than with the knowledge and skills of a specialist. We need, however, to clarify the nature of this stock of knowledge and to explain how it was adapted to the requirements of the bureaucratic organization as it functioned in the Chinese social milieu.

The Confucian classics are oriented toward the achievement of *t'ai-p'ing* (Great Peace) through knowledge of the general social order based on a harmonious system of human relations and moral norms. Regulation of the social order thus became the chief business of the bureaucracy, regulation in the sense of coordinating the activities of the people and the statuses of groups in accordance with the principles of nature and the moral norms of society. The Great Peace will obtain when things and people are structured into the smoothly operating order of these principles and norms, ideally with all frictions and obstructions eliminated. This essence of Confucian political knowledge was succinctly expressed by Lü K'un (1534–1616):

The life of the superior man is dedicated to reproducing the achievement of Yao and Shun, and gaining the wisdom of Confucius and Mencius. Some have asked how to approach these two goals. The answer is, treat the myriad things between heaven and earth as a grand unity, this is the wisdom of Confucius and Mencius; enable the myriad things between heaven and earth to obtain their proper places, this is the achievement of Yao and Shun.[10]

In a broad sense, the system of Confucian knowledge may be said to center upon the proper ordering of people and their activities as a means of achieving the main administrative goal, peace and harmony in an extensive empire. In sociological terms, the proper ordering of people and their activities involves the understanding of individual and group goals, the arrangement of roles and statuses, and the operation of behavioral norms. Anyone with the most cursory acquaintance with the Confucian classics knows that they deal with precisely these topics. The proper social order was understood in the classics as being based on the principles of nature, both cosmic and human. Officials were to use these principles as the basic norm or standard (*ching*, literally meaning "the classics"), and they could devise expedients (*ch'üan*, literally meaning to weigh) to implement the norm according to circumstances.

Because of the abstract nature of the principles of social relations, an official could move from level to level or even from department to department with facility, with a pronounced degree of independence from the specialized nature of the office. This being the case, it is understandable that Lü K'un should have said, "With a deep acquaintance with the principles of human relations and worldly affairs, one can take up any official position, however high; with adaptation to the principles of nature and the inclinations of men, one can accomplish any task."[11] Here, skill in bureaucratic administration is equated with mastery of the basic principles of social relations, with the bureaucrat playing the role of coordinator and regulator of these relations. Hence, many of the guides to proper administrative behavior concern the ideal model for such a role, as for example: "One must be grave in stance, steadfast in purpose, gentle in expression, calm in emotion, brief and precise in speech, kind in heart, courageous and persistent in ambition, and discreet in official secrets."[12] This is not the portrait of an efficient specialist.

Bureaucracy is theoretically the most efficient mechanism for executing a policy that can be expressed in terms of a series of specific tasks for which specific operatives are available; orders can be set down in clear terms, and the specialists can take it from there. But when the policy or goal is diffuse and the official's duties are of a multi-functional character, men of general ability seem better equipped to handle the situation, men whose efficiency cannot be measured by the order-result criterion that applies to the specialist. This consideration explains the characteristic emphasis on the generalist's knowledge in the Chinese bureaucracy.

It has been pointed out that the overall objective of government in the Confucian tradition was to bring about the Great Peace in the empire, and with it, general prosperity and happiness. Not only did this objective underlie the elaborate discussions on the vital subject of *chih-kuo* (ruling the kingdom) and *p'ing t'ien-hsia* (tranquilizing the empire) in Confucian writings, but it ultimately became an ingrained political desideratum among the people, and it has so remained, even in the recent decades of wars and strife.

But this objective, set up for all levels of local government and for the empire as a whole, was not a specific assignment but an all-inclusive, multi-functional goal, or a diffuse objective; its realization involved everything needed in building a good society. On the county level, the magistracy had the following functions, as stated by Ch'en Hung-mou from his successful administrative experience and as suggested in the "Imperial Directive on Prefectural and County Affairs": (1) judicial work—attending to litigation, suppressing litigation-mongers, punishing local bullies and violators of justice, administering the jail, purging rapacious members from the yamen staff; (2) public safety work—apprehending robbers and thieves, suppressing heretic sectarian organizations, suppressing prostitution and gambling; (3) financial work—collecting taxes and distributing the tax burden fairly among the people; (4) educational work; (5) helping farmers—e.g., by developing and reclaiming cultivable land; (6) public welfare work—giving relief to destitute widows, aged persons and orphans, feeding victims of famine, operating the ever-normal granaries; and (7) administering the imperial postal system, which involved keeping up the postal relay stations, the post horses, and the post roads and bridges.[13]

This list immediately suggests a system of division of labor along specialist lines, and indeed specialists or the equivalent were assigned to each of these specific duties. But the magistrate was the formal member of the bureaucracy; the specialists were only his aides who enjoyed no official rank. The magistrate was expected to be acquainted with the full range of these tasks and to perform many of them personally, especially as they concerned judicial and financial matters. Tasks that he did not personally perform he had to organize and coordinate. His personal acquaintance with specialized tasks, especially in judicial and financial matters, was in fact imperative, since he was frequently required to render verbal accounts to his superiors on questionable points.[14] In addition, since there were very few formal positive rules on how to go about accomplishing a given task (though there were fairly elaborate rules governing punishment for bad results), officials were needed who could make proper use of their latitude on this score. Specialists were too narrow; a good official was one who had built up a generalist's fund of knowledge from books and experience covering a variety of fields.

When the official, guided by his general knowledge and aided by his specialist assistants, was able to perform the wide variety of tasks well, an approximation of the administrative goal of *t'ai-p'ing* was considered attainable. The following picture, though it comes from the Sung period, was regarded as a model of successful government in one of the leading reference works for nineteenth-century officials, the *Ts'ung-cheng I-kuei*. In describing the good administration of P'ing-hsiang hsien, a military officer, Fan Yen-kuei, said, "When I entered the territory, I saw the post roads and bridges all in good repair. All arable lands were under cultivation, and there were no idle peasants in the countryside. When I entered the city, I saw that there was no gambling in the market place, and transactions were conducted with no quarrels. When I stopped at the official residence at night, I heard the drum striking the hours with clarity and regularity. So I knew the administration was good."[15]

A recommended way to attain this diffuse goal of good government was to let the local communities operate by their own social standards and moral tradition with a minimum of government interference, except to strengthen them whenever necessary. Repeatedly encountered in writings on administration current in the nineteenth century are the following quotations:

Yang I-ch'ing (Ming period):

What is needed in administration at the present time is to keep troublesome business at a minimum, not to add to it; to preserve the rules, not to change them; to bring about tranquillity in all situations, not to stir them up; and to relax and simplify the control of the people, not to tighten and complicate it.

Lu Shu-chien (Ming period):

"Maintenance of moral tradition is the main task in government."[16]

And contemporary works on the art of government repeatedly emphasize the use of *chiao* ("educating") and *hua* ("transforming") to strengthen the social and moral order and to simplify government.

"Education and transformation" included such measures as establishing public schools, holding public lectures on imperial edicts, glorifying the "filial and chaste" in the community, paying ceremonial honor to local scholars and elders, and convoking mass gatherings at trials to demonstrate the standards of right and wrong.[17] Schools served the function of "transforming vicious custom by literary influence. If one or two out of every thousand students matured into leaders and in turn transformed others around them, the good influence would spread, reaping slow but enduring benefits."[18]

All these were elaborations of Confucius' familiar statement that the best way to settle lawsuits is to prevent them from arising. In other words, the basic policy of government was to let society operate spontaneously by strengthening its social and moral order. This was possible because traditional Chinese society was basically of the *gemeinschaft* type: the main regulatory force was the moral order, not formal law or a highly specialized administrative apparatus. But men who tried to conduct government on this basis would have to understand the basic principles governing the structure and operation of the social and moral order. It was this understanding that men sought in Confucianism, for it was the Confucian type of general knowledge that had proven effective in regulating a diffuse pattern of social life.

Specialists, of course, had their place as well as generalists in the traditional bureaucracy. Both the size and the qualitative complexity of the administrative tasks involved in governing such an extensive empire made a certain amount of specialization inevitable. In fact, both the central and the provincial administrations had a functionally departmentalized structure. Peking had its six boards (of Justice or Punishment, Civil Office, Rites, War, Revenue, and Public Works) and other specialized agencies, and the provinces had closely corresponding offices. The prefectures and county magistracies were multi-functional offices in a formal sense, but many of their duties were entrusted to specialist staff members of informal status. Magistrates' aides, for instance, were assigned to judicial work, revenue collection, record-keeping, and secretarial jobs,[19] while lesser functionaries specialized in police work, in keeping the public granaries, in maintaining the postal relay stations, etc.[20]

Some acquaintance with practical specialized knowledge and skills was obviously required of the bureaucrat for him to operate the functionally differentiated structure, and indeed, in some instances, to preserve his self-respect and the respect of his subordinates. The bureaucracy tried with varying degrees of success to meet this situation by: (a) maintaining the controlling position of the generalist's tradition, (b) acquiring technical knowledge through in-service training, and (c) employing specialized personnel in subordinate and often formally unrecognized positions. The first two of these points will be considered here, leaving the last for examination later.

(a) For centuries intermittent attacks had been launched on the impracticality of mere bookish knowledge as a basic qualification for administrative office. But the eighteenth and nineteenth centuries still found the general knowledge of the classics reigning supreme. The scholar-officials made their stand on two formal grounds. One was the argument that those who found the classics impractical failed to study them in terms of social realism and erroneously associated them with the empty art of literary formalism, in which terms the wisdom of the sages "deteriorated into verbal platitudes for the scholars and a mere steppingstone to status in the eyes of the people. This is the main cause for the degeneration of contemporary writing and the emptiness and impracticality of present-day scholarship."[21] The fault thus lay not with the content of the classics but with the wrong orientation of those who did not know the proper way to study them.

The other ground (or a re-statement of the first) was the *t'i-yung* concept, the analysis of a situation into its essence or principle (*t'i*, literally meaning the body) and its practical manifestations or implementations (*yung*, literally meaning use or application). Which, for example, is the proper means of ridding an area of robbery: rigorous police measures or sound economic measures so that the people "find it unnecessary to rob for a living"? Are we to treat the symptoms or the disease, to concentrate on the *yung* or on the *t'i*?[22] In settling lawsuits, is it better to perfect the technique of fact-finding to establish evidence (*yung*), or to bend every effort toward properly applying moral and social principles (*t'i*) to the situation?[23] Clearly there is something to be said for both approaches; the point is that the bureaucrats could argue, and did, that *t'i* took precedence over *yung*. To their way of thinking, even the distinctly specialist task of public finance had an overriding generalist requirement, for it called not merely for budgetary accounting technique, but above all for the knowledge to weigh and decide on items of expenditure in the light of the long-term benefit of society.[24] This knowledge, of course—and insight into *t'i* in general—could be attained only by studying the Confucian classics.

A protracted debate took place on this subject, and philosophically speaking no settlement was ever reached. Practically speaking, however, the generalist, the man with the general "principle," remained firmly in control of the bureaucratic structure, while the specialist, the man with the "implementing" technique, remained a "mere expert." The substratum of practical and specialized personnel, though organized into an informal structure and actually performing administrative operations, never attained policy-making status.

(b) Having to coordinate and direct specialized tasks and being required on occasion to perform some of them personally, the official was compelled to acquire a certain amount of practical knowledge himself while in service. In the central government, regulations provided for a year's practice for the novice in a department before cases were assigned to him.[25] In the provincial and prefectural administration, officials were promoted from among experienced men who already had had their internship in other, usually lower, positions, and their assignment to special departments was often directed by their reputation or aptness at certain lines of work as developed in their previous service. Kuei Ch'ao-wan, for example, who eventually became provincial judge in Fukien in 1863, had already established a reputation for judicial work during his long service in such places as Luan-hsien in Hopei, and Soochow and Ch'ang-chou in Kiangsu.[26]

Nevertheless, hierarchical status in the bureaucratic structure placed a restriction on in-service training and handicapped even the experienced man as he moved into an unfamiliar new post. Lü K'un spoke from personal experience when he made the following criticism of bureaucratic practice:

Scholars in the ancient days shared their knowledge. Nowadays, among colleagues, the novice dare not inquire about the affairs of the experienced, and men in one office dare not find out the duties of those in the next office, lest they be suspected of interfering with others' duties or branded as ambitious. Hence, one cannot prepare oneself before moving into a new post, and it is too late to learn after one is appointed. As a result, one is compelled to muddle through in haste and to make a mere formality of fulfilling the duties of the office.[27]

If such considerations affected men already well along in an official career, the position of many of the county magistrates was worse. The magistracy was the initial appointment for successful candidates from the national examinations. Most of them were fresh from their abstract studies and completely unfamiliar with practical administrative duties, yet they embarked on those duties with no such practice period as was allowed to newcomers in the central government. The problem is well expressed in an edict:

Local problems have their origin in prefectures and counties, where affairs are complex and intrigues take a hundred forms. Those shouldering such responsibilities are mostly newcomers to the roster of officials, totally without previous experience and suddenly set to work. It is no wonder that they are at a loss. Even if they seek advice, others may not advise them without reservation . . .[28]

In view of this long-recognized handicap in the efficiency of the bureaucracy, one wonders—as countless earlier reformers wondered[29]— why some sort of education in practical subjects or pre-appointment training was not instituted. It would seem that there were several reasons.

First, there were not many usable texts on practical administrative subjects, especially on local administration, since systematic empirical study in the administrative field was relatively undeveloped. The issuing of the *Ch'in-pan Chou Hsien Shih-I* ("Imperial Directive on Prefectural and County Affairs") in the eighteenth century was prompted by this need.[30] The rapid and wide circulation of Wang Hui-tsu's *Tso Chih Yao Yen* ("Salutary Advice on Assisting in Administration") and *Hsüeh Chih I-shuo* ("Learning to Govern"), and Ch'en Hung-mou's *Ts'ung-cheng I-kuei*, soon after they were written, indicates the dearth of such practical materials even in the last century of Ch'ing rule.

Second, there was the handicap of hierarchical rank and official secrecy, which operated against training through practice in the manner indicated by the quotation from Lü K'un.

Third, if specialized practical knowledge were to be stressed in the training of prospective officials, as many reformers urged, candidates who failed to obtain official appointment would remain unemployed, since the state was the only conceivable employer for administrative specialists in a society where specialization of functions and large-scale organizations were relatively undeveloped. By contrast, a man trained in the classics could teach school or become a community leader should he fail to become an official.[31]

It seems likely that despite these handicaps, in-service training served its function with a reasonable degree of adequacy. The impractical scholar, the bookworm, and the inept devotee of literary form were met most frequently at the low level of county magistrate, thanks to the Ch'ing system of reviewing officials' accomplishments every three years and selecting only the most promising men for promotion. On the prefectural and provincial levels we rarely encounter an unrealistic scholar, though the picture in the central government departments was rather uncertain. In short, since only the generalist with proven practical ability was promoted, the administration of the country tended to run smoothly, and the generalist remained in command of the situation despite his initial lack of practical training.

(c) Finally, the need for practical specialized knowledge was met to a certain degree by the development of an informal group of specialized operatives. We shall discuss the service of these specialists in the last part of this paper.

Another thing that strengthened the generalist's position was the relative simplicity of an administrative mechanism, especially at the local level, designed to rule a society in which the self-regulating social and moral order minimized formal government. The size and qualitative complexity of most bureaucratic offices were still comprehensible to the non-specialist, and their number was comfortably small. The empire as a whole, in the nineteenth century, had only about 40,000 official posts, incomparably fewer than a modern bureaucracy ruling a state of comparable area and smaller population.

Unfortunately, we have few data on the size of staff and the volume and nature of business in a department on the central or provincial level, but scattered data on the prefectural and county levels suggest a rather simple picture. Litigation furnished the bulk of a magistrate's formal business, and the number of cases, varying with the locality, did not seem to be uncontrollably great even in a busy post. When Kuei Ch'ao-wan took over the magistracy of Ch'ang-chou prefecture in Kiangsu, a very busy post, in the early part of the nineteenth century, he complained about the "unusual" accumulation of unfinished cases he inherited, which was "over 1,200."[32] This is a fraction of the docket of the courts in a medium-sized American city. The cases fell mostly into a few classes, namely troubles involving kinship relations (e.g. marital and inheritance problems), disputes over ownership of property, bodily injury and loss of life, and robbery. Both the nature of the majority of

the cases and the characteristics of the law demanded more consideration of moral norms and situational needs than mastery of legal techni-
cality, though the latter was a part of the picture, as will be seen.

The next heaviest item of administrative business was finance. Luan-
hsien in Hopei was a busy center, the converging point of a system of
roads leading to five provinces, and yet, under Kuei Ch'ao-wan's administration, the official revenues totaled only 16,000 taels of silver, out
of which about 9,000 was retained for expenditure and 7,000 handed
over to the central government.[33] In terms of monetary units, the size
of the budget was rather small, well within the ability of an intelligent
and experienced layman to comprehend and control. The total staff of
a county yamen, though varying with the locality, was correspondingly
small. The number of aides, for instance, ranged "from two to three in
a small place to over ten in a large locality."[34] In short, the office of the
prefect or county magistrate was neither too big nor too complex to be
adequately filled by a generalist trained in the concepts of coordination
and unity, roles and status, behavioral norms, and individual and social
objectives.

FORMAL RULES AND MORAL NORMS

Bureaucracy is theoretically distinguished from other types of political structure by its pervasive system of formal and abstract rules governing official conduct.[35] In the Weberian conception, the aim of such a
system is to produce a uniform treatment of cases, to facilitate the coordination of tasks, and to develop the rational character of the bureaucratic organization: the predictability of means toward the ends. Acting
under the system of formal rules, "the ideal official conducts his office
. . . in a spirit of formalistic impersonality, without hatred or passion,
and hence without affection or enthusiasm."[36] "For rational standards
to govern operations without interference from personal considerations,
a detached approach must prevail within the organization and especially
toward clients."[37]

A system of formal rules was a well-developed feature of the Chinese
bureaucracy. In fact, institutional pressure on officials to act according
to formal rules and semi-formal norms (li, or rites) left a proverbial
stamp of formalism on Chinese bureaucratic behavior—witness the use
of the expression ta kuan ch'iang ("talking in an official tone") to describe someone speaking in a formally correct style. But formal rules
and impersonality were not characteristic of the traditional Chinese
social system, which was based on the dominance of the moral order
and personal primary-group relationships. Since, as we have seen, the
bureaucratic subsystem was obliged to function within the framework

of the general social system, these moral and personal values, though they were dysfunctional to the rational quality of bureaucracy, had to be taken into account. In the following pages we shall consider the place of formal rules and their operation under the influence of moral norms and primary-group relations.

The formal aspect of the normative system was developed to a fairly high degree in the Chinese bureaucratic structure to assure uniformity and coordination of official action on a national scale. There were elaborate codes like the *Ta-Ch'ing Lü Li* and the *Hui Tien* (a collection of rules based on precedents). There were also the voluminous *Liu-pu Tse-li* ("Rules of the Six Boards"), and especially the *Li-pu Tse-li* ("Rules of the Board of Civil Office"), which set forth formal specifications on such matters as assuming a new post, transferring an office to a successor, proper conduct in office, and proper style in official documents. These were supplemented by a variety of lesser references, among them the *Huang-cheng Ch'üan-shu* ("Cyclopedia of Famine Relief Administration"), *Liang-cheng Ch'üan-shu* ("Cyclopedia of Revenue Administration"), and a variety of *mu-ling shu* (reference works for magistrates). Though not comparable to the modern Western legal codes in size or in precision and objectivity, these compilations did provide a formal framework to facilitate uniformity, coordination, and predictability of official actions, making bureaucracy an organization rationally superior to its historical precedent, the personal rule of feudalism.

This is not to imply that the system of formal rules had completely eliminated rule by personal will and choice in nineteenth-century China. In fact, the age-old issue of rule by good men and rule by good law (*chih jen, chih fa*) still smoldered throughout the Ch'ing period. But there was unmistakable recognition and acceptance of formal rules as a vital instrument for administration. Opinions on this point abound in volumes such as Ho Ch'ang-ling's (1785–1848) *Huang-ch'ao Ching-shih Wen Pien* ("Collection of Ch'ing Writings on Statesmanship"), but for succinct statements we may choose a paragraph or two from Lü K'un's *Shen-yin Yü Chieh-lu* ("Some Moaning Words"):

Nature operates by regular rules, and men must follow these rules to accomplish things . . . When government operates by definite rules, subordinates performing their duties will know where they stand. The uniformity of instructions will minimize errors. If [an official] rules by whim and unbridled temperament, others will not be able to guess at his intentions . . .[38]

In Lü's opinion, reliance on men and not on law is possible only in a Golden Age under the rule of sages:

Exclusive reliance on men under any other circumstances will inevitably end in chaos . . . In later times, mediocre rulers and commonplace officials failed to employ the great principles so as to bring about good government, and tyrannical rulers and wicked officials dared to indulge in evil deeds and treachery. Hence, laws with broad outlines and detailed stipulations were made to control them, to guide them . . . Mediocre rulers and common-place officials would still observe the laws and would not dare to change them, and the laws thereby attained a part of their objective. Even tyrannical rulers and wicked officials would hesitate before trying to change or disre-gard them . . . It is thus obvious that we cannot do without laws.[39]

But it is of course true that in the Confucian tradition great emphasis has been placed on the importance of getting good men in office. Lü must try to meet objections:

Good officials and good laws are equally needed . . . Good officials would make good laws . . . and would allow these laws to stand until at some later time other good officials come forth to enforce them.[40]

It is argued that each new law will bring a new abuse. This is correct. But it is not correct to do without law merely because law is abused. Using law to inhibit evil is like building dikes to prevent floods. It is possible that a dike will break because of flimsy construction, but because one dike has broken we do not cease building dikes. Even Yao and Shun could not produce a flawless law . . . Hence the sage . . . does not abandon a good law because of a small abuse, or abandon a durable law because of temporary abuse.[41]

Contemporary Chinese writings on administration show a general appreciation not only of the importance of law, but also of administrative objectivity as a condition for the successful functioning of law. Ad-ministrators are proverbially admonished to cultivate *hsü* (impartiality), *kung* (openness), *hsiang* (thoroughness), *shen* (carefulness), and self-control.[42]

But bias, arrogance, and temperamentalism, so characteristic of per-sonal rule and contrary to rational administrative requirements, marred the behavior of many officials who formed a part of society's status group.[43] Yen Kuang-ch'ung (Ming period) remarked:

Officials are accustomed to displaying arrogance and intolerance toward all. Trying cases is for them more an occasion for exhibiting arrogance and temper than for finding out the right and wrong; thus they allow the crafty [litigant or criminal] to win and the clumsy one to lose.[44]

Hence, Lü K'un stressed that "superior men control their emotions and observe the rules."[45] He gave a good illustration of the irrelevance of emotional factors to the rational administration of the law in a vivid description of typical administrative behavior:

[The official] sat in court, severe in gesture and word, flanked by soldiers and threatening instruments of torture; he might let [the litigant or criminal] live or let him die, he might do anything to him with little restraint. Secure and complacent was the state of his feeling. But soon a courageous man of learning arose and spoke the truth, pointing out the official's errors without fear for his solemnity and arrogance, and the great dignitary was deflated. At this juncture, the dignitary still had power to put the man to death, but it had become obvious that to do so would be to use force to suppress reason, that the dignitary could kill him but could not convince him of his guilt. When a notorious bandit holds a sharp knife against a man's neck at night, that man will be afraid, whoever he may be. The irrational employment of power to suppress people compares with the robber's act, and is unworthy of an official . . . Therefore, when an official uses power, it should be to vindicate reason, not to impose superiority of status.[46]

This same discernment of the distinction between reason and irrational use of power led Lü to assert that the good official would render judgment "according to the merits of the case and not according to his personal feeling, following the standard of right and wrong and disregarding any praise or blame that he may receive. In this way he will satisfy the people's sense of justice and prevent rebellion."[47] Emotional factors are irrelevant to the formal principle of the law, an extraneous element introduced into the operation of the bureaucratic machinery, making it less efficient in attaining its ends (justice and order).

It is important to note that this irrelevant and extraneous factor of emotion was introduced into the situation not fortuitously but following an established pattern, as will be obvious to anyone who knows anything about the traditional Chinese court. Arrogance was built into the status system of the traditional social structure; it was an institutionalized prerogaive of the high-status group of scholar-officials, a part of their personality pattern in normal social life. They were hardly likely to drop their domineering traits when they entered the bureaucracy where the added power and prestige would only enhance such traits. Their arrogance was contradictory to the rational orientation of bureaucracy, but arrogant they remained. Once again we see the general social system impinging upon the bureaucratic subsystem.

Interference from the social status system, of course, was not the only source of emotional obstruction to the objectivity and detachment needed in the rational administration of law. Another source was the possible bias, venality, or stupidity of the official's assistants. The seasoned bureaucrat Wang Hui-tsu put the matter thus:

A proud, self-confident official often likes to rely on personal assistants, to regard them as his eyes and ears in the matter of collecting evidence for a case. But these assistants are not all reliable, for they may be tempted by private gain or blinded by ignorance . . . When the official attends to his business, he enjoys the advantage of detachment from the case. Once he relies on reports from his personal assistants, he becomes personally involved with the case and encounters obstructions [in his effort to do justice].[48]

This self-involvement was contradictory to the rational requirement of detachment, or the norm of impersonality. This again was not accidental, but was the result of a confirmed characteristic of the general social system: the pervasive influence of personal, primary-group relations, from which the official could seldom extricate himself. The primary-group orientation caused other difficulties also, as will be seen presently.

Finally, the rational functioning of the law was obstructed by common corruption, the appropriation of the law as a personal possession. This well-known feature of bureaucracy is incisively analyzed in the following passage from Lü K'un:

> The treasurer guards the ruler's wealth, and the official guards the ruler's law; the duty of guardianship is the same in both cases. The treasurer becomes a thief when he steals the ruler's wealth for private business. When the official abuses the law in return for personal favors, should he not be called a thief too? How deplorable it is to sell public law for private favor, to rob the people in order to cement a personal friendship, and to regard such conduct as perfectly normal![49]

> The law is a sacred instrument for ruling the world and controlling things. Rulers formulated it in accordance with the principles of nature and human relations, and officials were to guard it for the empire and for posterity. It does not belong to me, so how could I dare to treat it as a private possession? But it is different nowadays; people use the law for personal gain. They request favors openly, and officials respond by granting their requests in return for favors. And crafty fellows subvert right principles by making their appeal in the name of generosity, kindness, returning a service, or honoring a superior. But generosity and kindness must be practiced without violating the law; a service may be returned or a superior honored only where the law permits. Why use the public law of the imperial court to meet personal obligations and to obtain personal benefits? This is a matter calling for serious caution from those traveling on the roads of officialdom.[50]

The intrusion of individual goals into the operation of the law is inconsistent with the formal public purpose of the bureaucratic apparatus. It is a result of the personal obligations imposed on the official by the general social system.

Even in a theoretical construct, a completely rational bureaucratic system is impossible—"a law without gaps" simply cannot be designed. "The conception of the modern judge as an automaton into which the files and the costs are thrown in order that it may spill forth the verdict at the bottom along with the reasons, read mechanically from codified paragraphs—this conception is angrily rejected, perhaps because a certain approximation to this type is implied by a consistent bureaucratization of justice."[51] We are here concerned not so much with the automation of justice as with the problem of how the inevitable "gaps" in the system of formal rules are filled.

In the Chinese case, it appears that (1) the law stressed negative inhibition of offense more than positive direction for correct action, thus leaving much room for non-legal judgment; (2) gaps abounded in both the negative and positive aspects of the law, as shown in "borderline cases"; and (3) the gaps permitted a certain amount of normless "arbitrary action and *personally* motivated favor and valuation."[52] Moral norms greatly helped to curb this last threat and it is this that made the moral tone prominent in the operation of the Chinese bureaucratic system of formal rules. The "valuational" nature of judgments made on the basis of moral norms may be regarded as an adaptation of the bureaucratic procedure to the characteristically fundamental position occupied by moral premises in the functioning of the traditional social order.

Since the law clearly could not specify every minute act in the conduct of office, it was necessary to supplement the law with the moral conscience of the official. Reminiscing over the tragic fall of the Ming dynasty, Ku Yen-wu (1613–82) declared in his famous *Jih-chih Lu* ("Learning Day by Day"):

As *li* (rites) and *i* (righteousness) are the great rules for the control of men, so *lien* (financial honesty) and *ch'ih* (sense of shame) are the great criteria for the establishment of character. For without *lien*, one would not hesitate to appropriate anything, and without *ch'ih*, one would not hesitate to do any wrong. When the common people behave this way, there will inevitably be calamity, defeat, chaotic strife, and finally destruction of the state. Just consider, then, what must occur when high officials do not hesitate to appropriate anything or to do any wrong.[53]

The function of moral conscience in the control of an official's behavior is again well elucidated by Lü K'un:

Good men are not always rewarded, and evil men do not always incur misfortune; the superior man knows this well, but he would rather suffer misfortune than do evil. The loyal and the honest are poor, the obsequious and the deceptive are prosperous; the superior man knows this well, but he would rather stay poor than deceive. He understands the logical outcome of the situation, but his conscience will not tolerate any other course.[54]

In this connection, it is interesting to read the "inaugural declaration" of Liu Heng (middle Ch'ing) when he assumed the office of magistrate: ". . . Anyone who dares to implicate me in personal dealings and tempt me with bribery is treating me as a prostitute and a thief . . . Whoever he may be, I will immediately report him for punishment."[55] The sig-

nificance of this statement lies in the fact that it centers attention not
on the law, but on the moral standards by which Liu proposed to govern
his official actions as a magistrate.

The moral conscience does more than simply fill the gap left by the
law. Moral values were understood and accepted more widely in traditional society than law; hence the effectiveness of these values in controlling the official's behavior, especially toward his constituents (as
opposed to his subordinates). When an official dealt with his constituents, the moral or behavioral aspects of the situation were understood
and accepted by both parties, while the legal aspects were understood
mainly by the official.

Turning from the official's behavior to the administration of law
over the people, we find moral norms occupying an equally important
position. Thus Hsüeh Hsüan (early Ming) declared in his *Yao Yü*
("Vital Words"): "It has been said that written stipulations are only
eight-tenths of the law. The codified paragraphs of the law are all intended to control men's desires and to help the functioning of the principles of nature."[56] The implication is that one must know how to control men's desires and understand the functioning of the principles of
nature in order to interpret the unwritten two-tenths of the law; moreover, there was considerable latitude for independent action beyond the
letter of the law, and such action must be dictated by moral considerations. Wang Hui-tsu expressed this quite clearly:

There is no hard and fast rule about the administration [of the law]; much
depends on the administrator. If an official bases an administrative action on
genuine kindness, then the action will be a kind one whether he properly lets
a man live or properly puts a man to death. If he does otherwise, then if he
is overindulgent, he will nourish evil; if he is obstinate, he will let his own
temperament lead him; if he is vain, he will be likely to act so as to please
others; and if he is an intriguer, he will work only for his own benefit. When
there is no sincerity of intention . . . administrative action amounts to mere
ostentation.[57]

In the actual handling of legal cases the guidance of the moral norm
became particularly significant, owing to the borderline nature of most
of the cases. Recounting his own experience, Wang Hui-tsu said:

To "let live" has in all ages been a vital principle for specialists in the law.
If the law absolutely stipulated the death punishment, it would not be open
to the aide to let a man live by wrongly interpreting the law. But when a
case offers a choice between heavy and light punishment, dispute over just
one sentence may be fraught with grave consequences. In such circumstances,
one must sincerely search for a solution by putting oneself into the situation of
the case, and one is then likely to be able to find a thread leading to life [for
the criminal]. In the twenty-six years I served as aide in criminal law, only
six persons received the death penalty . . .[58]

It was the basic intention unexpressed in the letter of the law and the considerable latitude for interpretation that gave the moral norm its importance. This issue has its Western counterpart in the familiar controversies over the letter and the spirit of the law. The uncertainty of the letter of the law, the variety of possible interpretations, was so great that even as seasoned an administrator of law as Wang himself preferred to put his trust in moral judgment: "any misinterpretation of the letter of the law may harm human lives. Therefore, the mark of keen understanding of the spirit of the law lies in one's ability to avoid using the law and not in one's ability to quote the law."[59]

The same rationale lay behind many widely quoted maxims on the administration of the law, among them the Ming writer Hsiung Mienan's admonition: "The imperial court must be severe in formulating laws, and the officers must be forgiving in executing the laws";[60] and the statement by Ts'ui Jen-shih (Ming period) that "the administration of criminal law must be based on kindness and forgiveness."[61]

In the broader issues of devising a normative system to attain the organizational goal of peace and tranquillity for the empire, the Chinese bureaucratic mind tended to rely on the moral norm as the mainstay, with formal law as a supplemental instrument. This was the opinion of Lü K'un, who had a clear recognition of the function of law:

In the Great Ancient Age, the rulers and the people unconsciously trusted each other without resorting to explicit statements. In the Middle Ancient Age, the rulers and the people still trusted each other. But in Later Ages, the rulers and the people tried to overcome each other. The rulers used law to overcome the people, and the people employed deception to circumvent the law. The people devised tricks to overcome the rulers, and the rulers used wit to prevent tricks. How can good government be attained in this way? To return to the ancient principle, we must treat the people with sincerity; where sincerity proves insufficient, supplement it with law.[62]

Mutual trust between officials and the people, regarded as so vital here, assumed a complete understanding and agreement on the norm of conduct by both parties; and the norm, as we have seen, was not formal law, which only the literate officials understood, but the corpus of moral values.

Generally speaking, the law cannot take into account special circumstances, or the situational context of an act. Here once again the functional requirements of the general social system compelled a modification of the formalistic principle. Since legal interpretation of an act in isolation from its situational context was disruptive of a social order in which the intimate personal relations of the primary group played a dominant role, some adjustment was necessary. Only one was possible:

to supplement the system of formal rules by a situational orientation in which moral judgment prevailed over legal distinctions. This was another characteristic of the operation of the Chinese legal system.

One difficulty of the system of formal rules is that, while it is designed to group individual acts into distinct categories for standardized legal treatment, a corresponding categorization has not been successfully accomplished for the great variety of situational contexts in which a given type of act can occur. A prescribed legal treatment for an act may have widely differing effects on different related situations not intended by the spirit of the law.

Seasoned administrators such as Wang Hui-tsu were always seeking to overcome the limitations of the law by giving due consideration to the social situation related to an act:

When I served as an aide, I always asked the magistrate to give special consideration to offenders who had wedding or funeral obligations, unless the cases were serious ones . . . In 1767 or 1768 there was a capable official in Kiangsu named Chang who emphasized the rigidity and severity of the law. In a county examination, one student carried a hidden essay prepared beforehand, and he was punished with the cangue in public as prescribed by law. The student's relatives and friends appealed on their knees for one month's deferment of punishment on the ground that the student had just been married a day. Chang refused to listen. The bride committed suicide, and the student drowned himself. The law prescribes the cangue for carrying hidden essays, and it is not wrong to execute the law. But had Chang heard about the statement [by Cho Mou (Ming period)], "The law demands uniform ruling, but the *li* (rites) make allowance for human situations"? Deferment of the cangue until a month after the wedding would give due consideration to the situation without distorting the law. Why was this not possible? It is cruel indeed to use such an occasion to demonstrate one's power . . . *The law is a uniform standard, but situations take on a thousand variations* [italics added]. To use the law with reference to the situation involved is to avoid disturbing the harmony of the natural order.[63]

Chang, incidentally, was later executed—for corruption.

In the light of this incident, Wang added a general observation: "In a case where the law tolerates no evasion, one should not encourage evil by giving the law a distorted interpretation. But where the situation permits leniency, it is not wrong to give greater consideration to the situation than to the law."[64] This was the basic rationale for the late Ch'ing official Weng Ch'uan-chao's policy of deferment for five types of offenders: drunks, travelers far from home, those subjected to unusual pressure from circumstances, newlyweds, and the newly bereaved.[65]

In a social order dominated by primary-group relations, most legal cases involved members of the same social group, and as we have seen, any strict application of the letter of the law was likely to disturb that healthy functioning of the group which was so basic to the bureaucracy's goal of maintaining the social order. This point is clearly elucidated in the following paragraphs by Wang Hui-tsu:

Cases involving loss of life, rape, robbery, and bullying [i.e., cases that call for rigid legal treatment] do not happen often. The rest are quarrels and conflicts arising mostly from small matters of kinship and property affairs. *The parties involved are either relatives or old friends, either members of the same clan or neighbors* [italics added]. Their relationship has endured for generations, but their conflicts arise from a moment's excitement. There is basically no ineradicable hatred between them. One ought to select some vital points from their statements, talk to them earnestly and determine what is reasonable in this situation, so that the weaker party receives satisfaction, and the aggressive party becomes humbled. Other details will be settled by relatives and neighbors . . . This is to preserve harmony between relatives and friends.[66]

. . . Cases that turn on no absolute distinction between right and wrong and that can be reconciled are best settled with the help of relatives and friends. Adjudication is based on law, but reconciliation is based on the situation. Law must distinguish between right and wrong, but the situation may allow moderation of the strict standard of right and wrong. The right party's position will be endorsed by relatives and friends, and the wrong party will avoid punishment by the court . . .[67]

. . . When two parties in conflict over small matters are relatives, making clear the distinction between right and wrong will decide who is the winner and who is the loser. Any punishment in addition to this sows the seeds of further conflict . . .[68]

In addition to fostering the healthy social relations that were basic to the political order, this situational orientation served another function: it made the law flexible enough to meet heterogeneous local conditions in a widely extended empire administered by a centralized bureaucracy. Wang Hui-tsu, whose long administrative career took him to a variety of localities, has a passage on this function.

Studying the law is most important in learning to be an aide. But the art of using the law boils down to skill in grasping human situations. Customs and traditions often vary from place to place. One must personally inquire into them without bias, and adapt administrative measures to them, employing the law as a supplemental aid. This will bring harmony between the officials and the people . . .[69]

Rationally speaking, China's centralized bureaucracy needed uniformity in its rules in order to achieve coordination and predictability of action in its widely distributed agencies. Emphasis on the more flexible moral norms and on situational considerations interfered with this uniformity, and consequently with the efficiency of the law in terms of its immediate objectives. But, as we have previously pointed out, the law and the bureaucratic structure do not function in isolation but as part of the general social system, to which bureaucratic behavior must adapt itself. This adaptation is not necessarily to be deplored. If in China it reduced the bureaucracy's theoretical efficiency in terms of precision and predictability of action, it perhaps served with reasonable efficiency the overall organizational goal of maintaining peace and order in a vast empire under pre-modern technical limitations.

PERSONAL AND INFORMAL ORIENTATION IN
BUREAUCRATIC BEHAVIOR

Bureaucracy, as we have seen, calls for "formalistic impersonality" in the official's conduct of his office. Theoretically, formalism is the prescription of action in full so as to assure precision or correctness of performance, and impersonality is necessary in order to exclude the disruptive influence of personal and emotional attachments. But formalistic impersonality, like the other rational requirements of ideal bureaucratic behavior, comes under pressure from the general social system, with the result that informal and personal patterns of behavior are developed within the formalistic framework. The fact that this was so in China is well known to Sinologists and needs little elaboration. My present purpose is only to demonstrate how the adaptation of bureaucratic behavior to the general social system led to the development of characteristics not envisioned in the formal structure.

The mentors of the Chinese bureaucracy clearly recognized the principle of formalistic impersonality as a requirement for the operation of government. "The official entertains no personal friendship" was one of many bureaucratic platitudes.[70] Lü K'un and others repeatedly stressed that the official must follow reason and fixed rules instead of relying on personal relations in the conduct of his office.[71] This conceptual recognition of the value of formalism was consistently exhibited in the interpretation of concrete behavioral situations. Wang Fengsheng (mid-Ch'ing), for instance, observed that guiding one's official action by formal principles was the only way to carry out the duties of one's office, and that any personal relationship with one's colleagues and superiors would put one under obligations which would interfere with the proper performance of these duties.[72] Wang Hui-tsu, from his rich bureaucratic experience, makes the same point:

It is the duty of an official to serve his superiors. An official task assigned by one's superior must not be refused, regardless of the hardships and difficulties involved. But when one's superior commands one to do him a personal favor, one must stay away from him. One must act this way not only with regard to obviously personal matters, but even when personal intentions are merely implied in an official assignment, since any catering to such intentions will cause one to act against one's conscience . . . leading eventually to corruption of the law. One must sincerely make this understood when one's abilities first become appreciated by one's superior, by expressing a complete devotion to public duty to the exclusion of any private dealing. Should the superior take this as an inability to appreciate expediency, one should resign to preserve one's own character.[73]

Wang also appealed to this principle of impersonality in discussing the familiar subject of personal favors from superiors to lesser officials:

When an official receives favored consideration from his superior, he indeed has gained an opportunity to realize his ambitions. But those already in a favored position will fear him; those about to receive favors will be jealous of him; those who fail to obtain favors will watch for an opportunity to push him out. A secret may leak out; rumors will follow. Superiors vary in their feelings about their subordinates. Even should all my present superiors like me, there is no certainty that my later superiors will feel the same way. Lo T'ung said, "The deeper the dislike, the craftier the slander." The man who receives favors walks in fear and trembling; those who have had the experience will know what I mean.[74]

Thus, the only dependable guide for an official's behavior was the principle of impersonality. But to remain impersonal, he had to combat environmental pressure from a society in which personal relationships were not merely ethically valued but also the only medium the common people had for getting things done. The average official was unable to resist this pressure. We get a good idea of the situation from Li Pao-chia's (1867–1906) famous novel *Kuan-ch'ang Hsien-hsing Chi* ("An Exposé of Officialdom"), depicting official life at the end of the Ch'ing period, when informal personal relationships dictated the course of a bureaucratic career. The development of the informal personal factor in bureaucratic behavior despite recognition of the impersonality principle may be regarded as a response to three factors: (a) organized pressure from social groups, notably kinship groups, where relationships were completely personal; (b) the informal personal relationship as a socially accepted operational value; and (c) structural gaps in the bureaucracy.

(a) The pressure from social groups—stable circles of friends, fraternal bodies, localistic associations, and above all, kinship organizations —was usually a matter of claiming privileges from a member who had achieved official rank by appealing to the sense of obligation recognized among members of such groups. An official who refused to honor such claims or requests risked alienating himself from the whole system of social relations based on the informal personal bond. The average official could hardly afford to take this step because of the transitory nature of his official position. His office of the moment carried no guarantee of a life-time career; and there was, of course, no provision for pensions. In fact, his personal primary groups were his permanent base of social life, the society from which he sprang, which he brought with him when he entered officialdom, and to which he must return when his official career came to an end. In comparison, the bureaucratic organization had only transitory significance to him.

The official, then, was in continuous conflict between two incompatible organizational systems, to both of which he owed loyalty. They were incompatible in goals (one public, the other private) and in operational norms (one formal and impersonal, the other informal and personal). Wang Hui-tsu indicates the dimensions of the problem in endorsing the proverbial caution against employing the "three kinds of relatives" (son, son-in-law and brother-in-law)—a common practice and indeed socially an almost obligatory one:

Follow the law and you will destroy personal affection; follow personal affection and you will abuse the law. The problem is the same with all three [types of relatives], but it is worst with a son. Nothing need be said about the son who sacrifices his father for his own interests. But even the son who meticulously works for his father's benefit out of filial affection will inevitably subvert the father's proper performance of his duty . . . Punish a son-in-law and you will alienate your daughter; punish a brother-in-law and you will alienate your wife. Should the official sacrifice affection and dismiss his relatives, he has already suffered much from the complication. It is better to choose aides from among friends. The relationship between the official and his aides is based on duty. He treats them with respect only as long as they are loyal to their duties. If they are disloyal to their duties, there is nothing wrong in severing the relationship, or even punishing them by law.[75]

What could an official do to resist such pressure and keep his conduct formal and impersonal? The logical solution was to sever personal relations from official conduct and treat the two as separate operations. This indeed was what Wang Hui-tsu did. He refused to employ any relatives in his office, giving them instead money from his own salary in order to keep on good terms with them. When he was an aide, he refused to serve under any official having sons in his own office.[76] And an enlightened father like Nieh Chi-mo could tell his son in government service not to be concerned with any family affairs while in office.[77] But the average bureaucrat was not a Wang Hui-tsu, nor the average father a Nieh Chi-mo. Some tried to effect a compromise: Wang Feng-sheng, for example, employed relatives but gave them no power and kept them under careful surveillance and control. But there was still no way of preventing relatives from usurping power secretly, especially when others regarded them as having power because of their kinship with the official. Even Wang Feng-sheng, a successful administrator with a good reputation, had to admit that "it is not easy to be loyal to both affection and duty."[78]

Why were there no formal rules against employing relatives? Most likely because of the recognized importance of the kinship system to the social and moral order upon which the peace and stability of the state rested. In addition, the system of formal rules honored kinship values in many ways, such as by conferring titles upon the parents, wife, and sons of an outstanding official, and by granting officials in Peking leaves of absence with pay to go home and visit their parents and attend to family affairs.[79] Under the requirement of logical consistency in a body of formal law, it would be difficult to rule out an official's personal relationship with his kin in the conduct of office unless there was a violation of duty—thus, there could be, and was, a law specifying punishment for an official who permitted members of his family to usurp his power and use it to oppress the people.[80] On the whole, however, the age-old contradiction between the kinship system and the state stood unresolved, despite attempts to "translate filial piety into loyalty to the state."[81]

(b) The informal personal relationship as a prevailing and ethically approved operational norm in traditional Chinese society intruded into the formalistic and impersonal system of bureaucratic behavior in two ways: through the inertia of habit and through the adaptability of the informal norm to the personal aspect of bureaucratic office.

The effect of habit is obvious. The bureaucrat was conditioned to respecting and utilizing personal relationships in conducting his personal business, and he carried this habit with him when he took office. Moreover, the common people with whom he dealt had the same habit, and in most instances would have been difficult to deal with on any other basis.

By "the personal aspect of bureaucratic office" we refer to the distinction indicated in Lü Shu-sheng's (Ming period) incisive analysis: "Emolument and rank are an official's status, and the assigned office is his duty."[82] In the actual operation of the office, status and duty were intricately intertwined. Subjectively, for both the bureaucrat and his public, the status component of his office had a strong personal aspect; for his emolument and rank, unlike the duties of his office, belonged to him personally. Hence his personal temperament, his private material interests, his social prestige and power, entered fully and easily into the functioning of status with social approval, if not with formal legitimacy. And the relatively flexible informal norm of personal relations was more adaptable to the operation of these elements of status than the rigid norm of formalistic impersonality.

In a highly status-conscious society, the informal norm of personal relationship is likely to be operative on all levels of bureaucratic activity. To see that this was so in China, we need only consider a representative account of the promotion system:

An evil habit among officials is to guess at a situation without regard for facts. A man's promotion is interpreted as a result not of his administrative accomplishments, but of his superior's being personally pleased by something he has done, or of somebody's putting in a good word for him. A man's impeachment is regarded as a result not of failure in his duty, but of some act that offended his superior, or of someone's unfavorable criticism. How can we assume that all superiors know no public criteria of right and wrong and act only on their likes and dislikes?[83]

It is fairly clear from this passage that these "misconceptions" were as likely as not to have some basis in fact. Even a respectable and successful bureaucrat like Kuei Ch'ao-wan dwelt at length in his memoirs on how a provincial governor's personal dislike of him had delayed his advancement in the early part of his career.[84] Later on, as magistrate of Ch'ang-chou prefecture in Kiangsu, he was able to straighten out a tax-evasion situation by arresting several powerful local figures; his two predecessors in the post had failed in the same task because, unlike Kuei, they did not enjoy the personal confidence of the provincial governor. The personal connection led to success where the formalistic impersonal procedure had proved impotent. Wang Hui-tsu himself charged that his official career had been ended by the unjustified personal anger of a provincial judge, who wrongly accused him of evading duty at a time when he was laid up with an injured foot.[85]

Small wonder that all sensible bureaucrats sought to circumvent the formalistic framework and placed their hopes in personal relationships, until, as even Lü K'un admitted, "most of the official's time was taken up by running around trying to please his superiors, going to parties," etc.[86] The few rules in the *Li-pu Tse-li* against permitting personal connections to influence promotions had little or no effect.[87] There was more than a grain of truth in Li Pao-chia's bitter charge that officials "show no administrative accomplishment beyond welcoming and sending off superiors, and possess no other ability than a talent for managing these occasions in grand style."[88]

(c) The lower echelon of the bureaucracy was even more influenced than the upper by personal considerations, owing to the almost total absence of formal legal provisions for the organization and operation of the lower posts. Among such functionaries the informal personal norm fully asserted itself; where the law did not pronounce, habit took command.

By "lower posts" we mean minor staff positions in the specialized departments of the central and provincial governments, and, most important, in the offices of prefectural and county magistrates. It is beyond the scope of this paper to analyze this segment of the Chinese bureaucracy, but we can perhaps get an idea of its functions and problems by briefly considering the staff of the county magistracy.

The staff of the county magistracy comprised three main sections: aides, operatives (clerks, deputies, police, etc.), and servants. This order represented their rank, but there was no formal hierarchy or chain of command beyond the fact that they were all under the command of the magistrate. Thus they may be regarded as only informally structured with regard to the internal functioning of the staff as a whole. We have discussed the aides' duties. Servants included the doorman, the keeper of the official seal, the cook, the keeper of the granary, the postal relay station attendants, and the personal servants of the magistrate.[89] Thus aides, operatives and servants were the actual producers of work at the yamen, a fact which led Shao Erh-yün (mid-Ch'ing) to remark: "Administration nowadays is carried on by three kinds of people, with the official bearing only an empty title."[90]

Despite the functional importance of these three groups, there were few formal stipulations for their recruitment, conditions of employment, or organization. The aides and the servants were personally recruited by each magistrate who came to the yamen, and the periodic change of magistrates made them a rather unstable group, though some of them might remain through the terms of several magistrates. The operatives remained with the yamen and were more stable as a group.

There were various ways in which prospective aides and servants might obtain an appointment. The "leading aides," notably the legal and the financial aides, generally were carefully selected by the magistrate, but other appointments were made at the behest of colleagues and superiors (who would grant favors in return), or to appease friends and relatives.[91] The imperial edict of 1831 prohibiting officials from forcing servants upon newly appointed subordinates[92] obviously had little effect on this practice. In short, the recruitment procedure rested on a purely informal and personal basis, ungoverned by any formalistic impersonal standard.

Actually the magistrate did not have complete personal control of his appointments. Appointments were often made to pay off social and financial indebtedness. More important, minor aides were often appointed on the recommendation of the "leading aides." When this happened, there was an informal organization among the aides based on the minor aides' obligation to the leading aides, an obligation that was often strengthened by the teacher-pupil relationship among the aides, both within the yamen and beyond its walls. Aides learned their trade by a sort of apprenticeship under experienced men, who usually recommended them for jobs when they had completed their training. As teachers and pupils manned positions in different places and on different levels of government, they formed an organized system that often controlled the settlement of important cases independently of the legitimate power of the officials. Aides from the county magistracy to the provincial governor's office would follow a case as it passed from level to level for legal action.[93]

The operatives were also organized after a fashion, as men tend to be who live and work together under relatively stable conditions. The deputies or police were likely to have close ties with the local underworld and the local bullies. When this association gave rise to some scandal and the magistrate fired the operatives involved, their replacements were usually found to be just as bad or worse, being members of the same crowd.[94] There was no point in trying to appoint a man of moral character who was not a member of the circle, since all working connections and facilities would be denied him and obstacles regularly thrown in his way. In effect, the operatives ran an informal closed shop, and there was not much the transient magistrate could do about it.[95]

Finally, the aides, the operatives, and the servants were linked with each other in an informal alliance. In short, the entire staff of the magistracy formed a loosely integrated system which had developed informally out of a situation left ungoverned by formal law, a system based mainly on informal personal relationships.

Thus, on the lower echelon of the (at least in principle) formalistically and impersonally oriented bureaucracy existed a legally unregulated and organizationally incompatible structure. From this quarter originated most of the corruption that marred the traditional conduct of local government.[96] The basic difficulty lay in the fact that the formally organized officials and the informally oriented substratum each had their own goals and their own norms of operation; as this worked out, it was possible for the latter to circumvent nearly all efforts at control by the former.

Broadly speaking, magistrates tried to control this substratum in three ways: (1) by tightening up law enforcement; (2) by performing critical parts of the clerical work themselves, to reduce the functional importance of the staff (such was the practice of Wang Hui-tsu); and (3) by encouraging staff members, especially the operatives and servants, to study the classics and to believe in spiritual reward and punishment.[97] The first and second methods had no more than a temporary effect because of the transiency of the effective administrator. The third method was more ambitious: an attempt to extend to the less educated and uneducated staff members the principles of intellectual enlightenment and moral conscience that marked the good magistrate. The limitation of this method lay in the social and economic restriction on the common man's opportunity to acquire the necessary learning. Fundamentally, the solution perhaps lay in the extension of the formal bureaucratic system to the staff organization, with necessary modifications. This was not done, however, and the lower echelons of local government remained informally structured and personally oriented right down to the end of the empire.

CONCLUSIONS

In this discussion, we have examined how traditional Chinese bureaucracy developed its characteristics in adaptation to the requirements of the general social system. We have studied the subject from three aspects: the type of knowledge and ability that stocked the bureaucrat's mind, the relative importance of the system of formal rules and the system of moral norms, and the effects of formalistic impersonality and the informal personal orientation on bureaucratic behavior. We may summarize our findings:

1. Contrary to the general assumption that functional specialization is a necessary feature of bureaucracy, in the Chinese bureaucracy the generalist held a position superior to the specialist. This was due partly to the diffuse nature of the Chinese social pattern and partly to the importance of the territorial unit in the Chinese administrative system.

2. The need for standardization in operating a bureaucracy administering a vast empire led to the development of an operational framework based on a set of formal rules. But, because of the functional importance of informal norms in a society oriented to the primary group, the system of informal moral norms also played a prominent and often a contradictory part in bureaucratic conduct.

3. While formalistic impersonality was recognized as a basic norm in Chinese bureaucratic behavior, its functioning was seriously disrupted by the constant pressure of the bureaucrat's informal social and personal relationships. Here again, the explanation is the basic importance of the primary group in the general social structure.

Since theoretically these characteristics of the Chinese bureaucracy were deviations from the rational requirements of a bureaucratic structure, they might be expected to have reduced the efficiency that a bureaucracy is theoretically capable of yielding. And it is indeed true that historically the Chinese bureaucracy has periodically broken down, causing widespread corruption, banditry, floods from neglected dikes, mass economic misery, and rebellions, and generally making a mockery of its traditional objective of bringing peace and tranquillity to the empire. On the other hand, these features of the Chinese bureaucracy were adaptations to a social order which could operate by itself, with a minimum of assistance from the formal political structure, and as such may actually have given the bureaucratic structure an elasticity which helped it to revive after each breakdown. Paradoxically, it seems possible that the remarkable durability of the Chinese bureaucracy through history was a consequence of the very factors which made it often inefficient and prone to periodic collapse.

James T. C. Liu

SOME CLASSIFICATIONS OF
BUREAUCRATS IN CHINESE
HISTORIOGRAPHY

Recent scholars have analyzed and classified Chinese bureaucrats or officials of various periods according to their social origins,
geographic distribution, economic position, class interests, schools of
thought, and the like, but have paid little attention to their political behavior. In the past, the situation was very different: classifying officials according to their political behavior was a serious concern of Chinese historians. It is instructive to consider why this was so, and what
classifications were proposed.[1]

"Classification" in this connection does not have as rigorous a meaning as it has in the contemporary social sciences; it merely refers to a
general set of distinctions between various kinds of officials based on
differences between them in certain respects to which the classifier attached value. Such classificatory schemes were relatively simple, for the
classifiers did not consider detailed or complicated classifications to be
desirable. Liu Chih-chi (661–721), the father of Chinese historiography
of the T'ang period, pointed out that one might go on classifying officials into an endless number of categories without serving any particularly useful purpose.[2]

Scanty as they were, these classificatory schemes were consistently
developed and applied by the Confucianists over many centuries. They
were used to assess the political behavior of an enormous number of
officials, contemporary and past, and inevitably exerted a normative influence upon innumerable later officials. In this respect, these schemes
constitute a singular feature in Chinese intellectual history; parallels can
hardly be found in the history of other countries.

The basic pattern of these classifications, as might be expected, is
the reliance placed upon the use of a moral criterion. A moral criterion
is usually stated in idealized, and sometimes abstract, terms; hence its
application to political behavior, which is essentially a matter of de-

tails and variables, often leads to difficulties. Moral qualities may remain the same, but their meanings change under various political circumstances. Theoretical standards frequently suffer from depreciation in practice. And their influence upon the political behavior of the officials may not be altogether what has been intended.

The present inquiry has drawn mainly upon three groups of data. The first group is the theoretical teachings of Confucianism, beginning with the ancient classics, which classify officials according to ideal types. The second group consists of historical writings and compilations, which adopt the ideal types but develop in addition their own historical types. The third group is composed of encyclopedias dealing with government (*cheng-shu*) and sections on official conduct in general encyclopedias (*lei-shu*). These present more detailed and realistic classifications, which may be described, for lack of a better term, as functional types.

These three groups of source materials themselves form in a sense three layers of Confucianism. The first layer, consisting of pure theories, is the foundation; next comes the layer of historical interpretations based on political theories; and finally, dealing in more specific detail with the realities of government operation, comes the third layer of functional theories. The classifications of officials vary from one layer to another, for the classifiers approach their work from different viewpoints and are concerned with different aspects of their subjects' political behavior.

In order to keep our inquiry within manageable limits, we shall concentrate principally on the Sung period (960–1279), which made significant contributions to all three groups of source materials. This was a period abundant in theoretical discussions and reformulations, a period in which historical writings and compilations advanced in quality as well as volume, and a period which produced monumental encyclopedias which became respected models for the reference works of later periods. Furthermore, the increasing complexity of the bureaucratic structure of the Sung state led many Confucian scholars to take a greater interest in both the pure theory of good government and the practical problems of the bureaucracy.[3] It was clear to Sung scholars that the old classifications of officials had to be re-evaluated and reformulated.

THE IDEAL CLASSIFICATION IN THEORETICAL TEACHINGS

Basic in Confucian thought are the well-known ideal type of "virtuous man" (*chün-tzu*, usually translated as "superior man," which essentially means morally superior man), and its contrasting type of "unworthy person" (*hsiao-jen*). To the virtuous man are ascribed all the desirable moral qualities, especially moral leadership in influencing other people. To the unworthy person are ascribed the undesirable opposites. The two types form the yardstick by which the Confucian theory judges all men. But the same yardstick has also been used frequently as an ideal classification of officials, for the Confucian political philosophy postulates that only a morally upright person can be a good official and a capable administrator. It is especially important for an official to exert moral leadership in government administration. From this viewpoint, political activities and administrative operations are in no way different from private conduct; they are essentially the manifestation of moral qualities or the lack of them.

This ideal classification of officials is so well known that it needs no elaboration. Some discussion of its applications is necessary, however.

First, this classification had a constant application in the education and the self-discipline of individual officials. With its simple black-and-white contrast, the moral ideal of the virtuous man was a powerful one. Most officials were inspired in their student days to regard themselves as virtuous men, and many were affected deeply enough to remain within moral bounds in spite of temptations and pressures in their political life. At times the bureaucracy was attacked by idealistic critics, from both within and without, for departures from the ideal. The weakness of this classification also lies in its simplicity. A black-and-white theoretical scheme such as this cannot be readily translated into a practical public policy.

Second, an insistent application of this classification in practical affairs when no generally acceptable behavioral basis for it could be found usually produced political division or political apathy in the bureaucracy. This may be illustrated by two reform controversies during the Northern Sung period. In the reform of 1043–44, initiated by Fan Chung-yen (989–1052), a group of leading scholar-officials supported the reform program, regarded themselves as virtuous men, and denounced their opponents as unworthy persons. In this instance, their application of the moral classification was to a certain extent meaningful, for their contention was to a significant extent justified—i.e., the reform leaders were on the whole both morally and politically superior to their opponents. Even so, by claiming for themselves the prestige of virtuous men and branding their adversaries with the opprobrium of unworthy persons, they plunged the bureaucracy into a bitter factionalism. In the reform of 1070–76, led by Wang An-shih (1021–86), a reform of far greater magnitude and significance, the majority of scholar-officials stood in opposition, considered themselves to be virtuous men, and denounced the reformers, with the singular exception of Wang himself, as unworthy persons. In this second instance, the application of the moral classification is highly questionable. The self-righteous scholar-officials were not on the whole superior morally or politically to the condemned reformers. Their insistence upon an ill-founded distinction led to a wave of political persecutions, to the detriment of the entire bureaucracy.[4]

Obviously, the distinction between virtuous man and unworthy person cannot rest simply on subjective opinion. Even the prevailing opinion among a majority of leading scholar-officials, no matter how morally upright and politically idealistic they were, would not be sufficiently reliable. The difficulty of applying this moral classification without an acceptable basis of behavioral distinction was recognized quite early. During the first reform controversy, Ou-yang Hsiu (1007–72) suggested a new and interesting theoretical solution in his famous essay entitled "P'eng-tang lun" ("On Factions"), which begins as follows:

Your humble official learns that factions have existed since ancient times. The only hope is for the emperor to distinguish between virtuous men and unworthy persons. Generally speaking, virtuous men are friends or form one faction, for they hold the same principles; while unworthy persons are friends or form another faction, for they share the same interests. This seems natural. Your humble official believes, however, that unworthy persons, unlike virtuous men, have no real friends or faction. Why is that so? What unworthy persons like is emolument and profit. What they covet is wealth. When their interests happen to be the same, they temporarily form a faction to befriend one another, but only in pretense. When they see some advantage, they fight among themselves to get ahead. When there is nothing to be gained, they become cool toward one another. Then they turn upon one another and do not even have enough decency to stand by their own brothers and relatives. This is why your humble official maintains that unworthy persons have no real friends or factions, and that their temporary friendship or partisanship is a bogus one. Virtuous men are different. They abide by principles and righteousness. They behave in accordance with loyalty and honesty. They cherish reputation and integrity. In self-cultivation, having the same principles, they strengthen one another. In serving the state, they have the same aim and complement each other. Virtuous men thus become friends and a faction and remain so. Therefore what the emperor should do is dismiss the bogus faction of unworthy persons and rely upon the genuine faction of virtuous men. If this is done, the country will be well governed.[5]

Ou-yang Hsiu is clearly attempting to define the two contrasting types not just in their conventional moral connotations but also in political and behavioral terms. The unworthy persons are the self-seeking opportunists who have a tendency to turn against each other. The virtuous men are the ones who act in the public interest and therefore readily co-operate with each other. They have a moral affinity which forms the basis of their political affinity, and their affinity is a recognizable behavioral distinction.

Unfortunately, Ou-yang Hsiu's new theory was not supported by facts. More often than not, the learned and upright scholar-officials of his time failed to stand together. The differences among them stemmed not so much from policy matters or political issues as from personal antagonism and mutual lack of respect. For example, Chang Fang-p'ing (1007–91) was a generally well-regarded official. Su Shih (1036–1101), a famous scholar-official, praised Chang as a man of great virtue; but Ssu-ma Kuang (1019–89), another scholar-official of high prestige, denounced Chang as an unworthy person. Ch'eng I (1033–1107) was a philosopher active in politics at one time. Su Shih detested Ch'eng; Ssu-ma Kuang admired him. Moreover, all of them were against those who supported the second reform.[6]

When the moral classification was applied largely as a tool of mutual criticism in factional and personal controversy, without careful regard for its justification on behavioral grounds, it rapidly degenerated into name-calling. The results were not only a badly divided bureaucracy, but a widespread political apathy. One way to avoid the risk of being labeled an unworthy person and thus to stand a better chance of becoming known as a virtuous man was to remain politically inactive except in the matter of routine responsibilities. Such was the observation of Li Ch'ing-ch'en (1032–1102):

In ancient times officials were judged by their ultimate accomplishments rather than by what they did at the beginning of their administration. They were held responsible for major items rather than minor details. . . . Nowadays, officials are judged by their small faults and not by their important activities, by the irresponsible criticism prevalent in official circles and not by an examination of their actual administration. . . . Only those who carefully protect their personal career interest by avoiding controversies and following the prevailing trend can go on safely without blame. Consequently, only mediocre officials will rise steadily by promotion.[7]

Third, a meaningful application of this moral classification is found in instances of political agitation—sometimes in the bureaucracy but more often outside—against a notoriously corrupt administration. In such circumstances the behavioral distinction between the virtuous and the unworthy is crystal-clear. Such was the case during the Southern Sung period when a group of dissatisfied scholars who claimed to stand for the "orthodox learning" (*tao-hsüeh*) were suppressed by the government for advocating "bogus learning" (*wei-hsüeh*). A far more significant instance occurred toward the end of the Ming period, when

the Tung-lin Academy became the center of the political opposition
known as the Tung-lin faction.[8] There was hardly any doubt about who
were the virtuous men and who were the unworthy persons; a clear-cut
polarization already existed in reality. We note, however, that in such
cases the virtuous men function rather as independent ideological critics
of the government than as moral leaders within the bureaucracy. In
other words, the moral classification applies largely in extreme cases in
which Confucianism happens to exert only a minimum influence during
the malfunctioning of state affairs, rather than in the normal case in
which Confucianism does help to maintain a tolerable standard of behavior in the government.

THE CLASSIFICATIONS IN HISTORICAL WRITINGS AND COMPILATIONS

The ideal classification of mankind into virtuous men and unworthy
persons had a strong influence upon the historical interpretation of the
rise and fall of dynasties in terms of good and bad elements, and of
political struggles as conflicts between these elements. The canonical
rule of "bestowing praise and blame" (*pao-pien*) from the moral point
of view finds an especially rigorous application in a class of biographies
written essentially for the purpose of judging officials. The term for
biography, *chuan,* carries the connotation of its verbal form, *ch'uan,*
meaning to establish moral examples and lessons for the benefit of posterity.[9]

While following the ideal classification in principle, the early Chinese
historians undertook to study political realities, and from these studies
they derived their own classification according to historical types. One
well-known classification is that of local administrators—and bureaucrats
in general—into "principled officials" (*hsün-li*) and "oppressive officials"
(*k'u-li*). Another essentially classificatory term is "famous statesman"
(*ming-ch'en*), used to designate the more impressive (to the historian or
compiler) of the high-ranking officials at the court.

The classification of principle and oppressive officials originally had
little to do with the concepts of virtuous man and unworthy person. It
began with the *Shih-chi,* the first of the twenty-four dynastic histories,
which defines the principled officials as those who "perform their duties
in accordance with principles as *one* way to achieve good administration" (italics mine). This original definition indicates a combination of
the Confucian moral qualities with administrative qualities.

An annotation in the *Ch'ien Han Shu,* the next dynastic history, speci-
fies the mode of administration of such principled officials as "following
the law from above as well as the disposition of the people below."[10]
This explanation cannot be understood without a brief reference to the

historical context. The Han government at first placed a great emphasis upon the strict enforcement of law, especially in the interest of centralization. Judicial and criminal matters received so much attention that the leading division of the government was not the personnel division, as was the usual case in later dynasties, but the police division.[11] Under this system, many aggressive local government officials were especially strict in interpreting and enforcing the law. Since these men were seeking to extend the power of the sovereign, they were understandably regarded as oppressive officials by many people. They followed the Legalist practice more than they did the Confucian principle.

Thus the appearance of principled officials, men who administered with due regard to the disposition of their constituents, was a development of considerable significance. These principled officials abided by the Confucian philosophy of government, with an admixture of the Taoist spirit. They fulfilled the essential purpose of the law by giving the letter of the law more flexible and considerate interpretation. They demonstrated an administrative mode which served the state interest and was kind to the people at the same time.[12] What earned them the honorable name of principled officials was not a moral leadership in the Confucian theoretical sense, but specifically a functional moral leadership in the practical sense which succeeded in bringing about superior administrative results.

Principled officials are given increasing prestige in the subsequent dynastic histories, notably in the *Hou Han Shu* and the *Liang Shu*, which single out for praise those who "guide the people by virtues," "restrain the people by propriety," and "apply the principles of the classics to their administration." But the meaning of the term "principled officials" began to change as political conditions became worse. The *Sung Shu*, in lamenting the lack of principled officials during a chaotic period, introduces a substitute category of "good officials" (*liang-li*) to designate those "who owing to the pernicious interference of their superiors cannot be good administrators" but nevertheless "maintain noteworthy moral standards themselves." The *Pei Ch'i Shu* is even more explicit in saying that "amidst widespread corruption, the good officials have kept their own high standards and refused to follow the crowd."[13] In later historical works, the term "principled official" and the term "good official" become interchangeable. Both tend to stress personal moral qualities rather than active moral leadership.

By the time of the Sung period, the distinction between principled officials and officials of no more than average merit became blurred. A conforming official, without being particularly outstanding as an administrator would claim that he was abiding by the principles of Confucianism. So long as he was virtuous enough to refrain from corruption and abuses, he was likely to be accepted as a principled official. Wang Ming-sheng (1722–97), in his critical study of the dynastic histories, points out that by the original standards of the Han period many later officials should not be included in the biographies of principled officials at all, since their alleged achievements in administration were at best "vague and mediocre."[14]

A similar change also took place in the usage and the meaning of the term oppressive officials. The *Shih-chi* in introducing this historical type explains with due care that while some oppressive officials happen to be dishonest, a large number of them are morally upright. Even their oppressiveness has a justification, for "If they were not militant, strong, strict, and cruel, how could they carry out their responsibilities satisfactorily?" The *Hou Han Shu*, likewise, does not consider oppressive officials immoral; it confines itself to expressing regret that "they have neglected the fundamentals" of moral leadership. The *Wei Shu*, dealing with a period of disunity when centralizing measures again became necessary and desirable, praises officials who regard "strictness and severity as the fundamentals of administration."[15]

The crucial change comes in the *Sui Shu*, which was compiled during the T'ang period, when Confucianism was in high favor. The T'ang historians were especially prejudiced against the rapid centralization undertaken by the Sui empire. This work therefore takes the position that "the oppressive officials are motivated not by a desire to suppress the villains and to get rid of the scoundrels, but by a desire to oppress the helpless people." It thus redefines the oppressive official as the abusive official. And the subsequent dynastic histories consistently follow this new definition.[16]

Thus the historical types of principled and oppressive officials, although originally based upon an administrative criterion, with time became more and more similar to the virtuous men and unworthy persons of the theoretical teachings. This change came about partly as a result of the intense influence of the Confucian theories upon historical works, and partly as a result of the increasing emphasis, especially from the Sung period on, upon the personal morality of the individual officials, irrespective of their administrative records.

The term "famous statesman" was commonly given in pre-Sung times to high-ranking officials at the court who had rendered distinguished service to the state or who had been conspicuously successful in their careers. It was necessary, of course, that their service or success should be morally commendable, but the appellation was bestowed primarily for political rather than moral merit. To the Confucian historians of the

Sung period, however, the political criterion was not satisfactory, and they accordingly introduced two noteworthy modifications of it. First, since they believed very strongly that political accomplishments should be explained in terms of moral qualities, they felt that candidates for the designation "famous statesman" should be judged by the moral criterion as well as the political. Second, as a result of their concern with the preservation of a stable social order, they ranked contributions to the stability of the state highest among the possible accomplishments of a statesman.

The most influential work on this subject is the *Sung Ming-ch'en Yen Hsing Lu* ("A Record of the Words and Conduct of Famous Statesmen of the Sung Period"), compiled by Chu Hsi (1130–1200), the leading Confucianist of the Southern Sung. In emphasizing the moral qualities of his subjects, Chu Hsi deliberately presents them in a favorable light. He even fails to mention some of their faults, faults that are noted in other historical sources and even in some other works by Chu Hsi himself.[17] In short, he practically converts his famous statesmen into shining moral examples, patterned after the ideal type of virtuous man. His justification is that this work on the famous statesmen is meant to be not an objective history, but a normative history.

On the other hand, no matter how a normative history stresses moral qualities, it is not pure theory and has to deal with concrete political situations. In assessing the political accomplishments of these famous statesmen, Chu Hsi tends to place the need for political stability before the need for reform. This is shown in his treatment of the two reform leaders. He pays high tribute to Fan Chung-yen's moral character, exemplary behavior, high ideals, and leadership among the scholar-officials. Yet he not only fails to stress the significance of Fan's reform efforts but tends to deplore Fan's outspoken belligerence and eagerness to assume leadership in the political struggle. He praises Wang An-shih for his outstanding virtues and profound learning. Yet he introduces a number of unfavorable comments made by Wang's opponents, and remarks that in spite of Wang's superior qualities and the emperor's trust in him, his reform policy was a grave mistake.[18]

Chu Hsi's conservative political outlook is best revealed in his treatment of Lü I-chien (977–1043). Many Confucianists criticized Lü for his discrimination against Fan Chung-yen and other morally upright officials in favor of the reform. In fact, Chu Hsi in his writings elsewhere made the same criticism. However, he still includes Lü among the famous statesmen, on the ground that Lü displayed considerable moral excellence in not suppressing the reform leaders with excessive severity, in trying to conciliate Fan later on, and especially in giving the empress-dowager some morally sound advice on her strained relationship with the emperor. In view of these accomplishments and his long service as the chief minister, Lü is regarded as having contributed to the stability of the state.[19]

These changes in the delineation of famous statesmen are not without profound implications. Under the powerful influence of this work by Chu Hsi and other historical writings thereafter, most Confucianists in the succeeding centuries tended to interpret the term famous statesman as meaning a model of moral but conservative leadership. By implication, high-ranking officials should cultivate their personal morality and use their moral influence to improve political conditions, but largely within the limits of political stability and without attempting drastic changes. There is a further implication: once the existing state institutions are accepted as being qualitatively normal and even permanent, the only goal left for Confucianism is a *quantitative* one, the goal of producing a larger number of morally upright officials to work within the fixed institutional setting. This was in effect a main goal of Confucianism in later periods, with the notable exception of the early Ch'ing.

THE CLASSIFICATIONS IN THE ENCYCLOPEDIAS
DEALING WITH GOVERNMENT

The encyclopedias dealing with government, by the very nature of their subject matter, are more realistic in approach than both the Confucian theories and the historical writings. We shall confine our discussion to two important encyclopedias. The first one is the *Ts'e-fu Yüan-kuei* ("Primary Reference for Government Office"), an early Sung compilation, commissioned by the court and compiled under the personal supervision of the Emperor Chen-tsung (reigned 997–1022). As originally planned, this official publication was to include only items of information selected from the classics and formal histories. In its final form, however, it includes selections from works outside the Confucian school and from numerous informal historical sources.[20] This departure from the original intention indicates that the compilers, in dealing with various practical aspects of the bureaucracy, found it impossible to confine themselves strictly to what the Confucian theories sanctioned.

The second encyclopedia, more noteworthy than the first, is the *Ching-shih Pa-pien Lei-chuan* ("A Classified Compilation of Eight Works on Statecraft"). It was not an official compilation like the *Ts'e-fu Yüan-kuei*. Its compiler, Ch'en Jen-hsi (1580–1636), was a Ming official well known for both his scholarship and his practical knowledge of government and political affairs. Although some sources from earlier times are included, most of the materials deal with the period from the Sung to the Ming. The chief interest of this encyclopedia is not in its discussion of Confucian theoretical standards, but in its treatment of administrative matters and political realities, including expediencies and exigencies. Perhaps for that reason, it was suppressed during the literary inquisition under the Manchu Emperor Ch'ien-lung (reigned 1736–95).[21]

While following the general orientation of the Confucian theories, the classifications of officials in these two encyclopedias are to a significant extent realistic and functional. The *Ts'e-fu Yüan-kuei* begins by listing the various kinds of officials—court ministers, army commanders, ministerial and departmental chiefs, fiscal officials, judicial officials, policy critics and censors, literary officials, palace functionaries, and so on. Then, under each group of officials, it enumerates the specific desirable and undesirable qualities by which officials in this group should be judged. It has no simple classification applicable to all officials independent of their responsibilities. However, we may reconstruct its classificatory scheme by indicating the kinds of desirable and undesirable qualities it lists. These qualities fall into four categories: (1) From the standpoint of personal morality, virtuous conduct and dignity, among other qualities, are termed desirable; vicious conduct and dishonesty, among others, are undesirable. (2) From the standpoint of professional qualification, principally the knowledge and the ability required of a particular office, experience and influence in shaping policy are desirable, ineptitude and ignorance undesirable. (3) From the standpoint of administrative behavior, such traits as reliability in confidential matters, judiciousness in dealing with critical issues, and devotion to duty are desirable; exceeding proper jurisdiction, duplicity, and indecision are undesirable. (4) From the standpoint of political behavior, chiefly a matter of relations with other officials and scholars, respect for talents and eagerness to recommend the worthy for offices are desirable; nepotism, factionalism, and betrayal of friends are undesirable.[22]

In this classificatory scheme, we see a clash between two antithetical modes of administrative operation. On the one hand, this encyclopedia praises officials who are kind to the people, who exercise moral influence, and who are gentle in their administration. On the other hand, it pays tribute to officials who punish abusive elements, who are strict against corruption, who are forceful, who are effective tacticians, and who are active in carrying out official policies.[23] There is of course a certain degree of correlation between the moral qualities and the functional qualities. Kindness toward the people demands the punishment of abusive elements. Moral influence should lead to the elimination of corruption. In practice, however, the morally superior officials tend to be too mild and persuasive, while the capable administrators tend to be too strong and assertive. Here lies a basic problem of Confucianism in action. What precisely is the combination of moral qualities and functional qualities that yields the best mode of administration?

The encyclopedias do not provide a categorical answer to this question. The theoretical teachings emphasize a mild and persuasive mode of administration. The historical concept of principled officials, from being in Han times more or less a functional concept, came in the course of time, as we have seen, to accord more and more with the virtuous man of Confucian theory. Concurrently, however, the needs of state necessarily placed a premium on a strong and assertive mode of administration. Shortly after the appearance of the *Ts'e-fu Yüan-kuei*, Ou-yang Hsiu offered one of the best answers:

Someone asked how it was possible to administer with leniency and simplicity without falling into laxity. Ou-yang replied: "If license were to be mistaken for leniency and neglect for simplicity, laxity would naturally result and the people would suffer from it. What I mean by leniency is not to be harsh and urgently pressing. What I mean by simplicity is to refrain from imposing burdens that are either excessive in number or too minute in detail."[24]

The implication of this answer is important. Contrary to the conventional Confucian interpretation, the best administrator is not an altogether mild and persuasive one. The ideal administrator converts his moral virtues into a practical and reasonable considerateness, which he uses to restrain and offset the functional severities of a strong and assertive mode of administration.

The second encyclopedia, like the first, advocates a combination of moral qualities and functional qualities without specifying any particular combination as better than any other. It stipulates that good officials should be incorruptible, cautious, just, diligent, enterprising, and eager to carry out measures beneficial to the people; and moreover that they should have executive talent and administrative ability.[25] In a word, good officials should be both upright and capable. However, at various points the second encyclopedia is closer to the position of Ou-yang Hsiu. It maintains that leniency and mildness are desirable in administration in so far as they are practical, but calls for strict enforcement of the law when moral persuasion and pressure fail. Strictness is not to be confused with harshness; strict officials are just and straightforward (*kung chih*).[26]

In short, while the second encyclopedia regards moral virtues as necessary to a good administrator, it does not regard them as sufficient. It cites the comment of Su Hsün (1009–66) of the Sung period that many so-called good officials were content merely to refuse bribes and refrain from exceeding their jurisdiction while their administration achieved no satisfactory results. It also mentions that the Sung court, after the dismissal of the energetic reform leaders in 1044, tended to favor sincere, simple, honest, and careful officials, many of whom spent their time poring over the classics without a thought to improving the state administration. It quotes an edict of the Emperor Jen-tsung (reign: 1425 only) of the Ming period admonishing officials who merely disciplined themselves well but failed to perform their administrative duties well.[27] Here we see a clear departure from the conventional Confucian attitude. Between morally superior officials with little administrative ability and morally average officials with superior administrative ability, the *Ching-shih Pa-pien Lei-chuan* would probably prefer the latter. Its tendency is consistently to relax the moral standards of Confucianism where they conflict with pragmatic standards.

Similar to the problem of moral qualities and functional qualities is the problem of moral qualities and political realities. This is again a fundamental problem of Confucianism in action. To what extent do moral qualities lead to political success? With this question in mind, let us examine the classification of high-ranking officials in the *Ching-shih Pa-pien Lei-chuan*: officials who have helped emperors in formulating policies, especially in the founding of an empire (*hsiang-ch'en*); officials who qualify as famous statesmen (*ming-ch'en*); officials who have contributed successful strategies and tactics (*mou-ch'en*); officials who have been responsible for military victories or for preserving the stability of the regime (*kung-ch'en*); officials who qualify as principled officials (*hsun-li*); officials who have courageously remonstrated with emperors (*chien-ch'en*); and on the other hand, officials who have been favorites of emperors (*hsin-ch'en*) and officials who have been treacherous (*chien-ch'en*).[28]

We note first that among the politically successful officials—notably those who achieved renown as policymakers, strategists, and military leaders—by no means all were morally outstanding, and some were known to have sacrificed moral principles more than once to political expediency. The fact that men of this sort are nonetheless included on such a list is a tacit recognition of the cold fact that moral qualities are not necessarily essential to political achievement. Moreover, in discussing the officials who have courageously remonstrated with emperors, the encyclopedia takes pains to point out the difficulties they faced: if the remonstrance is not put in emphatic terms, it could hardly move the emperor, whereas if it is, it might come dangerously close to *lèse-majesté*.[29] This amounts to a warning that the morally admirable desire to give the emperor good advice must be given effect only within limits and with political skill.

Finally, in dealing with famous statesmen, this encyclopedia stipulates the following traits: integrity and righteousness, fairness, straightforwardness, ability to deal with judicial and fiscal matters, and administrative capacity. Note the difference from Chu Hsi's work on the Sung famous statesmen, the far greater emphasis on functional qualities. But even such a combination of moral qualities and functional qualities will not ensure the success of a statesman. The encyclopedia cites Tu Yen (977–1057), a famous statesman in what was probably the most enlightened and well-governed period of the Sung, on the necessity of circumspection even in the daily circumstances of political life:

The most important thing for an official is to remain pure at heart and vigilant, without seeking to have others know of his merits. If his merits are made known, unscrupulous colleagues will be sure to attack him behind his back. It usually happens that a man's superiors are not wise enough to see through such attacks, and misfortune will fall upon him. Hence, one should appear to be leisurely and calm in official circles, get things done quietly, and be satisfied with one's own conscience.[30]

This encyclopedia cannot openly depart from Confucian principles or revise the Confucian political theories, but the above points are evidence of its struggle to reconcile principles and theories with experience. The same struggle goes on in the minds of many aspiring officials. A good official should be a virtuous man, yet he must modify his moral virtues to a certain extent in adapting himself to political realities. When moral virtues are so modified, they tend to function negatively, as moral restraints on political behavior, rather than positively, as the attributes of moral leadership envisioned in the Confucian theoretical teachings.

THE RATING OF OFFICIALS IN CIVIL SERVICE REGULATIONS

There is an affinity between the encyclopedias dealing with government and the actual civil service regulations. Both are essentially concerned with defining the qualifications of a good official; both have to deal with the same disparity betwen Confucian theories and practical necessities. Clearly, changes in the value schemes of the civil service regulations are pertinent to our discussion.

The Han system, as we have seen, rated officials according to their administrative performance; it gave little recognition to moral qualities as such. On the other hand, it had the "Six Rules," injunctions against six kinds of illegal and immoral behavior: (1) the illegal use of power to oppress others; (2) illegally exploiting the people for selfish gains; (3)

injustice, undue severity, and other conduct tending to cause unrest among the people; (4) favoritism and nepotism in appointing subordinates; (5) permitting relatives to interfere with government functions; and (6) collusion in corrupt practices with subordinates or influential persons.[31]

The system of the T'ang period gave a much fuller expression to the Confucian moral values. It evaluated officials according to four general merits and a specific merit. The four general merits were, briefly, (1) virtue and righteousness; (2) purity and caution; (3) justness and fairness; and (4) sincerity and diligence. The specific merit was ability to perform the specific duties of an office. This four-to-one ratio is deceptive, however; actually, the four general merits which embodied the Confucian moral values were not nearly so important as the specific merit. Only officials with the specific merit received a high rating. To be sure, if they had in addition some of the general merits, they received an even higher rating; but those who had only the general merits—the Confucian virtues—were given no more than medium rating.[32] In other words, functional qualities were valued above moral qualities.

The Confucian influence increased during the Sung period. In the sponsorship system of the civil service, great stress was placed upon personal character. However, as Professor Kracke points out in his definitive study of the early Sung civil service, the moral qualities stressed by Confucianism were translated into more concrete and practical traits in the merit rating, so that they could be weighed on a more objective basis. For example, an official was said to have "moral discipline" if he had committed no misuse of authority and no impropriety. Among all traits, the greatest emphasis was upon a record free from corruption and penal offenses.[33] In other words, though the moral qualities were emphasized, the emphasis tended to have a negative connotation. Moral behavior largely meant the absence of immoral behavior.

The Confucian orientation of the civil service rating system became somewhat weakened when the Southern Sung government, facing national hardship, turned its attention to administrative exigencies. An outstanding example of this trend was the rating of officials in the Hupeh area. In the absence of corruption and failure in routine responsibilities, which would disqualify them, they were rated simply by the size of the population under their jurisdiction, on the assumption that able officials would promote prosperity and attract more people to their areas. This trend continued to the Yüan period during which local officials were rated by five merits: (1) population increase; (2) increase in cultivated land; (3) decrease in legal cases; (4) absence of bandits and thieves; and (5) fair administration of taxation and labor service.[34]

To make a long story short, the rating system in its final form was that of the Ch'ing period—once again a combination of Confucian orientation and practical regard for administrative performance. Generally speaking, the Ch'ing ratings were based on four major criteria: (1) integrity; (2) ability; (3) diligence in administration; and (4) age. Integrity largely meant the absence of corruption and other immoral behavior, but officials with a high rating in integrity also had to have high ratings in the other three items before they qualified as first-rate officials. Those with a medium rating in integrity, if they were able and diligent, were classified as second-rate officials; if their ability and diligence were average, they were classified as third-rate officials, barely fulfilling their duties and with little prospect of promotion.[35]

The pattern is clear and consistent. Over the centuries the government persistently valued functional qualities higher than moral qualities. The Confucian emphasis upon moral qualities made little headway against this tendency, except in the form of negative injunctions designed to establish certain minimum standards of morality and conduct. There was little encouragement either of moral qualities as such or of the moral leadership in politics which is so emphasized in Confucian political theory. Such is the extent to which Confucian morality was embodied in the bureaucratic institutions. And even this summation is misleading, since the theoretical standards of Confucianism were of necessity compromised by realistic considerations to a greater degree than is admitted in the encyclopedias or the civil service regulations.

CONCLUDING REMARKS

The various classifications of officials discussed in the preceding pages are to a certain extent indicative of the general problems which Confucianism as a whole has often encountered. We see among these classifications theoretical schemes, historical schemes, and functional schemes. The theoretical schemes tended to dominate the historical schemes to the point where the two became indistinguishable in their persistent emphasis upon moral qualities. The functional schemes devalued moral qualities and upgraded administrative and political qualities. Yet they never abandoned the general theoretical orientation of Confucian morality, nor did they work out very satisfactorily on the practical level.

On the one hand, all these classificatory schemes were influential. Their normative values, in so far as they were accepted as the standards of political behavior by the scholar-official class, helped to encourage good conduct and to restrain bad behavior, especially from the moral point of view. On the other hand, they all had their practical limitations. When the theoretical schemes were applied, as they often were, without regard to realities, they led to conflict and confusion, and ultimately to hypocrisy and apathy. When the theoretical standards were lowered for one reason or another, the leading Confucianists became dissatisfied, and in time their dissatisfaction generated a new demand to restore the theoretical standards to their proper place and to apply them more earnestly. When this was done, the able but not particularly virtuous officials protested. Thus the struggle between theory and practice went on incessantly.

This perpetual struggle may be projected to the large canvas of Confucianism as a whole. Confucianism is a morally-oriented body of thought, whereas the state is a power structure. The Confucian emphasis on moral qualities is more readily applicable to the face-to-face social relationships of primary groups[36] such as the family, the clan, and the small community than it is to the impersonal and complex political institutions of the state, which are never predominantly moral, are in many respects amoral, and in some respects immoral. However, it is to the credit of Confucianism that, by adapting itself to political realities to a considerable measure, it succeeded in effecting a fusion of its theories, including their moral emphasis and normative values, with the laws and practices of the state institutions. This fusion was not always stable and never total; there always existed a tension between Confucianism and the state. The problem of classifying officials is an illustration which reflects *the fusion as well as the tension* in the dynamic complexities of the Confucian state through its historical evolution—an essential fact which studies in Chinese intellectual and political history, using a static approach or frame of reference, often tend to overlook.

Charles O. Hucker

CONFUCIANISM AND THE CHINESE CENSORIAL SYSTEM

Students of China have long been in the habit of labeling as Confucian all the traits, attitudes, practices, and institutions that have given to the Chinese people their distinctive Chineseness. We do this despite recognizing that each of these things is associated with its own separate ideological complex and that each of these ideological complexes—separate "Confucianisms," so to speak—is in turn derived only in part from the teachings of Confucius and his immediate disciples. The problem of developing a system of terms that will clearly differentiate these Confucianisms from one another and from the Confucianism of Confucius himself has long perplexed us, as is indicated by several contributions to the present volume.

We are perhaps especially inclined to speak of the Confucian state, referring by this term to the centralized, non-feudal, bureaucratic, imperial governmental system that appeared under the Ch'in dynasty in 221 B.C. and persisted thereafter without many basic changes until it disappeared with the Ch'ing dynasty in 1912. We call this system a Confucian state because, through much of its history, the imperial government supported the ethical teachings of the classical Confucian thinkers and their later interpreters as an official orthodoxy and because the scholar-bureaucrats who staffed the government mostly considered themselves to be Confucians. We nevertheless recognize that the Confucianism that is manifested in the so-called Confucian state is necessarily a distorted reflection of the views on government that were held by Confucius, who lived in pre-imperial antiquity. It has become a truism that this "Imperial Confucianism" is, as a matter of fact, a mixture of elements from many philosophical traditions.

Other papers in this volume demonstrate in different ways the eclectic character of Imperial Confucianism. The present paper attempts to do so by examining the ideological implications of one of the Confucian state's most characteristic institutions, the censorial system, with special reference to its workings during the Ming dynasty (1368–1644).

IDEOLOGICAL FOUNDATIONS OF THE CONFUCIAN STATE

The two major philosophical systems that contributed significantly to the formation of the so-called Confucian state both developed in the latter part of the feudalistic Chou dynasty (1122?–256 B.C.), in a chaotic period of multi-state competition that preceded unification under a Ch'in emperor. These were classical Confucianism, as founded by Confucius (551–479 B.C.) and expounded by Mencius (373–288 B.C.) and Hsün-tzu (fl. third century B.C.), and Legalism, as developed principally by Kung-sun Yang ("Lord Shang," fl. fourth century B.C.) and Han Fei (d. 233 B.C.). Both were products of their time to such an extent that each in its own fashion is primarily a theory of government, offering the promise of social stability. Legalism is almost exclusively so, and Confucianism is concerned with human problems of a more general sort only because its conception of government is a moralistic and hence a broadly inclusive one. Neither system of thought in its early form emphasizes metaphysics or other abstract concerns.

As they are applicable to state administration, the Legalist and classical Confucian doctrines differ markedly. The Legalists maintain, on the one hand, that:

1. Man is amorally self-seeking.

2. The people exist for the sake of the state and its ruler.

3. The people must therefore be coerced into obedience by rewards and harsh punishments.

4. Law is a supreme, state-determined, amoral standard of conduct and must be enforced inflexibly.

5. Officials must be obedient instruments of the ruler's will, accountable to him alone.

6. Expediency must be the basis for all state policy and all state service.

7. The state can prosper only if it is organized for prompt and efficient implementation of the ruler's will.

Conversely, in direct contrast, the classical Confucians maintain that:

1. Man is morally perfectible.

2. The state and its ruler exist for the sake of the people.

3. The people must therefore be encouraged toward goodness by education and virtuous example.

4. Law is a necessary but necessarily fallible handmaiden of the natural moral order and must be enforced flexibly.

5. Officials must be morally superior men, loyal to the ruler but accountable primarily and in the last resort to Heaven.

6. Morality—specifically, the doctrines of good government expounded in the classics and manifested in the acts of worthy men of the past—must be the basis for all state policy and all state service.

7. The state can prosper only if its people possess the morale that comes from confidence in the ruler's virtue.

In even more generalized terms, it might be said simply that classical Confucianism stands for the claim of the people against the state, for the supremacy of morality. At the other pole, Legalism stands for the supremacy of the state and its inflexible law.

In 221 B.C. the state of Ch'in was able to unify all China into the imperial pattern that predominated thereafter by utilizing Legalist ideas. But the regime's harsh and totalitarian policies provoked great resentment, and popular rebellions overthrew the Ch'in in 207 B.C. Subsequent Chinese rulers, while perpetuating the Ch'in imperial structure of government and many Legalist-like attitudes that were inseparably associated with that structure, dared not openly espouse Legalist doctrines. Under the Former Han dynasty (202 B.C.–A.D. 9) it was specifically ruled that no adherent of Legalism could even be employed as an official, and Confucianism was accepted as the orthodox philosophical justification of the state. From that time on, Chinese dynasties practiced Confucian-approved ceremonies and entrusted administration to scholar-officials versed in the literature of classical Confucianism.

The Confucianism that was thus adopted as the state ideology was not, however, identical with classical Confucianism. It was an interpretation by the Han-dynasty scholar Tung Chung-shu (179–104 B.C.). His Imperial Confucianism, for one thing, is more strongly theistic and metaphysical than the original. Moreover, it glorifies the ruler almost to the point of negating the anti-statism of the classical doctrine. That is to say, it compromises with the inescapable fact that the Chinese had to live with and under an autocratic, centralized government on the Ch'in pattern. It is consequently an amalgam of classical Confucian and Legalist ideas.

This official state ideology, furthermore, was by no means a static thing. It was modified anew from time to time. Some Taoist and even Buddhist ideas eventually came to be added to the mixture, though Confucian and Legalist elements remained at all times predominant. So great a change was wrought in the ideological alignment during the Sung dynasty (960–1279) that Western writers habitually label the new mixture Neo-Confucianism, to differentiate it clearly from classical Confucianism. We make further refinements by speaking freely of Han Confucianism, Sung Confucianism, or Ming Confucianism, for example, as identifiable subcategories within the broadly inclusive category of Imperial Confucianism.

Imperial Confucianism in all its varities represents a compromising of certain basic principles in classical Confucianism. The process of change is particularly evident in the case of law. The early Confucian distrust of law simply could not persist once all of China was united under a centralized, bureaucratically administered government. The very vastness of the empire and the ever-increasing complexity of governmental responsibilities, coupled with an inevitable desire for uniformity and consistency in relations between state and subject, required some degree of compromise with the Legalist insistence on codification. Before long imperial Confucianists were compiling voluminous law codes and commentaries. But this was not a complete Confucian surrender to Legalist principles; rather, it has been called the Confucianization of Chinese law. The Legalist form of law was retained, but the laws were infused with a Confucian spirit. Confucian ideas were consistently brought into battle to "temper the rigor of the law" by injecting into juristic considerations the classical Confucian emphases on ethics and *li*, propriety.[1] Thus law, though elaborately codified, remained the instrument of morality. A differentiation between Legalist and classical Confucian influences in Imperial Confucianism consequently cannot be based on whether or not legal sanctions are relied upon. It must rather be based on the purposes for which legal sanctions are sought. Reliance on law to promote the state at the expense of the people might represent the persistence of a Legalist spirit, and excessive punishment in any case can be attributed only to Legalist influences. But reliance on law to promote equity and popular well-being clearly suggests the persistence of a Confucian spirit within a Legalist-like apparatus.[2]

In imperial times there was no opportunity for classical Confucian ideals to persist unmodified. State subsidization of Confucianism forced would-be bureaucrats of all persuasions, whether or not they were Confucian by personal conviction, to become at least nominal Confucians in order to pass the civil-service examinations that qualified one for office. It was inevitable that the bureaucratic ranks would include some men whose personal convictions resembled Legalist principles more than classical Confucian ones. But no one labeled himself a Legalist, and Legalism was not perpetuated as a philosophic tradition. Since everyone was Confucian, Confucianism necessarily assimilated certain Legalist elements. On the other hand, those bureaucrats whose personal convictions genuinely resembled classical Confucian principles had no choice but to adapt themselves to prevailing conditions of government service. This required that they manifest in practice certain attitudes consonant with Legalist principles and not consonant with classical Confucian ones, since the structure and much of the rationale of the state they served was Legalistic. They did so unwittingly, no doubt. Thus the seventeenth-century scholar Ku Yen-wu could justifiably lament that self-styled Confucians of his time righteously denounced Ch'in Legalism while being unaware that they still served it.[3]

Inasmuch as these bureaucrats owed their official status to demonstrated competence in the classical Confucian literature, sincerely considered themselves to be latter-day protagonists of classical Confucianism, and would have rejected in alarm any intimation that they were un-Confucian, it would be presumptuous indeed to suggest that some of them were little more than Legalists in Confucian dress. The bureaucratic ideology did include a spectrum of ideas ranging from Legalist-like realism at one extreme to unchallengeably Confucian idealism at the other, it is true; but they were all within the expanded mainstream of Imperial Confucianism. It has been proposed, consequently, that in referring to the ideas and motivations of bureaucrats in imperial times we should replace the words Legalism and Confucianism with such terms as "rigorist Confucianism" and "humanist Confucianism." In the following account of how these poles of thought manifested themselves in the organization and functioning of the imperial censorial system, I shall continue to refer to them as Legalism and Confucianism, but only for the sake of convenience and without meaning to imply that the early doctrines persisted as separate and competing traditions.

CHINA'S CENSORIAL SYSTEM

The traditional Chinese censorship that concerns us here has nothing to do, characteristically, with governmental control of private publications and entertainments. It is not a normal police activity. Rather, it represents an organized and systematic effort by the government to police itself. The scope of this effort was very broad, encompassing all levels of administration, all governmental personnel, and both policy-formulating and policy-implementing processes. Against the formulators of policy, its weapon was remonstrance; against the implementers, impeachment.

As in most other governmental systems, control powers in traditional China were widely exercised. Officials of every status, and non-officials also, did commonly impeach (or at least denounce) governmental personnel and remonstrate with their governmental superiors. In China, as we shall subsequently see, there were special sanctions for the general exercise of the right or obligation to criticize; and we shall take note of this general diffusion of the right to criticize to the extent that

Legalist or Confucian principles are related to it. But criticism of this sort—unorganized and unsystematized—is not the type of censorship that primarily concerns us. Our concern is rather with specialized censorship: highly organized, highly systematized, and highly institutionalized, concentrated in particular governmental agencies and officials whose prescribed function was to impeach or remonstrate or both, vested with high prestige and special sanctions, providing a routine surveillance over all governmental activities. It is this censorship that is distinctively Chinese and that has specially important ideological implications.

By Ming times the system had attained a high degree of complexity, both in its organization and in its functioning. It included hundreds of censorial officials grouped in three categories of agencies: (1) a Chief Surveillance Office or Censorate at the capital, (2) six Offices of Scrutiny also at the capital, and (3) thirteen Provincial Surveillance Offices, one located at each provincial capital. Within these three types of agencies were concentrated the powers and obligations of what the Chinese traditionally called surveillance officials (*ch'a-kuan*) and remonstrance officials (*yen-kuan*). Censors, supervising secretaries, and surveillance commissioners all had specified surveillance and impeachment functions of general scope. The supervising secretaries also exercised specially prescribed controls over the flow of documents to and from the respective ministries; virtually all state documents passed through their hands, whether memorials to the throne or decrees from the throne, and were subject to a kind of editorial veto by the supervising secretaries. Specialized remonstrance functions were not so widely diffused, however, being the prescribed additional duty of the censors and supervising secretaries only—in Chinese terms, "the avenues of criticism" (*yen-lu*).[4]

The roots of this censorial system go deep into Chinese history, and the manner of its evolution reveals something of the conception that underlay it. What is particularly apparent is that the amalgamation of surveillance and remonstrance functions into one agency, whether the Censorate or the combined Offices of Scrutiny, was a relatively late development. In origin and early evolution, the two functions were quite distinct.[5]

The term by which Chinese censors have always been known, *yü-shih,* probably has had longer continuous use as an official title than any other in any language; for it appears as a title in oracle bone inscriptions of the Shang dynasty (traditional dates 1766–1122 B.C.) and was used thereafter until A.D. 1912. Until Ch'in times, the title seems principally to have been associated with men who were court recorders and chroniclers.[6] Then it was adopted for use in the imperial Censorate, which was a creation of the Ch'in and Han rulers. The *yü-shih* of early imperial times may indeed have engaged occasionally in remonstrance, as was every official's wont, but their prescribed and characteristic function as *yü-shih* was to provide disciplinary surveillance over the bureaucrats, as instruments of monarchical—or at least of central administrative—control.[7]

Specialized remonstrance functions developed separately, being associated with the titles Supervising Secretary (*chi-shih-chung*, literally "palace attendant") and Grand Remonstrant (*chien-i ta-fu*), which seem to have been originated by the Ch'in dynasty. For many centuries both these titles, or near equivalents, were reserved for eminent dignitaries considered suitable companions and mentors for the emperors. The early supervising secretaries, therefore, did not exercise the clerkly control over documents that occupied their successors in Ming times. But by the T'ang era (618–907) both titles had come to designate normal bureaucratic positions. The supervising secretaries then did control documents as later, and the grand remonstrants bore the heavy assigned responsibility of criticizing the emperor himself.[8]

The first tendencies toward amalgamation of the surveillance and remonstrance functions appeared early in the Sung period, when special policy censors (*yen-shih yü-shih*) were established in the Censorate to "speak out about affairs." For a time newly appointed censors were even punished if, within a short time following appointment, they failed to submit criticisms of important matters. But this first Censorate invasion of the remonstrators' preserve was short-lived, and the traditional distinctions were quickly restored.[9]

Full-scale amalgamation of the surveillance and remonstrance functions came about under the "barbarian" Yüan dynasty (1260–1368), which succeeded the Sung and directly preceded the Ming. The Mongol rulers promptly abolished the title and office of remonstrator. They also converted the supervising secretaries from document inspectors to court annalists. The Censorate—the supreme instrument of monarchical control—was, on the other hand, greatly expanded in staff and scope. Its net of disciplinary surveillance was now thrown more efficiently over the bureaucracy than ever before, through the creation of branch Censorates and the establishment of Provincial Surveillance Offices ancestral to those of the Ming period but directly subordinate administratively to the metropolitan Censorate. This was probably the most highly centralized and most widely pervasive control system of Chinese history. Apparently as a sop to the native tradition, the Mongol rulers assigned to censors the additional duty of remonstrance. Kubilai Khan (reigned 1260–94), for instance, once announced: "The duties of the Censorate's officials lie in speaking out straightforwardly. If We should by chance commit improprieties, let them speak out vigorously, without concealment and without fearing others."[10] Hence the absorption of the remonstrance function into the surveillance organization was complete, undoubtedly to the detriment of its effective exercise. With the exception of a few years early in the Ming period, the office of remonstrator was not again reconstituted. But supervising secretaries were restored to their old document-control functions by the founder of the Ming dynasty, and thenceforth they and the censors, equally, shared both remonstrance and surveillance functions.

When we consider the censorial system and its history in the light of the Legalist-Confucian tension within Imperial Confucianism, a few significant correlations suggest themselves. For one thing, I am inclined to believe that the very existence of the censorial establishment manifests Legalist concepts of state organization; it appears to me that only Legalist-inclined minds, with a bureaucratic passion for impersonality, organizational clarity, and efficiency, could have produced such an elaborate mechanism. On the other hand, the presence within the system of specialized remonstrance agencies, agencies whose very existence calls into question the inviolability of the ruler's will, clearly suggests a genuinely Confucian influence. Further, it would seem that the evolution of the system—the progressive extension and systematization of censorship and the progressive curtailment of its remonstrance functions—indicates an increasing stress on Legalist principles at the expense of classical Confucian ones. This accords well with the prevailing interpretation of Chinese institutional history, which emphasizes the steady growth of despotic absolutism.

THE FUNCTION OF SURVEILLANCE

There can be no reasonable doubt, I think, that the censorial functions of disciplinary surveillance and impeachment must be viewed as manifestations of Legalist rather than classical Confucian ideas.

The classical Confucian thinkers and the early Legalists equally emphasized the need to obtain proper men for government office. But, whereas the Legalists were also very concerned with the problem of controlling men once in office, the Confucian thinkers had no worries on this score. They seemed to feel that once a morally superior man had been placed in authority, he could be trusted to do what was right. As a matter of fact, the whole spirit of classical Confucian political thinking clearly implies that he should not be interfered with. In attempting to place superior men in office to restrain the rapacious rulers of their time, Confucius and his followers could not concede, for strategic reasons, that the officials themselves might require restraints. And there was a principle involved, too. Confucius said, "If the ruler himself is upright, all will go well even though he does not give orders. But if he himself is not upright, even though he gives orders, they will not be obeyed."[11] Thus officials should be restrained, not by coercive surveillance, but by the virtuous example of their superiors. This principle was clearly cited in a great policy debate between Confucian-minded scholars and Legalist-minded ministers at the Han court in 81 B.C. The scholars indignantly rebuked the ministers for having put to death two magistrates, saying: ". . . when members of the reigning clan are not upright, then laws and regulations are not enforced; when the ruler's right hand men are not upright, then treachery and evil flourish. . . . Thus, when a ruler commits a mistake, the minister should rectify it; when superiors err, inferiors should criticize them. When high ministers are upright, can magistrates be anything else? It is indeed highly remiss of you who are in actual control of administration to find fault with others instead of turning to examine your own persons."[12] Criticism should be directed by inferiors at superiors, not vice versa.

Especially, classical Confucian thought does not condone informers. Confucius said that a superior man "hates those who point out what is hateful in others," and one of his immediate disciples said, "I hate those who mistake tale-bearing for honesty." "The gentleman," in Confucius' definition, "calls attention to the good points in others; he does not call attention to their defects. The small man does just the reverse of this." And Mencius' contempt for informers is plain: "What future misery have they and ought they to endure," he exclaimed, "who talk of what is not good in others!"[13]

The attitude of the Legalists was quite the reverse. They not only condoned informers; they would have the ruler encourage them and rely on them. Disciplinary surveillance was in fact a foundation stone in the Legalist-conceived state, and it was under the Legalist-dominated Ch'in dynasty that censorship of this sort was first institutionalized. The Legalists specifically maintained that criticism should be directed by superiors at inferiors: "In case of transgression of the law," Kung-sun Yang said, "then those of higher rank criticize those of lower rank and degree."[14]

Kubilai Khan once said of his three top-level governmental organs that "the Secretariat is my left hand, the Bureau of Military Affairs is my right hand, and the Censorate is the means for my keeping both hands healthy."[15] This was the Legalist conception manifested also in the censorial system of Ming China: both the Censorate and the Offices of Scrutiny were intended primarily to check on the performance of duties by officials and to denounce those who were remiss. The functions of all governmental agencies were carefully prescribed, in great detail, in such codifications as the voluminous 228-chapter "Collected Institutes of the Ming" (*Ta Ming Hui-tien*). The number and nature of impeachment entries in the day-by-day chronicles called "The True Records of the Ming" (*Ming Shih-lu*) make it quite clear that the censorial officials ordinarily devoted most of their time and energy to seeing that these functions were in fact performed, and performed as prescribed. The censorial officials were numerous and ubiquitous, and their surveillance processes were themselves voluminously prescribed and carefully routinized. The censors, supervising secretaries, and provincial surveillance commissioners—one or another—routinely examined all state documents; they routinely inspected all state files and accounts; they routinely received and checked activity reports from other agencies; they routinely visited and interrogated every official in the emperor's employ; they accepted and investigated complaints from the people. In consequence of their investigations, they impeached officials high and low for violations of the law: for being indolent and inefficient, for delaying or otherwise hindering the execution of state business, for keeping improper records, for being ignorant of state regulations, for failing to observe prescribed administrative routine, for failing to enforce state policies or regulations, for unprescribed expenditures, for freeing the guilty or punishing the innocent, for exceeding their authority, etc.[16] A very large proportion of all their recorded activities reflects a striking, and strikingly Legalist, concern for legality and efficiency not only in the thinking of those who prescribed the censorial rules but in the thinking of those who wielded censorial powers.

Empowered and expected to find fault with their bureaucratic colleagues, the censorial officials must necessarily have gained great satisfaction from the exercise of their surveillance and impeachment functions, especially since they were ordinarily young and new to the civil service. It was established Ming policy to appoint neophytes, apparently in the expectation that, being merely on the threshold of government careers, they would have little to lose and much to gain by the zealous prosecution of their assigned duties. And it was certainly true that a censor or supervising secretary who made a name for himself as a zealous investigator and impeacher could expect to rise rapidly into high civil-service ranks. The dedicated impeacher was a kind of ideal. Probably the most renowned censor-in-chief of the whole Ming period, Ku Tso, who conducted a great purge of the Censorate itself in 1428, was known awesomely as "Sit-alone Ku" because of the detached, unfriendly scrutiny that he daily inflicted on his fellow participants in court assemblies.[17]

Considering the circumstances, it is not surprising that these officials at times had to be dissuaded from excesses of Legalist zeal. In 1434, for example, a censor impeached a provincial official for punishing a criminal too lightly, only to be rebuked mildly by the Hsüan-te Emperor (1425–35) on the decidedly non-Legalist premise that "punishing too lightly and punishing too severely are not the same."[18] And even the tyrannical Yung-lo Emperor (1402–24) lost patience at his supervising secretaries' penchant for denouncing petty clerical errors in documents: "You have all recently made an endless fuss," he complained to a group of them, "about trifling errors in memorials, and rejected the memorials for this reason. This is really too much! Paperwork annoyances accumulate in bureaucratic work, and one's energy is sometimes exhausted by them, so that it is difficult to avoid errors. Hereafter, whenever memorials include erroneous characters in numbers, dates, and so forth, just block them out and rectify them in marginal notations. There's no need to inform me!"[19]

Thus the very existence—and certainly the elaborateness—of the censorial surveillance processes would seem justifiable only on Legalist and not on classical Confucian premises; and censorial officials, in carrying out their duties, consistently acted in accordance with Legalist ideas. They were called upon to uphold the law and tried to do so, being literal about it at times to the point of pettiness.

But Confucian ideas did make some inroads into this sphere of Legalist influence. This is largely because in imperial times Chinese law, as we have seen above, was no longer the amoral law conceived by the early Legalists, but had become Confucianized and hence moralistic. While upholding the law, therefore, censorial officials at the same time upheld morality, which was prescribed by law. Their impeachments clearly reveal this dual concern, and to that extent they manifest a Confucian influence. Officials were denounced not only for their illegalities in a narrow sense, but for personal immorality as well: for licentiousness, for venality, for improprieties of all kinds. The great authoritarian grand secretary of the sixteenth century, Chang Chü-cheng, for example, was denounced by censors and other officials for failing to observe the mourning rituals prescribed by Confucian tradition after his father's death in 1577.[20]

Confucian influence is similarly observable at times in what the censorial officials did not do. A good example is another instance of a censorial denunciation of Chang Chü-cheng, this one in 1576. A scathing broadside denunciation of Chang was submitted by a censor named Liu T'ai. Liu had originally won entry into the civil service at examinations presided over by Chang, and it had been on Chang's recommendation that he had subsequently been appointed to the Censorate.

In the view of Ming Confucians, these circumstances created a master-disciple bond between the two men. Liu's denunciation of Chang consequently provoked counteraccusations that Liu's act was one of gross impropriety. Chang himself seems to have been shocked most by this un-Confucian aspect of the attack, reflecting that no such "disciple" had attacked his patron throughout the two centuries of the Ming dynasty's prior existence. And Liu himself, in his denunciation, felt it necessary to apologize for and justify his breach of Confucian propriety, for which he was ultimately dismissed from the civil service.[21]

This incident suggests how classical Confucian ideas—emphasizing morality and the importance of personal relationships—consistently intruded into censorial operations. But it is particularly instructive in demonstrating that these Confucian ideas remained entangled with Legalist ones. For Liu's justification of his impropriety is stated as follows:

When I attained my doctoral degree Chang Chü-cheng was chief examiner, and when I was serving in a ministry it was Chang Chü-cheng who recommended my selection as a censor. I have therefore been abundantly favored by Chang Chü-cheng. The reason why I now attack him so presumptuously is that *the ruler-minister relationship is so important a one that it excludes consideration of personal favors.* I hope that Your Majesty, taking note of my unenlightened earnestness, will curb the minister's power so as to prevent him from disrupting the proper course of events and *impeding the state.* Then, though I should die, I shall not have died in vain.[22]

Here Liu appealed to the Legalist doctrine that loyalty to one's ruler overrides the obligations inherent in other relationships. Moreover, though Liu had in passing accused Chang of personal immorality, the argument on which he relied most heavily in denouncing Chang is not a Confucian, moralistic one but a strictly Legalist one: that Chang's growing authority endangered the state. In an earlier section of his impeachment he had pointedly called the Emperor's attention to the fact, as he saw it, that people were coming to stand more in awe of Chang than of the throne. There could hardly be a more naked appeal to the Legalist inclinations of an emperor.

THE FUNCTION OF REMONSTRANCE

On the conceptual level, the censorial function of remonstrance is even more clearly linked to classical Confucian doctrines than those of surveillance and impeachment are linked to Legalist doctrines. And it is because censorial officials were at their dramatic best in remonstrating that the whole censorial system can easily be misinterpreted as an essentially Confucian institution.

The recorded history of the feudal Chou period abounds in examples of ministers—recorders among others—who doggedly remonstrated with rulers, often at great cost to themselves. The early Confucian thinkers, always interested in imposing their own notions of good government on the rulers of their time, patterned themselves after these models. Confucius often rebuked the powerful to their faces, as when he told a grandee who had complained that his people were committing burglary, "If only you were free from desire, they would not steal even if you paid them to."[23] And Mencius, in his wide travels, repeatedly said such bold things to rulers that they "changed countenance" or hastily changed the subject.[24] The early Confucian thinkers, therefore, became through their own conduct examples to be emulated by later remonstrators.

Some classical Confucian doctrines seem at first glance to contradict the notion that morally superior men must remonstrate with their superiors. The great Confucian emphasis on loyalty and filial piety, for example, would seem to discourage remonstrance. And some of Confucius' own statements add to the apparent confusion. He once said, "A ruler in employing his ministers should be guided solely by the prescriptions of ritual. Ministers in serving their ruler, solely by devotion to his cause." When a disciple asked how one's friends should be dealt with, Confucius said, "Inform them loyally and guide them discreetly. If that fails, then desist. Do not court humiliation."[25]

These are by no means the only statements attributed to Confucius that are difficult to reconcile with the general tenor of his doctrines. Whether or not it can be considered that Confucius actually said such things does not concern us here. The statements, genuine or spurious, exist in the Confucian lore that was part of every Ming minister's intellectual baggage. Taken in isolation, they could be understood to sanction certain kinds of ministerial subservience and opportunism as being Confucian, despite their being clearly out of harmony with general Confucian principles and in essential accord with the Legalist view of ministership. It must also be admitted that the authoritarian Chu Hsi form of Neo-Confucianism, which was the officially orthodox Imperial Confucianism of Ming times, might have dissuaded remonstrators by emphasizing loyalty to the ruler even more strongly as a cardinal virtue.

Subservience and opportunism, however, are quite clearly not ministerial qualities that the early Confucians admired and advocated. Their own conduct and an overwhelming proportion of their comments on what ministers ought to be make this clear. When asked by a disciple how a prince should be served, Confucius said, "Do not deceive him, but when necessary withstand him to his face." Confucius also told a grandee that "if a ruler's policies are bad and yet none of those about him oppose them, such spinelessness is enough to ruin a state."[26] The great early compendium "Record of Ceremonial" (*Li-chi*) quotes Confucius in the same vein repeatedly. For example, "for one whose place is near the throne, not to remonstrate is to hold his office idly for the sake of gain."[27] And Mencius mourned, "Now-a-days, the remonstrances of a minister are not followed, and his advice is not listened to, so that no blessings descend on the people."[28]

The Confucian precepts about being loyal and those about remonstrating were easily reconciled; for loyalty was defined as being more than subservience. "How can he be said to be truly loyal," Confucius asked, "who refrains from admonishing the object of his loyalty?"[29] And Mencius said, "He who restrains his prince loves his prince." Mencius expanded on this concept often, notably in the following passage:

Among the people of Ch'i there is no one who speaks to the king about benevolence and righteousness. Are they thus silent because they do not think that benevolence and righteousness are admirable? [No, but] in their hearts they say, "This man is not fit to be spoken with about benevolence and righteousness." Thus they manifest a disrespect than which there can be none greater. I do not dare to set forth before the king any but the ways of [the idealized legendary emperors] Yao and Shun. There is therefore no man of Ch'i who respects the king as much as I do.

Mencius also explained that "to urge one's sovereign to difficult achievements may be called showing respect for him. To set before him what is good and repress his perversities may be called showing reverence for him."[30]

Even parents, to whom in classical Confucianism one owes primary loyalty, cannot be immune from remonstrance: "to remonstrate with them gently without being weary . . . may be pronounced filial piety"; "when they have faults, to remonstrate with them, and yet not withstand them . . . —this is what is called the completion [by a son] of his proper services."[31] The Confucian primer, "The Classic of Filial Piety" (*Hsiao-ching*), stipulates that one should serve a superior by assenting to his good inclinations but rescuing him from his evil inclinations. It also reports that when a disciple asked if filial piety meant for the son to obey the father's orders, Confucius said, "How can you say this! How can you say this! . . . When confronted with unrighteousness, the son cannot but remonstrate with his father and the minister cannot but remonstrate with his ruler. Therefore, when confronted with unrighteousness, remonstrate against it! How could merely obeying the father's orders be considered filial piety?"[32]

The Confucian-minded scholars who in 81 B.C. debated state policy with Han ministers put this problem of remonstrance, as so many others, in clear perspective. When rebuked by one of the ministers for their trenchant criticisms, they replied:

Benighted provincials that we are, who have seldom crossed the precincts of this great court, we realize that our wild and uncouth speeches may indeed find no favor here even unto offending the authorities. Yet, so it seems to us, as a medicinal tonic, though bitter to the palate, still is of great benefit to the patient, so words of loyalty, though offensive to the ear, may also be found beneficial to mend one's morals. A great blessing is to be able to hear straightforward denial; it cheapens one to hear nothing but adulatory praise. As swift winds are raging through the forest, so flattering words encompass the rich and powerful. After hearing daily at this court controlling myriads of *li* [Chinese miles] of territory nothing but servile aye-aye's, you hear now the straightforward nay-nay's of honest scholars. 'Tis indeed a great opportunity for you, Lord High Minister, to receive a well-needed physic. . . .[33]

So strong was the classical Confucian insistence on this aspect of the loyal minister's service that remonstrance became not only the right but the duty of all officials in the Confucian state. "Such criticism not only served the people—it prolonged the life of the dynasty."[34] Emperors consistently, therefore, actually called upon their officials to remonstrate. And, as we have seen, remonstrance was institutionalized by the establishment of special remonstrance officials.

This theoretical concept of remonstrance, as I have already suggested, draws little support from Legalist ideas. The Legalist view of kingship has no place for the moralistic criticisms of the rulers that classical Confucianism advocates, and it would seem to imply a distaste for the very fact of remonstrance. Nevertheless, remonstrators in practice could gain considerable inspiration from the Legalist teachings; for the Legalists did advocate remonstrance of certain sorts.

Legalist writings, as a matter of fact, often sanction the remonstrance principle in general terms. Han Fei listed paying no heed to remonstrance among ten common faults of rulers and praised at great length some of the remonstrators of ancient times.[35] He warned rulers against ignoring advice and alienating "frank and straightforward speakers." He particularly warned that "if the ruler takes advice only from ministers of high rank, refrains from comparing different opinions and testifying to the truth, and uses only one man as a channel of information, then ruin is possible."[36]

This last-mentioned warning, especially, could well have been used by later censorial officials against any attempt to curtail the censorial "avenues of criticism." As a matter of fact, the very concept of an institutionalized system of remonstrance, like that of an institutionalized system of surveillance and impeachment, is apparently more Legalist than Confucian in its implications. When one concedes an advantage in the ruler's having an abundance and variety of opinions available, one implies that no one adviser can be trusted to have opinions that are consistently right or to express them sincerely. Original Confucianism, by contrast, would seem to imply that it is perfectly proper for the ruler to be guided by only one adviser, if this adviser is the best man available by Confucian standards. It is in this sense that classical Confucianism is authoritarian and Legalism egalitarian. What is right, in Confucianism, has no necessary correlation at all with majority opinion—except, of course, in the very vague premise that the mass of the people somehow manifests the will of Heaven.

It is precisely in regard to this basic premise, however, that Legalism's special bias regarding remonstrance appears. Han Fei reported, "They say that, of old, Pien Ch'iao [a legendary physician], when treating serious diseases, pierced through bones with knives. So does the sage *on rescuing the state out of danger* offend the ruler's ear with loyal words."[37] This makes explicit a basic difference in the Legalist and classical Confucian views of ministerial remonstrance. The Legalist-minded remonstrator rebukes the ruler for neglecting his own selfish interest, whereas the Confucian-minded remonstrator rebukes the ruler for deviating from the natural moral order and the interests of the people. The difference lies in the content of remonstrance, not in the fact of remonstrance.

An even more notable difference lies in the contrasting manners of remonstrance advocated by the two schools. Confucius urged his disciples to be ready, if attacked, "to die for the good Way," and warned that "to see what is right and not to do it is cowardice."[38] The Confucian-minded remonstrator must therefore stand firm for his principles, remonstrating bluntly, unflinchingly, and without compromise, whatever the cost to himself. This view of remonstrance is ridiculous in Legalist eyes. According to Han Fei, the Legalist remonstrator, being thoroughly opportunistic, "must carefully observe the sovereign's feelings of love and hate before he starts persuading him."[39] Whatever end the minister may wish to attain, he amorally phrases his remonstrance as an appeal to the ruler's self-interest and self-esteem, allowing no possibility of a reaction injurious to himself. "In general," Han Fei said, "the business of the persuader is to embellish the pride and obliterate the shame of the persuaded." Han Fei devoted a long essay to a detailed discussion, in an utterly Machiavellian spirit, of the techniques that a minister must employ if he hopes to impose his will on a ruler. "The dragon is a creature which is docile and can be tamed and ridden," he concluded. "But under its neck are reversed scales which stick out a full foot, and anyone who comes in contact with them loses his life. A ruler of men is much like the dragon; he too has reversed scales, and an adviser who knows how to keep clear of them will not go far wrong."[40] This opportunism contrasts sharply with the Confucian ideal. The Confucian must not only remonstrate about morality; he must do so in a moral manner.

Officials of necessity had to compromise this classical Confucian ideal once a centralized empire had been established. The early thinkers had served and taught in a social context that permitted them more freedom of movement than bureaucrats were later to enjoy. When their remonstrances went unheeded—or when they felt that, in general, the moral Way did not prevail—Confucius and Mencius merely left the court in question and wandered to another in search of more congenial surroundings. Both repeatedly urged that this was the only course open to a moral minister.[41] Especially in late Chou times, the competition between states was so keen that a renowned adviser could get a hearing and a substantial emolument almost anywhere, and this circumstance naturally emboldened such men as Mencius to speak very frankly to their temporary patrons, in a spirit of independence and detachment. But after all China had been brought under one rule by the Ch'in and Han regimes, the bureaucrat found himself in a much less enviable position. He might remonstrate, and if his remonstrances went unheeded or if his principles were consistently violated he might indeed withdraw from service. But where could he go? There was no escaping the state; there was only one ruler and only one governmental structure. The bureaucrat had the choice of giving loyal service to a ruler whom he might consider evil or of abandoning entirely the sense of political responsibility that is imbedded in the whole Confucian ideology.

Faced by this choice, some frustrated Confucians abandoned bureaucratic careers in favor of the anchorite self-cultivation that had always been advocated by China's anti-government Taoist thinkers.[42] Other Confucians resolutely upheld the traditional ideal of political service by remonstrating fearlessly, at the risk of disgrace and perhaps death for themselves and their families. The typical Confucian of imperial times, however, was neither a die-hard moralist nor a resigned hermit, but a practicing bureaucrat in circumstances which frustrated attempts to embody all the classical Confucian virtues. He kept himself alive and prospering, and hence able to provide the filial service to his parents that classical Confucianism demanded, by being prudently subservient to his ruler in much the way Legalism had prescribed. On the other hand, his subservience was so modified by moralistic considerations as to make him much less than an ideal Legalist minister and at times to bring disgrace and hardship upon his family, in contravention of a basic Confucian principle.

The practice of remonstrance in Ming times illustrates both the dangers that forthright remonstrators encountered in China's imperial history and the extent to which Legalist influence had affected this Confucian-hallowed institution.

At the outset it must be noted that the Ming government was especially ill-suited to forthright remonstrance. Its tightly centralized structure was unusually conducive to autocracy, and its emperors as individuals tended to be unusually despotic and tyrannical. The tradition was created by the founder of the dynasty, the Hung-wu Emperor (1368–98), who had risen from the status of an illiterate commoner. Almost fanatically jealous of his imperial power, he tried to secure and preserve it by ruthless Legalist means. He eventually exterminated many of the powerful men who had helped him gain the throne, together with thousands of their relatives and friends, and reorganized the government so as to centralize all control in his own hands.

The Hung-wu Emperor had a particular aversion to some aspects of the classical Confucian heritage. He honored Confucius himself, apparently because Confucius seemed to favor loyalty, stability, and order. The "True Records," as a matter of fact, show the Hung-wu Emperor to have been an unwearying lecturer on the subject of Confucian-style ministerial responsibilities. But Mencius infuriated him. He thought Mencius was disrespectful to rulers (this was undoubtedly true), and he said that if Mencius were still alive he would have to be punished severely. In 1394 he created a special board of scholars to edit the text of Mencius' writings, purging those passages that spoke disparagingly of the position of rulers and those that urged ministers to remonstrate against rulers' errors. In all, eighty-five passages were struck out. The emasculated edition that resulted was printed and circulated for official use in all schools.[43]

The Hung-wu Emperor's successors were, for the most part, of the same breed. Occasionally a Confucian-minded ruler such as the Hsüan-te Emperor (1425–35) emerged, and all Ming emperors, in accordance with the now long-established custom, recurringly mouthed the phrases that enjoined officials to speak their minds freely. The acknowledged dogma was that "since antiquity sage emperors and enlightened kings have established remonstrance officials in the desire to hear of their own shortcomings."[44] Nevertheless, the Ming emperors were characteristically intolerant of criticism; and the codified regulations as well as the successive imperial exhortations of the Ming period, while showing the greatest care for systematic and effective censorial surveillance over the bureaucracy, give little evidence that censorial officials were seriously encouraged to engage in remonstrance at all.

The Ming emperors specifically deprived censorial officials of at least one of their traditional privileges, that of submitting statements based on hearsay evidence. This seems to have been a valuable privilege in prior periods, in regard to both remonstrating and impeaching. The Hung-wu Emperor once demoted a censor for criticizing an official on the basis of what he had "heard in the streets."[45] Later emperors repeatedly rebuked censorial officials for "making vexatious demands based on rumor."[46] In a nostalgic manner, Ming officials sometimes reminded emperors of this lost privilege of protecting their sources of information, but in vain.[47]

That many censorial—and other—officials of the Ming dynasty nevertheless withstood emperors to their faces in the best Confucian manner testifies to the vitality of the tradition. The Ming dynasty, as a matter of fact, had a disproportionately large number of China's most famous remonstrators, perhaps because Ming remonstrators were so likely to be martyred. Censorial duty was very hazardous duty. "Of all the inner and outer offices," one Ming source testifies, "none is more difficult than that of the censorial personnel; moreover, none is more dangerous than that of the censorial personnel."[48] The fifteenth-century censor Li Shih-mien may have survived (barely) after rebuking the Hung-hsi Emperor (1424–25) for consorting with concubines during the prescribed period of mourning for his father.[49] And the early-sixteenth-century censor Chang Ch'in may have gone unpunished when, by bolting a frontier gate and guarding it with a sword brandished before the Emperor's astonished outriders, he prevented the Cheng-te Emperor (1505–21) and all his entourage from touring beyond the Great Wall.[50] But the historical record generally is a sad one for Ming remonstrators.

The tide of remonstrance advanced and receded in accordance with the personalities of the emperors—or of those who dominated the emperors. During the decade 1424–35, when the liberal and tolerant Hung-hsi and Hsüan-te Emperors reigned, there was very little remonstrance, apparently because there seemed little need for it. The sixteenth century saw a notable increase, and by the 1620's the "True Records" give the impression that censorial officials did little else but remonstrate. This rising tide was a censorial response to challenges posed by particular emperors: the Cheng-te Emperor (1505–21), the Chia-ching Emperor (1521–67), the Wan-li Emperor (1572–1620), and especially the T'ien-ch'i Emperor (1620–27).

The Cheng-te Emperor was a frustrated bravo. He loved gaiety and adventure, and he often wandered about the capital in disguise, seeking thrills. Military adventures pleased him especially; he staged special campaigns for no purpose other than to give himself the thrill of field leadership. In consequence of fancied victories, he then conferred upon himself ever more distinguished military titles: for example, the Chen-kuo Duke, Grand Defender, Controller of the Troops, August Martial Generalissimo, Supreme Commander of All Military Affairs (all one title). Court ministers often protested against his inanities, which were both wasteful and undignified. In 1519, on the eve of a grand "campaign" in South China, censorial officials led a host of ministers in vigorous remonstrance. As a result at least 33 officials were imprisoned, 107 were forced to prostrate themselves in ranks outside the palace gate for five days, and 146 men (with some duplications) were subjected to floggings in open court, of which eleven men died.[51]

The Cheng-te Emperor had no son, and a cousin succeeded him as the Chia-ching Emperor in 1521. A great ceremonial dispute immediately arose. It originated in the new emperor's wish to honor his natural father in sacrificial worship with the title "imperial father." Censorial officials and others objected, insisting that the Emperor recognize his actual uncle, the Hung-chih Emperor (1487–1505), as "imperial father" and relegate his own father to the status of uncle for the purpose of imperial sacrifices. The controversy lasted for several years, becoming almost impossibly confusing in a welter of proposals, counterproposals, and compromises. Court ministers, with censorial officials consistently in the vanguard, submitted remonstrances wholesale: 31 men at a time, 64 at a time, more than 100 at a time, 32 at a time, etc. At one point 220 officials went en masse to chant remonstrances outside the palace, pound noisily on its gates, and prostrate themselves weeping and wailing at the entrance, all in protest against a new proposal by the Emperor. The record shows that 134 of the remonstrators were promptly imprisoned, that a large number of others were flogged in open court, that some were dismissed from service, and that others were exiled to frontier guard duty as common soldiers. At least nineteen men are reported to have died of their punishments.[52]

The long reign of the Wan-li Emperor was marked by numerous controversies in which groups of officials for the most part attacked other officials rather than the Emperor himself. But the Emperor's intolerance of remonstrance provoked one great court storm comparable to those just described. This was a controversy over what was called "the root of the state." The Emperor did not have a son by his empress but had several sons by concubines. When the two eldest sons were still children, censorial and other officials began insisting that the

Emperor nominate the elder as heir apparent so as to make secure "the root of the state"—that is, the imperial succession. The Emperor refused. The resulting battle of wills between the Emperor and the officialdom lasted from 1586 until 1601, when the Emperor at last gave in. In the meantime dozens of officials had been degraded or banished for their temerity in remonstrating, and foundations had been laid for the bitter court factionalism that was to disrupt the Emperor's remaining years.[53]

The T'ien-ch'i era was characterized by almost incessant remonstrance. The T'ien-ch'i Emperor was indecisive and indolent and came increasingly to be dominated in all things by flattering, self-seeking palace intimates—especially an ambitious wet-nurse named Madame K'o and the most powerful eunuch of all Chinese history, Wei Chung-hsien. Palace intrigues were viewed with special alarm because China was just then being threatened seriously by the Manchus and because popular rebellions were becoming a serious domestic problem. Censors and supervising secretaries submitted remonstrances almost daily warning the Emperor against eunuch influence, and finally Wei Chung-hsien in 1624–26 conducted a great purge of the administration designed to quell all such opposition. Hundreds of officials lost their posts or were otherwise punished; fourteen ringleaders of the remonstrators lost their lives.[54] Eight of these were censors, and two were supervising secretaries. One list of 319 men who were punished one way or another for opposing Wei Chung-hsien includes a total of 76 censorial officials (censors and supervising secretaries combined)—more men than were listed in any of seven other categories.[55]

Such "remonstrance disasters" as these reveal that Ming censorial officials unquestionably did remonstrate forthrightly at great cost to themselves. Innumerable examples of individual remonstrators could be added. As regards the fact of upright remonstrance, consequently, there can be no doubt about the influence of the classical Confucian ideal. But it is equally clear that, in some of these cases and in others not yet discussed, Confucian-style remonstrance served ends that were consonant only with Legalist principles and, furthermore, was carried out in a distinctively Legalist manner.

It is particularly noteworthy that two of the great remonstrance controversies had to do with problems of imperial succession. I cannot pretend to understand all the subtle nuances of the "Great Ceremonial Debate" provoked by the Chia-ching Emperor. Shorn of its less important ramifications, however, the controversy pitted the Emperor and a few advisers (denounced as sycophants by Confucian-minded historians) against the mass of the officialdom over a problem in the peculiarly Confucian sphere of filial piety. The remarkable thing is that the officials gave precedence to the imperial succession over natural succession—that is, they insisted that the Emperor owed greater honor to his imperial predecessor than to his own father. That the debate took place at all reflects a Confucian penchant among the officials for moralistic problems which old-time Legalists would have considered trivial. But what the officials argued for seems to reflect Legalist conceptions of kingship and the state and is not consonant with classical Confucianism's conception of filial duty.

The case of the "root of the state" reflects the Ming entanglement of Legalist and classical Confucian ideas even more markedly. The Wan-li Emperor, whatever his actual motivations, took the seemingly Confucian stand that he would not designate an heir apparent until his sons had matured sufficiently to enable him to evaluate their potentialities. Against this, the officials consistently advocated compliance with "the laws of the dynastic founders," which they understood to require early recognition of the eldest imperial son as heir apparent. I have not observed any appeal in the officials' arguments to what is right or wise in moral terms; they merely invoked, in Legalist-sounding fashion, the sanction of law. The fact that the law involved here was the household law or precedents of the Ming emperors permits the rationalization that the officials were being Confucian in outlook after all, by urging the Emperor to show filial respect for the wishes of his ancestors. However, the officials' insistence that the imperial succession was the "root of the state" clearly violates a cardinal Confucian maxim, that the root of the state is the people.

The censorial attack on the eunuch Wei Chung-hsien during the 1620's culminated Ming officials' many warnings against eunuch influence. Eunuchs had contributed to the ruin of earlier dynasties, notably the Han and the T'ang; and the tyrannical Hung-wu Emperor had been clear-sighted enough to insist that palace eunuchs be limited in numbers and restrained from administrative activities. But his successors did not comply with these particular "laws of the dynastic founders," and authority repeatedly fell into eunuch hands. Historians agree that eunuch influence was significantly facilitated by the establishment in 1429 of a palace school for eunuchs. This violated the Hung-wu Emperor's doctrine that eunuchs should be kept illiterate, and it made possible the extensive eunuch interference in administration that marked the whole last half of the Ming era. So far as I can ascertain, no official protested against the establishment of the school. Perhaps officials at this time put their trust in the Confucian doctrine that education brings moral improvement. But as the eunuchs' influence on government increased, the officials did increasingly protest against it. They accused individual eunuchs of personal immorality, and they objected on moral grounds to many of the things eunuchs did. In general remonstrances against eunuch influence, however, they seldom relied on Confucian arguments—for example, that eunuchs, being by their nature the most unprincipled, subservient, and self-seeking of state employees, could be expected to exploit the people mercilessly rather than provide moral examples for them. Instead, they relied on the Legalist arguments that had been so well understood by the Hung-wu Emperor. They argued that eunuchs by their nature tended to usurp imperial authority and hence endangered the dynasty (as distinct from the people).[56] "They ought altogether to be kept at a distance, not being permitted to get control of affairs," one early official warned. "The events of Han and T'ang provide clear warnings."[57] The seventeenth-century denunciations of Wei Chung-hsien were in the same vein. His immorality was denounced, true; but the argument relied on most heavily was that he had usurped imperial authority.[58]

Similar Legalist-sounding arguments can be found, intermixed with Confucian-sounding ones, in the proposals for new policies and for more effective implementing of existing policies with which censorial officials deluged the throne throughout the Ming period.

Many censorial proposals, as well as direct remonstrances, reveal a genuinely Confucian concern for the popular well-being. Censorial officials, for one thing, often urged tax remissions for the people in areas where there had been natural disasters.[59] In the 1620's, when defense needs brought about general tax increases, censorial pressure for reductions and remissions became intense. The T'ien-ch'i Emperor responded that the censors and supervising secretaries—like the Confucian-minded scholars of 81 B.C. in the view of the Han ministers—were unrealistic and refused to recognize the practical problems of national defense. And the Emperor was similarly unimpressed by censorial suggestions that new financial needs be met, not by new taxes imposed on the people, but by palace economies.[60]

The treatment of prisoners was another subject that consistently aroused censorial officials to plead for humaneness in accordance with the Confucian tradition. They objected to the use of such torture instruments as the infamous cangue, and they repeatedly asked for medical assistance to sick prisoners.[61]

But Legalist attitudes were also regularly manifested in censorial proposals. They consistently appeared, for example, in proposals about national defense. The T'ien-ch'i Emperor may have thought his officials were impractical in this regard, but the "True Records" show that censors and supervising secretaries were in fact staunch champions of military preparedness—not only preparedness against outside invasion but preparedness against domestic rebellions. The old Confucian doctrine that moral virtue triumphs over force had apparently been completely discarded; not a single censorial proposal that I have encountered is based even indirectly on this doctrine. Instead, the censorial officials repeatedly urged that public order be forcibly maintained and the dynasty preserved. Though they generally seemed to believe that these ends could be achieved without increasing the people's burdens, as we have just seen, they adamantly demanded more defense funds, more effective recruitment and training, more effective checks against troop desertions, and so on. One censor in 1622 even proposed that taxes be specially increased to provide for an empire-wide local militia system, a proposal that is reported to have delighted the Emperor.[62]

Even as early as the 1420's and 1430's, when there was no significant outside threat to China and there was a notably high level of domestic contentment, censorial officials nevertheless were constantly harping on military preparedness and the possibility of domestic rebellion. Though much "banditry" could be attributed to popular distress and hence, according to Han Confucianism, interpreted as manifestations of Heaven's displeasure with the government, the censors and supervising secretaries generally advocated severely repressive policies. In 1428, for example, a censor-in-chief submitted the following proposal:

For the capture of fierce bandits there already are rules about promotions and rewards, but the law for catching bandits should emphasize severity. If it is severe, then men will not dare to become bandits and the catchers on their part will entirely exhaust their strength. Henceforth, whenever fierce bandits plunder and pillage an area, officials and lesser functionaries of the guards and civil offices and also the village and neighborhood chiefs should all be sent out to serve as soldiers so that captures might be effected. If they make captures within two months they will escape punishment, but if they have failed to do so when the time limit has expired, then, in accordance with the rules, they should be turned over for punishment. Moreover, when fierce bandits have been captured they should be asked during trial to identify the guards or battalions or subprefectures or counties in which they were formerly registered. If they had been soldiers, then those in charge of the appropriate troops should be punished. If they had been civilians, then the appropriate civil officials, lesser functionaries, village elders, and neighborhood chiefs should be punished. If this is done then men will know what to dread.[63]

The proposal shows an obvious correlation with the Legalist doctrine of handling men by rewards and, especially, punishments; and of meting out punishments rigorously according to fixed principles of group responsibility.

Another sphere in which Ming censorial officials showed a Legalist bias is that of administrative procedures. In general, the extreme systematization of procedures and the inflexible, objective standards of performance that characterize the Legalist doctrines were consistently advocated by Ming censors and supervising secretaries. Again and again we find them proposing elaborate procedural rules to be imposed on the officialdom[64]—understandably enough, since such rules (together with the objective evaluation techniques they would give rise to) would immensely simplify their own job of denouncing wrongdoing. This is perhaps one of the most obvious instances of the prevalence of Legalist-like attitudes in the bureaucracy.

The result of the Confucian-Legalist mixture that thus dominated censorial thinking was often a proposal to obtain ends sanctified by classical Confucianism by means advocated in Legalism. In 1624, for example, the censor-in-chief Kao P'an-lung proposed detailed regulations about local government that were prefaced with these remarks:

. . . If the subprefectures and counties are worthily administered, then the people are contented. If not, then the people are not contented. However, the empire includes 221 subprefectures and 1,166 counties. How is it possible in all cases to obtain those who are worthy of employment? Those who are worthy regard the ruler as Heaven, which cannot be deceived, and regard the people as their sons, who cannot be injured. Their observance of the law and performance of duty proceed from the fact that what the mind cannot endure is not done. Lesser men, being given something to admire, are stimulated to do good; being given something to dread, they *do not dare do what is not good*. But totally inferior men do not know what their duties are or what the regulations are; they merely give rein to their desires. This is preying on the people. Therefore, in governing, one should select those who are worthy and talented, get rid of those who prey on the people, and restrain mediocre men. *Mediocre men are the most numerous in the empire. They should be restrained by laws*, which do no harm to the worthy. Thus the prefect restrains the subprefectures and counties; the circuit intendants restrain the prefectures; and the governor and regional inspector restrain all without exception. These restraints cause everyone to observe the law, as in the case of farmlands having dividing lines which no one thinks to overstep. Then the empire is well governed![65]

Kao's emphasis on the contentment of the people, and a large proportion of the terminology he employs, reflect classical Confucian ideals. But his assumption that the masses of people are amoral and must be restrained by laws so that they "do not dare do what is not good" is altogether Legalist.

The same Legalist cynicism was dominant, in a different context, in a suggestion by the early-sixteenth-century supervising secretary Liu Ch'ih. When sweeping staff changes were being considered, Liu advised the Cheng-te Emperor to retain old hands in top-level administrative posts rather than bring in new blood. He did not argue that the existing executives were virtuous or that their experience was valuable. He merely suggested, curtly and cynically, that "it is better to keep a sated tiger than a hungry one"[66]—an apt maxim for any Legalist-minded employer of men, but hardly the voice of Confucian idealism.

CONCLUSION

China's traditional censorial institution has been extravagantly praised and extravagantly criticized. Some authorities have considered it an instrument of monarchical control over the bureaucracy, whereas others have considered it an instrument of bureaucratic control over the monarch. These conflicting evaluations naturally derive from the fact that the censorial system—like Imperial Confucianism as a whole—was based on discordant ideological premises. It was not the idealized creation of either Confucius or Kung-sun Yang; it was a complex of inherited practices that were influenced by both. From one point of view it was a Confucian institution, and from another it was a Legalist institution.

The individual censorial official was representative of the whole body of traditional Chinese bureaucrats in that, as an Imperial Confucianist, he was neither a genuine classical Confucian nor a genuine Legalist in outlook. His was not an either-or situation. His impeachment function stemmed from Legalist roots, but his manner of exercising it drew heavily on classical Confucianism. Conversely, his remonstrance function was primarily Confucian in origin, but his manner of remonstrating was often consonant with pure Legalism. We can do no more than speculate about his actual motivations.

Students of Ming documents are easily tempted to conclude that Ming censorial officials—and Ming bureaucrats in general—were in fact principally Legalist-minded in their motivations. The abject servility that characterized ministerial statements to the throne in this period is very striking. Not only were they filled with excessively humble terminology; they consistently attributed to the emperor—the "ruler-father" in their words—wisdom, goodness, and all other admirable qualities. However pointed the criticism, it was always sheathed in implications that the emperor, though wise and good, had been misled and deceived by unscrupulous attendants or advisers. However degenerate the emperor, he was always pictured in official documents as a paragon of virtue whose gracious benefits no minister could ever wholly requite. Thus, in practice, Ming ministers perfectly exemplified Han Fei's Legalist maxim that "the business of the persuader is to embellish the pride and obliterate the shame of the persuaded," and their servile expressions implied complete acceptance of the Legalist concept of ruler-subject relations.

Given the circumstances, these expressions of Legalist import could perhaps be dismissed as insincere conventions—as tactical devices employed by ministers with tongue in cheek because they could not be avoided. The evidence strongly suggests, however, that most of these protestations of abject devotion were perfectly sincere. Consider, for example, the case of the censor Tso Kuang-tou, who saw service under three emperors and was finally tortured to death in prison in 1625 at the instigation of the eunuch Wei Chung-hsien and by order of the T'ien-ch'i Emperor. After weeks of almost daily torture, on the point of death and apparently without any hope for his own survival or for his family's escape from ruin, he scribbled a series of private notes to his sons that include these statements:

At this moment my pain and distress are extreme; I can no longer even walk a step. In the middle of the night the pain gets still worse. If I want water to drink, none is at hand. Death! Death! *Only thus can I make recompense to the Emperor and to the two imperial ancestors.* . . . The bones of my whole body are broken, and my flesh is bloodlogged. . . . This loyal heart came to be at odds with powerful villains and brought about this sore calamity. All sorts of punishments I have willingly endured. Since I have already argued at the risk of my life, why need I shrink from running against the spear and dying? *My body belongs to my ruler-father.* I am lucky I shall not die in the arms of my wife and children; for I have found the proper place to die! *I only regret that this blood-filled heart has not been able to make recompense to my ruler,* and that my aged parents cannot once again see my face. This will be my remorse in Hades! . . . My misery is extreme; my pain is extreme. Why do I live on? Why do I cling to life? Death! Only thus can I make recompense to the Emperor and to the two imperial ancestors in Heaven.[67]

In the circumstances, hypocrisy is almost inconceivable.

The ruler-minister relationship envisioned by Confucius and Mencius had clearly succumbed; Tso's abject protestations of devotion to the throne are the badge of the Legalist sycophant. Paradoxically enough, however, any early Legalist would have repudiated Tso instantly, whereas Confucius would undoubtedly have acknowledged kinship with him. For Tso—and Ming ministers generally—did not mouth these phrases opportunistically. They *believed* them. And the capacity for selfless commitment that this implies is peculiarly Confucian and utterly foreign to the ideal minister in the Legalist conception.

Perhaps it is primarily in this sense that Imperial Confucianists remained Confucians at heart after all.

David S. Nivison

HO-SHEN AND HIS ACCUSERS: IDEOLOGY AND POLITICAL BEHAVIOR IN THE EIGHTEENTH CENTURY

> I turn my attention to a political state in which a ruler, jealous of his rights, and a live public opinion are in conflict with each other. The people are indignant against an official whom they hate, and demand his dismissal; and in order not to show that he is compelled to respect the public wish, the autocrat will expressly confer upon the official some great honour, for which there would otherwise have been no occasion.
>
> Sigmund Freud, *The Interpretation of Dreams*

During the last score of years in the eighteenth century, great power and influence in the Chinese state came into the hands of one Ho-shen, a Manchu favorite of the Ch'ien-lung emperor Kao-tsung. It is the general opinion of historians that Ho-shen was extremely corrupt. When his life ended in 1799 (by his own hand, and with the gracious permission of Kao-tsung's successor, the Chia-ch'ing emperor), he had amassed a personal fortune second only to that of his imperial master.

Meanwhile, the chroniclers record for our instruction a distressing tale of misfortune for China. The Chinese bureaucracy during these twenty years and more was rocked by case after case of official malfeasance. Vast sums were embezzled by officials under constant pressure to secure themselves by gifts and bribes to Ho-shen and his immediate subordinates. Everywhere local treasuries were depleted. The groaning people, goaded to desperation by the rapacity to which their magistrates were driven, turned to revolt. By 1800, a half-dozen provinces in the center of the country were torn by rebellion which for five years had raged out of control. The glory of the Ch'ing had passed. It was the beginning of the long way down.

So history has it.

In this paper I propose to do three things. First, I shall attempt to delineate Ho-shen as his contemporaries and subsequent historians have seen him. This effort raises a question. Why did a man so harshly judged continue in power as long as he did with very little significant opposition?

Second, I shall explore what I take to be the necessary basis for an intelligent answer to this question. This will lead me to examine the ideology governing the relationship between "prince" and "minister" in the particular form it took in the Ch'ing period, and the attitude toward this relationship taken by Ch'ing emperors in the eighteenth century.

Finally, in the hope of throwing light on this relationship in the actual behavior of the officials and the emperor, I shall examine a number of episodes in which Ho-shen was directly or indirectly attacked or criticized.

Ho-shen, a Manchu of the Plain Red Banner, was born in 1750. In 1775, when he was twenty-five (and the emperor sixty-four), he was an officer in the Imperial Equipage Department and a guard at the palace gate. He had been a student in a government school, and had read, it is said, the Four Books and the Five Classics, though we are assured that this was and remained the extent of his education. His duties brought him into frequent personal contact with the emperor, and he quickly attracted His Majesty's attention (according to one anecdote, by recognizing a quotation from the *Lun-yü* which the emperor had used).[1] There are darker accounts of the emperor's interest in Ho-shen. Ho-shen was young, handsome, smooth-tongued. In personal appearance he resembled (it was rumored) a certain concubine in the menage of Kao-tsung's father, the Yung-cheng emperor. Kao-tsung had entered into a liaison with this lady when a young man; his empress had later brought about her destruction.[2] Such stories by their nature cannot be checked. But their existence indicates the way in which Ho-shen's reputation has developed.

Ho-shen's rise was startlingly rapid. He was at once taken into the emperor's immediate entourage. Early in 1776 he was named to a vice-presidency in the Board of Revenue, and then appointed to the Grand Council. In 1780, he became president of the Board of Revenue, and his son was betrothed to the emperor's favorite daughter, the Princess Ho-hsiao. By 1784, he was in the Grand Secretariat, and had been shifted to the presidency of the Board of Civil Office. In the course of this career he held many concurrent literary and military posts as well as posts in the Imperial Household, and advanced through a succession of titles of nobility, reaching the grade of duke in 1798. Ho-shen quickly showed himself to be without military talent; indeed his performance in the suppression of a Mohammedan revolt in Kansu in 1781, and his subsequent attempts to shift blame onto others, caused the emperor momentarily to censure him.[3] But this inadequacy may actually have been to his advantage. Subsequently, when there were disturbances in the realm or campaigns abroad—and military activity of one sort or another was almost constant during this period—Ho-shen could count on being able to stay at the capital, where he was able to do much better for himself.

His position in the emperor's confidence was such that he is said to have been able "to cause the advancement or ruin of officials almost at will."[4] Sir George Staunton, who accompanied MacCartney's embassy to Jehol in 1793, writes of Ho-shen that "he might be said to possess, in fact, under the Emperor, the whole power of the empire."[5] Although Ho-shen was not actually a titular board president after 1787, he was often directed by the emperor to "handle the affairs" of important boards concurrently with his other duties. For a brief time during the years 1797–98 he was in this way in de facto control of the Board of Civil Office, the Board of Punishments, and the Board of Revenue; and it is in fact one of the accusations made against him by the Chia-ch'ing emperor that at this time he took into his own hands the management of the imperial finances, submitting reports from the Board of Revenue himself and "refusing to allow his associates on the Board to consult with him on a single word."[6]

Ho-shen is said to have placed his "henchmen" at once in key positions throughout the empire and to have put virtually the entire civil service in such dependence on his pleasure that they could maintain themselves only with lavish bribes, which eventually reached Ho-shen's own pocket—a state of affairs which obliged officials to embezzle funds constantly from the public treasuries and to multiply the normal exactions upon the people. Even military commanders in the field, men busy suppressing rebellions that this harsh treatment of the people provoked, are said to have been forced to draw upon their supply funds for presents to Ho-shen, thus dangerously weakening the imperial armies.[7] His movable property alone, at the time his estate was confiscated, amounted to 80,000,000 taels (Staunton gives this as the equivalent of £23,330,000), or more than the entire stand-by treasury surplus of the state at the time of his rise to power.[8] The presumption is that this wealth was ill-gotten, simply because there can be no other explanation.

Ho-shen is presented as a man without culture or refinement, incapable by nature of an interest in anything less ignoble than the accumulation of material goods. Of the institutionalized gift-tribute (*kung*) which high provincial officials throughout the realm were obliged to

send to the Imperial Household, it is said that the better half ended in
Ho-shen's hands. Anecdotes indicate that he had the run of the palace.
Sun Shih-i (1720–96), who is said by some to have been one of Ho-
shen's "clique,"[9] was reporting in person to the throne after his unsuccessful campaign in Annam (i.e., in 1789), and while waiting for audience outside the palace he encountered Ho-shen. Sun of course had
with him a present for His Majesty. Ho-shen was curious and Sun
showed it to him—it was a snuff box, carved out of a pearl the size of an
egg. Ho-shen marveled at it and said, "Do you suppose I could ask you
to give it to me?" Sun replied, "I've already told the emperor about it
and I'm about to present it to him; I am afraid it's impossible." Ho-shen
smiled slyly: "I was only joking. What do you take me for?" Several
days later, both happened again to be waiting in front of the palace,
and Ho-shen said, "The other day I too got a pearl snuff box, but I don't
know how it compares with the one you gave the emperor." He produced it (it was the identical piece that Sun had presented to the
throne); Sun, puzzled, supposed that the emperor had given it to him,
but on checking found this not to be the case.[10] That Ho-shen had his
own way in the Imperial Household is the implication of the fourth of
the "great offenses" charged against him by his imperial accuser in 1799:
"The young females that were educated for the service of the palace
he took from thence, and appropriated to himself as concubines, without any sensation of shame or regard to decorum."[11]

Another story is related by the scholar and philosopher Chiao Hsün
(1763–1820). A pearl dealer whom he encountered showed him a small
box containing a satin pouch, in which there was a pill made of gold.
Broken open, the pill turned out to contain a large pearl. These were
prepared, the dealer explained, as presents for Ho-shen, and were
always quickly bought up by eager customers. Ho-shen, it seems, took
one of these pills every morning, believing that they greatly sharpened
his powers of memory. Only the newest pearls could be used in the
fashioning of these costly aide-mémoires; old ones, or pearls that had
already been pierced, lacked the mysterious effect.[12]

That Ho-shen was a man of scant cultivation, indeed almost a court
jester type, capable of extreme inelegance if not outright vulgarity, is
suggested by another near-contemporary source, namely the miscellaneous notes of that haughty, quick-tempered, disaffected Manchu
prince, Chao-lien (1780–1833). "Although no minister ever attained a
higher position than Ho-shen," Chao-lien writes, "nonetheless he was
singularly deficient in the qualities and bearing of a great official. He
was fond of using the language of the market place to try to be amusing.
Once he was giving a lecture on ceremonial in the Ch'ien-ch'ing palace

(the "Palace of Celestial Purity"), before a large number of prominent and cultured high officials and princes. He grinned and said 'Today we'll do like Sun Wu-tzu when he taught the girls to be soldiers.'" (Sun Wu, who lived in the sixth century B.C. and is traditionally supposed to have written the *Ping Fa*, an ancient work on military tactics, is said once to have attempted on a dare to train a group of girls from the harem of the prince of Wu. He appointed two of the prince's favorite ladies as leaders of the troop and began to drill them; the girls giggled; he at once executed the two leaders and restored order.) Again, writes Chao-lien, "Annam sent to the court as a tribute-gift a golden statue of a lion, which was hollow at the base. Ho-shen showed amazement and said, "Too bad it's hollow in the middle; if it weren't, we'd get an awful lot of gold!' —making the foreign officials sneer at him for being so crude and shallow."[13]

Ho-shen's brother, Ho-lin (d. 1796), inevitably shared in the family good fortune and enjoyed important military positions and high noble rank. Even Ho-shen's household stewards and more tenuous dependents were able to acquire wealth and assume a degree of swagger which seems to have provoked much talk and resentment. This provided the opportunity, in 1786, for a censor, Ts'ao Hsi-pao (1719–92) to arrest and flog one of Ho-shen's stewards on charges of displaying "in his clothing, equipage, and residence" luxuries not permitted for a man of his station.[14] (This incident, which was an open thrust at Ho-shen, will be examined further on.)

In 1791 Ho-shen heard a false report that Wang Lun (d. 1774), a sectarian leader who had rebelled and briefly assumed the imperial title in Shantung in 1774, was still alive.[15] Working the report for whatever it might be worth, Ho sent eleven Peking constables as his personal agents to Shantung to investigate secretly. In Po-shan district, two of these constables became drunk and disorderly. When the recently appointed magistrate, Wu I (1745–99), had them arrested, they arrogantly claimed immunity because of their connection with Ho-shen. Wu I nonetheless had them flogged. The governor of Shantung, fearing reprisals from Ho-shen, thereupon recommended to the capital that Wu be dismissed, and Ho, in virtual control of the Board of Civil Office although not then its president, saw to it that Wu's dismissal was effected (on the conveniently vague charge of "arbitrarily exercising the cudgel," although Wu in fact had been legally exercising his authority). This incident must have been talked about very widely, for Wu was well-known as a scholar and was a personal friend of many prominent literary men of the day.[16]

In 1796 the censor Hsieh Chen-ting (1753–1809) arrested and ordered the flogging of a younger brother of one of Ho-shen's concubines, who was in the habit of driving a carriage recklessly through the streets of Peking, heedless of the safety of pedestrians and in violation of sumptuary regulations. Unfortunately, Hsieh chose to have the incriminating carriage burned publicly in the street; so that when, at Ho-shen's behest, an investigation was ordered, Hsieh was in the embarrassing position of having destroyed the only evidence supporting his case. Consequently he was dismissed, though this incident too apparently became speedily famous, winning for Hsieh the sobriquet "the carriage-burning censor" (*shao-ch'e yü-shih*). Unlike most of the handful of men who dared to attack or bait Ho-shen, Hsieh outlived him, and had the satisfaction of being reinstated in 1799 by the Chia-ch'ing emperor after submitting a long memorial on the ills of the country under Ho-shen's domination.[17]

Another story portrays Ho-shen as a man who would and did go to any extreme to suppress criticism of himself. In 1793, a certain salt commissioner of Liang-Huai was prosecuted for illegally transferring 220,000 taels of salt-tax funds. When his private accounts were examined, they were found to contain an entry of a gift of 1,000 taels "to his excellency Mr. Fu." The gift (or bribe), it is said, was actually made to Fu-ch'ang-an (d. 1817), a brother of the Manchu general Fu-k'ang-an (d. 1796) and a close associate of Ho-shen in the Grand Council. It was necessary for Ho-shen to cover up for Fu-ch'ang-an. Conveniently enough, the governor of nearby Chekiang province, a man for whom Ho had a long-standing dislike, was a Manchu named Fu-sung; Ho accordingly had one of his "henchmen," another salt commissioner, testify that the bribe had gone to this "Mr. Fu" and no other. Fu-sung was thereupon arrested and ordered to the capital to be questioned by the emperor. One would naturally expect Fu-sung, given audience under these circumstances, to have a few things to say about Ho-shen; unfortunately, he let it be known that he intended to make his forthcoming conversation with the emperor an interesting one. Ho-shen was alarmed, and managed, by rewording the accusation, so to arouse the emperor's anger that he ordered Fu-sung to commit suicide at once. This grim tale happens to be fictitious (Fu-sung was in fact recalled from the Chekiang governorship in 1786, and so could hardly have been on the scene in 1793); when it was invented one can only guess. But its currency shows the extreme of evil which people were willing to ascribe to the emperor's favorite.[18]

Some accounts suggest that Kao-tsung was aware of Ho-shen's character, and even of his criminal culpability, implying that Ho-shen maintained some peculiar and unnatural hold on his master. At the time of the prosecution of Kuo-t'ai in 1782 (see p. 233), according to one story, the emperor had documentary evidence that Ho-shen was attempting to thwart the investigation; yet not only was he not censured, but he was shortly afterward made Grand Guardian of the Heir Apparent. The account in question has the tone of hearsay; but it is likely, at least, that it was widely believed; and it must be granted that the occasional mild reproofs administered by the emperor to Ho-shen were often followed by lavish honors.

In view of the prevalence of this picture of Ho-shen as a man of unlimited power, vast greed, and no compensating abilities or personal qualities, a man, moreover, with a strange hold over an aged and probably senile emperor, it is not surprising that contemporaries and historians alike have charged him with virtually sole responsibility for the misfortunes that were more and more obviously besetting the Chinese state in the last years of the eighteenth century. These misfortunes were not inconsiderable. Financially the empire was nearly exhausted; officials had become so venal that it was not clear to what extent the court could control its own officers; and internal rebellions were becoming more frequent, more serious, and exceedingly costly. The White Lotus rebellion, which raged through the provinces of Szechwan, Hupeh, Honan, Kansu, and Shensi from 1795 to 1803, had cost the state 100,000,000 taels by 1800 (and it must be supposed that actual expenses ran far higher than those officially recorded). It was reasonable to see these aspects of the deteriorated state of the country as interrelated. "Officials force the people to revolt" was one of the rebels' slogans. Official venality and the cost of suppressing revolt were obviously both causes of the emptiness of the treasuries. "The deterioration in the civil service," a moral collapse on the part of the whole governing group in the country, seemed to be the root of the matter.[19]

This, at least, was the way it appeared to one highly articulate contemporary observer, Chang Hsüeh-ch'eng (1738–1801). Chang lived in Hupeh during much of the 1790's while the White Lotus rebellion was brewing. He was a friend of Wu I and of others who had directly felt Ho-shen's power. In 1799, after Ho-shen's forced suicide, the Chia-ch'ing emperor proclaimed his desire to receive freely given advice on the country's problems. Chang had no position and was not entitled to address the throne himself, nor did he feel able to trust any of the official "avenues of remonstrance"; he was slightly acquainted, however, with Wang Chieh (1725–1805), who had long been a member of the Grand Council and Grand Secretariat. So he composed a long "Letter to those in charge of the government, on the problems of the present time" and sent it, with a covering letter, to Wang. His thesis was that deterioration of standards of honor in the civil service was at the root of the problem of deficiencies and rebellion, and he opposed a superficial solution of either of these two problems. To force officials to make good the deficiencies would merely drive them to plundering the people, whereas rebellion could not be dealt with until the rebel leaders had been deprived of their main excuse—that "officials have forced the people to rebel." And what, in turn, was the cause of this deterioration in the civil service? The cause was Ho-shen, source of universal corruption:

Public funds have flowed from the treasuries until now they are bone dry; and the cause of all this can be indicated in the palm of one's hand. From 1780 through 1798 Ho-shen dominated the government, and for almost thirty years, officials high and low have covered up for one another, and have thought only of grasping for bribes and of personal gain. At first they nibbled away like worms, gradually taking more and more until they were gulping like whales. In the beginning, their embezzlements could be reckoned in hundreds and thousands of taels, but presently nothing less than ten thousand would attract notice. Soon amounts ran to scores of thousands, then to hundreds of thousands, and then to millions. . . . High officials, blackened with avarice and habituated to extravagance, have come to regard a present of ten thousand pieces of silver as if it were no more than a casual present of a box of food.[20]

And even before Ho-shen's fall there were dark hints. Chang's friend Wang Hui-tsu (1731–1807), in his book "Learning to Govern" (*Hsüeh-chih I-shuo*, preface dated 1793), has revealing things to say about the quality of the civil service farther down in the hierarchy. On "the difficulty of obtaining government aides of good character," he writes as follows:

Alas! Of ethics in the profession of aide it is difficult to speak. Formerly, when I was twenty-two or twenty-three and was first studying to be an aide, those who took positions as judicial aides or tax accountants conducted themselves with dignity as would a guest or a teacher in another's house. From dawn till dusk they would stay at their tables handling documents, not amusing themselves at dice and chess or wasting money drinking with one another. Whenever there was some public business, they would cite the law and talk the matter over, and if some higher official disagreed with them they would have the courage to defend their opinions. Their superiors treated them respectfully, and followed their advice with trust. If they were treated disrespectfully or had any of their advice rejected by their superiors, they would resign. If there chanced to be one or two who failed to take themselves seriously, all the others would point them out in ridicule; there were never any flatterers. When I reached the age of thirty-seven or thirty-eight, it was still like this; but shortly thereafter, people became slightly less strict in their relationship with their employers. A few years later, a man who remained personally upright was regarded as unrealistic and impractical, and throughout the land an aide who would stand firm under pressure could hardly be found. Finally it became so bad that business was arranged by bribery or unethical agreements, and men formed cliques and alliances to protect one another. Not even two or three out of ten behaved uprightly. New men entering this profession would usually pick up these evil ways from their mentors and would not know any better. . . .[21]

Arithmetic does the rest. Wang had "reached the age of thirty-seven or thirty-eight" in 1767–68; "a few years later" Ho-shen's rise to power began. Wang, it should be added, was himself a professional judicial aide.

If the picture of Ho-shen as exerting a poisonous and pervasively corrupting influence on official morals emerged almost at once, modern Chinese historians, looking back on the progressively more enfeebled condition of the Chinese state after 1800, have had even stronger judgments to make: "By the beginning of the Chia-ch'ing period," writes Hsiao I-shan, "the vigor of the K'ang-hsi, Yung-cheng, and Ch'ien-lung reigns had been almost completely destroyed by the hand of one man—Ho-shen."[22]

It is natural to ask whether this picture is wholly just or accurate. On a number of counts, certainly, it deserves to be suspected. The idea that China's difficulties could be blamed almost wholly on the evil character of a single man is too nearly in accord with standard modes of Chinese historical explanation to be passed over without scrutiny. Chinese historical causes have always been moral ones; even when relatively abstract tendencies are seen as explaining events, they tend to be moral essences. Did Ho-shen's greed cause the White Lotus rebellion, the military weakness, the treasury deficiencies, the prevalence of corruption at the end of the eighteenth century? There are too many other explanations clamoring for consideration, and some, certainly, deserving it.

Was Ho-shen the sort of uncultured buffoon that reports suggest him to be, or did some of his more salient disagreeable characteristics lead his detractors to misrepresent him as a stereotype of the detestable? (We will recall that the Sung statesman Wang An-shih has acquired, in traditional story, an uncouth manner and a habit of appearing in court without taking sufficient care of his personal appearance.) Members of the British embassy, who in 1793 had opportunity to observe Ho-shen at close range, reported that his "manners . . . were not less pleasing than his understanding was penetrating and acute. He seemed, indeed, to possess the qualities of a consummate statesman."[23] Staunton also reports a story that Ho-shen was once, when the emperor suspected him of some deceit, reduced to "his original low station for about a fortnight," until the matter was cleared up to the emperor's satisfaction.[24] Certainly Ho-shen was not completely invulnerable. Nor was his power complete in the civil service. The most derogatory stories about him

plainly imply that there were other, upright officials who were opposed
to him.

What we can be sure of is that Ho-shen was widely hated. Many
men who regarded themselves and one another as men of conscience
believed that he was utterly bad and that he was wrecking the country.
And whatever doubt may attach to the actual facts about Ho-shen, it
seems likely that he was evil enough to give these beliefs a respectable
amount of substance. We might expect, from what some of these men
wrote and said later, that they would have been highly articulate in
opposing him while he lived and held power. Yet the public moves
that were made against him were devious in the extreme; and even in
the private writing of the period, one has to settle for such cleverly
concealed adverse judgments as that of Wang Hui-tsu. How shall we
explain this? During the Ming, an age of often brutal autocracy, pro-
testing officials would have massed before the palace gates by the hundreds. Men educated in the tradition of Confucian political ideals have
not always been cowards; it seems hasty to suppose that they suddenly
became cowards in the 1780's. In answering this question we need to
examine more closely how Ho-shen's opponents actually behaved in
concrete instances; and, first of all, to consider with care what were the
tacit restraints, as well as the ideals and obligations, which would have
been accepted by a conscientious Confucian "subject" in Ho-shen's time.

THE IDEOLOGY OF THE EMPEROR-OFFICIAL RELATIONSHIP
IN THE EIGHTEENTH CENTURY

It is a very ancient assumption that a worthy and loyal official ought
to be able to speak out when his prince is acting under bad guidance
or from a wrong viewpoint, or is exhibiting personal weakness. Usually
this involves personal risk for the servitor, but loyalty to his prince demands that he take the risk. If the prince is utterly bad, reproving him
means certain death. In this case, death must be faced and accepted.
(Consider the retainers of Wei Wu-chi who advised him to return to
Ta-liang and defend his ancestral state, in spite of his threat to execute
anyone interceding for the King of Wei.) Sometimes loyalty, prompt-
ing outspokenness, is not to the *prince*, but to *principle*, either to one's
political philosophy or *tao* (symbolized in the story of Pien Ho), or
simply to truth (as in the story of Nan-shih). But the result is the same:
the good official braves the displeasure of the ruler and speaks the truth
as he sees it, regardless of consequences.

From the ruler's side, it is assumed that a good ruler should be able
to attract worthy men, and induce them to speak out without reserve.
If their principles prevent worthy men from coming forward, the ruler

will visit them, showing them the greatest respect. By this mutual offer of sacrifice—the ruler offering up his prestige and the servitor his very life—both servitor and prince gain unlimited virtue.

The foregoing is an ancient, pre-imperial ideal (not necessarily mirrored in practice), articulated at a time when many princes were competing for the services of men of talent. Under the empire, it became less possible to criticize the ruler directly, for his position and prestige were enormously magnified. One criticism of an evil ruler had been that he puts his trust in villains. The emperor, however, was in a more exalted position than earlier monarchs; he was a "later sage." It was accordingly more expedient to criticize the villains instead of the ruler, and to treat shortcomings in the ruler or his government as the effect of bad influence, bad advice, or ministerial misbehavior.

This was still dangerous, since shortcomings are after all shortcomings, and having one's failings or failures pointed out is painful, whatever the rationalization. Furthermore, to criticize a minister is to criticize the emperor's choice of that minister (a sage, even a "later sage," is supposed to be infallible in his judgments of men, though he may piously claim not to be). Since criticism of this sort was dangerous, it could be virtuous. As before, it meant an offer of sacrifice out of loyalty either to prince or to principle. It was doubly dangerous because officials in power had privileged access to the emperor, the source of authority, and often controlled a state apparatus through which they could strike back. A favorite minister would, of course, use his allies in the bureaucracy and in the emperor's entourage. A critic, likewise, could not hope to succeed unless he had friends. Whatever may have been true in more ancient times, it is clear that political criticism and political activity in an imperial bureaucracy had to function within a context of factional rivalry.

This situation was inevitably vexatious to a ruler pretending to be a prince of great virtue. All factions, in the nature of things, had one interest in common: seeing to it that the emperor was the least informed person in the state. Instead of speaking out forthrightly and without hesitation, dissatisfied persons of whatever clique kept counsel with their friends until the right moment arrived. Instead of being able to draw men out, the ruler found that they shrank back. Furthermore, factional rivalry meant confusion, potential disorder, tension, bickering, the opposite of the universal harmony which a sage was supposed to be able to bring about by the strength of his virtue.

Relevant to this problem was an institutional development of very ancient origin. The security and status of the subject performing the function of remonstrance were traditionally guaranteed by his being

given a position as a sort of official gadfly. Whatever the original intention may have been behind this development, it could have the effect
of enabling the critic to function independently of clique support. Moreover, the traditional sanctity investing high-minded criticism of the
throne was widely extended. Anyone whose qualifications for office
were intellectual—a degree holder, a han-lin, a grand secretary—might in
suitable circumstances be regarded as a *yen-kuan* ("speaking official")
or *chien-ch'en* ("remonstrating official"), even though these terms applied properly only to censors, "omissioners," etc., and only these more
official *yen-kuan* had the privilege of addressing remonstrances to the
throne directly without being expressly invited to do so.

But the *yen-kuan* institution had its shortcomings, precisely because
of the exclusive access to the throne enjoyed by a *yen-kuan* in the strict
sense. Persons wishing to achieve some political end but not entitled
to approach the throne had to act through a *yen-kuan*. A faction might
acquire power by getting control of one of these pipelines to the emperor's ear. And from the censor's own point of view, the office of
tweaker of the imperial whiskers was bound to have its precarious side,
no matter how institutionalized or sanctified it might be. It would always be more safely exercised if the censor had friends, inside or outside the palace, who would stand up for him if necessary.

We must now examine two related ambiguities. One has to do with
the Confucian ideal of loyalty, the other with the concept of a bureaucratic faction. Loyalty could imply, and on the whole Confucians have
preached, that the servitor should insist on what he believes to be right.
To do this is ultimately in the prince's best interest and hence loyal; to
remain silent for fear of censure or punishment is disloyal. But loyalty,
in China and even among Confucians, could have and from ancient
times often did have a common-sense meaning of a different sort: loyal
officers or ministers are those who accept their ruler's "likes and dislikes," defend his preferences in men and policies, and straightforwardly
try to carry out his wishes. Moreover, this common-sense notion of
loyalty is not just a value to be expected in any power structure. For
even by Confucian lights, the more high-minded loyalty of the loyal
critic has in it inescapably an element of *lèse majesté*. The emperor, as
Son of Heaven, is the one man ultimately responsible for the world's
problems. In effect, the loyal critic is claiming a share in this responsibility which by rights is the ruler's.

Turning to the faction concept, we note first that factions have usually
been held to be bad. A ruler, moreover, has practical as well as traditional reasons for suspecting them. Why, after all, should men feel a
need to form a faction unless they wish to defend and further policies

that are unpalatable to the prince? The Mohist chapters on government clearly express this view: allying with one's colleagues is antithetical to the conduct considered right and essential to good order, viz., to hold no information back from the ruler and to accept his preferences and opinions as one's own.

But factions can be defended, and not only because their ranks include so many men esteemed in tradition. For, surely, group defense of the right is theoretically as loyal as individual defense of the right. It has often been possible for historians, and no doubt more often possible for partisans, to see factional rivalry as a struggle between Good and Evil.

Carefully considered arguments in defense of "good" factions have been rare. One of the best is Ou-yang Hsiu's "P'eng-tang Lun," a short but pointed essay "On Factions," which he addressed to the throne in 1044 in the midst of a factional struggle at the Sung court. He asks the emperor not to condemn factional groupings out of hand, but to recognize that some are bad and some are good. "Inferior persons" join in temporary alliances when their material interests converge, but are just as likely to turn on one another later. Such "factions" are not lasting and not genuine, and are rightly suspected. But "superior men" also often form factions, and among such men there can be a real and permanent bond. They are held together by allegiance to a common *tao*; "they are loyal and trustworthy"; their association enhances their individual worth and their ability to serve the state. Historically, rulers who have drawn on the services of good factions have prospered, whereas rulers who have suppressed such factions have come to ruin. Thus, the suppression of the literati group in its struggle with the eunuch party at the end of the Han led to the collapse of that dynasty, and the execution of the leaders of the literati group in 906 was followed directly by the fall of the T'ang.[25]

Note that what binds such men together is loyalty to a self-justifying *tao*, a set of principles that are right because they are right, not because the ruler approves of them. It is the *chün-tzu*, not the *jen-chün*—the gentleman, not the ruler—who chooses this *tao* rather than another. It is this loyalty to principle, Ou-yang tries to imply, that makes such men "loyal and trustworthy" in the political sense.

But it is a paradox of Confucian thought that this traditional notion of loyalty as defense of the right has rarely been accompanied by a realistic awareness that defenders of the right have to act together if they are to be effective. Factional rivalry is almost always thought of as a sordid competition among groups bent merely on advancing their own worldly interests, or at best as characteristic of decadent times in which men have been unable to subordinate their own personal bias to the good of the dynasty and the people.

In the Ch'ing, this residual and not altogether concordant set of political notions was modified in a peculiar way by the logic of Chinese court politics in the seventeenth and eighteenth centuries, as well as by the personal predilections of a series of strong-minded Manchu rulers (and perhaps also by intellectual trends). The Ch'ing was a dynasty of conquest; and although this underlying fact was progressively allowed to become less obvious, the literati, whose prestige and abilities were indispensable to the court, were merely to be used; they were not to be allowed to use their masters. The really important business of government was in the hands of the emperor, his Manchu kinsmen and vassals, and such Chinese as they saw fit to call in as assistants. The importance of Chinese in the higher levels of the state structure steadily increased, but it was a very long time before the court widely sought advice on the problems of the country.

The Ch'ing government at once devoted close attention to the officially maintained schools and the system of instruction which prepared the Chinese for state service. In 1652, an edict regulating the conduct of licentiates reminded them of their privileged status and exhorted them to deport themselves with grateful humility, to respect their parents and teachers, to stay out of court, etc. One of the regulations is noteworthy. "Licentiates are not permitted to address letters to the authorities or submit opinions on any military or civil problem. If in a single instance a licentiate submits his views on such matters, he will be considered in violation of imperial law and will be deprived of his status and punished." A Ming dynasty list of regulations for students promulgated in 1382, in the Hung-wu reign (a period marked for its autocratic tone), is similar but milder. The Ming regulation corresponding to the foregoing prohibition says merely that "while members of the farming, artisan, and merchant classes may express themselves on matters of military and civil concern, licentiates may not." And in the Ming regulations there is another provision conspicuously absent from the Ch'ing set: "If there be worthy men living in retirement who have a refined understanding of the principles of government and who submit their views on the Kingly Way, the local authorities may include their statements in memorials forwarded to the capital, though they may not seal and forward their writings on their own."[26]

Robert Morrison in his *Dictionary* has observed that the Manchu rulers at first did not approve of the pride of the Chinese literati, "who assume a superiority over their fellow citizens, and who affect to guide the understanding and conscience of the nation, and of the sovereign."

And he cites in evidence the action taken by the Yung-cheng emperor in 1726, when the official literary examinations in Chekiang were suspended after two scholars were charged with criticizing the K'ang-hsi emperor. The emperor rounded off the punishment with a lecture: the state, he said, does not support scholars "merely in order to stimulate literary talent," which is useless, but in order to inspire "due respect in the people toward their rulers and ancestors."[27]

The Yung-cheng and Ch'ien-lung emperors used this ironic idiom with skill. They affected to take with utmost seriousness their role as "later sages"—the moral teachers and first intellects of the world. Their tactic for keeping the literati from lecturing the monarch was constantly to lecture the literati. The idiom was ironic because it had been used before. Since T'ang times, doubts had been expressed about the usefulness of mere formal literary skill in a government servant, along with regrets that most men of education thought of nothing else. But these doubts and regrets were ordinarily voiced either by officials criticizing the state examination system for emphasizing literary requirements, or by students and other persons outside the government who felt that the purely formal literary standards barred from the civil service those who had most to contribute in practical ability and political understanding. Now, however, the tables were turned. Manchu emperors could not only insist that students accommodate themselves to a more and more pervasively state-controlled educational system that prepared them for examinations requiring proficiency in rigid literary forms; they could also lecture these students for taking literary form and examination-passing too seriously, to the detriment of "real study"—steeping themselves in good Chu Hsi philosophy and becoming morally better men. Kao-tsung does this exquisitely in a fatherly edict to the Imperial Academy in 1740.[28]

The attitude of the Ch'ing emperors toward factions will come as no surprise. Licentiates were forbidden by the 1652 regulations "to associate with large numbers of others, or to form alliances or join societies." But the story is much larger than this. The Manchus, when they could manage it, shrewdly posed not as alien conquerors of China, but as reformers of a decadent and disordered Chinese state. The last convulsion of the Ming, in the minds at least of subsequent generations of Chinese, had been the protracted and violent struggle between the Tung-lin party and their enemies, notably the eunuch faction. But in spite of the stench the word "eunuch" had for a good Confucian, no "Good vs. Evil" interpretation of this historical era was made by the Ch'ing court (for the position of the Manchus in the state power structure was after all embarrassingly similar to that of the eunuchs under

the Ming). One of Kao-tsung's edicts early in 1781 illustrates the way
in which Ming factionalism was officially regarded. Ch'ien Tsai (1708–
93), vice president of the Board of Ceremonies, who had recently
represented the throne in sacrifices at the tombs of ancient emperors,
had memorialized tendering his opinion that the tomb of the ancient
(mythical) emperor Yao ought to be located not in P'ing-yang (Lin-
fen) in Shansi, as was generally thought, but in P'u-chou in Shantung.
A concourse of grand secretaries and other high capital officials had
discussed and rejected his argument. Ch'ien had not been silenced, but
had pressed his position in another memorial. The matter was gone over
again, and the emperor impatiently decided in favor of his grand secretaries. After going over the exegetical arguments himself (a "later sage"
is among other things the foremost philologist of his time), Kao-tsung
concluded by lecturing Ch'ien for his impertinence:

Ch'ien Tsai is essentially a man of slow understanding, and this matter moreover is merely of archaeological importance. Therefore We do not hold his
fault to be serious. But if he were guilty of this sort of incessant bickering
on administrative matters of importance, We would surely deal severely with
him. At the end of the Ming, whenever some incident occurred, the hubbub
among the officials filled the court. In their many litigations they made use
of their public position to serve their private interests. At first, each one set
up his own clique; this led to the founding of rival factions, with resulting
harm to the government and a constant deterioration in the activities of the
state. We cannot forbear to cite this as a pointed warning.[29]

We find the same disparaging reference to Ming factionalism in an edict
issued by the Yung-cheng emperor in the first year of his reign (dated
May 22, 1723): "Factionalism is an extremely bad pattern of behavior.
At the end of the Ming, cliques were set up and plotted against each
other, with the result that all suffered injury together. This tendency
has not yet been arrested."[30]

Nonetheless, while the pose of the Manchu emperors was that they
were reforming decadent Chinese morals, the truth is that the Ch'ing
had its own peculiar difficulties over factionalism, not (or not only)
among Chinese but among Manchus. Like many dynasties in which
power was consolidated (as it always was) under non-literati leadership, the Ch'ing in the early reigns showed tendencies of what could
crudely be called nascent feudalism. In the early years of the dynasty,
Manchu princes had great power. This power was basically military—
each had absolute control over a banner—but it was readily extended
into the realm of court intrigue. Early emperors were actually selected
by deliberation among members of the imperial clan. Manchu emperors
instinctively and realistically regarded clandestine groupings among

powerful officials and generals as presenting a dangerous threat to their position.

The problem of factionalism took on a slightly new aspect toward the end of the K'ang-hsi reign. Institutions were moving in the direction of more traditional Chinese patterns: the K'ang-hsi emperor attempted to name his own successor, but he was unfortunate in his first choice of an heir apparent. He had many sons, and for a long time it was highly uncertain which of them would succeed him. Each built up around himself a coterie of supporters whose futures were invested in the success of their candidate. The man who won this grim contest was Yin-chen, who became the Yung-cheng emperor (1723–36). He was the only one of the rivals present when the emperor died, and the only prince to witness his father's choice. His supporters in the capital and in the army enabled him to confirm his bid for power. The circumstances were suspicious, and evidence for what happened was mysteriously lacking. It was charged (the accusation set off the first of the cases of literary inquisition for which this and the following reign are remembered) that he had done away with his father to take his brothers by surprise.[31] When the new emperor assumed the throne hostile rumors were everywhere, and the bureaucracy was racked by mutual suspicions and bitterness. In the circumstances the emperor was obliged to assert his authority quickly and incontestably. This he did both by using his power to the full and by the adroit use of ideological measures.

Aware, from successful experience, of the power that could be built up in a faction, the Yung-cheng emperor showed an extreme sensitivity to this problem in the first years of his reign. In 1724 he wrote and promulgated a long essay titled "On Factions" ("P'eng-tang Lun"), stating his position on the matter and, in his capacity as moral teacher of the empire, giving this position the stamp of Confucian orthodoxy.[32] From the beginning, this essay is uncompromisingly authoritarian:

We reflect that just as Heaven is exalted and Earth is low, so are the roles of prince and minister fixed. The essential duty of a minister is simply that he be aware that he has a prince. For then his dispositions will be firmly disciplined and he will be able to share his prince's likes and dislikes; hence the saying, "One in virtue, one in heart, high and low are bound together." But sometimes people's minds harbor several interests, so that they are unable to accept the ruler's preferences, and as a result the sentiments of superiors and inferiors become opposed and the distinction between noble and base is subverted. This is what always comes of the habit of forming cliques and factions.[33]

The emperor complains that the K'ang-hsi emperor repeatedly warned his officials against factionalism but could not completely reform

them, and that even now, after repeated warnings by himself, the officials persist in their folly:

They have no concern for being impartial in their likes and dislikes, but
obstinately continue to follow the judgments of those with whom they are
intimate; so that when We employ a man, they all discuss the matter and
say "This man was recommended by so-and-so"; and with this they avoid
him as though he were unclean, saying "We will stay away from him; we
won't follow after him just because he is powerful"; and with envious hearts,
one after another they slander and revile him, and will not be happy till they
are rid of him.

Similarly, when the sovereign dismisses a man, people say that it is because someone has denounced him. Even his former enemies sym-
pathize with him and try to make up with him. "But you will not find
anyone who urges him to rectify his faults and reform himself; and so the
man ceases to be aware of his defects and is increasingly moved to express feelings of resentment against his sovereign." Hence the court's
ability to reward and punish no longer carries weight; "on the contrary
it is the sympathy and admiration of partisans that gives prestige, and
their carping and criticism that counts as disgrace." The result of such
partisanship is that "impartial standards of right and wrong are confused"; and the ruler's "handles" (his ability to "give and take back"),
by which he controls his officials, are quietly neutralized.[34] This has
very much of a Legalist ring. Note especially that in this argument what
distinguishes a faction is not the principles or policies it favors, not its
tao, but its judgments of this or that man in office.

The title the emperor chose for his political sermon made it immediately recognizable as a rejoinder to Ou-yang Hsiu's famous essay on
factionalism. Naming Ou-yang as the author of what he regarded as
political heterodoxy, the emperor proceeded to give him a pummeling:

Ou-yang Hsiu, in the Sung dynasty, once wrote an essay "On Factions,"
in which he invented a perverse theory. "Superior men," he said, "form
cliques because they share the same *tao*." But how can there be *tao* among
them when they deny their sovereign and work for their own interests?
Ou-yang Hsiu's "*tao*" is simply the *tao* of inferior persons. With this essay at
hand, inferior persons who form factions will all be able to pretend that they
have "the same *tao*" while in fact they are merely advancing their common
interests. Our opinion is that the superior man does not join factions; it is only
the inferior man who does so. Are we to suppose from Ou-yang Hsiu's essay
that if men stick together in a faction they are superior men, whereas if they
separate and do not stick together they are inferior men? If Ou-yang Hsiu
were alive today and wrote this essay, We would surely rebuke him for his
misconceptions.

Generally speaking, continued the emperor, when mere literary men (e.g., Ou-yang) "play with their pens or wag their tongues," all they try to do is display a lively skill with words, and as a result they are always heedlessly "offending against correct principles."[35]

The emperor protests that he does not mean to condemn friendship. But prior friendships must cease to influence one's acts when one takes office. Even the much stronger bond of son to parent must give way once a man takes office, for then "he gives himself to his prince, and can no longer consider himself as belonging to his father and mother." (Here, certainly, the emperor was treading on a thin edge of Confucian political theory.) Incredibly, but without visible embarrassment, the emperor offers himself as a model to his officials. When he was a prince, he says, he did not seek to form alliances with officials, either Manchu or Chinese, and sternly turned away those who tried to become too familiar with him. It was precisely for this reason that the K'ang-hsi emperor chose him as his successor.[36]

The ideological importance attached to this treatise, in the Yung-cheng reign and later, can be inferred from a decree issued in 1725, directing that the "P'eng-tang Lun" and the "Sheng-yü Kuang-hsün" (the "Sacred Edict" of K'ang-hsi with the Yung-cheng emperor's comments) be distributed to all schools throughout the empire. These two statements of official doctrine were to be read aloud by all officers of instruction on the first day and at the full moon of every month.[37] These documents must have been drummed into the minds of government students for generations. The official regulations for the imperial educational administration, in which the essay "On Factions" is contained, were published in 1810.

Of Yung-cheng edicts which deal with the problem of factionalism there are two which are particularly full: one dated May 22, 1723 (already cited), and another dated September 3, 1724. They present many of the arguments contained in the "P'eng-tang Lun," sometimes using the same language. We find the emperor again particularly exercised by the factional challenge to his own choice of his ministerial favorites: "When We employ a man who does not belong to a certain faction, the members of that faction despise him; when We punish a man who is of a certain faction, the members of that faction cover up for him, so that honor and disgrace do not depend on reward and punishment. What then is to become of the laws of the state?"[38]

The emperor insists that he wants neither blind and paralyzing criticism nor sycophantic praise of the men he selects. He has often, he protests, allowed even minor officials to approach him directly and has sent away his attendants so that advice could be offered in complete privacy. But "you high officials are regularly allowed to memorialize;

and yet you hide your views and do not state them, and then withdraw-
ing from Our presence you talk behind Our back, saying 'so-and-so
ought not to be employed,' or 'such-and-such a thing ought not to be
done.'" This insincere and petty behavior is linked, as the emperor
sees it, with the sort of self-serving which he identifies with the partisan
habit of mind. "Sometimes when We have trusted a man and charged
him to devote his entire mind and strength to the business of the state,
you turn about and say that he is usurping authority and lording it over
people. Who then will be willing to follow his lead and lay himself open
to your slandering?"[39]

Essentially what the emperor demands is that his officials trust him
utterly. This trust is to exclude their placing any trust in themselves
or in one another. Not only are they to trust his good faith and his ability to distinguish between sincere and insincere counsel; they are to
accept his "preferences" as virtually making the distinction between
right and wrong, good and bad:

Worthy men are the men of whom We approve, and you ought therefore to
approve of them; unworthy men are the men We dislike, and you ought therefore to dislike them. . . . A man's greatest duties are his duty to his prince
and his duty to his parents. Suppose a man's father has an enemy and the
son is friendly with him; or suppose the father is fond of someone and the
son takes him as an enemy. Is this the right course for a son? In sum, only if
each man takes his prince's likes and dislikes as his own will everyone be able
to reform his evil ways and turn to the good. For prince and minister to be
of one mind means good fortune for the state.[40]

This argument may do no more than make explicit one out of the many
conflicting moral and political implications of Confucian doctrine, but
there are probably very few Chinese emperors who have stated their
position so bluntly.

The Ch'ien-lung emperor Kao-tsung ascended the throne in 1735, at
the age of twenty-five *sui*. For the first dozen years, administration was
largely in the hands of two elder statesmen who had held the trust of
his father—O-er-t'ai (1680–1745), a Manchu who had acquired distinction for imposing Chinese rule on the Miao of Yunnan, and Chang
T'ing-yü (1672–1755), a Chinese who was said actually to have composed many of the imperial edicts of the Yung-cheng reign.

All did not go well. Within ten years, the young emperor was showing a strong desire to make his own decisions. His problem was not
merely that his government was dominated by two elder officials of his
father's choosing (his father had gone so far as to direct that O-er-t'ai's
and Chang's names were to be celebrated after their death in the imperial ancestral temple). In the course of their long public careers, each

had acquired a following of lesser office holders beholden to himself, relatives in office, and other satellites and admirers. Between these two groups a feeling of rivalry and animosity rather naturally developed.

Kao-tsung found this situation increasingly intolerable. From an edict issued in the fourth month of 1740, we get a very clear idea why. There was first of all the fact that O-er-t'ai was a Manchu and Chang a Chinese. If a Manchu party and a rival Chinese party did develop in the bureaucracy, the state of affairs, from the Manchu point of view, would obviously be highly unhealthy and precarious. Kao-tsung could not discuss so delicate a matter, but he does admit to the danger. While he carefully absolves O-er-t'ai and Chang from blame—*they* would not think of building up partisan followings of protégés around themselves— nonetheless "ignorant men foolishly fancy that, if they be Manchus, they are dependents of O-er-t'ai, and if Chinese, of Chang T'ing-yü; and this is the case not only of insignificant officials, but even of presidents and vice-presidents of boards."[41]

But this does not seem to have been Kao-tsung's chief vexation. A young man, sensing himself still under the shadow of his late strong-willed father, he not only felt under constraint in the exercise of his judgment but was outraged to discover that such decisions as he did make were attributed to his ministers. He could not make an appointment, he complained, without its being supposed that either O-er-t'ai or Chang had prompted it:

Since We have occupied the throne, We have never laid aside the appointive power. During the past several years, what persons have been appointed as a result of being recommended by these two ministers? What men have been degraded as a result of criticism by them? But as men generally imagine the matter, these two ministers are men of great power, who are able at will to effect the appointment or dismissal of others. What sort of ruler, then, do people regard Us to be?

Clearly, Kao-tsung was disturbed not only by the *fact* of partisan alignments, but also, and above all, by the very suggestion that *talk* of party divisions and affiliations might have any basis in the facts of power.

O-er-t'ai died in 1745, and Chang retired in obvious disfavor in 1750; but as late at 1749, Kao-tsung was still sensitive to this aspect of the problem of factionalism. In the twelfth month of that year, he found occasion to protest that "High officials have divided themselves into factions, as exclusive as so many religious sects; is this sort of thing proper in such an illustrious age as this? The imperial power of Our Ch'ing dynasty is securely held; surely, during the fourteen years of Our reign, there is no matter large or small which has not been decided by Us alone."[42] It is probably significant that both O-er-t'ai and Chang

T'ing-yü were implicated in cases of literary *lèse majesté*. The former's prestige was posthumously blackened by the execution of a member of his faction, Hu Chung-tsao (d. 1755), in some of whose poems the emperor pretended to see attacks upon Chang and his function and also (inevitable charge) slurring references to the Manchus; O-ch'ang (d. 1755), O-er-t'ai's nephew and a friend of Hu, was implicated in this case and obliged to commit suicide. And Chang, in the year of his retirement, was found to have a son-in-law involved in the case of literary sedition in which Lü Liu-liang (1629–83) had been posthumously prosecuted during the years 1728–32.[43]

The Ch'ien-lung emperor shared his father's suspicions not only of factional groupings among officials, but also of the traditional literati presumption in political matters. Ou-yang Hsiu had made the classic defense of factionalism, holding that like-minded defenders of "right principles" are morally justified in supporting one another, and the Yung-cheng emperor had been careful to refute this implied claim that the subject may be judge of his own rightness. One of the most extreme claims in Confucian literature for literati dominance over the emperor was made by another Sung statesman and philosopher. Ch'eng I (1033–1107), whose philosophical theories constitute a basic part of the synthesis of Chu Hsi, addressed three short memoranda to the throne, apparently while he was imperial tutor at the beginning of the reign of the young emperor Che-tsung (1086–1100). In these memoranda, "On Imperial Tutors in Classical Study," Ch'eng claims that the best governed era in history was the reign of King Ch'eng of Chou (1115–1079 B.C.). The reason, he says, is that King Ch'eng, who was still a minor at the beginning of his reign, was ably assisted in government and carefully educated in virtue by the Duke of Chou.

Just as important families at the present time engage men of outstanding virtue and uprightness to live with them and teach their sons, so should the emperor be constantly attended by upright teachers (Ch'eng is addressing the empress dowager as well as the emperor himself):

The principle of being assisted and educated [for a ruler] does not consist in his issuing directives that people speak out about his faults and then being criticized; it consists solely in the nourishing and cultivation of his virtue. Generally speaking, if in the course of a day the emperor is in the company of worthy men much of the time and is in the company of monks and concubines only a small part of the time, his character will automatically be transformed and his virtue will become perfect.[44]

"Since ancient times, no ruler has attained perfect sagehood who has not honored virtuous men and respected his ministers." It goes against proper ceremonial usage, Ch'eng adds, for an official instructing the emperor in the classics (*chiang kuan* or *ching-yen kuan*) to remain standing while he is teaching. This is so important that Ch'eng would have His Majesty hereafter provide the lecturer with an assistant to point to the text when necessary, so that the lecturer himself may not only remain seated at all times but also seat himself at a slight distance from the emperor's table. "This will not only show compliance with correct principles, but will foster in the ruler an attitude of respect for literati and esteem for the *tao*."[45]

And Ch'eng concludes by again linking the roles of minister and teacher (actually identified in the person of the Duke of Chou): "Your servant is of the opinion that the most important responsibilities in the empire are those of prime minister and imperial tutor in the classics. Order and disorder in the world depend on the prime minister; and the perfecting of the ruler's virtue is the responsibility of the imperial tutor."[46]

To this memorandum, and in particular to the last passage, the Ch'ien-lung emperor took vigorous exception:

Who after all employs a prime minister if it be not the sovereign? Suppose a sovereign merely dwells in lofty seclusion, cultivating his virtue and trusting the fortunes of the empire to his chief ministers rather than concerning himself with it. Then even if he is fortunate and chooses ministers like Han [Han Ch'i (1008–75)] and Fan [Fan Chung-yen (989–1052)], he will still not avoid contention among his high officials; and if he should be so unfortunate as to choose ministers like Wang [Wang Ts'eng (d. 1038)] and Lü [Lü I-chien (d. 1044)], how is the world to escape disorder? Surely this will not do. And if a chief minister habitually thinks of the world's welfare as his own sole responsibility, for all the world as if he had no sovereign, his conduct is surely intolerable.[47]

(All the officials mentioned held high office in the Northern Sung in times marked by factional strife; Wang and Lü quarreled so constantly that they were both dismissed.) Somewhat similarly the Yung-cheng emperor had objected to "those who hold that the ruler ought not to give personal attention to all the many problems of the realm." Men hold this view, he had argued, because "the factional habit of thinking has not yet been eradicated; and fearing that the ruler will look too closely into their affairs, they want to cover his ears and eyes, so that they may seek to indulge their own personal likes and dislikes."[48]

It seems clear that the Ch'ing emperors in the eighteenth century found it expedient, and were themselves personally disposed, to exalt the majesty of the throne both by playing up their own role and by curtailing that of their subordinates. On the one hand, Kao-tsung and his father were vigorous personalities; they were jealous of their prestige and convinced that any show of diffidence or torpor on their part would mark their reigns as weak and inglorious. There was little place in this picture, as they saw it, for subjects who honored the Confucian ideal by taking the world's problems upon themselves. The old ideals no doubt received a certain amount of unavoidable lip service, but the emperor kept the moral and intellectual advantage in his own hands.

On the other hand, factional politics was piously and indignantly denounced. It was never altogether suppressed, for the necessity of ingratiating oneself with others, of fortifying one's position by careful attention to personal relationships, was ineradicably built into Chinese society, and it was out of this matrix of normal behavior that networks of "friendships" and "master-disciple" relationships (for example, between examinee and examiner) constantly tended to take form. But in the political sphere, at least, there could be no honor attached to membership in a faction. To the Ch'ing, factionalism had but one origin: a tendency on the part of officials and gentry to scheme for the advancement of base personal interests by clandestine and presumably illicit means. (This view really soaked in. It was taken for granted, for example, by Chang Hsüeh-ch'eng and Wang Hui-tsu in their comments on political morality.) It was never conceded that men might band together out of *disinterested* motives—to defend the state, to protect the throne, to work for common "principles." The scholar-intellectual's contribution to government, if he made any, was to be a loyal official; if he had anything to say, he was to say it directly to the throne (if he was entitled to) and was to trust the emperor's judgment. In particular he was not to question the emperor's choice of men or suggest that he was abandoning his power to others. And so while factionalism, at least of the self-serving sort which officially was all it ever was, continued in fact, the fact had to be denied: factionalism could not be conceded to exist in such an illustrious era as Ch'ien-lung, the Age of Celestial Splendor.

OPPOSITION TO HO-SHEN: RESTRAINTS AND COMPULSIONS IN EIGHTEENTH-CENTURY POLITICAL BEHAVIOR

In the circumstances it was all but impossible to suggest that a high minister such as Ho-shen had packed the bureaucracy with his henchmen, or that he was squeezing bribes out of lower officials and driving them to embezzlement by his control over promotions and demotions. To make this charge would be not only to question the emperor's choice of a favorite, but to imply that his reign was marred by that sign of weakness and decay, factionalism; and it would further imply that the emperor had become so weak as to abandon the power of appointment.

To make any really strong move against Ho-shen would be even more difficult. An attack by a minister of high rank and prestige—such as A-kuei (1717–97) or Liu Yung (1720–1805), both of whom are remembered as upright officials—would be considered an expression of "dissension" among the emperor's ministers (recall Kao-tsung's lecture to Ch'ien Tsai), and would be as likely to bring down imperial anger on the attacker as on the attacked. And if an official bringing charges were supported openly by others, this would be positive proof that Ho-shen had become the victim of a cabal. He could be got at only indirectly, for example by some specific accusation against one of his subordinates, or against someone generally recognized as his "friend." Such a move would have the strategic advantage of creating or playing upon a suspicion that Ho-shen, rather than his accuser, was guilty of improper associations. A move of this sort would properly be within the role of a censor. But even this was uncertain and dangerous.

The nature of the difficulty can better be seen from a more careful examination of some of those few cases in which censors or other officials did take the risk of thrusting at Ho-shen.

The impeachment of Kuo-t'ai has already been mentioned. In 1781, reports reached the emperor that Kuo-t'ai, governor of Shantung, was guilty of corruption and of excessive severity toward people under him. Kao-tsung summoned the Shantung lieutenant governor, Yü I-chien (whose elder brother was the late grand councillor and grand secretary Yü Min-chung, 1714–80, one of Kao-tsung's earlier favorites); Yü assured the emperor that Kuo-t'ai was honest, and the emperor addressed a fatherly edict to the governor on how to handle his subordinates.[49]

But murmuring in Shantung persisted, and in May of 1782 the censor Ch'ien Feng (1740–95) accused both Kuo-t'ai and Yü of extracting bribes from lower officials at the ultimate expense of several local treasuries. An imperial commission was at once sent to investigate, including Ch'ien, Ho-shen, and Liu Yung, then senior president of the Censorate. The interest of the case lies in the fact that Kuo-t'ai and Yü, by the universal testimony of unofficial accounts, were Ho-shen's "henchmen." The governor, having been forewarned (perhaps by Ho-shen), attempted to transfer funds and refill the first treasury checked, but the attempt was detected and he confessed. Liu Yung and Ch'ien Feng are said to have worked together secretly in unspecified ways to prevent Ho from thwarting the inspection. Subsequent auditing in the province revealed that the deficits, before frantic attempts to make them good, had amounted to 2,000,000 taels silver. This so shocked the emperor that both the accused were ordered to commit suicide. The case of corruption had indeed not been firmly established against Yü I-chien, but the emperor considered that Yü had "covered up" for Kuo-t'ai and had deceived the emperor to his face the preceding year, making him appear ridiculous. It was this that sealed Yü's fate. In a formal sense, Ch'ien Feng was successful; but in a larger sense he failed, for the emperor either did not suspect Ho-shen of complicity or closed his eyes to the possibility.[50]

Ch'ien Feng, indeed, was probably in a more precarious position throughout the action than Ho-shen. At one point Kao-tsung questioned Ch'ien very sharply about his sources of information, plainly suspecting that the charge of corruption against Yü was unfounded.[51] And the attempt to cover up the evidence might, after all, have succeeded. If it had, it is certain that Ch'ien would have suffered dismissal or worse.

It is evident that Ch'ien, Yü, and other officials were constantly caught in a most unpleasant squeeze by the emperor's instinctive tactics. It was always assumed to be an official's duty to report malfeasance among his colleagues if he perceived it. And if malfeasance later came to light and were serious, the emperor would inevitably assume that it had been noticed. A censor's position was worse, for he was expected to notice everything. Failure to "speak" left him open to the charge of cowardice at the least, and at the worst, of connivance. As soon as the Shantung investigation was launched, Kao-tsung sent edicts to a number of Shantung officials, upbraiding them for not having reported on Kuo-t'ai earlier themselves, calling upon them to make full statements of what they knew, and threatening them with dire consequences if they held back anything which should subsequently come to light.[52] Yet if an official made charges which subsequent investigation did not substantiate, he would be guilty of "talking wildly" and suspected of the worst motives.

Another case, resembling Ch'ien Feng's venture but ill-planned and abysmally unsuccessful, makes an instructive contrast. In 1790, a sub-chancellor in the Grand Secretariat named Yin Chuang-t'u (1738–1808) submitted a memorial charging that corruption was general throughout the empire and that treasury deficiencies existed everywhere. According to some accounts, Ho-shen, taking this as a move against himself (and this, historians assure us, was Yin's intent), demanded that Yin be dismissed and punished; when this was refused he requested an investigation. But the emperor, for his part, took Yin's move as an affront not to Ho-shen but to himself. He demanded that Yin state his evidence. Yin had none, and requested that he and some Manchu official named by the throne investigate conditions in several localities. This course was followed. The emperor named Ch'ing-ch'eng, a board vice-president, as co-investigator. This man, it is said, was in Ho-shen's pocket, and saw to it that all the treasuries checked were refilled in time for the audit.

Yin was obliged to request punishment for making false charges, and early in 1791 the emperor angrily granted his request. Always, Kao-tsung protested, he had conducted his government with the greatest concern for the people's welfare. But they would be deluded by Yin's wild charges unless the emperor made his case plain. It was inconceivable that in this age of good government there could be officials who would dare to scheme for their own interests in violation of the law. Officials of this stamp had all been exposed and rooted out—witness Kuo-t'ai, and the case of Wang Tan-wang, an embezzler in Kansu whose exposure had resulted in 1781 in the execution of over fifty officials. Yin was brought back to the capital a prisoner and condemned to death, though he was later let off. In 1799 the Chia-ch'ing emperor restored him to honor, recognizing him as an official who had "dared to speak."[53] Yin's case illustrates the peril that an accuser put himself into, but it adds a new and important dimension. It was not Yin's false charges that made the emperor furious, but the reflection on his own virtue as a ruler.

Kao-tsung in fact shows himself chronically beset with two anxieties. On the one hand, he fears that his officials are holding back on him, covering up damaging facts. Kuo-t'ai, if guilty, is guilty of "scheming" for his own interests; likewise Yü. He repeatedly exhorts his investigators to "get to the bottom" of the case and report to him fully. At the same time, the emperor exhibits a strange compulsion to justify himself constantly to his officials. Even in the Kuo-t'ai case his edicts all end up as homiletics. How can his officials face him if they deceive him? Can't they see he is being lenient with them?

That this note of self-justification is not just a matter of tone is clear from an edict issued August 17, immediately after the close of the Kuo-t'ai case. Ch'ien Feng, so his biographers tell us,[54] had coupled his denunciation of Kuo-t'ai with an "outspoken" request that the emperor discontinue the practice of accepting "tribute" (*kung*) from his provincial officials at New Year's and on the celebration of the Imperial Birthday. The matter was certainly relevant. If there was room for the slightest suspicion that imperial favor was given in return for these gifts, the emperor was actually encouraging by his example the mischief at the root of the problem of official morality—bribery and de facto extortion. And the *kung* practice was going to extremes; the "gifts" were often very lavish—Ho-shen, it is hinted, built his fortune in large part out of his share of this imperial take. The emperor's edict on *kung* reviewed the matter in connection with the Kuo-t'ai case. Kao-tsung was very much on the defensive. The "tribute" was justified because "essentially its purpose is to establish a bond of good feeling between high and low." The emperor (since the Yung-cheng reign) granted officials an extra stipend, the *yang-lien* ("nourishment of integrity"), to enable them to do without bribe-taking. The "tribute" was supposed to be made by officials out of this stipend, in gratitude for the imperial generosity and "to demonstrate their loyalty." But, Kao-tsung protested, "this has no connection whatever with their promotion or demotion," and he counted off examples of officials who had obviously received no special consideration even though their "tribute" had been lavish. Last but not least was the case of Kuo-t'ai, who had been condemned even though his presents "were more splendid than others'." Kao-tsung deplored those officials who financed their tribute by squeezing their subordinates, for this would merely force lower officials to squeeze the people. Nonetheless he persisted in defending the system.[55]

Of this strange, guilty defensiveness, this sensitivity about his virtue and eminence as a ruler, we have had an anticipation in Kao-tsung's early concern to make it clear that he was exercising the full measure of his authority himself. This is not just a personality trait in Kao-tsung. Like his phobia of "connivance" (which was real enough), his fear of being deceived, it was a trait imposed on him by political ideology, in which in this respect emperor and officials were equally enmeshed. The Ch'ing emperors had made unlimited claims to political and moral authority. But he who makes great moral claims exposes himself painfully.

Sometimes a compulsion to justify oneself or a latent feeling of guilt can be alleviated by a convenient capacity to overlook unwelcome realities. Perhaps Kao-tsung had shown this disposition, also, in his attitude toward factions and the power of ministers early in his reign. Could this psychic complex have any bearing on his treatment of Ho-shen? Did Ho-shen perhaps enjoy even greater favor just because the emperor did not want to face the fact that he was being deservedly criticized?

Ch'ien Feng had made the logical move against Ho-shen: an effort to destroy an official in whose guilt, if it were established and if the emperor's eyes were open, Ho would be implicated. But sensitive as the emperor was to the danger of "connivance" among officials, as far as Ho was concerned his eyes apparently were not open. It was necessary to be more obvious.

The accusation made by the censor Ts'ao Hsi-pao in 1786 had the needed transparency. For this time the accused man—one Liu Ch'üan, whom Ts'ao charged with violating sumptuary regulations—was a person in Ho-shen's personal employ. The emperor grasped the censor's intent at once, and took the case very seriously. Indeed, with due allowance for the gentle exaggeration of official gossip, this may have been the incident which Staunton says caused Ho-shen's fortunes to hang in the balance for a fortnight. The emperor was in Jehol (it was the sixth month) and instructed the princes and officials in charge at Peking to conduct an immediate investigation. He did not, he said, want to punish Ho-shen if the charge was unfounded, nor did he want to let him off if there was substance to it. It would be wrong for the investigators to mistake his intent and try to intimidate Ts'ao "with the idea of finding flaws in his case so that the accuser should become the accused." Let the investigators proceed with an open mind, and if Ts'ao could produce evidence, let the matter be dealt with rigorously. "It would be wrong for you to cover up anything on Ho-shen's account. If you do, you will cause Ho-shen's downfall as well as your own." And while the investigation was in progress, realizing that Ts'ao's charges against Ho-shen's steward were intended merely as an entering wedge, Kao-tsung pressed the censor to "state the facts without reserve, if there be instances of scheming or malfeasance on Ho-shen's part. We will not fail to interrogate him Ourselves, find out the truth, and punish him."[56] The fat was in the fire.

Ho-shen, however, had been tipped off "by a certain court official" in time to have the evidence against his servant destroyed during the night. The Peking investigators found nothing, and advised the emperor that Ts'ao was merely trying to make a reputation for himself as a daring censor by making baseless charges. Ts'ao's position appeared grave. At this time, Ts'ao's biographers lament, Ho-shen had been in power over ten years, and although everyone talked about the case and some deeply sympathized with the censor, no one dared even to speak out in defense of his good character.[57] His "crime" was turned over to the Board of Punishments, which recommended that he be reduced two degrees in rank and transferred. The emperor, however, merely gave him a nominal discharge and kept him in his post, justifying this light treatment because Ts'ao was a "remonstrance official."

The emperor's behavior, so far, may have been mistaken in the light of history, but it seems to be straightforward. Was it?

The sequel to the case is extremely puzzling. On the one hand, during the next month Ho-shen was named a full grand secretary, the highest post he attained in his career. But while the emperor gave with one hand he took away with the other, by depriving Ho at the same time of his position as superintendent of customs at the Ch'ung-wen Gate— a lucrative plum, which Ho had held for eight years although it was usually held only for one. It was inexpedient, said Kao-tsung, for a grand secretary to be burdened with such responsibilities; indeed, he added, it may have been just this that led to Ts'ao Hsi-pao's accusation.

Kao-tsung was assuming, apparently, that Ho had been obliged to delegate his superintendent's duties to Liu Ch'üan as his personal representative, and had then been too busy to check up on his agent's behavior. But what else was the emperor assuming? Obviously, that Ts'ao, who had just been so magnanimously let off, was right after all! Ts'ao's honor was completely reestablished by the Chia-ch'ing emperor early in 1799.[58]

An incident in the summer of the following year (1787) provides an even more devious example of the imperial conscience at work. The price of grain was rising sharply in Peking and merchants were hoarding their supplies. At Ho-shen's advice a policy was instituted of limiting the amounts of grain a merchant might hold in stock. Ho had intended that stocks be seized and sold by the government at a reduced figure, but had not worked out appropriate regulations before he accompanied the emperor to the summer palace in Jehol. The officials left in charge in Peking soon memorialized on the difficulties in carrying out such a program, implying that it was impractical. Kao-tsung then announced that the merchants might be allowed to handle the sale of grain themselves at reasonable prices—reluctantly, for he was angered at the absurd appearance this reversal must present to the populace. Commenting on the report of the Peking officials, the emperor complained,

You have deliberately described the matter in a muddled way, as if, aware that Ho-shen was the man who started the business, you wanted to pass it over without getting to the bottom of it. Not only this, between the lines you seem to imply that We were not Ourselves completely innocent of an intention to cover up for Ho-shen. Is this reasonable? In our view, in the way you conduct this affair you are not protecting Ho-shen but actually harming him.[59]

What are we to make of this? The emperor, flailing about, was venting his indignation on all about him, Ho-shen not excepted. Yet Ho-shen suffered nothing from the affair; and the emperor's irritation, we begin to suspect, was due not so much to the loss of face to the government in Peking as to the delicate situation in which Kao-tsung found himself. For it was a fact that Kao-tsung could not bring himself to be severe with Ho-shen, and in the circumstances his officials could not afford to behave as if they were unaware of this fact. Yet Kao-tsung was ashamed of his weakness, and could not help seeing that his officials understood the situation only too well.

A few years after this, after years of service in other capacities, Ch'ien Feng again found himself a censor. In 1794 or 1795[60] he made another move against Ho-shen, this time almost a direct attack, which was both daring and skillful. Ho, it seems, during his many years as grand councillor, had found it convenient to discharge his duties not at the official Grand Council hall, but from his own private office; in fact he maintained several private offices. Ch'ien now memorialized to this effect. Of all the grand councillors only A-kuei, he noted, held office in the Grand Council hall itself. Others had their offices scattered about in different places, so that it was very difficult to forward documents to the council as a body. Moreover, Ho-shen's and Fu-ch'ang-an's offices, which were usually together, were located in improper proximity to imperial residences, or in places where it would be easy for their subordinates to strike up understandings with palace eunuchs.

"Your Majesty's celestial conduct of affairs is vigorous," wrote Ch'ien, "and your splendor is illustrious; all officials high and low are deeply imbued with your virtue and take to heart your admonitions." Surely, he added, the situation he describes "will not go so far as to lead to a development of partisanship and dissension." But it was precisely the existence of "partisanship and dissension" among the highest officers of state, with the crafty Ho-shen and his accomplices on one side and the upright A-kuei on the other, that Ch'ien was suggesting. Such a suggestion could be made only with the greatest delicacy, since it called into question both the imperial virtue and the motives of the memorialist. That there was tension between Ho-shen and A-kuei in the grand council is attested also by Hung Liang-chi, who wrote a few years later that A-kuei behaved very stiffly toward Ho-shen whenever the latter addressed him in the council. Hung adds that in his last years A-kuei's one hope was that he might outlive the emperor and be allowed to speak his mind about the former guards officer.[61]

Ch'ien asked that the emperor take steps; it would be best, he said, to return to the established procedures laid down in the Yung-cheng era and maintained for many years of Kao-tsung's reign, under which grand councillors always conducted their business together; if this were done, "the greater advantage will derive from their combined reflections," and "their authority will not be divided."[62]

This move had little likelihood of destroying Ho-shen, but it might (and may) have damaged him. The emperor was receptive enough to lecture the grand councillors and to assign Ch'ien to the council in a more or less investigative capacity. But Ch'ien died not long after, according to some accounts because Ho-shen assigned him the most exhausting duties of the council (other accounts have it that Ho poisoned him).[63]

In the last months of 1795, Kao-tsung named his fifth son, Yung-yen, as heir apparent and announced that he would "abdicate" on the new year following—ostensibly in order to avoid reigning longer than his grandfather, the K'ang-hsi emperor. This event, which was without precedent in Chinese history, raises questions. As early as 1793, British Embassy reports indicated that members of the imperial clan—and others—were concerned over Ho-shen's marriage alliance with the emperor and feared that he might try to manipulate the succession. As it happened, however, the new heir apparent was Ho-shen's implacable enemy. Ho probably had no illusions on this score. In 1797, Yung-yen's close friend Chu Kuei (they were fellow poets) was demoted from the governor-generalship of Kwangtung and Kwangsi to the governorship of Anhwei, ostensibly because of his failure to suppress pirates on the South China coast. But sub rosa accounts of his demotion are more readable. It is said that actually Chu was to be promoted, to the Grand Secretariat; and that the "emperor," on hearing the news, wrote Chu a poem of congratulation. This was intercepted by Ho-shen and shown to the "ex-emperor," who was so angered at this improper intimacy that he demoted Chu instead.[64] If Ho-shen's object was to block Chu's advance, he was being very foolhardy. But if his real object was to provoke Kao-tsung into dethroning the emperor? We can then at least credit him with a desperate but intelligent gamble. Perhaps his opponents had not been so ineffective after all.

Surely, after Kao-tsung's death in 1799 and Ho-shen's destruction which quickly followed, the political atmosphere should have changed dramatically; it would then have been frankly admitted that Ho-shen had built up an evil combination around himself, and worthy officials who opposed and hated him would have been appointed to prominent positions and solicited for their advice on the many problems of state that had been building up during the latter part of Kao-tsung's reign. Was this indeed what happened?

Matters began promisingly. One of the Chia-ch'ing emperor's first acts was to call his friend Chu Kuei to Peking and make him president of the Board of Civil Office. After the emperor moved against Ho-shen, there was a virtual open invitation (and in some cases pressure) for all to join in denouncing him. Wu I, Hsieh Chen-ting, Ts'ao Hsi-pao, Yin Chuang-t'u, and others were reinstated or posthumously honored (perhaps at Chu's urging), and if still living were urged to speak. Upon assuming personal control of the government, the new emperor issued the traditional invitation to all officials qualified to memorialize, urging them to offer advice on problems of the realm.[65] In addition, however, and as part of his move against Ho-shen, he decreed that all memorials would henceforth be addressed directly and solely to himself; submission of copies to the Grand Council would not be necessary, nor would it be allowed. Any qualified official having something to say, he asserted, could have direct access to the throne and assurance of the emperor's confidence.[66] This was of course a move against "connivance." But under the circumstances it gave the emperor some justification for saying, as he repeatedly did, that he had "opened wide the avenues of remonstrance."

It looked as if he were prepared to view the Ho-shen experience as a "Good vs. Evil" cleavage in the bureaucracy. Soon, however, he unmistakably shied away from this idea. Perhaps—he was apparently a man of mild temper—he had no stomach for a rigorous purge of the bureaucracy and the inevitable confusion that would follow. Perhaps the idea of helping one group overthrow another made him uneasy. In any case, after Ho-shen and the grand councillor Fu-ch'ang-an, whom the emperor regarded as Ho's closest accomplice, were disposed of, no very extensive attempt was made to bring charges against Ho's lesser minions. Indeed, even Fu-ch'ang-an had his sentence commuted. Presently the emperor announced his intentions in a general edict. Ho-shen, he observed, had held power so long that the practice of gaining favor by "illicit and corrupt donations" to him must have become very general. Many of Ho-shen's "adherents and connections," the emperor realized, must have shared his guilt. But the emperor did not wish to encourage a wave of accusations against these people:

If the officers and magistrates of our dominions should misconceive Our views . . . and proceed in consequence to a severe scrutiny of past transactions, at the instigation of personal animosity and dislike, . . . although these reports should prove just and faithful, it would be inexpedient to enter into inquiries which would be almost endless in themselves, and but too probably suggested to Us from unworthy motives.

In short, the emperor proposed to go no further, and to view Ho-shen not as the leader of an evil group in the bureaucracy but as a "monstrous contriver of iniquity" who at the top of the structure had exercised a more or less general corrupting influence. With Ho-shen gone, and with adequate imperial admonition, the hearts of all the officials could be brought back to a state of virtue.[67]

This attitude toward Ho-shen that the emperor now elected to take must have been disappointing to many. Late in September, one man decided to risk his political fortunes and speak out. Hung Liang-chi (1746–1809), a han-lin who had been working on the "veritable records" of Kao-tsung's reign, was a close friend of many of Ho-shen's bitterest opponents, and had very strong views about the fallen minister himself. Since Hung was not entitled to address the emperor directly, he wrote a letter to the grand councillor Prince Ch'eng, requesting that it be forwarded to the throne. At the same time he sent copies to two board presidents, Liu Ch'üan-chih and his own and the emperor's friend Chu

Kuei. In this letter Hung urged in effect that the Ho-shen problem be treated as factional—that Ho's associates and protégés (he gave a number of names) be punished or posthumously disgraced. This was not all; he went on to criticize the emperor himself, suggesting that there were still undesirable persons around him who were distracting his attention from problems of state.[68]

Prince Ch'eng took the letter at once to the emperor, who was outraged by it. Hung was removed from his post on September 24, and the Board of Punishments rendered a recommendation that he be decapitated for "extreme disrespect." The emperor set about to defend himself. For one thing, he observed, Hung was guilty of refusing to accept the emperor's earlier edict of amnesty to persons implicated with Ho. For another, his recommendation was foolish: the persons he named either were dead and did not matter—Sun Shih-i, for example—or were not in important positions anyway. As for the suggestions about the emperor himself, they were ridiculous. But what angered the emperor most was the way Hung had proceeded. What he should have done was memorialize directly (even though he was not entitled to) or ask another official to forward a memorial for him. Instead, he wrote a letter, and worse, distributed it to several officials. This amounted to talking behind the emperor's back. It is an indication of the emperor's sensitivity on this point that Chu Kuei was actually degraded three ranks for retaining his copy of the letter and not forwarding it till the emperor demanded it.[69]

But there was a curious reverse side to the emperor's reaction. He could not kill Hung, since he did not want to frighten off other officials who might otherwise speak freely and give him good advice. He would merely exile Hung to I-li, to show that there were extremes of impropriety and irresponsibility that could not be tolerated. But having made this decision, the emperor added that he would keep Hung's letter near him for its value as a warning to himself![70]

The episode had an amusing conclusion. Hung turned his exile to good account. He was interested in geography, and the long trip provided the material for another book. And in the following spring, not long after Hung reached I-li (for he took his time), there was a protracted drought in and about Peking. The emperor prayed, performed ceremonies, and finally turned to issuing amnesties. Eventually he thought of Hung, and dispatched a pardon to the general in command at I-li, publicly reproaching himself for having punished a "speaking official." On the afternoon of the day this action was taken, Heaven sent down rain in such abundance that the ground was saturated to a depth of three inches, the rainfall continuing through the night and extending as far as Pao-ting prefecture. The emperor, overwhelmed, wrote a poem in honor of the occasion, which is included at the beginning of one of Hung's collections of prose.[71]

Ho-shen had left the scene, and with this resolution of Hung's difficulties his ghost was exorcised: he could now become matter for the moralistic historian, or he could be forgotten. What have we learned from his story?

Why was Ho-shen able to appear, to entrench himself for over twenty years, and to remain virtually untouched? I have tried to link this phenomenon both to imperial motivations and to restraints upon the behavior of officials and subjects. The Yung-cheng and Ch'ien-lung emperors strongly resented criticism, particularly of their choices of ministers and favorites; their feeling in this matter was reinforced by a suspicion, which they inherited from earlier reigns, of literati participation in government, and of factons within the bureaucracy. This imperial viewpoint was fixed in official ideology in the 1720's and 1730's; and the ideology was sufficiently in line with earlier Confucian political thinking—and with the realities of political power—to be quite effective. The result was that large-scale, outspoken protest ceased to be either politically or morally possible.

For Kao-tsung's part, the exalted and isolated position ideology accorded him not only assisted Ho-shen's rise but also appears to have strengthened in the emperor certain psychological characteristics of which his officials were no doubt aware: an extreme sensitivity about his virtue as a ruler and a defensiveness which impelled him to suppress in himself any suspicion that the criticism he would not countenance might be merited. Even the emperor's doubts, it would seem, reinforced his trust in his minister and increased the risk that an unlikely critic of Ho-shen must take. And Ho-shen, no doubt, was clever enough always to soothe the emperor's self-esteem. He had no embarrassing prestige as a man of learning; and even when the emperor scolded him, by serving as a scapegoat he contrived to put his master at ease.

But by 1800 the climate was changing. The Chia-ch'ing emperor was still uneasy about factionalism and would not brook undue liberties, but his treatment of Hung Liang-chi would have been inconceivable in his two imperial predecessors. More important, the dynasty was weakening. This did not prevent the malfunctioning of despotic rule which had produced Ho-shen; and corruption, of course, continued to flourish. But as difficulties of state became more and more serious in following generations, factions and parties could take shape around serious issues; and as the power of the Manchu throne faltered, the influence of Confucian scholar-officials inevitably increased.

Joseph R. Levenson

THE SUGGESTIVENESS OF
VESTIGES: CONFUCIANISM
AND MONARCHY AT THE LAST

Hommes de l'avenir souvenez-vous de moi
Je vivais à l'époque où finissaient les rois . . .
Apollinaire, *Alcools*

THE HUNG-HSIEN EMPEROR AS A COMIC TYPE

In 1914 Yüan Shih-k'ai, trying to be the strong man not by muscle alone, but by mystique, contrived a bit of ceremonial. He still called his state the *min-kuo*, the Republic, and he still called himself a president, not an emperor, but he meant to be a president with a quite remarkable staying power, and he looked for some awe to reinforce his political arrangements. Accordingly, he embellished his presidential election law (which was frankly designed as a guarantee that Yüan would succeed himself and succeed himself) with a ritualistic rigmarole to add a touch of suspense—three names, the president's private and secret choices, put in a gold box kept in a stone house in the presidential palace enclosure, the president with the one key to the gold box, the president and two of his appointees with the three keys to the stone house, the dramatic disclosure to a safe electoral college of the three names three days before the election, the thoughtful addition of the president's name to his roster of tame candidates, etc.[1] It was a cunning plan.

However, he never used it. His real aim was to invoke a sanctity, not to create one, and the comical complexity of his "republican" devices—his mummery for presidents and his plethora of schemes for treadmill rounds of provisional parliaments and provisional constitutions—were better made to mock the Republic than to make it seem legitimate. Total discredit of the Republic was the preamble; then, the body of the tale might be a new dynastic history.

Yet, when Yüan finally inaugurated the Hung-hsien reign on January 1, 1916, the parody of a republic yielded to only a parody of the empire. And this was perhaps inevitable, the result not of some failure of dignity in Yüan himself, but of a condition of modern Chinese history in the large: the vitiation of old conventions, an invincible staleness which not all the evident futilities of the republican alternative could dispel. Goethe's Faust had seen his emperor's court as a world of masks for emptiness, and court and carnival as one.[2] And the question that needs to be asked about Yüan's imperial masquerade, about all the vestigial monarchism in the Chinese Republican era, is the question that Mann's Faust-as-the-artist put to himself: "Why does almost everything seem to me like its own parody? Why must I think that almost all, no, all the methods and conventions of art today are good for parody only?"[3]

The imperial office in 1916 could not be taken seriously because the Republic, while a failure, was not a mistake. Its failure lay in its social meaninglessness; the revolution seemed to have had no substance. But the Republic, however insubstantial, did have meaning as a symbol: by its mere existence after thousands of years of monarchy, it offered license to new thought, the solvent of Chinese pieties. When Yüan Shih-k'ai, by trying to make himself stick as emperor, asserted in effect that no political revolution had occurred in 1911 and 1912—only at most a traditional rebellion intervening between dynastic periods—his monarchism, in defiance of this interpretation, was fatally compromised by the revolution which *had* occurred, the intellectual revolution. When the Republic, devoid of social achievement though it may have been, shameless political fake though it may have seemed, nevertheless stood for something—iconoclasm—its rival, monarchy, had to stand for something (and something, in the circumstances, equivocal), traditionalism.

In Yüan's gentle demurrers at the offer of the throne in early December, 1915 ("Our sage-master emerged with destiny . . . the people submit to your virtue, the whole country of one mind," pronounced his Council of State, humbly petitioning that he "graciously indulge the feelings of the people"),[4] and in his discreet extraction of a formal blessing from the Ch'ing ex-emperor ("In accordance with the command of the Ch'ing emperor: with regard to changing the form of state and raising the president to imperial honors, the Ch'ing royal house deeply approves"),[5] he conformed to the pattern of *shan-jang*, cession and seemly initial rejection, which derived from the *Shu-ching* lore of Yao and Shun. When modesty ceased to forbid him, Yüan accepted the offer ("For the empire's rises and falls the very commoner has responsibility; shall my love of country lag behind others?")[6] in Chinese phrases of classical cadence and in part, at least, in direct echo of the seventeenth century's Ku Yen-wu.[7] The republican bureaucracy's *ch'eng* ("submit" [a document]) gave way to the grand old *tsou* ("memorialize"); the ancient monarchical *ch'en*, for "official" (the Ch'ing mark of Confucian distinction between the Chinese official and the Manchu *nu*, or "slave"), sup-

planted the current *kuan* in the bureaucratic nomenclature.[8] And on the
last day of 1915, when the next year was proclaimed as Hung-hsien I,
Yüan gave to the *Yen-sheng kung,* the "Holy Duke," K'ung Ling-i, direct
descendant of Confucius, the brevet rank of *chün-wang,* a feudal title
of Han devising and long in imperial use.[9] In these and a hundred other
ways old legitimacies were solicited for Yüan Shih-k'ai. But when the
Emperor Yüan was traditionalistic, as he had to be, he ran through an
emperor's lines, he followed the ancient stage directions, but he was not
(nor could anyone else then be) an authentic, traditional emperor.

LATE CH'ING: CONFUCIANISM REDEFINED AS THE COUNTER
TO MODERN THOUGHT

Actually, monarchy was lost when the Ch'ing were forced to im-
provise after the Boxer debacle of 1900, and the untraditionally traditionalistic monarchy was preordained for Yüan Shih-k'ai by his Ch'ing
dynastic predecessors. For the Ch'ing were in a hopeless dilemma in
their last decade. Modernization was necessary if they were to avoid
being held responsible for continued Chinese disasters. But their sponsorship of modernization, the abandonment of traditional Chinese ways,
would end their only claim, as an ethnically foreign people, to legitimacy
as Chinese rulers, a legitimacy which prenationalistic culturalism had
once accorded them, but which Chinese nationalism, necessarily spreading as Chinese culture changed, found inadmissible. In short, in their
last decade the Ch'ing had a discouraging choice between going down
in a traditional way, out of simple cyclical weakness in a world of outer
pressures and inner strains, or going down as moderns, aspiring, at least,
to strengthen China and strengthen their hold and thereby extend their
title to the traditional mandate, but running afoul of the nationalism
which modern, foreign strengthening methods entailed. Quite naturally,
no clear-cut choice was made. Given a situation in which the best of
both worlds in another light was the worst, they tried to be modern
enough to defend their traditional status and traditional enough to take
the curse off modernism.

And so one finds the anomalies of a 1906 decree about the new educational system—a sharp departure from the examination system, which
was centuries old and of incalculable significance for the traditional
social order and cultural values. The new education was to have military spirit, industrial spirit, and public spirit generally among its main
objectives—so much for the leanings to modernism—and loyalty to the
emperor and reverence for Confucius as vital bequests from the past.
At the same time, as if to reinforce the latter strain, the Ch'ing decreed
that sacrifices to Confucius were raised to the grade of *ta-ssu,* "great

sacrifices," the highest grade of three.[10] But this Confucian zeal of the Manchus (always apparent in Ch'ing history as a means of their growing into China on a principle other than ethnic, and heightened, if anything, at the last) only intensified Confucianism to the point of its exhaustion. For Confucianism, when "worked at" for a social purpose—as something to spoil the potentialities, anti-Manchu, of implicitly nationalistic modern thought—was deprived of almost its last intellectual substance and left as mainly a symbol of resistance to revolution. And when revolution came, and the Republic, justified by Sun Yat-sen as the "latest thing" politically in a universal progressive evolution (and thus implying, if not compensating for, denial to China of her long-assumed Confucian autonomy), opened the lid on the latest things in every other sphere, people with vested interests in the old regime, or simply nostalgia, clung fiercely and particularly to Confucianism, which was, after all, an early thing itself, and a glorifier of early things.

THE REPUBLIC: CONFUCIANISM AND MONARCHISM NARROWED AND INTERWOVEN

It was an attenuated Confucianism, then, more a sentiment than a teaching, which confronted republican skepticism about the value of the past and which gravitated unerringly to any monarchical movement that seemed to have a chance. Prominent among the petitioners for monarchy in 1915 were the *K'ung she,* Confucian societies, of Chihli and Honan.[11] Yen Fu, one of Yüan Shih-k'ai's "six *chün-tzu*" (to quote a contemporary sardonic analogy between Yüan's monarchical inner circle and the "six martyrs" of 1898, whom Yüan Shih-k'ai was alleged to have sold to the Empress Dowager),[12] made a clear and characteristically untraditional statement of the new traditionalism's associations: "Chinese honor the prince and venerate the ancient; Westerners honor the people and venerate the modern."[13]

What is untraditional here is the identification of Chinese monarchism with intellectual traditionalism pure and simple. This was a change from the live imperial days, when the monarchy, or its centralizing agents, often strained against the conservatism of the bureaucratic intelligentsia; from their very beginnings the traditional Chinese bureaucratic and monarchical institutions had existed in a state of mutual and ambivalent attraction-repulsion (of which more below). What is characteristic here, in the contemporary context of Yen's untraditional assumption, is the air of conscious response to a serious foreign challenge, that of democratic thought and other intellectual novelty. The intellectually subversive revolutionary nationalists had injected the *min,* "the people," into modern political consciousness, and the *min* (or their self-styled representatives) not only had ousted the old monarchy, but had forced their way into the new monarchical thinking—indeed, had made it new.

Wu T'ing-fang (1844–1922), Sun's representative in conversations with the Ch'ing camp in late 1911, made a statement on December 20 to the effect that the new republican government would be based on *jen-min i-chih*, the people's "will."[14] On February 1, 1912, the dynasty itself ordered Yüan, its last agent, to come to terms with the revolutionary *min-chün*, "people's army": "The people's will has become clear . . ." And in the first edict of abdication, on February 12, came the sad renunciation: "By the indications of men's minds the mandate of Heaven is known."[15] Here was the contradiction of the principle of heavenly selection, to which popular control and ratification were essentially irrelevant. In the ensuing contradiction of republicanism, "the people" could not be exorcised from the monarchists' apologies. Sometimes "the people's will" was retained, in the Bonapartist sense, as in Yüan's amusingly hyper-successful plebiscite for monarchy in the fall of 1915; more often the Chinese people's "spirit," not their will, was emphasized as the guarantor of the imperial institution. The famous Goodnow memorandum along these lines inspired or released a flood of Chinese writings on *kuo-t'i* and *kuo-ts'ui* and *kuo-ch'ing*, the people's proper form of state, the national "spirit" or temperament, which implied not that this Chinese republic was puerile but that no Chinese republic was possible, that monarchism was inexpungeable from the Chinese people's spirit.

Why must the idea of "the people" as the source of political authority be seen as essentially modern in China, and therefore appropriate enough to an untraditional republic, but not to a monarchy needing to trade on authentic traditional lineage? After all, it has been a familiar enough suggestion in the last half-century or so that Western democratic theory was anticipated in ancient China, where the imperial idea (as it is alleged) demanded the people's happiness as the test of fulfillment of the will of Heaven by the Son of Heaven.[16] But such suggestions confuse the priorities in classical Chinese thought. A modern appeal to "the people" for validation denies, not derives from, the old imperial sanctions.

To say that *vox populi* is *vox dei* is not to define the latter but to displace it; the "voice of God" is metaphorized out of current acceptance, and now no more than lends emphasis through historical tone to the acknowledgment of a new supreme authority. In imperial China the *t'ien-tzu* held the *t'ien-ming* as long as he expressed the *t'ien-i*.[17] Heaven's son, mandate, and will were unequivocally the classical founts of supremacy, and the people's will, when it was worked at all by Confucian thinkers into political theory, was purely symbolic, not effective, in establishing legitimacy. Heaven's hand could not be forced.[18]

In traditional monarchical theory, that is, popular discontent did not itself invalidate an emperor's claims—nor, by the same token, did popular approbation legitimize him. Popular discontent was a *portent,* as a flood might be a portent, of the loss of the mandate; it was a sign, perhaps, of the loss of the imperial virtue. But a flood was not to be greeted with fatalistic acceptance. While an emperor should read the signs aright, he still should try to check the flood. And just so, the outbreak of a popular rebellion was no guarantee of its success or of its Confucian acceptability (far from it). It might be a portent, but it, too, should be and legitimately might be resisted. For the famous "right to rebel" was a contradiction in terms. People rebelled not because they had any legal right, but because actually existing legal arrangements left little scope to their lives. Until they succeeded, rebels had no right, and the people's will, if they claimed to express it, had to wait on Heaven's choosing.

If he had the name, the "rectified name," of Son of Heaven, the ruler had the *te* which the Ju (Confucian) school thought intrinsic to him—a *te* which was power on the outside and virtue, the *tao i hsing,* in his inner nature, a *te* which would bring no harm to the people's lives.[19] But popular satisfaction was one thing only in the classical political ideal: a sign of some higher ratification of the emperor's legitimacy. It was another thing in the modern aura of secular democracy: the legitimizer itself.

And just as vestigial monarchy derived, allegedly, from the people's will, instead of simply according with it while reflecting Heaven's, so vestigial Confucianism took the people's will as its novel justification. "If our parliamentarians really want to represent the people's will, then they cannot but establish Confucianism as the national religion," wrote a petitioner in 1917, the year after "Hung-hsien" and unpropitious for Confucian special pleaders. "Catholics oppose the idea of a state religion," he went on, "but some three million Catholics are not the people's will."[20] Mass identification with Confucianism, then, established by the evidence of history, was the ground of Confucian authority for this thinker and many others. It was the same sort of ground Yüan had sought as the basis of his dynasty.

But post-Ch'ing monarchism and Confucianism were linked more directly than by their merely invoking in common an identification with the people's will. The writer of this memorial for Confucianism (*not* a Confucian memorial), coming after Yüan's fiasco, had an embarrassed recognition of general opinion, which held Confucianism implicated in the discredited monarchical effort. It was hard to reconcile Confucianism with the symbolically modern Republic, but he did as well as he could. He admitted the charge of the Yüan affinity, dismissed it as a foible of Confucianists rather than a necessity of Confucianism, and suggested an act of oblivion. Christian churches, too, he pointed out, had launched prayers for Yüan's success. Christians, he alleged, were Yüan's loudest extollers, and took part in his government. Buddhists and Mohammedans repeatedly cheered him on. Yüan, he acknowledged, had fabricated a "people's will" for his own monarchical purposes. But the genuine people's will was with Confucianism, and Confucianism, if established as the national religion of the Republic, would be the indispensable institution for the state's consolidation.[21]

In short, quite plausibly under the circumstances, this Confucian partisan was really trying to make Confucianism independent of polity. Republics or monarchies were uncertain but Confucianism was permanent while a Chinese people lived, for it was particularly (historically) a part of the Chinese people, its very essence. "Every country has a form which is natural to it and it alone. Our country ought to establish Confucianism as the national religion . . . especially to protect the national essence."[22] When Norway split off from Sweden in 1905 (ran another expression of opinion), many changes were made in the constitution, but Lutheranism, long the state religion, remained so, as the link with the people's past. Moral: "As the physical body without the spirit must die, so must the nation without a national religion."[23] "Other countries, in some numbers, have established national religions. Is there not still more reason for us to do likewise? For Confucianism is our religion by nature."[24]

It is true that rationalistic as well as romantic apologia were still put forward, like the commendation of Confucianism above religions of the outside, Confucianism being termed a *jen-tao chiao*, a humanistic creed, and thus allegedly an advance over the *shen-tao chiao*, theologies, "superstitions," of the non-Chinese world.[25] Yet, in the context of Republican iconoclasm, such statements of rational conviction may represent romantic particularism in a special form—one which emphasized not that foreign bodies would die if grafted onto the Chinese organism (hence, for example, the hopelessness of the Republic) but that the Chinese organism might die of the intrusion, an intrusion which could indeed take place. Consequently, rational argument, depending on appeals to universal criteria, may rather derive from a feeling for the national essence than challenge it, so that a special concern for "our" religion would drive one to establish it as generally "better."

"Our religion": Chinese, that is, characteristically and exclusively

so, as long as any people could be called Chinese. This allegation of permanence—an unshakable attribute of essence, and safer as an approach to "the people's will" than any electoral soundings of what was, after all, a manipulable public—was the real trump (and the last card) of Confucianists under the Republic. And whatever their ultimate tactical wish to disengage from Yüan, it had been monarchy's card, too. The particular spirit of the Chinese people, not the universal reason of the way of Heaven, became an emperor's justification.

By this doctrine of romantic determinism, then, free choice among values of whatever historical origin, the premise of republicans' detachment from tradition, was ruled out. Chinese traditionalism became a relative, not an absolute, principle, a charge upon China, not upon man; compulsion to preserve the gifts of the Chinese past was psychological now, from a feeling of individuality threatened—not philosophical, as of old, from the mind's conviction of the general value of Chinese classic experience. Conservatism and monarchy were welded together, but when novelty was repelled on grounds of the limitations of the Chinese genius rather than on grounds of its fullness or universality, this conservatism was novelty itself, and—equally paradoxically—this monarchy, trading on the symbols of the past, was itself, no less than the Chinese Republic, a symbol of revolution.

For truly traditional, not merely traditionalistic, Chinese monarchy was ideally monarchy for the world, though centered in one intellectually self-sufficient society. Now, when republican nationalistic iconoclasts defined the world as larger than China, and Chinese society as very far from intellectually self-sufficient, monarchist traditionalists, finding it simply impossible in modern times to sustain Chinese cultural pretensions to universality (a Lutheran Norway as justification for a Confucian China!), could preserve the ideal of Chinese monarchy only as monarchy for China alone, and the ideal of intellectual self-sufficiency (i.e., renewal of Confucian dominance) only as (something new to Confucianism) "spirit-of-the-people" imperviousness to new ideas. Yüan Shih-k'ai could not be the "son of Heaven"; he could only, possibly, be king of China. And Yüan at the winter solstice, miming in the Temple of Heaven (and contemplating plowing in the spring) was a parody—and not just because he pulled up to the Temple in an armored car.

THE CONFUCIANISM-MONARCHISM COMPLEX BEFORE ITS MIN-KUO TRANSFORMATION

Yüan ends, then, supported by a Confucianism turned inside out, a Confucianism, that is, which for the most part no longer initiated a philosopical commitment to tradition, but which itself derived from a psychological commitment to tradition: when the people's Chinese identity seemed threatened by Republican Westernization, the "Chineseness" of Confucianism, more than its own traditionalist message, made it an object of traditionalists' reverence and a pillar of the throne. Thus, as suggested already, the cement of the "national spirit" joined the new monarchism and the new Confucianism in a new sort of partnership, new in its rather simple, uncomplicated character in contrast with the devious, uncertain partnership of pre-Western days. For the classical imperial system, for which Confucianism became the philosophy *par excellence*, was founded by Ch'in (221 B.C.) on anti-Confucianist Legalist principles, and this paradox, right from the start, remained at the core of Chinese history; a bureaucratic intelligentsia, while it cherished the social stability attending imperial centralization, yet was recurrently centrifugal, hence dangerous to a dynasty, by reason of acquisitive tendencies. The ancient imperial paradox, whose existence distinguishes true Confucian monarchy from its parody, deserves to be examined.

Over the long span of imperial Chinese history, there developed a Confucian literati-type; the figure of the emperor failed to conform to it. In many of his cultural and institutional affinities, he offended literati taste. The literati were eclectic enough philosophically, of course, and for any period from the Warring States (403–221 B.C.) on, Confucian texts may be shredded into all sorts of ingredients—Taoist, Buddhist, and what-not—but Chinese history does know intellectual confrontations, not just a happy melange, and relatively pure distillations of non-Confucian ideas had tendencies to seem at least in part imperial. Nonphilosophical Taoism, for example, jarred on fundamentally rationalistic Confucianists not only in its form of popular "enthusiasm" but in its connection with the elixir lore often strongly associated with emperors. Buddhism, too, had not only popular backing (often, from late T'ang on, as an anti-gentry, i.e., anti-Confucian, symbol) but imperial patronage as well, in times when its standing was extremely low or at best equivocal among the literati.[26] What could cause more revulsion in Confucianists, with their code of ethical relationships, than the patricidal or fratricidal episodes that disfigured so many imperial family histories? Eunuchs, whom Confucianists scorned and often hated and coupled with monks as "bad elements," were characteristic members of imperial retinues. Trade, which Confucianists affected to scorn (while Buddhism gave it impetus),[27] was a matter of imperial interest—given a court society's demands for luxury, not Confucian-approved—an interest manifest in such various phenomena as the eunuch Cheng Ho's voyages (1403–33), which Confucian historians buried;[28] eunuchs' prominence, protested by officials, in trading-ship control organs;[29] and the Canton system of trade

(1759–1839), in which the superintendent, the "Hoppo," was a specifically imperial appointee and outside the regular bureaucratic chain of command.[30] And the history of aesthetics in China records the distinction, Sung and later, between the "officials' style" (*shih-ta-fu hua*) and the style of the court academy (*yüan-hua*), a distinction which may be blurred by artistic eclecticism but is nonetheless significant, for it speaks of the self-detachment of the literati critic, his sensing of a dissonance of gentry and palace tones.[31]

Now, cultural rifts like these were far from extreme, for, after all, the social roles of bureaucracy and monarchy were only clashing, not incompatible, and were complementary even as they clashed. To put it another way: at least from the reign of Han Wu-ti (140–87 B.C.), monarch and civil official had a common stake in anti-feudalism (and in this their interests were complementary), while at the same time each had leanings (and here they clashed) to just that side of feudalism which was poison to the other. The ambivalence of bureaucracy toward monarchy and of monarchy toward bureaucracy was comprehended in the ambivalence of each toward feudalism: bureaucracy had some, at least, of the dynamics of feudalism without the statics; monarchy had the reverse.[32]

The imperial state was the proper milieu for bureaucracy (emperor and official, that is, were to this extent drawn together) in the following sense: a pre-Ch'in feudal nobility exploited land withdrawn from the reach of the public power, the state, which thus became a nullity; but the instability attendant on China's fragmentation reduced the private feudal power itself, and in the post-Ch'in empire the feudal nobility was superseded by a bureaucracy, which exploited the power of an anti-feudal state. The centralized state, as the universal tax-gatherer, inhibiting instability, had a basic though ambiguous value to a power-seeking bureaucracy—it provided something rich and real that could be eaten away in the feeding of private power. And it was eaten away recurrently. The process began anew each time the imperial state was reconstituted, after such attrition had brought it toward an impossible (because self-dissolving) feudal dissolution. Bureaucracy, then, perennially suspicious of imperially-backed suspect-radical strong men, with their various ideas for checking private aggrandizement in land (the *hsien-t'ien*, or "limit-the-fields," central-government policies), was, though abortively, a "feudalizing" force.

But it was never feudal. Needing the centralized state as it did, after its fashion, the Confucian corps had very serious anti-feudal commitments. As a type, Confucian intellectuality runs counter to the feudal admiration of martial vigor. War is mainly for the young, and Confucian opposition to a chivalric code of heroes was a turn to the elders, to learning over courage, and to a system of examinations of learning as the ideal road to power and prestige, circumventing those juridical guarantees of status which feudalism accorded to birth. And the examinations stressed a *traditional* learning, not original thought, because age over youth means not only counselor over warrior but old over new— the rule of precedent, the rule of example. Such reverence for precedent may sound close to feudalism, but feudal spokesmen for the most part dwell extensively on tradition only when feudalism is coming to be obsolete and under fire.

However, this Confucian hostility to the "static" attributes of feudalism implied tension, too, with monarchy. It was a tension explainable socially by the monarch's resistance to that erosion of public power which bureaucracy furthered dynamically, in its own gesture toward feudalism; and it was explainable intellectually by monarchy's leaning to just those feudal attributes that Confucianism countered. For in a feudal system, after all, monarchy had its familiar place at the pinnacle, and, with the marked exception of the feudal propensity for draining the central power (the Confucian bureaucracy's side of feudalism), many feudal associations were Chinese-imperial as well. Dynasties were not Confucian-pacifist but military like the feudalists, always trying to keep a grip on the Confucian-suspect military organs.[33] The Confucian ideal, embodied in the examination system and the model-emperor lore, of uninherited qualification for political standing, was inapplicable to hereditary monarchy, as it was to a feudal system in the round[34]—and to the simulated feudal systems which dynasties successively created and literati continually condemned.[35]

From the monarchy's side, too, the priority of family might be deplored: the Confucian *hsiao*, filial piety, was potentially irreconcilable with *chung*, political loyalty, an imperial requirement as well as originally a feudal conception;[36] while on their side Confucianists (especially of the Sung variety), at least in their ideals, tended to moralize *chung* as they had moralized other originally feudal concepts. They accepted loyalty as an obligation, but they meant to impose their definition of loyalty upon the emperor, not simply to have a blind requirement imposed upon themselves. As the Neo-Confucianist Ch'eng Hao (1032–85) put it, the emperor must distinguish between those who are loyal and those who are disloyal.[37] This imperative distinction implies a Confucian sense of discrimination. The onus is on the emperor. Loyalty may not be defined as unquestioned obedience to his (perhaps improper) wishes. Rather, the advice or example (the same thing) of a true Confucianist expresses it, and the emperor should recognize that those who agree with such sage advice are the loyal ones.

And when it came to the rule of law (more acceptable in feudal than in Confucian political theory), Ch'in Shih Huang-ti (reigned 246–210 B.C.) was the Legalist and truly the First Emperor, the prototype, for the codes were imperial and their very existence an implied rebuke to emperors, whose virtue, thought Confucianists, was evidently not enough to make for a flawless (law-less) social order.[38] A Stoic parallel in the Greek and Roman world (the Stoics, like the Confucianists, stressed harmony rather than action) corroborates the logic of this anti-legalist deprecation of actual monarchical power. Like the Confucianists again, the Stoics were far from admitting the unqualified legitimacy of contemporary absolute monarchy. Only the Sage, they felt, is capable of absolute royal rule, and he rules by calling others to imitation of himself (see Cicero, *De Legibus* and *De Republica*). Possessing reason in himself, he can dispense with written laws; he is the living law.[39] In China, when the Sung scholar Ch'en Liang (1143–1194) professed to discern sage-king patterns not merely in classical high antiquity but in the prosaically historical Han and T'ang dynasties, Chu Hsi (1130–1200), incomparably more influential, denounced him, and with appropriate emphasis stressed *hsiu-chi*, self-cultivation—the "inner" pole of a famous Confucian dichotomy—over the "outer" pole, *chih-jen*, ruling men.[40] Morality, the inner test which non-ideal, actual monarchs do not pass, transcends the legally constituted externals.

The over-all distinction between the necessary partners, Confucian literati and monarchy, and the basic condition of the tension between them, lay in their respective attitudes toward tradition. Here Ch'in Shih Huang-ti again, at the beginning, and the *T'ien-wang* of the Taipings (1850–64) near the end, seem the purest representatives of anti-literati, anti-traditional, undiluted monarchy. They were too pure to survive, too unequivocally unrestricted, without that blurring of the timeless monarchical abstraction which could make them historically viable; dynasties in general had to make the adjustments these disdained with traditionalist Confucianism. But the adjustments came from practical necessity, not from the genius of the institution of Chinese monarchy itself. One who contemplates the relation of monarchy to bureaucracy from this standpoint may reverse a familiar emphasis: perhaps the real issue is not the degree to which alien dynasties proved acceptable to Chinese literati, but the degree to which native dynasties proved alien to the same. In the total complex of Chinese political society, foreign dynasties may well have been nothing peculiar, only native dynasties to a higher power; and ethnic distinction no bureaucratic-dynastic problem in itself, only an exacerbation of the endemic problem of the division of powers. A foreign conquest-people and its chiefs might well in their hearts be culturally out of touch with the ideals of the literati. But so, to some extent, would any Chinese court. What Manchu prerogatives represented to Ch'ing Confucianists, the prerogatives of eunuchs may have represented to their predecessors under the Ming. And eunuchs or no, Manchus or no, Ming and Ch'ing were dynasties that Confucianists could live with. The Taipings' anti-Manchuism—symbolic, perhaps, of a proto-nationalistic revulsion from gentry culture—was a sham as an anti-Ch'ing weapon; for the gentry-literati-Confucianists, who were ostensibly more likely than any other Chinese to respond to the anti-Manchu call (since they suffered from the unfair proportion of Manchus to Chinese in high governing circles, while nineteenth-century peasants could barely have known Manchus as such), were loyal. They felt no special ethnic revulsion from the Manchus, but simply an expected strain between monarchical and bureaucratic bodies, a strain far less traumatic than the Taiping break appeared.

By this token, the familiar statement that prenationalistic culturalism legitimized any patrons of Confucianism, whatever their ethnic background, can be stated more precisely as follows: Any dynastic establishment, whatever its ethnic background, had the same need to patronize *but also the same need to qualify* Confucianism. It was not that foreign dynasties met a minimum of expected cultural conformity; it was rather that foreign dynasties practiced no more nonconformity than the maximum expected of rulers in general and grudgingly allowed them. It is because this was the state of affairs that we find Confucianism, for its part, always needing monarchy and always assuming its existence, but always implying restraints on its innate waywardness.

For what monarch could be justified in his pride of place when Confucius, the sage, had not been king? Kingship was not despised by Confucianists, but what the world saw as the king's "position," the outer trappings (and that meant kings in history, not the ideal conception), was hardly precious when the true king in his own day was the uncrowned Confucius, a *su-wang*, a "monarch unadorned."[41] "*Su-wang*" implied a possible separation between *wang-tao*, the Confucian ideal of the hidden royal "way," and *wang-i*, the monarchy's statement of visible royal rank. It was the impulse to restrain this natural tendency of monarchy to be *visible* that gave point to some of Confucianism's most vital conceptions.

Inescapably, everywhere, splendor and spectacle attach themselves to monarchy. As the ultimate leader of society, and as one not to be scrutinized for human frailties (for in that case, he might not pass), a monarch requires acceptance as something more than man, something related to divinity; majesty is the visible reflection in society of a divine splendor.

But it is a special conception of divinity—the transcendental—which spectacle connotes. Just as it sets the monarch apart, so it speaks of a divine power that is truly "other," and truly power, the combination that spells Creator. A creator, however, is alien to Confucian thought as the literati came to profess it. However much a transcendental sentiment may be recognized in popular Chinese religion or suspected in the Classics, in a perhaps irrecoverable stratum of meaning, buried far beneath the commentaries, the literati's Confucianism — certainly by Sung, the civil bureaucracy's time of fulfillment—was committed unequivocally to immanence. Scholars have recently suggested that in the period of the Warring States, in the time and region of Confucianism's first emergence, the *Huang* of *Huang [t'ien shang] ti* (sovereign heavenly emperor) had passed over into its homonym, in *Huang-ti*, the "Yellow Emperor."⁴² What had been heavenly became a supposedly historical monarch, and the first one, thereafter, in the Confucian list of the five model sage-kings. This would represent etymologically the Confucian transfer of emphasis from the celestial to the earthly-political sphere—a shift from a vision of transcendental power to one of the monarch as exemplar.

Philosophically, no Creator meant no "in the beginning," hence no progressive concept of time threatening the Confucian ideal of equilibrium and the non-"time-ridden" historical theory (more paradigmatic than process-oriented) that accorded with it. The corollary in political theory was a Confucian ideal of an emperor radiating virtue, magically reflecting harmony to society, not logically interfering with it to move it; he should be sympathetically stabilizing an eternal cosmos, which had never been once created and should never be freshly tampered with by some mock-transcendental earthly ruler, acting, creating anew.

In the *Shuo-wen*, where the *Tso-chuan* is given as *locus classicus* (*cheng i cheng min*), *cheng*, "to govern," is a cognate of *cheng*, "to adjust." The emperor's role is government, its definition "adjustment" of the people's transgressions and errors.⁴³ The assumption here is of an eternal pattern; *cheng* is the process of restoring conformity to it. The Sung Neo-Confucianist Ch'eng Hao, memorializing his emperor, saw the "way" of Yao and Shun as the perfecting of the five social relationships, achieving adjustment to heavenly reason.⁴⁴ This is essentially the task of a silent one, a sage in concealment (the immanent is always hidden, never spectacular). The very idea of it clashed with a real emperor's natural place as a focal point for spectacle, and with his natural penchant for wielding power to change the world, not for emanating perpetuation of a changeless pattern.

In the most completely austere of transcendentalisms, with idolatry under an absolute ban, the monarchical idea is fundamentally discouraged: if God is King, there ought to be no king to play at God (see I Samuel 8: 4–7, before the enthronement of Saul in Israel). For that is surely what kingship carries with it. To the Byzantine philosopher Themistus (fourth century A.D.), the ruler's primary attribute, the divine *philanthropia* (love of man), made the emperor God-like, with God's prerogative of mercy being the emperor's prerogative, too, marking for both transcendence over what they give the world—the legal codes of justice.[45] For dominant Christianity in the Byzantine Empire, this was the ground for submission to imperial authority; for dominant but very different Confucianism in China, this imperial link with formulated law, with its transcendental implications, was, we saw, a ground of conflict. From the standpoint of Samuel's terrible warning of what a king would really mean in exercise of power (I Samuel 8: 11–18), the Byzantine's active *philanthropia* was a myth to gloss over the true potential of monarchy. From the same standpoint, the Confucian ideal of sage-like non-activity was a myth, too: the king does not stay hidden. The difference between the myths is that the Byzantine coincided with an emperor's naturally transcendental pretensions, and strengthened his hold; while the Confucian was at odds with the character of the throne, and stood as a reproach. Byzantines conceived of imperial government as a terrestrial copy of the rule of God in Heaven.[46] Confucianists had no God in Heaven, no autonomous Voice that spoke from the outer and above; and in so far as monarchy inevitably approached that model, the Confucianists strained against it—not condemning it (in the Hebraic fashion, out of an utter transcendentalism unvitiated by the Greek idea of incarnation), but correcting it, as far as they could, toward silence.

Perhaps the nearest approach a Chinese emperor made to this quasi-Taoist non-activity[47] which Confucianists commended to the throne was in the imperial ineffectualness which often accompanied social breakdown. But in that case, one may be assured, there was no Confucian accolade. Instead, the emperor's virtue was disparaged (usually from the safe vantage point of a later dynasty), since he had evidently not fulfilled his symbolic responsibilities as holder of Heaven's mandate. Clearly, the Chinese emperor was subject to checks: material noncooperation in his own day and at least posthumous moral reproach.

I have already suggested (in discussing "the people's will"), and Wittfogel has also emphasized, that these moral reproaches, for whatever they were worth, were no testimony to "the innate democracy of Chinese political thinking."[48] But what still needs to be emphasized—and Wittfogel, preoccupied with a model of absolute despotic power, neglects to dwell on it—is that the immanentist *t'ien-ming* (mandate)

doctrine really was an expression of conflict with the emperor (Byzantine Christian officials, much more than Chinese Confucianists, were a
despot's faceless men), though a bureaucratic, not democratic, expression. Bureaucratic historians, in their Confucian moralism, charged up
to the emperor symptoms of social decay which were actually effects of
the normal functioning of the bureaucracy itself.

Confucianists had to have an emperor as a reflector of morality (in
social terms: officials needed a state), but by the system of morality he
capped, the emperor could be indicted to cover the part which officials
played in wasting the state they needed. "Mandate" theory was no defense of the people, mitigating absolutism, but it was a defense of gentry-
literati in their conflict-collaboration with the emperor in manipulating
the state.

I have no wish to imply here any organized cynicism, or conscious
cabals to fool the people and bind the emperor. This is a statement of
the logic of a world, not an assumption of cool detachment and logical
calculation on the part of the world's leaders. What we see in the Confucian political order is an inner consistency—something not depending
on the exercise of rational cunning or on any other melodrama—a consistency of intellectual theory and the intellectuals' social concerns. A
conservative social group, opposed above all else to revolution while it
contributes provocation to that end, favors an almost exquisitely appropriate doctrine: by making an explanation of the workings of the
social system moral, inner, rather than social, outer, it makes the system
sacrosanct, untouchable intellectually. Dynasties, the Confucianists'
lightning rods to draw off the fury of social storms, go through *ko-ming*,
exchanges of the mandate, but bureaucracy goes on and on, not subject
to revolution.

Finally there was a revolution in China, establishing the Republic,
and its participants called it *ko-ming*. But was it the same old term? It
seems rather a translation back into Chinese, as it were, of the modern
Japanese *kakumei*, which had used the "mandate" characters metaphorically to convey the idea of revolution. It could have been nothing
but metaphor in Japan, where a monarchist theory, stressing descent, not
heavenly election, genealogical qualifications, not moral ones, had never
been Confucian.

For the primordial heroes in Confucian myth are men, not gods or
descendants of gods; but the Japanese myth begins with the sun-goddess
and her Japanese warrior-offspring. Thus a Chinese monarch is legitimate when he repeats the example of sage-kings of independent lineages,
while a Japanese monarch is legitimate when he descends from divinity,
which bequeaths his line eternity; *his* mandate is irrevocable. Only revo-

lution, which explicitly denies the old legitimacy, can bring it to an end, and "change of mandate," which a Chinese Confucianist could contemplate with equanimity, as a perpetuation of legitimacy, could not be reconciled with the Japanese monarchical system. One of the most highly esteemed of Ming writings published in Japan (Hsieh Chao-chi [*chin-shih* 1593], *Wu Tsa Tsu* ["The Five Assorted Vessels," there being five sections, on heaven, earth, man, objects, and events]) had its passages from Mencius deleted; as a modern scholar explains it, the *ko-ming* conception was thought inappropriate to the Japanese form of state.[49]

Ko-ming, then, had no natural place in the Japanese vocabulary as long as its literal Confucian sense, which was nonsense in Japan, was the only sense it had. But when modern Japan, moving from Chinese traditions to Western for foreign influences, enlarged her vocabulary to encompass Western ideas, the *ko-ming* compound had enough flavor of sharp political break to be assigned the meaning of revolution. Modern Chinese, enlarging their vocabulary in their turn, and finding in the Japanese language a repository of modern terms in characters, reached for "revolution" and made the same transformation, from literal to figurative, in *ko-ming* (Sun Yat-sen accepted himself as leader of a *ko-ming tang* only when [1895], in a flash of revelation of new meaning in the old term, he read in a Kobe newspaper that that was what he was.)[50] The phrase was not stripped of its old associations; its historical depth was recognized. But this very recognition reduced an ancient Confucian concept to something quaint and "period." For a modern, to say that Hsüan-t'ung lost the mandate in 1911 was to strive with conscious anachronism for allusive effect. Once-serious Confucian content was turned into rhetoric. And Yüan Shih-k'ai, the Hung-hsien Emperor, buckling on his virtue where the Ch'ing had dropped it and implicitly denying the anti-traditional purport of the republicans' *ko-ming* (as his followers explicitly countered anti-traditionalism in general), was an anachronism, a farceur, a period piece come to life.

It was a starved life and it had to be. The royal latecomer was forced to look back to a sacred past, in which his brand of traditionalism and his Confucian supporters', unfortunately, was not prefigured, and in which Confucian support for monarchy, anyway, was not so straightforward. How could "the spirit of the people," the basis of traditionalism for modern monarchists and modern Confucianists, have any place in the earlier Chinese complex, in which a foreign dynasty, patently unassimilable to the "spirit" of the Chinese people, was always, nevertheless, an orthodox possibility? And where was the old tension between essentially Legalist, anti-traditionalist dynastic monarchy, whether Chinese or foreign in ethnic and cultural origin, and literati-Confucian traditionalism?

In the great imperial ages some Confucian ideals, sacrificed in practice to the need for accommodation with the throne, had remained in force implicitly as restraints on imperial power, while, *mutatis mutandis,* the same may be said on the other side. But now, when revolutionaries were occasionally helping themselves to some of the old Confucian-bureaucratic specifics against the pretensions of the throne (Yao and Shun as "democrats," for example, since they were anti-dynastic),[51] such checks had to be dropped by Confucian-traditionalist anti-republicans (though not by Confucianists who were defeatist about monarchy and tried to make a go of the Republic).[52] Now the old tension was released. Yet it was a release that brought only the rest of death, as a wraith-like monarchy and a wraith-like Confucianism faded into a final association, untroubled at last by each other, but untroubled, also, by very much of life.

FORM AND CONTENT

Thus, the apparent emptiness of the Chinese Republic did nothing for monarchy. The monarchical symbols were just as thoroughly drained, and this in itself reminds us that the new form of republican China was not only form but content; the Republic was really new, and *sui generis* in Chinese history. If literal monarchy was a hollow shell, then the supposition that figurative monarchy has been the setting of post-Ch'ing history is hollow, too. The early republican period should not be viewed as just one more warlord pendant to an imperial era, with the Nanking government of Chiang K'ai-shek as the Ch'in or Sui type of abortive dynasty, unifying and preparing the way for a longer-lived bureaucratic centralized regime. If the Hung-hsien movement was monarchical in form only (because its justifications and associations had to be new), the Republic could not have been monarchical in all but form.

For radical depreciation of the significance of "form" in comparison with "content" (a depreciation involved in suggestions that things are "really" the same as ever in what is merely formally the Republican era in Chinese history) is both trite and misleading. If form has any "mereness," it is not in its unimportance when it changes; it is in its failure to hold a specific content when it, form, remains the same. The forces revising monarchy's content likewise made the Republic more than superficially new: if Yüan Shih-k'ai was a parodist as Emperor, he was not in essence Emperor as President.

What was really involved in Yüan's effort to reinstate *ch'en* as the word for "official" in his reign? There was the simple fact of its monarchical affinities, of course: there were the classic pairs of *chün* and *ch'en,* prince and minister, a relationship found in such famous catalogues as the *Tso-chuan's* "six *shun*" and "ten *li*," the *Li-chi's* "ten *i*" and "seven *chiao*";[53] and *wang* and *ch'en*, monarch and minister, bound together as firmly as the *Ch'un-ch'iu* and *Tso-chuan*, for of the two reputed authors, when Confucius was called a *su-wang*, Tso Ch'iu-ming was a *su-ch'en*.[54] But there was something more deeply significant about *ch'en* than any merely verbal associations. It was something relating not just to monarchy but to the cultural air of Confucian, imperial China, so that its banishment from the Republic (and consequently, Yüan's effort to restore it) symbolized a genuine change of social and intellectual climate.

Kuan, the Republic's term for official which Yüan wished to displace, was a very old one, too, but in the pre-republican, Confucian bureaucratic world it had a sense quite distinguishable from *ch'en*'s. *Kuan* denoted the bureaucrat in his technical, functional, impersonal capacity. It had no connection with personal cultural dignity and individuality. For example, *kuan-t'ien*, set apart from *min-t'ien* in the Ming tax system,[55] was not "officials' land," the land of officials as persons; it was "official land," i.e., public land as opposed to private. *Kuan* suggests the state apparatus and *min*, here, the private sector. If "people" and "official" were being counterposed as human types, "official" would be *ch'en*.

For the outstanding attribute of *ch'en* (and this made it a "grander" word) was personal status, free of technical, professional connotations. Not the task but the personal tie defined him: "The loyal *ch'en* does not serve two princes."[56] An official was *kuan* in his job, something akin to being a tool, a means—and *ch'en* in his position, an end.

One of the outstanding, all-pervasive values of Confucian culture was its anti-professionalism. The Confucian ideal of personal cultivation was a humanistic amateurism, and Confucian education, perhaps supreme in the world for anti-vocational classicism, produced an imperial bureaucracy, accordingly, in which human relations counted for more than the network of abstract assignments (just as in Confucian society generally, human relations counted for more than legal relations). In these respects—not by accident—it differed from bureaucracies of the modern industrial West and, at least in conception, from that of the Chinese Republic.[57] A comparison of the Ch'ing dynasty's *mu-liao* or *mu-yu* and the Republic's *k'o-chang mi-shu* may be illustrative. All these designations, on both sides of the great divide, applied to the private secretary-advisers of administrative heads. There was nothing fundamentally dissimilar in their roles, but there was a great difference in their relationships with their respective seniors and in their legal status: the Republic's secretary-adviser was formally an official (*kuan-li*); his Ch'ing counterpart was the official's friend and technically not attached to the *pu*, the office, or paid from the public granaries.[58] As Chang Chien, a modern-minded industrialist (and later one of Yüan's supporters, though out of "strong man" sympathies, not out of archaism), caustically observed, all Ch'ing officials, provincial and local, could appoint their own assistants, as in the Han and T'ang *mu-chih*, government by staffs of intimates.[59]

The Republican emphasis on *kuan*, then, to the exclusion of *ch'en*, was the mark of a specifically modern commitment, to a professionalized, anti-literati world in which science, industry, and the idea of progress (all of them having impersonal, hence un-Confucian, implications) claimed first attention. This was not just the preference of a faction. It was really the world which for some time had been making over and taking over China, not only manfacturing iconoclasts but transforming traditionalists, in ways we have seen. The *ch'en*, the nonspecialized free man of high culture as the master-creation of civilization, who relegated to the *kuan* category the "jobs," the "business" of government (necessary even in the old regime, of course, but faintly unsavory, more the price paid than the prize won with prestige), was a figure of the unredeemable past. The Republic of *kuan* meant a genuine change from the Empire of *kuan* and *ch'en*.

The Empire dissolved in *ko-ming*. *Ko-ming*, itself drained of its traditional literal meaning and metaphorized into modern "revolution," freed men's minds and made them aware of the changing content of Chinese civilization. Chinese imperial forms became anachronisms. And *ch'en*, one of them, had its meaning changed like the *ko-ming* that had destroyed its proper world.

For *ch'en*, as we early suggested, had been paired not only with *kuan*, but in the Ch'ing dynasty with *nu*, "slave." *Nu* was the term for Manchu officials, relating them to the Ch'ing as Manchu monarchs, while the Ch'ing as Chinese emperors left Chinese officials the Confucian status of *ch'en*, in the classically noble relationship of minister to throne. Revolutionary republicanism, however, extended the application of the term "slave," and in this way, also, marked the obliteration of the world of *ch'en*. By doctrinaire republicans, "slave" was stripped of its literal, technical significance (which it had had for the Manchu officials, who were *nu* in a juridical sense for all that their use of the term may seem to be simple etiquette) and made expressive, metaphorically, of all subjects of supreme monarchs. As the republican minister, Wu T'ing-fang, put it in 1912, in a placatory cable to anti-republican Mongol princes, all had suffered the bitterness of slaves under the Ch'ing crown—Chinese, Manchus, Mongols, Moslems, Tibetans—and all would be brothers in the one great republic.[60] From the republican standpoint, then, to have been *ch'en* was not to have distinguished oneself from slaves but precisely to have been a slave. For there was no *ch'en* without his *wang* or *chün*, no Confucian gentleman outside a realm—at least an ideal one, however much the actual may have strained against Confucianism (Confucianists *had* required the Empire, even if they execrated Ch'in Shih Huang). *Ko-ming* as change of mandate would have struck off *nu* and left *ch'en* in a continuing imperial bureaucracy. But the *ko-ming* revolution, anti-imperial and in more than form, retroactively confounded *ch'en* and *nu*, struck them off together, and in this alone set a seal on the end of the Empire.

Nevertheless, just as for Mao Tse-tung and his regime today, so for Yüan Shih-k'ai in his lifetime (and the same theoretical issue is at stake: changing content behind changing form, or not?), some contemporaries saw analogies with patterns of the old monarchical past. A Japanese observer in 1914, Sakamaki Teiichirō, fixed Yüan as the Wang Mang in a late version of the fall of the former Han. Yüan, as rumor had it, was implicated in the death of the Emperor Kuang-hsü (1908), just as Wang Mang was involved in the murder of the Emperor P'ing (A.D. 5). Subsequently, Yüan's engineering the transfer of power to himself from Kuang-hsü's young successor was precisely the story of Wang Mang and the Emperor P'ing's successor. Yüan's *Chung-hua min-kuo*, to sum up, stood in the same relation to regular dynastic history as the *Hsin-kuo* of Wang Mang.[61]

Two of Yüan's puppets (one of them his "sworn brother" Hsü Shih-ch'ang, who had been brought up by Yüan's father, Yüan Chia-san) became "Grand Guardians of the Emperor" in November 1911, after the Prince Regent retired.[62] Sakamaki was not the only one to feel that Yüan, in imperial fashion, was easing out the Ch'ing. There is a note of innuendo in some of Sun Yat-sen's expressions in late January, 1912, when Yüan was proceeding, in sweet independence of the Nanking Kuomintang, to set up a government in Peking, a city Sun feared for its imperial associations.[63] "No one knows whether this provisional government is to be monarchical or republican," said Sun on January 20. "Yüan not only specifically injures the Republic, but is in fact an enemy of the Ch'ing emperor," said Wu T'ing-fang, at Sun's direction, on January 28.[64] By 1913, though Yüan had crowned the occasion of the Ch'ing abdication in February 1912 with a statement that monarchy would never again function in China,[65] Sun was sure that Yüan was imperial as well as imperious. The very term "Second Revolution" for the Kiangsi rising in the summer of that year had anti-monarchical overtones, and Sun's provocative public cable to a variety of addressees, on July 18, read

Yüan out of the Republic, right back to the ranks of Chinese absolute monarchs. Public servants, said Sun, should be subject to the people's appraisal. This was the case even in constitutional monarchies—how much more should it be so in a republic![66]

VESTIGIAL MONARCHISM AND THE MEANING OF
JAPANESE SPONSORSHIP

Yet, despite the pedantic or polemical impulses of the moment which moved men to interpret Yüan's republic as a monarchical regime, Yüan himself knew that his republic was not his empire—knew it emotionally, at the level of desire for an emperor's baubles and trappings, and knew it intellectually, at the level of tactics, in his grasp of the need to shift his base of support. Nationalism, with its iconoclastic implications, was the Republic's grain of novelty. As at least the ostensible exponent of the nation's cause against Japan in the 1915 crisis of the "Twenty-one Demands," Yüan, the president, had the most solid public support of his life. But immediately thereafter Yüan was a would-be emperor, and he tried to feel his way to Japanese support, tried this reversal quite plausibly, in a search for something to replace the nationalists' backing, which had been available to him as a nationalistic president, but would necessarily be withdrawn from a traditionalistic emperor.

Yüan succeeded only imperfectly in gaining useful Japanese support. He was too old a foe of Japanese diplomacy to be rehabilitated in that quarter overnight, and his monarchical chances, it was soon apparent, seemed too dim to proclaim him at the last a likely protégé. Given the Japanese aims in China, and Yüan's billing, for so many years, as China's strong man, Japanese leaders quite naturally found their habit of hostility to Yüan hard to break.

Yet Yüan as emperor, by his forfeiting of the support of modern-minded nationalists, actually had potentialities as China's weak man, potentialities for exploitation by expansionist Japan, since he needed aid to make himself strong enough to survive, and, once surviving, to recognize his debt. Japanese support of Chinese monarchy would bring Japan at least a minority Chinese backing, minor enough to need Japan to protect its cause in China, not major enough to threaten Japan with Chinese independence. Japanese who looked on China as empty of vitality and devoid of national feeling (as many did in 1916, more than were able to later) might think this solicitude for Chinese monarchism unnecessary, and resent Yüan as an ambitious flouter of these anti-nationalist Chinese virtues. But when Chinese nationalism was invoked against Yüan as emperor, invoked in its aspect of anti-traditionalism, its sanction for the free thought and open prospects which the latter-day monarchists' historicism denied, some few Japanese recognized at last the impending maturity of Chinese nationalism (which must ultimately work against Japan, though Japan had helped tremendously to bring it to birth), and turned pro-Yüan in the end.

The balance was still against him, in Japan as in China. But the Hung-hsien movement was the turning point for Japan in China and Japanese influence on Chinese culture. From being the school of Chinese radicals and nationalists, Japan became the temple of the deepest Chinese traditionalism. And Chinese monarchy was ultimately relegated to foreign sponsorship, foreshadowed in the ambiguous Japanese attitude toward Yüan in 1915, and culminating in the Japanese revival of the Ch'ing dynasty in Manchuria. When nationalism implied both iconoclasm culturally and anti-Japanism politically, the cause of Chinese monarchy quite plausibly qualified for Japanese backing; for with its imprisonment in cultural traditionalism, latter-day Chinese monarchy committed itself to anti-nationalism, and to a political ambience, accordingly, at least passively pro-Japanese.

THE JAPANESE AND CHINESE MONARCHICAL MYSTIQUES

Ironically enough, Chinese monarchism not only ended as bankrupt with Japanese receivers, but had marked its panic long before with a desperate reaching out for Japanese procedures. The Ch'ing and their supporters, back in the days of the post-Boxer "Manchu Reform Movement" and right down to 1911, had taken to insisting on Ch'ing eternity in the midst of the myriad changes that the Ch'ing were forced to bless, and they did it by reiterating "Wan-shih i-hsi," the *Bansei ikkei*, "One line throughout ten thousand ages," that celebrated Japan's imperial house. It hardly belonged in China, with the latter's long centuries of nonfeudal imperium, in which the mandate was not necessarily inheritable.

It is this difference between the premodern societies, Chinese bureaucratic and Japanese feudal, that accounts for the different fates of the Chinese and Japanese monarchies. In modern Japan, monarchy has been no parody; the mystique of the throne has been strengthened, not dispelled (the repercussions of the recent war are not considered here). For in Japan, unlike China, a postfeudal regime could cite prefeudal precedents against the feudal intermission. The Japanese revolution, that is, could strike against the *de facto* Tokugawa feudal shogunate in the name of Nara, and Meiji, *de jure* imperial control: modernization could be combined with myth-making about antiquity. But in China the modern breach with things as they were was a breach precisely with a *de jure* situation, a dynastic and bureaucratic regime which was, in general terms, as tradition had accepted it, and modernization required myth-breaking. Compare only the early-modern contemporaries, the Chinese "Han Learning," with its probing for forgeries and its ultimately revolutionary and republican implications, and the Japanese "Pure Shintō," with its writing of forgeries and its ultimately revolutionary but monarchist implications. The Japanese could combine a prefeudal form with postfeudal content; the strengthening of Japanese monarchy was compatible with modernization. But the strengthening —or the mere reestablishing—of Chinese monarchy was incompatible with modernization. Indeed, as we have seen, Yüan Shih-k'ai's effort to reestablish monarchy was undertaken deliberately as an anti-modernist counterthrust.

Kokutai, or "national form," intimately individual polity, was an ancient Japanese term with tremendous modern and nationalist-monarchist currency. But its Chinese counterpart, with the same characters, *kuo-t'i,* was just another of those terms proper to Japan, exotic in China, which were rushed to the aid of a Chinese monarchism having none of the favorable circumstances of monarchy in the modern age in Japan. Liang Ch'i-ch'ao (1873–1929), rebuffing Yüan's son's *kuo-t'i* monarchical blandishments in 1915, with their invitation to see the *kuo-ch'ing* or "national spirit" in just this form of state, preferred to speak, he said, of *cheng-t'i,* of the practical question of the workings of government rather than the more metaphysical, "essential" question of the location of national authority[67]—this distinction having first been made as a Japanese distinction, between *kokutai* and *seitai,* in the *Kokutai Shinron* of Katō Hiroyuki in 1874.[68] *Kokutai* was a living word; *kuo-t'i* was a contrivance.[69] To speak a living language, one must say that the Hung-hsien reign was supposed to be the revival of Chinese *kokutai.* But how could a Chinese *revive* in China a new and foreign importation? What was this traditional national form which tradition had never named and nationalists could hardly accept? It was paradox which made of Yüan a parodist.

For the kings were truly finished — *wang* and *su-wang* both, the merely royal and the Confucian sage-ideal. Monarchism and Confucianism, which had belonged together in their own way and run dry together, were garbled together in a new way now that failed to elicit the old responses. When republican "men of the future" set the pace, they not only abandoned traditionalism on their own account but transformed the traditionalism of those who never joined them, turning it into nostalgia—which is thirst for the past, not a life-giving fluid itself.

John Whitney Hall

THE CONFUCIAN TEACHER
IN TOKUGAWA JAPAN

In 1608, when Tokugawa Ieyasu appointed Hayashi Razan Confucianist to the Shogunate, he put an official stamp on a movement which within a few decades was to make Confucianism the "strongest intellectual and ethical force in Japan"[1] and was to have a lasting influence upon Japanese thought.

The broad outlines of the story of the spread of Neo-Confucian philosophy and institutions in Tokugawa Japan have become part of all standard histories of the period. But beyond the introductory level, the story has been told only inadequately. What purport to be histories of Tokugawa Confucianism turn out to be either collections of biographies of Confucian scholars arranged chronologically,[2] or interpretations, often of a Marxist nature, which identify Confucianism with what was "feudal" in the political and social institutions of the time.[3] The biographies, typically the work of men so close to the movement as to be concerned above all with problems of scholarly continuity and doctrinal controversy,[4] make little effort to relate the Confucian movement to other historical developments or to consider Confucianism in the light of its influence upon contemporary society. The theoretical works, which date largely from the 1920's, go to the other extreme: they tend to ignore the lives and thoughts of individual scholars, or rather to generalize such details into a single ideological system exerting a massive conservative pressure upon the Japanese of the time.

From these two sterile and one-sided historical traditions, scholarship both in Japan and in the West is only now extricating itself. What is needed is a clearer emphasis on Confucianism *in action* and on its demonstrable effect within society. As Benjamin Schwartz has observed, the task of the intellectual historian is to determine the nature of "men's conscious responses to the situations in which they find themselves."[5] In the following pages we shall examine the responses of a particular set of men, the prime agents through whom Neo-Confucianism was introduced and disseminated in Japan—the *jusha,* or professional Confucian teachers.

My purpose has been to relate the lives, thoughts, and actions of individual jusha to the phenomena of political and social action. For this reason I have concerned myself primarily with the relationship of the Confucian teachers to the members of the politically dominant class, the samurai.

THE ORIGIN OF THE JUSHA

The rise of the jusha is intimately related to the process of political reorganization which during the early seventeenth century resulted in the establishment of the Tokugawa Shogunate and the daimyo domains. In fact it has been suggested that it was only by conscientiously and openly espousing Confucian principles that shogun and daimyo were able to make the difficult transition from continuous warfare to peacetime rule.[6] The conditions which gave rise to the acceptance of Confucian thought as the favored official philosophy of the Tokugawa period have frequently been described, and there is little cause to quarrel with the accepted versions. In very general terms, this acceptance was a product of political and intellectual changes which occurred in Japanese society during the sixteenth century.

First of all, the emergence of the large daimyo domains brought into being new and more clear-cut distinctions in the political and social functions of the various segments of society. In particular the separation of the military-administrative class (*bushi* or samurai) from the land required the daimyo to direct his attention to the organization of a formal administrative apparatus to deal with civil affairs. To the Japanese of the late sixteenth century, it took no great effort of the imagination to see similarities between the emerging social order and that of Chou times in China, the age when Confucianism had come into being.

At the same time the intellectual climate in Japan was itself undergoing change. It had become increasingly clear that a politically overextended and spiritually bankrupt Buddhism had no solutions to offer to the pressing problems faced by the administrative class. It was under these circumstances that the Japanese made their dramatic turn to Neo-Confucianism. What is perhaps most remarkable about the subsequent upsurge of Neo-Confucianism was that it depended in almost no way on missionary effort from the mainland. It was an indigenous movement stimulated by indigenous conditions.

The study of Confucian texts and their interpretations by Sung commentators, it should be recalled, was nothing new to the Japanese. Con-

fucian studies had a definite place in the scholarship of the Buddhist
monasteries as a branch of practical learning. What happened in the
sixteenth century was that they were emancipated from the monastic
confines and the monopoly control of certain court families. With the
freeing of the doctrine, the Confucian specialist became differentiated
from the Buddhist priest and took his place as a new variety of intellectual leader, the jusha. Three men in particular can be singled out as
illustrating in their careers the early history of the Confucian movement.
They are Fujiwara Seika, Hayashi Razan, and Nakae Tōju.

Fujiwara Seika (1561–1619) exemplifies in his life and thought the
shift in allegiance from Buddhism to Confucianism which was taking
place among Japan's political and intellectual leaders.[7] He was trained
as a priest in one of the foremost Zen monasteries of Kyoto; but like
many others of his training, he entered feudal service, becoming tutor
and adviser to Lord Akamatsu of Harima. While in Harima, Seika appears to have turned increasingly to the teachings of Chu Hsi as a source
of guidance in administrative and economic matters. His ultimate revulsion against the monastic world was confirmed during the years of
the Japanese campaigns in Korea, when he had the opportunity to
mingle with Chinese envoys and Korean captives. From them he learned
of the ascendancy of Confucianism in China and Korea and of the declining fortunes of Buddhism on the continent.

Seika can be thought of most appropriately as a transitional figure.
Though he pioneered in the effort to extricate Confucianism from the
dominance of the Buddhist monasteries, and although he defied tradition by publicly lecturing on the Classics (using Neo-Confucian
commentaries), he did not totally reject Buddhism. In his early career
he loyally served his feudal patron, but in his later years, when a position
in the service of the Tokugawa Shogunate was offered him, he declined
it in the interests of preserving his intellectual independence.

The identification of the Confucian scholar with the new political
order was ultimately achieved by the man Seika recommended to the
Shogun in his place, Hayashi Razan (1583–1657).[8] Razan came from a
minor samurai family and entered a monastery as a means of securing an
education. When pressed to take the tonsure, he rejected the offer indignantly and returned to his home to study Neo-Confucian texts. As
lecturer to the Shogun, Razan was in the end obliged to wear the Buddhist tonsure and take a Buddhist title, in order to retain the favor of
Tokugawa Ieyasu. Eventually the Hayashi house became attached to
the Tokugawa family as goyō gakusha (scholars in service). Although
others, notably Yamaga Sokō (1622–85), were to go farther than Razan
in interpreting Confucianism to fit the uses of the Tokugawa political
order, he went as far as any man of his generation. He acted not from

cowardice or cupidity, but from conviction. A believer in the need for firm political authority and in the power of good example, he sought to reform society through the agency of the prime political power in the land. Razan was equally authoritarian in his selection of Chu Hsi as the one source of doctrinal truth.

If Hayashi Razan can be considered the first jusha of the Tokugawa period, he was not alone in his generation to preach the Neo-Confucian doctrine or to apply Confucian principles to the political problems faced by the ruling houses of the early seventeenth century. In other parts of Japan as well, especially in the local cultural centers of central and western Japan, scholars were shaking off the dominance of the Buddhist establishment to advocate the superiority of the Sung philosophers. In Satsuma, Neo-Confucian studies had been stimulated as far back as the middle of the fifteenth century by the Zen priest Keian. During the sixteenth century, Satsuma priests availed themselves of opportunities to improve their understanding of Confucian texts through contacts with the continent and the Ryukyus. One such priest is reported to have listened to Fujiwara Seika in Kyoto only to return to Satsuma saying, "His interpretations originated in Satsuma."[9] In Chōshū, where the Mōri family continued the patronage of letters begun by the Ōuchi, the study of Neo-Confucian texts is said to have begun in the 1540's.[10] In Tosa the pioneer work of Minamimura Baiken inspired Tani Jichū (1598–1649) and later Nonaka Kenzan (1605–63) to found an independent line of Neo-Confucianism known as the Southern School.[11] In each of these locations the process of transition from Buddhist priest to jusha had begun by the turn of the seventeenth century.

For most other parts of Japan, however, the acceptance of Confucian doctrines and the patronage of jusha appear to have come more slowly, following the Tokugawa lead and the stimulus of the missionary work of Hayashi Razan. In the domains of Owari, Kii, Mito, Bizen, and Kaga, Confucian teachers were first employed during the second or third generation after the time of Ieyasu. In many domains Neo-Confucianism was not introduced until the internal affairs of the domain were stabilized and the daimyo could turn to the problems of civil affairs. As a consequence, during the middle decades of the seventeenth century, the eyes of many daimyo were turned simultaneously upon the source of Confucian scholars. In these years, before the Hayashi school in Edo had begun to turn out acceptable official Confucianists, the source was largely Kyoto. From Kyoto came a long list of jusha who served daimyo in various parts of Japan. Matsunaga Shakugo and Kinoshita Junnan in Kaga, Hori Kōan in Owari, Kumazawa Banzan in Bizen, Yamazaki Ansai in Aizu, all received their original training in Kyoto.

By the end of the seventeenth century Edo had become the major gathering and training place for jusha. Kyoto's position remained unique, however, as a center for such private scholars as our third major figure, Nakae Tōju (1608–48).[12] Not all Confucian scholars entered or aspired to official service, for it was possible in Tokugawa Japan for the independent Confucian teacher to make a living by writing and taking in pupils. Men like Nakae Tōju or somewhat later such men as Itō Jinsai (1627–1705) and Itō Tōgai (1670–1736) played a distinctive role in the Tokugawa Confucian movement. Their interests were not confined to the samurai but extended to the merchant class as well. In them we see a reaction against the undue accommodation of Neo-Confucianism to the social and political interests of the samurai. In many respects Nakae Tōju, living quietly in Ōmi outside of Kyoto, typified the dedicated Confucian teacher, detached from public service but a constant critic of the life of the times—a living conscience, as it were, for the age.

By the middle of the seventeenth century the career possibilities of the jusha had become well defined. Either in the service of feudal lords or as private instructors, the jusha had become a part of the samurai's world, performing necessary functions in the new political and social order. Broadly speaking, these functions were four in number. First, as a ritualist and a philosopher-moralist, the jusha became the champion of the Confucian world view in his society. Second, as an authority on the Confucian texts, he was looked to for advice in governmental affairs. Third, as keeper of the basic educational texts, he was given the responsibility of developing educational institutions. Fourth, as a scholar and a writer, he became a respected leader in cultural activities. In the following pages we shall examine these four functions and their importance to the new regime.

THE JUSHA AS RITUALIST-MORALIST

Although Confucianism in Japan did not give rise to a religious establishment comparable to that of organized Buddhism, it served a number of functions in samurai society which were fundamentally religious. To this extent, the Tokugawa jusha acted as ritualists on behalf of a specific world view and social ethic.

The Tokugawa jusha were not subtle students of Chinese cosmology. But their efforts in this area were sufficient to provide a satisfying framework for the social principles which were their primary concern. At all events, they found in Chu Hsi a system laid out with such authority that they were able to defend with assurance their new social doctrines in a world still dominantly Buddhist. Thus Fujiwara Seika could say, "For a long time I devoted myself to Buddha but my heart was in doubt. Upon reading the books of the Sages I believed and did not doubt. The Way is indeed in them."[13] Thus also Nakae Tōju, preaching the superiority of Confucianism to Buddhism, could claim that Buddha had never penetrated to the true meaning of virtue.[14] Although in 1614 Hayashi Razan was publicly defeated in his debate with the Buddhist priest Tenkai, the jusha were already beginning to displace the Buddhist priesthood from positions of political and intellectual influence in the samurai world.

Secure in the conviction that the books of the Sages revealed the ultimate truth, the jusha entered the realm of their prime concern—the realm of human relations, of state and society. Their contributions in this field were, for the Japan of their day, vital and creative. The pioneers of the movement saw in the Classics Heaven's laws for human society. Thus in the works of the early jusha, Hayashi Razan, Yamaga Sokō, Nakae Tōju, and Kumazawa Banzan we find taking shape a systematic rationalization of Tokugawa society, its structural and moral basis. This application of Confucian principles to the newly emerging social order in Japan was worked out at several levels. At the top it provided a philosophical and moral basis for the political hierarchy of emperor, shogun, and daimyo. At the bottom it affrmed a social hierarchy of samurai, agriculturalist, artisan, and merchant.

One of the jusha's major concerns was to devise a satisfactory rationalization of the Tokugawa political order. It was to this end that Hayashi Razan and his successors, in their essays and particularly in the great historical work *Honchō Tsugan*, applied Confucian moral ideas to the history of the imperial house and the relationship between emperor and shogun. Thus Razan, by explaining the sacred regalia of the imperial house as symbolizing the ideals of intellect, humanity, and duty, gave a moral foundation to the position of the emperor; and the Shogunate official Hirayama Yoshitada offered the following justification of the shogun's right to rule:

The Divine Prince won [the rule of] the country solely and naturally by his high virtue; he did not [simply] inherit the work of the Minamoto and their successors. His statesmanship was broad, and his prowess was great, beyond all things since the beginning of the country; all people obeyed him, as the rivers flow to a lower level, and all classes rejoiced, as if clouds had parted and the sun had been revealed. It was but natural justice that the emperor rewarded his merit with the office of *tai-kun*, which had come down from the house of Minamoto.[15]

The daimyo, who had recently fought their way to precarious supremacy in their locales, were also supplied with satisfying assurances of their position in the scheme of things. Thus Ikeda Mitsumasa, daimyo of Bizen, could announce:

The shogun receives authority over the people of Japan as a trust from Heaven. The daimyo are entrusted with the people of one province by the shogun. The daimyo's great lords and retainers should aid the daimyo in bringing peace and harmony to the people.[16]

Beneath this idealized framework of political institutions the jusha saw a natural order of social classes and social functions. Hayashi Razan provided the most direct and simplest explanation of this order: "When we look at the multitude of things we see that everywhere there is the distinction between high and low. To say that there is no distinction between high and low is to be ignorant of the law of Heaven [li]."[17] Hayashi's explicit views on the social hierarchy are well expressed by his patron, Tokugawa Ieyasu:

The emperor, with compassion in his heart for the needs of the people, must not be remiss in the performance of his duties. . . . Second, the shogun must not forget the possibility of war in peacetime, and must maintain his discipline. . . . Third, the farmer's toil is proverbial—from the first grain to a hundred acts of labor. . . . Fourth, the artisan's occupation is to make and prepare wares and utensils for the use of others. Fifth, the merchant facilitates the exchange of goods. . . .[18]

If such expressions had become little more than platitudes to the Chinese, they were being discovered afresh by the Japanese of the seventeenth century. At a time when Japanese society was undergoing a thorough regimentation and formalization into status groups, Confucian concepts played a vital part in providing the theoretical basis for the acceptance of a social hierarchy as naturally ordained.

One of the major accomplishments of the jusha in this respect was the formulation of a justification for the existence of the samurai class. This they did by fusing Japan's feudal traditions with the Confucian ethical system, i.e., by explaining the warrior's social mission as one of devotion to the welfare of the non-warrior classes. Confucianism was drawn upon both to reinforce the traditional practices of loyalty and performance of duty and to provide the civilizing ideals of self-cultivation and scholarship. According to Kumazawa Banzan, a samurai turned jusha, "The bushi of today, if he educates himself, learns the law of things, and beyond this performs well in his military calling, is the equivalent of the chün-tzu of old."[19] Yamaga Sokō worked out the first systematic statement of what was to become the Way of the Warrior (bushidō), a code heavily weighted with Confucian ideals.

It should not be inferred that Confucian social and moral principles were adopted merely to rationalize the existing patterns of authority.

To be sure, Japanese rulers were attracted to Confucianism because of its usefulness, but its adoption had consequences beyond the mere rationalization of the status quo. The moral order required the exercise of morality on the part of its members. Only if the leaders of society, emperor and shogun, fulfilled their ideal roles would "high and low help each other and the people have peace."[20] The social dream of the jusha was indeed an ideal world which required effort on the part of ruler and subject alike. It obliged the samurai to carry his social privileges with humility, to dedicate himself to Heaven and society. Thus the Daimyo of Bizen expressed his obligation publicly:

If the people of the province are not secure, the blame falls upon the daimyo. Moreover, if one person within the land is without his place, this reflects discredit upon the shogun. Thus, if the daimyo permits misfortune to come to his people, this also diminishes the shogun's benevolence and hence is an act of unprecedented disloyalty. Though a daimyo who has been disloyal to his shogun and unbenevolent to his subjects be put to death, the harm he has done cannot be rectified.[21]

The samurai, too, must dedicate himself to social leadership. As Yamaga Sokō put it, "One cannot succeed in applying military principles alone but must achieve complete self-cultivation, rectification of the heart, regulation of the state, and pacification of the world."[22]

The expression of these social ideals, as we have seen, was not limited to the jusha alone. While the Confucian teachers were instrumental in originating and systematizing certain basic concepts, their public expression and inculcation became a matter of governmental concern as well. Shogun and daimyo inserted phrases in support of Confucian values in their public statements and in their basic codes and laws, and the creation of institutions for the support of Confucian principles was largely their work. Two practices in particular indicate the close support given to Confucianism by political institutions. These were the monthly or yearly public Confucian lectures and the periodic awards for good conduct.

Among Tokugawa shogun, Tsunayoshi (1680–1709) was most active in sponsoring formal public lectures on the Confucian classics. He himself on occasion lectured to his assembled vassals. In Tsunayoshi's day several types of lectures were given, each designed for specific groups within the Edo court: the *shimpan* (collaterals), daimyo, high-ranking officials, lower officials, etc.[23] Eventually public lectures by the head of the Hayashi house became a regular feature of shogunal ceremonial, being held on the tenth day of each month.[24] Most domains instituted similar practices on a monthly or yearly basis.

The encouragement of virtuous conduct by shogun and daimyo also seems to have been adopted fairly generally. The *Tokugawa Jikki* frequently lists awards for good conduct at the end of the year.[25] Undoubtedly the most conspicuous effort along these lines was made by Ikeda Mitsumasa. During the three years 1665–68 alone, 1,684 persons of all classes in Bizen were commended for such virtues as filial piety (219), loyalty (52), truthfulness (226), ability at literary and military arts (111), and good performance of official duties (214).[26]

In this way Confucian values were given institutional support by government authorities, and shogun, daimyo, and samurai, as they fulfilled their administrative functions, served to a certain extent as moralists or Confucian exemplars. In these matters, however, the jusha remained in a special position; among other things, their presence as lecturers or doctrinal authorities was always necessary on state occasions.

They also had more specifically religious functions. The first official effort to provide a separate institutional foundation for Confucianism as a system of belief was made in 1632, when Tokugawa Yoshinao, Ieyasu's ninth son, provided the funds for the erection of a Sages' Hall in the Hayashi Establishment in Edo. The next year Hayashi Razan performed the first public ceremonies in honor of Confucius. About the same time the Shogun Iemitsu paid official respect to Confucius by visiting the Sages' Hall. In 1690 the Shogun Tsunayoshi built a much more imposing Paragon Hall (Taiseiden) on Shōhei Hill. Here the head of the Hayashi family served as master of ceremonies, and the Shogun attended Spring and Autumn ceremonies along with the assembled daimyo. This was the high point of Tokugawa patronage of Confucianism. Later shogun took such ceremonies less seriously, but the ritual functions of the Hayashi family continued to the end of the regime.[27]

No adequate record exists of the number of Confucian temples built during the Tokugawa period. Of those which were erected as separate buildings, architecturally based on Chinese models, some fifteen have received the attention of historians. Of these, nine were already in existence by the end of the seventeenth century. The daimyo most active in promoting Confucian ceremonies were the Tokugawa of Owari and Mito, and the masters of Bizen, Hizen, Chōshū, Aizu, and Sendai.[28] Most of these buildings were incorporated into the domain school compounds. By the end of the Tokugawa period nearly all domains (*han*) possessed schools, and it is probable that every school had at least some sort of facility for the worship of Confucius. In Bizen, ceremonies to Confucius were regularly carried out by the students of the domain school with the jusha presiding.[29] In Mito it was under the Ming refugee Chu Chih-yü that students at the domain school first conducted the Spring and

Autumn ceremonies in 1672.[30] Here, then, although in less imposing fashion than the Buddhists had done, Confucianism achieved a spiritual existence of its own and the jusha was recognized as its ritualist. The religious aura surrounding the jusha's activities was clear. Indeed, like the Buddhist priest, he claimed the care of the dead. Although Confucian burial was not widely practiced, Ikeda Mitsumasa of Bizen adopted it for a time in his domain, and jusha frequently insisted upon it for themselves.[31]

THE JUSHA AS OFFICIAL

As we have seen, it was not always easy to draw a clear line of distinction between the professional Confucianist and the samurai official fulfilling his ideal role. In the eyes of the jusha, this was as it should be. In Kumazawa Banzan's words, "The Way of the Sages is the Way of the Five Human Relationships. This is the Way which all five classes of men—sovereign, great lords, officials, samurai, and commoners—should practice. There is no separate class of jusha who follow the Way."[32] The Shogun Tsunayoshi is recorded as saying, "The Sages of old, Yao, Shun, Yü, T'ang, Wen, and Wu, were all jusha. That some men now make a separate profession of reading books is a development of later generations. It is a great mistake."[33] Nonetheless the jusha of the Tokugawa period was a specialist, and it was as such that he served the feudal government.

The position of the jusha who entered the service of the Tokugawa is revealed, first of all, in the career patterns of such pioneer Neo-Confucianists as Hayashi Razan. At the outset the position of the Tokugawa jusha was little different from that of the earlier priest-official (*sōkan*),[34] i.e., that of a scribe and an adviser in spiritual and occasionally political matters. Hayashi Razan, in order to secure Tokugawa patronage, actually assumed the guise of a priest, and it was not until 1691 that his son was permitted to let his hair grow out and take his place among the samurai.[35]

Eventually the positions and functions of jusha became fairly well standardized within the Shogunate and various domains, although great variety remained in matters of specific titles and official treatment. Hayashi Razan and his successors won for the house of Hayashi the office of jusha, the official status of *koshōgumi-bangashira-gaku*, ("Rank Equivalent to Captain of the Inner Guard"), a stipend of 3,500 *koku*, the title Daigaku-no-kami ("Rector of the College"), and court rank of junior fifth rank, lower grade.[36] This placed the Hayashi among the upper 10 per cent of the shogun's direct vassals (*hatamoto*)[37]—a position of some consequence, though below the policy-making level, which was staffed largely with officials of daimyo rank. The other jusha in the Shogunate did not fare nearly so well. In 1706 the so-called *jusha-shū* ("Corps of Confucianists") contained sixteen men with stipends ranging from 450 to 150 bales (*hyō*) of rice.[38] A special post, that of personal Confucian lecturer to the shogun (*oku-ju*), for many years held by members of the Narushima family, carried a stipend of 200 bales of rice and an additional income of 200 bales.[39] Except for the Hayashi, therefore, the jusha were placed in the shogunal bureaucracy at the bottom of the *hatamoto*, a status that nonetheless carried with it the privilege of shogunal audience.

Within the Shogunate the general term of *juin* ("Confucian official") was sometimes applied to a number of other functionaries, notably scribes, librarians, ceremonialists, teachers, lecturers on literature, and the like. But since such positions carried specific functional titles we have no way of determining how many were filled by professional Confucianists.

The situation in the domains is also not fully clear. In the biographies of local Confucian scholars the terms *juin* and *jushin* are loosely applied and seldom refer to specific posts. Moreover, not all domains employed the title of jusha. For instance, while the Ikeda of Inaba used it, the Ikeda of Bizen did not.[40] When used, it generally applied to the highest class of Confucian officials within the domain—in most instances senior lecturers in the domain school.

The jusha in the domains held a status equivalent, relatively, to that of the shogunal jusha, except that few families achieved a hereditary position comparable to that of the Hayashi. In most domains the senior jusha came somewhere in the upper section of the middle group of samurai, and the lesser jusha in the lowest group having the right of audience. Although the incomes commensurate with these status levels differed considerably according to the size of the domain, some figures for the Bizen domain may help to indicate the jusha's relative status. In 1765 in Bizen 5,142 samurai retainers were listed under the daimyo. Of these, 118 were high officials, with salaries ranging from 33,000 to 120 *koku*. Another 853 were of middle rank, with a minimum salary of 40 *hyō*. Another 1,010 were lesser officers, with incomes ranging from 40 *hyō* to ration allotments only. The remaining 3,161 men were foot-soldiers paid in rations.[41] How many in each category were jusha we are not told, but we know that in 1838 one superintendent of schools qualified as a high official with a salary of 230 *koku*, and that four lecturers were among the officers with incomes of 40 *hyō* and four rations. Other officials engaged in education or other scholarly pursuits fell below the level of officers.[42]

Thus in both the shogunal and domain bureaucracies nearly all jusha occupied official positions which placed them low among the middle group of retainers. The Hayashi house was a conspicuous exception. Members of this house traditionally served the Shogunate as (1) rector of the Tokugawa College, (2) tutor and lecturer to the Tokugawa family, (3) chief Confucian ritualist, (4) chief historian, (5) consultant on the phrasing of laws and documents, and (6) official in charge of diplomatic correspondence.[43] Other jusha aided the Hayashi in these duties but were more restricted to educational, ceremonial, and research functions. The duties of jusha in the domains were somewhat less comprehensive than those of the Hayashi family but of the same order. They were probably most heavily weighted toward education.

Not all jusha stayed within the limitations of their status or office. The path of advancement to other levels of the hereditary feudal hierarchy was no more difficult for them than for other samurai of their general status, and their ability to influence their superiors by their suggestions and advice worked strongly in their favor. Some jusha obtained high office and entered directly into the making of policy. Kumazawa Banzan was taken into the Bizen domain and given the rank of Captain (*bangashira*) and a stipend of 3,000 *koku*.[44] In the Aizu domain Abei Hitoshi rose to the "unprecedented" rank of Chamberlain (*soshaban*).[45] Yamada Hokoku reorganized the finances of the Matsuyama domain as Magistrate of County Affairs (*kōri-bugyō*).[46] Jusha may have attained high rank in the smaller domains more frequently. Those who took part in government, however, did so in an acquired official capacity, not as jusha.

Most jusha exerted only such influence on government as might reasonably be expected to emanate from lecturers and consultants on Chinese texts. In some instances, this influence was considerable. In the early years of the Neo-Confucian movement, Confucian tenets of government were taken up with an air of excitement and discovery by Japan's rulers, and Ieyasu himself acknowledged the fundamental importance of the Classics as a basis of statecraft.[47] Many daimyo suddenly awoke to the virtues of Neo-Confucianism. Hoshino Masayoshi of Aizu, for instance, is said to have discovered the "Lesser Learning," Chu Hsi's commentary on the "Great Learning," in 1652 at the age of forty-two. Throwing away the Buddhist texts he had been reading, he became a vigorous patron of Confucianism. His first act was to send copies of the "Lesser Learning" to all his senior officials.[48] The public avowal of Confucian ideals became a common practice of Tokugawa rulers.

The main theme of the jusha's exhortations was *jinsei* (Chinese *jen-*

cheng), "benevolent rule," an ideal that was readily adopted by shogun and daimyo. Few Tokugawa officials attained the heights of benevolence, but a number gained reputations for their adherence to Confucian principles. Uesugi Harunori, following the advice of Hosoi Heishū, reformed his domain's economy and administration along model Confucian lines,[49] and Matsudaira Sadanobu, the Shogunal reformer, prepared himself by assiduous reading of the Classics.[50] Ikeda Mitsumasa, who conscientiously attempted to live by the principles he had learned from his Confucian mentor, summed up his philosophy as follows:

The ruler must regard his own filial behavior as the most important thing. . . . The filial ruler is one who governs his land well, treats samurai and farmers with benevolent love, and causes the country to prosper. . . . The truly learned man is one who reads books constantly, reveres the ancient men of wisdom, makes clear the causes of political instability, both ancient and modern, practices etiquette and makes straight his path, . . . and cultivates himself before trying to rule others.[51]

Although the ideal of *jinsei* was to produce the sage ruler, the application of Confucian principles in government more often was the result of advice from Confucian advisers. Often the advisers were lecturers or tutors to the administrator or his family, but it was not unusual for renowned scholars to be consulted or requested to present treatises on political subjects. The best known unofficial jusha adviser in the shogunal bureaucracy is Arai Hakuseki (1657–1725), who served two shogun, Ienobu and Ietsugu. Arai reports vividly in his autobiography:

After the new year of 1695, I began lectures on the *Shu-ching* on the 24th and lectures on the *T'ung-chien Kang-mu* on the 28th. That year I lectured approximately 71 days. . . . Usually after the lecture I was offered a seat, and my lord asked questions about the history of Japan and China. He was especially interested in the history of the period in which his ancestors came to power.[52]

Hakuseki, the meticulous scholar, states that in all he lectured 1,299 times before his lord in the course of nineteen years. Most of his writings on history, ceremony, economics, and jurisprudence were prepared for his lord, and many matters of state policy were decided according to his recommendation.

Because of the jusha's ability to handle ancient texts, both Japanese and Chinese, he was regarded by the feudal authorities as an authoritative source of information on legal and administrative precedents, and hence as indispensable in the writing of laws. This was an especially important function during the early years of the Tokugawa period, when patterns of administration were still flexible and new laws and procedures were in the making. We know, for example, that Hayashi Razan had a hand in Tokugawa legislation during the rule of the first three shogun, if not so great a hand as his biographies claim; and the exhortation toward learning in the *bushi* code is clearly a product of jusha activity. There were less direct products as well. Within a surprisingly short time after the consolidation of Tokugawa power, official moral exhortations had taken on a distinctly Confucian cast, and Confucian social and economic concepts had become part of the conscious or unconscious approach of feudal administrators throughout Japan.

THE JUSHA AS EDUCATOR

As we have seen, many of the ritual and governmental functions of the jusha had an educational component, in the sense that they had as their ultimate aim the moral and intellectual edification of the samurai. The more formally educational activities of the Confucian scholars fell into three main categories: tutoring, teaching in officially sponsored schools, and private instruction.

Despite the availability of formal schools and colleges, the tutor continued to hold a central position in the educational system of Tokugawa times. In all classes the earliest steps in education were entrusted to a tutor—a professional tutor if the family could afford one, but otherwise a parent, some other close relation, or a learned person of the neighborhood. For the lower levels of the samurai class the early stages of tutoring might well provide the only education, but children with some academic ability were generally able to enter the small, private or publicly supported local schools (*juku* or *shijuku*) or the shogunal or domain colleges. Children of daimyo and high-ranking samurai, however, commonly remained for many years under the guidance of a tutor or tutors.

The duties of tutor (*jidoku*) to the shogun were normally handled by the head of the Hayashi house and later the Narushima house. But most shogun and daimyo felt free to employ tutors of their choice. At this level the selection and hiring of a tutor was not a casual affair; it generally involved a formal agreement between student and tutor.[53] Even though the tutor held low official status within the feudal hierarchy, he was respected as a superior in the field of learning. Thus the daimyo of Saga fondly spoke of his tutor: "What is strongly impressed upon one's heart in early age remains there to the end of one's life. When I was a child I was tutored by Koga Tōba. Many of his words and deeds remain in my memory still."[54] Historians have suggested that Hayashi Razan had a special hold over the minds of the second and third shogun, who, as Ieyasu's sons, had been placed under his instruction. Two other sons of Ieyasu who later became the daimyo of Owari and Mito were also tutored by Razan, and both became avid patrons of Confucianism. Arai Hakuseki's intimate relationship with two shogun indicates that most shogun and many daimyo continued in their mature years the practice of receiving instruction in the Classics or literature.

Formal institutions of education received the serious attention of both the Shogunate and the various domains after the beginning of the Tokugawa period. The dawn of a new day of official education came in 1630, when the third shogun, Iemitsu, provided Hayashi Razan with the land on which to build a school. It was this school which eventually became the Shōheikō, the Tokugawa College, under the rectorship of the Hayashi family. Continually expanded under the patronage of the shogun in order to meet the growing needs of the shogunate, this college became the central educational institution for all *fudai* daimyo and direct retainers of the shogun. It provided a broadly conceived classical education of Confucian studies in political economy, history, poetry, and law.[55] The Shōheikō was radically improved after 1791 by Matsudaira Sadanobu, who tightened the curriculum and expanded facilities so that more young men could be trained. Also under Sadanobu a system of examining graduates of the school and assigning grades of excellence was begun. Examinations, held every three years, were taken by upwards of 200 candidates on each occasion, with only a small portion receiving honors. In the seventy-one years from 1794 to 1865, only 708 scholars were singled out for this distinction.[56]

Domain schools (*hankō*) modeled after the Tokugawa College soon sprang up in the larger domains, growing out of such humble beginnings as public lecture halls or private arrangements made by the daimyo for educating the children of their retainers. Out of such beginnings and in line with the development of the official Tokugawa College, daimyo began the establishment of formal schools with regular staffs and endowed incomes. Ishikawa gives the following statistics on the establishment of domain schools during the Tokugawa period:[57]

Period	Years elapsed	New schools
1624–1710	87	23
1711–1750	40	18
1751–1780	30	26
1781–1803	23	58
1804–1843	40	65
1844–1867	24	35
1868–1871	4	47

In all, there were 272 domain schools founded in the period 1624–1871, about half of them in two rapid spurts: from 1790 to 1810, and in the interval between the Restoration and the establishment of the new educational system in 1871.

One of the earliest domain schools was the Hanabatake-kyōba, which was established at Okayama in 1641 to instruct the daimyo's retainers in the classical Six Arts: etiquette, music, literature, mathematics, archery, and horsemanship.[58] In 1669 the school was renamed simply Gakkō. In 1680, the Shizutani-gakkō, a special academy for samurai and commoners, was established in the hills over a day's ride from the domain capital.[59] The combined enrollment of these two schools never exceeded 350 pupils—only a small portion of the children of the more than 5,000 samurai families in the daimyo's retinue.[60] No doubt many others attended private schools or remained with their tutors. Figures for other schools, taken at the end of the Tokugawa period, seem somewhat more reasonable. The Fukui domain college had 800 students, and the Kumamoto school had 378 in advanced studies and 934 elementary students.[61]

While there was considerable variety in the administrative arrangement of schools and in the method of instruction, in general all followed the pattern described in the following statement by a former head of the Matsuyama school:

> The staff of the Yūshūkan were, as I remember, the director, ten instructors, and twenty readers. The readers took the children of the *han* and instructed them in elementary reading. The instructors handled instruction in the explanation of texts for students beyond this level. The director listened to students who had progressed beyond the instructors. He also delivered lectures on the Classics for all the samurai in the *han*. Also when the daimyo was in residence the director was called in to give lectures before him.
>
> Instruction of the domain youths was performed at the school. But since the public lectures were attended by all from the elders (*karō*) on down, there was not enough room in the school, and the great hall of the palace was used. This was thus called the palace lecture. It was held once or twice a year. When the daimyo was in residence, he attended.
>
> The readers and instructors were all members of the teaching staff, but since they were still young, they also pursued their own education. When not teaching the less advanced students, they attended the classes in text criticism and received instruction from the director.
>
> There was a dormitory set up in the school compound where talented students lived so that they might study night and day. The instructors acted as dormitory masters and supervised the students in return for their keep.
>
> Instruction in literary and military subjects was graded into classes. In literature the simple reading of the Four Books and Five Classics was the first grade, the explanatory reading of the Four Books the second grade, and that of the Five Classics the third grade. In military training the first steps were ranked as grade one, the first certificate as grade two, and the diploma as grade three. It was *han* custom to give additional rations to the eldest son

of each house when he reached 16 or 17 years of age, but this custom was modified. No such ration was given unless he had passed the third grade in literary and military training. Those who were idle, even though they reached the age of 16 or 17, did not receive rations. Second and third sons who had not graduated were not desired for adoption into other houses. For a while there was a loud outcry of distress, but in the end the retainers submitted to the regulation. Thus the youth of the *han* were stimulated to exert themselves . . .

For military training, there was space for spear and sword drill in the school compound. Instruction in etiquette according to the Ogasawara school was handled in the lecture hall when it was not in use. Training in archery, horsemanship, and gunnery was conducted in several places outside the school. All these arts had their instructors. They were out of the jurisdiction of the directors of the Yūshūkan. Among the *han* elders one was named Superintendent of Training. He inspected the training in both literary and military subjects.

In the school in the inner room a tablet to Confucius was kept and Spring and Autumn ceremonies were performed. All school staff performed functions in the ceremonies. Among the *han* retainers those who had interest in classical music [*gagaku*] gathered to play music. The daimyo attended when he was in residence, and if he was absent an elder represented him.[62]

In addition to the official schools, there were a great many private schools, or *juku*. During the early Tokugawa period, as we have seen, Kyoto was the foremost center of such schools; Osaka was for a time its closest rival. Before long, however, with the development of the Hayashi school, Edo eclipsed them both. Here were the best opportunities for scholars who hoped to attract the attention of some daimyo and receive employment. Moreover, many of the employed jusha were able to take in private students on the side. Often when the Shōheikō was unable to accept further students, it was possible for aspirants to enter the private classes of members of the Hayashi family or other official jusha.

It has been estimated that there were over 1,400 private schools in Japan in 1870.[63] The majority of these schools were run by single instructors, who used the Confucian classics as the basis for the first steps of reading and writing. Some received official support, but most probably maintained themselves on fees.

At the lowest level of organized education were the *terakoya* ("temple schools"). Although established primarily for the education of commoners, they were attended by some children from the lower levels of the samurai. The first *terakoya* were attached to Buddhist institutions, but many later ones had no association whatever with Buddhism. By the middle of the nineteenth century, the *terakoya* provided a reasonably complete network of schools for the lower levels of society. Over 11,000 such schools existed in 1870, employing over 15,000 teachers, of whom only about one-sixth were Buddhist priests.[64] In general, these schools relied on the simpler Confucian texts as a basis of elementary instruction in reading, writing, and ethics.

Emerging into the rough and unlettered samurai world of the early seventeenth century, the jusha from the outset found themselves looked up to and patronized as men of learning. Two words in particular summarize the special cultural role of the jusha. These are *gakumon* (scholarship) and *bun* (art and literature). It was the Confucian who put the emphasis on *bun* into the samurai's code. At the same time he came to exemplify what was meant by the term.

The jusha's cultural emphasis was on the edifying arts—the study of the Classics, the writing of poetry in the Chinese style, the study and writing of history, "literati" painting, and calligraphy. Their concern with history is perhaps the most worthy of attention; as had happened so many times in China, the historical tradition of Confucianism and the particular needs of the emerging political regime conspired to produce a spate of historical research and writing. Members of the Hayashi family and other scholars set about recovering ancient texts, interpreting old laws, compiling and rationalizing the samurai genealogies, and generally rewriting Japanese history to the specifications of the new shogunate. Their motives were at once scholarly and political: they sought to refurbish the mirror of the past and justify the present for the Tokugawa samurai world.

The jusha was above all a scholar of things Chinese. The sources of his "learning" came in some measure out of Japan's past, but it was primarily his acquaintance with Chinese accomplishments in the fields of philosophy, poetry, political theory, and agricultural technology that gave his teachings their authority.

The jusha became the foremost cultural and intellectual leader of Tokugawa times. But to say this, and to say that Confucianism became the strongest ethical force of its day, does not in any way provide a quantitative evaluation of the elements, Confucian or otherwise, which made up the samurai way of life. We shall accordingly do well to look at the relationship of the jusha to the samurai in the wider context of the interaction between them.

Two preliminary observations may help to fix the boundaries of the jusha's role in samurai society. First, it should be evident that the jusha in no way expected to convert Japan into another China. He found Tokugawa society satisfactory in many respects; in other respects he accommodated himself to it; only in certain limited respects did he seek to alter it by preaching the higher wisdom of China. In most ways the jusha lived within the samurai world, subordinating himself to its fundamental structure and purposes. Second, we should recall that Confucianism as a system of beliefs, unlike Buddhism, never achieved the institutional independence that would have enabled its high priests to exert political and economic influence on their own. The jusha were thus dependent upon the society they served for its patronage and support.

Despite the wide variety of functions they performed within Tokugawa society, the jusha were essentially specialists, successors to the priest-officials of the previous era. Although the idealized Confucian view of society was that every samurai was, or should be, a jusha, those who were masters of the Chinese classics were a group apart. For one thing, there were relatively few of them. As we have seen, at the beginning of the eighteenth century the Shogunate's *jusha-shū* had only sixteen members. Daimyo such as the Maeda of Kaga generally maintained from six to eight Confucianists at any given time, the Ikeda of Bizen from three to five, and smaller daimyo often only one. To be sure, other officials of scholarly attainment were employed as teachers, scribes, historians, or doctors, but even if we added these to the numbers of jusha proper, our total would almost certainly be less than one per cent of the total samurai population.[65]

It seems fairly clear why this figure was so low: the game, in many instances, was not worth the candle. The training of a jusha was long and rigorous, and required both aptitude and application. Yet the upper limits of official service to which the jusha could aspire were not high. In Tokugawa society ascription was the main basis for selection, and the upper levels of the ruling class were largely a closed hereditary preserve. Consequently there was little motivation for members of the upper or even middle samurai class to go into the jusha's profession. At the other end of the social scale, economic necessity made an elaborate education impossible. Thus those who aspired to this career were in overwhelming numbers from the level of lower samurai or just below.

This observation is strongly supported by the information contained in standard biographical sources.[66] For instance, of the 270 followers of the Shushi (Chu Hsi) school listed in the *Tokushibiyō*,[67] biographical information is unavailable for 73. The remaining 197 came from the following backgrounds: samurai, 58; jusha, 55; physicians, 23; commoners, 8; priests, 3; unrecorded, 50. It is safe to surmise that few or none of the unrecorded backgrounds conceal a distinguished samurai status. Indeed, of the 58 men of stated samurai origin, over half came from the lowest levels of the class; and nearly all of the remainder should not be considered career jusha at all, but rather officials who became identified as Confucian scholars.

The ranks of jusha seem to have remained relatively open to talented aspirants. (The above figures, which show a large portion of Confucianists coming from jusha families, are heavily weighted toward certain exceptional families such as the Hayashi and the Narushima.) Here and there, a distinguished family of jusha held a teaching post in perpetuity, but a glance at the turnover of names in the educational institutions of the domains shows that heredity had far less weight than achievement in the selection of jusha.

This state of affairs was agreeable to both prospective jusha and their prospective employers. From the point of view of the feudal authorities, the jusha's function was a service function to be patronized but kept useful. He was not so essential as to demand the concession of hereditary privileges. In short, the career of jusha remained peripheral to the main lines of achievement to which the samurai aspired.

In general, then, we may conclude that the samurai had a higher regard for Confucianism than for the professional Confucianist. Confucianism was something to be respected; the jusha was someone to be used. He was not even necessarily accorded the respect that customarily is paid to the indispensable man, for, as we shall see, in many of his most important functions he had competitors in the eyes of the samurai.

THE SAMURAI'S IDEALS AND THE JUSHA

The mind of the Tokugawa samurai was served by three systems of thought, of which Confucianism was only one. The others were Buddhism and Shinto.

Despite the victory of Neo-Confucianism in the realm of social and political ideas, the Buddhist establishment retained a good deal of its religious influence and some of its economic support. The early years of the Tokugawa period, during which Neo-Confucianism and Buddhism competed for the patronage of Japan's rulers, was a time when throughout Japan new military powers were asserting themselves. Shogun and daimyo, whatever their particular personal attitudes toward specific priests or Confucian advocates, were involved fundamentally in the struggle to make religion serve their political order.

The confiscation and redistribution of temple lands by the first three Tokugawa shogun reduced forever the political and economic influence of Buddhism in Japan. But at the same time there was no intention of eradicating the religion. In the end Buddhist institutions retained something over one per cent of the tax-bearing land of Japan, a figure estimated at 144,000 koku during the 1660's.[68] Indeed, once the power of the old monastic orders had been crushed, the feudal authorities began a re-building process of considerable magnitude, encouraging the establish-ment of temples which would serve their interests. In their eyes, Bud-dhism was a force making for social stability. Ieyasu himself patronized the priest Tenkai and erected on Ueno Hill a "guardian temple" for the city of Edo, Kaneiji.

One well-known use of Buddhism for official purposes was the re-quirement that every household, commoner and samurai alike, had to be registered at a temple as a guarantee against Christian belief.[69] Daimyo were required to send in annual reports to the Shogun based on sta-tistics compiled by their inspectors of religious affairs. The enforced registration must have given the temples a certain hold over people, even though it was a formalistic arrangement involving no assurance of belief. And the pressure in favor of Buddhism which these policies tended to produce was exerted upon the samurai as well as others.

Buddhism exhibited remarkable staying power. Few assaults on it were as intense as the one launched by the first daimyo of Bizen, Ikeda Mitsumasa, a determined champion of Confucianism and Shinto. In 1655 he ordered the Buddhist ceremonies in honor of his departed an-cestors to be discontinued in favor of Confucian rituals. In 1666 he con-ducted a thorough purge of Buddhist institutions and temples, already considerably depleted by the actions of previous daimyo in the area. He abolished 583 of the 1,044 temples in existence at that time and de-frocked or expelled 847 priests, leaving only 1,110 priests, and 1,937 koku of temple land.[70] At the same time he put into effect a policy re-quiring all families in his domain to register with Shinto shrines instead of Buddhist temples as a mark of their non-Christian affiliation. During the year he also brought the remains of his grandfather, Terumasa, and his father, Toshitaka, from Myōshinji temple in Kyoto to be buried in a special Confucian-style grave at Waidani in the mountains of the remote Wake district.

Yet even Mitsumasa did not eradicate all Buddhist temples, and after his death his successor Tsunamasa reversed the Shinto registration order and adopted the Tokugawa practice of Buddhist registration. Also all succeeding burials of daimyo were made at Sōgenji, a branch temple of Myōshinji just outside Okayama. Later daimyo continued to patron-ize Buddhism, and temple lands increased to nearly 3,000 koku by the end of the Tokugawa period. Priests (both Shinto and Buddhist) and their families numbered 9,281 out of a total domain census of 375,724 in 1707;[71] probably well over half of these were Buddhist. At all events, Buddhist priests were far more numerous in Bizen than jusha.

A study of the yearly round of ceremonies of both shogun and daimyo reveals that the Buddhist ceremonies far outnumbered the Confucian.[72] Ironically, the first visit of a shogun (Iemitsu) to the Confucian temple in the Hayashi establishment was made on his return from worship at a Buddhist temple. All Tokugawa mausoleums were Buddhist, as were the graves of nearly the entire population of Japan. Shogun and daimyo received temple names after death and were generally referred to in later documents by these names. An increasingly close link between Buddhist temples and members of the high samurai tended to grow up as more and more departed members were buried in temple graveyards. Thus in Sendai, eleven of the thirty-eight temples in the city held graves of members of the daimyo family.[73] By the end of the Tokugawa period, the shogun and daimyo families had ten or fifteen generations of deceased ancestors for whom yearly memorial services had to be performed.

In the final analysis, the samurai attitude toward Confucianism and Buddhism as religions depended greatly on individual preference and conscience. The role of Confucianism as a religion was limited, and only an occasional fanatical daimyo attempted to assert its precedence over Buddhism as a religion for his domain. On the other hand, most Japanese of the time were not disturbed by the antagonism between Neo-Confucianism and Buddhism. Very often those very rulers who had done the most to encourage Confucianism became ardent Buddhists as they approached the ends of their lives. Tokugawa Tsunayoshi, for example, became almost fanatically Buddhist before his death, and Date Tsunamura, daimyo of Sendai, who had introduced Confucian ceremonies within his domain, turned to the patronage of Buddhism before his death.[74]

It has been observed that in the struggle with Buddhism, the jusha, among them Hayashi Razan, looked to Shinto for an ally. Confucianists were able to turn Shintoism to their own use, working out various amalgams of it and Confucian thought. In view of the limitations of Confucianism as a religion, some pro-Confucian daimyo (such as Mitsumasa of Bizen) sought to combine Shinto with Confucianism as the officially supported religion of their domains. This alliance with Shinto was eventually to work against the Confucianists, however, for Shinto emancipated itself from Confucian control to become yet another competitive religious and intellectual system. The danger of this was not fully evident until after the middle of the Tokugawa period. But thereafter, under the impetus of the Kokugaku scholars (scholars of "national learning"), Shinto as the basis of a nationalistically oriented world view became increasingly influential in the higher circles of the ruling class. And just as Confucianism had provided a rationalization of the political order (*koku-tai*), Shinto now became the basis of still another, and more indigenous, *kokutai* concept.[75]

The role of Shinto is frequently not considered important until its appearance as a rational system of thought in the works of the Kokugaku scholars. Actually as an institutional vehicle for the expression of deeply felt attitudes toward the homeland and the traditional social and political relationships, Shinto played a vital role from the beginning of the Tokugawa period. We refer here to Shinto in its political sense: a set of practices involving attitudes of reverence toward the national deities (*kami*) and respect for the hereditary relationships between aristocratic families, a source of ritual justification of the aristocratic concept of *kokutai*, giving order and meaning to the relationship between emperor, the noble families, and their deified ancestors.

The contribution of Neo-Confucianism to Tokugawa political theory was that it provided a *universal* rationale for the new order. But Confucian ideals and the actual political order in Tokugawa Japan were never in perfect accord. In particular, there were difficulties with the Japanese practice of dual sovereignty. If Confucian theory could hold that "the Shogun receives authority over the people of Japan as a trust from Heaven," it could also (as did the Mito school) support the traditional (and Shintoist) legal fiction that the authority came as a trust from the emperor. At any rate, the actual institutional and ceremonial relationship between emperor and shogun continued, in fact, to be ritualized in the practices of Shinto and in the familiar ceremonies of the Kyoto court. The rehabilitation of the imperial ancestral shrine at Ise and the elaborate ceremonial respect paid the imperial court by the Shogunate was clearly a recognition of the Japanese form of *kokutai* as a political order based not on supposedly universal values but on Japanese traditions and on reverence to the national deities.

The shogun also utilized a variety of religious practices to give sanction to his position within the country. The great shrine to Ieyasu at Nikkō, though established under the guidance of Buddhist priests, was basically Shintoist in its conception. The periodic progress to Nikkō carried out by successive shogun, and participated in by the daimyo and Tokugawa housemen, was an act of religious veneration toward the founder of the Tokugawa house. It implied a dedication to the political order which Ieyasu had created. Eventually miniature versions of the shrine were erected in the castle towns of the several daimyo so that each locality could celebrate the Festival of Ieyasu. In Bizen the celebration of the Festival occurred on the 17th day of the fourth and ninth months. These were events of great pomp, participated in by large numbers of the daimyo's retainers.[76]

Like the shogun, the daimyo too enshrined their founding ancestors and held yearly services to exalt the prestige of their families. Although these services were conducted by Buddhist priests, this sort of veneration for a "first ancestor" was an element of Shinto. In most domains also, as we discover in Bizen, there was an annual New Year's procession to the foremost local shrine, an important means of ritualizing the identification of political authority with the spirits of the local territory.

For the samurai, these ceremonies were infused with much more immediate political significance than the Confucian rituals honoring the Sages. In Tokugawa times, matters of lineage and ancestral status were of deep and pressing concern. Emperor, shogun, daimyo, family—these were all part of the immediate structure, the immediate *kokutai,* in which the samurai lived. And while Confucianism might provide a rational explanation of the social order, it was the traditional feudal and Shinto-based ceremonies and beliefs which gave emotional unity and meaning to it.

The typical Tokugawa samurai saw some value in each of the three world views that competed for his allegiance. Buddhism and Shinto provided for his religious needs; Confucianism gave him a rational cosmology and a social ethic; Confucianism and Shinto both contributed to his conceptions of the political order. To be sure, the professional advocates of these systems were constantly at odds, but the Tokugawa samurai found compatibility among them an easy matter. His attitude is nicely revealed in the words of Ikeda Mitsumasa:

According to the view of Lord Gongen [Ieyasu], Shinto, Confucianism, and Buddhism should all three be used. Shinto is the way of inner truth and of inner purity. Confucianism is the way of sincerity, love, and benevolence. Buddhism emphasizes selflessness and desirelessness, teaching forbearance and compassion.[77]

If we can identify any primary commitment in the samurai's approach to these world views, it would be to what we should call immediate political realities, to a sense of his class importance, a sense of his tradition, a sense of national pride. Out of this commitment a unique amalgam of Confucian values and a Shinto-based sense of national destiny emerged to become the samurai's inspiration.

THE SAMURAI'S GOVERNMENT AND THE JUSHA

It was a rare jusha who became an adviser to some person of high government status, and thus acquired a measure of political influence; rarer still was the jusha-adviser who enjoyed a secure position within the bureaucracy. Typically, the jusha-adviser owed his post to the personal favor of a feudal superior, and held it at the superior's pleasure. Furthermore, the jusha was obliged to compete for favor with other members of the ruler's retinue—chamberlains for example, or members of the bodyguard.[78] It seems likely that the jusha did not fare particularly well in this competition.

His ideas, as we have seen, fared better. Under the urging of the jusha, Confucianism became a part of the philosophical basis of Tokugawa government, supplying ideals, models of conduct, precedents, and technical administrative knowledge. But it was the samurai who had to convert theory into practice, and he did so within certain well-defined limits.

What is most impressive about the basic political institutions of the Tokugawa regime is that they owe little or nothing to Chinese models. The origins of Tokugawa political forms are clearly visible in the practices of the autonomous feudal houses which became the daimyo establishments of Tokugawa times. At the core of the daimyo system of government was the clan-like relationship between feudal lord and vassals, a relationship cemented by the vassal's oath and rendered visible in the public ceremonies of investiture and service. After the establishment of the Tokugawa hegemony, shogunal and daimyo bureaucracies became increasingly specialized. A certain amount of Chinese official terminology came into use; yet these bureaucracies remained essentially an elaboration of the house governments of the late feudal age. Names of offices and the functions of officials emerged naturally as military organization evolved into civil bureaucracy.

Legal developments took the same course. Each of the emerging daimyo governments of the warring states period found it expedient to set down directives for its own housemen and for the territory it controlled. A haphazard but practical body of customary law thus came into existence.[79] During the late sixteenth and early seventeenth centuries this law was dignified by the addition of elements from earlier Japanese codes. Tokugawa Ieyasu in his later years assigned his literary advisers the task of combing ancient Japanese texts—especially the *Jōei Shikimoku* of 1232—for precedents and rules of administration. Hayashi Razan figured prominently in this endeavor, along with other scholars, priests, and courtiers.[80] The resulting materials were then gone over by the Shogun's chief policy-making daimyo, using Hayashi Razan as consultant. The major collections of injunctions to come out of this system were crude but practical, and Confucian only to the extent of setting forth generalized moral principles and using Confucian terminology to add authority to or embellish existing practices.

We can see something of how Confucianism affected the political behavior of the samurai by inspecting two basic codes of conduct drawn up by the shogunate: *Buke Shohatto,* or rules for the daimyo, and *Shosamurai Hatto,* which applied to the lesser retainers of the shogun. The *Buke Shohatto,* formally enunciated in 1615 as a thirteen-article code, was subsequently modified several times. In its original version, Articles 1 and 13 carried a Confucian message.[81] Article 1 made the well-known exhortation that "learning (*bun*) as well as the arts of war (*bu*), particularly archery and horsemanship, are to be pursued with diligence." Article 13 stated that "the provincial lords should select officials with administrative ability." The opening article of the *Shosamurai Hatto* as set down in 1635 read: "The samurai will cultivate loyalty and filial piety, be correct in the practice of rules and ceremonies, apply himself constantly to learning and military training, be complete in his performance of duty, and not permit his conduct to deteriorate."[82]

The strictly utilitarian and traditional nature of the other articles in these two codes is made all the more obvious by the sometimes far-fetched attempts of commentators to provide explanations or justifications out of the Chinese classics. Take for instance Article 8 in the *Buke Shohatto,* which put forth the common prohibition that vassals should not contract marriage without the shogun's permission. This blunt statement is embellished as follows:

Marriage follows the principle of harmony between Yin and Yang and must not be entered into lightly. In the "Book of Changes," under the thirty-eighth hexagram [*k'ui*], it says, "Marriage should not be contracted out of enmity [against another]. Marriages intended to effect an alliance with enemies [of the state] will turn out badly." The Peach Blossom ode in the "Book of Poetry" also says that "When men and women are proper in their relationships and marriage is arranged at the correct time, then throughout the land there will be no loose women. To form an alliance by marriage is the root of treason."[83]

Here Confucian theory is clearly rung in to dignify accepted Japanese practices.

But let us return to those general principles of conduct which these codes enjoined upon the samurai. The regulation that men of administrative ability should be selected for office was a favorite theme of the jusha, who were quick to point out the shortcomings of the Tokugawa reliance on heredity. Here is a typical complaint:

From the times of the Genroku period [1688–1704] a great many scholars have been taken from among the humble and lowly and given incomes, and have mixed with the samurai of the Court. But they have been entrusted with nothing beyond the literary work of secretaries. None are entrusted with governing. Those who become officials are all from the houses of samurai and great men with inherited incomes.[84]

The complaint is just. The top offices were exclusively hereditary, in one sense or another, save only for an occasional favorite or a rare genius in the field of military or civil affairs. There were ways and means of selecting men of ability within broad class grades, but with the handful of exceptions just noted, promotion through grades was impossible. The practice of adoption, to be sure, was widespread. The prestige of a "house," after all, depended on its capacity to fulfill its duties and perpetuate itself; second and third sons of samurai families, if they showed bodily vigor and intelligence, were therefore frequently used to carry on families lacking capable heirs. But this practice scarcely resembled the system of selection through education advocated by the more orthodox jusha.

For the very low levels of the samurai class, scholarship had its attractions as a career, but even on these levels the path of advancement by military ability or skill in financial management was probably more certain and rewarding. It is significant that Article 13 of the *Buke Shohatto* was dropped from the code after 1635.[85] The injunction in favor of "learning" which remained in Article 1 was meant primarily to encourage the samurai to cultivate themselves so that they might better perform the duties which were theirs by heredity. It was largely in this spirit that the shogunal and domain educational programs were established.

In the samurai codes two other less specialized value terms, loyalty (*chū*) and filial piety (*kō*), were given prominence by their inclusion in the first articles. (Exhortations in favor of *chū* and *kō* were inserted into the *Buke Shohatto* in 1683.)[86] These moral concepts enjoyed great currency; their origin was admittedly Confucian, and they had been part of the vocabulary of the samurai from the early days of the Kamakura period. Their reemphasis in the Tokugawa period was part of the ideological conversion to a peacetime administration. The change in the *Shosamurai Hatto* between its first promulgation in 1632 and its second in 1635 reveals this changing emphasis. In the first text the opening clause still retained the vigor of wartime: "The way of the samurai is to take delight in the vigilant performance of military service."[87] No mention was made of *chū* or *kō*.

The actual impact of these two Confucian concepts should not be overstressed. There is reason to believe that the conduct referred to as *chū* and *kō* represented no change from the old patterns of samurai behavior—i.e., that Japanese values were read into the Chinese Neo-Confucian texts.[88] Moreover, loyalty and filial piety were only two of many concepts in the moral armamentarium of the Tokugawa samurai. His primary concern was with service (*hōon*), duty (*giri*), status (*bungen*), and honor (*na*), values derived from the feudal relationships of samurai society and the experience of a warrior class. Though these values found less expression in the texts of the jusha, they were the values that the samurai lived and died by.[89]

If the Tokugawa samurai lived largely in a world of his own making when it came to political and military organization and social values, he appeared less self-sufficient when it came to the formation of social and economic policy. Lacking at the outset of the Tokugawa period the experience and vocabulary of civil administration, he relied readily on Confucian sources. It is important to realize that the economic principles of the Confucian school were, at least during the early Tokugawa period, fully congenial to the political and economic environment in Japan. The jusha as experts on Chinese technology recommended themselves to the feudal rulers as masters of a new and "scientific" body of learning which was able to prove its efficacy in application. Confucian precepts on the relationship of agriculture to the state and of the class system to agriculture were not outmoded; on the contrary, they were welcomed as new discoveries in the art of government and human relations.

But if these precepts worked well at first, they worked less well as time went on. By the beginning of the eighteenth century, Japan's feudal government faced new and different problems. Signs of a disturbing economic imbalance began to worry scholars and officials, and in the ensuing debate over policy the bankruptcy of the old Confucian answers became increasingly apparent. As a result, Japan's rulers and administrators became more and more willing to listen to those who professed other points of view. On the one hand, there came into existence a whole group of realistic Confucian students of political economics whose attitude toward trade, money, and industry went far beyond the limits of traditional Confucian doctrines.[90] On the other hand, new branches of learning—"Japanese studies" (*kokugaku*) and "Western studies" (*yōgaku*)—were given stimulus.[91] The Prohibition of Heresies undertaken in 1794 by the shogunal minister Matsudaira Sadanobu is indicative of the defensive posture forced upon the orthodox Confucianists of the day.[92] During the last half-century of Tokugawa rule, the intellectual climate of Japan became even less responsive to orthodox Confucian principles. The Tokugawa administrator was increasingly inclined to look elsewhere for effective answers to his political and economic problems.

THE SAMURAI AND HIS EDUCATION

Tokugawa educational administration and policy appear unusually free from political controls. In reality, however, this freedom was considerably qualified, especially in government-supported schools. In the minds of the Tokugawa authorities, education was conceived of as a means of training better samurai. As an official of the Tokushima domain put it, an avid pursuit of learning, "Except for those who intend to make a career out of Confucian studies," was hardly to be desired: If a samurai becomes enamored of books and proficient in scholarship, he will forget the way of the samurai and will neglect his main calling. The purpose of schooling is the building of talented material for the state.[93] Educational institutions were supported for practical purposes and were expected to conform to the best interests of the Shogunate and domain governments. In most of these situations, therefore, official support was closely associated with official control.

In the early years of the Hayashi school, government control was indeed limited. But so was government support. During its first century and a half of existence, the school was actually regarded as the family school of the Hayashi house. It was not until 1797 that the school, renamed the Gakumonjo, was increased in size so as to handle more fully the needs of the Tokugawa vassals. As a result the finances of the college were separated from the family finances of the Hayashi house, but they were also brought under the audit of the shogunal finance bureau.[94] When in 1862 the office of Commissioner of Education was created and staffed with non-academic members of the shogunal bureaucracy, the basic administrative and policy functions of the government-supported educational system had been taken out of the hands of the jusha completely.[95]

The arrangement whereby educational administration, or at least supervision, was placed in the hands of career administrators was probably even more strictly adhered to in the domains. For example, the school system of the Aizu domain was placed under a commissioner (*gakkō-bugyō*) in 1791 who until that time had been the domain's chief disciplinary officer (*ōmetsuke*). In 1797 five officials (*metsuke*) were attached to the school as "disciplinarians" (*gakkō-metsuke-yaku*).[96] In Bizen the commissioner of education was generally a career samurai. In Matsuyama we noted that one of the domain elders had the task of superintendent.[97] In all these instances, the fact that the jusha did not hold the highest educational planning and policy-making posts is most significant. The primacy of political considerations is obvious.

We must never forget that the objective of education for the samurai class was competence in the civil *and* military arts. While the jusha maintained that civil accomplishments should come before military, the political authorities often had other ideas. Individual shogun and daimyo were indeed induced to come out in favor of civil education.

But in time of crisis the cry for military training was quickly revived; and in the training of the young samurai, military discipline was always a pervasive ingredient. In Chōshū the domain college founded in 1710 established a basic allocation of instructional time as follows:

1. The school year will begin on the 12th of the first month and end on the 10th of the 12th month.

2. Lectures on Confucian texts will be held for 16 days out of each month at the lecture hall.

3. Lectures on military texts will be held for 6 days out of each month at the drill ground.

4. Lectures will begin at 8 A.M. As soon as they are finished, students will engage in military exercises.

5. Military drill will be held on 5 days each month. . . .

6. On clear days students will conscientiously practice horsemanship. Every day from the 2nd to the end of the month, students will drill in reading from 6 A.M. to 8 A.M. The practice of reading should not be limited to the classroom, but should engage the student constantly even when he is alone.

* * *

9. Literary studies should be started young or the student will not achieve success in them. Hence from the age of 8 or 9 training in reading should begin. From about age 14 the student should concentrate on books. Then when physical maturity is reached, military training should be the ultimate objective.[98]

In the Aizu domain the heavy emphasis on military training is indicated by a count of instructors and the subjects taught by them at the college during the 1860's:[99]

Confucianism	3	Military texts	2
Literature	2	Archery	9
Calligraphy	6	Horsemanship	5
Shinto	2	The lance	6
Japanese studies	2	Swordsmanship	28
Etiquette	1	Swimming	2
Mathematics	3	Gunnery	16
Music	2	Wrestling	11
Medicine	1	Other military arts	27
Total	22	Total	106

Of significance also is the fact that many of the instructors in military subjects were men of high rank in the domain hierarchy, which suggests that military training carried greater prestige than literary study. The result of this particular type of education is well described in an intimate view of domain education written by W. E. Griffis in 1870. Griffis, an American brought in to instruct at the Fukui domain college, reported his first impression of the samurai students:

At the tapping of the clapperless bell, the students put away their brushes, inkstones, and sticks of ink, wrapped up their books and portable matter in square pieces of silk or calico, making neat bundles; put their short swords, which lay at their sides, in their girdles; and each and all bowing low, with faces to floor, to their teachers, rose up and went, first, to the sword room to put on their long swords. . . . Thrusting it in his girdle, and adjusting the pair, each scholar passed to the clog room, where several hundred pairs of clogs or sandals were stowed in numbered order. . . . The scraping and clatter of hundreds of wooden clogs over the long stone bridge were deafening. All were bare headed, with the top knot, queue, and shaven midscalp, most of them with bare feet on their clogs, with their characteristic dress, swagger, fierce looks, bare skin exposed at the scalp, neck, arms, calves, and feet, and with their murderous swords in the belts, they impressed upon my memory a picture of feudalism I shall never forget.[100]

Here indeed is a picture of education unique to Tokugawa Japan. Confucian in its early stages, and based upon Confucian moral principles, it was in its deepest motivation militant and practical.

Not only did the samurai impose upon the jusha an unfavorable balance between the military and the civil arts, they also obliged the jusha to share their curriculum with advocates of other intellectual systems. Schools which started in the early Tokugawa period with two basic curricula, literary and military, began to add other subjects in increasing numbers after the middle of the period. The Shogunate, for instance, supported a medical college (Igakkan) after 1765 and a school of native learning (Wagaku-kōdansho) after 1785.[101] In 1855 a school of Western learning (Yōgakusho) was set up, primarily to teach the Dutch and English languages. In the final years of the Shogunate, this school gradually expanded its instruction to include Western-style mathematics and science.[102] Even so, Tokugawa policy tended to be somewhat behind developments within the domains and in the large cities such as Edo and Osaka. The Shogunate authorities remained essentially conservative in their emphasis on civil training as against military and in their attempt to maintain the prestige of orthodox Neo-Confucianism. Because of the inability of the various domains to support multiple educational facilities, the domain schools give a more comprehensive picture of the various interests competing for a place in samurai education.

Most domains (224 out of 283 at the end of the Tokugawa period) provided in one way or another for sending their exceptionally talented young men to advanced schools or special educational institutions outside of the domain.[103] The best advanced schools were in Edo, Kyoto, Osaka, and Nagasaki. Edo offered instruction by leading Confucianists, the most famous masters in military skills, and a few masters of Western learning. In Kyoto one could find scholars in Japanese studies and in the unorthodox Kogaku school of Confucianism. In Nagasaki there were opportunities for the study of Western learning, Western medicine, and military science. One is struck by the great interest and expense the domain authorities put into the encouragement of such outside study and the practical results they expected from it.

Two new branches of learning gained widespread recognition during the late years of the Shogunate: Western studies and Japanese or Imperial studies. Educational statistics compiled in the first year after the Restoration show that most domain schools devoted part of their curriculum to Japanese studies. The Fukuoka domain showed the following distribution of students in its literary school: Japanese studies, 200; Confucian studies, 750; Western studies, 180; mathematics, 105; medicine, 120.[104]

The story of the spread of interest in Western learning is well known. Writers on Tokugawa intellectual history have brought into prominence a number of Tokugawa men who pioneered in the new fields of Western learning or who, in one way or another, broke with the Confucian tradition.[105] What has never been adequately brought out is that these men were quickly followed by many others. In the last years of the Tokugawa, between the coming of Perry and the Restoration, the career patterns of young samurai included more and more frequently a period of Western learning in Nagasaki or Osaka. It was not considered proper for any samurai to express too great an interest in Western subjects, but the opportunities for study were there. The picture of Fukuzawa Yukichi secretly pursuing prohibited subjects has probably magnified the obstacles in the way of the student with unorthodox aspirations. Western learning was an accepted part of the curriculum of many of the domain schools by 1867. The Fukui college in 1870, as described by Griffis, was not unusual:

I was surprised to find it so large and flourishing. There were in all about 800 students, comprised in the English, Chinese, Japanese, medical, and military departments. A few had been studying English for two or three years under native teachers who had been in Nagasaki. In the medical department I found a good collection of Dutch books, chiefly medical and scientific, and a fine pair of French dissection models, of both varieties of the human body. In the military school was a library of foreign works on military subjects, chiefly in English, several of which have been translated into Japanese. . . . The school library, of English and American books . . . was quite respectable. In the Chinese school I found thousands of boxes, with sliding lids, filled with Chinese and Japanese books.[106]

In increasing numbers the samurai of the late Tokugawa period were discovering that Japan had to create for herself a new world view as a nation and as a people in the world. Thus the students of Western studies and of Japanese studies were brought together. The former were able to discover the practical realities of Japan's position, especially with regard to the Western nations; the latter created out of Japan's past a sense of nationalism which was to give the Japanese the energy and the courage to fight for their position in the world. In 1869, when the new government established what was to become Tokyo University, the official announcement of educational policy was stated in a way that made the utilitarian view of Japan's leaders abundantly clear:

Divine scriptures and national codes, which call for respect for the imperial cause and which clarify the national entity are the objectives of this empire. They must be regarded by the students as of primary importance. The Chinese teaching of filial respect and social morality and the Chinese doctrine of harmonizing the nation and pacifying the world, as well as recent Western scientific inventions and progress are all important branches of knowledge.[107]

THE JUSHA AT THE END OF THE TOKUGAWA PERIOD

The long years of the Tokugawa period in many ways modified the samurai's way of life and his dominant concerns. One of the most obvious changes, of course, was the very imprint of Confucianism on his thinking. At the end many of the fundamental aims of the jusha had actually been achieved. Japan's leaders had become a well-educated, rationally thinking, socially oriented group whose professed ideals in government, society, and letters were strongly Confucian. Even in those aspects of samurai activity which were farthest from the Neo-Confucian experience, such as military training, Confucian thought and values had made their mark.

But the very fact that the samurai had absorbed so much of the Confucian substance made them less dependent on the jusha. In the early seventeenth century the field of letters was largely confined to Buddhist priests and Confucian scholars; the later age was one of infinitely greater richness and complexity. The Confucian scholar was still a respected member of the cultural elite, but by now the samurai themselves had taken over many of the cultural roles previously performed by the jusha. In the realm of history, for example, so clearly the preserve of Confucianists in the early days, amateur historians from among the samurai were active in almost every domain. In various branches of "scientific" study in which the jusha had once led the way because of their ability to handle Chinese sources, the primacy of Chinese studies was being questioned. The Chinese-style physician was challenged by the physicians with knowledge of Western medicine. The Confucian-trained military strategist was giving way to the man with knowledge of Western tactics and equipment. In astronomy, botany, geography, and a host of other subjects, the strictly Chinese traditions were put on the defensive.

Daimyo who once eagerly sought in Kyoto or Edo for Confucian scholars to staff their schools or to take up the study of domain history now as eagerly sent their young retainers to the Western-oriented schools in Nagasaki or to the Shinto-oriented military schools of Edo.

If what had happened to the jusha in the samurai's world was not evident by 1800, it was obvious by 1870. The jusha had entered that world in command of many fields. He brought with him a new world view, a new social ethic, and a new "science" in the form of Chinese theory and technology. He was listened to by his samurai patrons. Yet he remained basically subservient to the world of his patrons. By the end of the Tokugawa period these patrons had absorbed much of what the jusha had taught, but they had begun to doubt the invincibility of the Confucian system. The national crisis that followed 1853 converted much of what was the jusha's strength into weakness. His world view was superseded by a more nationalistic *kokutai*. His "science" was superseded by that of the West. His system of education was encroached upon. All that remained to him was the area of social ethics. Here, in what had always been the most universally applicable aspect of the jusha's system, was the residue that he and his pupils were to carry into the new world of Meiji.

Donald H. Shively

MOTODA EIFU: CONFUCIAN LECTURER TO THE MEIJI EMPEROR

The restoration of political power to the Imperial Court in 1868 launched Japan headlong upon a process of modernization and westernization which, in two decades, transformed a feudal country into a modern nation-state on the European model. The program was broadly outlined in the Charter Oath of 1868, which concluded with the statement: "Knowledge shall be sought throughout the world so as to strengthen the foundations of imperial rule." This was the signal for the wholesale importation, not only of all branches of Western science and technology, but also of Western political and moral philosophy. The Confucian world view and the Confucian classics were to be discarded in favor of Western texts. Confucianism was repudiated by the eager students of Western civilization as being part of the shameful past—the feudal age of barbarous customs and insular ignorance. The once honored Confucian scholar was now derided for the impracticality of his knowledge and was called a "rice-eating dictionary." There was no place for him in this age of enlightenment.

Actually, of course, this change did not come about overnight. During the first four or five years of the Restoration, the Confucian tradition remained strong in the areas of political theory and education. This was the time when the Restoration looked like a restoration, when the political offices of the seventh century were reconstructed, when the fiefs were returned to the Throne, when the Imperial position was elevated and Imperial edicts were again law, and when, in education, Confucian ethics was acknowledged to be the basic subject.

From about 1872, however, the tide of westernization gained force, submerging more and more of the traditional past. Government ministries were reorganized, somewhat modernized, and renamed with bewildering frequency, representative assemblies came into being, agitators for people's rights demanded parliamentary government on the English model. School textbooks based on Confucian ethics were replaced by translations of American and French readers, and Confucian moral education was no longer the core of the proliferating curriculum.

The experiments in westernization led in the late seventies to the propagation of radical ideas which alarmed both palace and government. The oligarchs, after some deliberation, countered with an orderly series of measures designed to create a sound authoritarian political structure, a structure which was to stand essentially unchanged for half a century. Political theories and institutions suitable for this purpose were found in the more conservative states of Europe, and were buttressed and supplemented by elements of traditional Japanese thought. By Imperial ordinance the government established the peerage, the cabinet system, the Privy Council, the General Staff, the Imperial Household Law, and the Constitution of 1889, and crowned its work with the Imperial Rescript on Education in October 1890. A month later, when the Diet was convened for the first time, the bureaucratic machine was in full operation, out of the reach of popular controls.

Even in some of these modern-sounding developments, the force of traditional ideas, Confucian and Shinto, played an important part. Confucian ideas in particular were drawn upon in raising the status of the Imperial Household, as may be seen in the following developments:

(1) Although during the seventies there was no clear concept of the Emperor's powers, and even among the oligarchs serious consideration was given to a division of sovereignty between the Emperor and the people, the Constitution of 1889 placed sovereignty in effect, if not nominally, with the Emperor.

(2) The position of the Emperor was increasingly elevated and sanctified by rituals and taboos, by the employment of Chinese Imperial terms, and by the issuance of edicts and rescripts cast in more heightened language. A peerage was established as a bulwark to the throne, borrowing its titles from the Chou dynasty.

(3) Emphasis was placed on the familistic pattern of the state, the Emperor as the father of the people, ruling not only with benevolence, but also with love.

(4) The Emperor emerged as the moral preceptor of the people, designating loyalty and filial piety as the cardinal virtues, and prescribing Confucian moral principles as the basis of education for the entire nation.

The contribution which Confucian ideas made to these developments amounts to rather an impressive record for a creed that many had given up for dead after 1872. Our concern in these pages will be with the man who more than any other was responsible for this resurgence of Confucianism—Motoda Eifu (or more properly, Nagazane [1818–91]), tutor and personal adviser to the Meiji Emperor.

At the time of the Restoration, Motoda was one of many Confucian scholars, too old and too inflexible to change with the times, who seemed destined to be discarded with the old regime. He had just made up his mind to retire from his provincial office when in 1871 he was summoned to serve as the Emperor's lecturer on Chinese books, a function that he interpreted, as we shall see, in the broadest possible sense. At this time the Emperor was eighteen, Motoda was fifty-three. He remained with the Emperor for twenty years, seeing him almost every day.

Motoda wrote an autobiography,[1] in which he pictures himself as the ideal Confucian minister, speaking out only when called upon or when it would be disloyal to remain silent. Be this as it may, it would seem that he was rarely silent. Whether out of loyalty or by request, he found occasion to advise the Emperor on every subject from marital relations and personal habits to questions of cabinet appointments, the reorganization of government institutions, drafting the constitution, foreign loans, the education system, rehabilitating the peerage, and relief for the ex-samurai. He spoke out against the dangers of rapid westernization, the partiality and arrogance of the oligarchs, and the bad personal character of some of the cabinet ministers. He repeatedly urged the Emperor to exercise his Imperial right of personal decision, overriding the cabinet when necessary, and never tired of adjuring the young sovereign to model his conduct on the sage-emperors Yao and Shun. The Emperor apparently took all this in good part and came back for more. There is no doubt that until Motoda's death, he was the Emperor's closest and most trusted adviser.

Motoda's autobiography gives us considerable information on his relationship with the Emperor and the advice he gave, especially until 1883. An autobiography, however, even one as seemingly modest and forthright as Motoda's, can hardly be considered a disinterested evaluation. Moreover, the only witness to much of what Motoda relates was the Emperor himself, of whose personality and ability we as yet know very little.[2] Finally, the practice of corporate decision in Japanese government, and the large number of ministers and advisers involved in many government decisions, makes it hard to evaluate any one man's influence in almost any matter; it seems clear that most of the decisions ascribed to the Emperor were very much in line with Motoda's advice, but no more than this can be said.

It seems more rewarding, therefore, to study him, not as a political figure of indeterminate power, but rather as a professional Confucianist who filled, in the new age of enlightenment, all the functional roles which John W. Hall has distinguished for the Tokugawa *jusha*: creator of a world view, political adviser, educator, and writer of poetry and prose in Chinese. Although he was appointed only to read Chinese books with the Emperor, his concept of the universal applicability of Confucian knowledge was too broad for these narrow bounds. Confucianism was not just a matter of Chinese books; it was the ultimate authority in all affairs, the key to all mysteries, the source of all virtue. This was the message for the Emperor—an impressive message; and in all likelihood impressively delivered. It was perhaps through the force of his personality as much as through his Confucian knowledge that he gained the Emperor's confidence.

Motoda's career is of particular interest as being one of the last significant demonstrations, historically, of Confucianism in action at the highest levels of government. It is a kind of index of the rapidity of Japan's development that a Tokugawa Confucianist could survive long enough to give political advice, exclusively in Confucian terms, to the ruler of a modern state.

MOTODA'S BACKGROUND

During the Edo period (1600–1868), the Chu Hsi school was officially designated by the Tokugawa Shogunate as the official school, but other schools, such as the Wang Yang-ming school and the *kogaku* (Ancient Learning) school were tolerated. Motoda, although formally classified as a follower of the Chu Hsi tradition, was educated according to a method of study known as *jitsugaku* (Practical Learning), which had gained considerable popularity. Motoda's teacher, Yokoi Shōnan (1809–69), one of the most original and powerful thinkers in the two decades immediately preceding the Restoration, contended that the classics should be read for the practical insight they afforded into the true nature of things. Through this method one developed wisdom and the ability to act; other methods led only to futile pedantry. As Shōnan said: "When I have read a book and fully understood its principles, the principles become my possessions and the book immediately becomes dregs. When the principles have become my possession, they can be applied . . ." And again: "If you decided to study Chu Hsi, you should consider what it was that Chu Hsi studied. Unless you do this, when you come in contact with Chu Hsi's books you will become Chu Hsi's slave . . ."[3] His search for basic principles took him beyond the Confucian classics to the reigns of Yao, Shun, and the three ancient dynasties.

Although the influence of Shōnan's ideas can be clearly seen in Motoda's writings, the disciple was not able to keep pace with the rapid development of his master's ideas at the time of the Restoration. When in 1862 Shōnan advocated the opening of Japan and parliamentary government, Motoda accepted his plan without any real understanding of its implications. Above all, he did not understand his master's restless interest in universal principles, an interest which ultimately caused Shōnan to become curious about Christianity and led to his assassination in 1869.

By birth and upbringing, Motoda was a typical member of the warrior-official class of the late Tokugawa period.[4] The Motoda family had served for generations as officials under the daimyo of Kumamoto domain (han). The family observances which Eifu describes during his early life seem to have served as the model for the practices he advocated sixty years later for all Japanese. He was told stories about loyal subjects, filial children, and brave warriors, and was shown pictures of these paragons. He reports that the solicitude with which his grandparents cared for his great-grandmother won such admiration among the people of the community that they petitioned the authorities to bestow a reward upon the family. He was taught that the family members owed everything to generations of ancestors and to the lord of the domain, and that he must never be remiss in loyalty and filial piety. He gathered with the other family members every morning to bow before the ancestral deities on the god-shelf, and was taught to report to them whenever leaving or entering the house, and to visit the ancestral graves three times a month.

Eifu's grandfather started the boy's education by teaching him Japanese and Chinese poems, and during his tenth year he completed the twenty chapters of the Analects. The next year he was sent to a teacher to study Mencius. He was introduced to the Practical Learning method at the domain school when he was fourteen, and remained an adherent for the rest of his life.

During the next ten years of study at the domain school, Eifu came particularly under the influence of two young scholars of the Practical Learning method, Shimotsu Kyūya and Yokoi Shōnan, both of whom stressed wide reading in Japanese and Chinese history. When Eifu was about twenty-three, Shōnan, who had been the head of the school, left for Edo, the policies of the school changed, and Eifu withdrew. He continued to study privately, reading Ogyū Sorai's Seidan and Kenroku, Kumazawa Banzan's Shūgi Washo and Shūgi Gaisho, the Sung Ming-ch'en Yen-hsing Lu, Han Fei-tzu, Mencius, the Analects, and the Great Learning.[5]

The next year Shōnan returned to Kumamoto. He formed a study group, in which he and Shimotsu Kyūya at thirty-three were the oldest.

The others were Nagaoka Kemmotsu (1812–59), Ogi Kakubei, and Motoda Eifu, who was the youngest member. They met every two or three days to read and discuss books. They also discussed with admiration the achievements of Tokugawa Nariaki (1800–1860) and Fujita Tōko (1806–55) of the Mito school, who criticized the Tokugawa government for lack of respect for the Emperor and advocated a program of governmental reform. Because Shōnan was in communication with Tōko, the senior officials of the domain became fearful that the activities and growing strength of the Practical Learning school might bring reprisals by the Shogunate against Kumamoto as they had against Mito. The lord advised Eifu's father to direct his son to withdraw from the group. After that Eifu did not attend their meetings, but he remained a lifelong friend of its members.

He spent the next years in travel and private study. He went to Nagasaki in 1844 to see the Dutch ships, and from talking to retainers of the Saga *han* he learned with surprise of the progressive developments in that domain in the study of foreign books, of the new ironworks they had built, and of their plan to construct iron ships. He also learned more of the activities of the patriots of the Mito *han*. He was surprised at how little he and his associates knew of what was going on outside their *han*. Even the opening of Japan a decade later had little effect on his life.

His opportunity to participate in the affairs of the domain finally came in 1858, after the death of his father, when he succeeded to the headship of the family with a stipend of 550 *koku*. Thereafter he was appointed to various *han* offices which took him to Edo and Kyoto. His domain did not take a major role in the political agitation and plots which led to the overthrow of the Shogunate and the Restoration of the Emperor, but Motoda followed the course of events with interest. In early 1868 he twice urged his lord to declare his allegiance to the Emperor and send his forces to join the triumphant Imperial army in their march to the east, but his advice was rejected. He then retired from public life to open a private school called the Gorakuen. In 1870, however, his lord (by this time the Governor of Higo) recalled him to duty to serve as his tutor with the title of Reader (*jidoku*). Early the next year he was ordered to Tokyo on *han* business, and it was during this stay in the capital that he was summoned to the post of Reader to the Emperor.

THE EMPEROR'S READER

Concerning the events which led to his appointment, Motoda wrote in his autobiography:

Because my family, relying upon the precepts of loyalty, filial piety, benevolence, and duty, fostered obedient and loyal natures, my mind was turned early to reverence for the Emperor and to statecraft. However, I did not wish to go beyond my station in life, leave my rank, compete for advancement, and act forcefully. . . . I evaluated my own ability, considered my talents, and adhered to my principles in retirement without asking for a post. When, by order of the *han,* I went to Tokyo to take part in political affairs as an assistant to our lord the *han* governor, I hoped to be able to serve the Court, but I did not venture to push myself forward and compete with the men of the day. That year I was fifty-four [*sai*] . . . Saigō and Ōkubo were both forty-three or forty-four and Kido, Itagaki, and the others were mostly men of the same age. . . . How could I venture to curry favor with them in order to seek fame?

Not being invited to take a prominent role in the national government or even in the affairs of his domain, Motoda had just decided to return to Kumamoto when his call came.

One day I was discussing national affairs with Yoneda and Yasuba [Yasukuzu (1829–99)] at the home of the venerable [Shimotsu] Kyūya. In the course of the conversation, Yasuba said to Kyūya: "Something good happened recently which has made me extremely happy. Yesterday I saw Finance Minister Ōkubo, and he said to me: 'The Court needs a Reader. . . . Do you know of anybody?' Thinking to myself what good fortune this was, I suggested Master Motoda, saying, 'He is a colleague of mine and the Governor's Reader. He follows the Ch'eng-Chu teachings.' Ōkubo said, 'Ch'eng-Chu teachings—excellent. . . .'" When, sitting to one side, I heard this, I was greatly surprised and reproached Yasuba, saying: "Why do you want to put me to shame? I am deficient in learning, bigoted, and old. Thanks to the assistance I receive from all of you I am barely able to struggle along in this world, but how could I presume to present myself at the new Court, stand alone, and defile the title of His Majesty's Reader?"

According to Motoda, he was pushed forward against his will by his compatriots and the Governor, and they were summoned as a body to the residence of Prime Minister Sanjō Sanetomi.

He received us courteously, and when the entertainment was at its height asked me to write something. Not venturing to refuse, I wrote a poem in Chinese which I had once composed for a book:

> The minister loves the sovereign
> The sovereign likewise loves the minister.
> With natures mutually allied
> They administer the government.
> In the entire court there is not dissatisfaction;
> Twenty-two men are like one.

The Minister praised it. Perhaps he privately hoped for a relationship between sovereign and ministers in this age comparable to that of the time of Yao and Shun.

Five days later Motoda was summoned for an Imperial audience.

Wearing court dress, I approached on my knees, bowed to the floor, saw the Dragon Countenance three *ken* away [18 feet], and withdrew on my knees. On this, my first close approach to the Emperor, there was nothing in my heart but awe and joy, and I could not repress my emotion.

His first lecture was on the first chapter of the "Kung-yeh Ch'ang" in the *Analects,* which he took up where the Emperor's previous Reader had left off. After expounding the essential meaning and the language used, he explained:

"When a sage looks at men to select those with talent, he is fair and unbiased, regardless of the world's criticism or praise. . . . If the ruler of men today looks upon the men of the realm as did the sage upon Kung-yeh Ch'ang and Nan Yung, there will be no wasted talent inside or overlooked wisdom outside the government, and all will be joyful obedience within the realm. Now, although the innate sagacity of the ruler of men does not seem to depend upon study, reliance on one's own wisdom means that one's knowledge will be restricted and that errors of excess and deficiency will be unavoidable. Accordingly, sage-emperors and enlightened kings invariably prefer to make sages their teachers and to abide by their rules. In remote antiquity the Emperor Ōjin made Wani his teacher and studied the *Analects,*[6] and other examples in Japan and China have not been few. Your servant is overcome with admiration that in the present flourishing era Your Majesty is performing the splendid work of carrying on the ancestral precepts by again studying the *Analects* and following the example of the sages . . ."

Ah! What a day was that! . . . By studying the Ch'eng-Chu teachings in company with Nagaoka Atsuyoshi, Yokoi, Shimotsu, and Ogi, I had acquired faith in the Way of the sages when I was twenty-five [*sai*]. I believed without reservation that morals and statecraft lay in this Practical Learning, but because it had become an object of dislike and jealousy in the domain, I had been checkmated for almost thirty years. Now, for the first time, I went to Court, entered the Imperial presence, and expounded these teachings to the Emperor himself. What joy could exceed this?[7]

The scholar whom Motoda replaced as Reader, Nakanuma Kien (Ryōzō) (1829–96), was a Confucian scholar of the Chu Hsi school, who had served for two years and then resigned. The other principal lecturers were Fukuba Bisei (1831–1907), a scholar of Japanese studies (*kokugaku*), and Katō Hiroyuki (1836–1916), who represented Western studies. At this time Motoda lectured not only on the Confucian classics, but also on a history of Japan by Rai San'yō (presumably his *Nihon Gaishi*) and works on Chinese history such as the *Chen-kuan Cheng-yao* and *T'ang-chien.* Fukuba lectured on works of Japanese history including *Kōchō Shiryaku* and *Jinnō Shōtōki.* Katō lectured on German legal history, and for a time also taught German to the Emperor. All three lectured on a survey of Japanese history called the *Kokushi Sanron* and on the most popular book of the day, Nakamura Keiu's translation of Samuel Smiles' *Self-Help.* Motoda felt that the Emperor had not advanced very far in his education. He conferred with

Fukuba and Katō, and they agreed that there should be regular daily hours of instruction and an increase in subject matter.[8]

In 1873 the Emperor was also being lectured by two other members, besides Katō, of the Meirokusha, the "Meiji Six Society," formed by prominent scholars of Western studies to hold lectures and discussions for the public. They were Nishi Amane (1829–97), who had studied at the University of Leiden, and Nishimura Shigeki (1828–1902), always a Confucianist, but also a keen student of the West, who lectured to the Emperor on French law and world history. As Motoda said in his autobiography:

From 1873 on, the fashion among people was to follow the Western education. Esteeming knowledge and skills, they regarded morality, benevolence, and duty as bigotry. They concentrated on reading Western books and translations, abandoning almost completely Chinese books such as the Four Books and Five Classics. The books used by the Readers also, aside from some Japanese books and histories, were for the most part only trivial translated things. At this time Fukuba used mostly Japanese books and Katō mostly Western books. . . . Regardless of what book I used, I always discussed the essential points of the sovereign's virtue, the importance of duty, . . . reverence for the national polity [kokutai], the purity of the Confucian Way, the harm of Christianity, the errors of Buddhism and vulgar studies, the differences between Eastern and Western customs, the reasons that Imperial and republican constitutions must not be the same, and so forth. I explained these repeatedly until I was certain that he believed firmly. His Majesty was extremely fond of these discussions, and always listened carefully. I never noticed him to become tired of them.[9]

We have no way of estimating the number of formal Court lectures, not to mention the private ones, which Motoda delivered to the Emperor during his twenty years of service. He had the honor of giving the New Year's Lecture every year from 1872 to 1890. Most of these lectures were on the Analects, the Doctrine of the Mean, and the Book of History. In January 1878 he began a series of lectures on the Analects, twelve a month, and many of these have been preserved.[10] They are generally repetitive and dogmatic, following the traditional progression from classical theme to current application; one lecture is an attack upon the Western-style education system, another an exhortation to appoint a frank and sincere man as Minister of Foreign Affairs. Although Fukuba and Katō resigned as regular lecturers in 1875, and the other lecturers changed from time to time, Motoda continued year after year to reiterate his views. The title of Reader was changed to Lecturer (jikō) in 1875, and Motoda was later appointed Palace Councillor (1886) and Privy Councillor (1888), but he was always the main lecturer.

MOTODA'S THOUGHT

To Motoda the central core of education meant training in Confucian ethics. This was the root or trunk; all other learning followed naturally from this, and was merely the branches—the secondary and external aspects of education. Motoda said that if the Emperor's virtue were cultivated, he could match the accomplishments of the greatest Japanese emperors of the past. If the people were trained in Confucian ethics, they would be loyal subjects of the Emperor and dutiful members of society. The premises from which he proceeded in expounding these views can best be understood by examining his explanation of the development of Confucian principles in China and Japan.

Motoda explained that at the beginning of heaven and earth the one harmonious principle was simply sincerity. To it was added *yin*, *yang*, and the five elements. Thus all human qualities came from natural laws. Human nature is innately good. In early times, in the age of Yao and Shun, the people's sincerity and harmony were immediately manifest. In later times, with the awakening of selfish desires, it became necessary to give men moral instruction so that the innate good in their natures could be developed. It became necessary to clarify human ethics by explaining the Way.

The only comprehensive and balanced presentation of this Way is to be found in the writings of Confucius, which should thus form the basis of education for the Emperor, the ministers, and all the people. The method of study must be that of Practical Learning. One must always keep in mind that the purposes of study are "to develop one's innate good nature, expel selfish desires, clarify human ethics, and reveal the workings of heaven."[11] Motoda explained that the early emperors of China and the Confucian sages were by nature benevolent and wise and did not need to read books. From the Han dynasty on, however, many Confucian scholars emerged who

developed skill in poetry and prose, engaged in detailed metaphysical discussions in commentaries, and established each his own school on the basis of his explanations of morality and scholarship. . . . As a result, . . . practical learning finally became unknown in the world. The teachings of Yao, Shun, Confucius, and Mencius turned into the pedantry of useless scholars and a prostituted learning; it was of no assistance in maintaining peace, the Great Way declined, and China came to her present condition.

Japanese Confucianists must see through this pedantry and apply the measuring rods of Yao, Shun, Confucius, and Mencius by drawing directly on the classics.[12]

However the student of Chinese thought may feel about these remarks, it is clear that Motoda can only be called a Confucianist. Not only did he base his philosophy squarely upon the Confucian classics, but he regarded them as the only written repository of the Way. The Japanese works sacred to Shinto beliefs he rarely, if ever, mentioned. The few Japanese books which are mentioned in his writings are written by Confucianists, and are histories, commentaries on the Chinese classics, or morals texts.

Motoda, however, was not just a Confucianist; he was also a Japanese. He had to take account in his philosophy of the divine descent and transmission of virtue of the Japanese Imperial family. Most Confucianists of the Chu Hsi school in the Tokugawa period had disposed of this problem by regarding Shinto mythology as a local and rather primitive manifestation of the universal Way of Confucius. Some less orthodox Confucianists, however, under pressure from the revival of "pure" Shinto by the kokugaku (national studies) scholars during the eighteenth century, worked out a way of combining the Japanese Confucian tradition, ideas of divine descent and virtue, and political allegiance to the Emperor into a single doctrine which gave equal reverence to Confucian and Shinto beliefs. This was a prevalent view among scholars of Mito and the western domains at the time of the Restoration.

In a statement to his *han* lord when he was his Reader in 1870,[13] Motoda explained the development of moral teachings in Japan in the following way. In remote antiquity the Sun Goddess, being by nature sagacious and wise, took care to establish clear precepts for all posterity. Since there was no method of writing at this time, her teachings could not be transmitted in books. She lodged them, therefore, in the three sacred regalia, which according to Motoda symbolize the three virtues of wisdom, benevolence, and duty. These three virtues, received by the people of Japan when their life on earth began, were transmitted and exemplified by the emperors; they spread through the realm, and the entire empire was in every way well governed and peaceful.

Motoda explained the transmission of the teachings more fully in a lecture he delivered to the Emperor (ca. 1878):

As we have learned from ancient texts, Ninigi-no-mikoto [grandson of the Sun Goddess] first established the country and, in compliance with the instructions of the Heavenly Progenitrix, cultivated virtue and guided the people. Succeeding ancestors, inheriting the rule from generation to generation, spread the teachings and administered the government, but in every case they possessed the virtue of being born with knowledge and acting with natural ease, and used the excellent method of using the heart to transmit to the heart. . . . [In later generations] men turned to cleverness and this gave rise to the danger that the . . . Great Way might lose its purity. It therefore became unavoidably necessary to rely upon books and exposition in order to elucidate and amplify this Way . . . Fortunately the *Analects* was available, having been obtained from Kudara when that territory was under our jurisdiction, and since its explanations were in harmony with our Way, the Emperor thereupon accepted and studied it.

He said further: "This book, being a book transmitted by the Emperor, is to be revered as an exposition of the Imperial Way; no book of our Court can be ranked above it."[14]

A golden age followed. Thanks to the practical learning taught to the people by ancient Japanese Emperors by word and by example, "all held the three virtues, all unconsciously followed the Way of the five relationships. High and low, noble and base, all had the same teachings, and the beauty of their customs, the purity of their education, were preeminent in the universe."[15] In these idyllic days "religious observances, government, teaching, and learning were one, and benevolence, duty, loyalty, and filial piety were honored by the Emperor and people alike, as history proves unmistakably . . ."[16]

Later, however, there was "a decline of Imperial influence and the study of the teachings lost its clarity, the three sacred teachings becoming something lofty and mysterious which none could fathom." Confucianism degenerated into frivolity and pedantry, causing Shōtoku Taishi to espouse Buddhism, "the heretical path of sudden enlightenment," a disastrous move from which Japan did not recover for centuries.[17] Thereafter political power was monopolized by the Regents, and then it was usurped by the military.

Happily, in spite of the confusion in political order in the period of the Tokugawa usurpers, Confucian teachings of loyalty, filial piety, benevolence, and duty were encouraged. "Mitsukuni of Mito, basing himself primarily on the national polity [*kokutai*], clarified the Imperial Way and taught the Confucian doctrine. Accordingly, the education of ancient times appeared brightly in the world again . . ." In this way men were prepared to come forward to accomplish the great work of the Meiji Restoration.[18]

Now the Imperial rule has been restored and within the four seas there has been a renovation. It is to be hoped that by clarifying the sovereign's virtue, settling the people's hearts, and expounding the principles of government, we can come forth ahead of all the nations. This is nothing other than expounding the learning of Yao, Shun, and the three dynasties, and again clarifying the divine teachings.[19]

We might ask whether, thanks to the guidance of the divine ancestors, there were any other respects in which the Way in Japan differed from that of Confucius. Motoda points to one. He says that in the age of Yao and Shun the relationship between father and son was established as the first of the five relationships (Confucius placed it

second to the relationship between lord and subject). Because Japan
from the beginning has been ruled by an Emperor descended from the
Heavenly Progenitrix, the Way begins with the lord-subject relationship:

The ruler looks upon his subjects as his own children; the subjects look up to
the ruler as to their parents. Lord and subject, ancestor and descendant, are
one body and one spirit, united and inseparable. This union of the loyalty
between lord and subject with the love between father and son is a perfection,
a triumph of the Way and its principles without parallel in the world, something undreamed of even by Yao and Shun, something even Confucius was
unable to postulate.[20]

Essentially, then, the formula used by Motoda to reconcile the
native traditions with Confucianism was as follows: the Sun Goddess
was peerless in virtue, but Confucianism was needed to restore and
expound her teachings. He said as little as possible about Japanese
mythology, nor did he make any real examination of the Japanese tradition and the *kokugaku* texts. He merely asserted that the Japanese
imperial traditions were in harmony with the earliest Confucian traditions. This he could easily claim, because these traditions came down
through the hands of eighth-century historians who were thoroughly
imbued with Chinese ethical and political ideas, and whose main concern was to give the Japanese imperial family an aura of Confucian
legitimacy. In doing this, they described the existence in early Japan
of an ideal order such as existed in China in the age of the sage-emperors.
To Motoda, whose indoctrination and ends strikingly resembled theirs,
this order was ideal in every sense of the word.

Having made these concessions to Shinto, Motoda disposed of the
other competition by insisting that the only method of cultivating the
Way was in the study of the classics, and only if the study was conducted
according to practical principles. All other systems of moral education
were one-sided and incomplete:

The studies of punctuation and vocabulary made by various heterodox and
mediocre scholars, as well as Buddhism, Christianity, and the hundred
branches of Western studies—all are one-sided, factional studies rather than
studies in the Confucian sense. Furthermore, although people at present generally apply the term *kangaku* [Chinese studies] to the study of Chinese letters,
and equate it with Confucian studies, this urgently requires correction. "Chinese studies" is a field of literary endeavor which involves a knowledge of
China's history, past and present institutions and culture, as well as proficiency in Chinese. Confucian teaching is the study of perfecting the individual's moral character, attaining to truth, and practicing the Great Way
of the realm. Accordingly, although in the case of China it is called the Way
of Yao and Shun and the teachings of Confucius and Mencius, in the case of

this country it ought to be called the Way of the Divine Ancestors and our moral teachings. Although what is called *kokugaku* . . . studies old books and ancient matters, and emphasizes reverence for the gods and respect for the emperors, it is predominantly one-sided. It is not sufficient to give practical effect to the supreme virtue and Great Way of the former emperors, and therefore is not the same as our Way of the Divine Ancestors or the learning of Confucius.[21]

THE EMPEROR'S VIRTUE

Motoda brought all these beliefs and prejudices relentlessly to bear on his primary concern—cultivating the Emperor's virtue. Virtue, defined as "the practice of the Way of benevolence, duty, loyalty, and filial piety, and their acquisition and perfection by the individual," was the sole principle and instrument of government, defined as "a comprehensive term for rites, music, education, laws, prohibitions, and all means of governing the people." In a word, "the countless methods of governing the people are all applied by means of virtue alone."

Moreover, Motoda told the Emperor, virtue specifically includes wisdom. The modern inclination to separate the two, to distinguish between "subject-matter education and moral education," was erroneous and pernicious.

The advocates of enlightenment completely mistake the basic meaning of virtue when they contend that whereas the province of wisdom is broad and boundless, the sphere of virtue is narrow and limited. Originally, virtue was a name which embraced myriad excellences, while wisdom was one part of virtue with no province outside it.[22]

Motoda made his fullest statement concerning the cultivation of the Emperor's virtue in a document which he presented to Minister of the Right Iwakura Tomomi in September 1873, two years after his appointment as Reader.[23] In summary, this statement said that nothing is of more urgent importance to the country than the cultivation of the Emperor's virtue. If the virtue of the Emperor is not perfected—and "at present the sovereign's wisdom is not yet extensive and his benevolence is not yet comprehensive"—all the attempts to strengthen Japan by westernization and modernization will lead but to disaster. The most urgent business for chief ministers of state, therefore, is not in administrative matters, but in helping to develop the Emperor's mind. This must be the responsibility of the ablest men in the country, and not left to second- and third-rate teachers as at present. The ablest men of the day have become Prime Minister, Ministers of the Left and Right, and Councillors, but these men rarely consult the Emperor on political matters. Under the circumstances how can the Emperor develop wis-

dom and evince benevolence? Palace and government must be united.
To this end the following program should be followed:

The Prime Minister, the Ministers of the Left and Right, and two or three
Councillors should attend in the Imperial chamber daily, closely observe the
Son of Heaven's activities and actions, share in and hear of all important
matters within the palace, occasionally beside the Jewel Seat discuss the mind
of lord and subject and success and failure in the conduct of government,
. . . attend in the palace lecture room and ask questions concerning doubtful points in the classics and histories, go along to the parade ground and
expound the merits and deficiencies of strategy and military techniques, attend banquets in the inner palace, participate in the private conversations of
palace officials, ride in the same carriage with the sovereign to visit the homes
of ministers of state, and go on Imperial progresses through towns and villages. The Son of Heaven worries if he does not see his assisting ministers
during the day; the assisting ministers dread being away even briefly from
the Emperor's side. In all cases there is the pleasure of ease and tranquillity
of mind with no trace of troublesome formalities; there is the benefit of
thoroughness of training of the mind without blunt admonishing. The advancement of the Imperial wisdom and the development of the Imperial
virtue reside exclusively herein.

Motoda pointed out also that more care should be taken in the selection of palace officials, for only they are informed of what happens at
the palace when the chief ministers are away. Their position is important because "the basis of morality lies within the women's quarters.
If rectitude is lost in this respect, the ultimate disorders will be impossible to imagine." In conclusion Motoda contended that if his plan were
faithfully followed, the Imperial virtue could be expected to mature in
ten years. Then "why should we worry lest ours not be a sovereign like
Jimmu or Ōjin? Why should we doubt our ability to stand alongside
any nation of the world?"

A more immediate means of improving the Emperor's virtue was by
lecturing him on the wise emperors of the past. Quoting Chu Hsi's
advice to "imitate what was done by pioneer spirits," Motoda urged the
Emperor to take as his pioneer spirits the classical Emperors of China
and Japan.

As regards the magnanimity which makes the four seas your family, takes the
myriad people as your children, and places implicit trust in others, you must
make the Emperor Jimmu your teacher. As regards revering the gods, tranquilizing the people, and opening the way to benefit and welfare, you must
make the Emperor Sujin your teacher. . . . [And so on, through the emperors Keikō, Nintoku, Tenchi, and Go-Sanjō.] In addition there is nothing
which is not an example for a sovereign of men in the supreme virtue and
great exploits of Yao, Shun, and Yü related in the Book of History, or in the
words of Confucius in the Analects.[24]

After lecturing on emperors of the past, Motoda would lead the discussion to the present day. In one instance, after observing that the achievements of Meiji's reign to date had been undertakings on a scale comparable to those of the Emperor Jimmu, the subject of that day's lecture, Motoda asked the Emperor which of Jimmu's able assistants he regarded as the most outstanding. When Meiji named Umashimade no Mikoto, Motoda noted that in terms of modern offices Umashimade had duties comparable to the Commander of the Imperial Guards and the additional function of Home Minister, and added:

I would like to see ministers of similar versatility today . . . If your Majesty wishes to obtain an Umashimade no Mikoto today, nothing could be better than to bring together, trust, and be intimate with Saigō, the former Commander of the Imperial Guards, and Ōkubo, the present Home Minister. Combining wisdom and courage, perfect in civil and military matters, these are your Majesty's Umashimade.[25]

Motoda next asked Meiji which of the emperors of Japanese history he admired most. He named Jimmu and Keikō, for their martial exploits and "extension of the national influence." Motoda observed that the accomplishments of Meiji resembled those of these two emperors in scope and spirit. He pointed out, however, that there were other serious problems facing present-day Japan, where "the name of enlightenment is present but the wisdom of the people is not yet awakened; the form of Imperial rule is present but many of the people have not yet enjoyed its blessings." It would be better, he suggested, if in the future the Emperor were to model himself more on the emperors Ōjin and Nintoku. Ōjin had spread education and fostered the proper teachings, while Nintoku, with his deep affection for the people, had governed with benevolence and led the people to self-reliance. Only when these matters had been accomplished, he said, would the real essence of the scope and spirit of Jimmu and Keikō be achieved.

On another occasion Motoda pointed out to the Emperor that every one of the eleven wise and just Japanese emperors from Ōjin to Go-Kōmyō (1644–55) not only was an adherent of Confucian principles, but was tutored by Confucian scholars who instructed him in the Confucian classics and the Way of good government. The lesson was clear:

In the successive reigns since the Emperor Ōjin, the rulers who are known as sage-emperors and enlightened sovereigns all revered and believed in Confucius and cultivated real virtue with the result that the realm came to be well governed and peaceful; but during reigns in which Buddhism received Imperial patronage and literature flourished, powerful subjects brought disorder to the court's decrees, and disturbances followed one upon the heels of another. The evidence of this is clearly visible in historical annals.[26]

Certainly the Meiji Emperor could only conclude that the success of his reign depended solely upon following the teachings of his Confucian Lecturer.

THE PALACE ADVISERS

A vital part of the plan which Motoda put forward in 1873 to prepare the Emperor to take personal charge of government was his scheme to develop the Emperor's political ability through intimate contact with the chief ministers and consultations on governmental decisions. Several attempts to enlist the cooperation of Iwakura, Sanjō, and Kido Kōin brought no results. Finally in 1877 Ōkubo Toshimichi, the Home Minister, gave some support to the plan by agreeing to the appointment of a number of special consultants, called *jihō*, who were to be in constant attendance on the Emperor to offer remonstrances and correct any omissions or deficiencies in his actions. The office was established in September 1877, and eight *jihō* were appointed, among them Motoda, Sasaki Takayuki (1830–1910), Yoshii Tomozane (1828–91), and Hijikata Hisamoto (1833–1918). All eight were inexperienced in political matters, and since they did not receive information on the deliberations and decisions of the government, they were unable to advise the Emperor on any but minor matters concerning the palace. This was a great disappointment to the *jihō*, who had accepted their appointments with high hopes of helping the Emperor take over the direction of political affairs.[27]

After sizing up the situation, the *jihō* conceived the plan of enlisting an influential minister to devote all of his time to guiding the Emperor, and they persuaded Ōkubo to accept the post of Imperial Household Minister and undertake this mission. Iwakura, Sanjō, and Itō gave their approval,[28] but before the appointment could be made Ōkubo was assassinated. The *jihō* felt that none of the other ministers was suitable to serve in this role, and they resolved to work as a group to carry through their program. Only four days after Ōkubo's death they formally demanded that the Emperor be given the right to make political decisions, and that the *jihō*, as his advisers, be permitted to participate in cabinet deliberations. The oligarchs—Iwakura and Itō, in particular—were indignant. They agreed to include the Emperor in cabinet meetings and to keep him informed of the work of the ministries, but they refused to include the *jihō*, not only because of the need for secrecy, but also because of the necessity in modern government to keep palace and government separate — witness the noxious political activities of the palace eunuchs in Chinese history. The *jihō* were shocked by this comparison, and considerable bitterness seems to have developed between them and the government.[29] The following year the government abolished the office of *jihō*. Of the eight men who had served in this capacity, only Motoda, who had continued to hold his appointment as Lecturer, remained close to the Emperor.

One outcome of the agitation of the *jihō* was that whereas formerly the only high officials whom the Emperor saw frequently were Iwakura and Sanjō, now the Councillors also came to inform him of their work and consult with him. They attended the Court at specified times and in addition began the institution of holding Court dinners once or twice a week, attended by ministers and important civil and military officials, and also Court luncheons after the weekly cabinet meeting.[30]

ADVICE ON GOVERNING

When the *jihō's* bid for power ended in their dismissal, Motoda's role at the palace increased in importance, for he was now one of the few men to whom the Emperor could turn to discuss matters of state. There is no question but that Motoda spent a great deal of time with the Emperor. In July 1885, when Itō was engaged in the onerous task of drafting the Constitution, the Imperial Household Law, and plans for reorganizing government offices, he complained that Motoda and the Grand Chamberlain, Tokudaiji, spent so much time with the Emperor every day that there was not enough time left for Ministers like himself to report on governmental matters. He asked that they see the Emperor only in the morning so that the Ministers and Councillors could see him in the afternoon.[31]

When Motoda was ill—as he was, for example, while various constitutional proposals were being considered in 1881 and again during the formulation of the new peerage system in 1884—the Emperor sent courtiers to consult him and bring back his suggestions. Iwakura and Itō, Japan's two most influential statesmen, took care to clear many of their proposals with Motoda. He says in his autobiography:

Whenever Iwakura and Sanjō intended to present some secret matter to the Emperor, Iwakura spoke to me about it privately so that I could speak to the Emperor when there was an opportunity in order to assist the Imperial decision. Therefore as the occasion required he called me to his residence or talked to me at the palace.[32]

We can imagine that Motoda was consulted without reluctance, for, dogmatic and hidebound though he was, he was at all times a Confucian gentleman, respected by all for his integrity, and trusted implicitly by the Emperor. His loyalty to the Emperor was of the highest order, and he judged men and proposals primarily in terms of their service to the Throne. There is no evidence of his seeking office, favors, wealth, or power, in contrast to many of the ministers of the day. Because of his modest rank at court, ministers could not regard him as a political adversary; moreover, his position close to the Emperor rendered him immune from attack. If he was stubborn, he was stubborn in the interests of the Emperor and the nation. Dedicated to guiding the Emperor's virtue and preserving the national polity, he felt it his righteous duty to speak out against anything that was not in these interests.

He made a revealing statement about himself when, in 1879, the Emperor followed his advice and rejected Councillor Kuroda Kiyotaka's demand that Soejima Taneomi be dismissed as Lecturer:

I had repeatedly pleaded this case, and what I said was valued by the Emperor. Because I am Lecturer, I receive favored treatment from the Emperor. I am able to hear about secret matters which I should not hear about, and I am able to speak about these matters, which, since they exceed my authority, I should not speak about. When, as the Emperor's adviser, I see something which I regard as disgraceful, so that it would be disloyalty on my part not to speak and speak fully, I express my innermost mind completely, even though I may cause displeasure. My wish is only that the Emperor may forgive me and find something to select from my advice.[33]

One of the means by which Motoda furthered the causes he believed in was to write a statement after he had had a discussion with the Emperor on some political problem, entitling it "The Imperial Opinion on . . ." There are several such statements on problems of education, and also on treaty revision and other subjects. Sometimes he would send the document to the minister whose policy needed correcting, and sometimes he would speak to the minister concerning the Emperor's wishes. It is likely that at such times the Emperor consented to his Lecturer's speaking for him, but the choice of words and the ideas themselves are clearly Motoda's.

Although Motoda's political advice to the Emperor apparently followed no formal plan, he seems to have been capable of thinking beyond daily crises toward a long-range program. There is some evidence of such a program in his petition of 1873 on the Imperial virtue and in his individual lectures, and there is still better evidence in a document of May 1877 addressed to the Emperor, setting forth ten broad principles of political strategy for the Emperor's attention. This was a by-product of lectures he had been delivering during the Satsuma Rebellion on a book by Li Kang (1085–1140),[34] a leader of Sung resistance to the Tartars. In presenting his ten-point memorial to the Emperor, he was modeling himself on Li Kang's ten points to Kao-tsung, which in turn were modeled on ten points that Yao Ch'ung of the T'ang dynasty had expounded to Ming Huang.

The ten points are the following:

"One, winning the hearts of the people. The *Book of History* says: 'The people are the root of a country; the root firm, the country is tranquil.'[35] The life of the nation is in the people; the life of the people depends on food. Accordingly, when food is abundant, the hearts of the people are obedient . . ." Motoda developed this into an argument for the necessity of easing the tax burden on the people. "Although an Imperial order has been issued calling for tax reductions and decreased expenditures this year, it has not yet been put into effect." He concluded each of his ten discussions with a sentence similar to the following: "If His Majesty will act at once to make benevolent rule a reality and thereby win the hearts of the people of the realm, it will be a great blessing for the realm."

"Two, providing purpose for men of education [*shih*, "samurai"]. Mencius said: 'They are only men of education who, without a certain livelihood, are able to maintain a fixed heart.' "[36] Dispirited and beset by poverty, the unemployed samurai was one of the most serious problems faced by the new government in the early Meiji period. In addition to the steps taken by the government, Motoda took his own by drafting an Imperial order on this subject, which directed the Ministry of Education to counteract the "discontented men delivering quick-tempered and radical speeches" by inaugurating a program of lecture meetings throughout the country to expound moral principles, and recommended that samurai of good character be organized into reserve units or employed as policemen and guards.[37] Motoda also wrote recommendations to the Emperor in 1880 and to Iwakura in 1882 pointing out the importance of financial aid to the samurai, which, in turn, would strengthen their allegiance to the Imperial Household.

"Three, nurturing military spirit. Soldiers are like fire; when properly used they nurture man, when improperly used they harm man. The present rebellion in the west arose from the arrogance of the soldiers . . ." Motoda had little to say elsewhere about this problem. After the Rebellion, perhaps it no longer worried him.

"Four, decreasing building and repairs. The *Analects* says 'economy in expenditures, and love for men.'[38] . . . No waste at present is as shocking as the building and repair of government offices and residences . . ." Motoda persuaded the Emperor to issue an Imperial rescript on frugality in March 1879 and an Imperial order to the ministries and government offices the following year to reduce expenses.

"Five, being acquainted with prefectural officials. The task of the Son of Heaven is to shepherd the people, and the deputies used for shepherding the people are the prefectural officials." Motoda pointed out that local administration would be improved if the Emperor paid as much attention to prefectural officials as he did to those of the central government. He mentioned in his autobiography a few years later that when local officials came to Tokyo, Iwakura invited them to his official residence to question them about conditions in their prefectures. Motoda attended these discussions, and later in his lectures presented the information to the Emperor.

"Six, creating public discussion. The *Book of History* says: 'Throw open all the doors [of communication between the Court and the empire]. . . . See with the eyes and hear with the ears of all.'[39] When avenues of expression are open, the feelings of those below are communicated; when avenues of expression are closed, the feelings of those below are blocked off. Peace and disturbance in the realm depend upon whether the feelings of those below are communicated or blocked off. . . . The government should weigh the good and bad proposals, select the best discussions and most reasonable opinions, subject them to discussion in the cabinet, and have the decision made by the Emperor himself." Motoda's views on constitutional government are discussed in detail in the following section.

"Seven, stressing the importance of the cabinet. There is a saying that although the king of the realm is one man, the realm cannot be well governed by one man.[40] . . . Because of this, we establish a cabinet." Motoda goes on to recommend personal intimacy between the Emperor and his ministers along the lines of his 1873 proposal. The appointment of the *jihō* was announced only a few months after this document was written.

"Eight, making the four seas a house. There is a saying: 'The Son of Heaven makes the four seas his house.'[41] When, within the four seas, even one man does not achieve his place, the Son of Heaven cannot escape responsibility. . . . At present, the revolt in the west and the actions of the rebellious subjects are, needless to say, criminal, but in essence these men are His Majesty's children. . . . If His Majesty will make the four seas the Imperial domicile, take tours occasionally, and thus set the minds of his children at ease, it will be a great blessing for the realm." The Emperor had, in fact, made a tour of northeast Japan the previous year, followed by a trip to the Kyoto area, where he remained because of the outbreak of the Rebellion. After this time the Emperor took more extensive tours, notably a tour of the northeast from August to November, 1878, which brought forth a number of expressions of Imperial solicitude for the welfare of the people, especially in matters of education and frugality. This trip and one to Hokkaido two years later took the Emperor to areas which no previous emperor had ever visited.

"Nine, studying the proper teachings. . . . Of late, although learning and accomplishment in law and the various sciences are progressing daily, the proper teachings—morals and human feelings—are losing ground with every passing month. It is for this reason that gentlemen and scholars are fickle and frivolous, conduct is improper, and customs are extravagant." To remedy this deplorable situation, the Emperor and his chief ministers must "personally lead the masses by expounding the study of morals and human feelings." Motoda's educational policies are discussed at length below.

"Ten, cultivating the sovereign's virtue. The sovereign of men is he to whom the myriad people look. Moreover, they look only where virtue resides. Therefore, with virtue one can be the sovereign of men; without virtue one cannot be the sovereign of men. . . ." This tenth point was, of course, Motoda's primary concern from the beginning.

These were not the only political topics on which Motoda expressed his views to the Emperor. He often spoke about the importance of choosing honest, well-behaved ministers, and occasionally criticized ministers who did not meet his standards, notably Inoue Kaoru and Kuroda. And in the late 1880's, during the course of the government's intensive negotiations to secure revision of the unequal treaties, Motoda was extremely critical to the Emperor and to others about the terms being considered by the cabinet. He urged that the attempt be postponed for fifteen years until Japan would be in a stronger position to negotiate—a policy which ultimately had to be followed.

With the exception of these two subjects, most of the matters on which Motoda gave advice to the Emperor might be considered as falling within the range of the ten points. Two of these merit further discussion: the sixth, "public discussion," which led to the question of assemblies and a constitution, and the ninth, "proper teachings," which dealt with moral training as the root of education.

CONSTITUTIONAL GOVERNMENT

Motoda had the opportunity to express his views on constitutional matters not only in private to the Emperor, but also after 1888 as a member of the Privy Council, which discussed and approved the Imperial Household Law and the Constitution of 1889. We have considerable information on the views he expressed to the Emperor between 1878 and 1881, but unfortunately his autobiography and papers yield very little information on this subject for the following years.

As we have seen, Motoda advocated a national assembly on the basis of a passage from the *Book of History*. He also justified it on the basis of expediency. In a proposal he wrote to the Emperor in June 1879 concerning the establishment of a constitution,[42] he asserted that the popular agitation for a diet and for people's rights, as well as the revolts of the last few years, were all protests against the despotism of the cabinet. Because of these circumstances the creation of a diet was inevitable, and it would be wisest to convoke one before being compelled to do so by public opinion. Quoting the saying, ". . . forestall others and rule them; follow others and be ruled by them,"[43] he urged the Emperor to take steps at once toward issuing a constitution. He made the same point with even greater urgency two years later:

If we put these matters aside today and defer them until later, the mad outpourings of mistaken Western ideas, growing worse daily, will finally become uncontrollable and the harm to the Imperial Household will be incalculable. This is why I consider it essential to establish a constitution today.[44]

Motoda said that the national polity must never be changed. By national polity he meant direct rule by the Imperial line descended from the Sun Goddess and ruling the nation as a family. Changes in the form of government to meet the special needs of the times, however, could be recommended, provided they were designed to preserve the national polity. Indeed, there had been such changes in the past: Shōtoku Taishi's Seventeen-Article "Constitution," the system of the Taika Reform, the Taihō laws, etc.

Popular sovereignty was a very different matter, a concession in principle that must never be made. Motoda pointed out that many of the people had misinterpreted the Charter Oath of 1868 and the proclamation of 1875 establishing the Genrō-in (Senate) to mean that the Japanese constitution would provide for joint rule by the Emperor and the people. This would be an imitation of Western ways which would violate the national polity. A proper Japanese constitution would be one granted by the Emperor to the people out of his benevolence. It would be "based on the correct Way of heaven and earth, founded in the correct Way of the ancestors and the national polity, and appropriate to the customs and conditions of the people, high and low, in the past and in the present."[45]

During these years there had been a great deal of discussion within as well as outside the government concerning the type of constitution and system of representative government which should be established in Japan. In 1881 the Emperor instructed seven of the Ministers and Councillors—Ōki, Ōkuma, Itō, Yamagata, Inoue, Yamada, and Kuroda—to submit their proposals concerning these matters and passed them to

Motoda for his comments. Motoda read them very carefully and found that each differed from all the others on almost every matter of importance. He then drafted a document in which he stated his approval of various suggestions, and also set down his own ideas. Before he finished, he had an attack of cerebral hyperemia and had to rest for three weeks.[46]

Motoda's comments on the seven proposals are often negative and almost always qualified. His interest seems to have been focused primarily upon whether they placed the sovereignty with the Emperor or divided it with the people, and upon the suggestions for the reorganization of the Genrō-in into an upper house. Giving little attention to proposals for a popularly elected lower house, he discussed strengthening the upper house as a body to support the Imperial prerogatives, all of its members being appointed by the Emperor. In fact, he seems to have conceived of any deliberative assembly in Japan as essentially a means of strengthening the Throne, on one hand curbing the arbitrary actions of cabinet ministers, on the other providing the Emperor with a sounding board for useful opinions from the people. Motoda had no confidence that the opinion of a majority should be followed in deciding national affairs. He made this clear in a discussion of the difference between mass opinion (*shūron*) and correct public opinion (*kōron*). By this time the term *kōron* seems to have been generally used in Japan in its modern meaning of "public opinion" as that concept is understood in Western societies, but Motoda persisted in using it in its classical meaning of impartial opinion which is in the public interest, as contrasted to private or self-interested opinion.

Mass opinion, because held by many people, is not necessarily correct public opinion. Although the eight hundred nobles met at Meng-chin, correct public opinion in the empire in later generations rallied to two men who died of hunger.[47] While the Emperors Hui and Ch'in were advocating peace with the Tartar Court, only two or three people like Li Kang and Chao Ting wanted to fight,[48] but it cannot be said that the ideas of the majority were correct public opinion, and the ideas of one or two men were private opinions. This is the difference between mass opinion and correct public opinion. Even if a national diet is established and the opinions of the masses are brought together, the only way to decide what constitutes correct public opinion is for the Emperor to choose from among them. Although the people in the country who advocate popular rights argue volubly, imitating Western ways of talking about political regulations, they advance their ideas without differentiating clearly between the national polity and the form of government, and without distinguishing between correct public opinion and mass opinion.[49]

Motoda's conception of representative government was clearly so far behind Japanese aspirations that his advice could have been of little service in preparing the Emperor for participation in government.

Motoda's concern for the Imperial dignity is illustrated by other statements he made to the Emperor concerning a constitution. In 1880 he prepared a document entitled "Kokken Taikō" ("Main Principles of a National Constitution"),[50] consisting of seven "articles":

1. The Japanese nation is ruled by one divinely descended Imperial line unbroken for ages eternal.
2. The people of Japan revere their Emperor of one line unbroken for ages eternal. Whatever disturbances may occur, they cannot oppose the Emperor.
3. The national teaching takes as its principles benevolence, duty, propriety, deference, loyalty, filial piety, uprightness, and honesty. Sovereign and people, high and low, constitution and laws, none can depart from these principles.
4. The Emperor is sacred and inviolable. Whatever disturbances may occur, his person is not affected.
5. The Emperor wields the power of government and education for the entire nation.
6. The Emperor wields the power of reward and punishment, promotion and demotion and life and death over the people of the entire nation. He disposes in accordance with the Constitution and laws.
7. The people possess the rights of freedom of person, residence, and property. These rights may not be circumscribed arbitrarily without reference to the law.

Motoda concluded this text by saying: "Numerous other articles ought to be included. They will depend upon the recommendations to the Throne of the responsible persons. The foregoing seven articles are the ones needed with respect to the relationship between sovereign and people in Japan." Motoda's first and fourth articles correspond closely to Articles 1 and 3 of the Constitution the Emperor granted in 1889.[51] His third and fifth articles, which in effect prescribed a Confucian curriculum for Japan's schools and entrusted its supervision to the Emperor, were rejected by the framers of the Constitution.

THE ROOT OF EDUCATION

After 1880 Motoda frequently used the term *kokkyō,* "national teaching." The character *kyō* (in Chinese, *chiao*) can, in different contexts, cover the range represented by the English words education, learning, teachings, doctrine, and religion. To Motoda this range of meaning of the character was a single concept which had as its core Confucian moral training. The Emperor had received the national teaching from the Imperial ancestors, and should propagate it among the people in his role as preceptor. This would bring uniformity of mind and a common purpose to the whole nation.

Motoda considered the national teaching to be completely different in nature from *shūkyō* ("religion"), which was at once contemptible and dangerous: "While the errors of Buddhism and Christianity render them unworthy of belief, their concern with life and death, misery and happiness, and gain and loss strikes a kindred note in the human mind, people become superstitious, and the disease becomes rooted and immovable."[52] These religions could only be combated, he said, by teaching all children up to the age of thirteen or fourteen to revere the teachings of the divine ancestors and respect the national polity. This could be done through training in Confucian ethics.[53]

Motoda's crusade began when the Ministry of Education decided in 1872 that it was a waste of time to teach Confucian ethics in the courses in moral training (*shūshin*), and replaced Confucian textbooks with translations of American and French primers. Motoda spoke about the matter often to the Emperor, criticizing not only these courses, but the entire structure of the new educational system, which emphasized law, economics, science, and technology. He said in a lecture (ca. 1878) that although well-informed and versatile men might be produced by this curriculum,

this is outward show. Outstanding in imagination and technical accomplishments, they are deficient in the spirit and soul of our country, their foundation in morals and in courage for righteous causes is shallow, and one would try in vain to make pillars of the nation out of them. . . . Efforts are being made to convert Japanese into facsimiles of Europeans and Americans. All this is due to a confusion between the root of education and its branches.[54]

During the summer of 1879, Motoda wrote a document entitled "Kyōgaku Taishi" ("The Great Principles of Education"), which purported to be the Emperor's sentiments concerning what he had seen during his inspection of schools in northeast Japan the previous year. This document severely criticized the Western-style ethics texts as responsible for the decline in public morals. The Japanese family system and loyalty to the state were being destroyed; students were being taught high-sounding academic theories and empty arguments, which would make them useless as government officials and troublemakers as citizens. Disaster could be averted only if education were "founded upon the Imperial ancestral precepts, benevolence, duty, loyalty, and filial piety, and Confucius were made the cornerstone of our teaching of ethics."[55] Itō wrote a rebuttal in which he objected that the imposition of ethical principles was outside the province of political officers.[56]

Undeterred, Motoda set about writing an ethics text, based on Confucian principles, which he claimed was written at the Emperor's command and contained the Emperor's views. This book, *Yōgaku Kōyō* ("Essentials of Learning for the Young"), was published by the Imperial Household Ministry and forwarded to all schools with an Imperial endorsement. Because of the difficulty of the language, school children were unable to understand it, but Motoda suggested that they could memorize it: when they were older, its meaning would become clear.

Motoda expected that there would be strong opposition to his textbook from the Ministry of Education, but by the time the book was completed in 1881, the Minister of Education and some of the Ministry's other officials had been transferred.[57] Motoda often discussed educational matters with the new Minister, Fukuoka Takachika (1835–1919), who agreed with his views. There are a number of communications written during the early eighties by Motoda to indicate to the Ministry the Emperor's wishes concerning education. In 1881 the Ministry formally declared that the guiding principles of the educational system would be loyalty, filial piety, and patriotism. It banned the Western-type ethics texts, including some which it had endorsed several years earlier. The ardent westernizer, Fukuzawa Yukichi (1834–1901), was most indignant about this change of policy:

Around 1881–82, the government began to advocate in education the queer policy of Confucianism. For the alleged purpose of examining school texts, the Ministry of Education gathered up the general run of original books and translations in the country, and its officials met and decided whether to approve or to reject them. It also brought together old-fashioned Confucianists to compile readers, and otherwise staged the farce of trying to restore past customs in a civilized world. The books written and translated by me were adjudged to be harmful and without value as school texts; ridiculously enough, not one passed the inspection.[58]

A farce it was, but not to Motoda. Five years later he wrote with pride: "Since the compilation of *Yōgaku Kōyō* by Imperial order, the evils produced by American education have steadily been corrected, the nation has again turned to the principles of loyalty to the sovereign and love of the country, and people have come forward who advocate benevolence, duty, and morality."[59]

Unfortunately for Motoda, advocates of more pressing considerations were in the wings. At this time the oligarchs were attempting to make Japan look as Western as possible for purposes of treaty revision. Against the wishes of Motoda and the Emperor, Itō insisted on the appointment of Mori Arinori as Minister of Education in 1885. (Itō was so essential in these years of reorganization that he could not be denied.) Mori, under strong German influence, was the most unconventional, if not iconoclastic, of the Meiji leaders. He banned all ethics texts, and rejected Confucian teachings as too old-fashioned, too unscientific to use as a basis for building a really strong authoritarian state. He laid plans for ethics instruction based on the principles of Kant and Herbart.

Motoda complained that Japanese and Chinese studies were again on the verge of extinction. But he was dogged: this was one area in which German influence was not to sully the purity of the Imperial Restoration. When the Emperor inspected the Tokyo Imperial University, Motoda again put the Emperor's views on paper, in a document called the "Seiyuki" ("Record of Sacred Instructions"). Finding no courses given at the University on Confucian ethics, the root of education, the Emperor in effect ordered the University to make Japanese and Chinese ethics basic in the training of all students. The following disingenuous passage probably deceived no one:

I should like to take the liberty of reprimanding Minister of Education Mori and President of the University Watanabe in accordance with Your Majesty's commands. However, when I turn the matter over in my own mind, I realize that it is a matter of common knowledge that I, a scholar of Chinese studies, occupy a position close to Your Majesty. For that reason, anything I say, even though it is a repetition of Your Majesty's heartfelt utterances, may be suspected of being something suggested to the Throne by me, and I therefore respectfully refrain from venturing to accept this mission.[60]

Instead of admonishing the President himself, Motoda had Tokudaiji do it.

Nishimura Shigeki, who was appointed a Palace Councillor together with Motoda in 1886, began to develop the idea of having the Imperial Household Ministry take over the direction of moral education in Japan, removing it from the jurisdiction of the Minister of Education. Nishimura had been in charge of the compilation of textbooks in the Ministry of Education, but left this post shortly after Mori was appointed Minister. He suggested that new morals textbooks should be compiled within the Imperial Household, following the example, he said, of the K'ang-hsi and Yung-cheng Emperors, who had issued admonitions as guides to the moral conduct of the people.[61] Nishimura made this proposal early in 1888, but Mori was so angered by it that no further steps were taken. In February of the next year, Mori was assassinated, and Nishimura forthwith proposed the establishment of a department within the Imperial Household Ministry with the Confucian-sounding name of Meirin'in,[62] for the purpose of supervising and inspecting moral education, examining current textbooks, and beginning the compilation of new ones. Although no action was taken on this proposal either, Nishimura's suggestion that an Imperial pronouncement should be issued to "establish the basis of the people's morals wholly in the Imperial Household" was probably the first specific suggestion that there should be an imperial rescript on the subject.[63]

This idea coincided exactly with Motoda's wishes, and the new premier, Yamagata Aritomo, gave his support. Yamagata had been mainly responsible for the Imperial Rescript to Soldiers and Sailors eight years earlier. He felt that if the new Constitution was to operate in the manner desired by the government, it was essential to train the subjects to absolute loyalty to the Emperor, and to this end education would be the first step, conscription the second. Yoshikawa Akimasa (1841–1920) was appointed Minister of Education in May 1890, because it was felt that he would see the program through. The Emperor informed him that since the Japanese people were easily led astray and confused by foreign doctrines, it was essential to define the moral basis of the nation for them. The result was the Imperial Rescript on Education.

The Rescript was popularly believed to have been written by the Emperor himself and to contain his own thoughts for the guidance of his people. To emphasize that it was his personal and direct gift, it was not countersigned by a cabinet minister. However, the actual method of compilation was very different. Nakamura Keiu (1832–91), a professor at the Tokyo Imperial University, was directed to draft it. Although a Confucian scholar by background, he had never recovered completely from his experience of translating Samuel Smiles, and his draft was discarded as containing too many traces of Western individualism and utilitarianism. Yamagata then asked Inoue Kowashi (1844–95), a fellow clansman and associate of Motoda's, to undertake the task. For some weeks Inoue attempted to evade the assignment, recommending that the idea be dropped because any statement touching on religious and philosophical matters would bring criticism of the Throne. After repeated urging by Motoda, he submitted a draft, which Motoda found unsatisfactory. At this point Motoda himself wrote a long document, probably intended for Inoue's guidance rather than as a substitute draft. Inoue made a thorough revision along the suggested lines, which the Emperor then gave to Motoda for further revisions; this procedure was repeated several times. The surviving manuscripts of the Rescript show Motoda's extensive changes. Several others—Yamagata, Yoshikawa, and Mishima — seem to have made minor emendations. Parts of the central portions of the text were revised fifteen or sixteen times during a period of four months. It can be concluded that in the final document, Inoue was responsible for the style and most of the phraseology, but that Motoda actually contributed most of the content, for he knew, as it were, what the Emperor wanted.

The drafting was such a laborious task because it was imperative that an Imperial rescript invite a minimum of criticism, domestic and foreign. Blatant Confucian statements in the original were altered, among them the dictum that the aim of education was to inculcate the three virtues and the five relationships. This was changed to read "the precepts of the Imperial ancestors," but the three virtues and five relationships were spelled out. Motoda expunged all passages which he felt smacked of Western utilitarianism. However, his attempt to remove the phrase "respect the Constitution and observe the laws," on the ground that it detracted from the concentration of all allegiance in the person of the Emperor, was rejected by the Emperor himself after several days' contemplation.[64]

In many respects the Rescript, like the Constitution, was a delicate compromise between conflicting opinions about the balance that should be struck between traditional and new values in Meiji Japan. The final product was very much what the times demanded: a single page of text, general enough in tone, like the seventeen articles of Shōtoku, to forestall criticism and hopefully to endure the test of changing times. It was left to the commentaries to point out the specific applicability of its statements; so that this would not be left in doubt, Inoue Tetsujirō (1855–1944) was put to work to write the official commentary.

With the promulgation of the Imperial Rescript on Education on October 30, 1890, less than a month before the Diet opened, Motoda must have felt that his work was done. All four of his fundamental principles were embodied in the law of the land—two in the Constitution, two in the Rescript. Nothing more was necessary to ensure that the Imperial virtue would be manifest throughout the country. He died less than three months later, on January 22, 1891, at the age of seventy-two.

CONFUCIANIST IN THE MODERN WORLD

Motoda remained, more than two decades after the Restoration, a professed and practicing Confucianist. His vocabulary, his terms of reference, the progression of his argumentation, were all squarely in the Neo-Confucian tradition. He remained convinced that the Confucian heritage contained a complete set of prescriptions to guide Japan in any age. When elements from the West intruded upon his life, he fitted them into his Confucian scheme, even to naturalizing Samuel Smiles.

Although Motoda can only be called a Confucianist, his particular brand of Confucianism did not follow from a single tradition. In his condemnation of pedants from Han to Ming, in his call for a return to the classics, he is reminiscent of the *kogaku* school of Itō Jinsai. The influence of the Mito school is also strong in his view of Japanese history. Yet he identified himself with the Ch'eng-Chu school, and frequently cites Chu Hsi. His Confucianism must be described as a fusion of these and other traditions, caused by the intellectual pressures of the last dec-

ades of the Tokugawa period. If his thought seems eclectic, it was only
truly eclectic within the range of Confucian traditions. From *kokugaku*,
for example, he adopted what was orderly, useful, and compatible with
Confucian principles; he rejected what was irrational and mystical. A
characteristic of Neo-Confucianism has been its capacity to borrow in
this way from competing systems.

It was also typical of Neo-Confucianists that even in a period when
foreign influences could no longer be barred, when the development of
industry, military forces, and diplomatic relations were setting in motion
new social and political movements, they would seek guidance only in
examining the Confucian past. When Western solutions were advocated for Japan, Motoda did occasionally give his support, but only, as
in the instance of a constitution and deliberative assembly, when he
could find some precedent or some rationalization in the Confucian
tradition.

Motoda was one of the few men left in the 1880's who still maintained the ideal of a restoration in the full sense. To him it meant much
more than simply the return of political authority to the imperial government, and more also than the practice of personal rule by a virtuous
emperor. It meant the restoration of the entire social and political order
which was said to have existed in Japan from the fifth to the ninth centuries, a return after a millennium of aberrations to the Confucian harmony of the golden age.

In Motoda's view, substantial progress was being made toward this
goal during the last years of his life. But the decade in which he died
revealed with new meaning the pattern of modern Japan—constitutional government, party politics, industrial development, the Sino-
Japanese War. What had an old Confucianist like Motoda to do with
this modern Japan? What was he doing in the same century? Out of
step though he may seem, his activities did amount to a significant contribution, not to the modern innovations, of course, but to conditions
which made them possible. He played a part in two ways: in the development of the Meiji Emperor as an individual, and in strengthening
some of the forces which made for natural unity.

As the Emperor's tutor and guide for twenty years, Motoda seems
to have played a major role in helping him to gain the maturity and
strength of character to bear the strains and responsibilities of his office.
The Emperor was an important man, perhaps the most important, in
the Meiji scene. He was not directly responsible for political decisions,
but his influence counted, and he served as a court of appeal when there
were conflicts among the oligarchs. More important, perhaps, he was
the focal point of patriotic dedication during a reign of forty-six years

which transformed Japan from a weak country into a world power. The concentration of great prestige and influence in his person exposed the Emperor to pressures and dangers from all sides. His artificially exalted position, the sacredness attributed to his person, and his onerous religious and ceremonial duties, in addition to his political responsibilities, put severe strains upon him, strains that his early training and natural inclinations had not altogether prepared him to bear. By urging him to participate in decisions and guiding his thoughts, Motoda gave him confidence in himself and principles to proceed by.

Motoda's contribution to the forces of national unity took two forms: his efforts to strengthen the imperial institution and his part in the reintroduction of Confucian ethics as a basic subject in the school system. The Meiji leaders recognized the value of the Emperor as a symbol of national unity and a rallying point of loyalties. It was more difficult to achieve agreement on a system of values or beliefs which could be used as a binding force to strengthen the people for the sacrifices necessary in the effort of modernizing the nation. Motoda was convinced that the Confucian tradition provided from Japan's own past a system which met this need completely; to permit the intrusion of Western ideas would only disrupt the unity of the people.

In the short run, Motoda's policy had considerable value. The launching of a nation-building enterprise, however, involves hopes and expectations for the future which Motoda's philosophy did not take into account. Living in the community of nations of the modern world brought new opportunities and aspirations to men as well as to nations. In the long run, contradictions would arise between the new expectations and values based solely on the Confucian past. Even in the Imperial Rescript on Education, it was necessary to supplement Confucian ethics with more universal values.

Motoda died convinced that he had succeeded in both strengthening the imperial institution and reestablishing Confucian ethics, and that the foundations had been laid for a new golden age of order and tranquillity. Had he lived a few years longer, he might have had his doubts. Confucianism as he had known it was long dead, and the imperial institution was on its way to becoming the ideological basis of a modern imperialist state.

NOTES

NOTES TO INTRODUCTION

1. Ou-yang Hsiu and Sung Ch'i, editors, *Hsin T'ang Shu,* Po-na edition, ch. 11, p. 1a.
2. Ou-yang Hsiu, *Ou-yang Wen-chung-kung Wen-chi,* Ssu-pu Ts'ung-k'an edition, ch. 17, pp. 1b–2b.
3. *Hsin T'ang Shu,* ch. 11, p. 1a–b.
4. *Ou-yang Wen-chung-kung Wen-chi,* ch. 17, p. 1a–b.
5. *Ou-yang Wen-chung-kung Wen-chi,* ch. 67, pp. 10a–11a.
6. *Ou-yang Wen-chung-kung Wen-chi,* ch. 66, p. 1b.
7. See pp. 226–27.
8. Feng Ch'i (1558–1603), *Sung-shih Chi-shih-pen-mo* (Chung-hua Shu-chü, Peking, 1955), III, 647–48. For the correct date of Chu's memorial, see *Hui-an Hsien-sheng Chu Wen-kung Wen-chi* (Ssu-pu Ts'ung-k'an edition), ch. 11, p. 11a. This memorial was called to my attention by Mr. Conrad Schirokauer, who is completing a doctoral dissertation for the Department of History at Stanford University on Chu Hsi's political thought and behavior.

NOTES TO SOME COMMON TENDENCIES IN NEO-CONFUCIANISM

1. John K. Fairbank and others, "The Influence of Modern Western Science and Technology in Japan and China," *Explorations in Entrepreneurial History,* VII, no. 1 (April, 1955), 197.
2. J. K. Fairbank, *The United States and China,* Cambridge, Mass., 1948, p. 156.
3. We should, of course, recognize that Mr. Fairbank is thinking primarily of the whole socio-political order and the scholar-official class in general, rather than specifically assigning responsibility to their Confucian character.
4. "China's Response to the West: Problems and Suggestions," *Journal of World History,* III (1956), 391.
5. "East Asian Views of Modern History," *American Historical Review,* LXII (1957), 532.
6. *Japanese Religion in the Meiji Era,* translated by John Howes (Tokyo, 1956), p. 16.
7. Limited also in the sense that they were designed primarily for the training of officials and did not attempt to reach the vast majority of the population.
8. Of course the independence of these men is evidence of more than just the lack of total control; there is always the internal aspect to be considered along with the external. In several cases they displayed a strength

of character which made them difficult to intimidate! See, for instance, the example of Yamaga Sokō and Yoshida Shōin in R. Tsunoda, W. T. de Bary, and D. Keene, *Sources of the Japanese Tradition* (New York, 1958), pp. 394–410, 616–22.

9. In passing, something should perhaps be said about the rather widespread misconception that, as part of the iron curtain which the Shogunate hung around the Japanese mind, it was forbidden to import or study books from the West. Actually the ban, enacted in 1630, applied only to books in Chinese by Christians, and was rescinded in 1720. Cf. D. L. Keene, *The Japanese Discovery of Europe* (London, 1952), pp. 15–19.

10. As more aptly rendered by Franz Michael (*World Politics*, VII [1955], 424) than in my own earlier version in Arthur F. Wright (ed.), *Studies in Chinese Thought* (Chicago, 1953), p. 93.

11. *Studies in Chinese Thought*, pp. 81–111.

12. As Frederick Mote reminds me, a "return to the past" was a recurrent phenomenon in Chinese literary history during later times. There, however, it definitely takes the form of archaism rather than a creative revival. Ogyū Sorai, mentioned immediately below, was influenced by such an archaistic literary movement in the Ming (as exemplified by the sixteenth-century scholars Wang Shih-cheng and Li P'an-lung), but followed its implications beyond the mere adoption of an ancient prose style.

13. Cf. Nishijima Jun, *Jurin genryū* (Tokyo, 1934), pp. 163 ff.

14. Cf. Fujii Jintarō, *Ōsei fukko no dai-kyokumen* ("Restoration of Kingly Government as an Important Phase [of the Meiji Restoration]"), in *Meiji boshin* (Bummei Kyokai) (Tokyo, 1928).

15. It seems to me that something of the same idea is present in the ideology of the T'ai-ping Rebellion, where there was an attempt to associate the ancient social ideal (as found in the *Book of Rites*) with an adulterated Christianity which the Chinese were said to have lost in early times. I do not know, however, whether there are any definite links between this attitude and the type of Confucian revivalism we have been discussing.

16. "A Record of Drifting Across the Ocean" (*Pyohae-rok*). Columbia Ph.D. dissertation, 1958.

17. Readers of the famous *Chusingura* will remember that the vendetta of the Forty-seven Ronin arises out of the involvement of their master with the villainous Moronao, to whom he must go for instruction in the performance of certain rituals—a touch to the story which I suspect reflects a more conscious concern for such niceties in seventeenth-century Japan than had prevailed since Heian times.

18. Cf. Joseph Levenson, "The Abortiveness of Empiricism in Early Ch'ing Thought," *Far Eastern Quarterly*, XIII (1954), 155–66. The importance attached by Professor Needham to the late Ming and Ch'ing "naturalists" as individual representatives of Chinese scientific thought (*Science and Civilization in China*, II, 511–15) does not belie the fact that this particular strain of thought became submerged by other tendencies in Neo-Confucianism which the men in question also shared to a considerable degree.

19. Confucius himself would probably not have allowed such a distinction, but his relative emphasis is indicated by the passage in the *Analects* (I, 6): "A young man, when at home, should be filial, and abroad, respectful to his elders. He should be earnest and truthful. He should overflow with

love to all and cultivate the friendship of the good. When all that is done, if he has energy to spare, let him pursue learning." Even here, however, learning is understood traditionally to mean the polite arts of the gentleman, which are not wholly divorced from ethical training.

20. Ibn Khaldun is, of course, a major exception to this attitude. Cf. G. E. von Grunebaum, *Islam*, Memoir No. 81 of the American Anthropological Association, Chicago, April 1955, pp. 7–8, 111–19; *Medieval Islam* (Chicago, 1946), pp. 281–87. See also P. Hardy, "Islam in Medieval India," in W. T. de Bary (ed.), *Sources of Indian Tradition* (New York, 1958), pp. 390, 519 ff.

21. The noteworthy exception here is the *Gukanshō* (attributed to the monk Jien, ca. A.D. 1220), which does go beyond mere chronicling.

22. Certainly we should not exclude here changes in the relative emphasis on certain ethical values over others, such as the increasing importance attached to the virtue of loyalty in later times, which Mr. Mote points to in his paper for this conference (to appear in *The Confucian Persuasion*).

23. *A History of Chinese Philosophy,* translated by Derk Bodde (Princeton, 1953), II, 630–31.

NOTES TO AN ANALYSIS OF CHINESE CLAN RULES

1. Hui-chen Wang Liu, "An Analysis of the Chinese Clan Rules: A Study of Social Control" (Ph.D. thesis, University of Pittsburgh, 1956; University Microfilms, Ann Arbor, Michigan, Publication No. 18,242) (hereafter cited as Liu, *Analysis*). This is now revised and will be published shortly by the Monograph Series, The Association for Asian Studies, under the title *The Traditional Chinese Clan Rules*.

2. *Ibid.*, pp. 36–72.

3. Chang Tsai, *Ching-hsüeh Li K'u*, cited in the encyclopedia, *Ku Chin T'u shu Chi-ch'eng* (1884 ed.), section on *Tsung-tsu* ("clans"), "Tsung-lun" (general discussion), part 2, p. 2.

4. Chu Hsi, *Chin-ssu Lu*, cited *ibid.*, p. 8.

5. Mano Senryū, "Mindai no Kaki ni tsuite" ("Family Rules during the Ming Dynasty"), *Tōhōgaku*, VIII (1954), 83–93; Makino Tatsumi, "Sōshi to Sono Hattatsu" ("On the Ancestral Hall and Its Historical Development in China"), *Tōhōgakuhō*, IX (1939), 173–250; and Makino Tatsumi, "Peipin Toshokanzō Mindai Zempon Zokufu" ("On Various Family Monographs Belonging to the Ming Period Found in the Catalog of the Rare Books in the National Library of Peiping"), *ibid.*, VI (1936) [extra number], 169–202.

6. *Hung-tung Chin Shih Tsu-p'u* (1735), Vol. II; *Jen-ch'iu Pien Shih Tsu-p'u* (1772), Vol. II; *Huai-ning Ma Shih Tsung-p'u* (1876), Vol. I; *Ching-k'ou Shun-chiang-chou Wang Shih Chia-ch'eng* (1893), Vol. I. Generally, I have cited in these notes only the clan rules printed during the Ch'ing period, since those printed in 1912–36 are covered in my dissertation (see note 1).

7. *Wu-shan Hsi-chin-ts'un Wu Shih Shih-tsu-p'u* (1682), Vol. II; *Pan-yang Kao Shih Chia-mu Hui-pien* (1738); *Pi-ling Shih Shih Tsung-p'u* (1880), Vol. I; *Hsiao-shan Ch'ang-hsiang Shen Shih Tsung-p'u* (1893), Vol. VI; and *Hsiao-shan Wu Shih Tsung-p'u* (1904), Vol. I.

8. *Ku-jun Ching-k'ou Chu Shih Tsung-p'u* (1903).

9. Liu, *Analysis*, pp. 291–304.

10. "Family Instructions," in *Wan Huai Tsou Shih Tsung-p'u* (1796).

11. "Family Rules," in *Hung-tung Chin Shih Tsu-p'u* (1735), Vol. II.

12. "Rules by Common Decision," in *Lu-chiang Ho Shih Chia-ch'eng* (1848), Vol. I; "Ancestral Hall Rules" in *Pi-ling Hsieh Shih Tsung-p'u* (1921), Vol. I.

13. "Instructions of Ancestor Madame Wu," in *Hai-ning Chu Shih Tsung-p'u* (1879), Vol. IV.

14. "Clan Regulations," in *Yun-yang T'u Shih Tsu-p'u* (1930), Vol. II.

15. "Family Rituals," in *Hsiao-shan Tao-yuan T'ien Shih Tsung-p'u* (1837).

16. "Family Regulations," in *Ch'eng-chiang Hsiang-shan Hu Shih Tsung-p'u* (1872), Vol. I.

17. Wada Kiyoshi, "Min no Taiso no Kyōiku Chokugo ni tsuite" ("On the Educational Edict of Ming T'ai-tsu"), *Shiratori Hakushi Kanreki Kinen Tōyōshi Ronsō* ("Essays in Oriental History in Honor of Dr. Shiratori") (1925), pp. 885–904.

18. The Han period: Pan Chao (Ts'ao Ta-ku). The Northern Ch'i period: Yen Chih-t'ui. The T'ang period: Liu P'in. The Sung period: Chang Tsai, Chang Shih, Chang Hsiao-hsiang, Chang Chih-pai, Chen Te-hsiu, Ch'eng Hao, Ch'eng I, Chou Tun-i, Chu Hsi, Fan Ch'un-jen, Fan Chung-yen, Hu An-kuo, Hu Yüan, Lin Ho-ching, Liu An-shih, Liu K'ai, Lu Yu, Lu Chiu-shao, Lü Kung-chu, Lü Ta-lin, Lü Tsu-ch'ien, Ou-yang Hsiu, P'eng Chung-kang, Shao Yung, Ssu-ma Kuang, Su Shih, Wang Ke, Ying Chün, and Yüan Ts'ai. The Yüan period: Hsü Heng. The Ming period: Chan Jo-shui, Ch'en Chi-ju, Ch'en Hsien-chang, Fang Hsiao-ju, Hsia Yin, Hsü San-chung, Hsüeh Hsüan, Kao P'an-lung, Lu Shih-i, Lü K'un, Lü Wei-ch'i, Wang Yang-ming, Yang Chi-sheng, and Yen Mao-yu. The Ch'ing period: Chang Lü-hsiang, Chang Ying, Ch'en Hung-mou, Chiang I, Chu Yung-ch'un, Ch'ü Ch'eng-lin, Ku Yen-wu, Lu Lung-ch'i, T'ang Pin, Ts'ai Shih-yüan, Tseng Kuo-fan, Wang Chih-fu, and Yü Ch'eng-lung.

19. "The Ten Rules for Clan Harmony," in *Ning-chin Chang Shih Tsu-p'u* (1757), Vol. I.

20. *Ku Chin T'u-shu Chi-ch'eng* (1884 ed.), "Chia-fan-tien," ch. 1–116.

21. Ch'en Hung-mou, *Wu Chung I-kuei* ("The Five Collections of Rules") (1828 ed.).

22. "Clan Regulations," in *Lu Shih Feng-men Chih P'u* (1888), Vol. II.

23. "Ancestors' Instructions," in *Pan-yang Kao Shih Chia-mu Hui-pien* (1738).

24. "Instructions of Ancestor Yeh-kung" in *Wu-hsing Yao Shih Chia-ch'eng* (1911), Vol. IV.

25. "Family Instructions," *ibid.*

26. Obata Tatsuo, "Mindai Gōson no Kyōka to Saiban" ("Public Instructions and Village Elders' Instructions in the Ming Period"), *Tōyōshi Kenkyū*, XI (1952), 423–43; E. Chavannes, "Les Saintes Instructions de l'empereur Hong-wo, 1368–1398," *Bulletin de l'Ecole Française d'Extrême-Orient*, III (1903), 549–63; Wada Kiyoshi, "Min no Taiso no Kyōiku Chokugo ni tsuite," *loc. cit.* (note 17); and Sogabe Shizuo, "Min Taiso Rokuyu no Denshō ni tsuite" ("The Tradition of the 'Six Instructions' of T'ai-tsu of Ming"), *Tōyōshi Kenkyū*, XII (1953), 323–32.

27. Higashionna Hiroatsu, "Rokuyu Engi ni tsuite" ("On the Commentaries on the Six Instructions"), *Shigaku Zasshi,* XXXV (1924), 758–67.

28. Li Lai-chang comp., *Sheng-yü T'u-hsiang Yen-i,* in Li Li-shan, *Li-shan-yüan Ch'üan-chi;* Wu Yün-sun, comp., *Sheng-yü Kuang-hsün Chi-cheng* (1901); and Liang Yen-nien comp., *Sheng-yü Hsiang-chieh* (1681 comp., 1903 ed.).

29. See a memorial dated 1737 in *Huang-ch'ao Ching-shih Wen-pien* (1898), ch. 23, pp. 5–6.

30. *Ta Ch'ing Sheng-tsu Jen-huang-ti Sheng-hsün* ("The Imperial Edicts of the K'ang-hsi Emperor") (hereafter cited as *Sheng-tsu*), ch. 6, pp. 7b–8a; *Ta Ch'ing Shih-tsung Hsien-huang-ti Sheng-hsün* ("The Imperial Edicts of the Yung-cheng Emperor") (hereafter cited as *Shih-tsung*), ch. 26, p. 11; *Ta Ch'ing Kao-tsung Shun-huang-ti Sheng-hsün* ("The Imperial Edicts of the Ch'ien-lung Emperor") (hereafter cited as *Kao-tsung*), ch. 263, p. 5a.

31. *Shih-tsung,* ch. 26, pp. 1b–2a; *Kao-tsung,* ch. 261, pp. 3a, 5a.

32. *Shih-tsung,* ch. 26, pp. 14b–15a; *Kao-tsung,* ch. 261, pp. 13a–14a and ch. 264, pp. 4b–5a; and *Huang Ch'ing Tsou-i* ("Memorials of the Ch'ing Dynasty") (hereafter cited as *Tsou-i*), ch. 60, p. 15.

33. *Kao-tsung,* ch. 261, pp. 3a, 5; ch. 262, p. 5a; ch. 263, p. 5a.

34. *Ibid.,* ch. 264, p. 2a.

35. *Ibid.,* ch. 261, p. 9b.

36. *Ibid.,* ch. 262, p. 5b.

37. *Tsou-i,* ch. 25, pp. 8b–9b.

38. *Ibid.,* ch. 33, p. 34b.

39. *Ibid.,* ch. 55, pp. 1a–9a; Makino, "Sōshi to Sono Hattatsu," *Tōhō-gakuhō* (Tokyo), IX (1939), 197–201.

40. *Kao-tsung,* ch. 264, p. 6a.

41. "Instructions," in *Jen-ch'iu Pien Shih Tsu-p'u* (1772), Vol. II.

42. Liu, *Analysis,* pp. 249–52.

43. *Ibid.,* pp. 252–57.

44. *Ibid.,* pp. 16–17.

45. Ch'u Ch'eng-lin, *Hsi Shih Pien,* quoted in "Mottoes" of Hsia-p'u Hsu Shih Tsung-p'u (1921), Vol. I.

46. Yen Mao-yu, *Ti Chi Lu,* quoted in "Collection of Family Instructions" of *Shang-hai Ke Shih Chia-p'u* (1928).

47. Liu, *Analysts,* pp. 45–55; Niida Noboru, *Chūgoku no Nōson Kazoku* ("The Chinese Rural Family"), 2d ed. (1954) (hereafter cited as Niida, *Kazoku*), pp. 75–76.

48. "Charitable Land," in *K'uai-chi Chung-wang Shen Shih Chia-p'u* (1879), Vol. I.

49. "Charitable Estate Regulations," in *Chi-yang Chang-ch'ing Chao Shih Tsung-p'u* (1883), Vol. V.

50. "Ritual Land Regulations," in *Huai-an Yang-ch'iao Tu Shih Tsu-p'u* (1870), *chüan* 1, pp. 18a–18b.

51. "On the Restoration of the Ancestral Hall Property," in *Pi-ling Shen Shih Tsung-p'u* (1904), Vol. I.

52. Manchukuo, Ministry of Justice, *Manshū Kazoku Seido Shūkan Chosa* ("Customs of the Manchurian Family System") (1944), pp. 50–53, 511–13; and Ōyama Hikoichi, *Chūgoku-jin no Kazoku Seido no Kenkyū* ("A

Study of the Chinese Family System") (1952) (hereafter cited as Ōyama, *Kazoku*), pp. 30–34.

53. Liu, *Analysis*, p. 155.

54. *Ibid.*, p. 263; "Family Instructions," in *Wu-hsi Ch'ien K'un Li Shih Chia-p'u* (1888).

55. Liu, *Analysis*, p. 264.

56. *Ibid.*, pp. 263–64; "Clan Standard," in *Chiang-yin Ming-wei Kuo Shih Tsung-p'u* (1879); also "Family Instructions," in *Pi-ling An-shang-ch'iao Shao Shih Tsung-p'u* (1889).

57. Liu, *Analysis*, pp. 203–8.

58. "Charitable Granary Regulations," in *Shan-yin An-ch'ang Hsü Shih Tsung-p'u* (1884).

59. Liu, *Analysis*, pp. 204–6.

60. *Ibid.*, pp. 197–202.

61. *Ibid.*, pp. 178–79.

62. "Ancestral Hall Rules," in *Chieh-hsiu Chang-lan Ma Shih Tsu-p'u* (1843); "Record of the Management of the Common Land," in *Hai-ning Chu Shih Tsung-p'u* (1879), Vol. IV; "Clan Agreement," in *Pi-ling Sun Shih Chia-ch'eng* (1873), Vol. I; and "Ancestral Hall Regulations" in *Ching-chiang Tai Shih Chia-ch'eng* (1885).

63. *Ibid.*

64. Liu, *Analysis*, p. 175; cf. Niida Noboru, "Chūgoku Nōson Shakai to Ka-fu-cho Ken-i" ("Chinese Rural Society and Parental Authority") in *Kindai Chūgoku no Shakai to Keizai* ("Modern Chinese Society and Economy") (1951), pp. 259–60.

65. Record of the Ching-yin Charitable Estate," in *Wu-ch'ü Wang Shih Chih-p'u* (1910), Vol. I.

66. "Record of the Charitable Estate," in *Wu-chung Yeh Shih Tsu-p'u* (1911), Vol. I; "Regulations of the Charitable Estate" (1876), in *Wu-men P'eng Shih Tsung-p'u* (1923), Vol. III; "Clan Relief Association," in *Ssu-ming Ts'ang-chi Ch'en Shih Chia-p'u* (1934), Vol. II; cf. Liu, *Analysis*, pp. 176–77.

67. *Tsou-i*, ch. 33, pp. 32b–33a.

68. Liu, *Analysis*, pp. 209–13.

69. *Ibid.*, pp. 145–47, 193–94, 218–19.

70. Robert Redfield, *Peasant Society and Culture* (1956), pp. 75–76.

71. Liu, *Analysis*, pp. 172–73.

72. "Family Rules," in *Lo-p'ing Kao Shih Tsung-p'u* (1692), Vol. I; "Ancestors' Instructions on Self-cultivation," in *Hai-yü Tz'u-ts'un Chin Shih Chia-ch'eng* (1824); "Ancestral Hall Regulations" in *P'u-li Hsü Shih Chia-ch'eng* (1837), Vol. I; "Injunctions," in *Hsiao-shan Hsiang-feng-ts'un Chu Shih Tsung-p'u* (1870), Vol. I; and Liu, *Analysis*, pp. 113–15.

73. "Injunctions," in *Ti-hsi Tzu-yang Chu Shih Chia-ch'eng Hsu-hsiu* (1838), Vol. I; "Family Instructions," in *Yün-yang P'ei Shih Tsung-p'u* (1874), Vol. I; and Liu, *Analysis*, p. 237.

74. "Clan Injunctions on Sixteen Vices," in *Ching-chiang Liu Shih Tsung-p'u* (1891), Vol. I; and Liu, *Analysis*, pp. 283–85.

75. "Family Instructions," in *Yen-ling Ching-chiang Wu Shih Tsu-p'u* (1900); "Family Instructions," in *Chin-ling Cha-t'ou Liu Shih Tsu-p'u* (1905); Vol. I; and Liu, *Analysis*, pp. 285, 303.

76. "Ancestral Hall Regulations," in *Yen-ling Ching-ts'un Wu Shih Tsung-p'u* (1865), Vol. I; Liu, *Analysis*, pp. 226–29.

77. "Clan Agreement," in *Yü-yao Chiang Shih Chia-ch'eng* (1854), Vol. I.

78. "Clan Instructions," in *Ch'ien-yüan Hsi-li T'ang Shih Tsung-p'u* (1906), Vol. I.

79. Liu, *Analysis*, pp. 81–82.

80. "Three Types of Behavior Prohibited and Three Punished," in *Wan T'ung Hsi-hsiang Mao Shih Tsung-p'u* (1865), Vol. I.

81. "Family Instructions," in *Hsiang-yin Fu Shih Chih-p'u* (1845); "Clan Agreement," in *Yü-yao Chiang Shih Chia-ch'eng* (1854), Vol. I; and Liu, *Analysis*, pp. 81–88.

82. Niida, *Kazoku*, pp. 121–27, 136–43.

83. Liu, *Analysis*, pp. 91–95.

84. Martin C. Yang, *A Chinese Village* (1946), p. 129; Niida Noboru, "Chūgoku Nōson Shakai to Ka-fu-cho Ken'i" in *Kindai Chūgoku no Shakai to Keizai* (1951), p. 282.

85. Ōyama, *Kazoku*, pp. 93–94.

86. "The Six Articles Appended," in *P'u-li Hsü Shih Chia-ch'eng* (1837), Vol. I; "Family Instructions," in *Huang-kang Lü-yang-ts'un Hsieh Shih Tsung-p'u* (1865), Vol. I.

87. "The Sixteen Family Instructions," in *Shan-yin Niang-ch'uan Wang Shih Tsu-p'u* (1784), Vol. I.

88. Liu, *Analysis*, pp. 98–100.

89. "The Eight Items Added to Family Instructions," in *Shan-yin Chou-shan Wu Shih Tsu-p'u* (1840), Vol. I.

90. "Clan Agreement," in *Yü-yao Chiang Shih Chia-ch'eng* (1854), Vol. I.

91. Liu, *Analysis*, pp. 100–104; Manchukuo, *op. cit.* (note 52), pp. 40–41, 500–501; Niida, *Kazoku*, pp. 19–20, 104–16; and Niida Noboru, ed., *Chūgoku Nōson Kankō Chōsa* ("Chinese Rural Customs and Practices") (1952–55) (hereafter cited as *Kankō Chōsa*), IV, 70–93.

92. "Clan Agreement," in *Chao Shih Tsung-p'u* (1883), Vol. I.

93. Liu, *Analysis*, pp. 105–6.

94. Manchukuo, *op. cit.*, pp. 31, 492; and Ōyama, *Kazoku*, pp. 18–19, 20–21.

95. Liu, *Analysis*, pp. 126–30.

96. *Ibid.*, pp. 135–54.

97. *Ibid.*, p. 139.

98. *Ibid.*, pp. 137–40.

99. Niida, *Kazoku*, pp. 45–50, 243–310.

100. "Family Rules," in *Lo-p'ing Kao Shih Tsung-p'u* (1629), Vol. I.

101. "Regulations for Ancestral Hall and Ancestral Graveyard," in *Pi-ling Shih Shih Tsu-p'u* (1915), Vol. I.

102. Liu, *Analysis*, pp. 161–66.

103. *Kankō Chōsa*, III, 111, 149.

104. "On Aiding Clan Members," in *I-feng Ch'ü Shih Tsu-p'u* (1908).

105. Liu, *Analysis*, pp. 225–26.

106. *Ibid.*, pp. 244–46.

107. "Instructions of Ancestor Madame Wu," in *Hai-ning Chu Shih Tsung-p'u* (1879), Vol. IV.

108. "On Clan Harmony," in *Pi-ling Hsi-t'an Ch'en Shih Tsung-p'u* (1882), Vol. I.

109. Liu, *Analysis*, pp. 246–48.

110. *Ibid.*, pp. 237–41.

111. "Instructions of Ancestor Madame Wu," in *Hai-ning Chu Shih Tsung-p'u* (1879), Vol. IV; "Family Instructions," in *Wu-hsing Yao Shih Chia-ch'eng* (1911), Vol. IV.

112. Liu, *Analysis*, p. 289.

113. *Ibid.*, pp. 56–60.

114. *Ibid.*, pp. 273–75.

115. "Family Standard," in *Ch'i-i K'u-chu Wang Shih Tsung-p'u* (1696), Vol. I.

116. "Clan Regulations," in *Hsin-t'ien Shih Shih Tsung-p'u* (1877), Vol. I; "Ancestral Hall Regulations," in *Yün-yang Chang Shih Tsung-p'u* (1887), Vol. I.

117. "Family Instructions," in *Yen-ling Ching-chiang Wu Shih Tsu-p'u* (1900).

118. "Family Standard," in *Ch'i-i K'u-chu Wang Shih Tsung-p'u* (1696), Vol. I; "Family Instructions," in *Ts'ung-ch'uan Ch'ien Shih Shih-p'u* (1866), Vol. I.

119. "Clan Agreement," in *Yü-yao Chiang Shih Chia-ch'eng* (1854), Vol. I; "The Original Clan Regulations," in *Pi-ling Ch'en Shih Hsü-hsiu Tsung-p'u* (1876), Vol. I.

120. "Family Teachings," in *Shan-yin Ch'ing-hsi Hsü Shih Tsung-p'u* (1883), Vol. I; "Clan Regulations," in *Hsin-t'ien Shih Shih Tsung-p'u* (1877), Vol. I.

121. "The Original Clan Regulations," in *Pi-ling Ch'en Shih Hsü-hsiu Tsung-p'u* (1876), Vol. I; "Instructions in the Genealogy" in *Chiang-yin Kao Shih Tsung-p'u* (1881), Vol. I .

122. *Tsou-i*, ch. 9, p. 5a.

123. *Kao-tsung*, ch. 261, p. 5; ch. 262, p. 5a; ch. 263, p. 5; ch. 264, p. 2a.

124. *Ibid.*, ch. 264, p. 2b.

125. Liu, *Analysis*, pp. 272–76.

126. Uchida Tomoo, *Chūgoku Nōson no Kazoku to Shinkō* ("Chinese Rural Family and Beliefs") (1948), pp. 176 ff.

127. Liu, *Analysis*, pp. 276–77.

128. *Kao-tsung*, ch. 261, p. 3a.

129. *Shih-tsung*, ch. 16, p. 8b; ch. 26, pp. 1, 3; cf. Nieh Ch'ung-ch'i, "Nü-tzu Tsai-chia Wen-t'i ti Li-shih Yen-pien" ("The Historical Development of the Problem of Remarriage of Women"), *Ta-chung Yüeh-k'an* ("Ta-chung Monthly"), I, No. 4 (1942), 31–38.

130. "Family Regulations," in *Chin Shih Hsü-hsiu Tsu-p'u* (1884); and Liu, *Analysis*, p. 133.

131. "Family Regulations," in *Wan T'ung Hsi-hsiang Mao Shih Tsung-p'u* (1865), Vol. I; "Family Regulations," in *Pi-ling Ch'en Shih Hsü-hsiu Tsung-p'u* (1876), Vol. I; "Family Discipline," in *Hsin-t'ien Shih Shih Tsung-p'u* (1877), Vol. I; and "Family Regulations," in *Chin-sha Lu-chuang Shih Shih Tsung-p'u* (1877).

132. "Instructions of Ancestor Mien-wu-kung," in *Chin-ling Kao Shih Shih-p'u* (1915); and "Instructions in the Genealogy," in *Chiang-yin Kao Shih Tsung-p'u* (1881), Vol. I.

133. Liu, *Analysis*, pp. 147–48.

134. *Kankō Chōsa*, III, 111.

135. Liu, *Analysis*, pp. 145–47, 203–5.

136. Redfield, *op. cit.*, pp. 68–71, 91–96, 151.

137. *Ibid.*, pp. 124–25.

138. Niida, *Kazoku*, 122, 415–16.

NOTES TO THE FAN CLAN'S CHARITABLE ESTATE

Bibliographical Note

The principal sources for this study are the collected works of Fan Chung-yen and the *Fan Shih Chia-sheng*. For the latter I have employed the edition dated 1745 which is in the possession of the Tōyō Bunka Kenkyūjo, to whose Director, Professor Niida Noboru, I am indebted for a microfilm of the work. To judge from internal evidence, the book was reprinted and supplemented at least twice subsequent to the date on the title page, first in 1747 and again in 1758 or 1759. The 1745 edition was compiled by a large editorial board headed by Fan An-yao; the editors completely rearranged the material in previous versions, which derived from an edition dated 1577.

This 1577 version had been reprinted and augmented on several occasions. The editions of 1621 and 1643 contained 30 chapters. The new edition of 1745 divided the book into a *tso-pien* of 24 chapters comprising biographies, monographs, records and discussions of various topics, and a *yu-pien* of 16 chapters of branch genealogies. For reference I refer to the *tso-pien* as *FSCS*, and the *yu-pien* as *FSCS B*. The three sections directly related to the charitable estate are *FSCS*, ch. 14, "I-tse Chi," containing the documents relevant to the estate's fiscal position and a complete land register; *FSCS*, ch. 15, "Chia-kuei Chi," containing all the rules of administration; and *FSCS*, ch. 16, "I-Chuang Sui-chi," a full annual record of the administration with the names of the managers. This last chuan is printed in a peculiar format which precludes the convenient use of page references; I refer therefore to the year under which an event is recorded, e.g., "*FSCS*, ch. 16, under 1405."

The collected works of Fan Chung-yen, and in particular the numerous supplements which are included in all current editions, present a very complex bibliographical problem, since no two editions are identical either in contents or in arrangement. I have used three principal editions:

(1) The Ssu-pu Ts'ung-k'an edition, which reproduces a Ming copy (collated by Fan Chi-i and Fan Wei-yüan and printed by the charitable estate) of a Yüan edition of the T'ien-li period (1329–30). The Ming copy must have been printed before 1540, when Fan Chi-i was removed from office as ritual head of the clan, and was presumably issued during his period in office (1520-40). I cite this edition as *Works (SPTK)*.

(2) The lithograph edition published by the Sao-yeh Shan-fang in 1919, which is based on an edition with prefaces by Ts'ai Tseng-yü dated 1608, and by Mao I-lu dated 1622. The large board of editors included Fan Pi-yung, ritual head of the clan in 1609–17 and 1620–28, and Fan Yün-lin, the

outstanding scholar of the family in the early seventeenth century. This edition contains much material additional to that in the Ssu-pu Ts'ung-k'an text, a good deal of which is probably derived from early editions of the *Fan Shih Chia-sheng*. I cite this edition as *Works* (*SYSF*).

(3) The edition of Chang Po-hsing entitled *Fan Wen-cheng Kung Wen-chi*, originally published in the *Cheng-i T'ang Ch'üan Shu* and reprinted in *Ts'ung-shu Chi-ch'eng*, Vols. 2359–60. This edition reduces the chaotic material in the supplements to a semblance of order, and also includes documents by other scholars relating to the charitable estate. I cite this as *Prose Works*. The page references are to the *Ts'ung-shu Chi-ch'eng*, which is more generally available than the original print.

Much of the material in the *Prose Works* and the supplements is also included in the *Fan Shih Chia-sheng*. Although the latter often contains superior readings, I generally cite the collected works as being more accessible. However, in the case of the rules of administration, the text of the *Chia-sheng* is not only better but rather fuller than that in the current editions of the *Works*, and I refer throughout to the former.

In general, references to the histories are to the Po-na Pen edition, and references to collected works are to the editions in the *Ssu-pu Ts'ung-k'an* unless otherwise specified.

Notes

1. For a good analysis of the contents of the work, see Makino Tatsumi, *Kinsei Chūgoku Shūzoku Kenkyū* (Tokyo, 1950), pp. 121–34. This reprints with minor corrections an article which originally appeared in the *Hattori Sensei Koki Shutsuga Kinen Rombunshu* (Tokyo, 1936).

2. For example, the various studies in Makino Tatsumi, *Kinsei Chūgoku Shūzoku Kenkyū*; Hu Hsien-chin, *The Common Descent Group in China and Its Functions* (New York, 1948); Hui-chen Liu, "The Traditional Chinese Family Rules" (unpublished).

3. See *Chiu T'ang Shu*, ch. 190B, pp. 2a–b. His date of death is given as 690 by *Hsin T'ang Shu*, ch. 61, p. 15a.

4. See the genealogical tables in *Hsin T'ang Shu*, ch. 74A, p. 42a.

5. Preface to *Nien-p'u, Prose Works*, ch. 6, p. 57. Further information on the splitting up of the clan at the time of the Huang Ch'ao rebellion is to be found in the rare *Hsiu-ning Fan Shih Tsu-p'u* of 1597. The Fans of Hsiu-ning were also descendants of Fan Li-ping.

6. See Ou-yang Hsiu, *Shen-tao Pei-ming, Prose Works*, ch. 9, p. 115.

7. See Fan Chung-yen's original preface to the family genealogy printed at the beginning of *FSCS*.

8. *Prose Works*, ch. 6, p. 57. *Sung Shih*, ch. 314, p. 1a.

9. *Prose Works*, ch. 7, p. 89.

10. *Ibid.*, ch. 6, p. 57.

11. *Ibid.*, p. 60.

12. For general accounts of his career see J. Fischer, "Fan Chung-yen (989–1052), das Lebensbild eines chinesischen Staatsmannes," *Oriens Extremus* (1955), pp. 39–85, 142–56. Also James T. C. Liu, "An Early Sung Reformer: Fan Chung-yen," in J. K. Fairbank, ed., *Chinese Thought and Institutions* (Chicago, 1957), pp. 105–31.

13. *Prose Works*, ch. 7, p. 89.

14. *Prose Works*, ch. 6, p. 85.

15. See the passages cited by Hui-chen Wang Liu, "An Analysis of Chinese Clan Rules," pp. 63–96 above.

16. See the examples cited by Shimizu Morimitsu, *Chūgoku Zokusan Seido Kō* (Tokyo, 1949), pp. 98 ff. This list could be expanded indefinitely.

17. For example he sent a shipload of 500 *t'an* of wheat to the clan members in Su-chou. See *Prose Works*, ch. 7, p. 89.

18. See *Prose Works*, ch. 8, pp. 106–7.

19. *FSCS*, ch. 20. See also the pictures of the general lay-out of T'ien-p'ing shan, which are probably taken from an edition of the *Chia-sheng*, in *Works (SYSF)*, Vol. 12, "I-chi," pp. 5a–b.

20. *Prose Works*, ch. 7, p. 90; ch. 6, p. 59.

21. See Ennin's account of the monastery, in E. O. Reischauer, *Ennin's Diary* (New York, 1955), pp. 202–3.

22. *Works (SPTK)*, Vol. 10, "Ch'ao-chien Yu-ch'ung," pp. 1a–2a, and *Works (SYSF)*, "Pao-hsien Chi," ch. 2, pp. 1a–b. The latter gives the order authorizing changing the monastery's status to that of a private chapel.

23. See *Works (SYSF)*, "Pao-hsien Chi," ch. 2, p. 2a.

24. *FSCS*, ch. 14, p. 2b.

25. *Ibid.*, ch. 6, pp. 3b, 8b.

26. *Ibid.*, ch. 14, p. 3b; ch. 16, under 1744.

27. See Shimizu, *Chūgoku Zokusan Seido Kō*, pp. 101 ff.

28. See P'eng Shao-sheng's (1740–96) *P'eng Shih Jun-tsu-t'ien Chi*, quoted in *Su-chou Fu-chih*, ch. 137 (Tao-kuang edition).

29. *FSCS*, ch. 15, p. 10a. Hiring buildings for rent is also mentioned in the early thirteenth century. See *FSCS*, ch. 16, under 1210.

30. See *Prose Works*, ch. 6, p. 85.

31. See *FSCS*, ch. 15, pp. 12a–b.

32. *Prose Works*, ch. 6, p. 85.

33. *FSCS*, ch. 15, pp. 3a–5a.

34. *Ibid.*, p. 2a.

35. *Ibid.*, p. 2b.

36. *FSCS B*, ch. 1, p. 1a.

37. *FSCS*, ch. 15, pp. 2a–3a. *Works (SPTK)*, "I-chuang Kuei-chü," pp. 1a–b, has a rather different text.

38. *Sung Shih*, ch. 314, p. 16a.

39. Shimizu, *Chūgoku Zokusan Seido Kō*, pp. 78–79, cites two Ming cases in which charitable estates were granted tax exemption by imperial order, but here again the privileges were clearly exceptional. Under the Ch'ing a charitable estate could be registered as such only if it comprised at least 1,000 *mou*, and such official recognition did not carry with it the right to tax exemption. Most later charitable estates were of relatively small size, and the institution itself was rather uncommon. Of the 116 clans analyzed by Hui-chen Wang Liu, only 12 possessed charitable estates, although 57 held ritual lands.

40. *Prose Works*, ch. 8, p. 107.

41. *Sung Shih*, ch. 316, p. 7b.

42. See Wang Pi-chih, *Sheng-shui Yen-t'an Lu*, ch. 4, and Yü Yüeh, *Ch'un-tsai-t'ang Ch'üan-shu*, tsa-wen 4, p. 6b.

43. *Sung Shih*, ch. 331, pp. 25b–26a. Like Wu Kuei's estate this was in Shantung.

44. See the evidence collected in Niida Noboru, *Shina Mibun-hō Shi* (Tokyo, 1943), pp. 183–85; and Shimizu, *Chūgoku Zokusan Seido Kō*, pp. 39–47.

45. *Ming-kung Shu P'an Ch'ing-ming Chi,* "hu-hun men," *passim; Yüan Shih Shih-fan,* ch. A, p. 10a (in the later version, to be found in the *Pao-yen T'ang Pi-chi;* an earlier version, with preface dated 1178, is reprinted from the Yüan clan's family record in *Chih-pu-tsu Chai Ts'ung-shu,* and this text omits all mention of charitable estates). For an early case which was a deliberate imitation of Fan Chung-yen, see *Sung Shih,* ch. 437, p. 9b.

46. See *FSCS B,* ch. 2, pp. 3a–b, and *FSCS,* ch. 21, pp. 27a–38b, for details on Fan Shun-jen's involvement with the partisan struggles of the eleventh century. For the part played by his brothers, see the authorship attributed to the various supplementary rules from 1097 onwards in *FSCS,* ch. 15.

47. *FSCS,* ch. 15, pp. 6a–b.

48. Besides the common forms of desecration by grazing animals or cutting wood, which are frequently mentioned in the rules, during later centuries the Fans had great trouble with people quarrying the hillsides near the graves, and thus disturbing the *feng-shui* of the site.

49. See James T. C. Liu, in Fairbank, ed., *Chinese Thought and Institutions,* pp. 112–15. See also the documents on the subject collected in *Wen-hsien T'ung-k'ao,* Vol. 34, pp. 325a–c (Shih-t'ung edition of the Commercial Press, 1934).

50. *Sung Shih,* ch. 314, p. 29b.

51. *FSCS,* ch. 14, p. 2b.

52. Many scholars, among them Hu Hsien-chin, connect the origin of ritual lands with the *Wen-kung Chia-li,* the attribution of which to Chu Hsi was already doubted by the *Ssu-k'u* editors. Moreover, the work exists in two almost totally dissimilar rescensions, one in five chapters and one in eight, which present many difficult bibliographical problems. The actual passage cited by Hu Hsien-chin is completely different in the two versions.

53. The system envisaged separate ritual lands to provide for every deceased person's rites. Every parcel of ritual land was therefore vested in a different ritual community that was not necessarily coextensive with the clan, or with any single branch or family within it.

54. *FSCS,* ch. 15, pp. 6b–7a. The prevalence of landowning under the cover of nominees, usually tenants or some persons under an obligation to the occupier, is discussed in Sudo Yoshiyuki, "Sōdai no Kimeikisan to Gendai Kanjin no Token—Dengo-sei to no Kanren ni oite," *Tōyō Bunka Kenkyūjo Kiyō,* IX (1956), 65–127.

55. *FSCS,* ch. 15, pp. 7a–b.

56. *Ibid.,* p. 8a.

57. *Ibid.,* p. 7b.

58. *Ibid.,* pp. 8a–9b.

59. This is clear on the one hand from the use of the term in the rules in *FSCS,* ch. 15, and on the other from the description of the family buildings in *FSCS,* ch. 18.

60. *FSCS,* ch. 17, p. 10b.

61. *Ibid.* See also the plate showing the *i-chai* site in *Works (SYSF),* Vol. 12, "I-chi," pp. 3a–b.

62. *FSCS*, ch. 15, p. 9b.
63. *Ibid.*, p. 10a.
64. *Ibid.*, pp. 10a–b.
65. The practice was considered immoral since it might cause the true origin and surname of a child to be forgotten, with the result that he might contract an incestuous marriage. During the late eighth, ninth, and tenth centuries fictitious adoption had been widely practiced as a means of linking subordinates by a personal tie. This had resulted in wholesale confusion of true lines of descent.
66. *FSCS*, ch. 15, pp. 10b, 15a–b.
67. *Ibid.*, p. 10b.
68. *Ibid.*, p. 11a.
69. *Prose Works*, ch. 8, p. 107. The general disruption and destruction of property is borne out by a memorial submitted in 1210 by Fan Chih-ju, *FSCS*, ch. 15, pp. 12a–13b. Another account (*ibid.*, ch. 16, under 1095) reveals that much of the land of the estates was lost at the same time.
70. See *FSCS B*, ch. 1, pp. 6a–8b, for details of these three brothers. For their reestablishment of the estate, see *FSCS*, ch. 16, under 1195.
71. *Ibid.*, under 1196–97.
72. *Ibid.*, under 1195–96; *FSCS B*, ch. 1, p. 6a.
73. *FSCS*, ch. 16, under 1195–1207.
74. *FSCS*, ch. 5, p. 24a; ch. 14, p. 2b. *FSCS B*, ch. 1, p. 8b. *FSCS*, ch. 6, p. 6b.
75. *FSCS*, ch. 16, under 1208.
76. *Ibid.*, under 1200–1210.
77. *Ibid.*, ch. 17, p. 10b.
78. *Ibid.*, ch. 16, under 1210; ch. 15, p. 13b.
79. A list of holdings in *FSCS*, ch. 14, situates all the estate lands in *yü-t'ien* in the fertile area west and southwest of Su-chou. Unfortunately it is not clear whether the list refers to the original lands or to the lands held by the estate in 1758. On the reclaimed lands in the region in Sung times see Sudō Yoshiyuki, "Sōdai no Uden to Shōen-sei," *Tōyō Bunka Kenkyūjo Kiyō*, X (1956), 229–300.
80. For the supplementary rules see *FSCS*, ch. 15, pp. 14a–17b. The mention in the text of tax exemption (first granted in 1240) and of estate accountants (first appointed in 1276) shows clearly that the text as we have it had been further revised.
81. *Prose Works*, ch. 8, pp. 108–9.
82. *Ibid.*, p. 106.
83. *Ibid.*, p. 107.
84. *Ibid.*, p. 106.
85. *Chiang-su Chin-shih Chi*, ch. 13, inscription recording rents of endowment lands of a local school. See also Sudō Yoshiyuki, *Chūgoku Tochiseido Shi Kenkyū* (Tokyo, 1954), pp. 75–76. Much higher figures are recorded, ranging from 6 *tou* to 2 *tan* per mou. The average in 1263 was from 7 *tou* to 1.2 *tan*. *Ibid.*, pp. 140 ff., 580 ff. Modern rules from Kiangsu suggest that one *tan* was a very high figure for rent income.
86. On the general decline of the reclaimed lands in this area see the study by Sudō cited in note 79 above.
87. See *FSCS*, ch. 16, under these years.

88. *Ibid.*, under 1214, 1216–17.
89. *Ibid.*, ch. 14, pp. 4a–b.
90. *Ibid.*, p. 4a.
91. *Ibid.*, ch. 16, under 1243.
92. See the list of managers given in *FSCS*, ch. 16, under the given dates.
93. From 1236 to 1259, the powerful Yu-ch'eng branch alone filled 33 out of 69 possible annual appointments.
94. *FSCS*, ch. 16, under 1251.
95. *Ibid.*, under 1274; ch. 14, p. 2b.
96. *Ibid.*, ch. 16, under 1541, 1669.
97. For instance, Fan Yüan-li served from 1417 to 1460, and his successor Fan Ts'ung-kuei from 1461 to 1499.
98. Descendants in the ritual sense, that is. In fact both the senior lines failed to produce sons in early generations, and were continued only through adoption of sons from junior branches.
99. *FSCS*, ch. 16, under 1541.
100. *Ibid.*, under 1276.
101. *Ibid.*, under 1277.
102. *FSCS*, ch. 10, gives a list of all employed family members entitled "Teng-chin Chih."
103. See *FSCS*, ch. 16, *passim*.
104. See Mou Hsien's *I-hsüeh Chi* (*Prose Works*, ch. 8, p. 111), the compilation of which is mentioned under 1308 in *FSCS*, ch. 16.
105. *FSCS*, ch. 16, under 1277.
106. *Prose Works*, ch. 8, p. 111.
107. *FSCS*, ch. 16, under 1285.
108. *Ibid.*, under 1290.
109. *Ibid.*; ch. 14, pp. 5a–7a.
110. *Ibid.*, p. 5b.
111. *Ibid.*, pp. 7b–8a. Ch. 16, under 1294, reads *ssu-mai* instead of *ho-mai*, which is incorrect.
112. *FSCS*, ch. 16, under 1298.
113. *Ibid.*, ch. 14, pp. 7a–9a.
114. *Ibid.*, ch. 16, under 1310.
115. See *FSCS*, ch. 16, under 1311, 1312, 1317, 1327, etc.
116. *Ibid.*, under 1311.
117. *Ibid.*, under 1317.
118. *Ibid.*, under given dates.
119. *Ibid.*, under 1346; ch. 14, p. 1b.
120. *Ibid.*, ch. 16, under 1384; ch. 14, p. 3a.
121. There seems little reason to doubt that this was part of Ming T'ai-tsu's campaign against the gentry, which was severe in the Kiangsu region. It is also possible that the Fan clan had opposed the founder of the Ming empire in his pre-dynastic period. An account of the confiscation by an outsider exists in Wu K'uan's *Pao-weng Chia-ts'ang Chi*, ch. 52, which reads:
"Formerly Fan Wen-cheng established charitable lands in Wu-chung, and during the Sung and Yüan his clansmen annually consumed the income from these lands. At the beginning of the present [Ming] dynasty one of the clan offended against the law, and their lands were *all* confiscated by the state. All

the lands which they still possess to this day are not their old lands, but have merely been set up to continue the institution."

Now Wu K'uan (1435–1504) was a native of Ch'ang-shu County, in which the confiscated lands had been situated, and he thus had a very good chance to know the truth of the matter. But it is possible that he has confused their having lost all their land *in his native county* with their having lost all their lands.

122. See *FSCS*, ch. 24, which gives a list of all family members who migrated away from Su-chou.

123. *Ibid.*, under generations 10–13.

124. *FSCS*, ch. 24. Most of them married into local Kiangsu families. One case was that of a serving official who married into a clan in Shantung.

125. See the records of marriages included in the genealogies in *FSCS B*, chs. 1–16.

126. *FSCS*, ch. 10, under generation 13.

127. *FSCS*, ch. 10, and various entries in the genealogies in *FSCS B*, chs. 9 and 10.

128. *FSCS*, ch. 16, under 1416–17; ch. 14, p. 3a.

129. *Ibid.*, ch. 16, under 1429.

130. *Ibid.*, ch. 14, pp. 9a–11b; ch. 16, under 1432.

131. *Ibid.*, under 1432, 1436.

132. *Ibid.*, under 1453.

133. *Ibid.*, ch. 14, p. 3a. *FSCS*, ch. 16, records gifts of 89 *mou* in both 1444 and 1457, and these entries probably refer to the same donation.

134. See *FSCS*, ch. 16, from 1416 to the end of Ming times.

135. See *FSCS*, ch. 14, p. 11b; ch. 16, under 1461.

136. This reform was of course the *i-t'iao pien-fa*. For full reference see Wada Sei, *Minshi Shokkashi Shakuchū* (Tokyo, 1957), p. 214.

137. *FSCS*, ch. 16, under 1538.

138. *Ibid.*, ch. 14, pp. 11b–12a.

139. *Ibid.*, ch. 16, under 1569; ch. 14, p. 12a.

140. *Ibid.*, ch. 16, under 1471; ch. 4.

141. *Ibid.*, ch. 16, under 1541; ch. 4 tells how he had refused to make grants for weddings and funerals, and had confused the clan lineage by adopting persons of different surnames.

142. The treasures were pledged to the famous scholar Wang Shih-chen. See *FSCS*, ch. 16, under 1480, 1490.

143. *Ibid.*, under 1608, 1609, 1610.

144. His career is described in *FSCS*, ch. 5, pp. 66a–69a.

145. *Ibid.*, ch. 16, under the relevant dates; ch. 14, p. 12b.

146. *Ibid.*, ch. 16, under 1662.

147. *Ibid.*, ch. 14, pp. 12b–13a.

148. See lists of officers, *ibid.*, ch. 16.

149. *Ibid.*, under 1669; ch. 5.

150. *Ibid.*, ch. 16, under these dates.

151. The branch of the clan in Liaotung had already produced a President of the Board of War during the sixteenth century. In 1618, when the Manchus overran their family seat, Fan Wen-ch'eng (1597–1660) took service with Nurhaci, and quickly rose in the Manchu administrative service, in 1636 becoming one of the first four grand secretaries in the new government

centered at Mukden. The family were thus solidly entrenched even before the Manchu conquest of China. Wen-ch'eng's sons Fan Ch'eng-mo (1624–76) and Fan Ch'eng-hsün rose to high rank: Ch'eng-hsün became governor of Kwangsi (1685–86) and Yunnan (1686–94) and President of the Board of War (1699–1704). His own son Fan Shih-i (d. 1741) rose to be President of the Board of Works. The Liaotung branch were thus in much more influential positions than the members of the parent branch in Su-chou, and were unquestionably able to be of great service to their kinsmen. For details of the branch, see their own family record, the *Hua-yang Fan Shih Chia-p'u* (1883).

152. *FSCS*, ch. 16, under 1670–72.

153. He was appointed governor of Fukien in 1672, was captured by the rebels under Keng Ching-chung in 1674, and died in 1676.

154. See *FSCS*, ch. 16, under 1695, 1696, 1697, 1705, 1706, 1726, etc. Fan Ch'eng-hsün's benefactions were such that his epitaph was included in the *FSCS*. See ch. 21, pp. 146a–154a.

155. See list of officers, *ibid.*, ch. 16.

156. *Ibid.*, under 1669–74.

157. For the text, see *FSCS*, ch. 15, pp. 18a ff.

158. *Ibid.*, ch. 16, under 1729, 1744, 1750.

159. See *FSCS*, ch. 15.

160. See list of officers, *ibid.*, ch. 16.

161. *Ibid.*, under 1682, 1683, 1702, etc.

162. See edicts in *FSCS*, ch. 14, pp. 13a ff.; ch. 16.

163. *Works (SYSF)*, "Pao-hsien Chi," ch. 2, pp. 11a–14a.

164. See *FSCS*, ch. 16, under these dates. The *Ch'ing Shih-lu* does not mention these visits, though it has detailed accounts of the imperial progresses to Su-chou.

165. For instance, Fan Cheng-hsiang, a member of the Ju-lin branch who left Su-chou, is said (*FSCS*, ch. 24, under generation 23) to have become a renowned merchant in the Huai valley–Yangchou region.

NOTES TO SOME CHARACTERISTICS OF CHINESE BUREAUCRATIC BEHAVIOR

1. *From Max Weber: Essays in Sociology*, tr. by H. H. Gerth and C. Wright Mills (London, 1947), p. 209.

2. Max Weber, *The Theory of Social and Economic Organization*, tr. by A. M. Henderson and Talcott Parsons (New York, 1947), pp. 329–40.

3. *From Max Weber: Essays in Sociology*, p. 244.

4. This theme is at variance with Weber's notion that bureaucracy has developed an essentially similar form regardless of variations in social structures. See Alvin W. Gouldner, "Discussion of Industrial Sociology," *Am. Soc. Rev.*, XII (1948), 396.

5. Hsia Tseng-yu, *Chung-kuo Ku-tai She-hui Shih* ("History of Ancient Chinese Society") (Shanghai, 1927), p. 274.

6. Wang Hui-tsu, *Tso Chih Yao Yen* ("Salutary Advice on Assisting in Administration"), p. 11, printed as part of the collection of Hsü Nai-p'u (19th century), *Huan-hai Chih-nan Wu-chung* ("Five Guides to Sailing on the Sea of Officialdom"), published 1859.

7. Wang Hui-tsu, *Hsüeh Chih I-shuo* ("Learning to Govern"), Author's preface, p. 1, in Hsü Nai-p'u's collection *Huan-hai Chih-nan Wu-chung.*

8. See, for example, Peter M. Blau's interpretation of this Weberian concept in his *Bureaucracy in Modern Society* (New York, 1956), p. 106.

9. Herbert A. Simon, *Administrative Behavior* (New York, 1945), pp. 1–22.

10. Lü K'un, *Shen-yin Yü Chieh-lu* ("Some Moaning Words"), edited and annotated by Ch'en Hung-mou (1791), ch. 2, p. 56.

11. *Ibid.*, p. 23.

12. *Ibid.*, p. 30.

13. *Ts'ung-cheng I-kuei* ("The Administrative Tradition"), edited by Ch'en Hung-mou (1790 edition), ch. 1, pp. 54–56; also *Ch'in-pan Chou Hsien Shih-i* ("Imperial Directive on Prefectural and County Affairs"), in Hsü Nai-p'u's collection *Huan-hai Chih-nan Wu-chung.*

14. Wang Hui-tsu, *Hsüeh Chih I-shuo*, pp. 14–15.

15. Ch'en Hung-mou, *Ts'ung-cheng I-kuei*, ch. 1, p. 84.

16. Liu Heng, *Chou Hsien Hsü-chih* ("Guide to Prefectural and County Magistrates"), pp. 5–6, in Hsü Nai-p'u's collection *Huan-hai Chih-nan Wu-chung.*

17. Wang Hui-tsu, *Hsüeh Chih I-shuo*, p. 26.

18. *Ts'ai Wen-ch'in Kung Shu-tu* ("Letters of Ts'ai Shih-yüan [1682–1733]"), in Ch'en Hung-mou, *Ts'ung-cheng I-kuei*, ch. 2, p. 71.

19. Wang Hui-tsu, *Hsüeh Chih I-shuo*, p. 14.

20. Wen Ching-han (late Ch'ing), *Tzu-li Yen* ("From My Experience") (1897), p. 8.

21. "A Letter to Wang Hao [mid-Ch'ing]," in Ch'en Hung-mou, *P'ei-yuan T'ang Shou-cha Chieh-ts'un* ("Selected Personal Letters from the P'ei-yüan Hall"), ch. 1, pp. 21–22. "Letter to Lü I-yün [mid-Ch'ing]," *ibid.*, p. 41.

22. "Letter to Sun Chün [mid-Ch'ing]," *ibid.*, p. 25.

23. Ming Shan-hsi (mid-Ch'ing), *Che Yü Pien-lan* ("Handbook for Adjudicating Criminal Cases") (1859), pp. 4–24; Wang Hui-tsu, *Tso Chih Yao Yen*, p. 63.

24. "Letter to Te Ts'ung-ju [mid-Ch'ing]," in Ch'en Hung-mou, *P'ei-yüan T'ang Shou-cha Chieh-ts'un*, ch. 1, p. 28.

25. *Ch'in-ting Li-pu Ch'u-fen Tse-li* ("Official Penalty Regulations of the Board of Civil Office") (published in the 1950's), ch. 14, p. 8.

26. Kuei Ch'ao-wan, *Huan-yu Chi-lüeh* ("Brief Account of Life in Officialdom") (1873), ch. 10.

27. Lü K'un, *Shen-yin Yü Chieh-lu*, ch. 2, p. 56.

28. *Ch'in-pan Chou Hsien Shih-i*, p. 1.

29. E.g., Huang Tsung-hsi (1610–95) in *Ming-i Tai-fang lu.* Cf. W. T. de Bary, "Chinese Despotism and the Confucian Ideal," *Chinese Thought and Institutions* (J. K. Fairbank, ed., University of Chicago Press, 1957), p. 181.

30. *Ch'in-pan Chou Hsien Shih-i*, p. 1.

31. Ch'ü Tui-chih, *Wang Hui-tsu Chuan-shu* ("Biography of Wang Hui-tsu") (Shanghai, 1935), p. 5.

32. Kuei Ch'ao-wan, *Huan-yu Chi-lüeh*, ch. 7, pp. 8–11.

33. *Ibid.*, ch. 3, p. 10.

34. Wang Hui-tsu, *Tso Chih Yao Yen*, pp. 21–22.

35. Max Weber, *The Theory of Social and Economic Organization*, p. 331.

36. *Ibid.*, p. 330.
37. Blau, *Bureaucracy in Modern Society*, p. 30.
38. Lü K'un, *Shen-yin Yü Chieh-lu*, ch. 2, p. 33.
39. *Ibid.*, p. 39.
40. *Ibid.*, p. 48.
41. *Ibid.*, p. 47.
42. *Ch'in-pan Chou Hsien Shih-i*, p. 22.
43. *From Max Weber*, pp. 416–42.
44. Yen Kuang-ch'ung, *Kuan Chien* ("A Mirror for Officials"), in Ch'en Hung-mou, *Ts'ung-cheng I-kuei*, ch. 2, p. 54.
45. Lü K'un, *Shen-yin Yü Chieh-lu*, ch. 2, p. 54.
46. *Ibid.*, p. 50.
47. *Ibid.*, p. 30.
48. Wang Hui-tsu, *Tso Chih Yao Yen*, p. 19.
49. Lü K'un, *Shen-yin Yü Chieh-lu*, ch. 2, p. 31.
50. *Ibid.*, p. 65.
51. *From Max Weber*, pp. 219–20.
52. *Ibid.*
53. Ku Yen-wu, *Jih-chih Lu* (1902 abbreviated edition, Kuang-yüan T'ang, Shanghai), ch. 4, p. 11.
54. Lü K'un, *Shen-yin Yü Chieh-lu*, ch. 2, p. 67.
55. Liu Heng, *Chou Hsien Hsü-chih*, pp. 1–2.
56. Ch'en Hung-mou, *Ts'ung-cheng I-kuei*, ch. 2, p. 24.
57. Wang Hui-tsu, *Hsüeh Chih Hsü-shuo* ("More on Learning to Govern"), p. 88, in *Huan-hai Chih-nan Wu-chung*.
58. Wang Hui-tsu, *Tso Chih Yao Yen*, pp. 12–13.
59. *Ibid.*, p. 15.
60. Quoted in Liu Heng, *Chou Hsien Hsü-chih*, p. 10.
61. *Ibid.*, p. 1.
62. Lü K'un, *Shen-yin Yü Chieh-lu*, ch. 2, p. 39.
63. Wang Hui-tsu, *Hsüeh Chih Hsü-shuo*, p. 73.
64. *Ibid.*
65. Weng Ch'uan-chao, *Shu-sheng Ch'u-chien* ("Inexperienced Views of a Student") (1894), p. 11.
66. Wang Hui-tsu, *Tso Chih Yao Yen*, p. 28.
67. *Ibid.*, p. 30.
68. Wang Hui-tsu, *Hsüeh Chih I-shuo*, p .27.
69. Wang Hui-tsu, *Tso Chih Yao Yen*, p. 23.
70. See Li Chien-nung, *Chung-kuo Chin-pai-nien Cheng-chih Shih* ("Chinese Political History in the Last Hundred Years") (Shanghai, 1947), chs. 3 and 6.
71. Lü K'un, *Shen-yin Yü Chieh-lu*, ch. 2, p. 14.
72. Wang Feng-sheng, *Hsüeh Chih T'i-hsing Lu* ("Learning to Govern in Practice") (1823), ch. 1, pp. 8–9.
73. Wang Hui-tsu, *Hsüeh Chih I-shuo*, p. 19.
74. *Ibid.*, p. 18.
75. *Ibid.*, p. 40.
76. *Ibid.*, pp. 48–49.
77. Nieh Chi-mo, "Chieh Tzu Shu" ("A Letter Cautioning His Son"), in

Hsü Tung (19th century) (ed.), *Mu-ling Shu Chi-yao* ("Selected Works on County Administration") (1868), ch. 1, pp. 11–16.

78. Wang Feng-sheng, *Hsüeh Chih T'i-hsing Lu*, ch. 2, p. 4.

79. *Li-pu Tse-li* (1853), ch. 13, pp. 2–4.

80. *Ibid.*, ch. 15, p. 25.

81. Wang Chih (Ming), "Ch'ang-shih Yü ("Experimental Statements"), in Hsü Tung, *Mu-ling Shu Chi-yao*, ch. 1, p. 43.

82. Quoted in Liu Heng, *Chou Hsien Hsü-chih*, p. 7.

83. Ch'en Hung-mou, "Shen-shih Kuan-ch'en Shih" ("A Warning to Officials"), in Hsü Tung, *Mu-ling Shu Chi-yao*, ch. 1, p. 12.

84. Kuei Ch'ao-wan, *Huan-yu Chi-lüeh*, ch. 1, pp. 1–2.

85. Ch'ü Tui-chi, *Wang Hui-tsu Chuan-shu*, p. 42.

86. Lü K'un, *Shen-yin Yü Chieh-lu*, ch. 2, p. 24.

87. *Li-pu Chi-hsün Shih Tse-li* ("Rules of the Division of Merit Rating, the Board of Civil Office") (1853), ch. 2, p. 36, and chs. 3 and 4.

88. Li Pao-chia, *Kuan-ch'ang Hsien-hsing Chi* ("The True Picture of Officialdom") (Peiping, 1954 edition), Author's Preface.

89. Wen Ching-han, *Tzu-li Yen*, pp. 2–12; Wang Hui-tsu, *Hsüeh Chih I-shuo*, p. 16, and his *Tso Chih Yao Yen*, pp. 21–22.

90. Wang Hui-tsu, *Hsüeh Chih Hsü-shuo*, p. 81.

91. Wang Hui-tsu, *Tso Chih Yao Yen*, pp. 22–23, Weng Ch'uan-chao, *Shu-sheng Ch'u-chien*, p. 12; Wen Ching-han, *Tzu-li Yen*, pp. 3–4.

92. *Ch'in-ting Li-pu Ch'u-fen Tse-li*, ch. 15, p. 25.

93. Ch'ü Tui-chih, *Wang Hui-tsu Chuan-shu*, pp. 9–10, Wang Hui-tsu, *Tso chih Yao Yen*, pp. 22–23.

94. Wang Hui-tsu, *Hsüeh Chih I-shuo*, pp. 42, 80.

95. Ch'en Hung-mou, *Tsai-kuan Fa-chieh Lu Chai-ch'ao* ("Selections from Warnings to Officials") (1867 edition), Author's Preface.

96. See, for example, *Ch'in-pan Chou Hsien Shih-i*, pp. 11–20.

97. Liu Heng, *Chou Hsien Hsü-chih*, Author's Preface.

NOTES TO SOME CLASSIFICATIONS OF BUREAUCRATS IN CHINESE HISTORIOGRAPHY

1. There is practically no literature which discusses the subject systematically. These notes constitute in a sense a tentative bibliography. However, the dynastic histories are convenient sources for classifications of officials. Many biographies are arranged into groups. And the historians have expressed their value judgments in the "comment" (*lun-tsan*) at the end of each biography or each group of biographies. A recent work, Sung Hsi, *Cheng-shih Lun-tsan* (Taipeh, 1954), Vol. I, has conveniently put together these comments in the dynastic histories, without, however, analyzing the value systems underlying the comments. Some works on Chinese historiography discuss the value systems which prevailed among historians in the past, and such discussions sometimes include scattered comments which have a bearing on the subject. A prominent work of this description is Liu I-cheng, *Kuo-shih Yao-i* ("The Essential Principles of Chinese History") (1948).

2. Liu Chih-chi, *Shih-t'ung* ("A General Treatise on History"), Chi-san Shu-chü, ed. (1894), ch. 5, pp. 20–21.

3. Etienne Balazs, "Historical Compilations as Guides to Bureaucratic Practice," paper for the London Conference on Asian Historiography, 1956.

4. James T. C. Liu, "An Early Sung Reformer: Fan Chung-yen," in John K. Fairbank, ed., *Chinese Thought and Institutions* (Chicago, 1957), pp. 105–31. My book on Wang An-shih and his times will be published shortly by Harvard University Press, under the auspices of the Harvard Chinese Economic and Political Studies. In both instances, I have criticized the classifications of officials in Chinese historiography and attempted to construct, in contemporary social science terms, a specific typology of bureaucrats that will serve to clarify the given historical situation.

5. Ou-yang Hsiu, *Ou-yang Yung-shu Chi* ("Collected Works"), Wan-yu Wen-k'u, ed., III, 22.

6. Ch'ien Mu, *Kuo-shih Ta-kang* ("An Outline of Chinese History") (1947), II, 428.

7. Lü Tsu-ch'ien, ed., *Sung Wen-chien* ("Model Essays of the Sung Period"), 1929 ed., ch. 104, pp. 17–18.

8. Charles O. Hucker, "The Tung-lin Movement of the Late Ming Period," in *Chinese Thought and Institutions*, pp. 132–62.

9. D. Twitchett, "Chinese Biographical Writing," paper for the London Conference on Asian Historiography, 1956, pp. 2, 9–10.

10. *Shih-chi*, ch. 119, p. 262, and *Ch'ien Han Shu*, ch. 89, p. 585. All citations of dynastic histories are from the K'ai-ming edition.

11. *T'ung-tien*, ch. 23, p. 138. This and the related encyclopedias are cited from the Wan-yu Wen-k'u edition.

12. Etienne Balazs, *Le traité juridique du "Souei-chou"* (Leiden, 1954), pp. 185–92; and Kamada Shigeo, "Kandai no Junri to Kokuri" ("*Hsün-li* and *K'u-li* Officials in the Han Dynasty"), *Shigaku Zasshi*, LIX (1950), 322–37.

13. *Hou Han Shu*, ch. 106, p. 869; *Liang Shu*, ch. 53, p. 1837; *Sung Shu*, ch. 92, p. 1642; and *Pei Ch'i Shu*, ch. 46, p. 2259.

14. Wang Ming-sheng, *Shih-ch'i-shih Shang-ch'üeh* ("A Critical Study of the Seventeen Dynastic Histories") Kuang-ya ts'ung-shu ed., ch. 64, p. 6.

15. *Shih-chi*, ch. 121, pp. 264–66; *Hou Han Shu*, ch. 107, p. 871; and *Wei Shu*, ch. 89, p. 2093.

16. *Sui Shu*, ch. 74, p. 2518, and *Pei Shih*, ch. 87, p. 3011.

17. Chu Hsi, ed., *Sung Ming-ch'en Yen Hsing Lu*, 1661 ed. (hereafter "Famous Statesmen"). For a criticism of this collection, see Miyazaki Ichisada, "Sōdai no Shifū" ("The Morals of the Literary Class in the Sung Period"), *Shigaku Zasshi*, LXXII (1953), 139–48.

18. "Famous Statesmen," Section I, ch. 7, pp. 5–14 and Section II, ch. 6, pp. 2–19; cf. Chu Hsi, *Chu-tzu Yü-lei* ("A Topical Collection of Chu Hsi's Comments"), Cheng-i-t'ang Ch'uan-shu ed. (1876), ch. 130, pp. 1–8.

19. "Famous Statesmen," former section, ch. 6, pp. 1–6; *Chu-tzu Yü-lei*, ch. 129, pp. 2–4; and *Sung Shih*, ch. 311, p. 5321, which largely follows the opinion of Chu Hsi.

20. *Wen-hsien T'ung-k'ao*, pp. 1828–29.

21. Ssu-yü Teng and Knight Biggerstaff, *An Annotated Bibliography of Selected Chinese Reference Works*, revised ed. (1950), pp. 166–67.

22. Wang Ch'i-jo and others, eds., *Ts'e-fu Yüan-kuei*, 1814 ed., chs. 308–700.

23. *Ibid.*, chs. 674–78. Substantially, the same arrangement and ma-

terials have been adopted by the general encyclopedia, *Ku-chin T'u-shu Chi-ch'eng*, (compiled in 1725), ch. 771.

24. *Sung Shih*, ch. 319, p. 5340.

25. Ch'en Jen-hsi, ed., *Ching-shih Pa Pien Lei-chuan*, 1626 ed., chs. 184–86.

26. *Ibid.*, ch. 88, pp. 20–22; ch. 185, p. 22.

27. *Ibid.*, ch. 171, p. 19; cf. ch. 14, p. 10 and ch. 19, p. 16.

28. *Ibid.*, chs. 105–98 and 237–41.

29. *Ibid.*, ch. 157, p. 24.

30. *Ibid.*, ch. 172, p. 20; also *Sung Shih*, ch. 310, p. 5319.

31. *Wen-hsien T'ung-k'ao*, ch. 39, p. 370.

32. *Ibid.*, ch. 39, p. 372.

33. E. A. Kracke, Jr., *Civil Service in Early Sung China* (Cambridge, Mass., 1953), pp. 115–18.

34. *Hsü Wen-hsien T'ung-k'ao*, ch. 46, pp. 3199, 3202.

35. *Ta Ch'ing Hui-tien* ("Collected Regulations of the Ch'ing Empire"), 1813 ed., ch. 8, p. 9.

36. Robert K. Merton, *Social Theory and Social Structure* (1949), p. 159.

NOTES TO CONFUCIANISM AND THE MING CENSORIAL SYSTEM

Besides being indebted to the participants of the Fourth Conference on Chinese Thought at which the original draft of this paper was discussed, I am grateful to Professor F. W. Mote for many additional suggestions.

1. Etienne Balazs, *Le Traité juridique du "Souei-Chou"* (Leiden, 1954), p. 11.

2. Cf. A. F. P. Hulsewé, *Remnants of Han Law* (Leiden, 1955), p. 297; J. J. L. Duyvendak, *The Book of Lord Shang* (London, 1928), p. 129.

3. Hulsewé, p. 298.

4. Cf. C. O. Hucker, "The Traditional Chinese Censorate and the New Peking Regime," *The American Political Science Review*, XLV (1951), 1041–57; C. O. Hucker, "Governmental Organization of the Ming Dynasty," *Harvard Journal of Asiatic Studies*, XXI (1958), no. 1/2.

5. Cf. Kao I-han, *Chung-kuo Yü-shih Chih-tu tl Yen-ko* ("The Evolution of the Chinese Censorial System") (Shanghai, 1933). I disagree with several of the interpretations relating to censorial history given in Richard L. Walker, "The Control System of the Chinese Government," *The Far Eastern Quarterly*, VII (1947), 2–21.

6. Cf. Burton Watson, *Ssu-ma Ch'ien, Grand Historian of China* (New York, 1958), pp. 70 ff.

7. Cf. pp. 147 ff. of Wang Yü-ch'üan, "An Outline of the Central Government of the Former Han Dynasty," *Harvard Journal of Asiatic Studies*, XII (1949), 134–87; Sah Mong-wu, "The Impact of Hanfeism on the Earlier Han Censorial System," *Chinese Culture*, I (1957), 96.

8. Cf. Robert des Rotours, *Traité des fonctionnaires et traité de l'armée* (2 vols.; Leiden, 1947), I, 143–51.

9. Cf. E. A. Kracke, Jr., *Civil Service in Early Sung China, 960–1067* (Cambridge, Mass., 1953), p. 28; Sun Ch'eng-tse, *Ch'un-ming Meng-yü Lu*

("Memories from a Dream of the Capital") (Ku-hsiang Chai pocket ed.), ch. 48, pp. 21b–22a; *Sung Hui-yao Kao* ("Draft Institutes of the Sung") (photolithographic ed., 1936), *chih-kuan* section, ch. 17, pp. 16a–b.

10. *Yüan Shih* ("History of the Yüan") (Po-na ed., 1936), ch. 6, pp. 15b.

11. *Lun-yü*, 13.6; trans. by Arthur Waley, *The Analects of Confucius* (London, 1938), p. 173.

12. Esson M. Gale and others, "Discourses on Salt and Iron (*Yen T'ieh Lun*: Chaps. XX–XXVIII)," *Journal of the North China Branch of the Royal Asiatic Society*, LXV (1934), 85–86. This is a supplement to, and should be used in conjunction with, Esson M. Gale, *Discourses on Salt and Iron* (Leiden, 1931).

13. *Lun-yü*, 17.24, 12.16; trans. Waley, pp. 216, 167. *Mencius*, 4.2.9; trans. James Legge, *The Chinese Classics*, 2d ed. (7 vols.; Oxford, 1893–95), II, 321.

14. Duyvendak, p. 300. Cf. Duyvendak, pp. 121, 279; W. K. Liao, *The Complete Works of Han Fei Tzu*, I (London, 1939), 122–23; Derk Bodde, "Authority and Law in Ancient China," in *Authority and Law in the Ancient Orient* (*Supplement* to the *Journal of the American Oriental Society*, No. 17, July–September, 1954), p. 53.

15. Kao I-han, p. 43.

16. Cf. *Ta Ming hui-tien* ("Collected Institutes of the Ming"), chs. 209–11, 213.

17. Cf. Lung Wen-pin, *Ming hui-yao* ("Ming Precedents") (Kuang-hsü blockprint ed.), ch. 33, p. 9b; *Ming Shih* ("History of the Ming") (Po-na ed., 1937), ch. 158, pp. 2b–4b; and H. A. Giles, *A Chinese Biographical Dictionary* (London, 1898), item 997.

18. *Hsüan-tsung Shih-lu* ("True Records of the Hsüan-te Emperor") (photolithographic ed., 1940), ch. 112, p. 4a.

19. Lung Wen-pin, ch. 37, p. 2b.

20. Cf. C. O. Hucker, "The Tung-lin Movement of the Late Ming Period," in J. K. Fairbank, ed., *Chinese Thought and Institutions* (Chicago, 1957), p. 140.

21. Cf. Chu Tung-jun, *Chang Chü-cheng Ta-chuan* ("Biography of Chang Chü-cheng") (Shanghai, 1947), pp. 217–22.

22. Chu Tung-jun, p. 219. The italics are mine.

23. *Lun-yü*, 12.18; trans. Waley, p. 167.

24. For examples, cf. *Mencius*, 1.1.4; 1.2.6; 5.2.9; trans. Legge, *The Chinese Classics*, II, 133, 164–65, 392–93.

25. *Lun-yü*, 3.19, 12.23; trans. Waley, pp. 98–99, 170.

26. *Lun-yü*, 14.23, 13.15; translation and paraphrase from H. G. Creel, *Confucius the Man and the Myth* (New York, 1949), p. 160. Comma added.

27. *Li-chi* ("Record of Ceremonial") (Sung-pen Shih-san-ching Chu-shu ed., 1887), ch. 54, p. 6a; trans. James Legge in *Sacred Books of the East*, ed. Max Müller, XXVIII (Oxford, 1895), 345.

28. *Mencius*, 4.2.3; trans. Legge, *The Chinese Classics*, II, 319.

29. *Lun-yü*, 14.8; trans. Waley, p. 181.

30. *Mencius*, 1.2.4; 2.2.2; 4.1.1; trans. Legge, *The Chinese Classics*, II, 161, 212, 292.

31. *Li-chi*, ch. 51, p. 16b; ch. 48, p. 23a; trans. Legge, *Sacred Books of the East*, XXVIII, 290, 228.

32. *Hsiao-ching* ("Classic of Filial Piety"), chs. 17, 15.

33. Gale, Supplement (see n. 12), p. 106. Commas and semicolon added.

34. Kracke, p. 22.

35. Cf. Liao, pp. 69 ff., 78–85, 87–88, 88–89, 89–92, 216–17, 228–58.

36. *Han Fei Tzu* (Han Fei Tzu Chi-chieh ed.; Shanghai, 1897), ch. 5, pp. 3a, 1a; trans. Liao, pp. 142, 135.

37. *Han Fei Tzu*, ch. 8, p. 7b; trans. Liao, pp. 262–63. The italics are mine.

38. *Lun-yü*, 8.13, 2.24; trans. Waley, pp. 135, 93.

39. *Han Fei Tzu*, ch. 4, p. 7a; trans. Liao, p. 112.

40. *Han Fei Tzu*, ch. 4, pp. 4a–7b; cf. Liao, pp. 106–12 and Arthur Waley, *Three Ways of Thought in Ancient China* (New York, 1956), pp. 183–88. The translations quoted are from Liao, p. 108, and Waley, p. 188.

41. Cf. *Mencius*, 2.2.5 and 5.2.9; *Li-chi*, ch. 5, p. 30b and ch. 35, p. 15a. I am not concerned here with the problem of whether statements in *Li-chi* attributed to Confucius are genuinely his, since traditional Chinese bureaucrat-scholars accepted them as being his.

42. F. W. Mote has clarified the Imperial Confucian rationalization of such withdrawal in his "Confucian Eremitism in the Yüan Period," to appear in *The Confucian Persuasion*.

43. Cf. Wu Han, *Chu Yüan-chang Chuan* ("Biography of Chu Yüan-chang") (Shanghai, 1949), pp. 148–49.

44. Stated by the seventeenth-century grand secretary Yeh Hsiang-kao. *Hsi-tsung Shih-lu* ("True Records of the T'ien-ch'i Emperor") (photolithographic ed., 1940), ch. 17, p. 16b.

45. Lung Wen-pin, ch. 33, pp. 2a–b.

46. *Hsi-tsung Shih-lu*, ch. 5, p. 6a. Cf. *Kuang-tsung Shih-lu* ("True Records of the T'ai-ch'ang Emperor") (photolithographic ed., 1940), ch. 1, p. 22a.

47. Cf. Sun Ch'eng-tse, ch. 48, pp. 19b–21b.

48. *Ming Nan-ching Tu Ch'a-yüan T'iao-yüeh* ("Regulations of the Ming Nanking Censorate"), cited in Yü Teng, "Ming-tai Chien-ch'a Chih-tu Kai-shu" ("Survey of the Ming Dynasty Surveillance System"), *Chin-ling Hsüeh-pao*, VI (1936), 225.

49. Cf. *Ming Shih*, ch. 163, pp. 1a–4a; *Ming-ch'en Tsou-i* ("Memorials of Ming Officials") (Ts'ung-shu Chi-ch'eng ed.), ch. 2, pp. 20–22; Ku Chieh-kang, "A Study of Literary Persecution during the Ming," trans. L. C. Goodrich, *Harvard Journal of Asiatic Studies*, III (1938), 270–72.

50. Cf. *Ming Shih*, ch. 188, pp. 27a–29a; Wolfgang Seuberlich, "Kaiser-true oder auflehnung? Eine Episode aus der Ming-zeit," *Zeitschrift der Deutschen Morgenländischen Gesellschaft*, CII (1952), 304–14.

51. Cf. *Ming Shih*, ch. 16, p. 11a.

52. Cf. *Ming Shih*, ch. 17, p. 4b; Ku Ying-t'ai, *Ming-shih Chi-shih Pen-mo* ("Topical Analysis of Ming History") (Wan-yu Wen-k'u ed.), ch. 50.

53. Cf. Ku Ying-t'ai, ch. 67; Hucker, "The Tung-lin Movement," especially pp. 140–41; Lin Yutang, *A History of the Press and Public Opinion in China* (Chicago, 1936), p. 65.

54. Cf. Ku Ying-t'ai, ch. 71; Hucker, "The Tung-lin Movement," pp. 153 ff.; Lin Yutang, pp. 70–73.

55. *Tung-lin T'ung-chih Lu* ("Record of the Tung-lin Comrades"), in

Cho-chung Chih-yü ("Supplementary Treatise on Palace Life") (Cheng-chüeh-lou Ts'ung-k'e ed.), ch. 1, pp. 24–29.

56. For example, cf. *Hsi-tsung Shih-lu,* ch. 8, p. 12a.

57. *Ming Shih,* ch. 164, pp. 6b–7b.

58. For example, see the censor Yang Lien's famous denunciation of Wei's "24 great crimes" in *Yang Ta-hung Chi* ("Collected Works of Yang Lien") (Ts'ung-shu Chi-ch'eng ed.), pp. 1–7.

59. For example, cf. *Hsüan-tsung Shih-lu,* ch. 14, pp. 2b–3a.

60. For examples, cf. *Hsi-tsung Shih-lu,* ch. 21, p. 20b; ch. 24, pp. 15a–b; ch. 19, pp. 30a–b; ch. 21, pp. 20a–b; ch. 26, pp. 11a–b; ch. 32, pp. 9a–b.

61. For example, cf. *Hsi-tsung Shih-lu,* ch. 42, pp. 4a, 5a; *Hsüan-tsung Shih-lu,* ch. 47, pp. 12b–13a; ch. 51, pp. 7a–b; ch. 65, p. 9a.

62. Cf. *Hsi-tsung Shih-lu,* ch. 21, pp. 14b–15a.

63. *Hsüan-tsung Shih-lu,* ch. 36, p. 10a.

64. Cf. *Hsi-tsung Shih-lu,* ch. 50, p. 12b, for one example: a proposal that strict time limits be established within which newly appointed or transferred officials must arrive at their duty posts.

65. Hua Yün-ch'eng, *Kao Chung-hsien-kung Nien-p'u* ("Chronological Biography of Kao P'an-lung") (Kao-tzu I-shu ed.), pp. 24b–25b.

66. *Ming Shih,* ch. 188, p. 2a, in the biography of Liu Ch'ih.

67. Tso Tsai, *Tso Kuang-tou Nien-p'u* ("Chronological Biography of Tso Kuang-tou") (Pi-ts'e Ts'ung-shuo ed.), ch. 2, pp. 14a–b, 15b, 15b–16a.

NOTES TO HO-SHEN AND HIS ACCUSERS

Abbreviations and short titles used in the notes (this list excludes sources used only once, or twice in close succession):

CSCSPM: Huang Hung-shou, *Ch'ing-shih Chi-shih Pen-mo* (Shanghai, 1929; 1st ed., 1915).

HCCS: *Ch'in-ting Hsüeh-cheng Ch'üan-shu* (1810).

Hsiao: Hsiao I-shan, *Ch'ing-tai T'ung-shih,* 3 vols. (Shanghai, 1928).

Hummel: Arthur W. Hummel, ed., *Eminent Chinese of the Ch'ing Period* (1644–1912), 2 vols. (Washington, D.C., 1943–44).

ICWC: *I-ch'üan Wen-chi,* ts'e 5 of *Erh Ch'eng Ch'üan-shu,* Ssu-pu Pei-yao edition.

JTSL: *Ta-Ch'ing Jen-tsung Jui-huang-ti Shih-lu.*

KCCHLCCP: Li Huan (1827–91), *Kuo-ch'ao Ch'i-hsien Lei-cheng Ch'u-pien* (1890).

KCHCSL: Li Yüan-tu (1821–87), *Kuo-ch'ao Hsien-cheng Shih-lüeh* (1866).

KSCW: Hung Liang-chi (1746–1809), *Keng-sheng Chai Wen Chia-chi* in *Hung Pei-chiang Ch'üan-chi* (1877).

KSLC: *Kuo-shih Lieh-chuan.*

KTSL: *Ta-Ch'ing Kao-tsung Shun-huang-ti Shih-lu.*

KTSH: *Ta-Ch'ing Kao-tsung Shun-huang-ti Sheng-hsün.*

PCC: Ch'ien I-chi (1783–1850), comp., *Kuo-ch'ao Pei-chuan Chi* (1893).

STSH: *Ta-Ch'ing Shih-tsung Hsien-huang-ti Sheng-hsün.*

Staunton, *Embassy*: Sir George Staunton (1781–1859), *An Historical Account of the Embassy to the Emperor of China* (London, 1797).

Staunton, *Laws*: Sir George Staunton, tr., *Ta Tsing Leu Lee; Being the Funda-mental Laws, and a Selection from the Supplementary Statutes, of the Penal Code of China* . . . (London, 1810).

I am deeply indebted to Mr. Fang Chao-ying of the East Asiatic Library of the University of California, Berkeley, for making many valuable sugges-tions and corrections in various parts of this article. He is however, in no way responsible for errors I may have failed to eliminate.

1. Hsiao, II, 191; Hummel, p. 288; KSLC, ch. 34, p. 1a.
2. Hsiao, II, 198.
3. KSLC, ch. 34, p. 2b.
4. Hummel, p. 288.
5. Staunton, *Laws*, pp. 491–92; cf. also Staunton, *Embassy*, p. 335.
6. Staunton, *Laws*, p. 495; KSLC, ch. 34, pp. 6a, 7a–b.
7. CSCSPM, ch. 34, p. 2a.
8. Staunton, *Laws*, p. 492; Hummel, p. 370.
9. E.g., by Hung Liang-chi; JTSL, ch. 50, p. 42a.
10. Hsiao, II, 193–94.
11. Staunton, *Laws*, p. 495.
12. *Hsiao*, II, 194.
13. *Ibid.*, pp. 195–96.
14. KCHCSL, ch. 21, p. 10b.
15. For a detailed account of the Wang Lun revolt, see *Lettres édi-fiantes et curieuses* (Paris, 1783), XXVI, 418–28.
16. Sun Hsing-yen, Hung Liang-chi, Yao Nai, and Chu Kuei all wrote biographies in praise of him; cf. Hummel, p. 869; PCC, ch. 108, pp. 1a–5b; KSCW, ch. 4, pp. 17b–18a; Hsiao, II, 195.
17. Hsiao, II, 195; KCHCSL, ch. 21, p. 11b.
18. CSCSPM, ch. 34, p. 1b; *Ch'ing Shih Kao*, ch. 208, pp. 33a–35b.
19. Hummel, pp. 222–24.
20. *Chang-shih I-shu*, Chia-yeh-t'ang edition, ch. 29, pp. 39b–40a. See also Paul Demiéville, review of Hu Shih, *Chang Shih-chai Hsien-sheng Nien-p'u*, in *Bulletin de l'École Française de l'Extrême-Orient*, XXIII (1923), 487–88.
21. Wang Hui-tsu, *Hsüeh-chih I-shuo*, Ts'ung-shu Chi-ch'eng, ed. (#0892), p. 2. I am indebted to Mr. Fang Chao-ying for calling my atten-tion to this passage.
22. Hsiao, II, 197.
23. Staunton, *Laws*, p. 492; cf. Staunton, *Embassy*, p. 342.
24. Staunton, *Laws*, p. 491.
25. *Ou-yang Wen-chung-kung Wen-chi*, Ssu-pu Ts'ung-k'an edition, ch. 17, pp. 6b–8a. See quotation, p. 168.
26. HCCS, ch. 4, p. 2a; Omura Kyōdō, "Shinchō Kyōiku Shisōshi ni okeru 'Seiyu Kōkun' no Chii ni tsuite," in Hayashi Tomoharu, ed., *Kinsei Chūgoku Kyōikushi Kenkyū* (Tokyo, 1958), pp. 242–44.
27. Edouard Biot, *Essai sur l'histoire de l'instruction publique en Chine* (Paris, 1847), pp. 504–5. Robert Morrison, *A Dictionary of the Chinese Language* (1815–22), Part I, Vol. I, p. 762.
28. Omura, p. 245; HCCS, ch. 4, pp. 11a–12b.

29. KTSH, ch. 192, pp. 10a–11a.
30. STSH, ch. 19, p. 1b.
31. Hummel, pp. 748, 916, 918.
32. STSH, ch. 19, p. 10a.
33. HCCS, ch. 4, p. 5a.
34. *Ibid.*, pp. 6a–b.
35. *Ibid.*, pp. 7b–8a.
36. *Ibid.*, pp. 8a–9b.
37. *Ibid.*, pp. 4b–5a.
38. STSH, ch. 19, p. 11a.
39. *Ibid.*, pp. 2b–3b.
40. *Ibid.*, pp. 3a–b.
41. Hsiao, II, 16.
42. *Ibid.*
43. Hummel, pp. 56, 602.
44. ICWC, ch. 2, pp. 2a–b.
45. *Ibid.*, p. 3b.
46. *Ibid.*, p. 4a.
47. Quoted by Ch'ien Mu, *Chung-kuo Chin-san-pai-nien Hsüeh-shu-shih* (Taipei, 1957; 1st ed., 1937), author's preface, p. 2.
48. HCCS, ch. 4, pp. 8b–9a.
49. KTSH, ch. 192, pp. 11a–13a; KTSL, ch. 1156, pp. 11a–13a.
50. KTSL, ch. 1160, pp. 19a–20b; ch. 1154, p. 4b. KCCHLCCP, ch. 100, pp. 25b–26a, 20b–21a.
51. KTSL, ch. 1154, pp. 19a–23a.
52. *Ibid.*, pp. 6a–7a, 10b–11b, 12a–13a.
53. CSCSPM, ch. 34, p. 1b; Hsiao, II, 204–5; KCCHLCCP, ch. 100, p. 21a; Hummel, p. 151; JTSL, ch. 38, pp. 28a–b.
54. KCCHLCCP, ch. 100, p. 25b.
55. KTSL, ch. 1160, pp. 24a–25b.
56. KSLC, ch. 34, p. 3b.
57. KCHCSL, ch. 21, p. 10b; PCC, ch. 56, p. 16a.
58. KSLC, ch. 34, p. 4a; JTSL, ch. 38, p. 27b.
59. KSLC, ch. 34, pp. 4a–b. See also KTSL, ch. 1281, p. 4b ff.; ch. 1282, p. 11a ff.
60. The date is not easy to establish. Cf. PCC, ch. 56, pp. 18a–19a.
61. KSCW, ch. 4, p. 2a.
62. Hsiao, II, 196–97.
63. *Ch'ing Shih Kao*, ch. 328, pp. 5a–6a.
64. Staunton, *Embassy*, p. 342; Staunton, *Laws*, p. 492–93; Hummel, p. 185; CSCSPM, ch. 34, p. 2a.
65. JTSL, ch. 37, pp. 21b–22b.
66. *Ibid.*, pp. 27a–b; ch. 38, pp. 9a–b.
67. Staunton, *Laws*, pp. 502–4.
68. JTSL, ch. 50, pp. 40a–44a.
69. *Ibid.*, pp. 40a–44a, 35a–b.
70. *Ibid.*, p. 44a.
71. *Hung Pei-chiang Shih-wen Chi*, Ssu-pu Ts'ung-k'an edition, Nien-p'u, pp. 30b–31a, 32b–33b; KSCW, beginning of first volume; Hummel, p. 374.

NOTES TO CONFUCIANISM AND MONARCHY AT THE LAST

1. *North-China Herald*, CXIV (Jan. 9, 1915), 87.
2. *Faust*, Part II, Act 1, Scene 3.
3. Thomas Mann, *Doctor Faustus* (New York, 1948), p. 134.
4. Kao Lao, *Ti-chih Yün-tung Shih-mo Chi* ("An Account of the Monarchical Movement") (Shanghai, 1923), p. 17.
5. *Ibid.*, p. 19.
6. *Ibid.*, p. 18.
7. Ku Yen-wu, *Jih-chih Lu* ("Record of Knowledge Day by Day"), ed. Huang Ju-ch'eng (1834), ch. 13, pp. 5b–6.
8. Kao, pp. 20–21.
9. *Ibid.*, p. 22.
10. Imazeki Hisamaro, *Sung Yüan Ming Ch'ing Ju-chia Hsüeh Nien-piao* ("Chronological Tables of Sung, Yüan, Ming, and Ch'ing Confucianism") (Tokyo, 1920), p. 216 (in Chinese). The other Ch'ing *ta-ssu* were the rites for Heaven and Earth, the Celestial Emperor (Shang-ti), the imperial ancestral temple, and the gods of the land and grain.
11. Kao, p. 7.
12. T'ao Chü-yin, *Liu Chün-tzu Chuan* ("Biographies of the 'Six Martyrs'") (Shanghai, 1946), p. 2.
13. Chou Chen-fu, "Yen Fu Ssu-hsiang Chuan-pien chih P'ou-hsi" ("A Close Analysis of the Changes in Yen Fu's Thought"), *Hsüeh-lin*, No. 3 (1941), p. 117.
14. Sakamaki Teiichirō, *Shina Bunkatsu Ron: Tsuki, "Gen Seikai"* ("The Decomposition of China: Supplement, Yüan Shih-k'ai") (Tokyo, 1914), p. 183.
15. *Ibid.*, pp. 228, 229.
16. E.g., "Rinji Taiwan Kyūkan Chōsakai Dai-ichi-bu Hōkoku" ("Temporary Commission of the Taiwan Government-General for the Study of Old Chinese Customs, Report of the First Section"), *Shinkoku gyōseihō* ("Administrative Laws of the Ch'ing Dynasty"), kan 1, revised (Tokyo, 1914), I, p. 46.
17. Cf. Tung Chung-shu, *Ch'un-ch'iu Fan-lu*, "Shen-ch'a ming-hao," ch. 10, pp. 1–4: "The monarch who has received the mandate is given the mandate by the will of Heaven; therefore he is called the son of Heaven . . ." (This reference comes from Vincent Shih, "The Ideology of the T'ai-p'ing T'ien-kuo," ms.)
18. A proper corrective to the authority cited in note 16 is Hara Tomio, *Chūka Shisō no Kontai to Jugaku no Yūi* ("The Roots of Chinese Thought and the Preeminence of Confucianism") (Tokyo, 1947), p. 183, which emphasizes that in classical Chinese thought *t'ien-i* was independent and self-existent. That is, it was not derived from *min-i* and was certainly not reduced, in the modern metaphorical fashion, to being simply a rhetorical equivalent of the latter term.
19. Sagara Yoshiaki, "Toku no Go no Igi to Sono Hensen" ("The Meaning of the Word *te* and Its Evolution"), in Tsuda Sokichi, *Tōyō Shisō Kenkyū* ("Studies in Asian Thought"), No. 1 (Tokyo, 1937), pp. 290–91.
20. Wang Hsieh-chia, "Chung-hua Min-kuo Hsien-fa hsüan ch'uan chang ting K'ung-chiao wei kuo-chiao ping hsü jen-min hsiu chiao tzu-yu

hsiu-cheng an" ("Proposal that the constitution of the Republic of China promulgate a special clause establishing Confucianism as the state religion and permitting modification of the freedom of religion"), pp. 1, 4–5, in Tsung-sheng hsüeh-pao (publ.), *K'ung-chiao Wen-t'i* ("The Problem of Confucianism") (Taiyuan, 1917). (Hereafter, KCWT).

21. *Ibid.*, pp. 1–3.

22. *Ibid.*, p. 10.

23. "Hu-pei kung-min Liu Ta-chün shang ts'an chung liang yüan ching ting kuo-chiao shu" (Letter from Liu Ta-chün of Hupeh to the parliament requesting establishment of a state religion), in KCWT, pp. 4–5.

24. Wang Hsieh-chia, in KCWT, p. 1.

25. Li Wen-chih, "Ching ting K'ung-chiao wei kuo-chiao ti erh-tz'u i-chien shu" ("Second communication of views favoring establishment of Confucianism as the state religion"), in KCWT, pp. 2–3.

26. For example, cf. Jacques Gernet, *Les Aspects économiques du Bouddhisme dans la société chinoise du Ve au Xe siècle* (Saigon, 1956), pp. 293–94 et seq., for the exploitation of Buddhism to support the imperial power. To cite a later period: Ming imperial indulgence toward Buddhism was marked. Even while Confucian scholars biased in favor of their master, the Yung-lo emperor (reigned 1403–24), taxed his predecessor (whose throne he had usurped) with favor to Buddhists, Yung-lo himself retained his ties with the monks who had helped him to power; see David Chan, "The Usurpation of the Prince of Yen, 1398–1402," unpublished Ph.D. dissertation, University of California, 1957.

27. For the Buddhist contribution to trade and capital formation, see Gernet, esp. pp. 138–90.

28. J. J. L. Duyvendak, *China's Discovery of Africa* (London, 1949), pp. 27–28.

29. For Ming, see Charles Whitman MacSherry, "Impairment of the Ming Tributary System as Exhibited in Trade Involving Fukien," unpublished Ph.D. dissertation, University of California, 1957.

30. For the Hoppo's appointment by the "inner court" (imperial) rather than the "outer court" (general bureaucratic), see William Frederick Mayers, *The Chinese Government* (Shanghai, 1886), p. 40; and for his practice of sending memorials directly to the emperor, not through normal channels, see *Shinkoku Gyōseihō*, kan 5 (Tokyo, 1911), pp. 311–12.

31. See the chapter, "The Amateur Ideal in Ming and Early Ch'ing Society: Evidence from Painting," in Joseph R. Levenson, *Confucian China and Its Modern Fate* (Berkeley and Los Angeles, 1958), pp. 15–43. It is interesting to note that a Chinese Communist critic, in the interests of isolating the literati tradition as "the enemy," has set the "academic" style apart (the Sung Emperor Hui-tsung is specifically praised) as the anti-Confucian precedent for the Communist-sponsored "realism" in art; see Chang Jen-hsia, "Flower-and-Bird Painting," *China Reconstructs*, III (1953), 51.

32. As an interesting analysis of how a monarchy may naturally strain against an association which is nevertheless essential to it and inseparable from it, see, for comparison with China, Alexis de Tocqueville, *The Old Regime and the French Revolution* (New York, 1955), p. 8: he cites Mirabeau's letter to Louis XVI in 1790, pointing out the elements in the developing Revolution which should be reassuring to monarchy because of their

centralizing, rationalizing contributions to the liquidation of feudal institutions, including those against which the crown had historically struggled. Yet, as Joseph Schumpeter shows in "The Sociology of Imperialism," in *"Imperialism" and "Social Classes"* (New York, 1955), pp. 57–58, the French monarchy's struggle against the feudal aristocracy had been such as to bind the former to the now modified feudal system. Thus, it is not surprising that the Revolution, which may be seen as completing the work of the monarchy against feudalism, should have marked the two together for destruction.

Although French historical issues are by no means the same as Chinese, this French example may encourage one to recognize, and not simply be mystified by, paradox and ambivalence in Chinese institutional relationships.

33. As Pow-key Sohn has pointed out in "The Theory and Practice of Land-systems in Korea in Comparison with China" (ms., University of California, 1956), the Koryŏ victory of military over civil interests played a large part in defeating the trend in Korea toward a private-property system; it encouraged, rather, a return to a strict system of state ownership and state allocation—a system, be it noted, which T'ang and other rulers in China favored at times, but which civil-official recalcitrance broke down.

34. It is probably in this connection that the Confucian sage-emperor lore (of which more below, in text) has its greatest significance. The Yao-Shun period preceding the Hsia is sometimes referred to as the "Yao Shun *shan-jang* era"; and the *shan-jang* convention for solemnizing an imperial abdication and succession was a convention for transmission of the throne to one of a different surname (see Tezuka Ryōdō, *Jukyō Dōtoku ni Okeru Kunshin Shisō* ("The Sovereign-minister Idea in Confucian Ethics") (Tokyo, 1925), p. 112; and Miyakawa Hisayuki, "Zenjō ni Yoru Ōchō Kakumei no Tokushitsu" ("The Special Quality of Dynastic Overturns Depending on *shan-jang*"), *Tōhōgaku*, No. 11 (1955), p. 50.

What was the *shan-jang* idea (projected into the past by Confucianists) but an expression of Confucian anti-dynastic feeling? It is after Yao and Shun, who chose their successors by the Confucian criterion of virtue, not the feudal criterion of hereditary right, that dynasties begin: a falling-off.

35. See Shih ms. (*op. cit.* note 17) for this literati opinion. *Ming-shih*, Shih-huo chih, ch. 77, pp. 11a–11b: "Nothing did more harm to the people than the *huang-chuang* and *chuang-t'ien* (villas) of the princes and princesses, eunuchs and nobles." Note the emphasis on eunuchs and aristocrats, both nonbureaucratic types, and both having corporate existence only as imperial affiliates. We may assume that post-Ch'in enfeoffment did not represent any genuine monarchical sentiment for retrogression to a stage of feudal fragmentation of the state power. Rather, the monarch permitted what was after all a shadow feudal structure—never with a weight of power to threaten the bureaucracy's—to exist because the state was bureaucratically centralized enough to survive it; and the monarchy willed this feudal structure to exist because bureaucratic centralization had its inner seed of impermanence. The imperially patronized nominal feudal system—mainly an extended imperial family affair—was of such a character as to be safe for the emperor as long as gentry-literati-officials were with him, while it symbolized his awareness of their potential defection.

36. As Shih points out, the Taiping state stressed the motto *i hsiao tso chung*, "transform filial piety into loyalty." The Taipings seem to me to repre-

sent in Chinese history (among other things) the assertion of a pure monarchical spirit, i.e., a spirit of unqualified autocracy, a refusal to compromise
with bureaucratic ideals. A regime which understandably alienated the Confucian literati unequivocally, the Taiping state was trying to rule out the possibility of the traditional intrabureaucratic conflict between private and public
impulses.

37. Carsun Chang, *The Development of Neo-Confucian Thought* (New
York, 1957), p. 203.

38. See R. H. van Gulik, tr., *T'ang-Yun-Pi-Shih*, *"Parallel Cases from
under the Pear-Tree"* (Leiden, 1956), p. vii, for the oft-quoted statement
applying to the scholar-official, "One does not read the Code," and its bearing
on theories of the ideal state and ideal ruler.

39. Louis Delatte, *Les Traités de la royauté d'Ecphante, Diotegène, et
Sthénidas* (Liège and Paris, 1942), pp. 140–42.

40. Shōji Sōichi, "Chin Ryō no Gaku" (The Thought of Ch'en Liang),
Tōyō no Bunka to Shakai, V (1954), 98–100.

• 41. According to Tung Chung-shu (second century b.c.), Confucius received the "imperial mandate" in principle; see Fung Yu-lan, *A History of
Chinese Philosophy* (Princeton, 1955), II, 63, 71, 129. For Confucius as
su-wang see Tu Yü (222–84), *Ch'un-ch'iu Tso-chuan Hsü* (Preface to *Ch'un-
ch'iu*, with *Tso-chuan*): cf. *Tz'u-hai*, II, 61.

42. Toda Toyosaburō, "Gogyō Setsu Seiritsu no Ichi Kōsatsu" (Reflection on the Formation of Five-Element Theory"), *Shinagaku Kenkyū*, XII
(1956), 44.

43. Hara (*op. cit.* note 18), p. 233.

44. Ch'eng Hao, "Lun Wang Pa Cha-Tzu" (Memorial on *wang* and *pa*),
Erh Ch'eng wen-chi ("Collection of Writings of the Two Ch'engs") (Chang-
sha, 1941), p. 4.

45. Norman H. Baynes, "The Byzantine State," in *Byzantine Studies and
Other Essays* (London, 1955), pp. 55–57.

46. Baynes, "Eusebius and the Christian Empire," *ibid.*, p. 168.

47. The *su-wang* as the true sage and implied rebuke to the politically
visible royal incumbent figures in the Taoist *Chuang-tzu* (T'ien-tao section);
see *Tz'u-hai*, II, 61; also Inoue Gengo, "Juka to Haku I Tō Seki Setsuwa"
("Confucianism and the Tales of Po I and Tao Chih"), *Shinagaku Kenkyū*,
No. 13 (1955), p. 21, where *Kung-yang* Confucian influence on Chuang-tzu
is seen in the *su-wang* concept. In so far as we speak of Taoism as politically
anarchistic, we identify it with an *essential* Confucianism which affects Confucianism-in-action but is not coterminous with it. The Confucianism which
is implemented, visible in history, is the credo of officials, who are naturally
no anarchists. But the Taoist boycott of the world of affairs (as by hermits,
who flout the values of Confucianism-in-action, i.e., Confucianism-cum-
Legalism, but confirm them, too, by abandoning the world to Confucianists—
and dynasts—alone) dramatizes the theoretical principle which Confucianists
invoke, in their Confucianism-cum-Taoism, to rebuke emperors.

48. Karl A. Wittfogel, *Oriental Despotism: A Comparative Study of Total
Power* (New Haven, 1957), p. 103.

49. Ojima Sukema, "Shina Shisō: Shakai Keizai Shisō" ("Chinese
Thought: Social and Economic Thought"), in *Tōyō Shichō* ("Far Eastern
Thought-Tides") (Tokyo, 1936), pp. 23–24.

50. Ch'en Shao-pai, "Hsing Chung Hui Ko-ming Shih Yao" ("Essentials of the Hsing Chung Hui's Revolutionary History"), in *Hsin-hai Ko-ming* (Documents on the 1911 Revolution) (Shanghai, 1957), I, 32: "We saw the characters 'Chung-kuo ko-ming tang Sun Yat-sen.' . . . Hitherto our cast of mind had been such as to consider *ko-ming* something applying to the will to act as emperor, with our movement only to be considered as rebelling against this. From the time we saw this newspaper, we had the picture of the three characters *ko-ming tang* imprinted on our minds."

51. E.g., Sun Yat-sen on Yao and Shun ("The name was monarchy, the fact was the rule of democracy"), and on Confucius and Mencius as "pro-people's-rights" on the strength of their praises of Yao and Shun; cf. Kuo Chan-po (Kōya Masao, tr.), *Gendai Shina shisō shi* ("History of Modern Chinese Thought") (Tokyo, 1940), p. 108.

52. E.g., Wang Hsieh-chia, in KCWT, p. 2, for the admission that Confucianism uses a heavily monarchical language—but—"What is the origin of *ko-ming?*" A "people's rights" version of Confucianism had, of course, been worked up by K'ang Yu-wei and his Reform group, and was frequently refurbished by men like Wang, here adapting himself to the republican environment and quoting, without referring to K'ang, some of the latter's old proof-texts in the Li-yün section of *Li-chi*. Liu Ta-chün (see note 23, above) does the same (KCWT, pp. 1–2). The thinness of Confucianism in this "republican" version is apparent, not only from its highly special selectivity but from the fact that authority has clearly been stripped from it; Confucianism, instead of dictating the polity, must be interpreted by its defenders so that it conforms to a polity established on other authority. The rhetorical question "What is the origin of *ko-ming?*" suggests, at bottom, not that the Republic is Confucian, but that Western standards have invaded even Confucianism: *ko-ming* as revolution was from the Western political vocabulary, out of Japan.

53. Tezuka (*op. cit.* note 34), pp. 17–19.

54. Tu Yü: see note 41.

55. *Ming-shih*, ch. 77, p. 4a, cited in Sohn ms. (see note 33).

56. Tezuka, p. 130. Note that the connection between *chün* and *ch'en* (and *ch'en* is located only in this or an equivalent connection) is always denoted by *lun*, human relationship; see *Li-chi*, Mencius, etc., *passim*.

57. I have explored this subject more fully in "The Amateur Ideal . . ." (see note 31).

58. Chang Ch'un-ming, "Ch'ing-tai ti Mu-chih" ("The Private-Secretary System of the Ch'ing Dynasty"), *Lingnan hsüeh-pao*, IX (1950), 33–37.

59. *Ibid.*, p. 47.

60. Sakamaki, (*op. cit.* note 14), p. 210.

61. *Ibid.*, pp. 54–55.

62. *Ibid.*, p. 139.

63. Kuo Pin-chia, "Min-kuo Erh-tz'u Ko-ming Shih" ("History of the Republic's 'Second Revolution' "), part 2, *Wuhan Quarterly*, IV (1935), 843.

64. Sakamaki, pp. 214–15. Sun's friend Huang Hsing, trying to win over the Ch'ing loyalist, General Chang Hsün, to the anti-Yüan cause in the summer of 1913, declared: "Not only is Yüan Shih-k'ai abhorrent to the Republic, he was a robber of the Ch'ing house." Cf. Kuo, part 1, *Wuhan Quarterly*, IV, 650.

65. Li Ting-shen, *Chung-kuo Chin-tai Shih* ("Recent History of China") (Shanghai, 1933), p. 312.
66. Kuo, part 2, *Wuhan Quarterly*, IV, 642.
67. T'ao Chü-yin, *Chin-tai I-wen* ("Anecdotes of the Recent Era") (Shanghai, 1930), p. 2.
68. Heibonsha: *Seijigaku jiten* ("Dictionary of Political Science") (Tokyo, 1957), p. 449.
69. *Kuo-t'i* had some vague ancient usage, as in the *Ku-liang chuan*, irrelevant to modern monarchists, and a colorless existence in occasional documents thereafter. The monarchists' *kuo-t'i* had as much novelty infused in it from Japan as the republicans' *ko-ming*.

NOTES TO THE CONFUCIAN TEACHER IN TOKUGAWA JAPAN

1. Edwin O. Reischauer, *Japan Past and Present* (New York, 1953), p. 87.
2. See works such as Inoue Tetsujirō, *Nihon Shushigakuha no Tetsugaku* ("The philosophy of the Shushi school in Japan") (Tokyo, 1915); Yasui Kotarō, *Nihon Jugaku Shi* ("History of Japanese Confucianism") (Tokyo, 1939); and R. C. Armstrong, *Light from the East* (Toronto, 1914).
3. For instance, Bamba Masatomo, *Nihon Jukyō Ron* ("Japanese Confucianism") (Tokyo, 1939), and Matsushima Eiichi, "Nihon Hōken Shakai no Shisō" ("The Thought of Japan's Feudal Society"), in Rekishigaku Kenkyūkai, *Nihon Shakai no Shiteki Kyūmei* (Tokyo, 1949), pp. 107–36.
4. See works such as Hara Nensai, *Sentetsu Sōdan* ("Stories of Past Philosophers") (Edo, 1817) and its successors; and Nishijima Jun, *Jurin Genryū* ("Sources of the Confucian Tradition") (Tokyo, 1934).
5. Benjamin Schwartz, "The Intellectual History of China: Preliminary Reflections," in *Chinese Thought and Institutions*, ed. J. K. Fairbank (Chicago, 1957).
6. Itō Tasaburō, "Kinsei Daimyō Kenkyū Josetsu," ("Introduction to the Study of the Modern Daimyo"), *Shigaku Zasshi*, LV (1944), 919–23.
7. Sagara Akira, *Kinsei Nihon Jukyō Undō no Keifu* ("The Pedigree of the Confucian Movement in Early Modern Japan") (Tokyo, 1955), pp. 3–22.
8. Sagara, pp. 14–26.
9. Yamada Taku, "Satsuma no Jugaku" ("Confucianism in Satsuma"), in *Kinsei Nihon no Jugaku*, ed. Fukushima Kashizō (Tokyo, 1939), p. 741.
10. Yamaguchi Ken Bunkashi Hensan Iinkai, *Yamaguchi Ken Bunkashi* ("Cultural History of Yamaguchi Prefecture") (Yamaguchi, 1951), p. 383.
11. Kobayashi Nobuaki, "Nangaku no Tokushitsu" ("The Characteristics of Nangaku") in *Kinsei Nihon no Jugaku*, pp. 753–67.
12. Sagara, pp. 26–39.
13. Quoted in Sagara, p. 12.
14. Nakae Tōju, *Okina Mondō* ("Dialogues of the Old Man") in *Tōju Sensei Zenshū* ("Collected Works of Nakae Tōju") (Tokyo, 1940), III, 220.
15. Quoted as translated from the diary of Hirayama Yoshitada, in Asakawa Kanichi, *The Documents of Iriki* (New Haven, 1929), pp. 373–74.
16. Ikeda Archives, *Hōreishū* ("Collected Laws"), *kan* 7.
17. Quoted in Sagara, p. 18.
18. *Sources of the Japanese Tradition*, compiled by Ryusaku Tsunoda, Wm. Theodore de Bary, and Donald Keene (New York, 1958), pp. 338–39.

19. Quoted in Sagara, p. 63.

20. Quoted from Fujita Yūkoku of the Mito school in Sakata Yoshio "Tennō Kan no Hensen" ("Changes in the Concept of the Emperor"), *Zimbun Gakuhō*, VIII (1959), 69.

21. Ikeda Archives, Hōreishū, *kan* 7.

22. Quoted in Sagara, p. 73.

23. Katō Toranosuke, "Tsunayoshi to Jugaku" (Tsunayoshi and Confucianism"), in *Kinsei Nihon no Jugaku*, pp. 39–41.

24. Ono Kiyoshi, *Tokugawa Seido Shiryō* ("Materials on Tokugawa Institutions") (Tokyo, 1927), II, 39–41.

25. For instance Narushima Motonao, *Tokugawa Jikki* ("The True Records of the Tokugawa House") (Kokushi taikei ed.), X, 175.

26. Ikeda Archives, Ikeda-ke Rireki Ryakki, ("Abridged History of the Ikeda House"), *kan* 7 (Kambun 8).

27. Katō Toranosuke, pp. 47–51.

28. Iida Sukashi, "Edo Jidai no Kōshibyō Kenchiku" ("The Architecture of Confucian Temples during the Edo Period"), in *Kinsei Nihon no Jugaku*, pp. 947–1013.

29. Ikeda Archives, Kokugaku Kiroku ("Records of the Domain School").

30. Asaka Kaku and Imai Kosai, *Shunsui Sensei Kōjutsu narabini Ryakufu* ("Biography and Genealogy of Shu Shunsui"), in *Zokuzoku Gunsho Ruijū* (Tokyo, 1906), III, 419–25.

31. Mizuno Kyōichirō, "Bizen-han ni okeru Jinshoku-uke Seido ni tsuite" ("On the System of Temple Registration in Bizen-han"), *Okayama Daigaku Hōbungakubu Gakujutsu Kiyō*, V (1956), 74.

32. Quoted in Sagara, p. 67.

33. Quoted in Katō Toranosuke, p. 43.

34. Nishimura Tenshu, *Nihon Sōgaku Shi* ("History of Sung Studies in Japan") (Tokyo, 1951), p. 206.

35. Jingū Shichō, *Koji Ruien* ("Record of Ancient Matters") (Tokyo, 1935), XVII, 149.

36. *Ibid.*, p. 153.

37. Suzuki Hisashi, "Hatamoto Ryō no Kōzō" ("The Structure of a Hatamoto Fief") *Rekishigaku Kenkyū*, CCVIII (1957), 14.

38. Jingū Shichō, XVII, 152.

39. *Ibid.*, p. 153.

40. Tottori Archives, Tottori Hanshi Kōhon, Shokuseishi, Gakkan ("Manuscripts of Tottori *Han* History, Essay on Offices, The School").

41. Taniguchi Sumio, "Han Kashindan no Keisei to Kōzō," ("The Formation and Structure of a *Han* Corps of Housemen"), *Shigaku Zasshi*, LXVI (1956), 607.

42. Ikeda Archives, Samurai Chō ("Roster of Samurai") (Tempo 9).

43. Jingū Shichō, XVII, 147.

44. Okayama Shiyakusho, *Okayama Shishi* ("History of Okayama City") (Okayama, 1938), p. 3771.

45. Ogawa Wataru, *Aizu Han Kyōiku Kō* ("A Study of Education in Aizu Han") (Tokyo, 1941), pp. 506–9.

46. Nagayama Usaburō, *Okayama Ken Tsūshi* ("History of Okayama Prefecture") (Tokyo, 1930), p. 824.

47. Yamaguchi Saijō, "Ieyasu to Jugaku," ("Ieyasu and Confucianism"), in *Kinsei Nihon no Jugaku*, p. 28.

48. Ogawa, pp. 57, 60.

49. Saitō Tokutarō, *Nijūroku Daihan to Shifū* ("Martial Spirit in Twenty-six Large *Han*") (Tokyo, 1944), pp. 651 ff.)

50. Matsudaira Sadamitsu, "Matsudaira Sadanobu wo Chūshin to Suru Shokō no Kyōyō" ("Cultural Activities of the Daimyo Centered on Matsudaira Sadanobu"), in *Kinsei Nihon no Jugaku*, p. 155.

51. Ikeda Archives, Zoku Ikeda-ke Rireki Ryakki ("Abridged History of the Ikeda Family, Continued"), *kan* 4.

52. Arai Hakuseki, *Hyōchū Oritaku Shiba no Ki* ("Autobiography Annotated") (Tokyo, 1881), p. 57.

53. Ogawa, pp. 117–18.

54. Saitō, pp. 124–25.

55. Fushimi Takeji, *Sōgō Nihon Kyōiku Shi* ("Complete History of Japanese Education") (Tokyo, 1951), p. 230.

56. Kondō Masaharu, "Shōdō to Shōheizaka Gakumonjo" ("The Shōdō and the Shōheizaka School"), in *Kinsei Nihon no Jugaku*, pp. 210–13.

57. Ishikawa Ken, *Nihon Shomin Kyōikushi* ("History of Popular Education in Japan") (Tokyo, 1929), pp. 120–21.

58. Ishikawa Ken, "Okayama Han Gakkō" ("The Okayama *Han* School"), in *Kyōikugaku Jiten* (Tokyo, 1938), p. 146.

59. Shizutani Chūgakkō, *Shizutani Tokuhon* ("A Shizutani Reader") (Okayama, 1938), Appendix, p. 1.

60. Ishikawa, "Okayama Han Gakkō," p. 146.

61. W. E. Griffis, *The Mikado's Empire* (New York, 1906), II, 431; Saitō, p. 58.

62. Nagayama, pp. 824–25.

63. Ishikawa, *Nihon Shomin Kyōikushi*, pp. 174–75, 216–20.

64. *Kyōikugaku Jiten*, p. 1678.

65. Ikeda Archives, Samurai Chō; Ogawa, pp. 335–41; Nagayama, pp. 824; Jingū Shichō, XVII, 172–80.

66. For instance, Takebayashi Kan'ichi, *Kangakusha Denki Shūsei* ("Collected Biographies of Kangakusha") (Tokyo, 1904).

67. Tōkyō Teikoku Daigaku Shiryō Hensanjo, *Tokushi Biyō* ("Handbook of History") (Tokyo, 1933), pp. 1037–41.

68. Itō Tasaburō, "Haibutsu Kishaku no Shakaishiteki Kōsatsu" ("A Socio-historical Study of the Anti-Buddhist Movement"), *Shakai Keizaishigaku*, II (1933), 1142.

69. Ikeda Archives, On Tazune no Shinajina Kakiage ("A Report on Sundry Questions") (Meiwa 1); Shimmi Yoshiharu, *Kakyū Shizokū no Kenkyū* (Tokyo, 1953), pp. 290–305.

70. Mizuno, pp. 77–83.

71. Ikeda Archives, Biyōki ("History of Bizen"), Hōei 6.15.

72. Ono, II; Ikeda Archives, Nenchū Gyōji ("Yearly Ceremonial"), Kaei 4.

73. Sendai Shishi Hensan Iinkai, *Sendai no Rekishi* ("History of Sendai") (Sendai, 1949), pp. 75–78.

74. *Ibid.*, p. 75.

75. Nagata Hiroshi, *Nihon Hōkensei Ideorogi* ("The Ideology of Feudal Japan") (Tokyo, 1947), pp. 258–60.

76. Okayama Shiyakushō, p. 3663.

77. *Ibid.*, p. 3472.

78. J. W. Hall, *Tanuma Okitsugu* (Cambridge, Mass., 1954), pp. 34 ff; W. G. Beasley, "Councillors of Samurai Origin in the Early Meiji Government, 1868–69," *Bulletin of the School of Oriental and African Studies*, XX (1957), 89–103.

79. Kumazaki Wataru, *Sengoku Jidai no Buke Hōsei* ("Laws of the Military Houses of the Sengoku Period") (Tokyo, 1944), pp. 3–27.

80. Shibunkai, *Nihon Jugaku Nempyō* (Chronology of Japanese Confucianism") (Tokyo, 1921), p. 267.

81. Shihō Chō, *Tokugawa Kinrei kō* ("Tokugawa Prohibitions and Ordinances") (Tokyo, 1931), pp. 90–104.

82. *Ibid.*, pp. 104–7.

83. Translated in *Sources of the Japanese Tradition*, p. 337.

84. R. J. Kirby, "Translation of Dazai Jun's Essay on Gakusei," *Transactions of the Asiatic Society of Japan*, XXXIV (1907), 136–38.

85. Shihō Chō, pp. 92–95.

86. *Ibid.*, p. 96.

87. *Ibid.*, p. 103.

88. Ariga Kizaemon, "On the Relationship between Loyalty and Filial Piety in Japan" (Paper prepared for the Fourth Conference on Chinese Thought, 1958); Tsuda Sōkichi, *Shina Shisō to Nihon* ("Chinese Thought and Japan") (Tokyo, 1938), pp. 83–86.

89. Sakurai Shōtarō, *Nihon Hōken Shakai Ishiki Ron* ("A Study of Japanese Feudal Thought") (Tokyo, 1949).

90. Nomura Kanetarō, *Tokugawa Jidai no Keizai Shisō* ("Economic Thought of the Tokugawa Period") (Tokyo, 1939) pp. 106–30.

91. Umetani Noboru, "Bakumatsu Nihon Kindaika no Seishinteki Kiso ni Tsuite" ("On the Ideological Base for Modernization in Late Tokugawa Japan") *Zimbun Gakuho*, I (1950), 147–72.

92. Morohashi Tetsuji, "Kansei Igaku no Kin," ("On the Prohibition of Heresies of the Kansei Era"), in *Kinsei Nihon no Jugaku*, pp. 157–78.

93. Saitō, p. 306.

94. Kondō, pp. 208–14.

95. Jingū Shichō, XVII, 154–55.

96. Ogawa, p. 119.

97. Nagayama, p. 824.

98. Saitō, pp. 81–82.

99. Ogawa, pp. 400–409.

100. Griffis, pp. 433–34.

101. Fushimi, p. 235; Jingū Shichō, XVII, 161.

102. Fushimi, p. 236.

103. Watanabe Minoru, "Kinsei Shohan ni Okeru Yūgaku" ("The Practice of Extra-*Han* Education in the Early Modern Period"), *Nippon Rekishi*, LIV (1952), 2–8.

104. Saitō, p. 176.

105. G. B. Sansom, *The Western World and Japan*, pp. 248–78; *Sources of the Japanese Tradition*, pp. 552–77, 603–37.

106. Griffis, pp. 431–32.

107. Kokumin Seishin Bunka Kenkyūjo, *Nihon Kyōikushi Shiryōsho* ("Documents on the History of Japanese Education") (Tokyo, 1937), Document 2138.

NOTES TO MOTODA EIFU

I should like to acknowledge the extensive assistance contributed by Mrs. Helen Craig McCullough in the preparation of the materials on which the paper is based. I am indebted to Professors Kaigo Tokiomi and Watanabe Ikujirō and to many other Japanese scholars for discussions as well as materials which were helpful in this study. I should also like to thank members of the Committee on Chinese Thought for their suggestions, and in particular W. T. de Bary for a number of observations which contributed to the last part of the paper.

Abbreviations

Kaigo: Kaigo Tokiomi, *Motoda Nagazane* (Tokyo, 1942). Nagazane is an alternative reading for Eifu.

"Kanreki": "Kanreki no Ki" ("Record of Sixty Years"), ms., Motoda family (see note 1).

"Koki": "Koki no Ki" (Record of the Seventieth Year"), ms., Motoda family (see note 1).

Tokutomi: Tokutomi Iichirō, *Motoda Sensei Shinkō Roku* ("Record of Lectures Delivered to the Emperor by Motoda") (Tokyo, 1910).

Watanabe 1931: Watanabe Ikujirō, *Kyōiku Chokugo no Hongi to Kampatsu no Yurai* ("The Fundamental Meaning of the Imperial Rescript on Education and the History of Its Promulgation") (Tokyo, 1931).

Watanabe 1936: Watanabe Ikujirō, *Meiji Tennō to Hohitsu no Hitobito* ("The Meiji Emperor and His Assistants") (Tokyo, 1936).

Watanabe 1937: Watanabe Ikujirō, *Nihon Kempō Seitei Shikō* ("Historical Study of the Making of the Japanese Constitution") (Tokyo, 1937).

Watanabe 1941: Watanabe Ikujirō, *Meiji Tennō no Seitoku* ("The Sacred Virtue of the Meiji Emperor") (6 vols.; Tokyo, 1941).

Zuroku: *Kyōiku ni Kansuru Chokugo Kampatsu Gojūnen Kinen Shiryō Tenran Zuroku* ("Illustrated Catalog of an Exhibit of Materials in Commemoration of the Fiftieth Anniversary of the Promulgation of the Imperial Rescript on Education") (3 vols.; Tokyo, 1941).

1. The "autobiography," which exists in manuscript in the possession of the Motoda family, is in two parts: "Kanreki no Ki" ("Record of Sixty Years"), which covers until June 1877 and is dated February 12, 1889, and "Koki no Ki" ("Record of the Seventieth Year"), which was begun on December 3, 1889. The only biography is that by Kaigo, which deals with Motoda in the field of education. Motoda's important papers on educational matters have been published in Kaigo and *Zuroku* and in *Kyōiku Chokugo Kampatsu Kankei Shiryō Shū* ("Collection of Materials Pertaining to the Promulgation of the Imperial Rescript on Education") (3 vols.; Tokyo, 1940). Ten of his lectures to the Emperor on the *Analects,* probably all delivered in 1878, are published in Tokutomi. Most of his correspondence and papers pertaining to political matters are still in manuscript in the possession of the Motoda family, in the Kensei Shiryō Shitsu ("Archives on Constitutional Government") in the Diet Building, Tokyo, and in certain other private and official collections of materials on early Meiji political and Court history. There is a study in English by N. Asaji and Rev. J. C. Pringle, "Lectures Delivered in the Pres-

ence of His Imperial Majesty the Emperor of Japan by the Late Baron Motoda," *Transactions of the Asiatic Society of Japan,* XL (1912), 45–113, which contains numerous errors in data and in translation.

2. A Court history of the Meiji reign has been compiled by the Imperial Household Ministry, but it is not available for use by the public, nor are many of the materials on which it was based. There are indications in Motoda's writings and elsewhere to the effect that the Emperor as a young man was unconcerned with matters of state and given to frivolity.

3. Kōsaka Masaaki, *Shisō Genron Hen,* in *Meiji Bunka Shi,* IV (Tokyo, 1955), p. 41, quoting *Yokoi Shōnan Ikō,* pp. 899, 932, a source unavailable to me.

4. The essential biographical material on Motoda's early life is summarized in Kaigo, pp. 10–25.

5. Kaigo, p. 19. *Seidan* is a critique by Ogyū Sorai (1666–1728) of the political and economic problems of his day with suggestions to the shogun for their solution. *Kenroku* is his handbook on military administration and strategy. *Shūgi Washo* and *Shūgi Gaisho* are instructional books by Kumazawa Banzan on many aspects of Japanese and Chinese knowledge. *(Sung) Mingch'en Yen-hsing Lu,* a compilation of biographies of eminent Sung officials begun by Chu Hsi and completed by Li Yu-wu, was used as a textbook by the Yamazaki and Mito schools.

6. Motoda follows the account in the *Kojiki* (712?), which says that the King of Kudara sent Wani to Japan with the *Analects* and the *Thousand Character Classic* as tribute, by the traditional chronology in 285. This date is usually corrected by two sexagenary cycles to 405. The more reliable *Nihon Shoki* (720) does not give the titles of the books Wani brought. The present text of the *Thousand Character Classic* was not compiled before the sixth century.

7. Quoted in Kaigo, pp. 168–71.

8. Watanabe 1931, pp. 88–99; "Kanreki," pp. 229b, 297b, 271b–272a.

9. "Kanreki," pp. 273a–b.

10. "Koki," pp. 83a–84b, 2b; "Kanreki," pp. 297b–298a; Watanabe 1936, p. 194. Texts in Tokutomi.

11. "Igaku no Yō" ("The Essentials of the Pursuit of Learning") (25th day, 9th month, 1871), in Kaigo, p. 172.

12. *Ibid.,* pp. 172–73.

13. "Kyōgaku Taii Shigi" ("Personal Opinion on the Greater Meaning of Education") (10th month, 1870), in Kaigo, pp. 189–96, especially pp. 193, 189.

14. Tokutomi (Lecture 1), pp. 2–3. In the same lecture he quoted Kumazawa Banzan as saying in *Daigaku Wakumon* that the *Doctrine of the Mean* is a commentary on the sacred regalia.

15. "Kyōgaku Taii Shigi," in Kaigo, pp. 190–91.

16. "Kyōiku-gi Fugi" ("Another Opinion on 'An Opinion on Education'") (1879), in *Zuroku,* p. 92b.

17. "Kyōgaku Taii Shigi," in Kaigo, p. 191.

18. Tokutomi (Lecture 6), p. 92.

19. "Kyōgaku Taii Shigi," in Kaigo, pp. 191–92.

20. Tokutomi (Lecture 6), p. 90.

21. Tokutomi (Lecture 1), pp. 7–8.

22. Tokutomi (Lecture 10), pp. 123–26.

23. "Iwakura Udaijin e Jōsho. Kuntoku Hodō no Yō" ("Memorial to Minister of the Right Iwakura: Essentials for the Guidance of the Sovereign's Virtue") (September 1873), in Tokutomi, pp. xx–xxvi. Concerning a similar petition on the same subject which Motoda submitted to Iwakura the next year, Motoda records that Iwakura said to Yasuba: "Since the Restoration, I have seen a great many petitions submitted by persons within and outside the government, but never yet such a petition as this. His loyalty and sincerity are truly admirable. Even the composition is beautiful. Having respectfully received this [proposal], we must put it into practice at once." "Kanreki," pp. 261b–262a.

24. Tokutomi (Lecture 1), pp. 12–13. The Emperors Jimmu to Nintoku antedate the earliest Japanese written records. Their deeds are described in the *Kojiki* and *Nihon Shoki*; and in the latter text in particular, the account is embellished with long passages cribbed from the Chinese classics and histories. We may assume that the Japanese emperors' exploits as well as the verbiage were imported, and are therefore indeed Confucian.

25. "Jikō Sōtō" ("A Lecturer's Report to the Throne") (ca. 1874), in Kaigo, p. 152; "Kanreki," pp. 276a–277a. If the date of this document is 1874, as internal evidence indicates, Saigō Takamori had recently resigned from the government and was sulking in Satsuma.

26. Tokutomi (Lecture 1), pp. 5–6.

27. Watanabe 1936, pp. 151–53, 156–62; "Kanreki," pp. 281b–282b, 283b–284b.

28. "Koki," pp. 40a–42b; Watanabe 1936, pp. 172–73; "Kanreki," p. 303b.

29. Watanabe 1936, pp. 175–79.

30. Watanabe 1936, pp. 184–85.

31. Watanabe 1937, p. 179.

32. "Koki," p. 64b.

33. "Koki," pp. 45b–46a; see also pp. 8b, 32b, 34a, 39b, 42b.

34. The text Motoda used was *Ri Hakugi Chūgi Hen* ("Li Kang's Writings on Loyalty") (publ. 1809), a selection made by Tsukada Ko from Li Kang (Po-i), probably his *Li Chung-ting Chi* ("Collected Works of Li Kang"). Motoda's document does not have a title, and is unpublished.

35. James Legge, *The Chinese Classics* (Hongkong, 1861–72), III, 158.

36. Legge, II, 147.

37. Kaigo, pp. 124–25.

38. Legge, I, 140.

39. Legge, III, 41.

40. I have not been able to identify the source of this saying.

41. *Shih-chi* (K'ai-ming ed.), I, 0036d.

42. "Meiji Jūninen Rikkensei Kakuritsu ni Kansuru Motoda Nagazane Jōso" ("Memorial to the Throne by Motoda Nagazane in 1879 Pertaining to the Establishment of Constitutional Government") (June 1879), ms. in Kensei Shiryō Shitsu. An abridged version appears in Miyakoshi Shin'ichirō, ed., *Nihon Kensei Kiso Shiryō* (Tokyo: Gikai Seiji Sha, 1939), pp. 259–65.

43. A saying found in Chinese and Japanese literature, e.g., *Shih-chi*, I, 0029b.

44. "Rikken Seiji ni Kansuru Kaku Sangi no Kengi ni Tsuki Gokamon Hōtō (Meiji Jūyonen)" ("Reply to the Emperor's Inquiry Concerning the Pro-

posals of the Various Councillors Pertaining to Constitutional Government [1881]") (June 1881), ms. in Kensei Shiryō Shitsu.

45. Ms. cited in note 42.

46. "Koki," pp. 21a–22a. His comments are set down in the ms. cited in note 44.

47. Eight hundred nobles met at Meng-chin to join Wu Wang when he overthrew the Shang and established the Chou dynasty (*Shih-chi*, I, 0012b), but rather than serve under the usurper, Po-i and Shu-ch'i wandered in the mountains and died of hunger; according to the *Analects* "the people, down to the present time, praise them" (Legge, I, 315, 181).

48. Li Kang (1085–1140) and Chao Ting (d. 1147) advocated a policy of military resistance to the Chin Tartars, but the Emporers Hui-tsung and Ch'in-tsung, who ceded territory and attempted to negotiate with the Chin, were both carried into captivity in 1126.

49. Motoda's marginal annotation on the ms. cited in note 42.

50. Of the several variant drafts, I quote the ms. in Kensei Shiryō Shitsu dated September 1880. The identical text, undated, is in *Zuroku*, pp. 32b–33b, and Kaigo, pp. 145–46.

51. Article 1. The Empire of Japan shall be reigned over and governed by a line of Emperors unbroken for ages eternal. Article 3. The Emperor is sacred and inviolable. (Official translation.)

52. "Kyōiku-gi Fugi," in *Zuroku*, p. 92.

53. "Kokkyō-ron" ("Discussion of the National Teaching") (June 14, 1884), in *Zuroku*, pp. 96b–98a.

54. Tokutomi (Lecture 6), pp. 93–94.

55. "Kyōgaku Taishi" in *Zuroku*, p. 4a.

56. "Kyōiku-gi" (September 1879), in *Zuroku*, pp. 89a–91a.

57. "Koki," pp. 19b–20b.

58. Quoted from *Fukuzawa Zensho* in Watanabe 1931, p. 209. Fukuzawa wrote in *Jiji Shimpō* of January 18, 1883: "From what we hear, the current effort to chart a new moral course based on a resuscitation of the precepts of the Duke of Chou and Confucius is due to the belief that, in the one field of morals and conduct, China occupies a unique position. The flower *par excellence* is that of the cherry tree, the Way is that of the Confucianist, and virtue stops at the pigtail. It is incredible that there is this effort, this utterly unreasonable effort, to create a monopoly in the one field of morals." Quoted in Watanabe 1931, p. 210.

59. "Seiyuki" ("Record of Sacred Instructions") (November 5, 1886), in Kaigo, p. 187.

60. Text in Kaigo, pp. 185–88, especially p. 187.

61. Watanabe 1931, p. 252. The reference is presumably to the "Sacred Edict" issued by K'ang-hsi and elaborated by Yung-cheng. See F. W. Baller, *The Sacred Edict* (Shanghai: American Presbyterian Mission Press, 2d ed., 1907).

62. The name Meirin'in ("Clarifying Ethics Institute") reflects the terms *meirindō* and *meirinkan*, used as names of Confucian schools during the Edo period. In China *ming-lun-t'ang* (*meirindō*) was the hall of a school in which Confucius was honored.

63. Watanabe 1931, p. 253.

64. On the process of drafting the Rescript, see Watanabe 1931, pp. 257–88, and Kaigo, pp. 87–96.

Index

No attempt has been made to include Chinese characters for names found in Arthur W. Hummel, ed., *Eminent Chinese of the Ch'ing Period* (Washington, 1943–44).

Abei Hitoshi, 279

Administration, 181; Chinese writings on, 144, 148; finance, 146; Han Dynasty, 170, 171, 178; Manchu, 349; Ming, extensive eunuch interference in, 203; moral consideration in, 152; situational consideration in, 155; Sung Dynasty, 179; T'ang Dynasty, 171

Administrative behavior, ideal model for, 139

Administrative procedures, Ming Dynasty, 205, 206

Administrative system, importance of the territorial unit in, 163

Adoption, 347

Aides (*li 吏*), 135, 136, 140, 142, 149, 150, 154, 155, 158, 161–63, 216, 217; *see also* Bureaucracy

Aizawa Seishisai 會澤正志齋 (1782–1863), 47, 48

Aizu domain, 279; emphasis on military training in, 297; school system of, 296

Akamatsu, Lord, of Harima, 270

Akō, Lord of, 31

A-kuei (1717–97): opposed Ho-shen, 233; tension between Ho-shen and, in the Grand Council, 239

An Lu-shan, Rebellion of, 101

Analects (*Lun-yü*), 36, 52, 54, 55, 58, 68, 306, 310, 312, 313, 316, 321, 336, 356, 357, 370, 371, 373

Ancestral hall, 79, 80

Arai Hakuseki (1657–1725), 40, 280, 282; annotated autobiography of, 368; his critical version of Japanese history, 43

Ariga Kizaemon, 369

Armstrong, R. C., 366

Asaji, N., 370

Asaka Kaku 安積覺 , 367

Asakawa Kanichi, 366

Balazs, Etienne, 354, 355

Bamba Masatomo 萬羽正朋 , 366

Bansei ikkei 萬世一系 , 266

Baynes, Norman H., 364

Beasley, W. G., 369

Biot, Edouard, 359

Bizen, 278; Daimyo of, 275, 276; educational administration in, 296; Neo-Confucianism in, 271

Blau, Peter M., 351, 352

Bodde, Derk, 356

Bodhisattva ideal, in Neo-Confucianism, 33, 34

Book of History (*Shu-ching*), 310, 316, 321, 322, 324

Boxer movement, 246

Buddhism, China: decline of, 270; imperial patronage of, 252; influence on clan rules, 67; influence on trade and capital formation, 362; use in state ideology, 184

Buddhism, Japan: decline of, 269; institutions of, 284, 287; official policies, 288, 289

Buddhism, and Neo-Confucianism, 33, 34, 38, 44, 45, 46, 252, 270, 273, 289

Buke Shohatto 武家諸法度 , 293, 294

Bureaucracy, 134

Bureaucracy, China, 113, 114, 159, 166, 246, 253; Ch'ing Dynasty, 209; Ch'ing Dynasty, review system, 145; classification of officials, 165, 166, 167, 168, 176, 177, 178; codes, 147; conservatism of, 247; corruption in, 11, 21, 23, 77, 116, 150, 156–63, 175, 178–80, 192, 206, 207, 209–18, 232–43, 253; efficiency in, 144; factionalism, 167, 168, 219, 220, 221, 222, 232; factionalism, Ming Dynasty, 223, 224; functional structure, 141, 142, 157; generalist orientation of, 16, 17, 139–42, 145; goals, 155, 156; influence of primary-group orientation on, 150; lower echelon of, 160, 161; Ming Dynasty, 207; Ming Dynasty, indoctrination of, 18; moral standards, 166, 167; newcomers in, 143, 144; policy-making functions, 143; political apathy in, 167; promotion system in, 160; in the social system, 134, 135, 136; the specialist's role, 138, 141, 145; specialization in, 137, 163; training for, 142, 143, 145, 167; *see also* Aides, County magistrates

Bureaucracy, Japan, 292

Bureaucratic behavior, 156, 157, 162, 163

Bureaucratic ideology, 18, 147, 180, 186

Bushi, 269, 274; *see also* Samurai

Bushidō, 38, 39, 274; Yamaga's system of, 46

Censorate: and Confucianism, 189; functions of, 187, 188, 189, 190, 191; Han Dynasty, 355; ideology of, 207; Ming Dynasty, 15, 16, 187, 190, 191, 192, 200; origins of, 187, 188, 189

Ch'a-kuan 察官 ("Surveillance officials"), 187

Chan, David, 362

Chang, Carsun, 364

Chang Chien 張謇, 263

Chang Ch'in 張欽 (16th century), 200

Chang Chü-cheng 張居正, denounced by censors, 192, 193

Chang-chuang 長莊, 115

Chang Fang-p'ing 張方平 (1007–91), 169

Chang Hsüeh-ch'eng (1738–1801): on the deterioration of the civil service, 215, 216; on factionalism, 232

Chang Hsün 張勳, 365

Chang-kuan jen 掌管人, 106, 107

Chang Po-hsing, 344

Chang-shih I-shu 章氏遺書, 359

Chang T'ing-yü (1672–1755), 228–29, 230

Chang Tsai 張載, 64, 337, 338

Ch'ang-chu t'ien 常住田, 102, 104

Chao-lien (1780–1833), on Ho-shen, 212, 213

Chao Ting (d. 1147), 325, 373

Charitable estates (*i-chuang*), 10, 19, 69, 82, 93; administrative rules of, 129; Buddhist origin of, 102, 103; buildings of, 113; exemption from taxation, 123, 127, 128, 345; external business of, 113; of Fan Chung-yen, imitations of, 110; financial position of, 119, 120, 122, 123; functions of, 113; "gentry" and, 133; in improving social customs, 119; as legal institutions, 109; in maintaining the position of the clans, 110, 111; in maintaining social homogeneity, 133; management of, 83, 102, 125, 126, 128; in Northern Sung, 109; official recognition in Ch'ing period, 345; the original model of, 102; preferential treatment of, 127; prevalence of, 131; role of, in shaping Chinese traditional society, 133; size and number of, 82, 83; in Southern Sung, 109; in Yüan times, 109; *see also* Fan charitable estate

Charitable land (*i-t'ien*), 82

Charitable schools (*i-hsüeh*), 81, 122, 130, 131

Charter Oath of 1868, 302, 324

Che Yü Pien-lan 折獄便覽, 351

Chen-kuan Cheng-yao 貞觀政要, 309

Ch'en 臣 ("minister," "servitor," etc.), 14, 245, 261, 262, 263, 264

Ch'en Hung-mou (1696–1771), 71, 136, 338, 351, 352, 353; on administration, 144; on the county magistrate, 139, 140

Ch'en Jen-hsi 陳仁錫 (1580–1636), 174, 355

Ch'en Liang 陳亮 (1143–94), 255

Ch'en Shao-pai, contemporary writer, 365

Cheng 政 ("government"), 55, 257

Cheng Ch'iao 鄭樵 (1104–60), historical writing of, 42

Cheng Ho 鄭和, the voyage of, 252

Cheng-i T'ang Ch'üan-shu 正誼堂全書, 344

Cheng-shih Lun-tsan 正史論贊, 353

Cheng-shu 政書, 166

Cheng-t'i 政體, 267

Ch'eng, Prince, 241

Ch'eng-Chu school, 39; commentaries of 36; in Japan, 331; rationalism in, 41, 44; reactions to rationalism of, 44, 45; rejected by Ogyū Sorai, 46; in Southern Sung, 33; teachings of, 39, 40, 308, 309; *see also* Neo-Confucianism

Ch'eng Hao (1032–85), 338, 364; on the five social relationships, 257; on loyalty, 254

Ch'eng I (1033–1107), 12, 64, 65, 169, 338; on literati dominance over the emperor, 230, 231

Chi-shih-chung 給事中 ("supervising secretary"), 188

Chi-t'ien 祭田 ("ritual land"), 111

Chia-ch'ing Emperor (reigned 1796–1820), 239; against Ho-shen, 209, 211, 241

"Chia-fan-tien" 家範典, 70

Chia I 賈誼, 68

Chia I 家儀, 69

Chiang Fan (1761–1831), 45

Chiang Kai-shek, the government of, 261

Chiao 教 ("instructions," "doctrine"), 9, 141

Chiao Hsün (1763–1820), on Ho-shen, 212

Chiao Nü I-kuei 教女遺規, 71

Chien-ch'en 諫臣 ("remonstrance official"), 177, 220

Chien-ch'en 奸臣 or 姦臣 ("treacherous official"), 177

Chien-i ta-fu 諫議大夫 ("grand remonstrant"), 188

Ch'ien Feng (1740–95), 233, 234; censorial attack on Ho-shen, 238, 239

Ch'ien Han Shu, 170, 354

Ch'ien I-chi (1783–1850), 358, 360

Ch'ien Kung-fu 錢公輔 (1023–74), 101, 109, 114

Ch'ien-lung Emperor (reigned 1736–96), 70, 74, 209, 228; anti-superstition edict of, 92; attitudes and anxieties of, 235, 236, 243; and factionalism, 224, 228, 229, 230, 236; literary inquisition, 29, 175; on the literati, 223, 230, 231; on powerful clans, 76

Ch'ien Mu 錢穆, 354, 360

Ch'ien Tsai (1708–93), 224, 233

Chih Chia Ke-yen 治家格言 ("motto on family discipline"), 69

Chih-kuo p'ing t'ien-hsia 治國平天下 ("ordering the state and pacifying the world"), 52

Chin-ssu Lu 近思錄, 337

Ch'in-pan Chou Hsien Shih-i 欽頒州縣事宜, 136, 144, 351, 352, 353

Ch'in-ting Hsüeh-cheng Ch'üan-shu 欽定學政全書, 227, 358, 360

Ch'in-ting Li-pu Ch'u-fen Tse-li 欽定吏部處分則例, 351, 353

Ch'in-tsung, Emperor (reigned 1126), 325, 373

Ching-hsüeh Li K'u 經學理窟, 337

Ching-shih Pa-pien Lei-chuan 經世八編類纂, 174–78, 355

Ching-t'ien 井田, pattern of land tenure, 6

Ching-yen kuan 經筵官, an official who instructs the emperor in the classics, 231

Ch'ing Dynasty (1644–1911), Japanese revival of, in Manchuria, 266; *see also* Manchus

Ch'ing-shih Chi-shih Pen-mo, 358, 359, 360

Ch'ing Shih Kao, 360

Ch'ing Shih-lu, 350

Ch'ing-tai hsüeh-shu kai-lun 清代學術概論, 35

Ch'ing-tai T'ung-shih 清代通史, 358

Chiu T'ang Shu, 344

Ch'oe Pu 崔溥, Korean traveler, 15th century, 38

Chōshū: the domain college in, 297; Neo-Confucian studies in, 271

Chou Chen-fu, contemporary scholar, 361

Chou Hsien Hsü-chih 州縣須知, 351, 352, 353

Chou-li, 68

Chou period, the idealized social order of, 54, 55, 57, 269

Chou Tun-i (1017–73), 53, 338

Chū 忠 ("loyalty"), 294

Chu-chi 主計 ("auditor"), 122

Chu Chih-yü 朱之瑜, 276

Chu-feng 主奉, the ritual head of a clan, 121

Chu Hsi (1130–1200), 57, 64, 69, 70, 194, 230, 316, 331, 337, 338, 346, 354, 371; and *chi-t'ien,* 111; commentary of, on the "Great Learning," 279; condemned as "fame-seeker," 21, 23; on education, 81; on the emperor, 20, 21; and his enemies, 60; the ethical ideas of, 18; on Fan Chung-yen, 173; historical writings of, 42; on idealistic Confucian thought, 18; as interpreter of the Confucian Classics, 28, 29; and Japanese Confucianists, 270, 271, 272; on knowledge and action, 61; on Lü I-chien, 173; the metaphysics of, 41, 45; in the Ming period, 20; on the moral qualities of officials, 173; the objective learning of, 41; on the ordering of society, 60; and Ouyang Hsiu compared, 21; on partisan behavior, 20, 21; the philosophy of, 32; the philosophy of, rejection by Ogyū Sorai, 31; the philosophy of, in Tokugawa period, 30; political conservatism of, 173–74; on principles of reality, 59; on ritual and ceremony, 37; on self-cultivation, 255; and the Tung-lin school, 44; and Wang An-shih, 57, 173

Chu Hsi school of thought, 59, 305, 312

Chu Kuei (1731–1807), 359; as Chia-ch'ing Emperor's fellow poet, 240, 242; the demotion of, 242

Chu Tung-jun 朱東潤, 356

Chu Tzu Chia-li 朱子家禮, 37, 38, 69, 70; *see also* Wen-kung Chia-li

Chu-tzu Tseng-sun Lü shih Hsiang-yüeh 朱子增損呂氏鄉約, 69, 70

Chu-tzu Yü-lei 朱子語類, 354

Chu Yüan-chang 朱元璋, 357, *see also* Ming T'ai-tsu

Chu Yüeh 朱說, 99; *see also* Fan Chung-yen

Chu Yung-ch'un 朱用純 (Chu Po-lu 朱柏廬), 69

Chuang-t'ien 莊田 ("villa"), 363

Chuang-yüan 莊園 ("estate"), 102

Chung 忠, the Confucian concept of loyalty, 254; *see also Chū*

Ch'un-ch'iu, 262

Ch'un-ch'iu Fan-lu 春秋繁露 , 361

Ch'un-tsai-t'ang Ch'üan-shu 春在堂全書 , 345

Chün 君 ("prince," "ruler"), 261, 264

Chün-t'ien 均田 , land equalization, 102

Chün-tzu 君子 ("superior man"), 35, 39, 45, 52, 53, 54, 221, 274; moral leadership of, 166; self-cultivation of, 60

Ch'u Tui-chih 瞿兌之 , 351, 353

Civil service: Ch'ing, deterioration of, 209, 215–16; early Sung, 355; rating system, Ch'ing, 180; rating system, Confucian orientation, 179; rating system, in Southern Sung, 179; rating system, in the Yüan period, 179; regulations, 178, 179, 180; *see also* Bureaucracy

Clan (*Tsu* 族): absurd conceptions of, 131, 132; class differentiation in, 88, 89; a Moslem, 66; mutual responsibility in, 132

Clan cohesion, attitudes detrimental to, 89

Clan community, obligations to, 131

Clan-consciousness, 133

Clan institutions, proliferation of, 131

Clan organizations: changes in, 131; contribution of, to stability, 132; economic barriers of, 83; in Kiangsi and Kwangtung, 75; revival and strengthening of, 10

Clan prestige, 81

Clan relationships, 88

Clan rules: ambivalence of, to Buddhist and Taoist practices, 91; anti-political nature of, 76; on brotherly love, 85, 86; Buddhist sayings in, 71; Confucian interpretation of Buddhist concepts in, 72; Confucian values in, 70; folk-religion element in, 67; on geomancy, 92; Han writings cited in, 68, 69; influence of, 94, 95; legal basis of, 67; in Manchuria, 80; on marriage, 87; Neo-Confucian values in, 70; on parent-children relationships, 84; on personality and character, 90, 94–95; pre-Han writings cited in, 68; on promotion of education, 81, 82; on the role of the wife, 87, 88; and social customs, 93; unwritten, 80; value scheme of, 90

Clan stability, and individual family stability, 131

Clan system, Sung, 100

Clans: disintegration of, 130; feuds between, 74; as organs of social control, 11; of the T'ang period, 65

Confucian, abuse of the word, v, vi, 3, 25, 26

Confucian classics, 283, 302, 312; in civil service examinations, 28, 29; for instruction in official schools, 28

Confucianism: and anti-professionalism, 262; and art, v; authoritarian character of, 27, 30, 197; and Buddhism, 42, 44, 45, 46, 51, 252; Ch'ing Dynasty, 26, 27, 48, 247; classical, 183, 185; classical doctrines on state administration, 183, 184; conflicting moral and political implications in, 228; decline of, 42, 247, 249, 267, 302, 313; and familism, 49, 98; and feudalism, 254; and feudalism in Japan, 274; future of, 49; Han Dynasty, 3, 4, 5, 39, 69, 184; and historical writing, v, 42, 173, 285; humanism of, 186, 250; humanistic amateurism in, 262; in Korea, ascendency of, 270; and law, 185; and Legalism, 17; and literature, v; model-emperor lore, 13, 14, 254; and models, 43; and monarchy, 22, 28, 181, 184, 232, 252, 254, 258, 260; and monarchy in Japan, 317; mythology of, 259, 267, 363; as a national religion, 48, 249, 250; under new dynasties, 256; rationalistic strain, 40, 41, 42, 44, 252; "restorationism," 36, 37; "revivalism," 336; "revivalism" in Japan, 46; and revolution, 247; and "rigorist" officials, 186; and Shinto, 37, 41, 47, 289, 312; social-political effects of, 37, 249, 250, 268; and Taoism, 39, 44, 46, 51, 252; Yüan Shih-k'ai and, 249, 250; *see also* Neo-Confucianism

—ethics of, 42, 93, 151–55, 163, 164, 177, 311, 333; effect on social stability, 28; filial piety (*hsiao*), 254; filial piety (*hsiao*), in clan rules, 84, 85; filial piety, classic (*Hsiao-ching*), 68, 85, 195, 357; in late Tokugawa Japan, 47; and samurai code, 46

—ideals of: equilibrium, 257; loyalty (*Chung or Chū*), 220, 221; self-cultivation, 8, 9, 19, 20, 52, 53, 262; sociopolitical, 43, 52, 120, 174, 182, 247, 259

—Imperial, 182, 184, 185, 186, 207–8; Ming, 184; philosophical traditions of, 182; Sung, 184

—Japan, 3, 4, 45, 47, 268, 270, 273, 275, 295, 303, 305; and Buddhist monasteries, 270; chronology of, 369; Motoda Eifu, 304, 310–12, 313, 315, 316, 331; and samurai class, 289, 293, 294; temples (Edo Period), 367; Tokugawa patronage of, 276; training centers, Edo, 271; training centers, Kiyoto, 271, 272

Confucius, 51, 207, 311, 313, 314; and classical Confucianism, 183; ethical precepts of, 34, 39; on filial piety, 195; on government, 57; on the ideal order of the early Chou, 55, 58; on learning, 336; and *li*, 55; life of, 52–53; on remonstrance, 194, 195; sacrifices to, 246, 247, 276; as *su-wang* ("uncrowned king"), 256; vision of, 48, 49; the Way of, 58

Corruption, 127, 128; *see also* Bureaucracy

County magistrates (China), 139–40, 161–62; *see also* Bureaucracy

Creel, H. G., 356

Daigaku-no-kami 大學頭 ("Rector of the College"), 277

Daimyo domains, emergence of, 269

Dai-Nihon-shi 大日本史 , 43

Date Tsunamura 伊達綱村 , daimyo of Sendai, 289

de Bary, W. Theodore, 27, 336, 337, 351, 366, 370

Demiéville, Paul, 359

Doctrine of the Mean, 58, 310, 371

Duyvendak, J. J. L., 356, 362

Education: of emperors, 230, 231 (*see also* Motoda Eifu); of Fan Chung-yen in a Buddhist monastery, 103; of Ho-shen, 210; Japan, of commoners, 284; Japan, utilitarian views on, 300; *li* 禮 in Hsün-tzu's philosophy of, 55, 56; *see also* Ideology, *Jusha,* Motoda Eifu, Self-cultivation, Schools, Teachers

—China: clan efforts to promote, 70, 75, 76, 81, 82, 98, 110, 111; Ou-yang Hsiu on ancient education, 6, 7; relation between examinee and examiner, 193–94, 232; training of aides, 155, 162, 216; training of officials, 28, 142–45, 167; of women, 71

Educational system: in China, decree of 1906, 246; in Japan, 283

En 恩 ("Grace," "favor"), 111, 118, 131

Erh Ch'eng Ch'üan-shu 二程全書 , 358

Erh Ch'eng Wen-chi 二程文集 , 364

Erh-ya, 68

Eunuchs: prerogatives of, 256; scorned by Confucianists, 252

Examination system, 246, 254, 282; *see also* Civil service

Factional politics; *see* Bureaucracy, China, factionalism; Ch'ien-lung Emperor, Yung-cheng Emperor; Ou-yang Hsiu

Fairbank, J. K., 25, 26, 335, 366

Famous statesmen, 172, 174; *see also Ming-ch'en*

Fan An-yao, 343

Fan charitable estate, 116, 126, 128; anti-commercial attitude, 105; Buddhist emphasis on charity in, 104; collective responsibility in, 116, 117; confiscation of land of, 124, 348, 349; codification of rules of, 114; destruction of property of, 347; financial state of, 127, 129; official recognition of, 110, 116; and other charitable estates, 132, 133; outside assistance to, 132; pattern of management of, 120–22; privileges of, 128; remission of taxes of, 119; rules of administration of, 104, 105, 106, 110–14, 116, 117; *see also* Charitable estate

Fan Cheng-ch'ing 范正卿 , 103

Fan Ch'eng-hsün (1641–1714), 350

Fan Ch'eng-mo (1624–76), 128, 350

Fan Chi-i 范啟義 , 343

Fan Chih-ju 范之柔 , 116–17, 347

Fan Ch'un-jen; *see* Fan Shun-jen

Fan Chung-yen 范仲淹 (989–1052), 65, 69, 98, 338; biography, 99, 100, 101, 103; and Buddhism, 103; in Chu Hsi's estimation, 173; collected works of, 343; the fame of, in the Ming, 126; on the family as a continuous organism, 100; as leader of the reform party, 19; lineage of, 98, 99; as a model for imitation, 346; *nien-p'u* of, 105; political career of, 118, 344; reform program of, 167; on support to clan, 105; the tomb of, 123

Fan clan: commercial activities of, 125; decline of, 108, 125, 126; genealogy of, 127; legislation of rules in, 110; marriage records of, 125; medical tradition of, 125; migration of, 130; professions of the members of, 129; social status of, 129

Fan Liang-ch'i 范良器 , 115

Fan Liang-sui 范良遂 , 115

Fan Pi-yung, 343

Fan Shih Chia-sheng (Fan Shih Chia-ch'eng) 范氏家乘 , 98, 104, 113, 119, 122, 125, 343–50 *passim*

Fan Shun-jen 范純仁 , 103, 107–12 *passim,* 117–18, 338, 346

Fan Ts'ung-kuei, 348

Fan Wei-yüan, 343

Fan Wen-cheng; *see* Fan Chung-yen

Fan Wen-cheng Kung Wen-chi 范文正公文集 , 344

Fan Wen-ch'eng (1597–1660), 349, 350

Fan Yen-kuei, on good administration, 140

Fan Yüan-li, 348

Fan Yün-lin 范允臨 , 127, 128, 343

Fang Chao-ying, 359

Feng Ch'i 馮琦 , 335

Feng-su T'ung-i 風俗通義 , 69

Fu-ch'ang-an (d. 1817), 214, 239

Fu-k'ang-an (d. 1796), 214

Fu-ku 復古 ("revival of antiquity"), 34, 35, 36; *see also Fukko*

Fu-sung 福松 , 214

Fujii Jintarō, 336

Fujita Tōko (1805–55), 307

Fujita Yūkoku 藤田幽谷 , 367

Fujiwara Seika 藤原惺窩 (1561–1619), 32, 47, 270–73 *passim*

Fukko 復古 ("revival of antiquity"), 36; *see also Fu-ku*

Fukko-gakuha, 36

Fukuba Bisei 福羽美静 (1831–1907), 309, 310

Fukui domain college, 283, 297, 299

Fukuoka domain, 299

Fukuoka Takachika (1835–1919), 328

Fukuzawa Yukichi (1834–1901), 299, 328

Fung Yu-lan, 45, 364

Fushimi Takeji 伏見猛彌 , 368, 369

Gakkō-bugyō 學校奉行 , school commissioner, 296

Gakkō-metsuke-yaku 學校目付役 , school disciplinarian, 296

Gakumonjo 學文所 , name of the Hayashi School, 296

Gale, Esson M., 356, 357

Genealogies: Ch'ing Dynasty, 65, 66; Ming Dynasty, 65; Sung Dynasty, 65

Genro-in ("senate"), 324, 325

Geomancy, Edict of 1735 against, 93

Gernet, Jacques, 362

Giles, H. A., 356

Giri ("duty," "obligation"), 294

Goodnow memorandum, 248

Goyō gakusha 御用學者 ("scholars in service"), 270

Great Learning (*Ta-hsüeh*), 52, 58, 306

Griffis, W. E., 297, 298, 299, 368, 369

Gukanshō, 337

Hall, J. W., 364, 395

Han Fei-tzu, 56, 183, 196, 197, 207, 306, 356, 357

Han-hsüeh shih-ch'eng chi 漢學師承記 , 45

Han Learning: the Chinese, 267; Ch'ing Dynasty school of, 45

Han Wu-ti (140–87 B.C.), 253

Han Yü (768–824), 34, 44; on ethical precepts of Confucius, 34

Hanabatake-kyōba, name of a domain school, 283

Hankō ("domain school"), 282

Hara Nensai, 366

Hara Tomio, 361, 364

Hatamoto ("direct vassals"), 277

Hayashi family, the, 287; Confucian college (Shō-heikō) run by, 30, 32, 43, 47, 271, 276, 284, 296; hereditary position of, 278, 279; ritual functions of, 276; tutoring duties of, 281

Hayashi Razan 林羅山 (1583–1657), 39, 40, 270, 271, 273, 277, 278; and ancient Japanese texts, 292; and Buddhism, 47, 289; and Confucian ceremonies, 276; as Confucianist to the Shogunate, 268; as consultant on policy making, 292; as founder of the official school, 32; as founder of the Tokugawa College, 282; Neo-Confucian belief of, 47; and the samurai code, 281; on Shinto religion, 47; on the social hierarchy, 274; and Ssu-ma Kuang, 43; and Tokugawa legislation, 281; as tutor of Ieyasu's sons, 282

Hayashi Tomoharu, 359

Hijikata Hisamoto (1833–1918), 318

Hirata Atsutane (1776–1843), 31

Hirayama Yoshitada, 273, 366

Historiography: Chinese, classifications of officials in, 354; Chinese, value systems of, 353; Ch'ing Dynasty, 41; Sung Dynasty, 42; traditional, moral didacticism of, 43

Ho Ch'ang-ling (1785–1848), 147

Ho-lin (d. 1796), 213

Ho-shen (1750–1799), 210–15, 237–38; in British embassy reports, 217, 240; censorial attacks on, 233, 239; corruption of, 233; his corruption as cause of rebellions, 216; in the opinion of historians, 209, 211, 215, 217

Honchō Tsugan 本朝通鑑 , 43, 273

Hōon, feudal service, 294

Hoppo, 253, 362

Hori Kōan, of Owari, 271

Hoshino Masayuki, 279

Hosoi Heishū, 280

Hou Han Shu ("History of the Later Han Dynasty"), 171, 172, 354

Hsi-tsung Shih-lu 熹宗實錄 , 357, 358

Hsia Tseng-yu 夏曾佑 , 350

Hsiang-ch'en 相臣 , officials assisting dynastic founders, 177

Hsiang-huo t'ien 香火田 ("incense fields"), 104

Hsiang-yüeh 鄉約 ("community pact"), 69

Hsiao I-shan 蕭一山 , 217, 358, 359, 360

Hsieh Chao-chi 謝肇淛 , 260

Hsieh Chen-ting (1753–1809), 213, 214, 240

Hsien-t'ien 限田 ("limit the fields"), 253

Hsin-ch'en 倖臣 ("favorite ministers"), 177

Hsin T'ang Shu 新唐書 , 335, 344

Hsing 性 ("nature"), 59, 69

Hsiu-chi 修己 ("self-cultivation"), 52, 255

Hsiu-shen 修身 ("self-cultivation"), 52

Hsiung Mien-an 熊勉菴 , on the administration of law, 153

Hsü Heng 許衡 , 338

Hsü Nai-p'u, 19th century writer on bureaucracy, 350–51

Hsü Shih-ch'ang (1858–1939), 264

Hsü Tung 徐棟 , 353

Hsü Wen-hsien T'ung-k'ao, 355

Hsüan-tsung Shih-lu 宣宗實錄 , 356, 358

Hsüeh Chih Hsu-shuo 學治續説 , 352, 353

Hsüeh-chih I-shuo 學治臆説 , 216, 351, 359

Hsüeh Chih T'i-hsing Lu 學治體行錄 , 353

Hsüeh Hsüan 薛瑄 , 152, 338

Hsün-li 循吏 ("principled officials"), 170, 171, 177

Hsün Su I-kuei ("Rules on Social Customs"), 71

Hsün-tzu, 54, 55, 68; as a founder of classical Confucianism, 183; on human nature, 55, 56, 58, 59; on social order and harmony, 56

Hu An-kuo 胡安國 , 338

Hu Chung-tsao (d. 1755), 230

Hu Shih, 359

Hu Yüan 胡瑗 , 338

Hua Yün-ch'eng 華允誠 , 358

Huan-hai Chih-nan Wu-chung 宦海指南五種 , 350

Huan-yu Chi-lüeh 宦遊紀畧 , 351, 353

Huang-ch'ao Ching-shih Wen-pien 皇朝經世文編 , 147, 339

Huang Ch'ao rebellion, 344

Huang-cheng Ch'üan-shu 荒政全書 , 147

Huang Hsing, 365

Huang Hung-shou 黃鴻壽 , 358

Huang Tsung-hsi (1610–95), 35, 351

Hucker, C. O., 355, 356, 357

Hui Tsung, Emperor (1101–1125), 325, 362, 373

Hulsewé, A. F. P., 355

Hummel, A. W., 358, 359, 360

Hung-hsien 洪憲 movement, 266, 267

Hung-hsien reign, 244

Hung Liang-chi (1746–1809), 358, 359, 360; on A-kuei and Ho-shen, 239; attacking Ho-shen's faction, 241; collections of prose of, 243; exile of, to I-li, 242

Hung Pei-chiang Ch'üan-chi 洪北江全集 , 358, 360

Hung-wu Emperor (reigned 1368–98): on eunuchs, 203, 204; on Mencius, 199; on ministerial responsibilities, 199; *see also* Ming T'ai-tsu

I-chai 義齋 , clan poorhouse, 113, 115

I-ch'üan Wen-chi 伊川文集 , 358, 360

I-chuang 義莊 , 65, 98, 113; *see also* Charitable estates

I-hsüeh 義學 ("charitable school"), 122

I-hsüeh Chi 義學記 , 348

I-t'iao pien-fa ("single whip tax"), 348

I-t'ien 義田 , 65, 98; *see also* Charitable estates

I-t'ien Chi 義田記 , 101, 109, 114

Ideology: in Ch'ing state schools, 223, 227; Chu Hsi philosophy as orthodoxy in Tokugawa schools, 31; "educational edicts" in China, 72–76; governing as instructing, in Ou-yang Hsiu's thought, 5–8; Ming and Ch'ing regulations governing licentiates, 222; *see also* Education, Motoda Eifu, School texts and curricula

Iemitsu, Shogun (1623–50), 276, 289

Ienobu, Shogun (1709–12), 280

Ietsugu, Shogun (1713–16), 280

Ieyasu, 39; Festival of, 290; shrine to, at Nikkō, 290; *see also* Tokugawa Ieyasu

Igakkan ("medical college"), 298

Igaku no Yō 爲學の要 , 371

Iida Sukashi 飯田須賀斯 , 367

Ikeda 池田 Archives, 366, 367, 368

Ikeda of Inaba, 278

Ikeda Mitsumasa 池田光政, daimyo of Bizen, 274, 276, 277, 278, 286; attacking Buddhism, 288; as champion of Confucianism and Shinto, 288; on principles of the ruler, 280; on the three world views, 291

Ikeda Terumasa, 288

Ikeda Toshitaka, 288

Ikeda Tsunamasa, 288

Imai Kosai 今井魯齋, 367

Imazeki Hisamaro, 361

Imperial Household Law, Japanese, 303, 323

Imperial Rescript on Education, 303; drafting of the, 330, 331, 373; official commentary of, 331; promulgation of the, 331; promulgation of the, 50th anniversary of, 370; universal values in, 333; *see also* Meiji Emperor, Motoda Eifu

Imperial Rescript to Soldiers and Sailors, 330

Inheritance system, Chinese, 102, 130, 132

Inoue Kaoru, 323, 324

Inoue Kowashi (1844–95), 330

Inoue Tetsujiro 井上哲次郎, 366; on the Imperial Rescript on Education, 331

Ishikawa Ken 石川謙, 282, 308

Itō Hirobumi, 12, 318, 319, 324, 327, 328

Itō Jinsai (1627–1705), 32, 272, 331; on Confucius and Mencius, 46; on Sung philosophers, 46

Itō Tasaburō, 366, 368

Itō Tōgai (1670–1736), 272

Iwakura Tomomi, 315, 318, 319, 321, 322, 372

Japan, constitution, 303, 324, 330, 331

Japanese emperor, as a Confucian monarch, 303, 312; *see also* Confucianism, Japan

Japanese studies, in the Tokugawa period, 299, 300

Jen-cheng 仁政 ("benevolent rule"), 279–80

Jen-chün 人君 ("ruler of men"), 221

Jen-tao chiao 人道教 ("humanistic teachings"), 250

Jen-tsung, Emperor (reigned 1425), 177

Jen-tsung, Emperor (reigned 1796–1820); *see* Chia-ch'ing Emperor

Jidoku 侍讀 ("tutor"), 281, 307

Jih-chih Lu 日知錄, 151, 352, 361

Jihō 侍補, special consultants to the Meiji Emperor, 318, 319, 322

Jikō 侍講, ("lecturer"), 310

Jikō Sotō ("A Lecturer's Report to the Throne"), 372

Jinnō Shōtōki, 309

Jinsei 仁政 ("benevolent rule"), 279, 280

Jitsugaku 實學; *see* Practical Learning

Jōei Shikimoku 貞永式目, 292

Juan Yüan (1764–1894): on Ch'ing scholarship, 48; on the Han school, 45

Juin 儒員 ("Confucian official"), 278

Juku 塾, publicly supported local schools, 281, 284

Jurin Genryū, 336

Jusha 儒者 ("Confucianist"), 12, 269, 270, 277, 286; and Buddhism, 289; bureaucratic functions of, 277–80, 281, 291–92; career pattern of, 287; and the Chinese literatus, 11; decline of, 300, 301; educational functions of, 281, 282; legislative function of, 280, 281; Motoda Eifu, as professional Confucianist, 304; ritual functions of, 272–77; and the samurai, 285–86; and Shinto, 11; social origins of, 286; as successors to the priest-officials, 286

Jusha-shū 儒者衆 ("corps of Confucianists"), 278, 286

Jushin 儒臣 ("Confucian official"), 278

Kada Azumamaro (1669–1736), 36

Kaga, Neo-Confucianism in the domain of, 271

Kaibara Ekken (1630–1714), 32, 40, 46, 47

Kaigo Tokiomi 海後宗臣, 370, 371, 372, 373

Kaiho Seiryō (1755–1817), on the principles of heaven and earth, 40

K'ang-hsi Emperor (reigned 1662–1722), 329; edicts of, 74, 373; and factionalism, 225; Sixteen Injunctions of, 73, 74, 92

K'ang Yu-wei (1858–1927), 13, 365

Kanreki no Ki 還曆之記, 370, 371, 372

Kao Chung-hsien-kung Nien-p'u 高忠賢公年譜, 358

Kao I-han 高一涵, 355, 356

Kao Lao 高勞, 361

Kao P'an-lung, Ming censor, 206, 338

Kao-tsung, Emperor, Ch'ing Dynasty (ruled 1736–1796); *see* Ch'ien-lung Emperor

Kao-tsung, Emperor, Sung Dynasty (reigned 1127–62), 320

Kao-tzu 告子, 54, 55

Katō Hiroyuki (1836–1916), 267, 309, 310; on German legal history, 309, 310

Katō Toranosuke, 367

Keene, Donald L., 336, 366

Keng Ching-chung 耿精忠 , 350

Keng-sheng Chai Wen Chia-chi 更生齋文甲集 , 358, 360

Kenroku, of Ogyū Sorai, *q. v.*, 306, 371

Kensei Shiryō Shitsu, 370

Kido Kōin, 308

Kii, Neo-Confucianism in the domain of, 271

Kinoshita Junnan 木下順庵 , in Kaga, 271

Kinship system, 159; *see also* Clan, Clan rules

Kirby, R. J., 369

Kishimoto Hideo, on Confucianism, 27, 28

Kitabatake Chikafusa, 43

Kō 孝 , 294; see also Confucianism, ethics of, filial piety

K'o-chang mi-shu 科長秘書 , secretary-advisers to administrators, Chinese Republic, 262

Ko-ming ("revolution"), 259, 260, 263, 264, 265

Kobayashi Nobuake 小林信明 , 366

Kōchō Shiryaku, 309

Koga Tōba, 281–82

Kogaku school of "ancient learning," 32, 305, 331

Kojiki, 43, 371, 373

Koki no Ki 古棋之記 , 370, 371, 372, 373

Kokken Taiko 國憲大綱 , 326

Kokkyō ("national teaching"), 326

Kokkyō-ron, 373

Kokugaku ("Japanese studies"), 295, 309, 312, 314, 315, 332

Kokugaku-ha, 32, 36

Kokugaku scholars, 289, 290

Kokushi Sanron, 309

Kokutai ("national form," "national polity"), 267, 290, 301, 310, 313

Kondō Masaharu 近藤正治 , 368, 369

Kōri-bugyō 郡奉行 ("Magistrate of County Affairs"), 279

Kōron 公論 ("public opinion"), 325

Kōsaka Masaaki, 371

Koshōgumi-bangashira-gaku 小性組番頭格 , 277

Kracke, E. A., Jr., 355, 357

Ku Chieh-kang, 357

Ku Chin T'u-shu Chi-ch'eng, 70, 337, 338, 355

Ku-liang chuan, 366

Ku Tso 顧佐 , 191

Ku Yen-wu (1613–82), 35, 51, 245, 338, 352, 361; on moral conscience of the official, 151; on Neo-Confucian metaphysics, 45; on real knowledge, 60; on self-styled Confucians, 186

Ku Ying-t'ai (d. after 1689), 357

K'u-li 酷吏 ("oppressive officials"), 170, 172

Kuan, republican term for official, 246, 262, 263

Kuan-ch'ang Hsien-hsing Chi 官場現形記 , 157, 353

Kuan Chien 官鑑 , 352

Kuan fang 關防 ("rule of isolation"), 135

Kuan-t'ien 官田 ("official land"), 262

Kuan-tzu, 68

Kuang-tsung Shih-lu 光宗實錄 , 357

Kubilai Khan, on the duty of the censorate, 189, 190

Kudara, 313

Kuei Ch'ao-wan 桂超萬 , 143, 145, 146, 160, 351, 353

Kumamoto domain, the daimyo of, 306

Kumamoto domain school, 283

Kumazaki Wataru, 369

Kumazawa Banzan (1619–91), 31, 46, 271, 273, 274, 306, 371; the career of, 279; on Five Human Relationships, 277; as model samurai, 46

Kung 貢 ("gift-tribute"), 211, 235, 236

Kung 公 ("openness"), 148

Kung-ch'en 功臣 ("meritorious officials"), 177

Kung Kuo Ke 功過格 , 72

Kung-sun Yang 公孫鞅, 183, 190, 207

K'ung-chiao Wen-t'i 孔教問題 , 362

K'ung Ling-i, descendant of Confucius, 246

K'ung-she 孔社 ("Confucian societies"), 247

Kuo-ch'ao Ch'i-hsien Lei-cheng Ch'u-pien 國朝耆獻類徵初編 , 358, 359, 360

Kuo-ch'ao Hsien-cheng Shih-lüeh 國朝先正事略, 358, 360

Kuo-ch'ao Pei-chuan Chi 國朝碑傳集 , 358, 360

Kuo Pin-chia 郭斌佳, 365, 366

Kuo-shih Lieh-chuan 國史列傳 , 358, 359, 360

Kuo-shih Ta-kang 國史大綱 , 354

Kuo-shih Yao-i 國史要義 , 353

Kuo-t'ai, impeached in 1782, 215, 233, 234

Kuo-t'i 國體 ("national form," "form of state"), 248, 267, 366

Kuroda Kiyotaka, 320, 323, 324

Kyō ("teachings," "doctrine," etc.), 326; *see also* Chiao

Kyōgaku Taii Shigi 教學大意私議 , 371

Kyōgaku Taishi 教學大旨 , 327

Kyōiku-gi 教育議 , 373
Kyōiku-gi Fugi 教育議附議 , 371
Kyoto: educational institutions in, 284, 298–99, 301; as training center of early Japanese Confucianists, 271, 272
Kyoto court, Shinto practices in, 290

Large joint family, 86–87
Law, 152–55, 185, 255
Legalism, 56, 183, 184, 190, 197, 198; and Confucianism, 15, 17, 56, 135, 252
Lei-shu 類書 ("encyclopedias"), 166
Li-chi 禮記 , 68, 87, 195, 262, 356, 365
Li 理 ("principles"), 39, 69; *see also Ri*
Li 禮 ("ritual," "ceremonial," etc.), 53, 54, 55, 57, 61, 68, 151, 185
Li-chia 里甲 , neighborhood unit system of the Ming, 72
Li Chien-nung 李劍農 , contemporary scholar, 352
Li Chih 李贄 (1527–1602), 30, 61
Li Ch'ing-ch'en 李清臣 (1032–1102), 169
Li Chung-ting Chi 李忠定集 , 372
Li Huan (1827–91), 358, 359, 360
Li Kang 李綱 (1085–1140), 320, 325, 372, 373
Li Kung (1659–1733), 30, 41, 45
Li P'an-lung 李攀龍 , 336
Li Pao-chia (1867–1906), 157, 160, 353
Li-pu Chi-hsün Ssu Tse-li 吏部稽勲司則例 , 353
Li-pu Tse-li 吏部則例 , 147, 160, 353
Li-shan-yüan Ch'üan-chi 禮山園全集 , 339
Li Shih-chen, compiler of *Pen-ts'ao Kang-mu*, 40
Li Shih-mien 李時勉 , Ming censor, 200
Li Ssu 李斯 , 56
Li Yu-wu, 371
Li Yüan-tu (1821–87), 358, 360
Liang-cheng Ch'üan-shu 糧政全書 , 147
Liang Ch'i-ch'ao, 35, 45, 267
Liang-li 良吏 ("good officials"), 171
Liang Shu 梁書 , 171
Liao, W. K., 356, 357
Licentiates, 222
Lien-t'ien 奩田 ("dowry land"), 104
Lin Yutang, 357
Literary inquisition, under Ch'ien-lung Emperor, 29, 175
Literati, 15, 20, 22, 222–23
Liu Ch'ih 劉菑 , early 16th century, 206, 207

Liu Chih-chi 劉知幾 , T'ang historian, 165, 353
Liu Ch'üan, in Ho-shen's employ, 236, 238
Liu Ch'üan-chih (1739–1818), 241
Liu Heng (1776–1841), 151, 351, 352, 353
Liu Hsi 劉熙 (Han Dynasty), 68
Liu Hui 劉輝 (11th century), 109
Liu-pu Tse-li 六部則例 , 147
Liu Ta-chün 劉大鈞 , 362, 365
Liu T'ai 劉臺 , Ming censor, 192, 193
Liu Yung (1720–1805), 233
Lou Ho 樓槍 (1137–1213), author of Fan Chungyen's *nien-p'u*, 105
Lü I-chien 呂夷簡 (d. 1044), 173, 231
Lü K'un 呂坤 (1534–1616), 138, 156, 160, 338, 351–53; on inservice training, 143, 144; on law, 148, 150, 153; on moral conscience of the official, 151; on official corruption and abuse of power, 148, 149, 150
Lü Liu-liang (1629–83), 30, 230
Lü Shu-sheng, on personal aspect of bureaucratic office, 159
Lü Ta-lin 呂大臨 , 69, 338
Lu-Wang 陸王 , School of the Mind, 44
Lun-heng, 68
Lun-tsan 論贊 , "comment" at the end of a biography, 353
Lun-yu; *see Analects*
Lung Wen-pin 龍文彬 , 350, 357

Ma Tuan-lin, historical writings of, 42
MacCartney's embassy, to Jehol in 1793, 211
McCullough, Mrs. Helen Craig, 370
MacSherry, Charles Whitman, 362
Maeda 前田 , the daimyo family of Kaga, 286
Makino Tatsumi, 337
Manchus, 128, 202, 210, 222, 223, 224, 229, 230, 256, 263, 266
Mano Senryū, 337
Marxist theory, 27, 50
Matsudaira Sadamitsu, 368
Matsudaira Sadanobu 松平定信 , 280, 282, 295
Matsunaga Shakugo 松永尺五 , in Kaga, 271
Matsushima Eiichi, 366
Matsuyama domain, educational institutions in, 283, 296
Meiji, Emperor, 266, 302–33
Meirin'in 明倫院 , 329, 373
Meirokusha ("Meiji Six Society"), 310

Mencius, 54, 183, 306, 311, 314, 321, 356, 357; censored in Japan, 260; censored under Ming T'ai-tsu, 199; exalted by Itō Jinsai, 46; on government and social order, 55, 57; on human nature, 45, 55, 58; as a model remonstrator, 194, 195

Merton, Robert K., 355

Meskill, John, 38

Metsuke 目付 , police officer, 296

Min-t'ien 民田 ("private lands"), 262

Minamimura Baiken 南村梅軒 , 271

Minamoto, 273

Ming-ch'en 名臣 ("famous statesmen"), 170, 177

Ming-ch'en Tsou-i 明臣奏議 , 357

Ming Hui-yao 明會要 , 356

Ming-i Tai-fang Lu 明夷待訪錄 , 35, 351

Ming-kung Shu P'an Ch'ing-ming Chi 名公書判
清明集 , 109, 346

Ming Nan-ching Tu Ch'a-yüan T'iao-yüeh 明南
京都察院條約 , 357

Ming Shan-hsi 明善熙 , , 351.

Ming Shih, 356, 357, 358, 363, 365

Ming Shih-lu 明實錄 , 191, 199

Ming T'ai-tsu, 338, 357; on the gentry, 348; Six Injunctions of, 73

Mito school, 31, 43, 47, 290, 307, 312, 337, 367, 371

Mito school, the, 31, 43, 47, 290, 307, 312, 337, 367, 371

Mitsukuni of Mito, 313

Mitsumasa of Bizen, 289

Miura Baien 三浦梅園 , 40

Miyakawa Hisayuki, 363

Mizuno Kyōichirō, 367, 368

Mohist theory of government, 221

Monarchism, Chinese, 247, 249, 267

Monarchy, Chinese, 249, 253, 257; despotic character of, 23, 189

Mori Arinori, 328, 329

Morohashi Tetsuji, 369

Morrison, Robert, 222, 223, 359

Mote, F. W., 357

Motoda Eifu 元田永孚 , 302-33, 370-73; autobiography of, 304, 307, 308, 322, 323; on Buddhism, 310, 314, 317, 327; Ch'eng-Chu school, Mito School, 331; on Christianity, 310, 314, 327; on Confucian values, 310, 311, 312, 315, 316, 327; on Confucianism, degeneration of, 313; on constitutional government, 322-26, 372; on education, 310, 311, 326-31, 333; and the Imperial Rescript on Education, 330; and Shinto, 312, 314; on sovereignty, 324-26; on Western customs, thought, education, etc., 310, 314, 325, 327, 330, 331

Motoda Nagazane; *see* Motoda Eifu

Motoori Norinaga 本居宣長 (1730-1801), 41

Mou-ch'en 謀臣 ("counseling official"), 177

Mu-chih 幕治 ("government by staffs of intimates"), 263

Mu-liao 幕僚 , aide, *q.v.,* 262

Mu-ling shu 牧令書 , reference works for magistrates

Mu-ling Shu Chi-yao 牧令書輯要 , 353

Mu-yu 幕友 , aide, *q.v.,* 262

Müller, Max, 356

Myōshinji (temple), 288

Na 名 ("honor"), 295

Na-shui 納稅, basic taxes, 123

Nagaoka Atsuyushi, 309

Nagaoka Kemmotsu (1812-59), 307

Nagasaki, as center of Western learning, 298, 299, 301

Nagata Hiroshi, 368

Nagayama Usaburō 永山卯三郎 , 367, 368, 369

Nakae Tōju 中江藤樹 (1608-48), 32, 46, 47, 270, 272, 273, 366

Nakamura Keiu (1832-91), 309, 330

Nakanuma Kien (Ryōzō) (1829-96), 309

Nan Kan Hsiang-yüeh 南贛鄉約 , , 70

Nara, 266

Narushima family, 278, 287; tutoring duties of, 281

Narushima Motonao 成島司直 , 367

Nationalism, Chinese, 246, 265

Needham, Joseph, 336

Neo-Confucianism, 17, 18, 23, 33, 43-46, 59, 98, 332, 336; authoritarian strain in, 14, 18, 194; and Buddhism, 33, 34, 38, 39, 41, 44, 59, 91; in clan rules, 67, 69, 71, 91; empirical strain in, 43; ethics of, 42, 46, 93; ethics of, 17th and 18th centuries, 12; and family rites, 101; "fundamentalism," 34, 35, 41, 42, 43; historical-mindedness in, 34, 41, 42, 43; historiography of, 42, 43; humanism, 34, 38, 42; idealism, 18, 20, 21, 23; and the Meiji Restoration, 46; as a philosophical system, 33, 59; the problem of orthodoxy in, 22, 44, 46; rationalism, 34, 38, 39, 40, 41, 43; rationalism, and the Shinto revival, 41;

"restorationism" in, 34, 35, 42; "revivalism" in, 34, 42; as state ideology, 22, 23; Sung Dynasty, 3, 4, 12, 23, 54, 184, 254, 257, 269; and Taoism, 33, 91; vision of, 18, 50; Yüan Dynasty, 33; *see also* Confucianism

—Japan, 12, 32, 38, 39, 268, 269, 294; and Buddhism, 33, 289; institutions, 268; the Mito school of, 43; philosophy, 268; and political theory, 290; and the samurai class, 38, 39; scholarships, 270, 271; and Shinto, 32, 40; the Southern School of, 271

Nepotism, 157–59, 179

Nieh Chi-mo 聶纙模 , 158, 352

Nieh Ch'ung-ch'i, contemporary scholar, 342

Nihon Gaishi, 309

Nihon Shoki, 371, 372

Nihongi, 43

Niida Noboru, 96, 339, 340, 341, 343

Nintoku, Emperor, 316, 317

Nishi Amane (1829–97), 310

Nishijima Jun 西島醇 , 336

Nishimura Shigeki (1828–1902), 310, 329

Nishimura Tenshu, 367

Nomura Kanetarō, 369

Nonaka Kenzan 野中兼山 (1605–63), 271

Nu 奴 ("slave"), 245, 263

Nü Chieh 女誡 , 69

Nurhaci, 349

O-ch'ang (d. 1755), 230

O-er-t'ai (1680–1745), 228, 229, 230

Officials, officialdom; *see* Bureaucracy, Civil service

Ogasawara school, instruction in etiquette according to, 284

Ogawa Wataru, 367, 368, 369

Ogi Kakubei, 307, 309

Ogyū Sorai (1666–1728), 31, 36, 46, 306, 336, 371; on Sung philosophy, 36, 46

Ojima Sukema, 364

Ojin, Emperor, 309, 316, 317

Okayama, 283, 288

Oku-ju 奥儒 , Confucian lecturer to the Shogun, 278

Okubo Toshimichi, 317, 318

Ometsuke 大目付 , chief disciplinary officer of a domain, 296

Ono Kiyoshi, 367, 368

Osaka, educational institutions in, 284, 298

Ou-yang Hsiu (1007–72), 12, 13, 22, 23, 34, 65, 338, 344, 354; on Buddhism, 8; and Chu Hsi compared, 21; on exile, 19, 20; on factions, 21, 168, 221, 226, 230; historical writing of, 19, 42; on principles of government, 6, 7, 176; and "ritual" utopian vision, 6–9; Yung-cheng Emperor's treatment of, 20, 226

Ou-yang Wen-chung-kung Wen-chi 歐陽文忠公文集 , 335, 359

Ou-yang Yung-shu Chi 歐陽永叔集 , 354

Owari: daimyo of, 282; domain of, Neo-Confucianism in, 271

Pan Chao, 69, 338

Pan Ku, 68

Pao-chia, system of mutual responsibility, 74, 75

Pao-yen T'ang Pi-chi 寶顏堂祕集 , 346

Pei Ch'i Shu (History of the Northern Ch'i Dynasty), 171

P'ei-yüan T'ang Shou-cha Chieh-ts'un 培遠堂手札節存 , 351

"Pen Lun" 本論 , 6, 34

Pen-ts'ao kang-mu, 40

"P'eng-tang Lun" 朋黨論 , 168, 221, 225, 227

Po-hu-t'ung, 68

Practical Learning, the, 306, 309, 311; *see also Jitsugaku*

Primogeniture, 88, 102; *see also* Inheritance system

Pringle, Rev. J. C., 370

"Pure Shinto," 267, 312

Rebellions: ideology of, v; 19th century, 209

Redfield, Robert (1897–1958), 83, 95, 96, 340, 343

Reform movement, post-Boxer Manchu, 266

Reform program, Sung, controversies in, 167, 168

Reischauer, Edwin O., 366

Remarriage, of widows, 93, 94

Remonstrance: controversies, 201, 202; disasters, 200, 201, 202; functions of, 195–98, 219, 220; in the Ming period, 199, 200

Republicanism, Chinese, 245, 248, 250

Restoration, the Meiji, 46, 283, 299, 302, 305, 306, 307, 312, 313, 329

"Restorationism": in Neo-Confucianism, 34, 35, 42; outside the Confucian tradition, 36, 37

Ri 理, 32; *see also* Li

Ri Hakugi Chūgi Hen 李伯紀忠義編 , 372

Ritual land, 121, 346; *see also Chi-t'ien*

Rotours, Robert des, 355

Saga: the daimyo of, 281, 282; domain, progressive developments in, 307

Sagara Akira, 366, 367

Sagara Yoshiaki, 361

Sah Mong-wu 薩孟武, 355

Saigō Takamori, 308, 317, 372

Saitō Tokutarō, 368, 369

Sakamaki Teiichirō, 264, 361, 365

Sakata Yoshio, 367

Sakuma Shōzan, 26, 31

Sakurai Shōtarō, 396

Samgha, the Buddhist Community, 103, 104, 105

Samurai, 269, 277, 278, 279, 281, 283, 286, 287, 291, 294, 295; and Buddhism, 289; career pattern of the young, 299; and Confucianism, 38, 39, 285, 287, 289; cultural role of, 274, 300; genealogies, 285; historians among the, 300; reformers, 36, 37; and Shinto ceremonies, 291; social status of, 275, 284; the training of, 296–99; values of, 272, 273, 285, 295

Sanjō Sanetomi, 308, 318, 319

Sansom, G. B., 369

Satō Nobuhiro 佐藤信淵 (1769–1850), 36, 37

Satsuma domain, Neo-Confucian studies in, 271

Satsuma Rebellion, 320

School texts and curricula: *Mencius* edited under Ming T'ai-tsu and used in official schools, 199; "P'eng-tang lun" to be read in Ch'ing government schools, 227; texts recommended in clan rules, 69, 70, 71, 72; Western learning, in the domain schools, 299; Western learning, in samurai training, 299

Schools; *see also* Education, Teachers, Jusha

—China: academies (*shu-yüan*), suppressed in the Ming Dynasty, 29; "charitable school" (*i-hsüeh* 義學) of the Fan clan, 110, 111, 122, 123, 130, 131; "charitable schools" maintained by clans, 81; palace school for eunuchs in the Ming, 203; public and private, late Sung Dynasty, 131; Wen-cheng Shu-yüan, 124

—Japan: domain schools, 282, 283; Edo, educational institutions in, 298, 301; Fukui Domain college, 283, 297, 299; *juku,* publicly supported local schools, 281, 284; in Kyoto, 271, 272, 284, 298, 299, 301; in Osaka, 284, 298; School of Western Learning, 298; Shizutani Chūgakkō, 368; Shizutani gakkō, 283; *terakoya* ("temple schools"), 284; Tokugawa College (Shōheikō), 279, 282,

284; Wagaku Kōdansho, 298; Yūshūkan, 283, 284

Schumpeter, Joseph, 363

Schwartz, Benjamin, 268, 366

Seidan, of Ogyū Sorai, *q.v.,* 306, 371

Seikyō Yōroku 聖教要録 , 46

Seiyuki 聖喩記 , 329, 373

Self-cultivation, 8, 9, 52, 53, 59, 60, 81, 95, 255, 262; in exile, 19, 20, 198; and the ordering of society, 52–54; *see also* Confucianism, Neo-Confucianism

Seuberlich, Wolfgang, 357

Shan-jang 禪讓 ("abdication"), 245, 363

Shao Erh-yun 邵二雲, 161

Shen 慎 ("carefulness"), 148

Shen-tao chiao 神道教 ("religious teachings"), 250

Shen-yin Yü Chieh-lu 呻吟語節録 , 147, 351, 352, 353

Sheng-shui Yen-t'an Lu 澠水燕談録 , 345

Sheng-yü 聖諭 ("imperial injunctions"), 72

Sheng-yü Kuang-hsun 聖諭廣訓 , 73, 227

Shidō, 46; *see also* Bushidō

Shih, Vincent, 361, 363

Shih-chi, 170, 172, 354, 372, 373

Shih-ch'i-shih Shang-ch'üeh, by Wang Ming-sheng, 354

Shih-ta-fu hua 士大夫畫 , "officials' style" of painting, 253

Shih-tsung, Emperor, Ching Dynasty, *see* Yung-cheng Emperor

Shih-t'ung 史通 , 353

Shijuku 私塾 , private local schools, 281

Shimotsu Kyūya, 306, 308, 309

Shin-ron, by Aizawa Seishisai, 47

Shinto, 37, 289–90; and Confucianism, 32, 40, 47, 312; mythology, 312; the political sense of, 290; registration, 288; revival, 36, 41; shrines, 290–91

Shizutani Chūgakko 閑谷中學校 , 368

Shizutani-gakkō 閑谷學校 , 283

Shogunate: authority of, 31, 32, 273; ban of Western books, 336; ideological conformity, 31, 32

Shōheikō 昌平黌 , 282, 284; *see also* Tokugawa College

Shōji Sōichi, 364

Shosamurai Hatto 諸士法度 , 293, 294

Shōtoku Taishi, 313, 324, 331

Shu-sheng Ch'u-chien 書生初見 , 352, 353

Shūgi Gaisho, by Kumazawa Banzan, 371
Shūgi Washo, by Kumazawa Banzan, 371
Shūkyō ("religion"), 326–27
Shūron 衆論 ("mass opinion"), 325
Shushi, school, 286; *see also* Chu Hsi, Ch'eng-Chu
Shūshin 修身 ("moral training"), 327; *see also* Hsiu-shen
Six Arts, 42, 283
Six Martyrs (*Liu chün-tzu*), 247, 361
Smiles, Samuel, 309, 331
Soejima Taneomi, 320
Sōgenji, 288
Sohn, Pow-key, contemporary scholar, 363
Sōkan ("priest-official"), 277
Soshaban 奏者番 ("chamberlain"), 279
Ssu Ch'ao Hsüeh-an 四朝學案, 70
Ssu-ma Ch'ien, 355
Ssu-ma Kuang (1019–89), 42, 43, 57, 69, 169, 328; historical writing of, 42, 43; imitated by Hayashi Razan, 43
Staunton, Sir George, on Ho-shen, 211, 217, 237, 358, 360
Su Hsün (1009–66), 65, 176–77
Su Shih (1036–1101), 169, 338
Su-wang 素王 ("uncrowned king"), 262, 267, 364
Sui Shu, 172, 354
Sun Ch'eng-tse 孫承澤, 355, 357
Sun Yat-sen, 260; on Yao and Shun, 365; on Yüan Shih-k'ai's intentions, 264
Sung Dynasty: classification of officials in, 166; familism in, 101; historical writing in, 42
Sung Hsi, contemporary scholar, 353
Sung Hui-yao Kao 宋會要稿, 356
Sung Ming-ch'en Yen-hsing Lu 宋名臣言行錄, 173, 306, 354, 371
Sung Shih, 345, 346, 354, 355
Sung-shih Chi-shih-pen-mo, 335
Sung Shu, 171
Superstition, edicts against, 74, 75
Suzuki Hisashi, 367

Ta Ming Hui-tien, 191, 356
Tai Chen (1724–77), 30, 31; on Chu Hsi's metaphysics, 45; on the Way, 59
T'ai-p'ing 太平, as objective of government, 138, 139, 140
T'ai-shang Kan-ying P'ien 太上感應篇, 72
Taihō laws, 324

Taika Reform, 324
Taiping (T'ai-p'ing) rebellion, 255, 335; Christianity in, 336; and clan organizations, 82; ideology of, 361, 363
Takebayashi Kan'ichi, 368
T'an Ssu-t'ung (1865–98), 13
T'ang-chien 唐鑑, 309
T'ang Yin 唐寅, Ming painter, 5
Tani Jichū 谷時中 (1598–1649), 271
Taniguchi Sumio, 367
T'ao Chu-yin 陶菊隱, 361, 366
Taoism: and clan rules, 67, 71, 72; and Confucianism, 33, 44, 45; nonphilosophical, 252
Taoist ideas, in state ideology, 184
Taoist thinkers, anti-government, 198
Teachers: Confucian, of the Fan Clan, in the Wencheng Shu-yuan, 124; teacher-pupil relationship between literati and throne, 23, 222, 223; teaching as an occupation for unsuccessful scholars, 81, 125, 144–45; teaching as role of a Confucian in unfavorable times, 53; Yamaga Sokō, unorthodox, 31; *see also Jusha*, Schools
Tenkai 天海, Buddhist monk, 273, 288
Terakoya ("temple schools"), 284
Tezuka Ryōdō, 363, 365
Thousand Character Classic, 371
T'i-yung ("substance and function"), 26, 142, 143
Tien-chi 典籍 ("registrar"), 126
T'ien-chi Emperor (reigned 1621–27), remonstrance in the reign of, 200, 204
T'ien-li Emperor (reigned 1328–32), 343
T'ien-ming ("Mandate of Heaven"), 248, 258
Tocqueville, Alexis de, 362
Toda Toyosaburō, 364
Tokudaiji, 319, 329
Tokugawa College, 279, 282; *see also* Shōheikō
Tokugawa Ieyasu, 39, 268, 270, 271, 274, 279, 282, 292
Tokugawa Japan: education in, 295, 296, 298; Six Injunctions in, 73
Tokugawa Jikki, 276
Tokugawa mausoleums, Buddhist, 289
Tokugawa Nariaki (1800–1860), of the Mito school, 307
Tokugawa shogun, as usurpers, 313
Tokugawa Shogunate, 31, 46, 47, 266, 269, 270, 273, 292

Tokugawa Tsunayoshi (1680–1709), 275, 276, 277, 289

Tokugawa Yoshinao, 276

Tokushibiyō, 286

Tokushima domain, 296

Tokutomi Iichirō, 370–73

Tokyo (Imperial) University, 300, 329

Tosa domain, Neo-Confucian studies in, 271

Tottori Archives, 367

Tsai-kuan Fa-chieh Lu Chai-ch'ao 在官法戒錄摘抄, 353

Ts'ai Wen-ch'in Kung Shu-tu 蔡文勤公書牘 , 351

Ts'ao Hsi-pao (1719–92), 213, 236, 237, 238, 240

Ts'e-fu Yüan-kuei, 174, 175, 176, 354

Tso Chih Yao Yen 佐治藥言 , 144, 350, 351, 352

Tso-chuan, 257, 262

Tso Kuang-tou, Ming censor, 23, 208

Tso Kuang-tou Nien-p'u 左光斗年譜 , 358

Tso Tsai 左宰, 358

Tsu-chang 族長 , ("clan head"), 88

Tsuda Sōkichi, 361, 369

Ts'ui Jen-shih 崔仁師 , 153

Ts'ui Shu (1740–1816), 43

Tsukada Ko, 372

Tsung-tsu 宗族 , 64, 65, 337, *see also* Clan

Tsung-tzu 宗子 , heir of main branch of clan, 88

Ts'ung-cheng I-kuei 從政遺規, 136, 140, 144, 351, 352; *see also Wu Chung I-kuei*

Tsunoda, Ryusaku, 336, 366

Tu Yen 杜衍 (977–1057), 178

Tu Yu 杜佑, 364, 365

Tung Chung-shu (179–104 b.c.), 184, 361, 364

Tung-lin: Academy, 170; faction, 61, 170; school, and Chu Hsi, 44, 45; school, and Wang Yang-ming, 44, 45

Tung-lin T'ung-chih Lu 東林同志錄 , 357

T'ung-tien, 354

"Twenty-one Demands," 265

Tzu-li Yen 自歷言 , 351, 353

Uesugi Harunori 上杉治憲, 280

Umashimade no Mikoto, 317

Umetani Noboru, 369

Van Gulik, R. H., 364

von Grunebaum, G. E., 337

Wada Kiyoshi, 338

Wagaku-kōdansho 和學講談所 , school of native learning, 298

Waley, Arthur, 356

Walker, Richard L., 355

Wan-li Emperor (reigned 1573–1619), 73; remonstrance in the reign of, 200–203; reviving the Six Injunctions, 73

Wang An-shih (1021–86), 35, 51, 60; accused of Legalist goals, 54; Chu Hsi's estimation of, 173; and opponents, 53, 54, 56, 57; on "real knowledge," 59, 60; the reform program of, 167, 168

Wang Ch'in-jo, 354

Wang Feng-sheng 王鳳生 , 156, 158, 159, 352, 353

Wang Hsieh-chia (20th century), 361, 362, 365

Wang Hui-tsu (1731–1807), 160, 232, 350, 351, 352, 353, 359; on administration, 136, 144, 152; against favoritism, 157; on bureaucratic practice under Ho-shen, 216, 217; on goals of bureaucracy, 155; on interpretation of law, 152, 154; as magistrate, 162; on nepotism, 17, 158; on the official's aides, 149, 150, 158; on principle of impersonality in official action, 156, 157; on the "rule of isolation," 135

Wang Hui-tsu Chuan-shu 汪輝祖傳述, 351, 353

Wang Lun (d. 1774), 213, 359

Wang Mang, 264

Wang Ming-sheng (1722–97), 172, 354

Wang Pi-chih 王闢之 , Sung writer, 345

Wang Shih-cheng (Wang Shih-chen, 1526–90), 336

Wang Tan-wang (d. 1781), 235

Wang Yang-ming (Wang Shou-jen, 1472–1529), 30, 51, 60, 70, 338; influence in the Ming Dynasty, 44; influence on the Restoration movement, 46; on intuition, 41, 44; on knowledge and action, 61; school, 30, 305; school, in Japan, 32, 46; and the Tung-lin school, 44, 45

Wang Ying-lin (1223–96), historical writing of, 42

Wang Yü-ch'üan, 355

Wani, 309

Watanabe Ikujirō, 370–73

Watanabe Minoru, 369

Watson, Burton, 355

Way of the Warrior, 274, 275; *see also Shidō, Bushidō*

Weber, Max, 350, 351, 352; on bureaucracy, 16, 134, 136; on the Chinese state, 134

Wei Chung-hsien (1568–1627), 202, 358; censorial attack on, 203, 204

Wei Shu, 172

Wen-cheng Shu-yüan 文正書院, 124

Wen Ching-han 文靜涵, 351, 353

Wen-hsien T'ung-k'ao, 346, 354, 355

Wen-kung Chia-li 文公家禮 , 346; *see also Chu Tzu Chia-li*

Weng Ch'uan-chao 翁傳照. (late Ch'ing), 154, 352, 353

Western learning, in the Tokugawa period, 299, 300

Western studies, in Meiji Emperor's education, 309

Westernization, of Japan, 302, 303

White Lotus rebellion, 215

Wittfogel, Karl A., 364

Wu Chung I-kuei 五種遺規, 71, 338

Wu Han 吳晗, 357

Wu I (1745–99), 213, 215, 240

Wu K'uan 吳寬 (1435–1504), 348, 349

Wu K'uei 吳奎 (1012–69), 109

Wu T'ing-fang (1844–1922), 248, 263, 264

Wu Tsa Tsu 五雜組 , 260

Yamada Hokoku, 279

Yamada Taku, 366

Yamaga Sokō (1632–85), 39, 46, 47, 270, 273, 336; philosophical revolt of, 31; on Sung philosophers, 46; on the Way of the Warrior, 274, 275

Yamagata Aritomo, 12, 324, 329, 330

Yamaguchi Saijō, 367

Yamazaki Ansai, 32, 40, 46, 47, 271

Yamazaki school, 371

Yang Cheng I-kuei 養正道規, 71

Yang I-ch'ing 楊一清, 141

Yang-lien 養廉 , extra stipend for officials, 236

Yang Lien (1571–1625), 358

Yao Ch'ung 姚崇, 320

Yao Nai (1732–1815), 359

Yao Yü 要語, 152

Yasuba Yasukuzu (1829–99), 308, 372

Yasui Kotarō, 366

Yeh Hsiang-kao 葉向高 , 357

Yen Chih-t'ui 顏之推, 69, 338

Yen Fu, 247

Yen-kuan 言官 ("remonstrance officials"), 187, 220

Yen Kuang-ch'ung 顏光袤 , 148, 352

Yen-lu 言路 ("avenues of criticism"), 187

Yen-shih Chia-hsün 顏氏家訓 , 69

Yen-shih yü-shih 言事御史 , policy censors (Sung), 188

Yen Yüan (1635–1704), 30, 41, 45

Yin 廕 ("privilege"), 111, 131

Yin Chuang-t'u (1738–1808), 234, 235, 240

Yin Shu 尹洙, 19, 20

Ying-tsung, Emperor (reigned 1436–49), 109

Yōgaku Kōyō 幼學綱要 , 327, 328

Yōgakusho 洋學所 ("School of Western Learning"), 298

Yokoi Shōnan (1809–69), 305, 306, 309

Yoshida Shōin (1831–60), 31, 336

Yoshii Tomozane (1828–91), 318

Yoshikawa Akimasa (1841–1920), 330

Yü I-chien (d. 1782), 233

Yü Min-chung (1714–80), 233

Yü Teng 于登 (contemporary scholar), 357

Yü-t'ien 圩田 , fields below river level protected by dikes, 116, 119

Yü Yüeh (1821–1907), 109, 345

Yüan Chia-san (1806–63), 264

Yüan-hua 院畫, painting style of the court academy, 253

Yüan Shih, 356

Yüan Shih-k'ai (1859–1916), 244–48, 250, 251, 260–62, 264–67; an anachronism, 260; Japanese support of, 265; *see also* Hung-hsien

Yüan Shih Shih-fan 袁氏世範 , 86, 109, 346

Yung-cheng Emperor (reigned 1723–35), 17, 18, 83, 136, 236, 329; on factionalism, 224–28, 231; on the literati, 222; on Ou-yang Hsiu, 226, 227; resenting criticism, 243; on the Sixteen Injunctions, 73; supplementary edicts of, 74

Yung-lo Emperor (reigned 1403–24), 18; favor to Buddhism, 362

Yūshūkan, 283, 284; *see also* Matsuyama domain, educational institutions in

Zen monasteries of Kyoto, 270

Zen monks, and Neo-Confucianism, 33

DATE DUE			
OCT 31 '94			
DEC 06 '94			
JAN 23 '95			
MAR 06 '95			
MAY 22 '95			
NOV 13 '95			
NOV 20 '95			
APR 22 '96			
NOV 18 '96			
DEC 0 4 1998			